PENGUIN CLASSICS

WILLIAM SHAKESPEARE: FOUR HISTORIES

WILLIAM SHAKESPEARE

Four Histories

RICHARD II
edited by STANLEY WELLS

HENRY IV, PART ONE
edited by P. H. DAVISON

HENRY IV, PART TWO
edited by P. H. DAVISON

HENRY V
edited by A. R. HUMPHREYS

PENGUIN BOOKS

PENGUIN BOOKS

Published by the Penguin Group
Penguin Books Ltd, 27 Wrights Lane, London w8 5tz, England
Penguin Books USA Inc., 375 Hudson Street, New York, New York 10014, USA
Penguin Books Australia Ltd, Ringwood, Victoria, Australia
Penguin Books Canada Ltd, 10 Alcorn Avenue, Toronto, Ontario, Canada m4v 3b2
Penguin Books (NZ) Ltd, 182–190 Wairau Road, Auckland 10, New Zealand

Penguin Books Ltd, Registered Offices: Harmondsworth, Middlesex, England

This edition of *Richard II* first published in the New Penguin Shakespeare 1969
This edition of *Henry IV, Part One* first published in the New Penguin Shakespeare 1968
This edition of *Henry IV, Part Two*, first published in the New Penguin Shakespeare 1977
This edition of *Henry V* first published in the New Penguin Shakespeare 1968
1 3 5 7 9 10 8 6 4 2

Introduction and notes to *Richard II* copyright © Stanley Wells, 1969
Introduction and notes to *Henry IV, Part One* copyright © P. H. Davison, 1968
Introduction and notes to *Henry IV, Part Two* copyright © P. H. Davison, 1977
Introduction and notes to *Henry V* copyright © A. R. Humphreys, 1968
This edition copyright © Penguin Books, 1968, 1969, 1977, 1994
All rights reserved

Set in 10.5/12.5 pt Monophoto Garamond
Filmset by Datix International Limited, Bungay, Suffolk
Printed in England by Clays Ltd, St Ives plc

Contents

These plays and the accompanying editorial apparatus are faithful reproductions of the original New Penguin Shakespeare editions. The text has been reset, with the textual notes placed at the bottom of the pages for ease of reference, but the text itself is unchanged.

RICHARD II

Introduction

Richard II is the most purely lyrical of Shakespeare's histories – perhaps of all his plays – and the role of King Richard is the most lyrical among the tragic heroes. The play is written wholly in verse, which except for occasional irregularities is entirely in ten-syllabled lines, whether rhymed or unrhymed. Considering the metrical virtuosity that Shakespeare had already displayed in *Love's Labour's Lost*, and his masterly use of varied styles of prose in both that play and others written before *Richard II*, we may suspect that he was here deliberately restricting – or concentrating – his resources. True, the verse of *Richard II* encompasses the bluntness of Bolingbroke and Northumberland, the irresolution of the Duke of York, the business-like scheming of the conspirators, and the allegorizing formalities of the Head Gardener, as well as the elegiac lyricism of Richard and his grief-stricken Queen. Yet the mode we feel to be most characteristic of *Richard II* is the elegiac. Our image of the play is primarily an image of Richard himself, a beautiful young man luxuriating in sorrow. We think of him, not as the judicial figure of the opening scenes, nor as the maliciously petulant one revealed in his encounters with John of Gaunt, nor even in the splendid anger of his death, but rather as the man whose suffering we share intensely from the moment he returns from Ireland and is compelled to divest himself of all that he valued most highly.

It is a process that seems to result from inner rather than external compulsion; and while we should perhaps censure him for inflicting punishment upon himself, for the weakness that causes him to renounce responsibility, yet we can forgive his

self-indulgence because of the reality of his grief and bewilder-
ment as he feels himself stripped away to a point where he
seems no longer to possess a self. We forgive him too because
he suffers so articulately, so expressively, and in such melodious
and perfectly controlled verse. We think of him as a voice, and
a voice with tears in it.

Actors who have succeeded as Richard have inevitably been
praised for beauty of speech. One – William Macready – said of
another – Edmund Kean – that he could 'never forget the
music of the musical passages of Richard II and the sublime
melancholy of their delivery'. Ellen Terry regarded Richard as
one of the two best roles of Edmund's son, Charles Kean,
because in it 'his beautiful diction had full scope'; Walter Pater
wrote that when Charles acted in it 'the play became like an
exquisite performance on the violin'. Of the American Edwin
Booth, William Winter wrote: 'It was luxury merely to listen,
with closed eyes, to the voice of Edwin Booth, when he spoke
the soliloquies in "Richard II", for his tones were music, and
his clear articulation and delicate shading of the words en-
chanted the ear.' These performances all belong to the nineteenth century, when the play was only moderately popular and
was performed in versions that were always severely shortened
and sometimes significantly altered. Since the turn of the
century the text has been treated with more respect, and
perhaps its most influential interpreter has been F. R. Benson,
who played it many times in the late nineteenth century and the
early years of the twentieth. C. E. Montague wrote a famous
review praising him for 'a fine sensibility to beauty in words
and situations and a voice that gives this sensibility its due'.
Since then the greatest interpreter of the role has understandably
been our finest verse speaker, Sir John Gielgud, who was
influenced by a letter from Harley Granville Barker in which
he wrote, after seeing an early performance, 'my chief grouse is
about the verse. It is a lyrical play. W. S. has not yet learned to
express anything except in speech. There is nothing much, I
mean, in between the lines, as there is in *Macbeth* (for an

extreme example). Therefore – I am preaching; forgive me – everything the actor does must be done *within the frame* of the verse. Whatever impression of action or thought he can get within this frame without disturbance of *cadence* or *flow*, he may. But there must be nothing, no trick, no check, beyond an honest pause or so at the end of a sentence or speech. And I believe you'll seldom find that the cadence and emphasis – the mere right scansion of the verse – does not give you the meaning without much of any further effort on the actor's part . . . Variety of pace – tone – colour of speech; yes, as much as possible, but within the *frame*.' And he complained that Gielgud had been inclined 'to play more and more astride the verse instead of in it'. This is valuable less as a final judgement on Gielgud's performance, which matured into one of the best pieces of verse-speaking imaginable, than as a wise comment on the nature of the verse in this play and the actor's problems in speaking it.

If we are so conscious of the style of the play, the beauty of its language, this may be partly because it is deliberately a play of character, thought, and emotion rather than action. It is remarkably passive. Events seem to occur of themselves or by a remote, divine will rather than as the result of human volition. The play constantly approaches action only to withdraw before it happens. The third scene is characteristic: the lists are set up, all is ready for a personal combat between Mowbray and Bolingbroke, yet violence is averted at the last moment as Richard throws 'his warder down'. Gaunt is held back from taking revenge on Richard for the murder of Gloucester. Bolingbroke, though he returns to England illegally, needs to take no action in order to gain the crown; his mere presence is enough to draw from Richard a submission that seems to satisfy something within himself as well as representing his defeat. Aumerle's conspiracy against Bolingbroke is thwarted in its early stages. Except for the pageant-like *Henry VIII* this is the only history play of Shakespeare that has no battle scenes. The one violent action in the play is the murder of

Richard, a deed which its instigator immediately claims to have wished not to happen.

When he wrote *Richard II*, Shakespeare had already composed at least four plays about English history. Three are devoted to the long and eventful reign of Henry VI, and are closely linked. They are among his earliest work. Another, written probably after an interval, is *Richard III*, which tells how the warring houses of York and Lancaster were finally reconciled in the person of the Earl of Richmond, later King Henry VII. It is closely related to the early plays, which form a necessary background to it. Its triumphant ending celebrating Henry VII, Elizabeth's grandfather, was a genuine climax, the culmination of what might well have been regarded as a historical process designed by God for the benefit of the English nation. In choosing to write about Richard II Shakespeare went back to an earlier period, though one that could easily be seen in relation to that which he had already dramatized. The reign of Richard II was a real starting-point, for Richard was the last king of England to rule by direct and undisputed succession from William the Conqueror. Bolingbroke's usurpation of his throne set in motion the train of events which was finally expiated only by the union of the houses of York and Lancaster celebrated in the last speech of *Richard III*.

There is thus some appearance of a 'grand design'. Shakespeare might have written a great and closely integrated cycle of plays on English history from Richard II to Richard III. But he did not. He wrote eight plays, each capable of standing by itself, though to varying degrees related to others. He wrote them in two groups of four, the earlier group dealing with the later period. The three concerned with the reign of Henry VI are closely connected. So are the two concerned with Henry IV; and *Henry V* falls easily into place after them. But on the whole Shakespeare seems to have been more concerned to give unity to the individual plays than to subordinate them to an overall design. To consider or perform them together as a national epic may increase our perception of relationships that truly exist. But we are liable to distort each play if we try to force it into too close a relationship with the others. Though, for instance, the events of *1 Henry IV* are foreshadowed in *Richard II*, the two plays differ greatly in style. Historically, Harry Percy is the same character in both; artistically and theatrically, he is not. It is more valuable to attempt to realize the individual design, structure, and mode of each play than to seek for consistency of design from one to another.

It is reasonable, then, to see *Richard II* as a new departure, an attempt to do something different from what Shakespeare had done in his earlier history plays. The story that he chose was one that may well have seemed to have contemporary relevance. He was writing, we believe, about 1595. Queen Elizabeth had been on the throne since 1558, and had never married. The question of the succession was a major political issue. Elizabeth had done much to unify England and increase the country's prosperity. It was important that the next monarch should not throw away what she had won. A weak ruler would have been a national disaster, and there were those who felt that her successor should be chosen and appointed for his merits rather than on hereditary principle. Elizabeth, for all her popularity, was not exempt from criticism, and a charge often brought against her was that she was excessively influenced by favourites. This was one of the reasons why she was liable to be compared to Richard II. And there is good reason to believe that Shakespeare's play had special significance for his politically minded contemporaries. When it was first printed, in 1597, the scene of Richard's abdication was omitted, probably as the result of official censorship directed against the representation of the deposition of a monarch, even though Shakespeare elicits such sympathy for the victim. The scene is absent from the two later editions printed during Elizabeth's lifetime, but was restored in the first edition to appear after her death.

If Elizabeth was often compared to Richard, the most obvious candidate for identification with Bolingbroke was the Earl

of Essex, a favourite of the Queen who was himself ambitious
for power. In 1599 John Hayward published a book called *The
First Part of the Life and Reign of King Henry IV*. It bore an ill-
judged dedication to Essex which was considered so inflammatory that within three weeks the Archbishop of Canterbury
ordered that it should be cut out, and copies of the book were
burnt. Hayward deals almost entirely with the history of Richard II and the reasons for his deposition, and many readers
must have been tempted to draw the obvious parallels between
Richard and Elizabeth, and Bolingbroke and Essex. Among
them was the Queen. When in 1600 Essex was on trial for
having returned from Ireland the previous year against the
Queen's orders, Hayward was examined and his book was
regarded as potential evidence of Essex's treacherous
intentions.

In the following year a play about Richard II, almost certainly
Shakespeare's, was used as an instrument in the political struggle.
A performance at the Globe Theatre by the company of
players to which Shakespeare belonged was arranged and paid
for by Essex's supporters, apparently as a gesture of encouragement and defiance. The actors complained that the play was 'so
old and so long out of use as that they should have small or no
company at it', but they were paid enough to justify their
putting it on, and Essex's supporters attended the performance
on 7 February 1601. On the following day Essex led his
abortive rebellion, and before the month was out he had been
tried and executed. The Queen clearly resented the identification
of herself with Richard, and disliked contemplating the resemblances. A rather enigmatic conversation has been preserved
between her and William Lambarde, the keeper of the records
of the Tower. In August 1601 he presented her with some of
the archives and she 'fell upon the reign of King Richard II,
saying "I am Richard II, know ye not that?"' Lambarde made
a diplomatic reply agreeing that Essex, 'the most adorned
creature that ever your majesty made', had made the identification, and his sovereign replied 'He that will forget God will

also forget his benefactors; this tragedy was played forty times in open streets and houses.' 'This tragedy' is not an undisputable reference to Shakespeare's play, particularly since the actors had complained that the play they performed was 'long out of use' (though it could be that the Queen referred to performances some years previously). But there is no doubt that Elizabeth was peculiarly sensitive about comparisons between Richard and herself, and that some of her subjects felt the comparison was damaging to her.

Still, nothing in Shakespeare's play suggests that he was specially interested in the topical parallels, or that he wrote with any immediate political intent. Nor does he seem to have been suspected of doing so, since he and his fellows were not punished when the play was used as a prologue to Essex's rebellion. Shakespeare was not concerned merely to present a documentary account of the facts. Certainly he was interested in the political aspects of Richard's reign and their bearing on the general topic of the position of a monarch in relation to God and to his people. The play raises many general issues, both political and personal. But Shakespeare does not specifically relate them to the situation at the time he was writing. Nor does he twist the facts so as to force his audience into an awareness of relationships with contemporary politics. This play is closer to history as Shakespeare knew it than most of his other plays about English history.

His main source was Raphael Holinshed's massive *Chronicles*, which had been first published in 1577 and of which Shakespeare used the second edition, of 1587. He may have been directly influenced too by an earlier chronicle, that by Edward Hall, first printed in 1548, which begins at precisely the same point as Shakespeare's play – the quarrel between Bolingbroke and Mowbray. Hall's overall scheme too seems to have influenced Shakespeare. It is revealed by Hall's full title: *The Union of the Two Noble and Illustre Families of Lancaster and York, being long in continual dissension for the crown of this noble realm, with all the acts done in both the times of the princes, both of the one lineage and of the other, beginning at the time of King Henry the Fourth, the first author of this division, and so successively proceeding to the reign of the high and prudent prince King Henry the Eight, the undubitate flower and very heir of both the said lineages.* If one wanted to produce a simplified description of Shakespeare's history plays as a group, it might read something like that.

Shakespeare seems to have worked hard to prepare himself to write this play. Oscar Wilde has the pleasant fancy that he looked carefully at Richard's tomb in Westminster Abbey where 'we can still discern on the King's robe his favourite badge – the sun issuing from a cloud'. Certainly Richard is often associated in the play with the sun. The correspondence between sun and king was commonplace. Still, Wilde's suggestion reminds us that more than books existed to stimulate Shakespeare's imagination. The influence of some writings that have been suggested as sources is doubtful, and not of the first importance to an understanding of the play itself. It is, for instance, conceivable that Shakespeare used two French chronicles, one in verse, Jean Créton's *Histoire du Roi d'Angleterre Richard II*, and the other an anonymous *Chronique de la Traïson et Mort de Richard Deux roi d'Angleterre*. Both existed only in manuscript in Shakespeare's time, but they were known in England. Shakespeare probably read Lord Berners's great translation of *The Chronicles of Sir John Froissart*, and may have been distantly influenced by it; he appears to have known an anonymous play that has survived only in a slightly incomplete manuscript and is generally known as *Woodstock*; and his last Act in particular seems to be coloured by memories of Samuel Daniel's long narrative poem *The First Four Books of the Civil Wars between the Two Houses of Lancaster and York*. This was published in 1595, and Shakespeare's play must have been written at about the same time. But unquestionably his main source of information was Holinshed's *Chronicles*, a compilation which drew heavily on the writings of earlier chroniclers and was for Shakespeare the obvious, most up-to-date reference book. The Commentary to this edition draws attention to some of the more interesting features of Shakespeare's use of his source material.

In his plays about British history of the comparatively recent past Shakespeare did not depart so freely from the chroniclers as he did in, for instance, *Macbeth* or *King Lear*. In dramatizing the reign of Richard II he followed Holinshed fairly closely, but even so he chose to use only the final pages of Holinshed's long account of the reign, and with that he took liberties. Harry Percy becomes younger and Prince Hal (who is referred to but does not appear) older than in reality; thus, whether consciously or not, Shakespeare prepares for their rivalry in *I Henry IV*. Queen Isabel too he transforms from the little girl that she really was at the time of the events of the play to a woman capable of full emotional sympathy with Richard's plight. He invents characters, especially ones whom he requires for symbolic effect such as the Welsh Captain (II.4) and the Gardeners (III.4). The attitudes that he takes towards the characters are not always the orthodox ones; he is more sympathetic with Richard in the later part of the play than most historians were.

Besides omitting much, Shakespeare creates a theatrical and verbal structure which tells its historical story in a manner that transcends particularity. *Richard II* is often spoken of in musical terms. This is an indication of the extent to which Shakespeare has turned actuality into art. There is something operatic about it. Actions are shaped into an intricate pattern, characters engage and conflict in significant ways, and they are given things to say and ways of saying them that create a greatly resonant structure of words and ideas so intricately inter-related that they play against and recall one another like the phrases in a complex piece of music.

In the first edition *Richard II*, like most of Shakespeare's plays, is printed continuously. The division into Acts and scenes was made in the Folio (1623), and we have no reason to believe that it has Shakespeare's authority. Structurally the major break

comes at the end of what editors have called III.1. The first part
of the play thus considered presents Richard rather unfavour-
ably, but also keeps us distanced from him. We watch him
performing his kingly functions, but are rarely conscious of
him as a man with feelings of his own. In his relationship to
John of Gaunt on the one hand, and to his favourites, Bushy,
Bagot, and Green, on the other, it is fair to see the influence of
the patterned structures of morality drama. All but Bagot are
dead at the end of the first part. With their departure Richard
emerges into full prominence as a dramatic character.

In the first line Richard addresses 'Old John of Gaunt, time-
honoured Lancaster', and this is suggestive of Gaunt's main
function. He is to represent values associated with the old
order, and Richard is to be judged partly by them. But though
Richard is on stage throughout the first scene, and as king
must be prominently placed, we are not told much about him.
He is only in the chair, as it were, exercising his official, public
function. He watches silent while the others speak: a situation
later to be notably reversed. When he speaks it is with formality.
Coleridge noted the display of 'that feature in Richard's character which is never forgotten throughout the play – his attention
to decorum and high feeling of the kingly dignity'. The actor
has to decide how far he should try to suggest Richard's true
personality under the kingly exterior. Richard's very inaction
can be turned to account. Benson played him here as a luxurious
lounger, caressing and feeding his hounds in bored indifference.
Gielgud has written that the actor 'must use the early scenes to
create an impression of slyness, petty vanity, and callous indifference'. Yet the quarrel between Bolingbroke and Mowbray is
about a matter in which the King is deeply implicated – the
murder of his uncle, Thomas of Woodstock, Duke of Gloucester. Some actors of Richard have silently conveyed consciousness of guilt, and fear that Mowbray may betray him. It has
been argued that the only reason Shakespeare did not write
these emotions into the play was that an Elizabethan audience,
familiar with history and its representation in *Woodstock*, would

have known full well that Richard was guilty; and also that it would not have needed to be told of his extravagant and pleasure-loving nature. This is possible, though it is by no means certain that Shakespeare could reasonably have expected such knowledge in his audience. There is no real evidence that *Woodstock* was ever performed, let alone printed. It is more likely that Shakespeare deliberately left the issue vague so that Richard would not be too much exposed to censure. In any case the accusation that Mowbray 'did plot the Duke of Glouces-ter's death', which might be interpreted as a covert accusation against the King, is only one of Bolingbroke's charges. The emphasis in this scene is on the quarrel itself, the enmity between Bolingbroke and Mowbray, and the ideas released as a result of it, rather than on the rights and wrongs of the case.

It is not until the second scene that characters in the play assert their belief in Richard's responsibility for the murder; and this scene, invented by Shakespeare, has the important function of consolidating John of Gaunt as a strongly virtuous character. The desire for vengeance expressed by Gloucester's widow is understandable, but her argument turns back upon itself, for the very stress she lays on the sanctity of Edward III's line justifies Gaunt's refusal to act: the King rules by divine authority, so his subjects have no right to judge him. Shakespeare departs from his sources here, for Holinshed records that Gaunt and York made proposals for revenge, and *Woodstock* shows them put into action. The audience is encour-aged to sympathize with Bolingbroke, both for his father's sake and because of the apparent justice of his charges against Mowbray as the King's agent, and this bias is maintained in the scene of the lists (1.3), in which again we see only the public side of Richard.

We are given our first glimpse of the private man in 1.4. Whereas thus far he has maintained a show of impartiality, seeming if anything to favour Bolingbroke rather than his accomplice Mowbray, now he reveals both scorn and fear of Bolingbroke and also some of the less admirable aspects of his own nature as both man and king. He admits that he has kept 'too great a court', and is cynically callous in his reactions to the news of his uncle Gaunt's illness. The measuring of Richard as a king against the standards represented by Gaunt reaches its climax in the scene in which Gaunt, dying, expresses his wish to counsel him. In Richard's absence his uncle, York, speaks contemptuously of his susceptibility to flattery, his vanity, and his self-will, and is answered by Gaunt in the best-known lines of the play, lines which help to justify the common assertion that England is herself one of the *dramatis personae*. They foretell Richard's impending downfall – 'His rash fierce blaze of riot cannot last' – set up an image of England as Gaunt feels it should be, and deplore what Richard is doing to his country. Gaunt's speech is a climax, and an eloquent one, giving full expression to one view of what a king should be able to accomplish.

Richard is not present to hear Gaunt; and the implied criticism of him is perhaps softened on his immediately following entry by York's emphasis on his youth. Yet Gaunt is highly critical of Richard to his face. His analogy between himself and Richard, claiming that 'Thy deathbed is no lesser than thy land', will be paralleled later in the play in the Gardener's likening of the land to an ill-tended garden. In a climax of anger Gaunt taxes Richard with Woodstock's murder, and goes off to his death. It is characteristic of the peace-loving York that, having defended Richard to Gaunt on the grounds of his youth, he should now defend Gaunt to Richard on the grounds of his sickness and age. Yet his patience is sorely taxed by Richard's confiscation of Gaunt's possessions, and he utters a dire warning that in violating the principle of inheritance Richard is denying the very principle by which he has come to the throne –

> *how art thou a king*
> *But by fair sequence and succession?*

Bolingbroke uses the same argument later (II.3.122–3).

In this section Shakespeare goes a long way towards alienating the audience's sympathies from Richard, and ii.i ends with severe criticism of him from those who favour Bolingbroke, mitigated only by Northumberland's attribution of some of the blame to Richard's favourites:

> *The King is not himself, but basely led*
> *By flatterers.*

The characterization of the favourites is slight. Either Shakespeare decided to leave much to his actors or he relied on his audience's preconceptions. In *Woodstock* the favourites are much more prominent and more obviously evil in their influence. At this low point in Richard's career the counter-action against him begins, as Bolingbroke's supporters in England learn from Northumberland of his plan to return, and agree to join him when he does so.

From then onwards sympathy with Richard is gradually built up, at first obliquely, in his absence. His Queen's grief and foreboding (ii.2) suggest a more attractive side to his character than we have seen so far, and this is balanced by a corresponding demonstration of less-than-admirable characteristics in Bolingbroke. He had left the play declaring himself 'a trueborn Englishman'. He returns accepting Northumberland's egregious flattery of his 'fair discourse' (ii.3.2–20), and diplomatically offering rewards in return for support (lines 45–50). York, overwhelmed by a 'tide of woes', epitomizes the moral dilemma out of which Shakespeare is making dramatic capital. York owes duty to both his nephews: to Richard as hereditary king, to Bolingbroke as one whom the King has wronged. In his encounter (ii.3) with Bolingbroke he berates him for breaking his exile and declares his own continued allegiance to Richard, saying that if his forces were strong enough he would arrest the rebels and compel them to submit; but in the next line he admits that as he is too weak to do this he will 'remain as neuter', and he follows this by inviting them to stay the night. Thus does the old order yield to the new. ii.4 is another scene of foreboding, and III.1, in which Bolingbroke seems already to have assumed royal power in his condemnation of Bushy and Green, throws on them much of the blame for Richard's irresponsibility.

The situation to this point is fully summed up in III.2, a scene of both recapitulation and realignment which marks the full emergence of Richard as the centre of dramatic attention in his double role of king and man. He has been off stage for 465 lines – more than one sixth of the whole play. So far we have seen him largely in his public role, with very little expression of his private feelings. He has been tested against a high ideal of kingship, and he has been found wanting. He has relied on the strength of his public position to compensate for private weaknesses which make him ill-fitted to hold that position. The weaknesses give some justification to the assumption of authority by Bolingbroke and his followers which we have watched during Richard's absence in Ireland. As Aumerle puts it:

> *we are too remiss,*
> *Whilst Bolingbroke through our security*
> *Grows strong and great in substance and in power.*
>
> III.2.33–5

Richard has been warned of the danger of his position, but has seemed confident in the security of his hereditary kingship. Now he expresses love for his country and confidence that she will take his part against rebellion. Now too just before the storm breaks he utters his strongest affirmation of the power of his public office, of the idea of kingship:

> *Not all the water in the rough rude sea*
> *Can wash the balm off from an anointed king.*
> *The breath of worldly men cannot depose*
> *The deputy elected by the Lord.*   III.2.54–7

He is to learn most painfully that the identification suggested here between the kingly office and the holder of that office is an illusion. Thoughts of the power of his name console him when Salisbury brings news that the Welshmen, believing him dead, have 'gone to Bolingbroke':

> *Arm, arm, my name! A puny subject strikes*
> *At thy great glory.*

But bad news continues to assail him, and believing himself betrayed by his favourites he compares them to Judas, implicitly initiating a comparison between himself and Christ which is to recur several times. Taking their cue from this, actors have often tried to suggest Christ in their make-up; but this surely is to take Richard too much at his own valuation. Learning that his favourites are dead he launches into the first of his great solo speeches (III.2.144–77), a meditation on mortality which gives classic expression to the theme of the vanity of human greatness. Richard is beginning to learn that the façade of kingship may offer inadequate shelter to the human being who dwells behind it.

Bestirred for a moment by Carlisle and Aumerle to the optimism of projected action, Richard is rapidly cast down again by Scroop's further revelation that even his uncle York has gone over to Bolingbroke, and he gives up hope of regaining his power.

> *Go to Flint Castle. There I'll pine away.*
> *A king, woe's slave, shall kingly woe obey.*
> *That power I have, discharge, and let them go*
> *To ear the land that hath some hope to grow;*
> *For I have none. Let no man speak again*
> *To alter this; for counsel is but vain.*

Though it is not heavily stressed, this might well be regarded as the true moment of Richard's capitulation. He gives way not to violence, not in direct confrontation with Bolingbroke, but to words; to the news that Scroop brings and his imaginings of what it may mean.

Words are important too at the beginning of the next scene.

Bolingbroke receives messages, and this leads into a quibbling
episode resulting from Northumberland's omission of the word
'King' in speaking of Richard. The quibbling might be considered trivial, yet it is related to a central concern of the play. On
one level kingship is no more than a verbal trick, a distinguishing of one man from his fellows by the addition of a prefix to
his name. Yet it can have other attributes too. In the previous
scene Richard's faith in the power of the mere idea of kingship
was affirmed, then tested, then destroyed. Now on his entry
both Bolingbroke and York are impressed by the majestic
appearance of kingship that he still retains.

> YORK
> Yet looks he like a king. Behold, his eye,
> As bright as is the eagle's, lightens forth
> Controlling majesty.

In appearance the man and his office are still at one. As in the
previous scene, Richard is given an affirmation of faith in the
power of his office. But now it seems a public statement rather
than an expression of personal belief. His actions are at variance
with his words. Having instructed Northumberland to tell
Bolingbroke

> That every stride he makes upon my land
> Is dangerous treason

he nevertheless capitulates to Bolingbroke's demand that his
rights shall be returned to him. An aside to Aumerle shows
that, behaving like this, he seems far less kingly to himself than
he had to York:

> We do debase ourselves, cousin, do we not,
> To look so poorly and to speak so fair?

Aumerle counsels him still to rely on the power of words:

> Let's fight with gentle words
> Till time lend friends, and friends their helpful swords.

Richard's consciousness of the division within himself between the actor and the role finds expression along with his chagrin that he has had to acquiesce in Bolingbroke's illegal return from banishment:

> *O that I were as great*
> *As is my grief, or lesser than my name.*

And in fearful expectation that he will have to give up the throne be envisages a new role for himself:

> *I'll give my jewels for a set of beads,*
> *My gorgeous palace for a hermitage,*
> *My gay apparel for an almsman's gown,*
> *My figured goblets for a dish of wood,*
> *My sceptre for a palmer's walking-staff,*
> *My subjects for a pair of carvèd saints,*
> *And my large kingdom for a little grave,*
> *A little, little grave, an obscure grave . . .*

They are marvellous lines, marvellous partly because they express the possibility of consolation as well as the experience of despair. To emphasize the first element of each antithesis falsifies the picture. Richard imagines himself renouncing the kingly way of life, with all its obvious attractions, for another that might be held to be better still. The austerities that he envisages are those associated with the way to the kingdom of heaven. That he will be able to embrace them is unfortunately yet another of his illusions. Sir John Gielgud has demonstrated how moving the speech can be, yet he has written too of Richard's 'utter lack of humour and his constant egotism and self-posturing', qualities that are felt in this speech as he elaborates his fantasy of grief till it is in danger of seeming ludicrous:

> *Well, well, I see*
> *I talk but idly, and you laugh at me.*

He recovers enough to make his splendid comparison of his

own descent to that of the falling sun-god, an imaginative vision quite beyond the capacities of his enemies, who think he speaks 'fondly, like a frantic man'. Nevertheless they pay him the homage of their knees, and he ends the scene, as he had begun it, with external dignity but, we feel, greater consciousness of emptiness within.

Our direct view of Richard's progress is interrupted by a scene of comment and expansion which invites us to consider the public implications of his plight. This is the garden scene, invented by Shakespeare and clearly symbolic in function. The Queen's grief maintains an overall emphasis of the play (see page 33). And her personal grief is a prologue to the generalized comments of the Gardeners. These characters are liable to suffer in the theatre from the fact that *Richard II* contains little comedy, some of which is uncertain in execution and as a consequence often omitted in performance. There is a temptation to remedy the deficiency by playing the Gardeners for low comedy, giving them heavily rustic accents and exaggeratedly personal characteristics which put them in the same world as the grave-diggers in *Hamlet*. This is unjustified, and unnecessarily emphasizes Shakespeare's purposeful departure from decorum in giving highly wrought language to characters of lowly rank. The stylization of the action calls for equally stylized presentation. The scene is as obvious in its artifice as the one in *3 Henry VI* when King Henry expresses grief as intense as that of Richard's Queen, and hears the plaints of a father who has killed his son and a son who has killed his father. There, as here, the emblematic predominates over the natural. The fact that these men are gardeners is itself part of the metaphor that Shakespeare employs also in their language, and the absence from their presentation of individualizing characteristics should cause us to respect what they say as general truth rather than idiosyncratic comment. At various points in the play England has been compared to a garden, and now the image is fully extended and developed. The servant's summary of the distressed state of the country resembles John of Gaunt's plaint

(II.1.31–68), and again the responsibility is shown to be Richard's. But while Gaunt spoke as a prophet, grieving over what was likely to happen, the Gardeners speak with pitiful regret of an irremediable state of affairs. Richard's 'rash fierce blaze of riot' has burnt itself out, and the Gardener rebukes his man for harshness, demanding sympathy for the King, who though he

> *suffered this disordered spring*
> *Hath now himself met with the fall of leaf*

His favourites, those 'caterpillars of the commonwealth' (II.3.165), are dead, and

> *Bolingbroke*
> *Hath seized the wasteful King.*

As a king, Richard is blamed for his failure to govern his country as conscientiously as these men tend their garden, and especially for his failure to control his nobles; but as a man he is pitied for his suffering. The Queen's imagery as she rebukes the Gardener for the harshness of his news extends the imaginative scope of the scene still further. As 'old Adam's likeness' (line 73) the Gardener is tending the Garden of Eden, and Richard's fate is 'a second Fall of cursèd man'. Whereas the Queen's grief expresses itself in bitterness, the Gardener, less personally involved, maintains in face of her rebukes the tender compassion that he had expressed for Richard.

The fourth Act begins with one of the play's less satisfactory episodes, though one which has its place in the overall design. Bolingbroke reopens the question of responsibility for Gloucester's death. We may wonder why he should permit suspicion of Aumerle to be entertained considering that he had been so vehement in accusing Mowbray of the same crime. A more serious fault results from the compression that Shakespeare has exercised on his historical material. Events that took place over several months have been conflated and patterned in a manner that is obviously intentional but liable to seem over-stylized. The scene would have most chance of succeeding if it were consciously played as an elaborate ritual; but as one lord after another throws down his gage the situation is in danger of becoming ludicrous. Conceivably the humour is deliberate, suggesting a decline in the dignity of the monarchy as an inevitable consequence of usurpation; but it is not easy to see how this could be conveyed in the theatre. There is a hint that the problem may have arisen in Shakespeare's day in the fact that the final challenge, that of the anonymous lord, was omitted from the Folio text. In performance the episode has generally been omitted or curtailed.

Richard II is at no point a play of clear-cut moral issues. Though we sympathize with Richard, it is not because we feel him to be wholly virtuous; and though we may condemn Bolingbroke, we cannot deny his many good qualities. Bolingbroke, having already declared that he will recall his enemy, Mowbray, from banishment, is allowed another display of magnanimity on the report of Mowbray's death. Shakespeare is careful to give us no excuse for adopting an over-simple attitude. Bolingbroke is moving acceptably towards the throne. He is seen to lack no qualification for the royal office except hereditary right. This, though intangible, seems supremely important to the Bishop of Carlisle, who fiercely demonstrates the strength of his feelings about it (IV.1.114–49), and thus acts as a spokesman for the traditional values. As in the scene of Richard's return from Ireland, and the one at Flint Castle, a strong statement of faith in regality is the prelude to a demonstration of its vulnerability; but this time the statement does not come from the holder of the office. Carlisle speaks with the authority of the Church and the force of one who feels impelled to proclaim his commitment to beliefs so dangerous that he is arrested on a charge of treason immediately after expressing them. As Gaunt prophesied disaster that would result from Richard's folly, so now Carlisle prophesies disaster that will result from Bolingbroke's deposition of Richard. His speech is appropriate here, but looks forward too to the events portrayed in the later plays about Bolingbroke as Henry IV.

The episode of abdication is another one in which action is suspended while a situation is explored in depth, a scene of retrospection, summary, and expansion. The technique is operatic, Richard holding the centre of the stage in what is virtually a solo *scena*. When he enters this time it is his private, not his public self that he struggles to define and assert in a difficult and bitterly painful process of re-education. He is the deviser, director, and central performer in the rite of renunciation which forms an emotional climax to the play. The first formality is his cry of 'God save the King!', to which he receives no reply – understandably, since none of the onlookers can be sure to whom he refers. Then he takes the crown and uses it symbolically to illustrate the reversal of fortunes that has brought about the present situation. Responsibility is being transferred from him to Bolingbroke; yet the passing from Richard of the cares associated with the crown does not leave him free from care. The complications of the situation are expressed in wordplay and paradox ('Ay, no. No, ay . . .') suggestive of a tension created by the opposition of equal pressures. It finds release in the movement from a complex style expressive of dilemma to a fluent series of simple one-line sentences as Richard resolves the situation and gives up the last remnants of regality. His public façade is crumbling away and he fears that soon he will have nothing and be nothing. He can look forward only to 'an earthy pit'. Though he can still accuse his enemies of heinous crime, and again compares himself to Christ by referring to the silent onlookers as Pilates who 'Have here delivered me to my sour cross', yet he acknowledges treachery on his own part, too, when (using an antithesis that occurs frequently in the play) he says:

> *I have given here my soul's consent,*
> *To'undeck the pompous body of a king.*

He lacks even a name, and, as another property of the rite, calls for a looking-glass as if to assure himself that his appearance at least still exists. In his grief he acknowledges sin (line 274) and

meditates on the discrepancy between his still-glorious appearance and the wretchedness of his state. As he casts the glass
down he shatters the last remaining pretensions and unrealities
of kingship. The true reality 'lies all within'; his laments are
mere reflections of

> *the unseen grief*
> *That swells with silence in the tortured soul.*

'There' (paradoxically) 'lies the substance.' The only boon he
seeks is to be permitted to leave Bolingbroke's presence. The
episode after his departure forms a structural parallel to that at
the end of II.1. There, Richard's harshness to Gaunt provoked
plans for rebellion against him; now Bolingbroke's harshness
to him provokes plans for a rebellion on his behalf.

The Queen's subsequent appearance (v.1) shows the reluc-
tance of the person most associated with Richard's private life
to accept the change in his public station. She clings to the idea
of Richard as king; unkinged, he is only a shell – 'tomb' and
'inn' are the images she uses – housing his grief. But Richard
has progressed enough in self-knowledge to tell her that she is
still living a dream:

> *Learn, good soul,*
> *To think our former state a happy dream,*
> *From which awaked the truth of what we are*
> *Shows us but this. I am sworn brother, sweet,*
> *To grim Necessity, and he and I*
> *Will keep a league till death.*

Acknowledging sin, he returns to the imagery of the religious
way of life in which he had envisaged his deposition:

> *Our holy lives must win a new world's crown*
> *Which our profane hours here have thrown down.*

He is himself permitted a prophecy. Rebuking Northumberland
for his share in the rebellion he prophesies strife between the
allies, and counter-rebellion. In a passage of great formality, yet

also of grace and tenderness, he parts in grief from his Queen.

The closing episodes emphasize Richard's grief and the pity that it evokes in others far more strongly than the faults in his past way of life. Nevertheless the change in the political situation is one that his countrymen must recognize. The Duke of York, uncle of both Richard and Bolingbroke, gives a most sympathetic account of Richard's entry into London, pitying his grief and admiring the patience with which he endured his humiliation. But just as John of Gaunt had refused to try to take vengeance on Richard for the murder of Gloucester – 'God's is the quarrel' (1.2.37) – so York believes that 'heaven hath a hand in these events' (v.2.37), with the result that he now owes duty to the new king. He has accepted the change in the *status quo*. But his son has not. On discovering the conspiracy, in which Aumerle is involved, to assassinate Bolingbroke he does not hesitate to act in accordance with his duty to the new king rather than to his family. Understandably his wife takes the more personal point of view, and the conflict is worked out in a scene which, like that of the gages (iv.1), is uneasily balanced between the serious and the comic. Until recently it has generally been omitted in performance, though it can be defended as having definable functions in the play's economy.

York is the nearest approach to a comic character in *Richard II*. He is potentially amusing because of his vacillations, his inability in the early part of the play to reconcile his disapproval of Richard's conduct with his respect for the office of king, his feeling of the injustice done to Bolingbroke with condemnation of the wrong he has committed in usurping the throne. In the later scenes the completeness of York's transference of loyalty to the usurper, which prompts him not simply to inform on his own son but actively to plead against Bolingbroke's offer to forgive Aumerle, also has within it the seeds of comedy. Yet he is the mouthpiece of serious thoughts and the upholder of high ideals, touching in his refusal to be shaken when he feels himself to be in the right. Undoubtedly Shakespeare was aware

of the possibility of comic effect, and at times deliberately
cultivated it. But it is difficult to feel that he has completely
succeeded in fusing the serious and the comic so that they
emerge as different aspects of the same, rounded character. Sir
John Gielgud has written: 'The character of York, used by
Shakespeare as a kind of wavering chorus throughout the play,
touching yet sometimes absurd, can be of great value, provided
that the actor and director can contrive between them a tactful
compromise between comedy and dramatic effect.' The problem
is most acute in the episode of Aumerle's conspiracy. The
sequence of knockings at Bolingbroke's door as first Aumerle
comes to confess and beg forgiveness, then York arrives to
urge that his son should be punished, then the Duchess of
York to beg that he should be forgiven, becomes ludicrous, as
Bolingbroke himself recognizes:

> *Our scene is altered from a serious thing,*
> *And now changed to 'The Beggar and the King'.*
>
> v.3.78–9

The kneeling competition that follows, as each visitor presses
his case, has the same kind of mechanistic over-patterning as
afflicts the episode of the gages. Even Bolingbroke is apt to
seem comically ineffective as he fails on three separate attempts
to persuade his aunt to rise from her knees.

Nevertheless, there are good reasons for performing the
scene if actors can find a satisfactory mode of playing it. As
early as 1773 George Steevens wrote to Garrick: 'If you revive
King Richard, I beg that proper regard may be paid to old *puss
in boots*, who arrives so hastily in the fifth act.' Why he was so
anxious to see him he does not make clear. Granville Barker
disapproved of Gielgud's omission of the episode, 'the dramatic
point of which is merely that it is a swift and excited interlude
between the *slow* . . . farewell between Richard and the Queen
and the slow, philosophical death scene'. The Duchess's assertions that her husband's 'words come from his mouth, ours
from our breast' (v.3.101), and her emphasis on the power of a

king's words, though they may seem like trivial quibbling, maintain a recurrent concern of the play (see page 34). And the actor playing Bolingbroke may well be anxious for the scene to be retained, since even if it does put the character in danger of seeming ridiculously ineffective in his dealings with his cousin, his uncle, and his aunt, at a more public level he is eventually given the opportunity to behave mercifully to Aumerle and to voice his determination to have the other rebels killed.

Though Richard speaks often and at length about himself during the course of the play, it is not until his final appearance (v.5) that we see him alone. So far his meditations have all been conducted in public, and with at least some consciousness of his audience. Now, in the imposed solitude of his prison cell, stripped of his office and all its trappings, he utters his only real soliloquy. With no audience, he has no role to play. Only he has to try to define his real self. He has thoughts of religious salvation, but counter-thoughts of the difficulty of attaining it. He thinks of escape, but recognizes his folly. He considers resignation to his fate, and in this thought finds 'a kind of ease'. Bolingbroke, going into exile, had refused even to try to use his imagination to lighten his suffering; Richard makes a great effort to do so. Yet none of the roles in which he casts himself can content him, for each carries its anti-type along with it. The discovery that even the role of king is one from which he could be dislodged has made him feel that contentment can come only with oblivion:

> But whate'er I be,
> Nor I, nor any man that but man is,
> With nothing shall be pleased till he be eased
> With being nothing.

These lines suggest a hard-won acceptance of the fact of death, and this, along with the process of painful self-investigation that has led up to it, is characteristic of Shakespeare's tragic heroes. Richard II is sometimes said not to be truly 'tragic'. No one would deny that he is pathetic, but some find him ultimately inadequate in stature. Admittedly he lacks the grandeur revealed by Macbeth in his final defiance of his fate, or the sublimity of King Lear in the last stages of his purgatorial journey. It may be felt that he has not learned enough as the result of his sufferings. But perhaps there is something about the manner in which he faces death that may justly increase our respect for him. Shakespeare was limited by history. Our feelings about Richard's stature are likely to depend not so much on what he does as on sentiments such as those he expresses in his parting with his Queen (see page 24), and still more on our response to the style of his final speeches and the relationship of this style to that which he has employed previously. It is a concentrated style, luxuriant no longer. It suggests a man facing up to reality, trying to encompass it with his imagination, even though he is powerless to change it. There is a toughness about Richard's language in his last scene; he speaks like one who has come through suffering rather than been overcome by it.

Nevertheless, in Richard's soliloquy, as in so much of the play, Shakespeare is working in a heavily stylized mode. The cast of the speech itself is consciously artificial. Its opening lines draw attention to the metaphorical technique – 'I have been studying how I may compare . . .' The style is not wholly externalized, for mental effort on Richard's part is strongly suggested – 'Yet I'll hammer it out'; but he does not speak with the approach to real speech patterns characteristic of Hamlet's soliloquies and adumbrated in, for instance, the Nurse's speech of recollection in *Romeo and Juliet* (1.3.17–49). Unrealistic too is the interruption of Richard's meditation by the sound of music. Clearly we are here in the world of imagination and symbol rather than reality. The music is part of the dramatic metaphor just as the garden has been. For Shakespeare's audience the music was perhaps more obviously symbolic of the kind of order violated both by Richard's irresponsibility and by his deposition than it is liable to be for us. Hearing it Richard immediately puts it to metaphorical use, meditating on the paradox that he can discern harmonic inequalities though he was unable to notice the discrepancy between his behaviour and his office. Retrospectively he remarks and laments his own failure. Once, shortening the period of Bolingbroke's exile, he had seemed to have time under his command:

BOLINGBROKE

> How long a time lies in one little word!
> Four lagging winters and four wanton springs
> End in a word – such is the breath of kings.   1.3.213–15

Even then, in response to his 'Why, uncle, thou hast many years to live', Gaunt had replied 'But not a minute, King, that thou canst give' (1.3.225–6). Now time is catching up with him. 'I wasted time, and now doth time waste me –' (v.5.49). Bolingbroke has taken over from him, usurping his time, and 'I stand fooling here, his jack of the clock' (line 60). The idea seems to be that when a man is in tune with his office, when the actor is fulfilling his role, when the public and the private functions coincide, then he is in tune with his time; otherwise 'The time is out of joint' (*Hamlet*, 1.5.189) and life runs to waste.

But consolations remain. Richard explains away the music as a sign of love to him. (Could Shakespeare have been recalling Richard I's minstrel, Blondel, singing to his imprisoned master?) The final twist of pathos occurs with the entrance of the Groom, who has with difficulty got permission to visit his former master, but who saddens him with the tale of how Richard's horse carried Bolingbroke to his coronation. Life goes on. The horse has changed allegiance as York has. Barbary too is made to carry symbolic significance as Richard compares himself to an animal, 'Spurred, galled, and tired by jauncing Bolingbroke' (v.5.94). The end is near, and comes in the play's solitary episode of violence as Richard resists his attackers, kills some of them, but dies with a last assertion of regality and a commitment to the values of the soul over the body:

> *Exton, thy fierce hand*
> *Hath with the King's blood stained the King's own land.*
> *Mount, mount, my soul. Thy seat is up on high,*
> *Whilst my gross flesh sinks downward here to die.*

In the last scene Shakespeare seems simply to be conscientiously tidying things up. The rebellion against Bolingbroke is quelled, he is established in the throne, promises rewards to his helpers, is merciful to the Bishop of Carlisle, and expresses regret at the death of his chief enemy. The tone at the end is one of grief, not triumph. Bolingbroke is, as Richard had prophesied, assuming the cares of kingship, and his last lines foreshadow the care-laden and penitent usurper who is to be at the centre of the next two plays of the history cycle.

So far we have been concerned mainly with the characters of *Richard II* and their actions. Even so, comment on their language has been unavoidable. We cannot finally distinguish between what someone is and what he says, since it is largely through what he says that we receive our impression of what he is. And in this play nuances of speech, the vocabulary, syntax, and imagery through which the characters express themselves, are of unusual importance. So too are the sentiments that they voice over and above the statements required to delineate the situation. From time to time action is suspended to allow for verbal expansion of the situation. This happens in the deposition scene, the play's most generally admired episode. Its omission from the early quartos, usually attributed to censorship, has also been defended on the grounds that it is dramatically redundant. But this is mistaken; the technique Shakespeare adopted is not, in his hands, undramatic. Movement can be of the mind as well as of the body. The actor playing Richard can hold and sway his audience as effectively in his meditations as in his more active moments.

The fact that Richard talks so eloquently about himself has caused him frequently to be spoken of as a poet. If one is a poet because one speaks verse, then all the characters in this play are poets. The poetry Richard speaks is of course Shakespeare's, not Richard's. Yet it is fair to call him poetic in temperament in that he is portrayed as a man of strong imagination who needs to put suffering into words, and who is intensely conscious of the power of words, though also of their ultimate inadequacy. In this he is strongly contrasted with Bolingbroke, who throughout is seen more than heard, and whose realistic attitude towards the imagination is made explicit in the scene of his banishment (1.3.294–303). Verbally *Richard II* is both immensely complex and unusually self-conscious. Its complexity might fairly be called inexhaustible. Many studies have been written of the patterns formed by the interrelationships and echoes of words and the ideas that they express, but even the subtlest and fullest of them do not succeed in capturing all the play's elusive harmonies and revealing all the strains in its counterpoint. There are too many overtones, too many latent patterns of sense and sound in what has been called the play's 'symphonic imagery'. But it may be worth drawing attention to a few of the dominant images, and suggesting a view of their functions.

Richard II is about men. Women are shown only in relation to them. And the men are seen almost exclusively in relation to public life. Almost all are noblemen, deeply concerned with affairs of state. We hear something of the common people, see practically nothing of them. The Queen's ladies are lay figures; the Gardeners, highly symbolic. The Groom (v.5) gives a hint of the loyalty that some of the common people felt for their King, but his role is tiny. There is no attempt to give a sense of the ordinary life of the country through figures such as the frequenters of the Boar's Head Tavern in the *Henry IV* plays. Neither Richard nor Bolingbroke feels such concern for his meanest subjects as Henry V evinces in especially the night scene before Agincourt. This may represent a deliberate design on Shakespeare's part, *Richard II* looking back to a formal, medieval class structure. However this may be, England is not absent from *Richard II*. Richard is conscious of responsibility to his country, and others (notably Gaunt in his great panegyric) blame him for neglecting it; but the country, instead of being represented by a variety of members of the commonwealth, is brought to our consciousness rather through references to it as a living being, or as something of natural purity which is in danger of being stained, most horribly by the blood of those who have been brought up in it. Richard speaks thus of it before banishing Bolingbroke and Mowbray (I.3.125–43). Bolingbroke, in the challenge he sends to Richard through Northumberland, threatens the bloodstains that Richard tried to avert (III.3.42–50). Richard threatens the same result if Bolingbroke persists in his insurrection (III.3.93–100). Carlisle prophesies similar horror in later times as the result of the deposition (IV.1.136–47). The image finds forceful use in Richard's dying speech:

> *Exton, thy fierce hand*
> *Hath with the King's blood stained the King's own land.*

And finally Bolingbroke regrets that 'blood should sprinkle me to make me grow' (V.6.46) – an image which he is to recall in the fifth and sixth lines of *I Henry IV*:

> *No more the thirsty entrance of this soil*
> *Shall daub her lips with her own children's blood.*

Richard's feeling for his land as a sentient being, capable of taking his part against his enemies, is fully expressed on his return from Ireland (III.2.4–26). In the great speech in which he envisages his own overthrow (III.3.143–75) the land is the source of his glory, his 'large kingdom', and also one day will easily swallow him up into 'a little grave'. The tension created between an imaginative man's awareness of his possibilities and the knowledge that sooner or later he will be no more than dust is a source of great poetic power, and the image of the land over which Richard now holds sway but in which before long he will be buried while the subjects 'hourly trample on their sovereign's head' embraces both the glory and the pathos of kingship, elsewhere polarized in images such as the crown and the skull, the soul and the body. The land has continuity; so does the nation; so does the office of king; but the King himself is a mortal man.

In the speech just referred to, Richard says that Aumerle and he will weep themselves graves. As the land receives the blood of those who fight on it, so it receives also the tears of those who grieve. Tears are another recurrent image, and the vocabulary of grief helps to form the play's dominant emotional tone. Indeed the language almost creates of grief a dramatic character associated especially, though by no means exclusively, with the women. The Duchess of Gloucester initiates this emphasis in 1.2 as she speaks of 'her companion, grief' (line 55), discourses on grief and sorrow, creates an image of herself as a desolate person in a derelict building, and departs weeping. This is the first of the play's many sad partings. The next, between Gaunt and his exiled son, also makes much of the grief of the parted. Bolingbroke will be able to

> *boast of nothing else*
> *But that I was a journeyman to grief.*   1.3.273–4

Dying, Gaunt complains:

> *Within me grief hath kept a tedious fast.*   II.1.75

The first episode in which the Queen is prominent (II.2.1–76) is an extended meditation on the grief that she entertains as the result of parting from Richard and the sorrow she feels to be approaching. Indeed, the imagery here goes through a process of bringing grief to birth: Isabel imagines an 'unborn sorrow' in 'fortune's womb', speaks of a grief which 'nothing hath begot', and, hearing that Bolingbroke has landed, gives birth to her woe. Green, the bringer of the news, is the midwife, and Bolingbroke the offspring of her sorrow (II.2.62–6). Thus, for her, grief is firmly identified with Bolingbroke's usurpation of her husband's place.

Shakespeare is labouring to create a sense of foreboding and imminent tragedy, increased by the bad news that the Queen receives of the desertion of Richard's supporters. When York hears of the Duchess of Gloucester's death he justly exclaims:

> *what a tide of woes*
> *Comēs rushing on this woeful land at once*

II.2.98–9

Richard's reunion with his country releases tears that are for once of joy (III.2.4), but the sequence of bad news that he receives culminates in his great expression of grief (lines 144–77). The Queen sustains the tone in the episode with her ladies and the Gardeners, and Richard's grief reaches its eloquent climax in the deposition scene, through which chime the words 'tears', 'sorrow', 'grief', and 'woe', as they do through the subsequent parting of Richard from his Queen. The scenes of Aumerle's conspiracy give some respite from the prevailing woefulness, and although Richard in prison is undoubtedly a grieving figure, speaking of his sighs, tears, and groans (v.5.51–8), he is far less indulgent in his grief than he had previously been. The effort at intellectual control displayed in his soliloquy may help us to feel that he has passed through the lachrymose to a more stoical and a nobler frame of mind. At the end of the play it is Bolingbroke's soul that is 'full of woe' (v.6.45), and he is grieving that (in another of the play's dominant images) 'blood should sprinkle me to make me grow'.

Richard's awareness of the power of words, and of his own dependence on them, is one of the many manifestations in this play of a direct concern with the functions of language. It was remarked earlier (page 17) that Richard capitulates to words, not deeds. This aspect of the action finds correspondences in details of the language. In the episode of Mowbray's banishment the emphasis on words is so strong that the word 'sentence' acquires the force of a pun, referring equally to the banishment and the fact that it is expressed in words. Mowbray's reaction takes the form of a lament that his native language and his skill in it are now of no use to him. Richard's 'sentence' means, paradoxically, 'speechless death' – Mowbray will be as good as dead because deprived of the use of his tongue. Just as he sees himself, in a country whose language he does not speak, as 'an unstringed viol or a harp' (I.I.162), so Northumberland reporting Gaunt's death says 'His tongue is now a stringless instrument' (II.I.149). 'Tongue' becomes a key-word, and is often paired with 'heart' in references to the possible disjunction between what men mean and what they say. Aumerle in his account of his parting from Bolingbroke says that his heart prevented his tongue from profaning the word 'farewell' (though he admits to having acted the hypocrite by assuming a false appearance of grief); however, if the word had had power to lengthen Bolingbroke's exile he would have used 'a volume of farewells' (I.4.18). Ross, doubtful whether to reveal his opinion of Richard's actions, fears that his heart

> must break with silence
> Ere't be disturbed with a liberal tongue . . .
>
> II.1.228–9

The Duchess of York, trying to defend her son against her husband's accusations, claims that York's 'words come from his mouth, ours from our breast' (v.3.101). And Richard's faithful Groom, as he leaves his master, declares 'What my tongue dares not, that my heart shall say' (v.5.97). The truest sympathy may find no expression.

Aumerle's rebellious regret that his words could not lengthen Bolingbroke's exile recalls and sets in relief Bolingbroke's exclamation at the moment when Richard shortened the period of his exile:

> How long a time lies in one little word!
> Four lagging winters and four wanton springs
> End in a word – such is the breath of kings.
>
> I.3.213–15

Yet even then the limitations of the King's power had been pointed out. Though Richard can shorten Bolingbroke's exile, and Gaunt's lifetime, he cannot give life; he may urge time on, but cannot stop its progress:

> *Thou canst help time to furrow me with age,*
> *But stop no wrinkle in his pilgrimage.*

> I.3.229–30

And though the King's words are powerful, they may be constrained, so that before long Richard is regretting

> *that e'er this tongue of mine,*
> *That laid the sentence of dread banishment*
> *On you proud man, should take it off again*
> *With words of sooth!*

> III.3.133–6

He himself has to rely on other men's words, such as the oaths that Mowbray and Bolingbroke swear on their banishment (I.3.178–92); and oaths may be broken. So Richard complains bitterly of Northumberland's 'cracking the strong warrant of an oath', an offence that is 'Marked with a blot, damned in the book of heaven' (IV.1.234–5). And he may be deceived by false words, the flattery of his favourites, the 'praises', 'lascivious metres', 'report of fashions' which, York complains, are 'buzzed into his ears' (II.1.17–26).

It is easy – and fashionable – to claim of many works of literature that they are in some sense 'about' language, that the true concern of the artefact is the art that has created it rather than the events and ideas that form its ostensible subject matter. We may be sceptical of the more extreme manifestations of this tendency, but it is hard to deny that within the texture of *Richard II* there lies a sense of life as a fiction which, while it may be regarded on one level as a natural metaphor for the characters to employ, is likely also to make us reflect upon the relationship between reality and art, and thus to distance us somewhat from the events of the play, expanding them from the representational to the emblematic. The dying John of Gaunt hopes that his 'death's sad tale' may convey more of the truth to Richard than his 'life's counsel' has done. In his despair, Richard wishes to

> sit upon the ground
> And tell sad stories of the death of kings.
>
> III.2.155–6

In the examples that he gives he recalls the chronicled lives and deaths of earlier kings, so that we have a sense of him, too, as one of the many who have receded from life into history or – like him – into a play, with his 'little scene' in which to monarchize. It is a speech which (like some of Shakespeare's epilogues) might almost be spoken by the actor in his own person rather than the character he is representing.

   In the abdication scene Richard speaks of himself as

> the very book indeed
> Where all my sins are writ   IV.1.273–4

and after his fall he envisages himself as the central figure of a 'lamentable tale' that his Queen will tell by the fireside 'In winter's tedious nights' (v.1.40). His tale will be sadder than all the others that have been told, so that even the

> senseless brands will sympathize
> The heavy accent of thy moving tongue,
> And in compassion weep the fire out;
> And some will mourn in ashes, some coal-black,
> For the deposing of a rightful king.

And just after he has died his murderer admits that 'this deed is chronicled in hell' (v.5.116). The notion of Richard's life as a tale in a chronicle – where Shakespeare found it – does something to lessen the pain of the story, and may relate too to the old, poignant, but consoling notion that the life of this world is a fiction, heavenly life the only reality. In a famous lyric which is part of his play *Summer's Last Will and Testament*, performed at about the same date as *Richard II*, Thomas Nashe wrote:

> *Heaven is our heritage*
> *Earth but a player's stage.*

Shakespeare lays less emphasis on the reality of the heavenly
life; but Richard, in renouncing his kingdom for 'a little grave',
in seeing his life as 'a little scene' from which the figure of
Death, like a character in a morality play, will soon remove
him, and in his final declaration that his soul's seat is up on
high', gives expression to the old enduring theme of the
transience of human glory and worldly beauty, a theme which
pervades the whole play, linking it in subject matter as well as
manner to a central tradition of lyrical verse.

Further Reading

Texts and Sources

The most comprehensive edition of *Richard II* is Matthew W. Black's in the New Variorum series (1955). The present edition is deeply indebted to it, and also to Peter Ure's new Arden edition (1956). John Dover Wilson's New Cambridge edition (1938) has an original introduction and useful notes. All these editions, especially Black's, include valuable summaries of earlier work on the play. W. W. Greg prepared a photographic facsimile of the first Quarto which has been issued with an introduction by Charlton Hinman (Shakespeare Quarto Facsimiles No. 13, Oxford, 1966). The most important study of the text is in *King Richard II: A New Quarto*, facsimile edition with an introduction by A. W. Pollard (1916). More recent work supplementing this includes Richard E. Hasker's 'The Copy for the First Folio *Richard II*' (*Studies in Bibliography*, 5, 1953) and Peter Ure's Introduction. Other helpful editions are Matthew W. Black's for the Pelican Shakespeare (1957) and Kenneth Muir's for the Signet Shakespeare (1963).

The sources of the play present complex problems which editors have discussed at length. Black and Ure reprint relevant passages, as does Geoffrey Bullough in *Narrative and Dramatic Sources of Shakespeare*, Volume 3 (1960), which also includes a carefully considered essay. In 'The Sources of Shakespeare's *Richard II*' (*Joseph Quincy Adams Memorial Studies*, edited by J. G. McManaway, Giles E. Dawson, and Edwin E. Willoughby, Washington, 1948) Matthew W. Black challenges Dover Wilson's argument that Shakespeare was dependent on an earlier play, and argues that he used multiple sources.

The standard edition of *Woodstock* is A. P. Rossiter's (1946);

the play is conveniently reprinted in *Elizabethan History Plays*, edited by William A. Armstrong (World's Classics, 1965). The historical background is helpfully expounded in Peter Saccio's *Shakespeare's English Kings* (1977).

Criticism

The most important early critic of *Richard II* is S. T. Coleridge, who was especially concerned with the character of Richard himself. His writings are reprinted in *Coleridge's Shakespearean Criticism*, edited by T. M. Raysor (1930; Everyman's Library, 1960). Part of Walter Pater's well-known essay from *Appreciations* (1889) is reprinted in the Signet edition. There are, of course, sections on the play in the many books concerned generally with Shakespeare's histories. E. M. W. Tillyard in his helpful and influential *Shakespeare's History Plays* (1944; Penguin Books, 1962) stressed the 'essential medievalism' of *Richard II* and its links with the other history plays. *Shakespeare's 'Histories': Mirrors of Elizabethan Policy* (San Marino, 1947) by Lily B. Campbell includes an excellent study of the play against the historical and political background of the last ten years of Elizabeth's reign. Irving Ribner's *The English History Play in the Age of Shakespeare* (1957, revised 1965) offers a sound survey with emphasis on its historical rather than literary and theatrical aspects. John Palmer writes about the play in *Political Characters of Shakespeare* (1945).

A. R. Humphreys's *Richard II* (Arnold's Studies in English Literature No. 31, 1967) is a thorough and sound critical guide. There is a fine chapter on the ideas of the play in Ernst H. Kantorowicz's *The King's Two Bodies: A Study in Medieval Political Theology* (Princeton, 1957). A. P. Rossiter has a characteristically idiosyncratic essay in *Angel With Horns* (1961).

A number of critics have concentrated on the play's style and language. They include W. H. Clemen in *The Development of Shakespeare's Imagery* (1951), M. M. Mahood in a perceptive chapter of *Shakespeare's Wordplay* (1957), R. D. Altick in his excellent article 'Symphonic Imagery in *Richard II*' (*Publications of the Modern Language Association of America*, 62, 1947; reprinted in the Signet edition), Winifred Nowottny in a brief but pithy discussion of Richard's soliloquy in *The Language Poets Use* (1962), and R. F. Hill in 'Dramatic Techniques and Interpretation in *Richard II*' (*Early Shakespeare*, Stratford-upon-Avon Studies 3, 1961), interesting as a discussion of the limitations of the rhetorical mode. Nicholas Brooke's *Richard II: A Casebook* (1973) is an admirable selection of writings on the play, reprinting (in full or in part) those by Coleridge, Pater, Tillyard, Kantorowicz, Mahood, and Rossiter mentioned above, and those by Montague and Gielgud mentioned below.

Stage History

Harold Child sketches the stage history in the New Cambridge edition. A. C. Sprague has a valuable chapter in *Shakespeare's Histories: Plays for the Stage* (1964). On particular productions, C. E. Montague's review of F. R. Benson's performance is in A. W. Ward's anthology *Specimens of English Dramatic Criticism* (World's Classics, 1945), and the play is discussed in *Shakespeare's Histories at Stratford, 1951* by John Dover Wilson and T. C. Worsley (1952). Sir John Gielgud's interesting essay, written as an introduction to the Folio Society edition, is reprinted in his *Stage Directions* (1963). Harley Granville Barker's letter to him referred to in the Introduction to the present edition (pages 4–5) is printed in C. B. Purdom's *Harley Granville Barker* (1955). In a chapter of *Shakespeare's Plays in Performance* (1966; Penguin Shakespeare Library, 1969) John Russell Brown discusses the play as a theatrical experience. John Barton's important production with the Royal Shakespeare Company is described in my *Royal Shakespeare: Four major productions at Stratford-upon-Avon* (1977).

An Account of the Text

Richard II was first printed in 1597, in the edition known as the first Quarto (Q1). It is described on the title-page as *The Tragedy of King Richard the Second. As it hath been publicly acted by the Right Honourable the Lord Chamberlain his Servants.* The Lord Chamberlain's was the acting company to which Shakespeare belonged. The play seems to have been printed from his own manuscript, and with an unusually high standard of accuracy. As no manuscript has survived, modern editions must be based on the quarto. But it lacks one important episode – that portraying Richard's abdication (IV.1.154–319). This was omitted most probably for political reasons, perhaps out of tact, or because the printers feared prosecution, or because they had been instructed to omit it. It contains nothing obviously inflammatory, but was certainly considered dangerous at a time of anxiety about the succession (see Introduction, pages 7–9). A little tinkering was done to bridge the gap but there was no real revision, and the fact that the Abbot's line 'A woeful pageant have we here beheld' (IV.1.320) was retained though the 'pageant' had disappeared is a good reason for believing that the cut was not theatrical.

Richard II was popular, and the quarto was reprinted twice in 1598 (Q2 and Q3). The abdication scene continued to be omitted. The fourth edition (Q4) appeared in 1608. By this time the succession problem had been resolved, and the printer was able to announce on the title-page *The Tragedy of King Richard the Second: With new additions of the Parliament Scene, and the deposing of King Richard, as it hath been lately acted by the King's Majesty's Servants at the Globe. By William Shakespeare.* Unfortunately the text of the added passages contains many obvious mistakes, and was printed probably from an unauthorized source. The next edition appeared in 1615, and is a reprint of the previous one.

The other important text is the one in the collected edition of Shakespeare's plays, the first Folio (F), of 1623. The printers seem to have worked from a copy of Q3 with the substitution of a few leaves from Q5. There are two main reasons why this text is important. One is that the quarto from which it was printed had been altered from a source that was obviously theatrical in origin. The natural assumption is that it had been checked against the theatre prompt-book, which would be a manuscript or printed copy annotated and marked in accordance with theatre practice. It would, for example, indicate trumpet calls that Shakespeare had not noted in the manuscript, and might mark cuts. The stage directions in F are notably more precise and businesslike than those in the quartos. They obviously reflect the stage practice of Shakespeare's company and are our main source of information about how the play was put on the stage in his time. They have been incorporated in the present edition. Other alterations were made, some of which may be considered improvements on Q1. We have no reason to suppose that F presents an authoritatively corrected text, and the present edition is conservative in adopting Folio readings where Quarto ones are acceptable. The Collations, however, record plausible readings from F among the Rejected Emendations.

The other main reason for F's importance is that it includes a good text of the abdication episode omitted from the early quartos. Modern editors therefore use F as their basic text for this passage, while adopting some readings from Q4. The present edition is closer to F than most modern ones.

Fifty-one lines of the play were omitted from F. They are: I.3.129–33; I.3.239–42; I.3.268–93; II.2.77; III.2.29–32, 49, 182; IV.I.52–9; V.3.98. Some of these omissions may be accidental, some may represent theatrical cutting.

In the present edition spelling and punctuation have been modernized, speech prefixes have been made consistent, and stage directions have been regularized and amplified where necessary. The Collations that follow record departures from Q1 (F for the abdication episode); places where the present edition preserves original readings that other editors have often altered; and the more important modifications of the original stage directions. Quotations from early editions are given in the original spelling, but long 's' [ʃ] has been replaced by the modern form. 'Q' indicates a reading common to all the early quartos (Q1–5). The more interesting textual points are discussed in the notes.

COLLATIONS

I

The following list indicates readings in the present edition of *Richard II* which depart from the first edition (Q1) or, in the abdication episode (IV.1.154–319), from the first Folio (F1). It does not list corrections of simple misprints. Alterations of punctuation are recorded when a decision affecting the sense has had to be made. When the emendation derives from a later quarto or the Folio, this is indicated. Most of the other emendations were first made by eighteenth-century editors.

THE CHARACTERS IN THE PLAY] *not in* Q, F

I.I.   3   Hereford] Q1 *often, but by no means regularly, spells* Herford

    15   presence. *Exit Attendant* Face] presence face

   118   my] F; *not in* Q

   122   subject, Mowbray. So] subject Mowbray so

   152   gentlemen] F; gentleman Q

  162–3   When, Harry, when? | Obedience bids] When Harry? when obedience bids, | Obedience bids

		Q1; When *Harrie* when? Obedience bids,	Obedience bids Q2–5, F
I.2.	47	sit] F; set Q
I.3.	33	comest] Q5, F; comes
	172	then] F; *not in* Q
	180	You owe] F; y'owe Q
	193	far as] fare as Q; fare, as F (*see textual note*)
	222	night] Q4–5, F; nightes Q1–3
	239	had it] had't
I.4.	20	cousin, cousin] F; Coosens Coosin Q
	52–3	*Enter Bushy*	Bushy, what news?] F; *Enter Bushie with newes.* Q
	65	ALL] *not in* Q, F (*which also omits* 'Amen')
II.1.	18	fond] found Q1
	48	as a moat] Q4–5, F; as moate Q1–3
	102	encagèd] F (incaged); inraged Q
	124	brother] Q2–5; brothers Q1, F
	177	the] F; a Q
	257	King's] Q3–5, F; King Q1
	280	The son of Richard Earl of Arundel] *not in* Q, F
	284	Coint] Coines Q; *Quoint* F
II.2.	16	eye] F; eyes
	147	BAGOT] *not in* Q (F *gives the line to Bushy*)
II.3.	9	Cotswold] Cotshall Q; Cottshold F
	36	Hereford, boy?] Q3; Herefords boy? Q1
	163	Bristol] Bristow
III.2.	31	not – heaven's offer we] not, heauens offer, we Q1
	32	succour] succors
	40	boldly] bouldy Q1
	72	O'erthrows] F; Ouerthrowes Q
III.3.	12–13	Would you have been so brief with him, he would	Have been so brief with you to shorten you] F; would you haue beene so briefe with him,	He would haue bin so briefe to shorten you Q

31   lord] |; Lords Q

59–60   rain | My waters – on] raigne. | My water's on
Q1–2; raine | My water's on Q3–5; raine | My
Waters on F

119   a prince and] (Sisson) princesse Q1–2; a Prince
Q3–5; a Prince, is F

140   Swellest thou, proud heart? I'll] F; Swellst thou
(prowd heart) Ile

III.4.   *Speech prefixes to* 3, 6, 10, 11 (second part), 19
(first part), 21] *Lady* Q; *La.* F

11   joy] griefe

21   weep, . . . good.] Q2; weep; . . . good? Q1

34   too] F; two
Speech prefixes to 40, 54 (first part), 67] *Man.* Q;
Ser. F

57   garden! We at] garden at

80   Camest] Q2; Canst

IV.1.   22   him] Q 3 (my Q2); them

43   Fitzwater] F; Fitzwaters

54   As may] As it may

55   sun to sun] sinne to sinne

62   true.] true (true, Q2; true: F)

76   my] Q3; *not in* Q1 (the Q2)

83–4   gage. | That] gage, | That

154–319   *This passage is not in* Q1–3. *See 'An Account of
the Text', page 42. In its place,* Q1 *has: Bull. Let it be
so, and loe on wednesday next,* | *We solemnly
proclaime our Coronation,* | *Lords be ready all.*

182   and] (Q4, 5) *not in* F

250   and] (Q4) a F

253   haught, insulting] (haught insulting Q4–5)
haught-insulting F

254   Nor] (Q4) No, nor F

259   mockery king] (Q4) Mockerie, King F

318   proclaim | Our coronation. Lords, be ready, all.]

Q1; set downe | Our Coronation: Lords, prepare
your selues. |

332 I will] Ile

v.1. 20 this.] this: Q1 *(where the colon could be the equivalent
of a modern fullstop)*

41 thee] Q2; the

88 off than, near,] *(unpunctuated,* Q) off, then neere, F

v.2. 11,17 thee] F; the Q *(where however 'thee' is often spelt thus)*

v.3. 35 that I may] Q2; that May

74 shrill-voiced] Q3; shril voice

110 KING HENRY] Q2; *yorke*

134-5 With all my heart | I pardon him] I pardon him
with al my heart.

v.5. 27 sit] Q3; set

v.6. 8 Salisbury, Spencer] |; Oxford, Salisbury Q

43 thorough shades] through shades Q1; through
the shade Q2-5, F

2

The list printed below gives readings of the authoritative
editions (Q1, and F1 for the abdication scene) which have been
preserved in the present edition but which are often emended.
The common emendations are given to the right of the square
bracket. The aim has been to list alterations affecting the sense,
especially those that are to be found in some of the editions still
current. Most of them derive from the Folio, which until the
early years of this century was generally considered the most
authoritative early text. As the Folio has a special interest in
spite of its generally inferior authority, some of its more
interesting variants are noted even when they have been generally rejected. When a reading derives from an early edition
(Q1-5, F) this is indicated. Most of the unattributed emendations were first made by eighteenth-century editors, many of
them in an attempt to regularize the metre. The temptation to

do this is strong, but Shakespeare may not have had the precise
rhythmic sense that many of his editors assume in him.

I.I.	97	Fetch] Fetcht Q3–5, Fetch'd F
	186	up] downe F
I.I.	187	deep] foule F
I.2.	62	thy] my F
I.3.	15	As] And
	20	my succeeding] his succeeding F
	26	ask] demand of
	84	innocence] innocency
	193	far as] fare as (*see textual note*)
I.4.	23	Ourself and Bushy] Ourself and Bushy, Bagot here, and Green
	59	the] his F
II.1.	70	raged] ragged; reined
	115	And thou – | KING RICHARD – a lunatic] And thou. | *King.* Ah lunatick Q3–5; And – | *Rich.* And thou, a lunaticke F
	254	noble] *omitted in* F *and by many editors*
	278, 285	Brittaine] Britain; Brittany; Bretagne
II.2.	12	trembles. At something] (trembles, at something Q1) trembles, yet at something
	25	more is] more's F
	31	on thinking] in thinking
	88	The nobles they are fled. The commons they are cold] The nobles they are fled, the commons cold
	110	disorderly thrust] thrust disorderly
	112	T'one] (Q: Tone) Th'one F
	113	T'other] (Q: tother) th'other F
	118	Berkeley] Barkley Castle F
	128	that is] that's F
	137	Will the hateful commons] The hateful commons will
II.3.	65	thank's] thankes F
	80	self-borne] self-born

	98	lord] the Lord F
	122	in] of Q2–5, F
	150	never] ne'er (ne're Q3–5; neu'r F)
	157	unto] to Q2–5, F
II.4.	8	are all] all are Q2–5, F
III.2.	30	neglected; else heaven] (Q1: neglected. Else heauen) neglected; else, if heaven
	38	that] and
	40	boldly] (bouldy Q1) bloudy Q2, bloody F
	133–4	Would they make peace? Terrible hell / Make war upon their spotted souls for this.] Would they make peace? terrible Hell make warre / Vpon their spotted Soules for this Offence. F
III.3.	17	mistake the] mistake; the; mistake. The; mistake: the
	100	pastor's] (pastors Q1) pasture's; pastures'
	121	thus. The King returns] thus the King returns:
	168	laid there] (laide; there Q1) laid – there
	177	you,] you;
	182	base-court. Come down – down] (Q1: base court come downe: downe) base court? Come down? Down
	202	hands] hand F
III.4.	27	They will] They'le F
	29	young] yon Q2
	67	you the] you then the
	80	this] these
IV.1.	13	mine] my F
	49	And if] An if
	89	he is] hee's F
	91	never] ne're F
	112	fourth of that name] of that Name the Fourth F
	165	knee] limbes? Q4
	182	thine] yours Q4
	209	duteous oaths] duties rites Q4
	214	are made] that sweare Q4

219   Henry] Harry Q4
275   that] the Q4
284   Is this the face which] Was . . . that Q4
285   That] And Q4
288   an] a Q4
295   manner] manners Q4
       laments] lament
318–19   proclaim / Our coronation. Lords, be ready, all.]
       set downe / Our Coronation: Lords, prepare
       your selues. F

v.1.   25   thrown] stricken F
       32   the correction] thy correction Q2
       correction, mildly] Correction mildly, F
       34   the king] a King Q2, F
       37   sometimes] sometime Q3, F
       43   quite] quit F
       44   tale] fall F
       62   He] And he
       64   urged another way,] urged, another way,; urged,
       another way; urged another way
       66   men] friends F
       71   Doubly divorced! Bad] (Doubly diuorst (bad)
       Q1; Doubly diuorc'd? (bad F
       84   RICHARD] North. F

v.2.   18   the one] one F
       28   gentle] not in F
       52   Do these justs and triumphs hold?] Hold those
       Iusts & Triumphs? F
       55   prevent not] prevent me not; prevent it not
       74   Some editors add the direction: Enter a Servant.
       (See textual note)
       78   by my life, by my troth] my life, my troth Q2,
       F; by my life, my troth
       113   Spur, post] Spurre post F

v.3.   10   Which] While
       20   Yet] But yet [with relineation, lines ending yet,

	hope, forth, means] (Harold Brooks, in Ure's edition)
30	my roof] the roof
40	Villain] *omitted* (Ure)
45	What is the matter,] *omitted* (Ure)
67	An] And F *and editors*
105	still] shall F
143	cousin,] Cosin too, Q6
v.4. 7	wishtly] wistly Q3, F
v.5. 56	which] that F
70	never] euer Q5, F
105	means] meanest

3

Stage directions in the present edition are based on those of Q1. The original directions have been normalized and clarified. They are often inadequate, failing for instance to indicate many obvious entrances and exits. Additional directions have been made from F, which is much more precise in its instructions to the performers, and often indicates the practice of Shakespeare's company. Further directions have been added where necessary to clarify the action. All directions for speeches to be given aside or addressed to a particular character are editorial. Below are listed some of the other additions and alterations to Q's stage directions. When these derive in whole or part from F, this is noted. Minor alterations such as the addition of a character's name to *Exit*, the change of *Exit* to *Exeunt*, the normalization of character names, and the provision of exits and entrances where these are obviously demanded by the context are not listed here.

I.1.   0   *Enter King Richard and John of Gaunt, with other nobles, including the Lord Marshal, and attendants*] *Enter King Richard, Iohn of Gaunt, with other Nobles and attendants.* Q, F

15 *not in* Q, F

69 *not in* Q, F

78 *not in* Q, F

149 *not in* Q, F

165 *not in* Q, F

195 F; *not in* Q

I.3. 6 *The trumpets sound and the King enters with his nobles,
including Gaunt, and Bushy, Bagot, and Green. When
they are set, enter Mowbray, Duke of Norfolk, in
arms, defendant; and a Herald*] The trumpets sound
and the King enters with his nobles, when they are set,
enter the Duke of Norfolke in armes defendant. Q;
*Flourish. Enter King, Gaunt, Bushy, Bagot, Greene,
& others: Then Mowbray in Armor, and Harrold.* F

25 *The trumpets sound. Enter Bolingbroke, Duke of Hereford, appellant, in armour; and a Herald*] The trumpets sound. Enter Duke of Hereford appellant in
armour. Q; *Tucket. Enter Hereford, and Harold.* F

54 *not in* Q, F

117 *A charge sounded. King Richard throws his warder into
the lists*] not in Q. *A charge sounded* F

122 *A long flourish. King Richard consults his nobles, then
addresses the combatants*] not in Q. *A long Flourish.* F

248 *Flourish. Exit King Richard with his train*] not in
Q. *Exit. Flourish.* F

I.4. 0 *Enter the King with Bagot and Green at one door, and
the Lord Aumerle at another*] Enter the King with
Bushie, &c at one dore, and the Lord Aumarle at
another. Q; *Enter King, Aumerle, Greene, and Bagot.* F

52 (*see textual note*)

II.1. 0 *Enter John of Gaunt sick, with the Duke of York, the
Earl of Northumberland, attendants, and others*] Enter
Iohn of Gaunt sicke, with the duke of Yorke, &c. Q;
Enter Gaunt, sicke with Yorke. F

68 *Enter King Richard, Queen Isabel, Aumerle, Bushy,
Green, Bagot, Ross, and Willoughby*] F; *Enter king
and Queene, &c.* Q

223   *Flourish. Exeunt King Richard and Queen Isabel.*
       Northumberland, Willoughby, and Ross remain]
       Exeunt King and Queene: Manet North. Q; *Flourish.*
       Manet North. Willoughby, & Ross. F

II.3.   82   *not in* Q, F

III.1.   o   *Enter Bolingbroke, York, Northumberland, with Bushy*
               and Green, prisoners] *Enter Duke of Hereford, Yorke,*
               Northumberland, Bushie and Greene prisoners. Q;
               Enter Bullingbrooke, Yorke, Northumberland, Rosse,
               Percie, Willoughby, with Bushie and Greene Prisoners.
               F

III.2.   o   *Drums; flourish and colours. Enter King Richard,*
               Aumerle, the Bishop of Carlisle, and soldiers] *Enter*
               the King Aumerle, Carleil, &c. Q; *Drums: Flourish,*
               and Colours. Enter Richard, Aumerle, Carlile, and
               Souldiers. F

III.3.   o   *Enter with drum and colours Bolingbroke, York,*
               Northumberland, attendants, and soldiers] *Enter Bull.*
               Yorke, North. Q; *Enter with Drum and Colours,*
               Bullingbrooke, Yorke, Northumberland, Attendants.
               F

          61   *The trumpets sound parley without, and answer within;*
               then a flourish. King Richard appeareth on the walls
               with the Bishop of Carlisle, Aumerle, Scroop, and
               Salisbury] *The Trumpets sound, Richard appeareth on*
               the walls. Q; *Parle without, and answere within: then a*
               Flourish. Enter on the Walls, Richard, Carlile, Au-
               merle, Scroop, Salisbury. F

          183   *not in* Q, F

          186   *not in* Q, F

          209   F; *not in* Q

III.4.   o   *Enter the Queen with two Ladies, her attendants*]
               Enter the Queene with her attendants Q; *Enter the*
               Queene, and two Ladies. F

          23   *Enter Gardeners, one the master, the other two his*
               men] *Enter Gardeners.* Q; *Enter a Gardiner, and two*
               Seruants. F

28   *not in* Q, F

72   *not in* Q, F

101   *Exit Queen with her Ladies*] *Exit* Q, F

IV.I.   0   *Enter Bolingbroke with the Lords Aumerle, North-umberland, Harry Percy, Fitzwater, Surrey, the Bishop of Carlisle, the Abbot of Westminster, an-other Lord, Herald, and officer, to Parliament*] *Enter Bullingbrooke with the Lords to parliament.* Q; *Enter as to the Parliament, Bullingbrooke, Aumerle, Northumberland, Percie, Fitz-Water, Surrey, Car-lile, Abbot of Westminster. Herauld, Officers, and Bagot.* F

1   *Enter Bagot with officers*] *Enter Bagot.* Q; *not in* F

24   *not in* Q, F

34   *not in* Q, F

48   *not in* Q, F

55   *not in* Q, F

70   *not in* Q, F

83   *not in* Q, F

157   F; *not in* Q4

161   *Enter Richard and York*] F; *Enter king Richard* Q4

267   *not in* F, Q4

274   *Enter attendant with a glass*] *Enter one with a Glasse.* F; *not in* Q4

287   *not in* F, Q4

319   *Exeunt all except the Abbot of Westminster, the Bishop of Carlisle, Aumerle*] *Exeunt. Manent West. Caleil, Aumerle.* Q1; *Exeunt.* F

V.I.   6   *Enter Richard and guard*] F; *Enter Ric,* Q

96   *not in* Q, F

98   *not in* Q, F

V.2.   71   *He plucks it out of his bosom, and reads it*] Q; *Snatches it* F

87   *not in* Q, F

V.3.   0   *Enter Bolingbroke, now King Henry, with Harry Percy and other lords*] *Enter the King with his nobles.* Q; *Enter Bullingbrooke, Percie, and other Lords.* F

37 *Aumerle locks the door. The Duke of York knocks at
the door and crieth*] *The Duke of Yorke knocks at the
doore and crieth.* Q; not in F

38 YORK (*within*)] *Yor.* Q; *Yorke within.* | *Yor.* F.

44 *King Henry opens the door. Enter York*] *not in* Q;
Enter Yorke. F

73 DUCHESS OF YORK (*within*)] *Du.* Q; *Dutchesse
within.* | *Dut.* F

81 *Aumerle admits the Duchess. She kneels*] *not in* Q;
Enter Dutchesse. F (*after line 85*)

96, 97 *not in* Q, F

135 *not in* Q, F

V.3.145–V.4.0 *Exeunt* | *Enter Sir Piers of Exton and a Man*]
Exeunt. Manet sir Pierce Exton, &c. Q; *Exeunt.
Enter Exton and Seruants.* F

V.4. 11 *Exeunt*] *not in* Q; *Exit.* F

V.5. 41 *The music plays*] Q; *Musick* (*at end of line 38*) F

94 *Enter Keeper to Richard with meat*] *Enter one to
Richard with meate.* Q; *Enter Keeper with a Dish.*
F

102 *not in* Q, F

104 *The murderers, Exton and servants, rush in*] *The
murderers rush in.* Q; *Enter Exton and Seruants.* F

106 *not in* Q, F

107 *He kills another servant. Here Exton strikes him
down*] *Here Exton strikes him downe.* Q; *Exton
strikes him downe.* F

112 *not in* Q, F

118 *Exeunt with the bodies*] *not in* Q; *Exit.* F

V.6 0 *Flourish. Enter King Henry with the Duke of York,
other lords, and attendants*] *Enter Bullingbrooke with
the duke of Yorke.* Q; *Flourish. Enter Bullingbrooke,
Yorke, with other Lords & attendants.* F

18 *Enter Harry Percy with the Bishop of Carlisle,
guarded*] *Enter H Percie.* Q; *Enter Percy and Carlile.*
F

44 *not in* Q, F

Genealogical Table

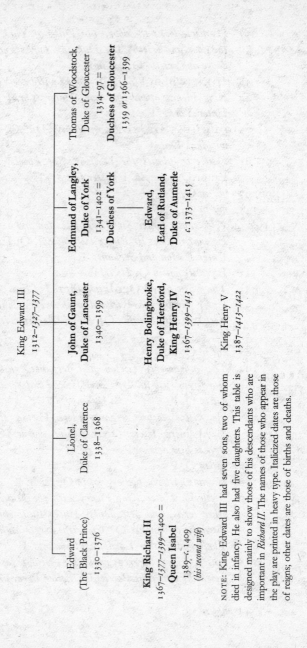

King Edward III
1312–1327–1377

- Edward
  (The Black Prince)
  1330–1376
  - **King Richard II**
    1367–1377–1399–1400 =
    Queen Isabel
    1389–c. 1409
    (his second wife)

- Lionel,
  Duke of Clarence
  1338–1368

- **John of Gaunt,
  Duke of Lancaster**
  1340–1399
  - **Henry Bolingbroke,
    Duke of Hereford,
    King Henry IV**
    1367–1399–1413
    - King Henry V
      1387–1413–1422

- **Edmund of Langley,
  Duke of York**
  1341–1402 =
  Duchess of York
  - **Edward,
    Earl of Rutland,
    Duke of Aumerle**
    c. 1373–1415

- Thomas of Woodstock,
  Duke of Gloucester
  1354–97 =
  Duchess of Gloucester
  1359 or 1366–1399

NOTE: King Edward III had seven sons, two of whom died in infancy. He also had five daughters. This table is designed mainly to show those of his descendants who are important in *Richard II*. The names of those who appear in the play are printed in heavy type. Italicized dates are those of reigns; other dates are those of births and deaths.

KING RICHARD THE SECOND

The Characters in the Play

KING RICHARD the Second
JOHN OF GAUNT, Duke of Lancaster, King Richard's uncle
Edmund of Langley, DUKE OF YORK, King Richard's uncle
HENRY BOLINGBROKE, Duke of Hereford; John of Gaunt's
    son; afterwards KING HENRY the Fourth
DUKE OF AUMERLE, Earl of Rutland; the Duke of York's
    son

THOMAS MOWBRAY, Duke of Norfolk
EARL OF SALISBURY
LORD BERKELEY
BAGOT ⎤
BUSHY ⎬ followers of King Richard
GREEN ⎦
Henry Percy, EARL OF
    NORTHUMBERLAND ⎤
HARRY PERCY (Hotspur), the Earl of ⎬ of Bolingbroke's
    Northumberland's son   party
LORD ROSS ⎦
LORD WILLOUGHBY

'Q' here refers to the first Quarto, 1597. Later quartos (see 'An Account of the Text', pages 00–0) are referred to as Q2, Q3, etc. 'F' refers to the text of the play in the first Folio, of 1623.

    Biblical quotations are from the Bishops' Bible, the version likely to have been best known to Shakespeare. Quotations from Holinshed's *Chronicles* have been modernized from the second edition, of 1587; those from *Woodstock* are from Rossiter's edition.

Title The title-page of Q calls the play *The Tragedy of King Richard the Second*. In F the play is *The Life and Death of King Richard the Second*.

BISHOP OF CARLISLE
SIR STEPHEN SCROOP
LORD FITZWATER
DUKE OF SURREY
ABBOT OF WESTMINSTER
SIR PIERS OF EXTON
LORD MARSHAL
CAPTAIN of the Welsh army

QUEEN ISABEL, King Richard's wife
DUCHESS OF YORK
DUCHESS OF GLOUCESTER, widow of Thomas of Woodstock,
    Duke of Gloucester (King Richard's uncle)
LADIES attending Queen Isabel

GARDENER
TWO GARDENER'S MEN
KEEPER of the prison at Pomfret
SERVINGMAN
GROOM to King Richard

Lords, two Heralds, officers, soldiers, and other attendants

*Enter King Richard and John of Gaunt, with other
nobles, including the Lord Marshal, and attendants*

KING RICHARD

Old John of Gaunt, time-honoured Lancaster,
Hast thou according to thy oath and band
Brought hither Henry Hereford, thy bold son,
Here to make good the boisterous late appeal –
Which then our leisure would not let us hear –
Against the Duke of Norfolk, Thomas Mowbray?

1.1 The matter of this scene is adapted
and compressed from Holinshed, according to whom the first accusations between
Mowbray and Bolingbroke were made
at Shrewsbury in spring 1398, followed
six weeks later by the formal 'appeal' at
Windsor.

Staging: A formal grouping is required, with the King centrally
seated.

(stage direction) *King Richard*. He was
known as Richard of Bordeaux,
was born in 1367, succeeded to the
throne in 1377, and died in 1400.
The play covers the last two years of
his reign. He had an army of 'livery
men' who wore the white hart as his
badge.

John of Gaunt. The fourth (third surviving) son of Edward III; he lived
from 1340 to 1399, and was Duke of
Lancaster. *Gaunt* is Ghent, his birthplace.

Lord Marshal. Mowbray himself was
the Earl Marshal at the time, but

Holinshed says that the Duke of
Surrey acted as his deputy on this
occasion. Surrey appears later in the
play (IV.1), but there is no reason to
think that Shakespeare cared about
the identity of the Lord Marshal; he
is important simply for his function.

1 *Old . . . time-honoured*. In 1398 John of
Gaunt was fifty-eight. Here and elsewhere Shakespeare contrasts the comparative age of Richard's uncles with
the King's own *youth* (II.1.69).

2 *band* (an alternative form of 'bond')

3 *Hereford*. In the play the name usually
has two syllables. In the early editions it is frequently spelt 'Herford'.

4 *boisterous* (two syllables; Q has 'bois-
trous', a common Elizabethan spelling) rough and violent
late recent
appeal accusation (of treason)

5 *our . . . us*. Richard uses the royal
plural, in keeping with the formality
of the occasion.
leisure (that is, lack of leisure)

JOHN OF GAUNT
  I have, my liege.

KING RICHARD
  Tell me, moreover, hast thou sounded him
  If he appeal the Duke on ancient malice,
10 Or worthily, as a good subject should,
  On some known ground of treachery in him?

JOHN OF GAUNT
  As near as I could sift him on that argument,
  On some apparent danger seen in him
  Aimed at your highness; no inveterate malice.

KING RICHARD
  Then call them to our presence.   *Exit Attendant*
                              Face to face,
  And frowning brow to brow, ourselves will hear
  The accuser and the accusèd freely speak.
  High-stomached are they both, and full of ire;
  In rage, deaf as the sea, hasty as fire.
          Enter Bolingbroke and Mowbray

8 *sounded* inquired of
9 *appeal* accuse
   on ancient malice because of long-
   standing personal enmity
12 This is an alexandrine. Most lines in
   the play are pentameters, but short
   and long lines are not uncommon.
   Editors have often attempted to regularize them, either by rearrangement
   or addition of extra words, but some
   of them can be justified dramatically
   (a short line may add emphasis).
   Others may represent an attempt to
   avoid monotony, or be the result of
   negligence.
   As near as I could sift him so far as I
   could discover by examining him
   argument subject
13 *apparent* obvious
15 (stage direction) *Exit Attendant*.
   This is not marked in Q; but it seems
   the most satisfactory way of manag-

ing the stage business.
presence. Face to face. Q reads 'presence face to face'. It is possible
(though not likely) that the passage
should be interpreted 'Then call them
to our presence face to face, and –
[they] frowning brow to brow –
ourselves . . .'
16 *ourselves* we (royal plural) ourself
18–19 These lines are sometimes spoken
   aside.
18 *High-stomached* proud, haughty
19 *deaf.* That is, to remonstrance; compare *King John*, II.I.451: 'The sea
   enragèd is not half so deaf.'
(stage direction) *Bolingbroke*. Henry Plantagenet, Gaunt's son by his first wife;
he lived from 1367 to 1413. *Bolingbroke* (often pronounced 'Bullingbrooke') was a nickname, from his
birthplace, in Lincolnshire.
Mowbray. Thomas Mowbray was

BOLINGBROKE

Many years of happy days befall   20
My gracious sovereign, my most loving liege!

MOWBRAY

Each day still better other's happiness
Until the heavens, envying earth's good hap,
Add an immortal title to your crown!

KING RICHARD

We thank you both. Yet one but flatters us,
As well appeareth by the cause you come,
Namely, to appeal each other of high treason.
Cousin of Hereford, what dost thou object
Against the Duke of Norfolk, Thomas Mowbray?

BOLINGBROKE

First, heaven be the record to my speech!   30
In the devotion of a subject's love,
Tendering the precious safety of my prince,
And free from other, misbegotten hate
Come I appellant to this princely presence.
Now, Thomas Mowbray, do I turn to thee;
And mark my greeting well, for what I speak
My body shall make good upon this earth
Or my divine soul answer it in heaven
Thou art a traitor and a miscreant,
Too good to be so, and too bad to live,   40

---

born about 1366, and died in 1399 at
Venice (IV.I.97–100). It seems likely
that in 1397 he was responsible for
the murder of Richard's uncle,
Gloucester, by Richard's command.
Mowbray in *2 Henry IV* is his eldest
son.
22 *Each day still better other's happiness*
may each day be happier than the
previous one
23–4 *Until . . . your crown.* In *Woodstock*
(1.1.37–8) it is said of the Black
Prince that 'heaven forestalled his
diadem on earth | To place him with
a royal crown in heaven.' Compare

V.I.24–5.
23 *envying*. The accent is probably on the
second syllable: 'heav'ns, envỳing'.
hap fortune
26 *cause you come* cause about which you
come
30 *heaven be the record to my speech!* This
might be regarded as a parenthesis.
record witness
32 *Tendering* watching over, being careful of
34 *appellant* in accusation
36 *greeting* address
38 *divine* immortal
40 *Too good* too high in rank

Since the more fair and crystal is the sky,
The uglier seem the clouds that in it fly.
Once more, the more to aggravate the note,
With a foul traitor's name stuff I thy throat,
And wish – so please my sovereign – ere I move
What my tongue speaks my right-drawn sword may
    prove.

MOWBRAY

Let not my cold words here accuse my zeal.
'Tis not the trial of a woman's war,
The bitter clamour of two eager tongues,
50   Can arbitrate this cause betwixt us twain.
The blood is hot that must be cooled for this.
Yet can I not of such tame patience boast
As to be hushed, and naught at all to say.
First, the fair reverence of your highness curbs me
From giving reins and spurs to my free speech,
Which else would post until it had returned
These terms of treason doubled down his throat.
Setting aside his high blood's royalty,
And let him be no kinsman to my liege,

41–6 Here, as often, the verse moves into rhymed couplets. This has often been objected to, and in the theatre the play's rhyming passages have sometimes been omitted or rewritten. There is of course no justification for this. In general, couplets signalize a higher degree of formality in the action, or a stronger emphasis on what is being said than on what is happening. Coleridge said of this passage: 'the rhymes . . . well express the preconcertedness of Bolingbroke's scheme, so beautifully contrasted with the vehemence and sincere irritation of Mowbray'.

41 *crystal* clear (as crystal), bright

43 *note* reproach, mark of disgrace

(from the Latin *nota*, a mark of censure)

46 *right-drawn* drawn in a just cause

47 *Let not my cold words here accuse my zeal* do not let my calm language cast doubt upon my ardour (or 'loyalty')

49 *eager* sharp

51 *cooled* (by death)

54 *reverence of* respect for

56 *post* hasten (continuing the riding metaphor of *curbs, reins and spurs*, and, perhaps, *free*)

57 *These terms of treason* (*traitor* and *miscreant* (line 39))

58–9 *his high blood's royalty,* | *And let him be no kinsman to my liege*. Bolingbroke was Richard's first cousin.

59 *let him be* assuming that he were

I do defy him, and I spit at him,   60
Call him a slanderous coward, and a villain;
Which to maintain I would allow him odds,
And meet him, were I tied to run afoot
Even to the frozen ridges of the Alps,
Or any other ground inhabitable
Where ever Englishman durst set his foot.
Meantime, let this defend my loyalty:
By all my hopes most falsely doth he lie.

BOLINGBROKE (*throws down his gage*)
Pale, trembling coward, there I throw my gage,
Disclaiming here the kindred of the King,   70
And lay aside my high blood's royalty,
Which fear, not reverence, makes thee to except.
If guilty dread have left thee so much strength
As to take up mine honour's pawn, then stoop.
By that, and all the rites of knighthood else,
Will I make good against thee, arm to arm,
What I have spoke or thou canst worse devise.

MOWBRAY (*takes up the gage*)
I take it up; and by that sword I swear
Which gently laid my knighthood on my shoulder,

---

63 *tied* bound, obliged
65 *inhabitable* not habitable, uninhabit-
    able. Similar expressions occur else-
    where, as in *Macbeth*, III.4.103: 'And
    dare me to the desert with thy
    sword.' A fight to the death is
    implied.
67 *this* (perhaps his sword; more prob-
    ably, the affirmation in the following
    line)
69 (stage direction) *gage* pledge. It was
    usually a glove or gauntlet, but ac-
    cording to Holinshed hoods were
    used on the occasion when Fitzwater
    accused Aumerle of causing Glouces-
    ter's death (IV.I). However, the

phrase *manual seal* (IV.I.25) in Shakespeare's version suggests that he
thought of the gage as a glove.
72 *except* set aside (compare line 58)
74 *honour's pawn*. The gage or pledge of
    line 69; the phrase recurs at IV.I.55
    and 70.
77 *What I have spoke or thou canst worse
    devise* the accusations that I have
    made, or any more heinous ones that
    you can think of
78 *I take it up* (and thus accept the
    challenge)
79 *gently* (perhaps 'conferring nobility'
    rather than 'with a light touch' or 'in
    friendly fashion')

80   I'll answer thee in any fair degree
       Or chivalrous design of knightly trial;
       And when I mount, alive may I not light
       If I be traitor or unjustly fight!

KING RICHARD
       What doth our cousin lay to Mowbray's charge?
       It must be great that can inherit us
       So much as of a thought of ill in him.

BOLINGBROKE
       Look what I speak, my life shall prove it true:
       That Mowbray hath received eight thousand nobles
       In name of lendings for your highness' soldiers,
90   The which he hath detained for lewd employments,
       Like a false traitor and injurious villain.
       Besides I say, and will in battle prove
       Or here or elsewhere to the furthest verge
       That ever was surveyed by English eye,
       That all the treasons for these eighteen years
       Complotted and contrivèd in this land
       Fetch from false Mowbray, their first head and spring.

---

80 *answer thee* give you satisfaction

80–81 *in any fair degree | Or chivalrous design of knightly trial* to any fair measure or any form of combat allowed by the laws of chivalry

82 *light* dismount, alight

85–6 *inherit us . . . of* put us in possession of

87 *Look what* whatever (a usage common in Shakespeare)

88 *nobles.* A noble was a gold coin, worth twenty groats, or 6s. 8d. in the currency of the time.

89 *lendings* (money paid to Mowbray for distribution to the soldiers, perhaps as advances when circumstances would not permit them to be given regular payments. Holinshed has

'Thomas Mowbray Duke of Norfolk hath received eight thousand nobles to pay the soldiers that keep your town of Calais.')

90 *lewd employments* improper use

93 *Or . . . or* either . . . or

95 *eighteen years.* The phrase is from Holinshed. Its significance (which Shakespeare did not necessarily recognize) is that the commons, under Wat Tyler and others, had risen in 1381.

96 *Complotted* plotted in combination with others

contrivèd (could mean 'plotted' or 'devised' as well as 'brought about')

97 *Fetch* derive. The metaphor is of drawing water from the *head* of a fountain, or a *spring.*

Further I say, and further will maintain
Upon his bad life to make all this good,
That he did plot the Duke of Gloucester's death,   100
Suggest his soon-believing-adversaries,
And consequently, like a traitor coward,
Sluiced out his innocent soul through streams of blood;
Which blood, like sacrificing Abel's, cries
Even from the tongueless caverns of the earth
To me for justice and rough chastisement.
And, by the glorious worth of my descent,
This arm shall do it, or this life be spent.

98–9 *maintain | Upon his bad life to make all this good.* Bolingbroke seems to mean that he undertakes to prove all this by taking Mowbray's *bad life.*

100 *he did plot the Duke of Gloucester's death.* Thomas of Woodstock, Duke of Gloucester, died at Calais in 1397 while in the custody of Mowbray, then captain of Calais. He was probably murdered by Mowbray or his agents at Richard's instigation. This view was commonly held in Shakespeare's time. Holinshed says 'The King sent unto Thomas Mowbray . . . to make the Duke secretly away', and reports that Mowbray 'caused his servants to cast featherbeds upon him, and so smother him to death, or otherwise to strangle him with towels (as some write).' Shakespeare leaves the matter open in this first scene but in the next one Gloucester's widow and his brother assert Richard's guilt. The Duke of York, too, implies belief in it (ii.2.100–102). In iv.i. Bolingbroke, taking it for granted that Richard was the instigator, inquires 'who performed | The bloody office', and Bagot seems to suggest that Aumerle, not Mowbray, was responsible. This episode, too, is based on Holinshed. The question is left unsettled. In portraying the varying views Shakespeare may have been concerned to suggest the uncertainties in our interpretation of the past; and the reopening of the question later in the play, with Aumerle's vehement denials, helps Richard's cause with the audience just before he makes big demands on their sympathy, in the deposition scene.

101 *Suggest his soon-believing adversaries* (incite Gloucester's enemies, who were predisposed to believe Mowbray. The enemies included Richard.)

102 *consequently* subsequently

104 *sacrificing Abel's.* The allusion is to the biblical story of Abel, who sacrificed 'the firstlings of his sheep' (Genesis 4.4), and to his murder by his brother, Cain. His blood cried from the ground (Genesis 4.10), and, unlike Christ's, called for retribution (Hebrews 12.24). It is echoed, ironically, in Bolingbroke's words to Piers of Exton (v.6.43–4), when he has murdered Richard at Bolingbroke's instigation.

105 *tongueless* dumb (though resonant)

106 *To me* (as his nephew – as Richard also is)

KING RICHARD

    How high a pitch his resolution soars!
110   Thomas of Norfolk, what sayst thou to this?

MOWBRAY

    O, let my sovereign turn away his face
    And bid his ears a little while be deaf
    Till I have told this slander of his blood
    How God and good men hate so foul a liar!

KING RICHARD

    Mowbray, impartial are our eyes and ears.
    Were he my brother – nay, my kingdom's heir –
    As he is but my father's brother's son,
    Now by my sceptre's awe I make a vow
    Such neighbour nearness to our sacred blood
120   Should nothing privilege him, nor partialize
    The unstooping firmness of my upright soul.
    He is our subject, Mowbray. So art thou.
    Free speech and fearless I to thee allow.

MOWBRAY

    Then, Bolingbroke, as low as to thy heart
    Through the false passage of thy throat thou liest!
    Three parts of that receipt I had for Calais
    Disbursed I duly to his highness' soldiers.

---

109 *pitch* (highest point of a falcon's flight before it swoops on its prey)

113 *slander of his blood* (disgrace to the blood royal, shared by both Richard and Bolingbroke)

115 *eyes and ears* (replying to *face* and *ears* in Mowbray's speech)

118 *my sceptre's awe* the reverence due to my sceptre

119 *sacred* (a hint of the theme of the divine nature of kingship, emphasized elsewhere)

120 *partialize* make partial, bias

122 *He is our subject, Mowbray. So . . .* We might equally read 'He is our subject. Mowbray, so . . .'

124–5 *as low as to thy heart | Through the false passage of thy throat thou liest!* This is a heightening of the common expression 'to lie in the throat', used menacingly.

126 *receipt* (sum received when Mowbray was captain of Calais)
Calais. The early editions use the spelling 'Callice', which represents the Elizabethan pronunciation.

The other part reserved I by consent
For that my sovereign liege was in my debt
Upon remainder of a dear account   130
Since last I went to France to fetch his queen.
Now swallow down that lie! For Gloucester's death,
I slew him not, but to my own disgrace
Neglected my sworn duty in that case.
(*To John of Gaunt*)
For you, my noble lord of Lancaster,
The honourable father to my foe,
Once did I lay an ambush for your life,
A trespass that doth vex my grievèd soul.
But ere I last received the sacrament
I did confess it, and exactly begged   140
Your grace's pardon; and I hope I had it.
This is my fault. As for the rest appealed,
It issues from the rancour of a villain,
A recreant and most degenerate traitor,

128 *by consent*. Holinshed does not record that Richard agreed that Mowbray should retain any of the money.

129 *For that* because

130 *remainder of a dear account* the balance of a heavy debt. *Dear* has a wide range of meaning, including 'important', 'of great value', and 'serious'. Heavy expenses were incurred in Mowbray's expedition to France to negotiate Richard's marriage.

131 *to fetch his queen*. In fact, Richard himself escorted his bride from France to England.

132 *For* as for

133–4 *to my own disgrace | Neglected my sworn duty in that case*. What his *sworn duty* was is obscure. He may mean that he should have killed Gloucester, but this is tantamount to an accusation against Richard. Alternatively his *sworn duty* may have been to guard Gloucester. Holinshed reports that

he 'prolonged time for the executing of the King's commandment, though the King would have had it done with all expedition, whereby the King conceived no small displeasure and sware that it should cost the Earl his life if he quickly obeyed not his commandment', and the point is repeated later. So probably Mowbray is here claiming to have saved Gloucester's life for a time, and perhaps taking refuge in the fact that he did not personally kill him.

137 *Once did I lay an ambush for your life*. In Holinshed, too, Mowbray admits having 'laid an ambush to have slain the Duke of Lancaster', and claims that he was forgiven. No details are known.

140 *exactly* 'expressly' or 'completely'

142 *appealed* alleged

144 *recreant* (could be an adjective – 'cowardly' – as well as a noun)

Which in myself I boldly will defend,
And interchangeably hurl down my gage
Upon this overweening traitor's foot,
To prove myself a loyal gentleman
Even in the best blood chambered in his bosom.
              He throws down his gage
150 In haste whereof most heartily I pray
Your highness to assign our trial day.

KING RICHARD
Wrath-kindled gentlemen, be ruled by me:
Let's purge this choler without letting blood.
This we prescribe, though no physician;
Deep malice makes too deep incision.
Forget, forgive, conclude, and be agreed;
Our doctors say this is no month to bleed.
(*To John of Gaunt*)
Good uncle, let this end where it begun.
We'll calm the Duke of Norfolk, you your son.

JOHN OF GAUNT
160 To be a make-peace shall become my age.
Throw down, my son, the Duke of Norfolk's gage.

KING RICHARD
And, Norfolk, throw down his.

JOHN OF GAUNT   When, Harry, when?
Obedience bids I should not bid again.

---

145 *Which in myself I boldly will defend* the
truth of which statement I personally
shall boldly defend
146 *interchangeably* reciprocally, in turn
hurl (present, not future, tense; Mowbray throws down his gage. Bolingbroke must pick it up at some un-
specified point, since at line 161 his
father tells him to throw it down.)
148–9 *prove . . . in* (probably in the sense
'demonstrate . . . by shedding')
149 *chambered* enclosed
150 *In haste whereof* to hasten which

153 *purge this choler without letting blood*
drain away anger (*choler*, or bile) without the letting of blood (playing on
the idea of bloodshed)
154 *though no physician.* The notion of a
king as his country's physician was
common.
156 *conclude* come to terms
157 *doctors* learned men, astrologers
this is no month to bleed. Some seasons
were supposed to be more favourable
than others to the medical practice
of blood-letting.

KING RICHARD

   Norfolk, throw down! We bid: there is no boot.

MOWBRAY (*kneels*)

   Myself I throw, dread sovereign, at thy foot.

   My life thou shalt command, but not my shame.

   The one my duty owes, but my fair name,

   Despite of death that lives upon my grave,

   To dark dishonour's use thou shalt not have.

   I am disgraced, impeached, and baffled here,   170

   Pierced to the soul with slander's venomed spear,

   The which no balm can cure but his heart-blood

   Which breathed this poison.

KING RICHARD   Rage must be withstood.

   Give me his gage. Lions make leopards tame.

MOWBRAY

   Yea, but not change his spots. Take but my shame

---

164 *We bid* (that is, 'since I, the King, bid')

   boot alternative, help for it

167 *The one my duty owes* my duty as a subject compels me to put my life at your disposal

167–8 *name, | Despite of death that lives upon my grave* name that will live on my tomb despite death. The awkward inversion of the natural word order is presumably a result of the use of rhyme.

170 *impeached* accused

   baffled treated ignominiously, publicly disgraced. To 'baffle' a knight found guilty of cowardice is explained in Hall's Chronicle: 'he was content that the Scots should baffle him, which is a great reproach among the Scots, and is used when a man is openly perjured, and then they make of him an image painted reversed, with his heels upward, with his name . . .' Sometimes the knight seems actually to have been hung up by his heels. Mowbray is not using

the word in its fullest literal sense.

172–3 *his heart-blood | Which* the heart-blood of him who

173 *breathed this poison* uttered this venomous slander

174 *his.* Bolingbroke's; King Richard repeats his demand.

   Lions make leopards tame. The analogy between the king and the lion (the king of beasts) is common. The lion was part of the royal coat-of-arms, and the crest of the Norfolks, worn by Mowbray, was a golden leopard.

175 *Yea, but not change his spots.* The modern proverb 'The leopard cannot change his spots' goes back to the Bible ('May a man of Ind change his skin, and the cat of the mountain her spots?', Jeremiah 13.23) and was probably proverbial by the time Shakespeare was writing. *Spots* has also the sense of 'stains (of shame)'. The line thus connects with line 166.

   Take but my shame simply remove the disgrace

And I resign my gage. My dear dear lord,
The purest treasure mortal times afford
Is spotless reputation. That away,
Men are but gilded loam, or painted clay.
180 A jewel in a ten-times barred-up chest
Is a bold spirit in a loyal breast.
Mine honour is my life. Both grow in one.
Take honour from me, and my life is done.
Then, dear my liege, mine honour let me try.
In that I live, and for that will I die.

KING RICHARD (*to Bolingbroke*)
    Cousin, throw up your gage. Do you begin.

BOLINGBROKE
    O God defend my soul from such deep sin!
    Shall I seem crest-fallen in my father's sight?
    Or with pale beggar-fear impeach my height
190 Before this outdared dastard? Ere my tongue
    Shall wound my honour with such feeble wrong,
    Or sound so base a parle, my teeth shall tear

---

177 *mortal times* human life
182 *in one* inseparably
184 *try* put to the test
186 *throw up your gage.* Richard tells Bolingbroke to relinquish Mowbray's
gage, which he is holding. *Throw up*
may indicate that Richard is situated
at a higher level than the disputants,
perhaps on a throne, possibly (on
the Elizabethan stage) on the upper
stage. F, however, reads 'throw
downe', which may represent a
method of staging different from that
first imagined by Shakespeare.
188 *crest-fallen* humbled
189 *beggar-fear* fear appropriate to a
beggar
    impeach my height disgrace my rank
190 *outdared* (both 'excelled in' and 'overcome by' daring)
    dastard coward

191 *such feeble wrong* the wrong of speaking so feebly
192 *sound so base a parle.* The metaphor
is, appropriately, from the sounding
of trumpets in combat to ask for a
truce.
192–5 *my teeth shall tear . . . even in Mowbray's face.* The image seems strained
and far-fetched. But behind it lies a
story of a philosopher who bit off
his tongue and spat it in a tyrant's
face. This story was reasonably well
known; also, neo-Senecan plays popular when *Richard II* was written sometimes required even the staging of
such horrific incidents. In Thomas
Kyd's *The Spanish Tragedy* (written
about 1587), for instance, the chief
character, Hieronimo, 'bites out his
tongue', provoking the comment
'See, Viceroy, he hath bitten forth

The slavish motive of recanting fear
And spit it bleeding in his high disgrace
Where shame doth harbour, even in Mowbray's face.

Exit John of Gaunt

KING RICHARD

We were not born to sue, but to command;
Which since we cannot do to make you friends,
Be ready as your lives shall answer it
At Coventry upon Saint Lambert's Day.
There shall your swords and lances arbitrate   200
The swelling difference of your settled hate.
Since we cannot atone you, we shall see
Justice design the victor's chivalry.
Lord Marshal, command our officers-at-arms
Be ready to direct these home alarms.   *Exeunt*

his tongue | Rather than to reveal what we required' (IV.4.193–4). And in Shakespeare's own *Titus Andronicus* the idea recurs when Titus, addressing his daughter, Lavinia, whose tongue has been horribly cut out, asks 'Or shall we bite our tongues, and in dumb shows | Pass the remainder of our hateful days?' (III.1.131–2).

193 *motive* instrument, organ (here, the tongue)

194 *in his high disgrace* (in disgrace of the tongue itself. Shakespeare regularly uses 'his' for modern 'its'.)

195 (stage direction) The direction is in F, but not in Q. There is no good reason why Gaunt should leave except that he is to re-enter at the beginning of the following scene. The Folio direction probably repre-

sents Elizabethan stage practice, and perhaps Shakespeare here fails to think in fully theatrical terms.

199 *Saint Lambert's Day* (17 September). Shakespeare takes the date from Holinshed, who however said: 'Here writers disagree about the day that was appointed; for some say it was upon a Monday in August; other upon Saint Lambert's day, being the seventeenth of September, other on the eleventh of September.'

202 *atone* reconcile

203 *design the victor's chivalry* indicate the winner in a combat of chivalry. The theory behind trial by combat is that the justice of God will reveal itself by causing the right man to win.

205 *home alarms* troubles at home (distinct from the Irish rebellion referred to later (1.4.38))

I.2   *Enter John of Gaunt with the Duchess of Gloucester*

JOHN OF GAUNT

    Alas, the part I had in Woodstock's blood
    Doth more solicit me than your exclaims
    To stir against the butchers of his life.
    But since correction lieth in those hands
    Which made the fault that we cannot correct,
    Put we our quarrel to the will of heaven
    Who, when they see the hours ripe on earth,
    Will rain hot vengeance on offenders' heads.

DUCHESS OF GLOUCESTER

    Finds brotherhood in thee no sharper spur?
10   Hath love in thy old blood no living fire?
    Edward's seven sons, whereof thyself art one,
    Were as seven vials of his sacred blood,
    Or seven fair branches springing from one root.

I.2 On this scene, see Introduction, page 13. It marks the difference in time between the first and third scenes, set in April and September.

(stage direction) *Duchess of Gloucester.* She was born in either 1359 or 1366, and died in 1399; but Shakespeare probably thought of her as an older woman.

1 *the part I had in Woodstock's blood* my blood-relationship to Thomas of Woodstock, Duke of Gloucester (Gaunt's brother)
  Woodstock's. F has 'Glousters', which would be easier for an audience unaware that they were the same person.

4–5 *correction lieth in those hands | Which made the fault that we cannot correct* the power to punish the murder is in the hands of the man (Richard) who committed the crime that we cannot undo

6 *Put we our quarrel* let us commit our cause

7 *Who, when they* which, when it. It is not uncommon in Shakespeare for 'heaven' to take a plural agreement.

11 *Edward* (Edward III)

12–13 *seven vials . . . seven fair branches.* Shakespeare preserves throughout the speech the double metaphor compounded of the medieval genealogical symbol of the Tree of Jesse, and the figure of the vials of blood. A typical Elizabethan genealogical table would represent a tree, the founder of a family being at the foot or root (and not, as in modern custom, at the head). Thus the sons are *branches springing from one root.* Altick, in the article referred to on pages 40–41, comments: 'The imposition of the figure involving the word *blood* (in its literal and therefore most vivid use) upon another figure which for centuries embodied the concept of family descent, thus welds together with extraordinary tightness the word and its symbolic significance.'

Some of those seven are dried by nature's course,
Some of those branches by the destinies cut.
But Thomas, my dear lord, my life, my Gloucester,
One vial full of Edward's sacred blood,
One flourishing branch of his most royal root,
Is cracked, and all the precious liquor spilt;
Is hacked down, and his summer leaves all faded,   20
By envy's hand, and murder's bloody axe.
Ah, Gaunt, his blood was thine! That bed, that womb,
That mettle, that self mould, that fashioned thee
Made him a man; and though thou livest and breathest
Yet art thou slain in him. Thou dost consent
In some large measure to thy father's death
In that thou seest thy wretched brother die,
Who was the model of thy father's life.
Call it not patience, Gaunt. It is despair.
In suffering thus thy brother to be slaughtered   30
Thou showest the naked pathway to thy life,
Teaching stern murder how to butcher thee.
That which in mean men we entitle patience
Is pale cold cowardice in noble breasts.
What shall I say? To safeguard thine own life
The best way is to venge my Gloucester's death.

JOHN OF GAUNT
    God's is the quarrel; for God's substitute,

---

15 *Some of those branches by the destinies cut*. The line recalls the epilogue of Marlowe's *Doctor Faustus*, written only a few years before *Richard II*: 'Cut is the branch that might have grown full straight.' *The destinies* are the Fates – Clotho, Lachesis, and Atropos.

21 *envy*. The word was stronger than it is now, and could mean 'malice' or 'hatred'.

23 *mettle* stuff, substance
   self same

28 *model* copy, image

29 *despair* (a sinful as well as pitiable state of mind)

30 *suffering* permitting

31 *naked pathway to thy life* 'undefended way by which your murderers can reach your life'; or perhaps 'that the way to your life is undefended . . .'

33 *mean* ordinary, common, not noble

36 *venge* (an old form of 'avenge')

37–8 *God's substitute*, | *His deputy* (a common way of thinking of the king)

His deputy anointed in His sight,
Hath caused his death; the which if wrongfully,
40   Let heaven revenge, for I may never lift
An angry arm against His minister.

DUCHESS OF GLOUCESTER
Where then, alas, may I complain myself?

JOHN OF GAUNT
To God, the widow's champion and defence.

DUCHESS OF GLOUCESTER
Why then, I will. Farewell, old Gaunt.
Thou goest to Coventry, there to behold
Our cousin Hereford and fell Mowbray fight.
O, sit my husband's wrongs on Hereford's spear
That it may enter butcher Mowbray's breast!
Or if misfortune miss the first career,
50   Be Mowbray's sins so heavy in his bosom
That they may break his foaming courser's back
And throw the rider headlong in the lists,
A caitiff recreant to my cousin Hereford!
Farewell, old Gaunt! Thy sometimes brother's wife
With her companion, grief, must end her life.

JOHN OF GAUNT
Sister, farewell! I must to Coventry.
As much good stay with thee as go with me!

DUCHESS OF GLOUCESTER
Yet one word more. Grief boundeth where it falls,

46 *cousin*. The word was often used to
mean no more than 'relative'. Hereford was the Duchess's nephew.
fell fierce, cruel (since she thinks of
him as the agent in her husband's
murder)
47 *sit*. Q reads 'set'; F 'sit'; but 'set' was
a common spelling of 'sit'.
49 *if misfortune miss the first career* if misfortune does not overcome (Mow-
bray) at the first encounter. To *career*

a horse was to run it at full speed
and then stop suddenly. In the following lines Mowbray is imagined over-
balancing at the stop and being
'thrown'.
53 *caitiff recreant* wretched coward
54 *sometimes* sometime ('wife of him who
was your brother' or 'she who was
your brother's wife')
58–9 *Grief boundeth where it falls,* | *Not
with the empty hollowness, but weight.*

Not with the empty hollowness, but weight.
I take my leave before I have begun;   60
For sorrow ends not when it seemeth done.
Commend me to thy brother, Edmund York.
Lo, this is all. – Nay, yet depart not so.
Though this be all, do not so quickly go.
I shall remember more. Bid him – ah, what? –
With all good speed at Pleshey visit me.
Alack, and what shall good old York there see
But empty lodgings and unfurnished walls,
Unpeopled offices, untrodden stones,
And what hear there for welcome but my groans?   70
Therefore commend me. Let him not come there
To seek out sorrow that dwells everywhere.
Desolate, desolate will I hence and die.
The last leave of thee takes my weeping eye.   *Exeunt*

Enter the Lord Marshal and the Duke of Aumerle   1.3

LORD MARSHAL
My Lord Aumerle, is Harry Hereford armed?

The Duchess is apologizing for adding *one word more*. The image is of a bouncing (bounding) tennis ball; but her grief bounces with the force of its weight, not because of its hollow lightness.

66 *Pleshey* (Gloucester's country house, near Dunmow in Essex)

68 *lodgings* rooms
unfurnished walls (possibly 'walls unhung with tapestry' which was taken down when the rooms were out of use; or the phrase may just mean that the rooms are unfurnished)

69 *offices* servants' rooms

1.3 The events represented in this scene took place at Coventry in September 1398. Holinshed describes an occasion of great splendour. The dukes came 'in great array, accompanied with the lords and gentlemen of their lineages. The King caused a sumptuous scaffold or theatre, and royal lists there to be erected and prepared.' Aumerle and the Marshal (Surrey) 'entered into the lists with a great company of men apparelled in silk sendal embroidered with silver, both richly and curiously, every man having a tipped staff to keep the field in order'. Bolingbroke entered to them, before the King arrived, accompanied by all the

AUMERLE

Yea, at all points, and longs to enter in.

LORD MARSHAL

The Duke of Norfolk, sprightfully and bold,
Stays but the summons of the appellant's trumpet.

AUMERLE

Why then, the champions are prepared, and stay
For nothing but his majesty's approach.

*The trumpets sound and the King enters with his
nobles, including Gaunt, and Bushy, Bagot, and
Green. When they are set, enter Mowbray, Duke of
Norfolk, in arms, defendant; and a Herald*

peers of the realm and 'above ten thousand men in armour, lest some fray or
tumult might rise amongst his nobles'.
Shakespeare makes Richard enter to his
seat, which according to Holinshed was
'richly hanged and adorned', before the
contestants, and then Mowbray before
Bolingbroke who, as appellant, should
have entered the lists first. In Holinshed
the Dukes arrived on elaborately cos-
tumed horses, dismounted, and sat on
their ceremonial chairs, Bolingbroke's of
green velvet, Mowbray's of crimson 'cur-
tained about with white and red damask'.
After they had received their lances
(lines 100–103) the chairs were removed, and the combatants were instructed to remount. At the sound of
the trumpet they moved towards each
other. Shakespeare simplifies the setting, though he mentions the chairs
(line 120). It can hardly be supposed
that horses were used, though they
have sometimes figured, more or less
prominently, in nineteenth- and twen-
tieth-century performances. In *2 Henry
IV* (IV.1.115–29) Mowbray's son describes the events of this scene, attribut-
ing Richard's downfall to his intervention in the combat.

(stage direction) *Duke of Aumerle.*
Edward of York; he lived from
about 1373 to 1415, and was York's
eldest son. *Aumerle* is Albemarle, a
town in France. In fact he became
the Duke of York whose noble death
at Agincourt is recounted in Shakespeare's *Henry V* (IV.6); but Shakespeare may not have realized this
when writing *Richard II*. He is
present here in his function as High
Constable. See also Commentary to
V.2.43.

2 *at all points* completely (that is, he is
wearing all the different pieces of his
suit of armour)

3 *sprightfully* spiritedly

5 *stay* wait

6 (stage direction) *Bushy.* Sir John Bushy
held a number of important offices,
and was Speaker of the House of
Commons for several years. He was
Richard's chief agent in the House,
and is said always to have advanced
before the King with obeisances, to
Richard's pleasure. He was beheaded
in 1399.

Bagot. Sir William Bagot, like Bushy,
held various offices of state. He escaped to Ireland after Bolingbroke

KING RICHARD
Marshal, demand of yonder champion
The cause of his arrival here in arms.
Ask him his name, and orderly proceed
To swear him in the justice of his cause.   10

LORD MARSHAL (*to Mowbray*)
In God's name and the King's, say who thou art
And why thou comest thus knightly-clad in arms,
Against what man thou comest, and what thy quarrel.
Speak truly on thy knighthood and thy oath,
As so defend thee heaven and thy valour!

MOWBRAY
My name is Thomas Mowbray, Duke of Norfolk,
Who hither come engagèd by my oath, –
Which God defend a knight should violate! –
Both to defend my loyalty and truth
To God, my King, and my succeeding issue   20
Against the Duke of Hereford that appeals me;
And by the grace of God and this mine arm
To prove him, in defending of myself,
A traitor to my God, my King, and me.
And as I truly fight, defend me heaven!

landed, and later was arrested and
released. He died in 1407.
Green. Sir Henry Green, a Member
of Parliament and follower of King
Richard, executed with Bushy at
Bristol.
When they are set . . . A separate flourish of trumpets should sound for
Mowbray's entrance.
set. The King and his nobles seat
themselves in state.
9 *orderly* according to the rules
10 *swear him in the justice of his cause.* A
knight entering the lists was required to swear that his cause was

just. One of them was thus likely
to commit perjury, and so deserve
defeat.
11 *say who thou art*. This was not a pure
formality, as the knight's visor would
be down.
13 *quarrel* cause of complaint
18 *defend* forbid
20 *my succeeding issue*. F reads 'his . . .'
Perhaps Mowbray would have been
more likely to swear by the King's
descendants than his own; but the
latter is not impossible and has the
generally superior authority of Q to
support it.

The trumpets sound. Enter Bolingbroke, Duke of
Hereford, appellant, in armour; and a Herald

KING RICHARD

Marshal, ask yonder knight in arms
Both who he is, and why he cometh hither
Thus plated in habiliments of war;
And formally, according to our law,
30   Depose him in the justice of his cause.

LORD MARSHAL *(to Bolingbroke)*

What is thy name? And wherefore comest thou hither
Before King Richard in his royal lists?
Against whom comest thou? And what's thy quarrel?
Speak like a true knight, so defend thee heaven!

BOLINGBROKE

Harry of Hereford, Lancaster, and Derby
Am I, who ready here do stand in arms
To prove by God's grace and my body's valour
In lists on Thomas Mowbray, Duke of Norfolk,
That he is a traitor foul and dangerous
40   To God of heaven, King Richard, and to me;
And as I truly fight, defend me heaven!

LORD MARSHAL

On pain of death, no person be so bold
Or daring-hardy as to touch the lists
Except the Marshal and such officers
Appointed to direct these fair designs.

BOLINGBROKE

Lord Marshal, let me kiss my sovereign's hand

---

28 *plated in habiliments* wearing plate-
armour
30 *Depose him* swear him, take his sworn
statement
42–5 *On pain of death, no person be so bold* |
Or daring-hardy as to touch the lists | *Ex-*
cept the Marshal and such officers | *Ap-*
pointed to direct these fair designs.
According to Holinshed a king-at-

arms (that is, a chief herald) 'made
open proclamation, prohibiting all
men in the name of the King, and of
the High Constable and Marshal, to
enterprise or attempt to approach or
touch any part of the lists upon pain
of death, except such as were appointed to order or marshal the
field'.

And bow my knee before his majesty;
For Mowbray and myself are like two men
That vow a long and weary pilgrimage.
Then let us take a ceremonious leave   50
And loving farewell of our several friends.

LORD MARSHAL (*to King Richard*)
The appellant in all duty greets your highness
And craves to kiss your hand, and take his leave.

KING RICHARD
We will descend and fold him in our arms.
    He leaves his throne
Cousin of Hereford, as thy cause is right,
So be thy fortune in this royal fight!
Farewell, my blood – which if today thou shed,
Lament we may, but not revenge thee dead.

BOLINGBROKE
O, let no noble eye profane a tear
For me, if I be gored with Mowbray's spear!   60
As confident as is the falcon's flight
Against a bird, do I with Mowbray fight.
(*To Lord Marshal*)
My loving lord, I take my leave of you;
(*to Aumerle*)
Of you, my noble cousin, Lord Aumerle;
Not sick, although I have to do with death,
But lusty, young, and cheerly drawing breath.
Lo, as at English feasts, so I regreet

51 *several* 'various' or 'respective'
55 *as* in so far as
58 *Lament we may, but not revenge thee dead.* Bolingbroke's defeat would indicate his guilt, so Richard would not be justified in seeking revenge.
59–60 *profane a tear | For me* misuse a tear in weeping for me
66 *lusty* strong, vigorous
    cheerly in good cheer

67 *as at English feasts.* This is an allusion to the English habit of ending banquets with elaborate sweet confections. The phrase seems to have been current; Bacon wrote: 'Let not this Parliament end, like a Dutch feast, in salt meats; but like an English feast, in sweet meats.'
regreet greet, salute

The daintiest last, to make the end most sweet.
(*To John of Gaunt*)
O thou, the earthly author of my blood,
70   Whose youthful spirit in me regenerate
Doth with a two-fold vigour lift me up
To reach at victory above my head,
Add proof unto mine armour with thy prayers,
And with thy blessings steel my lance's point
That it may enter Mowbray's waxen coat
And furbish new the name of John o' Gaunt
Even in the lusty haviour of his son!

JOHN OF GAUNT
God in thy good cause make thee prosperous!
Be swift like lightning in the execution,
80   And let thy blows, doubly redoubled,
Fall like amazing thunder on the casque
Of thy adverse pernicious enemy!
Rouse up thy youthful blood, be valiant, and live.

BOLINGBROKE
Mine innocence and Saint George to thrive!

MOWBRAY
However God or fortune cast my lot
There lives or dies true to King Richard's throne
A loyal, just, and upright gentleman.
Never did captive with a freer heart
Cast off his chains of bondage and embrace
90   His golden uncontrolled enfranchisement
More than my dancing soul doth celebrate
This feast of battle with mine adversary.

70 *regenerate* reborn
73 *proof* power of resistance
75 *waxen coat* (coat of mail as if it were made of wax)
77 *haviour* (an old form of 'behaviour')
81 *amazing* stupefying (the sense was much stronger than now)
casque helmet
84 *to thrive* I rely on for success
88 *freer* more willing
90 *uncontrolled enfranchisement* liberation from control

Most mighty liege, and my companion peers,
Take from my mouth the wish of happy years.
As gentle and as jocund as to jest
Go I to fight. Truth hath a quiet breast.

KING RICHARD
Farewell, my lord. Securely I espy
Virtue with valour couchèd in thine eye.
Order the trial, Marshal, and begin.

LORD MARSHAL
Harry of Hereford, Lancaster, and Derby,   100
Receive thy lance; and God defend the right.

BOLINGBROKE
Strong as a tower in hope, I cry 'Amen!'

LORD MARSHAL (*to an officer*)
Go bear this lance to Thomas, Duke of Norfolk.

FIRST HERALD
Harry of Hereford, Lancaster, and Derby
Stands here for God, his sovereign, and himself,
On pain to be found false and recreant,
To prove the Duke of Norfolk, Thomas Mowbray,
A traitor to his God, his king, and him,
And dares him to set forward to the fight.

SECOND HERALD
Here standeth Thomas Mowbray, Duke of Norfolk,   110
On pain to be found false and recreant,
Both to defend himself and to approve
Henry of Hereford, Lancaster, and Derby

93 Mowbray moves into couplets as he approaches the ritual of the combat.
95 *to jest* to go to a sport or entertainment
96 *Truth hath a quiet breast* (related to the proverb 'Truth fears no trial')
97 *Securely* confidently (*couchèd*)
100–103 *Harry of Hereford ... Duke of Norfolk.* 'The Lord Marshal viewed

their spears to see that they were of equal length, and delivered the one spear himself to the Duke of Hereford, and sent the other unto the Duke of Norfolk by a knight' (Holinshed).
102 *Strong as a tower in hope* (a biblical phrase: 'for thou hast been my hope, and a strong tower for me against the enemy', Psalm 61.3)

To God, his sovereign, and to him disloyal,
Courageously and with a free desire
Attending but the signal to begin.

LORD MARSHAL
Sound, trumpets; and set forward, combatants!

A charge sounded. King Richard throws his warder
into the lists

Stay! The King hath thrown his warder down.

KING RICHARD
Let them lay by their helmets and their spears
120 And both return back to their chairs again.
(*To his counsellors*)
Withdraw with us, and let the trumpets sound
While we return these dukes what we decree.

A long flourish. King Richard consults his nobles, then
addresses the combatants

Draw near,
And list what with our council we have done.
For that our kingdom's earth should not be soiled
With that dear blood which it hath fosterèd,
And for our eyes do hate the dire aspect
Of civil wounds ploughed up with neighbours' sword,
And for we think the eagle-winged pride

117, 122 (stage directions) 'The Duke of
Norfolk was not fully set forward
when the King cast down his warder
and the heralds cried "Ho Ho!" Then
the King caused their spears to be
taken from them, and commanded
them to repair again to their chairs,
where they remained two long hours
while the King and his council deliberately consulted what order was best
to be had in so weighty a cause'
(Holinshed). It is not easy to say
precisely what stage action Shakespeare imagined here. Probably Richard descends from his raised throne
as he throws down his warder, or

just after doing so. *Withdraw with us*
would be addressed to his councillors, and they would consult in a
cluster while the trumpets sounded
their *long flourish*. Richard could then
return to his throne to deliver his
decision.
117 (stage direction) *warder* (a truncheon
or staff to give the signal for the
beginning or ending of hostilities)
122 *While we return* until we tell
125 *For that* so that
129–33 These lines were omitted from
F, and though the passage does not
make very good sense without them
it is not surprising that clarification

Of sky-aspiring and ambitious thoughts   130
With rival-hating envy set on you
To wake our peace, which in our country's cradle
Draws the sweet infant-breath of gentle sleep,
Which so roused up with boisterous untuned drums,
With harsh-resounding trumpets' dreadful bray,
And grating shock of wrathful iron arms,
Might from our quiet confines fright fair peace
And make us wade even in our kindred's blood:
Therefore we banish you our territories.
You, cousin Hereford, upon pain of life   140
Till twice five summers have enriched our fields
Shall not regreet our fair dominions,
But tread the stranger paths of banishment.

BOLINGBROKE
Your will be done. This must my comfort be:
That sun that warms you here shall shine on me,
And those his golden beams to you here lent
Shall point on me, and gild my banishment.

KING RICHARD
Norfolk, for thee remains a heavier doom,
Which I with some unwillingness pronounce.
The sly slow hours shall not determinate   150
The dateless limit of thy dear exile.
The hopeless word of 'never to return'
Breathe I against thee upon pain of life.

MOWBRAY
A heavy sentence, my most sovereign liege,

was sought. The problem is that *peace* (line 132), having been aroused, goes on to *fright fair peace* (line 137). There may be some textual fault, but it is just as likely that Shakespeare lost control of his metaphors.

131 *set on you* set you on
142 *regreet* greet again (not merely 'greet', as in line 67)
143 *stranger* foreign (this is not a comparative, but the noun used adjectivally)
145 *That sun that warms you here shall shine on me*. The biblical 'he maketh his sun to rise on the evil and on the good' had acquired proverbial force.
148 *heavier doom* severer punishment
150 *determinate* bring to an end
151 *dateless limit* limitless period
     dear dire, grievous

And all unlooked-for from your highness' mouth.
A dearer merit, not so deep a maim
As to be cast forth in the common air
Have I deserved at your highness' hands.
The language I have learnt these forty years,
My native English, now I must forgo,
And now my tongue's use is to me no more
Than an unstringèd viol or a harp,
Or like a cunning instrument cased up –
Or being open, put into his hands
That knows no touch to tune the harmony.
Within my mouth you have engaoled my tongue,
Doubly portcullised with my teeth and lips,
And dull unfeeling barren ignorance
Is made my gaoler to attend on me.
I am too old to fawn upon a nurse,
Too far in years to be a pupil now.
What is thy sentence then but speechless death,
Which robs my tongue from breathing native breath?

KING RICHARD

It boots thee not to be compassionate.
After our sentence plaining comes too late.

MOWBRAY

Then thus I turn me from my country's light,
To dwell in solemn shades of endless night.

160

170

156 *A dearer merit* a better reward
159 *these forty years*. In fact Mowbray
was thirty-three in 1398; but 'forty'
was sometimes used as a round figure,
with no implication of exactness.
162 *Than an unstringèd viol or a harp*. Un-
stringèd refers to *harp* as well as *viol*.
The viol is a stringed instrument
played with a bow.
163 *cunning* 'skilfully made' or 'requiring
skill to play'
167 *portcullised* fortified (a portcullis is a

metal grating in a door)
170 *a nurse*. A nurse might have the
responsibility of teaching her charges
to speak.
172 *speechless*. The word is subtly chosen.
In death, speech is impossible; so
Mowbray's exile will be death to
him.
174 *boots* serves
to be compassionate (either 'to be sorry
for yourself' or 'to appeal for pity')
175 *plaining* complaining

KING RICHARD (*to Bolingbroke and Mowbray*)
    Return again, and take an oath with thee.
    Lay on our royal sword your banished hands.
    Swear by the duty that you owe to God –   180
    Our part therein we banish with yourselves –
    To keep the oath that we administer:
    You never shall, so help you truth and God,
    Embrace each other's love in banishment,
    Nor never look upon each other's face,
    Nor never write, regreet, nor reconcile
    This lowering tempest of your home-bred hate,
    Nor never by advisèd purpose meet
    To plot, contrive, or complot any ill
    'Gainst us, our state, our subjects, or our land.   190
BOLINGBROKE
    I swear.
MOWBRAY
    And I, to keep all this.
BOLINGBROKE
    Norfolk, so far as to mine enemy:
    By this time, had the King permitted us,
    One of our souls had wandered in the air,
    Banished this frail sepulchre of our flesh,
    As now our flesh is banished from this land.
    Confess thy treasons ere thou fly the realm.
    Since thou hast far to go, bear not along
    The clogging burden of a guilty soul.   200

181 *Our part therein* (that part of the
duty you owe to God that belongs
to me, as God's deputy)
188 *advisèd* deliberated
193 *so far as to mine enemy*. This is the
first time in the scene that either
combatant has spoken to the other.
These words seem intended as Bolingbroke's preface to what he is
about to say, intimating that though
he now deigns to address Mowbray,
he continues to hold him in enmity.
Some editors read 'fare' instead of
far (Q spells 'fare'), interpreting
'Bolingbroke bids Norfolk make
his way ("fare") through the world
in a fashion appropriate to an
enemy.'
196 *sepulchre* (accented on the second
syllable)

MOWBRAY

No, Bolingbroke, if ever I were traitor
My name be blotted from the book of life,
And I from heaven banished as from hence!
But what thou art, God, thou, and I do know,
And all too soon, I fear, the King shall rue.
Farewell, my liege. Now no way can I stray;
Save back to England, all the world's my way.   *Exit*

KING RICHARD (*to John of Gaunt*)

Uncle, even in the glasses of thine eyes
I see thy grievèd heart. Thy sad aspect
210   Hath from the number of his banished years
Plucked four away. (*To Bolingbroke*) Six frozen winters
       spent,
Return with welcome home from banishment.

BOLINGBROKE

How long a time lies in one little word!
Four lagging winters and four wanton springs
End in a word – such is the breath of kings.

JOHN OF GAUNT

I thank my liege that in regard of me
He shortens four years of my son's exile.
But little vantage shall I reap thereby;
For ere the six years that he hath to spend
220   Can change their moons, and bring their times about,
My oil-dried lamp and time-bewasted light
Shall be extinct with age and endless night.

---

202 *My name be blotted from the book of life*. This is a clear echo of Revelation 3.5: 'He that overcometh shall be thus clothed in white array, and I will not blot out his name out of the book of life.' It is appropriate to the solemnity of Mowbray's utterance.

205 *rue* (transitive: 'the King shall rue what thou art')

206–7 *no way can I stray*; | *Save back to England, all the world's my way* I cannot go astray now, since I can go anywhere in the world except England

208 *glasses of thine eyes* your eyes as mirrors (mirroring his feelings)

209 *aspect* (accented on the second syllable)

214 *wanton* luxuriant

220 *bring their times about* accomplish the cycles of their seasons

222 *extinct with* extinguished by

My inch of taper will be burnt and done,
And blindfold death not let me see my son.

KING RICHARD

Why, uncle, thou hast many years to live.

JOHN OF GAUNT

But not a minute, King, that thou canst give.
Shorten my days thou canst with sullen sorrow,
And pluck nights from me, but not lend a morrow.
Thou canst help time to furrow me with age,
But stop no wrinkle in his pilgrimage.   230
Thy word is current with him for my death,
But dead, thy kingdom cannot buy my breath.

KING RICHARD

Thy son is banished upon good advice
Whereto thy tongue a party-verdict gave.
Why at our justice seemest thou then to lour?

JOHN OF GAUNT

Things sweet to taste prove in digestion sour.
You urged me as a judge, but I had rather
You would have bid me argue like a father.

---

223 *My inch of taper will be burnt and done*. Shakespeare uses the same image elsewhere. The best-known example is *Macbeth*, v.5.23: 'Out, out, brief candle!' Here it links with *oil-dried lamp* (line 221).

224 *blindfold death*. Death is blindfold because there are no eyes in its traditional emblem, the skull, and also perhaps by analogy with Atropos, the blindfold destiny who cuts the threads of life (Milton's 'blind fury with the abhorrèd shears', *Lycidas*, line 75). The image is capable of other interpretations, and indeed may have had multiple associations for Shakespeare. Death's being blindfolded causes its impartiality. Dover Wilson ingeniously suggests that the image is of death wearing a hood which resembles in shape the extinguisher of a candle or *taper*. And it has also been suggested that death simply *is* the blindfold that will prevent Gaunt from seeing his son.

227 *sullen* gloomy, melancholy

230 *his pilgrimage* its journey

231 *current* valid

234 *party-verdict* one person's share of a joint verdict

236 *Things sweet to taste prove in digestion sour*. This is a proverbial expression deriving from Revelation 10.10, where it is said of a book that it 'was in my mouth as sweet as honey; and as soon as I had eaten it, my belly was bitter'.

O, had it been a stranger, not my child,
240   To smooth his fault I should have been more mild.
A partial slander sought I to avoid,
And in the sentence my own life destroyed.
Alas, I looked when some of you should say
I was too strict, to make mine own away.
But you gave leave to my unwilling tongue
Against my will to do myself this wrong.

KING RICHARD
Cousin, farewell – and, uncle, bid him so.
Six years we banish him, and he shall go.

Flourish. Exit King Richard with his train

AUMERLE
Cousin, farewell! What presence must not know,
250   From where you do remain let paper show.

LORD MARSHAL
My lord, no leave take I; for I will ride
As far as land will let me by your side.

JOHN OF GAUNT
O, to what purpose dost thou hoard thy words,
That thou returnest no greeting to thy friends?

BOLINGBROKE
I have too few to take my leave of you,
When the tongue's office should be prodigal
To breathe the abundant dolour of the heart.

---

240 *To smooth* in glossing over
241 *partial slander* the accusation of partiality
243 *looked when* expected that
249 *What presence must not know* what we shall not be able to communicate in person. It may be that Aumerle should depart after this leave-taking, especially as he enters at the beginning of the next scene. It is also a little odd that he should take such formal leave of Bolingbroke, since he accompanies him *to the next highway* (1.4.4).
251–2 The Marshal's friendly attitude to Bolingbroke here is one of the signs that Shakespeare was not concerned to identify him with the Duke of Surrey, one of Richard's supporters.
257 *To breathe* in breathing
dolour. There is a pun on 'dollar', in conjunction with *hoard* (line 253) and *prodigal*.

JOHN OF GAUNT
Thy grief is but thy absence for a time.

BOLINGBROKE
Joy absent, grief is present for that time.

JOHN OF GAUNT
What is six winters? They are quickly gone.   260

BOLINGBROKE
To men in joy; but grief makes one hour ten.

JOHN OF GAUNT
Call it a travel that thou takest for pleasure.

BOLINGBROKE
My heart will sigh when I miscall it so,
Which finds it an enforcèd pilgrimage.

JOHN OF GAUNT
The sullen passage of thy weary steps
Esteem as foil wherein thou art to set
The precious jewel of thy home return.

BOLINGBROKE
Nay, rather every tedious stride I make
Will but remember me what a deal of world
I wander from the jewels that I love.   270
Must I not serve a long apprenticehood

258–9 *grief ... grief* (both 'grievance'
and 'cause of sorrows')

262 *travel*. 'Travel' and 'travail' were in-
terchangeable in spelling and closely
related in meaning. M. M. Mahood
comments: 'When Gaunt bids him
call his exile "a *trauaile* that thou
takst for pleasure" and a "*foyle*
wherein thou art to set, The pretious
Iewell of thy home returne", Bolingbroke takes up *travel* in its harsher
sense of "travail" and *foil* in the meaning "frustration, obstacle" to fashion
the bitter wordplay of his reply'
(*Shakespeare's Wordplay*, page 78).

265 *sullen* melancholy (and 'dull in
colour')

269 *remember* remind
deal of world distance

271–4 *Must I not serve a long apprentice-
hood | To foreign passages, and in the end, |
Having my freedom, boast of nothing else |
But that I was a journeyman to grief?*
Bolingbroke expects to serve a long
apprenticeship in his foreign travels
and experiences (*passages*), and when
he gains his freedom, as an apprentice does, in the rank of *journeyman*
(qualified artisan, with a hint of 'one
who goes a journey'), and also his
freedom from exile, he will still be
subject to grief. The tense of the last
sentence causes difficulty because the
apprentice would normally become a

To foreign passages, and in the end,
Having my freedom, boast of nothing else
But that I was a journeyman to grief?

JOHN OF GAUNT
All places that the eye of heaven visits
Are to a wise man ports and happy havens.
Teach thy necessity to reason thus:
There is no virtue like necessity.
Think not the King did banish thee,
280   But thou the King. Woe doth the heavier sit
Where it perceives it is but faintly borne.
Go, say I sent thee forth to purchase honour,
And not the King exiled thee; or suppose
Devouring pestilence hangs in our air
And thou art flying to a fresher clime.
Look what thy soul holds dear, imagine it
To lie that way thou goest, not whence thou comest.
Suppose the singing birds musicians,
The grass whereon thou treadest the presence strewed,
290   The flowers fair ladies, and thy steps no more

journeyman on completion of his apprenticeship. It is as if *having my freedom* meant simultaneously 'having gained this amount of experience' and 'when, no longer in exile, I look back upon this period . . .' The sense would be easy if we could interpret *was* as 'have become'.

275–8 *All places that the eye of heaven visits | Are to a wise man ports and happy havens. | Teach thy necessity to reason thus: | There is no virtue like necessity.* A source for this passage has been seen in Lyly's *Euphues* (1578), in which Lyly is translating Plutarch's *De Exilio*: 'Plato would never account him banished that had the sun, fire, air, water, and earth that he had before, where he felt the winter's blast and the summer's blaze, where

the same sun and the same moon shined, whereby he noted that every place was a country to a wise man, and all parts a palace to a quiet mind.' 'A wise man makes every country his own' was proverbial; so was the phrase 'to make a virtue of necessity'.

279–80 *Think not the King did banish thee, | But thou the King.* Again Shakespeare seems to recall Lyly's *Euphues*: 'When it was cast in Diogenes' teeth that the Synoponetes had banished him Pontus, "Yea," said he, "I them of Diogenes."'

281 *faintly* faintheartedly

284 *pestilence* plague

286 *Look what* whatever

289 *presence strewed* (the King's presence chamber, strewed with rushes)

Than a delightful measure or a dance;
For gnarling sorrow hath less power to bite
The man that mocks at it and sets it light.

BOLINGBROKE
O, who can hold a fire in his hand
By thinking on the frosty Caucasus,
Or cloy the hungry edge of appetite
By bare imagination of a feast,
Or wallow naked in December snow
By thinking on fantastic summer's heat?
O no, the apprehension of the good   300
Gives but the greater feeling to the worse.
Fell sorrow's tooth doth never rankle more
Than when he bites, but lanceth not the sore.

JOHN OF GAUNT
Come, come, my son, I'll bring thee on thy way.
Had I thy youth and cause I would not stay.

BOLINGBROKE
Then, England's ground, farewell! Sweet soil, adieu,
My mother and my nurse that bears me yet!
Where'er I wander, boast of this I can:

291 *measure* stately dance
292 *gnarling* snarling
294–9 *O, who can hold ... fantastic summer's heat.* Again Shakespeare seems to recall Lyly's *Euphues*: 'he that is cold doth not cover himself with care, but with clothes; he that is washed in the rain drieth himself by the fire, not by his fancy; and thou which art banished oughtest not with tears to bewail thy hap, but with wisdom to heal thy hurt'. This is from the same passage as that quoted in the note to lines 275–8.
295 *Caucasus* (regularly thought of as cold by the Elizabethans, as in Lyly's *Euphues*: 'If thou be as hot as the Mount Etna, feign thyself as cold as the hill Caucasus')

296 *cloy* surfeit
299 *fantastic* imagined
300 *apprehension* conception
302–3 *Fell sorrow's tooth doth never rankle more | Than when he bites, but lanceth not the sore* cruel sorrow, which bites (line 292), makes his most festering wounds when he bites but does not pierce the skin, as does a physician's lance (on a boil or abscess). Bolingbroke seems to imply that Gaunt's consolations blunt a sorrow which it would be better for him to accept at its worst.
304 *bring* accompany
305 *stay* (perhaps 'away from England' – he would not accept banishment; or perhaps 'linger' – he would leave immediately)

Though banished, yet a trueborn Englishman! *Exeunt*

I.4   *Enter the King with Bagot and Green at one door, and
the Lord Aumerle at another*

KING RICHARD
We did observe. Cousin Aumerle,
How far brought you high Hereford on his way?

AUMERLE
I brought high Hereford, if you call him so,
But to the next highway; and there I left him.

KING RICHARD
And say, what store of parting tears were shed?

AUMERLE
Faith, none for me, except the north-east wind,
Which then blew bitterly against our faces,
Awaked the sleeping rheum, and so by chance
Did grace our hollow parting with a tear.

I.4 The main facts conveyed in this scene were available in Holinshed. The description of Bolingbroke's departure (lines 23–36) may have been suggested by him: 'A wonder it was to see what number of people ran after him in every town and street where he came before he took the sea, lamenting and bewailing his departure, as who would say that when he departed the only shield, defence, and comfort of the commonwealth was vaded and gone.' Shakespeare may also have derived a hint for Bolingbroke's *courtship to the common people* from Froissart's description of his return to London: 'and always as he rode he inclined his head to the people on every side'. The coolness of Aumerle to Bolingbroke is not in the sources; and the suggestion that Richard's farming of the realm was particularly to provide resources for his Irish campaign seems to be Shakespeare's.

(stage direction) Q's direction reads 'Enter the King with Bushie, &c at one dore, and the Lord Aumarle at another.' Probably Shakespeare originally intended Bushy to enter with the other favourites, but then decided to bring him on at line 52. F has 'Enter King, Aumerle, Greene, and Bagot.' See also notes to lines 23 and 52–3.

1 *We did observe.* Richard enters in the midst of a conversation. We learn from line 24 that what he observed was Bolingbroke's *courtship to the common people.*

2 *high.* As the apparent irony in Aumerle's reply suggests, various shades of meaning, including 'high-ranking', 'proud', and perhaps 'haughty', may be felt.

6 *for me* on my part
  except except that

8 *Awaked the sleeping rheum* made our eyes water (*rheum*, 'watery discharge')

KING RICHARD

    What said our cousin when you parted with him?   10

AUMERLE

    'Farewell' –

    And, for my heart disdainèd that my tongue

    Should so profane the word, that taught me craft

    To counterfeit oppression of such grief

    That words seemed buried in my sorrow's grave.

    Marry, would the word 'farewell' have lengthened hours

    And added years to his short banishment,

    He should have had a volume of farewells;

    But since it would not, he had none of me.

KING RICHARD

    He is our cousin, cousin; but 'tis doubt,   20

    When time shall call him home from banishment,

    Whether our kinsman come to see his friends.

    Ourself and Bushy

    Observed his courtship to the common people,

    How he did seem to dive into their hearts

    With humble and familiar courtesy;

---

13 *that* (his heart's disdain)

13–15 *taught me craft | To counterfeit oppression of such grief | That words seemed buried in my sorrow's grave* taught me the skill (*craft*) to pretend to be so stricken with grief that words seemed buried in my sorrow as in a grave

20 *cousin, cousin.* Richard, Bolingbroke, and Aumerle were each other's cousins. Q reads 'cousins cousin'; F, 'cousin, cousin'. The Q reading (meaning 'cousin's cousin') may be right, Richard reminding Aumerle of his relationship with Bolingbroke.

23 *Ourself and Bushy.* In F this line reads 'Our selfe, and *Bushy*: heere *Bagot* and *Greene*', which may be what Shakespeare first wrote. But Q's stage direction at the beginning of the scene includes Bushy among those who enter, though he is also required to enter at line 52. Probably Shakespeare originally intended him to enter at the beginning of the scene, but then he or the actors decided to use Bushy as the carrier of news. This may have resulted in the need to alter this line, though the version found in Q seems unsatisfactory. It sounds clumsy; and the absence of the second part of the line has the theatrical disadvantage of leaving Bagot and Green unidentified on this, their first speaking appearance. A harmless fabrication which would seem nearest to Shakespeare's intentions as well as providing a regular verse line would be 'Ourself and Bushy; Bagot here and Green', which is in fact the reading of the (unauthoritative) quarto of 1634.

What reverence he did throw away on slaves,
Wooing poor craftsmen with the craft of smiles
And patient underbearing of his fortune,
30 As 'twere to banish their affects with him.
Off goes his bonnet to an oyster-wench.
A brace of draymen bid God speed him well,
And had the tribute of his supple knee,
With 'Thanks, my countrymen, my loving friends',
As were our England in reversion his,
And he our subjects' next degree in hope.

GREEN

Well, he is gone; and with him go these thoughts.
Now, for the rebels which stand out in Ireland,
Expedient manage must be made, my liege,
40 Ere further leisure yield them further means
For their advantage and your highness' loss.

KING RICHARD

We will ourself in person to this war;
And, for our coffers with too great a court
And liberal largess are grown somewhat light,
We are enforced to farm our royal realm,

29 *underbearing* enduring
30 *banish their affects with him* take their affections (*affects*) into banishment with him
35 *As were our England in reversion his* as if my England were his in reversion (that is, would revert to him on my death). Richard means it sarcastically but there is a deeper irony.
38 *for* as for
    the rebels which stand out in Ireland. Holinshed records that 'the King being advertised that the wild Irish daily wasted and destroyed the towns and villages within the English pale, and had slain many of the soldiers which lay there in garrison for defence of that country, determined to make eftsoons a voyage thither, and

prepared all things necessary for his passage now against the spring . . . and so in the month of April, as divers authors write, he set forward from Windsor and finally took shipping at Milford, and from thence with two hundred ships and a puissant power of men of arms and archers he sailed into Ireland'.
    stand out resist, hold out
39 *Expedient manage must be made* speedy measures must be taken
43–4 *for our coffers with too great a court | And liberal largess are grown somewhat light.* Richard was notorious for extravagance.
43 *for* because
45 *farm our royal realm* let my land by lease. The procedure is explained by

The revenue whereof shall furnish us
For our affairs in hand. If that come short
Our substitutes at home shall have blank charters
Whereto, when they shall know what men are rich,
They shall subscribe them for large sums of gold   50
And send them after to supply our wants;
For we will make for Ireland presently.
    Enter Bushy
Bushy, what news?

BUSHY

Old John of Gaunt is grievous sick, my lord,
Suddenly taken, and hath sent post-haste
To entreat your majesty to visit him.

a passage in *Woodstock*, IV.1.180–93:
'These gentlemen here, Sir Henry
Greene, Sir Edward Bagot, Sir
William Bushy, and Sir Thomas
Scroope, all jointly here stand bound
to pay your majesty, or your deputy,
wherever you remain, seven thousand pounds a month for this your
Kingdom; for which your grace, by
these writings, surrenders to their
hands: all your crown lands, lord-
ships: manors, rents: taxes, subsidies,
fifteens, imposts; foreign customs,
staples for wool, tin, lead and cloth:
all forfeitures of goods or lands con-
fiscate; and all other duties that do,
shall, or may appertain to the king
or crown's revenues; and for non-
payment of the sum or sums aforesaid, your majesty to seize the lands
and goods of the said gentlemen
above named, and their bodies to be
imprisoned at your grace's pleasure.'

48 *blank charters*. Holinshed records that,
in order to placate the King after he
had been displeased with the City of
London, 'many blank charters were
devised and brought into the city,
which many of the substantial and

wealthy citizens were fain to seal, to
their great charge, as in the end appeared. And the like charters were
sent abroad into all shires within the
realm, whereby great grudge and
murmuring arose among the people;
for when they were so sealed, the
King's officers wrote in the same
what liked them, as well for charging
the parties with payment of money
as otherwise.' The author of *Woodstock* makes a good deal of this.

50 *subscribe them for* put them down for
51 *them* (the sums of gold)
52 *presently* immediately
52–3 *Enter Bushy | Bushy, what news?* This
is F's alteration from Q, which reads
'*Enter Bushie with newes*'. Probably the
manuscript from which the play was
printed gave the passage substantially
as it appears here, but without the
second *Bushy*, and with *what* abbrevi-
ated in such a way that it was mistaken for 'with' and thus was run on
with the stage direction. The confusion may be connected with a late
decision to use Bushy as the bringer
of news – see note to line 23.

KING RICHARD

Where lies he?

BUSHY

At Ely House.

KING RICHARD

Now put it, God, in the physician's mind

60   To help him to his grave immediately!

The lining of his coffers shall make coats

To deck our soldiers for these Irish wars.

Come, gentlemen, let's all go visit him

Pray God we may make haste and come too late!

ALL

Amen!   *Exeunt*

II.1   *Enter John of Gaunt sick, with the Duke of York, the*
            Earl of Northumberland, attendants, and others

JOHN OF GAUNT

Will the King come, that I may breathe my last

58 *Ely House*. This, the palace of the Bishops of Ely, was at Holborn, near London. It was often rented to noblemen.

59 *put*. This may be imperative, as interpreted here, or subjunctive, in which case the sense would be 'Now if God should put it . . .' and a lighter point after *immediately* would be required.

61 *lining* contents

II.1 Richard's visit to the dying John of Gaunt is Shakespeare's invention. The matter of the scene may be indebted to Froissart, who relates that Gaunt was displeased at his son's exile 'for so little a cause, and also because of the evil governing of the realm by his nephew King Richard; for he saw well that if he long persevered and were suffered to continue, the realm was likely to be utterly lost. With these imaginations and other the Duke fell sick, whereon he died; whose death was greatly sorrowed of all his friends and lovers. The King, by that he showed, took no great care for his death, but soon he was forgotten' (Lord Berners's translation). Richard's seizure of Gaunt's belongings comes from Holinshed, as does York's unfavourable reaction. (See note to lines 201–7 below.) The final episode is based on Holinshed's statement that 'divers of the nobility, as well prelates as other and likewise many of the magistrates and

In wholesome counsel to his unstaid youth?

YORK

Vex not yourself, nor strive not with your breath;
For all in vain comes counsel to his ear.

JOHN OF GAUNT

O, but they say the tongues of dying men
Enforce attention like deep harmony.
Where words are scarce they are seldom spent in vain,
For they breathe truth that breathe their words in pain.
He that no more must say is listened more
Than they whom youth and ease have taught to glose.   10
More are men's ends marked than their lives before.
The setting sun, and music at the close,
As the last taste of sweets, is sweetest last,
Writ in remembrance more than things long past.
Though Richard my life's counsel would not hear,
My death's sad tale may yet undeaf his ear.

---

rules of the cities, towns, and common-alty here in England, perceiving daily how the realm drew to utter ruin, not like to be recovered to the former state of wealth whilst King Richard lived and reigned, as they took it devised with great deliberation and considerate advice to send and signify by letters unto Duke Henry, whom they now called (as he was indeed) Duke of Lancaster and Hereford, requiring him with all convenient speed to convey himself into England, promising him all their aid, power, and assistance if he, expelling King Richard as a man not meet for the office he bare, would take upon him the sceptre, rule, and diadem of his native land and region'. (stage direction) *Duke of York.* Edmund of Langley, 1341–1402, fifth (fourth sur-viving) son of Edward III. The House of York took its name from him. *Earl of Northumberland.* Henry Percy, the

first Earl, 1342–1408. He does not speak till line 147, but as he there reports Gaunt's death his presence at the scene's opening seems likely.

2 *unstaid* unrestrained

5–6 *they say the tongues of dying men | Enforce attention like deep harmony.* The notion that last words have an oracu-lar quality was common, and Shake-speare makes much of it.

9 *listened* listened to, paid attention to

10 *glose* speak flatteringly (like Richard's favourites)

12 *music at the close* (the cadence, or clos-ing phrase of a piece of music)

13 *last taste of sweets* the last taste of sweet things (before the taste disappears)
    sweetest last (perhaps 'sweetest in its most recent manifestation'; or 'sweet-est because it comes last')

YORK

> No, it is stopped with other, flattering sounds,
> As praises, of whose taste the wise are fond;
> Lascivious metres, to whose venom sound
20   The open ear of youth doth always listen;
> Report of fashions in proud Italy,
> Whose manners still our tardy-apish nation
> Limps after in base imitation.
> Where doth the world thrust forth a vanity –
> So it be new there's no respect how vile –
> That is not quickly buzzed into his ears?
> Then all too late comes counsel to be heard
> Where will doth mutiny with wit's regard.
> Direct not him whose way himself will choose.
30   'Tis breath thou lackest, and that breath wilt thou lose.

18 *the wise are fond* even the wise are fond. Q reads 'found', and the line may be corrupt.

19 *metres* verses, poems

21 *fashions in proud Italy*. Italy was a traditional source of folly and wickedness. *Fashions* may refer to clothes or may extend to manners and behaviour. This passage is reminiscent of the lines in Act 1 of Marlowe's *Edward II* in which Gaveston imagines how he will win the King's favour:

Music and poetry is his delight;
Therefore I'll have Italian masques
  by night,
Sweet speeches, comedies, and
  pleasant shows.

A similar accusation against King Richard and his favourites is made in *Woodstock*, II.3.88–93:

They sit in council to devise strange
  fashions,
And suit themselves in wild and
  antic habits

Such as this kingdom never yet
  beheld:
French hose, Italian cloaks, and
  Spanish hats,
Polonian shoes with peaks a hand
  full long,
Tied to their knees with chains of
  pearl and gold.

22 *still* always
tardy-apish ready to ape fashions after they have become stale

25 *there's no respect* no one cares

28 *will doth mutiny with wit's regard* desire conflicts with the claims of intelligence

30–32 *breath . . . new-inspired . . . expiring.* Having been reminded of his shortage of breath, the fact that he will not breathe much longer, Gaunt imagines himself to be newly inspired (playing on the sense of 'given breath'), and so, expiring – that is, both 'breathing out' and 'dying' – foretells . . . This type of serious wordplay is particularly characteristic of Gaunt.

JOHN OF GAUNT

Methinks I am a prophet new-inspired,
And thus, expiring, do foretell of him:
His rash fierce blaze of riot cannot last;
For violent fires soon burn out themselves.
Small showers last long, but sudden storms are short.
He tires betimes that spurs too fast betimes.
With eager feeding food doth choke the feeder.
Light vanity, insatiate cormorant,
Consuming means, soon preys upon itself.
This royal throne of kings, this sceptred isle,   40
This earth of majesty, this seat of Mars,
This other Eden – demi-paradise –
This fortress built by nature for herself
Against infection and the hand of war,
This happy breed of men, this little world,
This precious stone set in the silver sea,
Which serves it in the office of a wall,
Or as a moat defensive to a house
Against the envy of less happier lands;
This blessèd plot, this earth, this realm, this England,   50
This nurse, this teeming womb of royal kings,
Feared by their breed, and famous by their birth,
Renownèd for their deeds as far from home

---

31 *Methinks I am a prophet new-inspired.*
Compare lines 5–6.
34–7 These lines all have a proverbial
ring. Behind the first lies the proverb
'Nothing violent can be permanent',
on which many writers played variations, as Shakespeare did in *Romeo
and Juliet*, II.6.9: 'These violent de-
lights have violent ends.' *He tires
betimes that spurs too fast betimes* was
an expression comparable to 'More
haste, less speed'.
35 *Small showers last long.* The four long

syllables show Shakespeare matching
the sound to the sense.
36 *betimes* soon, early
38 *cormorant* glutton
41 *This earth of majesty* this land which is
the proper seat of majesty
seat of Mars home of Mars (the god
of war)
45 *little world* world in little. Compare
Cymbeline, III.1.12–13: 'Britain is | A
world by itself.'
52 *Feared by* inspiring fear by

For Christian service and true chivalry
As is the sepulchre in stubborn Jewry
Of the world's ransom, blessèd Mary's son;
This land of such dear souls, this dear dear land,
Dear for her reputation through the world,
Is now leased out – I die pronouncing it –
60   Like to a tenement or pelting farm.
England, bound in with the triumphant sea,
Whose rocky shore beats back the envious siege
Of watery Neptune, is now bound in with shame,
With inky blots and rotten parchment bonds.
That England that was wont to conquer others
Hath made a shameful conquest of itself.
Ah, would the scandal vanish with my life,
How happy then were my ensuing death!
     Enter King Richard, Queen Isabel, Aumerle, Bushy,
     Green, Bagot, Ross, and Willoughby

55 *stubborn Jewry* (the land of the Jews, obstinate both in refusing Christianity and in resisting the crusaders)

59–60 *leased out ... Like to a tenement or pelting farm.* This may be a reference to *Woodstock*, IV.1.145–7, where Richard fears criticism because, he says, 'we ... to ease our wanton youth | Become a landlord to this warlike realm, | Rent out our kingdom like a pelting farm ...'

60 *tenement* estate held by a tenant
    pelting paltry

61–3 Shakespeare makes the Duke of Austria speak of England in similar terms in *King John*, II.1.21–30:

    to my home I will no more return
   Till Angiers and the right thou hast
     in France,
   Together with that pale, that white-
     faced shore
   Whose foot spurns back the ocean's
     roaring tides

   And coops from other lands her
     islanders,
   Even till that England, hedged in
     with the main,
   That water-wallèd bulwark, still
     secure
   And confident from foreign
     purposes,
   Even till that utmost corner of the
     west
   Salute thee for her king.

   bound in ... bound in surrounded by
   ... legally restrained by

64 *blots* (the blank charters)

68 (stage direction) If, as F suggests, King Richard's exit (line 223) is marked by a flourish, trumpets should sound too for his entrance here.
   Queen Isabel. At the time of the events of the play King Richard's wife was Isabel, daughter of Charles VI of France, whom he had married in

YORK

> The King is come. Deal mildly with his youth;
> For young hot colts being raged do rage the more. 70

QUEEN ISABEL

> How fares our noble uncle Lancaster?

KING RICHARD

> What comfort, man? How is't with agèd Gaunt?

JOHN OF GAUNT

> O, how that name befits my composition!
> Old Gaunt indeed, and gaunt in being old.
> Within me grief hath kept a tedious fast;
> And who abstains from meat that is not gaunt?
> For sleeping England long time have I watched.
> Watching breeds leanness; leanness is all gaunt.
> The pleasure that some fathers feed upon
> Is my strict fast – I mean my children's looks; 80
> And therein fasting hast thou made me gaunt.
> Gaunt am I for the grave, gaunt as a grave,
> Whose hollow womb inherits naught but bones.

KING RICHARD

> Can sick men play so nicely with their names?

1396, 'she being as then not past eight years of age' (Holinshed). Shakespeare does not give a name to Richard's Queen, and it is important to the scheme of the play that she should be presented as a woman who feels more than childlike love for her husband. Isabel was King Richard's second wife. The character in the play is closer to his first, Anne, to whom he had been deeply devoted and with whose portrayal in *Woodstock* Shakespeare's Queen has much in common.

Ross. Lord Ross sat in Parliament from 1394. He died in 1414.

Willoughby. Lord Willoughby sat in Parliament from 1397, and died in

1409. King Richard made him Knight of the Garter, but he joined Bolingbroke. He later married the Duke of York's widow.

73 *composition* state of both mind and body

75 *grief hath kept a tedious fast.* Fasts were sometimes observed as an expression of grief.

77 *watched* stayed awake at night (worrying over England *sleeping* in sloth or ignorance of what is happening)

78 *Watching* sleeplessness

80 *Is my strict fast* I must go without

83 *inherits* 'possesses' or 'will receive (at my death)'

84 *nicely* 'subtly' and 'triflingly'

JOHN OF GAUNT

No, misery makes sport to mock itself.
Since thou dost seek to kill my name in me,
I mock my name, great King, to flatter thee.

KING RICHARD

Should dying men flatter with those that live?

JOHN OF GAUNT

No, no. Men living flatter those that die.

KING RICHARD

90   Thou now a-dying sayst thou flatterest me.

JOHN OF GAUNT

O, no. Thou diest, though I the sicker be.

KING RICHARD

I am in health. I breathe, and see thee ill.

JOHN OF GAUNT

Now he that made me knows I see thee ill;
Ill in myself to see, and in thee seeing ill.
Thy deathbed is no lesser than thy land,
Wherein thou liest in reputation sick;
And thou, too careless patient as thou art,
Committest thy anointed body to the cure
Of those 'physicians' that first wounded thee.
100   A thousand flatterers sit within thy crown,
Whose compass is no bigger than thy head,
And yet, encagèd in so small a verge,

85 *misery makes sport to mock itself* it is
    misery (not sickness) which finds
    amusement in ridiculing itself
86 *to kill my name in me* (by banishing his
    son)
88 *flatter with* try to please
89 *flatter* (perhaps in the sense of 'try to
    cheer up')
93 *see thee ill.* The stress is on *thee.*
94 *Ill in myself to see, and in thee seeing ill*
    myself having poor power of sight,
    and seeing evil in you

98 *Committest thy anointed body to the cure.*
    This line appears to be alexandrine,
    but probably should be spoken as a
    pentameter by pronouncing 'com-
    mits' and eliding *thy* and *anointed.*
102 *verge.* Three senses are relevant: (1)
    compass; (2) the sphere of jurisdic-
    tion of the king's marshal, twelve
    miles round the royal residence; (3) a
    measure of land of from fifteen to
    thirty acres.

The waste is no whit lesser than thy land.
O, had thy grandsire with a prophet's eye
Seen how his son's son should destroy his sons,
From forth thy reach he would have laid thy shame,
Deposing thee before thou wert possessed,
Which art possessed now to depose thyself.
Why, cousin, wert thou regent of the world
It were a shame to let this land by lease.   110
But for thy world enjoying but this land,
Is it not more than shame to shame it so?
Landlord of England art thou now, not king.
Thy state of law is bondslave to the law,
And thou –

KING RICHARD
                    – a lunatic lean-witted fool,
Presuming on an ague's privilege,
Darest with thy frozen admonition
Make pale our cheek, chasing the royal blood
With fury from his native residence.
Now by my seat's right royal majesty,   120
Wert thou not brother to great Edward's son,
This tongue that runs so roundly in thy head
Should run thy head from thy unreverent shoulders.

103 *waste.* The legal meaning of 'a
tenant's destruction of his landlord's
property' is relevant.
104–5 *had thy grandsire with a prophet's
eye* | *Seen how his son's son should destroy
his sons* (that is, had Edward III seen
how his grandson, Richard, would
destroy his (Edward's) sons –
Gloucester and Gaunt)
107–8 *possessed . . . possessed* put in possession . . . possessed by a devil, mad
109 *regent* ruler
111 *for thy world enjoying but this land* as
this land is all the world that you
rule
114 *state of law is bondslave to the law* legal

status is now that of one who is
bound to obey the law (instead of
above the law, as a king should
be)
115 *a lunatic . . .* Richard interrupts
Gaunt's sentence, and turns it back
on him. It would be up to the actor
to make this clear, perhaps by pointing to Gaunt, or even by saying
'thou' simultaneously with him. F
gives 'thou' to Richard, not to
Gaunt. Q3 reads 'Ah lunatick . . .',
which is plausible but lacks
authority.
122 *roundly* 'bluntly' or 'glibly'
123 *unreverent* disrespectful

JOHN OF GAUNT

O, spare me not, my brother Edward's son,
For that I was his father Edward's son.
That blood already, like the pelican,
Hast thou tapped out and drunkenly caroused.
My brother Gloucester, plain well-meaning soul –
Whom fair befall in heaven 'mongst happy souls –
130   May be a precedent and witness good
That thou respectest not spilling Edward's blood.
Join with the present sickness that I have,
And thy unkindness be like crookèd age,
To crop at once a too-long withered flower.
Live in thy shame, but die not shame with thee!
These words hereafter thy tormentors be!
Convey me to my bed, then to my grave.
Love they to live that love and honour have.

Exit with Northumberland and attendants

KING RICHARD

And let them die that age and sullens have;
140   For both hast thou, and both become the grave.

YORK

I do beseech your majesty, impute his words
To wayward sickliness and age in him.
He loves you, on my life, and holds you dear
As Harry, Duke of Hereford, were he here.

124–5 *Edward . . . his father Edward* (the
  Black Prince, Richard's father; son
  of Edward III, who was also Gaunt's
  father)
126 *pelican* (an allusion to the common
  belief that the young pelican feeds
  on its mother's life-blood)
128 *Gloucester, plain well-meaning soul* (possibly influenced by the portrait of
  Gloucester as 'plain Thomas' in
  Woodstock)
129 *fair befall* may good befall
130 *precedent* example, proof
131 *thou respectest not* you do not scruple

to (the verb may be in the past tense
  – an elliptical form of 'respectedest')
133 *unkindness*. The word had a stronger
  sense to the Elizabethans than it has
  now: 'unnatural behaviour'.
135 *die not shame with thee!* may your ill-
  reputation live after you!
139 *sullens* sulks
140 *become* are fit for
143–5 *He loves you . . . so his*. York means
  that Gaunt loves Richard as much as
  he loves his son; but Richard embar-
  rasses him by taking him to mean 'as
  much as Bolingbroke loves you'.

KING RICHARD

   Right, you say true. As Hereford's love, so his.

   As theirs, so mine; and all be as it is.

                            Enter Northumberland

NORTHUMBERLAND

   My liege, old Gaunt commends him to your majesty.

KING RICHARD

   What says he?

NORTHUMBERLAND

              Nay, nothing. All is said.

   His tongue is now a stringless instrument.

   Words, life, and all, old Lancaster hath spent.   150

YORK

   Be York the next that must be bankrupt so!

   Though death be poor, it ends a mortal woe.

KING RICHARD

   The ripest fruit first falls, and so doth he.

   His time is spent, our pilgrimage must be.

   So much for that. Now for our Irish wars.

   We must supplant those rough rug-headed kerns

   Which live like venom where no venom else

   But only they have privilege to live.

   And for these great affairs do ask some charge,

   Towards our assistance we do seize to us   160

   The plate, coin, revenues, and moveables

   Whereof our uncle Gaunt did stand possessed.

---

149 *stringless instrument*. The image recalls that used by Mowbray at
1.3.161–2.

152 *death* (the state of being dead)

153 *The ripest fruit first falls* (proverbial)

154 *our pilgrimage must be* our pilgrimage
through life lies before us, and it too
will come to an end

156 *supplant* get rid of
rug-headed shaggy-headed. Edmund
Spenser in *The Present State of Ireland*
(1596) said of the Irish: 'They have
another custom from the Scythians,

that is the wearing of mantles and
long glibs, which is a thick curled
bush of hair hanging down over their
eyes and monstrously disguising
them.' (*Rug* is a shaggy material.)
kerns light-armed Irish foot-soldiers.

157–8 *live like venom where no venom else* |
But only they have privilege to live. This
is an allusion to the legend that
Saint Patrick banished snakes from
Ireland.

159 *charge* expense

YORK

How long shall I be patient? Ah, how long
Shall tender duty make me suffer wrong?
Not Gloucester's death, nor Hereford's banishment,
Nor Gaunt's rebukes, nor England's private wrongs,
Nor the prevention of poor Bolingbroke
About his marriage, nor my own disgrace,
Have ever made me sour my patient cheek
170   Or bend one wrinkle on my sovereign's face.
I am the last of noble Edward's sons,
Of whom thy father, Prince of Wales, was first.

164 *suffer* tolerate

166 *Gaunt's rebukes* the insults and shames offered to Gaunt (by Richard)

167–8 *the prevention of poor Bolingbroke | About his marriage.* This refers to an event not mentioned elsewhere in the play. It is explained by Holinshed, who writes that when Bolingbroke, during his exile in Paris, was about to marry the French King's cousin, Richard 'sent the Earl of Salisbury with all speed into France, both to surmise by untrue suggestion heinous offences against him, and also to require the French King that in no wise he would suffer his cousin to be matched in marriage with him that was so manifest an offender'.

168 *my own disgrace.* We do not know to what York refers. There may be significance in the fact that in *Woodstock*, III.2.4, Gloucester says to York and Lancaster that Richard has 'Disgraced our names and thrust us from his court'.

170 *bend on wrinkle* 'cause one frown to appear' or 'once frown (at you)'

172–83 This comparison between Richard and his father may owe something to one made by Gaunt in *Woodstock*, I.1.27–45:

A heavy charge good Woodstock
   hast thou had
To be protector to so wild a prince
So far degenerate from his noble
   father
Whom the trembling French the
   Black Prince called
Not of a swart and melancholy brow
(For sweet and lovely was his
   countenance)
But that he made so many funeral
   days
In mournful France: the warlike
   battles won
At Crecy Field, Poitiers, Artoise and
   Maine
Made all France groan under his
   conquering arm.
But heaven forestalled his diadem on
   earth
To place him with a royal crown in
   heaven.
Rise may his dust to glory! Ere he'd
   'a done
A deed so base unto his enemy,
Much less unto the brothers of his
   father,
He'd first have lost his royal blood
   in drops,
Dissolved the strings of his
   humanity

In war was never lion raged more fierce,
In peace was never gentle lamb more mild
Than was that young and princely gentleman.
His face thou hast; for even so looked he
Accomplished with the number of thy hours;
But when he frowned it was against the French,
And not against his friends. His noble hand
Did win what he did spend, and spent not that   180
Which his triumphant father's hand had won.
His hands were guilty of no kindred blood,
But bloody with the enemies of his kin.
O, Richard! York is too far gone with grief,
Or else he never would compare between.

KING RICHARD
Why, uncle, what's the matter?

YORK   O, my liege,
Pardon me if you please. If not, I, pleased
Not to be pardoned, am content withal.
Seek you to seize and grip into your hands
The royalties and rights of banished Hereford?   190
Is not Gaunt dead? And doth not Hereford live?
Was not Gaunt just? And is not Harry true?
Did not the one deserve to have an heir?
Is not his heir a well-deserving son?
Take Hereford's rights away, and take from Time

And lost that livelyhood that was
   preserved
To make his (unlike) son a wanton
   king.

173 *lion raged more fierce* (either 'lion
raged more fiercely' or 'a fierce (enraged lion')

177 *Accomplished with the number of thy
hours* at your age (*Accomplished with*,
furnished with)

185 *compare between*. Either York breaks
down, leaving his sentence incomplete, or this expression is complete

in itself, meaning 'draw comparisons
between them'.

186 *Why, uncle, what's the matter?* Richard
may be callously detached or genuinely bewildered.

188 *withal* none the less

190 *royalties* (rights granted to a subject
by the king; royal prerogatives)

192 *Harry* (Bolingbroke, Duke of Hereford). He is *true* in having accepted
exile.

195 *Take . . . and take* if you take . . .
you will take

His charters and his customary rights.
Let not tomorrow then ensue today.
Be not thyself; for how art thou a king
But by fair sequence and succession?
200   Now afore God – God forbid I say true –
If you do wrongfully seize Hereford's rights,
Call in the letters patents that he hath
By his attorneys general to sue
His livery, and deny his offered homage,
You pluck a thousand dangers on your head,
You lose a thousand well-disposèd hearts,
And prick my tender patience to those thoughts
Which honour and allegiance cannot think.

KING RICHARD

Think what you will, we seize into our hands
210   His plate, his goods, his money, and his lands.

201–7 *If you do wrongfully seize Hereford's rights,* | *Call in the letters patents that he hath* | *By his attorneys general to sue* | *His livery, and deny his offered homage,* | *You pluck a thousand dangers on your head,* | *You lose a thousand well-disposèd hearts,* | *And prick my tender patience* ... Holinshed has: 'The death of this duke gave occasion of increasing more hatred in the people of this realm toward the King, for he seized into his hands all the goods that belonged to him, and also received all the rents and revenues of his lands which ought to have descended unto the Duke of Hereford by lawful inheritance, in revoking his letters patents, which he had granted to him before, by virtue whereof he might make his attorneys general to sue livery for him of any manner of inheritances or possessions that might from thenceforth fall unto him, and that his homage might be respited with making reasonable fine; whereby it was evident that the King meant his utter undoing.

'This hard dealing was much misliked of all the nobility, and cried out against of the meaner sort; but namely, the Duke of York was therewith sore moved ...' The letters patent would have allowed Bolingbroke to institute suits to obtain his father's lands, which under feudal law would revert to Richard until it had been proved that the heir, Bolingbroke, was of age. When the lands were restored to the heir he was required to make an act of homage to the king. Richard is said to refuse (*deny*) this, which was to be 'respited with making reasonable fine' (presumably because the exiled Bolingbroke could not pay homage in person).

203–4 *sue* | *His livery* (institute suits for obtaining Gaunt's lands)

YORK

 I'll not be by the while. My liege, farewell.
 What will ensue hereof there's none can tell;
 But by bad courses may be understood
 That their events can never fall out good.   *Exit*

KING RICHARD

 Go, Bushy, to the Earl of Wiltshire straight,
 Bid him repair to us to Ely House
 To see this business. Tomorrow next
 We will for Ireland, and 'tis time I trow.
 And we create in absence of ourself
 Our uncle York Lord Governor of England;   220
 For he is just, and always loved us well.
 Come on, our Queen; tomorrow must we part.
 Be merry; for our time of stay is short.
    Flourish. Exeunt King Richard and Queen Isabel.
    Northumberland, Willoughby, and Ross remain

NORTHUMBERLAND

 Well, lords, the Duke of Lancaster is dead.

ROSS

 And living too; for now his son is duke.

WILLOUGHBY

 Barely in title, not in revenues.

NORTHUMBERLAND

 Richly in both if justice had her right.

213–14 *But by bad courses may be understood | That their events can never fall out good* (a not very elegant way of saying 'You cannot expect bad courses of action to have good results')

215 *the Earl of Wiltshire.* He was Richard's treasurer. He was executed at Bristol with Bushy and Green (see III.1.1–35), but does not appear in the play.
 straight immediately

216 *Ely House* (where Richard now is)

217 *see* see to
 Tomorrow next tomorrow ('morrow' originally meant simply 'morning')

218 *trow* believe

220–21 *York ... he is just, and always loved us well.* This appreciation of York seems surprising considering York's immediately preceding criticism of Richard. It is caused at least partly by Shakespeare's telescoping of events. In Holinshed some time passes between Gaunt's death and Richard's decision to go to Ireland.

ROSS

My heart is great, but it must break with silence
Ere't be disburdened with a liberal tongue.

NORTHUMBERLAND

230 Nay, speak thy mind; and let him ne'er speak more
That speaks thy words again to do thee harm.

WILLOUGHBY

Tends that thou wouldst speak to the Duke of Hereford?
If it be so, out with it boldly, man!
Quick is mine ear to hear of good towards him.

ROSS

No good at all that I can do for him,
Unless you call it good to pity him,
Bereft and gelded of his patrimony.

NORTHUMBERLAND

Now, afore God, 'tis shame such wrongs are borne
In him, a royal prince, and many more
240 Of noble blood in this declining land.
The King is not himself, but basely led
By flatterers; and what they will inform
Merely in hate 'gainst any of us all,
That will the King severely prosecute
'Gainst us, our lives, our children, and our heirs.

ROSS

The commons hath he pilled with grievous taxes,
And quite lost their hearts. The nobles hath he fined
For ancient quarrels, and quite lost their hearts.

WILLOUGHBY

And daily new exactions are devised,

228 *great* big with sorrow
229 *liberal* unrestrained
231 *speaks thy words again to do thee harm*
uses what you say in evidence against
you
232 *Tends that thou wouldst speak to* does
what you would say refer (favour-

ably) to
243 *Merely* purely
246–8 *The commons . . . lost their hearts.* This
echoes *Woodstock*, v.3.94: 'thou well
may'st doubt their loves that lost
their hearts'.
246 *pilled* plundered

As blanks, benevolences, and I wot not what.   250
But what o' God's name doth become of this?

NORTHUMBERLAND
Wars hath not wasted it; for warred he hath not,
But basely yielded upon compromise
That which his noble ancestors achieved with blows.
More hath he spent in peace than they in wars.

ROSS
The Earl of Wiltshire hath the realm in farm.

WILLOUGHBY
The King's grown bankrupt like a broken man.

NORTHUMBERLAND
Reproach and dissolution hangeth over him.

ROSS
He hath not money for these Irish wars —
His burdenous taxations notwithstanding —   260
But by the robbing of the banished Duke.

NORTHUMBERLAND
His noble kinsman! — most degenerate King!
But, lords, we hear this fearful tempest sing
Yet seek no shelter to avoid the storm.
We see the wind sit sore upon our sails

---

250 *blanks* blank charters (1.4.48; see textual note)
benevolences forced loans
wot know

252 *Wars hath.* The singular form of the verb with a plural subject is not uncommon in Elizabethan English. It may possibly be a northern dialectal form especially appropriate to Northumberland. He uses it again at II.3.5.

252–4 *warred he hath not,* | *But basely yielded upon compromise* | *That which his noble ancestors achieved with blows.* This probably refers to the giving up of Brest to the Duke of Brittany in 1397, which was a cause of dispute between Richard and Gloucester.

254 *noble.* This was omitted by F, and many editors follow suit, explaining it as an accidental anticipation of the same word in line 262. But Shakespeare may have written the alexandrine.

256 *in farm.* The 'farming' of the land is referred to at 1.4.45; see textual note.

257 *The King's grown bankrupt like a broken man.* Q reads 'King'. 'King's' is in all the early editions after Q2. But Shakespeare may have written 'King', intending Northumberland to complete Willoughby's sentence.

And yet we strike not, but securely perish.

ROSS

We see the very wrack that we must suffer,
And unavoided is the danger now
For suffering so the causes of our wrack.

NORTHUMBERLAND

270 Not so. Even through the hollow eyes of death
I spy life peering; but I dare not say
How near the tidings of our comfort is.

WILLOUGHBY

Nay, let us share thy thoughts, as thou dost ours.

ROSS

Be confident to speak, Northumberland.
We three are but thyself; and speaking so
Thy words are but as thoughts. Therefore be bold.

NORTHUMBERLAND

Then thus: I have from Le Port Blanc,
A bay in Brittaine, received intelligence
That Harry Duke of Hereford, Rainold Lord Cobham,

266 *strike* strike sail (perhaps also 'resist')
securely carelessly, with excessive
sense of security
268 *unavoided* unavoidable
269 *suffering* putting up with, doing nothing about
270 *eyes* eye-sockets
275 *are but thyself* share your feelings,
are of one mind with you
277–88 This is based on Holinshed:
'there were certain ships rigged and
made ready for him at a place in base
Brittaine called Le Port Blanc, as we
find in the chronicles of Brittaine,
and when all his provision was made
ready he took the sea together with
the said Archbishop of Canterbury
and his nephew Thomas Arundel,
son and heir to the late Earl of Arundel beheaded at the Tower Hill, as

you have heard. There were also with
him Reginald Lord Cobham, Sir
Thomas Erpingham, and Sir Thomas
Ramston, knights, John Norbury,
Robert Waterton, and Francis Coint,
esquires. Few else were there, for (as
some write) he had not past fifteen
lances, as they termed them in those
days, that is to say men-of-arms, furnished and appointed as the use then
was. Yet other write that the Duke
of Brittaine delivered unto him three
thousand men of war to attend him,
and that he had eight ships well furnished for the war, where Froissart
yet speaketh but of three.'
278 *Brittaine* Brittany, or Bretagne. No
modernized form of Q's spelling
seems wholly satisfactory.
intelligence information, news

The son of Richard Earl of Arundel   280
That late broke from the Duke of Exeter,
His brother, Archbishop late of Canterbury,
Sir Thomas Erpingham, Sir John Ramston,
Sir John Norbery, Sir Robert Waterton, and Francis
    Coint,
All these well-furnished by the Duke of Brittaine
With eight tall ships, three thousand men of war,
Are making hither with all due expedience,
And shortly mean to touch our northern shore.
Perhaps they had ere this, but that they stay
The first departing of the King for Ireland.   290
If then we shall shake off our slavish yoke,
Imp out our drooping country's broken wing,

280 *The son of Richard Earl of Arundel.*
This line is not in any of the early
editions, but was first added by
Edmond Malone in 1790. Something
like it seems necessary because Holinshed has 'the Earl of Arundel's son,
named Thomas, which was kept in
the Duke of Exeter's house, escaped
out of the realm'. Shakespeare is heavily dependent on Holinshed in this
passage.

    The Archbishop of Canterbury (line
282) was Richard Earl of Arundel's
brother. He was *late* Archbishop
because he had been banished in
1397, when his brother the earl was
executed as one of the Lords Appellant. It is possible that the line was
deliberately cut because Queen Elizabeth had had Philip Howard Earl of
Arundel executed in 1595, and she
did her best to deprive his young
son of his inheritance as well as his
title.

281 *broke* escaped

283 *Sir Thomas Erpingham.* He appears
as a character in *Henry V* (IV.I).
He was one of Richard's active
opponents.

Sir John Ramston. His real name was
Thomas. He became Warden of the
Tower when Richard was confined
there.

284 *Coint.* This is Holinshed's form of
the name. Q reads 'Coines'; F,
'Quoint', which Ure takes to be a
conscious correction of Q, perhaps
based on consultation of the prompt-
book. But it might (as Sisson suggests) be simply a variant spelling.

285 *Duke of Brittaine.* John de Montford,
who died in 1399 and whose widow,
Joan of Navarre, became Bolingbroke's second wife.

286 *tall* large, fine

287 *expedience* speed

289-90 *they stay | The first departing of
the King for Ireland.* Holinshed explains that Bolingbroke 'did not
straight take land, but lay hovering
aloof, and showed himself now in
this place and now in that, to see
what countenance was made by the
people, whether they meant envi-
ously to resist him, or friendly to
receive him'.

292 *Imp out* repair (a metaphor from
falconry)

Redeem from broking pawn the blemished crown,
Wipe off the dust that hides our sceptre's gilt,
And make high majesty look like itself,
Away with me in post to Ravenspurgh.
But if you faint, as fearing to do so,
Stay, and be secret; and myself will go.

ROSS

To horse, to horse. Urge doubts to them that fear.

WILLOUGHBY

300   Hold out my horse, and I will first be there.   *Exeunt*

II.2   *Enter the Queen, Bushy, and Bagot*

BUSHY

Madam, your majesty is too much sad.
You promised when you parted with the King
To lay aside life-harming heaviness,
And entertain a cheerful disposition.

QUEEN ISABEL

To please the King I did. To please myself
I cannot do it. Yet I know no cause
Why I should welcome such a guest as grief
Save bidding farewell to so sweet a guest
As my sweet Richard. Yet again methinks
10   Some unborn sorrow ripe in fortune's womb
Is coming towards me, and my inward soul
With nothing trembles. At something it grieves
More than with parting from my lord the King.

---

293 *broking pawn* (the possession of the King's moneylenders)
294 *gilt* (punningly)
296 *in post* in haste, travelling by relays of horses
    Ravenspurgh (a port on the Humber)
300 *Hold out my horse* if my horse holds out

II.2 The Queen's emotion both creates foreboding and suggests a more sympathetic view of the King. The events of the remainder of the scene are rearranged and developed from Holinshed.

3 *life-harming* (compare Ecclesiasticus 30.23: 'as for sorrow and heaviness, drive it far from thee; for heaviness hath slain many a man, and bringeth no profit')

BUSHY

    Each substance of a grief hath twenty shadows
    Which shows like grief itself, but is not so.
    For sorrow's eye, glazed with blinding tears,
    Divides one thing entire to many objects,
    Like perspectives which, rightly gazed upon,
    Show nothing but confusion; eyed awry,
    Distinguish form. So your sweet majesty,   20
    Looking awry upon your lord's departure,
    Find shapes of grief more than himself to wail,
    Which looked on as it is, is naught but shadows
    Of what it is not. Then, thrice-gracious Queen,
    More than your lord's departure weep not – more is not
        seen,
    Or if it be, 'tis with false sorrow's eye,
    Which for things true weeps things imaginary.

QUEEN ISABEL

    It may be so; but yet my inward soul

---

14 *Each substance of a grief hath twenty shadows* for each real cause of grief there are twenty illusory ones. This anticipates the imagery used by Richard at IV.1.294–8.

18 *perspectives* (pronounced with stresses on the first and third syllables). A perspective in this sense is a painting or drawing which from a normal point of view appears distorted, but which produces a clear image when looked at from a particular, and unusual, angle. There is a well-known example in the National Gallery in Holbein's portrait *The Ambassadors*, most of which is painted normally but which includes a weird object which when looked at *awry* is seen to be a skull. It is said to have been painted from the reflection of a skull in a curved mirror. Lines 16–17 are suggestive also of another kind of perspective, a multiplying glass cut into a number of facets, each one of which creates a distinct image. Queen Isabel's eyes, out of focus as the result of her tears, produce a similar effect.

20 *Distinguish form* show distinct forms

21–4 *Looking awry upon your lord's departure,* | *Find shapes of grief more than himself to wail,* | *Which looked on as it is, is naught but shadows* | *Of what it is not.* Here the two types of perspective mentioned in the note to line 18 become confused. Isabel, looking awry (which with the first type would produce a single, true image), sees a multiple image, as if she were looking at a multiplying glass. If, says Bushy, she looked at it from a normal angle (*as it is*), she would see that her cause of grief was all an illusion.

21 *Looking awry upon* considering mistakenly

27 *weeps* weeps for

Persuades me it is otherwise. Howe'er it be
30   I cannot but be sad – so heavy-sad
As, though on thinking on no thought I think,
Makes me with heavy nothing faint and shrink.

BUSHY

'Tis nothing but conceit, my gracious lady.

QUEEN ISABEL

'Tis nothing less. Conceit is still derived
From some forefather grief. Mine is not so,
For nothing hath begot my something grief,
Or something hath the nothing that I grieve –
'Tis in reversion that I do possess –
But what it is that is not yet known what,
40   I cannot name; 'tis nameless woe, I wot.

Enter Green

GREEN

God save your majesty, and well met, gentlemen.
I hope the King is not yet shipped for Ireland.

QUEEN ISABEL

Why hopest thou so? 'Tis better hope he is,
For his designs crave haste, his haste good hope.
Then wherefore dost thou hope he is not shipped?

GREEN

That he, our hope, might have retired his power,

---

29 This line has twelve syllables, but
can be spoken with five main
stresses: 'Per*suades* me *it* is *other*wise.
Howe'er it *be*'.
31 *though on thinking on no thought I think*
though I try to think about nothing
32 *with heavy nothing.* Isabel returns to
the thought of the *unborn sorrow*,
which in a sense is *nothing*, expressed
in lines 10–12.
33 *conceit* fancy
34 *nothing less* anything but that
34–40 *Conceit is still derived . . . 'tis nameless woe, I wot* a fancied grief always

(*still*) derives from a real one. Mine
cannot be fancied, because it derives
from an unreal one (the *nothing* of
line 12); or else the unreal one that
afflicts me exists somewhere, and I
own it as I might own an object that
as yet is in someone else's keeping.
But I cannot give a name to this
thing whose identity I do not yet
know; I think it must be 'Nameless
Woe'.

46 *retired his power* withdrawn his army
(from Ireland)

And driven into despair an enemy's hope,
Who strongly hath set footing in this land.
The banished Bolingbroke repeals himself,
And with uplifted arms is safe arrived   50
At Ravenspurgh.

QUEEN ISABEL   Now God in heaven forbid!

GREEN

Ah, madam, 'tis too true! And, that is worse,
The Lord Northumberland, his son young Henry Percy,
The Lords of Ross, Beaumont, and Willoughby,
With all their powerful friends are fled to him.

BUSHY

Why have you not proclaimed Northumberland
And all the rest, revolted faction, traitors?

GREEN

We have; whereupon the Earl of Worcester
Hath broken his staff, resigned his stewardship,
And all the household servants fled with him   60
To Bolingbroke.

QUEEN ISABEL

So, Green, thou art the midwife to my woe,
And Bolingbroke my sorrow's dismal heir.

---

49 *repeals* recalls from exile
50 *uplifted arms* brandished weapons
53–4 *Northumberland . . . Willoughby.*
These are all among the supporters
of Bolingbroke mentioned by
Holinshed.
53 *Henry.* This is printed as 'H.' in Q; it
may be that we should expand to
'Harry'.
57 *the rest, revolted faction, traitors.* The
exact interpretation of this line is
disputed. Some take 'rest revolted
faction' together as 'rest of the revolted faction'. Others interpret 'and
all the rest that are revolted, faction-
traitors'. The present reading assumes that *revolted faction* is in apposi-

tion to *rest.*
58 *the Earl of Worcester.* He was Thomas
Percy, the Earl of Northumberland's
brother, and steward of the royal
household. He becomes an important
character in *I Henry IV.* Holinshed
says: 'Sir Thomas Percy, Earl of
Worcester, lord steward of the
King's house . . . brake his white
staff, which is the representing sign
and token of his office, and without
delay went to Duke Henry. When
the King's servants of household saw
this – for it was done before them all
– they dispersed themselves . . .'
63 *heir* offspring

Now hath my soul brought forth her prodigy,
And I, a gasping new-delivered mother,
Have woe to woe, sorrow to sorrow joined.

BUSHY
Despair not, madam.

QUEEN ISABEL   Who shall hinder me?
I will despair and be at enmity
With cozening hope. He is a flatterer,
70   A parasite, a keeper-back of death
Who gently would dissolve the bands of life
Which false hope lingers in extremity.
          Enter York

GREEN
Here comes the Duke of York.

QUEEN ISABEL
With signs of war about his aged neck.
O, full of careful business are his looks!
Uncle, for God's sake speak comfortable words.

YORK
Should I do so I should belie my thoughts.
Comfort's in heaven, and we are on the earth,
Where nothing lives but crosses, cares, and grief.
80   Your husband, he is gone to save far off,
Whilst others come to make him lose at home.
Here am I left to underprop his land,
Who weak with age cannot support myself.
Now comes the sick hour that his surfeit made.
Now shall he try his friends that flattered him.
          Enter a Servingman

---

64 *prodigy* monstrous birth (the *unborn sorrow ripe in fortune's womb*, line 10)
69 *cozening* cheating
71 *Who* (death)
72 *lingers in extremity* prolongs to the utmost
74 *signs of war about his aged neck*. York is wearing the piece of armour called a gorget. It could be worn with civilian dress.
75 *careful business* anxious preoccupation
76 *comfortable* comforting
79 *crosses* troubles
85 *try* put to the test (some of the *friends* are of course on stage with York)

SERVINGMAN

    My lord, your son was gone before I came.

YORK

    He was? – why, so. Go all which way it will.

    The nobles they are fled. The commons they are cold,

    And will, I fear, revolt on Hereford's side.

    Sirrah, get thee to Pleshey to my sister Gloucester.   90

    Bid her send me presently a thousand pound –

    Hold: take my ring.

SERVINGMAN

    My lord, I had forgot to tell your lordship –

    Today as I came by I callèd there –

    But I shall grieve you to report the rest.

YORK

    What is't, knave?

SERVINGMAN

    An hour before I came the Duchess died.

YORK

    God for his mercy, what a tide of woes

    Comes rushing on this woeful land at once!

    I know not what to do. I would to God –   100

    So my untruth had not provoked him to it –

    The King had cut off my head with my brother's.

    What, are there no posts dispatched for Ireland?

    How shall we do for money for these wars?

---

86 *your son was gone.* Aumerle was with the King in Ireland.

88 *The nobles they are fled. The commons they are cold.* This is the reading of all the early editions. Some editors emend to 'The nobles they are fled, the commons cold', which may be correct, but long lines are not uncommon in this play.

90 *sister* sister-in-law

91 *presently* immediately

92 *Hold: take my ring.* The signet ring will be proof that he comes from York.

97 *An hour before I came the Duchess died.* Holinshed mentions the Duchess's death, but does not say where or when it happened, and attributes it to grief at her son's death. In fact it appears to have occurred in October 1399, later than the events of this scene. Shakespeare places it here to increase the *tide of woes*.

101 *So* so long as, provided that
    untruth disloyalty

Come, sister – cousin, I would say – pray pardon me.
Go, fellow, get thee home, provide some carts,
And bring away the armour that is there.
Gentlemen, will you go muster men?
If I know how or which way to order these affairs
110 Thus disorderly thrust into my hands,
Never believe me. Both are my kinsmen.
T'one is my sovereign, whom both my oath
And duty bids defend. T'other again
Is my kinsman, whom the King hath wronged,
Whom conscience and my kindred bids to right.
Well, somewhat we must do. (*To the Queen*) Come,
          cousin,
I'll dispose of you. Gentlemen, go muster up your men,
And meet me presently at Berkeley. I should to Pleshey, too,
120 But time will not permit. All is uneven,
And everything is left at six and seven.

                              Exeunt York and the Queen
                Bushy, Bagot, and Green remain

BUSHY
   The wind sits fair for news to go for Ireland,

---

105 *Come, sister – cousin, I would say.*
A. C. Sprague comments: 'He is
almost a comic character; a pitiful
one, by the same token, and very
real. "Come, sister ..." his mind
turning back, even as he speaks, to
the past; to that final piece of news,
which as yet he has scarcely taken in'
(*Shakespearian Players and Performances*, 1953, page 168).

108–9, 116–21 The metre is irregular.
Rearrangement is sometimes attempted, but a regular rhythm cannot
be obtained from these words. The
irregularity may reflect York's har-
assed state of mind. The present edition follows Q except that there lines
119–21 are printed as two lines, the

first ending with *permit*. The rhyme
demands rearrangement.

117 *dispose of* make arrangements for

118 *Berkeley*. F reads 'Barkley Castle'.
'Castle' may have been added in
performance.

122 The remainder of the scene is based
on Holinshed's 'The Lord Treasurer,
Bushy, Bagot, and Green, perceiving
that the commons would cleave unto
and take part with the Duke, slipped
away, leaving the Lord Governor of
the realm and the Lord Chancellor
to make what shift they could for
themselves. Bagot got him to Chester, and so escaped into Ireland. The
other fled to the castle of Bristol, in
hope there to be in safety.'

But none returns. For us to levy power
Proportionable to the enemy
Is all unpossible.

GREEN

Besides, our nearness to the King in love
Is near the hate of those love not the King.

BAGOT

And that is the wavering commons; for their love
Lies in their purses, and whoso empties them
By so much fills their hearts with deadly hate.   130

BUSHY

Wherein the King stands generally condemned.

BAGOT

If judgement lie in them, then so do we,
Because we ever have been near the King.

GREEN

Well, I will for refuge straight to Bristol Castle.
The Earl of Wiltshire is already there.

BUSHY

Thither will I with you; for little office
Will the hateful commons perform for us –
Except like curs to tear us all to pieces.
Will you go along with us?

BAGOT

No, I will to Ireland to his majesty.   140

122–3 *The wind sits fair for news to go for Ireland,* | *But none returns* the wind is favourable for news to go to Ireland, but not for it to come from there

126–7 *Our nearness to the King in love* | *Is near the hate of those love not the King* the King's affection for us makes us hated by those who oppose the King

127 *those love* those who love

132 *If judgement lie in them* if our fate depends on them ('the commons' or 'the commons' hearts')

133 *ever* constantly

136 *office* service

140 *No, I will to Ireland to his majesty.* According to Holinshed, Bagot 'got him to Chester, and so escaped into Ireland, the other [Bushy and Green] fled to the castle of Bristol'. Shakespeare follows this here. However, in II.3.164 Bagot, not Green, is rumoured to be at Bristol with Bushy. In III.1 Bushy and Green are executed at Bristol. It looks as if Shakespeare were rather confused or careless. The discrepancies would

Farewell. If heart's presages be not vain,
We three here part that ne'er shall meet again.

BUSHY

That's as York thrives to beat back Bolingbroke.

GREEN

Alas, poor Duke! The task he undertakes
Is numbering sands and drinking oceans dry.
Where one on his side fights, thousands will fly.

BAGOT

Farewell at once, for once, for all, and ever.

BUSHY

Well, we may meet again.

BAGOT   I fear me, never.   *Exeunt*

II.3   *Enter Bolingbroke and Northumberland*

BOLINGBROKE

How far is it, my lord, to Berkeley now?

NORTHUMBERLAND

Believe me, noble lord,

---

probably not be noticed in performance.

141–2 *If heart's presages be not vain, | We three here part that ne'er shall meet again.* Thomas of Woodstock takes leave of his brothers in similar words (*Woodstock*, III.2.102–6):

Adieu, good York and Gaunt,
    farewell for ever.
I have a sad presage comes suddenly
That I shall never see these brothers
    more:
On earth, I fear, we never more shall
    meet.
Of Edward the Third's seven sons
    we three are left . . .

141 *presages.* The accent is on the second syllable.

143 *That's as York thrives to beat* that's according to how far York succeeds in beating

145 *numbering sands and drinking oceans dry* (proverbial expressions for attempting the impossible)

II.3 In its fluidity of setting this scene is characteristic of the Elizabethan stage. It begins somewhere in Gloucestershire, on the way to Berkeley Castle where, according to Holinshed, Bolingbroke went from Doncaster, and where York had halted on his way to meet the King on his return from Ireland. At line 53 the action localizes itself outside the castle. The material of the scene is created by Shakespeare from facts given by Holinshed.

I am a stranger here in Gloucestershire.
These high wild hills and rough uneven ways
Draws out our miles and makes them wearisome.
And yet your fair discourse hath been as sugar,
Making the hard way sweet and delectable.
But I bethink me what a weary way
From Ravenspurgh to Cotswold will be found
In Ross and Willoughby, wanting your company,   10
Which I protest hath very much beguiled
The tediousness and process of my travel.
But theirs is sweetened with the hope to have
The present benefit which I possess;
And hope to joy is little less in joy
Than hope enjoyed. By this the weary lords
Shall make their way seem short as mine hath done
By sight of what I have – your noble company.

BOLINGBROKE
Of much less value is my company
Than your good words. But who comes here?   20
    Enter Harry Percy

NORTHUMBERLAND
    It is my son, young Harry Percy,
    Sent from my brother Worcester whencesoever.

---

4 *high wild hills.* Northumberland is
  referring to the Cotswolds. He, of
  course, comes from the north of
  England.
5 *Draws ... makes.* For the grammar,
  see note to II.1.252.
7 *delectable* (accented on the first and
  third syllables)
9 *Cotswold.* Q reads 'Cotshall', an old
  form of the name of the Gloucestershire hills. In *The Merry Wives of
  Windsor* it is spelt 'Cotsall', and in *2
  Henry IV* 'Cotsole'. Shakespeare's
  pronunciation was probably something like 'Cotsul'.
11 *beguiled* passed pleasantly

12 *tediousness and process* tedious process
16 *By this* by this hope (of enjoying Bolingbroke's company)
20 (stage direction) *Harry Percy.* He
   lived from 1364 to 1403, when he
   was killed at the Battle of Shrewsbury. He was known as Hotspur because of his daring in battle against
   the border clans. He is vividly characterized in *1 Henry IV*. There is no
   proof in *Richard II* that Shakespeare
   had yet conceived the idiosyncrasies
   of the character as he later portrayed
   it.
22 *whencesoever* from somewhere or
   other; wherever he may be

Harry, how fares your uncle?

PERCY

I had thought, my lord, to have learned his health of you.

NORTHUMBERLAND

Why, is he not with the Queen?

PERCY

No, my good lord, he hath forsook the court,
Broken his staff of office, and dispersed
The household of the King.

NORTHUMBERLAND   What was his reason?
He was not so resolved when last we spake together.

PERCY

30   Because your lordship was proclaimèd traitor.
But he, my lord, is gone to Ravenspurgh
To offer service to the Duke of Hereford,
And sent me over by Berkeley to discover
What power the Duke of York had levied there,
Then with directions to repair to Ravenspurgh.

NORTHUMBERLAND

Have you forgot the Duke of Hereford, boy?

PERCY

No, my good lord; for that is not forgot
Which ne'er I did remember. To my knowledge
I never in my life did look on him.

NORTHUMBERLAND

40   Then learn to know him now – this is the Duke.

PERCY

My gracious lord, I tender you my service,
Such as it is, being tender, raw, and young,
Which elder days shall ripen and confirm

26–8 (as reported at II.2.58–61)
36 *Have you forgot the Duke of Hereford,
boy?* (a rebuke to Harry Percy for not
greeting Bolingbroke. *Boy* is unhis-
torical, as in fact 'young' Percy was
two years older than Bolingbroke. In
1 Henry IV Hotspur is of the same

generation as Prince Hal – he was
actually twenty-two years older.)
38 *To my knowledge* so far as I know; to
the best of my knowledge
43–4 *Which elder days shall ripen and con-
firm | To more approvèd service and
desert* (ironical, considering what hap-

To more approved service and desert.

BOLINGBROKE

I thank thee, gentle Percy; and be sure
I count myself in nothing else so happy
As in a soul remembering my good friends;
And as my fortune ripens with thy love
It shall be still thy true love's recompense.
My heart this covenant makes, my hand thus seals it.   50

NORTHUMBERLAND

How far is it to Berkeley, and what stir
Keeps good old York there with his men of war?

PERCY

There stands the castle by yon tuft of trees,
Manned with three hundred men as I have heard,
And in it are the Lords of York, Berkeley, and Seymour,
None else of name and noble estimate.

Enter Ross and Willoughby

NORTHUMBERLAND

Here come the Lords of Ross and Willoughby,
Bloody with spurring, fiery red with haste.

BOLINGBROKE

Welcome, my lords. I wot your love pursues
A banished traitor. All my treasury   60
Is yet but unfelt thanks, which, more enriched,
Shall be your love and labour's recompense.

ROSS

Your presence makes us rich, most noble lord.

---

pened later, portrayed by Shakespeare in *1 Henry IV*)
45–50 *I thank thee ... thus seals it.* Hotspur recalls this conversation with disgust at Bolingbroke's treachery in *1 Henry IV*, I.3.236–51.
45 *gentle* noble, 'gentlemanly'
47 *As in a soul remembering* as having a heart which remembers
49 *still* continually, all the time

50 *my hand thus seals it.* They shake hands.
51–2 *what stir | Keeps* 'what event detains' or 'what is [he] doing'
56 (stage direction) *Enter Ross and Willoughby.* They actually joined Bolingbroke when he landed at Ravenspurgh, not at Berkeley.
61 *unfelt* intangible
which (refers to *treasury*)

WILLOUGHBY
 And far surmounts our labour to attain it.

BOLINGBROKE
 Evermore thank's the exchequer of the poor,
 Which till my infant fortune comes to years
 Stands for my bounty. But who comes here?
     Enter Berkeley

NORTHUMBERLAND
 It is my Lord of Berkeley, as I guess.

BERKELEY
 My Lord of Hereford, my message is to you.

BOLINGBROKE
70 My lord, my answer is to 'Lancaster'.
 And I am come to seek that name in England,
 And I must find that title in your tongue
 Before I make reply to aught you say.

BERKELEY
 Mistake me not, my lord. 'Tis not my meaning
 To raze one title of your honour out.
 To you, my lord, I come – what lord you will –
 From the most gracious regent of this land,
 The Duke of York, to know what pricks you on

---

65 *Evermore thank's the exchequer* 'thank
you' is always (or 'always will be')
the exchequer ... F has 'Euermore
thankes, th'Exchequer of the poor',
which many editors follow; but
'thank' as an expression of gratitude
is an authenticated usage. *Thank* is
the antecedent of *Which* in the following line.

66 *to years* to years of discretion, into its
own

67 *Stands for* represents, does duty for

(stage direction) *Berkeley*. He was a
baron, and sat in Parliament from
1381 till 1417, when he died.

70 *my answer is to 'Lancaster'*. Berkeley
has addressed him by his former title
of 'Hereford'. He replies that he answers only to the title of 'Lancaster',

which he has inherited from his
father. It may be that he begins to
reply with 'my answer is', and then
interjects 'to "Lancaster"', meaning
that this is the only title to which he
will reply; or perhaps he says simply
'I reply only in the name of Lancaster.' Northumberland referred to him
as 'Hereford' without rebuke at line
36.

75 *raze one title of your honour out* (Q has
'race', a variant form). The title is
imagined as an inscription, as at
III.1.25 where Bolingbroke complains that his enemies have *Razed
out my imprese*. There is probably also
a pun on 'tittle', meaning 'any part
of'.

To take advantage of the absent time
And fright our native peace with self-borne arms.   80
    Enter York

BOLINGBROKE

I shall not need transport my words by you.
Here comes his grace in person. My noble uncle!
    He kneels

YORK

Show me thy humble heart, and not thy knee,
Whose duty is deceivable and false.

BOLINGBROKE

My gracious uncle –

YORK

Tut, tut, grace me no grace, nor uncle me no uncle!
I am no traitor's uncle; and that word 'grace'
In an ungracious mouth is but profane.
Why have those banished and forbidden legs
Dared once to touch a dust of England's ground?   90
But then more 'why' – why have they dared to march
So many miles upon her peaceful bosom,
Frighting her pale-faced villages with war
And ostentation of despisèd arms?

79 *absent time* time of (King Richard's) absence

80 *self-borne*. This may mean 'born of' or 'originating in' yourself, or 'carried for your own cause', or 'carried by yourself', or may be a quibble on these meanings: 'begotten and carried on your own initiative and for your own ends'.

84 *duty* (the act of kneeling)
deceivable deceptive

86 *Tut, tut.* This extra-metrical exclamation has been suspected of being an actor's interpolation.
grace me no grace, nor uncle me no uncle! Shakespeare uses a similar contemptuous refusal of courtesy in *Romeo and Juliet*, III.5.152: 'Thank me no thankings, nor proud me no prouds.'

87–8 *'grace' . . . profane* (alluding to the religious connotations of 'grace', which would have been felt more strongly by Shakespeare's than by a modern audience)

88 *ungracious* wicked. The word was much stronger in Shakespeare's time than it is at present.

90 *dust* grain of dust

91 *But then more 'why'* but even if that can be answered there are more questions (and, perhaps, ones even more indicative of astonishment) to be asked

94 *ostentation* display

Comest thou because the anointed King is hence?
Why, foolish boy, the King is left behind,
And in my loyal bosom lies his power.
Were I but now lord of such hot youth
As when brave Gaunt, thy father, and myself
100   Rescued the Black Prince – that young Mars of men –
From forth the ranks of many thousand French,
O then how quickly should this arm of mine,
Now prisoner to the palsy, chastise thee
And minister correction to thy fault!

BOLINGBROKE
My gracious uncle, let me know my fault.
On what condition stands it, and wherein?

YORK
Even in condition of the worst degree,
In gross rebellion and detested treason.
Thou art a banished man, and here art come
110   Before the expiration of thy time
In braving arms against thy sovereign!

BOLINGBROKE
As I was banished, I was banished Hereford;
But as I come, I come for Lancaster.
And, noble uncle, I beseech your grace
Look on my wrongs with an indifferent eye.
You are my father; for methinks in you
I see old Gaunt alive. O then, my father,

---

98 *lord*. F reads 'the lord', which may be correct; but the irregular metre has strength.

98–101 There is no clear source of this incident.

100 *the Black Prince* (King Richard's father)

102–3 *arm of mine,* | *Now prisoner to the palsy.* Palsy is a paralytic condition. This may be no more than a general reference to York's advanced years, but it has been said that there is

historical warrant for the statement.

103 *chastise*. The accent is on the first syllable.

106–7 *condition . . . condition.* In its first use, the word refers to Bolingbroke's personal qualities; in its second, to the circumstances of the rebellion.

111 *braving* defiant, daring (adjectival rather than verbal)

113 *for* 'in the character of', 'as'; or 'to assume the title and rights of'

115 *indifferent* impartial

Will you permit that I shall stand condemned
A wandering vagabond, my rights and royalties
Plucked from my arms perforce, and given away   120
To upstart unthrifts? Wherefore was I born?
If that my cousin King be King in England
It must be granted I am Duke of Lancaster.
You have a son, Aumerle, my noble cousin.
Had you first died and he been thus trod down
He should have found his uncle Gaunt a father
To rouse his wrongs and chase them to the bay.
I am denied to sue my livery here,
And yet my letters patents give me leave.
My father's goods are all distrained and sold,   130
And these, and all, are all amiss employed.
What would you have me do? I am a subject,
And I challenge law. Attorneys are denied me,
And therefore personally I lay my claim
To my inheritance of free descent.

NORTHUMBERLAND (*to York*)
    The noble Duke hath been too much abused.

ROSS
    It stands your grace upon to do him right.

118–19 *condemned | A* condemned as a
119 *royalties* (rights granted to a subject
    by the king, as at II.1.190)
120 *arms*. The sense 'coat-of-arms' is
    felt.
121 *unthrifts* spendthrifts, prodigals
    (such as the King's favourites)
122–3 *If that my cousin King . . . Duke of
    Lancaster*. Compare York's argument
    to Richard on Bolingbroke's behalf,
    II.1.191–9.
122 *cousin King* cousin who is king;
    kingly cousin
125 *thus* (as I have)
127 *rouse . . . wrongs . . . bay*. The meta-
    phor is from hunting. *Rouse*, startle
    from the lair. The *wrongs* (presumably
    'wrongdoers') are the quarry. *Bay*,

last stand.
128 *denied* refused the right
128–9 *sue my livery . . . letters patents* (see
    Commentary to II.1.203–4)
130 *distrained* seized, taken possession of
    by crown officers
131 *and all* and everything else
132–5 Holinshed writes that when Bol-
    ingbroke arrived at Doncaster he
    swore 'that he would demand no
    more but the lands that were to him
    descended by inheritance from his
    father and in right of his wife'.
133 *challenge law* demand my rights
135 *of free descent* free from flaw; direct
137 *It stands your grace upon* it is incum-
    bent upon your grace

WILLOUGHBY
Base men by his endowments are made great.
YORK
My lords of England, let me tell you this:
140   I have had feeling of my cousin's wrongs,
And laboured all I could to do him right.
But in this kind to come, in braving arms,
Be his own carver, and cut out his way
To find out right with wrong – it may not be.
And you that do abet him in this kind
Cherish rebellion, and are rebels all.
NORTHUMBERLAND
The noble Duke hath sworn his coming is
But for his own, and for the right of that
We all have strongly sworn to give him aid;
150   And let him never see joy that breaks that oath.
YORK
Well, well, I see the issue of these arms.
I cannot mend it, I must needs confess,
Because my power is weak and all ill-left.
But if I could, by Him that gave me life,
I would attach you all and make you stoop
Unto the sovereign mercy of the King.
But since I cannot, be it known unto you
I do remain as neuter. So fare you well,
Unless you please to enter in the castle
160   And there repose you for this night.

138 *his endowments* the possessions with
   which he has (involuntarily) en-
   dowed them
   are (presumably this is accented; that is,
   'it is true that . . .')
142 *kind* manner
143 *Be his own carver.* The phrase seems
   to have been proverbial – 'help himself'. It gains point from the double
   sense of carving with a table-knife

and a sword.
144 *find out right with wrong* achieve your
   rights by doing wrong
150 *never* (probably to be pronounced
   'ne'er')
153 *power* army
   ill-left 'left ill-equipped' or 'left in
   disorder'
155 *attach* arrest
158 *as neuter* neutral

BOLINGBROKE

An offer, uncle, that we will accept;
But we must win your grace to go with us
To Bristol Castle, which they say is held
By Bushy, Bagot, and their complices,
The caterpillars of the commonwealth,
Which I have sworn to weed and pluck away.

YORK

It may be I will go with you, but yet I'll pause;
For I am loath to break our country's laws.
Nor friends, nor foes, to me welcome you are.
Things past redress are now with me past care.   170

Exeunt

Enter Earl of Salisbury and a Welsh Captain   II.4

CAPTAIN

My Lord of Salisbury, we have stayed ten days
And hardly kept our countrymen together,
And yet we hear no tidings from the King.

---

164 *Bagot.* At 11.2.140 (see note) he had declared his intention of going to Ireland.

165 *caterpillars of the commonwealth* parasites on society

166 *weed.* The word could be used of the removal of harmful creatures as well as plants. It is part of the recurrent image of England as a garden.

170 *Things past redress are now with me past care.* York gives vent to his divided feelings in a semi-proverbial expression.

11.4 This scene is based on Holinshed, who explains that because of storms Richard was late in hearing that Bolingbroke had landed in England, and that Richard did not set out immediately on hearing the news, but was persuaded to delay till his preparations were complete.

(stage direction) *Earl of Salisbury.* John de Montacute (or Montagu), 1350–1400.

Welsh Captain. In Holinshed the Welsh captain is Owen Glendower, who figures prominently in 1 *Henry IV.* The fact that the Welsh Captain speaks of omens and portents (lines 8–15), as Glendower does in the later play, gives some colour to the suggestion that Shakespeare identified the two. But he seems to have preferred not to give the captain a name. He is important rather for his representative quality than for any personal characteristics. See note to III.1.43.

1 *ten days.* According to Holinshed the Welshmen waited for fourteen days.

2 *hardly* with difficulty

3 *yet* still, so far

Therefore we will disperse ourselves. Farewell.

SALISBURY

Stay yet another day, thou trusty Welshman.
The King reposeth all his confidence in thee.

CAPTAIN

'Tis thought the King is dead. We will not stay.
The bay trees in our country are all withered,
And meteors fright the fixèd stars of heaven.
10   The pale-faced moon looks bloody on the earth,
And lean-looked prophets whisper fearful change.
Rich men look sad, and ruffians dance and leap –
The one in fear to lose what they enjoy,
The other to enjoy by rage and war.
These signs forerun the death or fail of kings.
Farewell. Our countrymen are gone and fled,
As well assured Richard their king is dead.   *Exit*

SALISBURY

Ah, Richard! With the eyes of heavy mind
I see thy glory like a shooting star

5–6 *thou trusty Welshman.* | *The King re-*
poseth all his confidence in thee. Holinshed
records that Richard 'had also no
small affiance [confidence] in the
Welshmen, and Cheshire men'.

8 ff. The expression of superstitious fear
in these lines is the main point of the
scene. Glendower in *1 Henry IV* (III.1)
speaks similarly. Whether or not the
Welsh Captain is Glendower, Shakespeare may have felt that such sentiments were specially appropriate in
the mouth of a Welshman. According to Holinshed the withering of
the bay trees happened in England,
not Wales: 'In this year in a manner
throughout all the realm of England
old bay trees withered, and afterwards, contrary to all men's thinking,
grew green again, a strange sight, and
supposed to import some unknown
event.' This passage occurs first in the

second (1587) edition of Holinshed,
and the parallel is part of the evidence for Shakespeare's use of this
edition. The bay tree was symbolical of
victory and immortality; its withering
was thus a particularly bad omen.

9 *meteors . . . fixèd stars.* Meteors, of
course, are 'unfixed' stars.

10 *The pale-faced moon looks bloody on the*
earth. Looks used of planets and stars
implies influence as well as appearance. This line may mean that the
normally pale-faced moon appears
bloody to earthly watchers, or that it
exerts a bloody influence.

11 *lean-looked* lean-looking
prophets soothsayers (rather than religiously inspired men)

14 *to enjoy* in hope of profiting

19–21 *I see thy glory . . . west.* These lines
anticipate Richard's imagery at
III.3.178–83.

Fall to the base earth from the firmament.   20
Thy sun sets weeping in the lowly west,
Witnessing storms to come, woe, and unrest.
Thy friends are fled to wait upon thy foes,
And crossly to thy good all fortune goes.   *Exit*

Enter Bolingbroke, York, Northumberland, with   III.I
Bushy and Green, prisoners

BOLINGBROKE

Bring forth these men.
Bushy and Green, I will not vex your souls,
Since presently your souls must part your bodies,
With too much urging your pernicious lives,
For 'twere no charity. Yet, to wash your blood
From off my hands, here in the view of men

22 *Witnessing* betokening
24 *crossly* adversely

III.I The basis of the scene is Holinshed's statement that 'the foresaid dukes with their power went towards Bristol where, at their coming, they showed themselves before the town and castle, being an huge multitude of people. There were enclosed within the castle the Lord William Scroop Earl of Wiltshire and Treasurer of England, Sir Henry Green, and Sir John Bushy, knights, who prepared to make resistance. But when it would not prevail they were taken and brought forth bound as prisoners into the camp before the Duke of Lancaster. On the morrow next ensuing they were arraigned before the Constable and Marshal and found guilty of treason for misgoverning the King and realm, and forthwith had their heads smit off.' Shakespeare omits Wiltshire, who makes no appearance in the play though at II.2.135 he is said to be at Bristol, and at III.2.141–2 and III.4.53 he is mentioned as having been executed along with Bushy and Green. It is possible that Shakespeare wrongly identified him with Bagot – see note to III.2.122.

(stage direction) F directs Ross, Percy, and Willoughby also to enter. They are not required by the action; but it may have been the custom to bring them on to dress the stage.

3 *presently* immediately
  part leave
4 *urging* stressing
5–6 *to wash your blood | From off my hands* to justify my condemning you. The phrase inevitably recalls Pontius Pilate's action, directly referred to by Richard at IV.1.238–41.

I will unfold some causes of your deaths.
You have misled a prince, a royal king,
A happy gentleman in blood and lineaments,
10 By you unhappied and disfigured clean.
You have in manner with your sinful hours
Made a divorce betwixt his Queen and him,
Broke the possession of a royal bed,
And stained the beauty of a fair queen's cheeks
With tears drawn from her eyes by your foul wrongs.
Myself – a prince by fortune of my birth,
Near to the King in blood, and near in love
Till you did make him misinterpret me –
Have stooped my neck under your injuries,
20 And sighed my English breath in foreign clouds,
Eating the bitter bread of banishment
Whilst you have fed upon my signories,
Disparked my parks, and felled my forest woods,
From my own windows torn my household coat,
Razed out my imprese, leaving me no sign

9 *A happy gentleman in* a gentleman fortunate in *blood and lineaments* birth and personal appearance
10 *clean* utterly.
11–12 *You have in manner with your sinful hours | Made a divorce betwixt his Queen and him*. This accusation does not appear to be borne out by the relations between Richard and his Queen in the rest of the play. It may have been suggested by Holinshed's 'there reigned abundantly the filthy sin of lechery, and fornication, with abominable adultery, specially in the King . . .' Shakespeare may also have been influenced by the clearly homosexual relationship of Edward and Gaveston in Marlowe's *Edward II*, though he does not necessarily imply sexual opposition between the King's favourites and the Queen. In *Woodstock* Richard displays intense affection for Greene. Perhaps the principal point

in *Richard II* is simply that the Queen stands at this point in the play as a symbol of the virtue from which Richard's favourites are diverting him.
11 *in manner* as it were
12 *divorce* (used metaphorically)
13 *possession* joint rights
20 *in* into (adding to them as well as mixing breath among them. So in *Romeo and Juliet*, 1.1.133: 'Adding to clouds more clouds with his deep sighs.')
22 *signories* estates, manors
23 *Disparked* (converted to other, less aristocratic, uses land in which game had been kept)
24 *From my own windows torn my household coat* broken the windows in which my coat-of-arms was emblazoned ('tear' could mean 'break')
25 *imprese* crest, heraldic device (this is the Italian plural of the singular *impresa*)

Save men's opinions and my living blood
To show the world I am a gentleman.
This and much more, much more than twice all this,
Condemns you to the death. See them delivered over
To execution and the hand of death.   30

BUSHY

More welcome is the stroke of death to me
Than Bolingbroke to England. Lords, farewell.

GREEN

My comfort is that heaven will take our soul
And plague injustice with the pains of hell.

BOLINGBROKE

My Lord Northumberland, see them dispatched.

Exit Northumberland with Bushy and Green

Uncle, you say the Queen is at your house.
For God's sake, fairly let her be intreated.
Tell her I send to her my kind commends.
Take special care my greetings be delivered.

YORK

A gentleman of mine I have dispatched   40
With letters of your love to her at large.

BOLINGBROKE

Thanks, gentle uncle. Come, lords, away,
To fight with Glendower and his complices.
A while to work, and after, holiday.   *Exeunt*

27 *gentleman* nobleman
36 *your house* (Langley)
37 *intreated* treated
41 *at large* in full (or 'in general terms')
43 *Glendower.* Owen Glendower is not
mentioned elsewhere in this play (but
see Commentary to II.4, opening
stage direction), though he is important in *1 Henry IV*. Holinshed says

that Glendower 'served King Richard at Flint Castle when he [Richard]
was taken by Henry, Duke of Lancaster'. Probably Shakespeare's main
reason for the choice of name here
was its obvious Welshness, though
he may have been thinking ahead to
the events of the reign of Henry IV.

III.2   *Drums; flourish and colours. Enter King Richard,*
                   Aumerle, the Bishop of Carlisle, and soldiers

KING RICHARD
   Barkloughly Castle call they this at hand?

AUMERLE
   Yea, my lord. How brooks your grace the air
   After your late tossing on the breaking seas?

KING RICHARD
   Needs must I like it well. I weep for joy
   To stand upon my kingdom once again.

III.2 The basis of this scene is Holinshed, who reports that the King 'landed near the castle of Barkloughly in Wales . . . and stayed a while in the same castle, being advertised of the great forces which the Duke of Lancaster had got together against him, wherewith he was marvellously amazed, knowing certainly that those which were thus in arms with the Duke of Lancaster against him would rather die than give place, as well for the hatred as fear which they had conceived at him.' He went to Conway, 'but when he understood as he went thus forward that all the castles even from the borders of Scotland unto Bristol were delivered unto the Duke of Lancaster, and that likewise the nobles and commons as well of the south parts as the north were fully bent to take part with the same Duke against him; and further, hearing how his trusty councillors had lost their heads at Bristol, he became so greatly discomforted that, sorrowfully lamenting his miserable state, he utterly despaired of his own safety and, calling his army together, which was not small, licensed every man to depart to his home.' Holinshed's later comment is interesting as an expression of the kind of sympathy which Shakespeare too begins to evoke; he writes how remarkable it is that Bolingbroke should have been advanced to the throne, 'and that King Richard should thus be left desolate, void, and in despair of all hope and comfort, in whom if there were any offence it ought rather to be imputed to the frailty of wanton youth than to the malice of his heart; but such is the deceivable judgement of man which, not regarding things present with due consideration, thinketh ever that things to come shall have good success, with a pleasant and delightful end'.

(stage direction) *colours* banners

Bishop of Carlisle. He was Thomas Merke, a friend and follower of King Richard. The Pope appointed him Bishop in 1397, at Richard's request. He was arrested in 1399 and pardoned in 1400, after which he became a country vicar, and died in 1409. Holinshed reports that he died 'shortly after' 1400.

1 *Barkloughly.* The name derives from Holinshed, where it seems to be an error for a form of Harlech.

2 *brooks* enjoys

Dear earth, I do salute thee with my hand,
Though rebels wound thee with their horses' hoofs.
As a long-parted mother with her child
Plays fondly with her tears and smiles in meeting,
So weeping, smiling, greet I thee, my earth,   10
And do thee favours with my royal hands.
Feed not thy sovereign's foe, my gentle earth,
Nor with thy sweets comfort his ravenous sense,
But let thy spiders that suck up thy venom,
And heavy-gaited toads, lie in their way,
Doing annoyance to the treacherous feet
Which with usurping steps do trample thee.
Yield stinging nettles to mine enemies;
And when they from thy bosom pluck a flower
Guard it, I pray thee, with a lurking adder,   20
Whose double tongue may with a mortal touch
Throw death upon thy sovereign's enemies.
Mock not my senseless conjuration, lords.
This earth shall have a feeling, and these stones
Prove armed soldiers ere her native king

6–7 *I . . . rebels.* The two words are contrasted.

6 *salute* greet. Richard bends to touch the ground.

8 *long-parted mother with* mother long parted from

9 *fondly.* The word implies a mixture of affection and slight folly. Shakespeare often uses the image of tears and smiles at once as in the description of Cordelia hearing news of King Lear: 'You have seen | Sunshine and rain at once: her smiles and tears | Were like a better way' (*King Lear*, IV.3.17–19). See also V.2.32.

14 *spiders that suck up thy venom.* It was believed that spiders were dangerously poisonous, and that they sucked their poison from the earth.

15 *heavy-gaited* (referring to the toad's clumsy movements)
toads. Like spiders, they were thought to be poisonous.

21 *double* forked

23 *senseless* (addressed to things which lack the sense of hearing)

24–5 *stones | Prove armed soldiers.* This seems like a reference to the myth of Cadmus, who sowed dragons' teeth which sprang up as soldiers. Gospel echoes are also possible: Luke 19.40: 'I tell you that if these would hold their peace then shall the stones cry immediately', and 3.8: 'God is able of these stones to raise up children unto Abraham.'

Shall falter under foul rebellion's arms.

BISHOP OF CARLISLE

Fear not, my lord, that power that made you king
Hath power to keep you king in spite of all.
The means that heavens yield must be embraced
And not neglected; else heaven would,
And we will not – heaven's offer we refuse,
The proffered means of succour and redress.

AUMERLE

He means, my lord, that we are too remiss,
Whilst Bolingbroke through our security
Grows strong and great in substance and in power.

KING RICHARD

Discomfortable cousin, knowest thou not
That when the searching eye of heaven is hid

30

---

27 *Fear not* do not doubt that. Or perhaps *Fear not, my lord* should form a
complete sentence.
29–32 These lines were omitted from F,
perhaps because they are obscure.
Perhaps they mean 'We must accept,
not neglect, the means that the heavens offer; otherwise we run counter
to heaven's wish – we refuse heaven's
offer . . .' The sentiment is common,
e.g. Prospero in *The Tempest*,
1.2.181–4:

my zenith doth depend upon
A most auspicious star, whose
influence
If now I court not, but omit, my
fortunes
Will ever after droop.

34 *security* over-confidence
36 *Discomfortable* disheartening. Shakespeare does not use the negative form
elsewhere; it may have been suggested by Holinshed's statement

that Richard became 'greatly
discomforted'.
37–8 *when the searching eye of heaven is hid* |
*Behind the globe, that lights the lower
world*. Richard again compares himself with the sun; his absence in Ireland is like the nightly departure of
the sun to light the other side of the
world (*the lower world*). The notion
that robberies are liable to take place
at night is commonplace enough, but
it may be worth comparing Falstaff's
'we that take purses go by the moon
and the seven stars, and not "by
Phoebus, he, that wandering knight
so fair" (*1 Henry IV*, 1.2.13–15).
The syntax of Richard's lines is obscure, and the sense difficult for the
actor to convey, but this is probably
what Shakespeare wrote. A common
emendation alters *that* to 'and', which
simplifies the sentence and makes the
meaning clearer.

Behind the globe, that lights the lower world,
Then thieves and robbers range abroad unseen
In murders and in outrage boldly here;   40
But when from under this terrestrial ball
He fires the proud tops of the eastern pines,
And darts his light through every guilty hole,
Then murders, treasons, and detested sins –
The cloak of night being plucked from off their backs –
Stand bare and naked, trembling at themselves?
So when this thief, this traitor Bolingbroke,
Who all this while hath revelled in the night
Whilst we were wandering with the Antipodes,
Shall see us rising in our throne, the east,   50
His treasons will sit blushing in his face,
Not able to endure the sight of day,
But self-affrighted, tremble at his sin.
Not all the water in the rough rude sea
Can wash the balm off from an anointed king.
The breath of worldly men cannot depose
The deputy elected by the Lord.
For every man that Bolingbroke hath pressed
To lift shrewd steel against our golden crown,
God for his Richard hath in heavenly pay   60
A glorious angel. Then if angels fight,
Weak men must fall; for heaven still guards the right.

---

41 *this terrestrial ball* (the earth)
42 *He* (the sun)
    fires (metaphorically) sets on fire
46 *at themselves* (at the revelation of their
    own wickedness)
49 *the Antipodes* (the people living on
    the opposite side of the earth. Rich-
    ard has only been as far as Ireland,
    but the metaphor is continued from
    line 38.)
54 *rude* rough, stormy

55 *balm* consecrated oil
57 *elected* chosen
58 *pressed* conscripted
59 *shrewd* harmful
59–61 *crown . . . angel.* These were both
    coins, on the names of which Shake-
    speare often puns. *In heavenly pay* es-
    tablishes the wordplay which leads to
    the curious notion of wage-earning
    angels.
62 *still* always

Enter Salisbury

KING RICHARD

Welcome, my lord. How far off lies your power?

SALISBURY

Nor nea'er nor farther off, my gracious lord,
Than this weak arm. Discomfort guides my tongue
And bids me speak of nothing but despair.
One day too late, I fear me, noble lord,
Hath clouded all thy happy days on earth.
O, call back yesterday – bid time return,
70   And thou shalt have twelve thousand fighting men.
Today, today, unhappy day too late,
O'erthrows thy joys, friends, fortune, and thy state;
For all the Welshmen, hearing thou wert dead,
Are gone to Bolingbroke – dispersed and fled.

AUMERLE

Comfort, my liege. Why looks your grace so pale?

KING RICHARD

But now the blood of twenty thousand men
    Did triumph in my face; and they are fled.
And till so much blood thither come again
    Have I not reason to look pale and dead?
80   All souls that will be safe fly from my side,
For time hath set a blot upon my pride.

AUMERLE

Comfort, my liege. Remember who you are.

---

63 *power* army (though Salisbury takes it
    in the more abstract sense)
64 *nea'er.* Q prints 'neare', which in Eliza-
    bethan English could mean 'nearer'.
    'Nearer' is required by the sense, and
    in speaking could be elided to form
    one syllable.
67–74 For Richard in relation to time,
    see Introduction, page 29.
76–81 Here the verse takes the form of
    the sestet of a sonnet.

76 *But now* just now
    twenty. Perhaps the requirements of
    metre are responsible for the discrep-
    ancy with *twelve* (line 70).
79 *dead* death-like
80 *fly.* This may be indicative – 'do fly';
    imperative – 'fly!'; or subjunctive –
    'let [them] fly!'

KING RICHARD

I had forgot myself. Am I not King?
Awake, thou coward majesty; thou sleepest.
Is not the King's name twenty thousand names?
Arm, arm, my name! A puny subject strikes
At thy great glory. Look not to the ground,
Ye favourites of a King. Are we not high?
High be our thoughts. I know my uncle York
Hath power enough to serve our turn. But who comes   90
    here?
        Enter Scroop

SCROOP

More health and happiness betide my liege
Than can my care-tuned tongue deliver him.

KING RICHARD

Mine ear is open and my heart prepared.
The worst is worldly loss thou canst unfold.
Say, is my kingdom lost? Why, 'twas my care;
And what loss is it to be rid of care?
Strives Bolingbroke to be as great as we?
Greater he shall not be. If he serve God
We'll serve Him too, and be his fellow so.
Revolt our subjects? That we cannot mend.   100
They break their faith to God as well as us.
Cry woe, destruction, ruin, and decay.

90 *power* (including the sense of 'army'.)
(stage direction) *Scroop.* Sir Stephen Scroop was a famous warrior, and was among the few who remained faithful to King Richard after his arrest. He died in 1408.
91 *betide* (subjunctive: 'may [they] betide . . .')
92 *care-tuned* tuned to the key of sorrow
93 *Mine ear is open.* Dr Johnson comments: 'It seems to be the design of the poet to raise Richard to esteem in his fall, and consequently to inter-

est the reader in his favour. He gives him only passive fortitude, the virtue of a confessor rather than of a king. In his prosperity we saw him imperious and oppressive, but in his distress he is wise, patient, and pious.'
95 *care* trouble
99 *his fellow* (Bolingbroke's equal)
101 *They break their faith to God as well as us* (because the King is God's deputy)
102 *Cry* (even if you) proclaim

The worst is death, and death will have his day.

SCROOP

Glad am I that your highness is so armed
To bear the tidings of calamity.
Like an unseasonable stormy day
Which makes the silver rivers drown their shores
As if the world were all dissolved to tears,
So high above his limits swells the rage

110   Of Bolingbroke, covering your fearful land
With hard bright steel, and hearts harder than steel.
Whitebeards have armed their thin and hairless scalps
Against thy majesty. Boys with women's voices
Strive to speak big and clap their female joints
In stiff unwieldy arms against thy crown.
Thy very beadsmen learn to bend their bows
Of double-fatal yew against thy state.
Yea, distaff-women manage rusty bills
Against thy seat. Both young and old rebel,

120   And all goes worse than I have power to tell.

KING RICHARD

Too well, too well thou tellest a tale so ill.

---

109 *his limits* its banks
110 *fearful* filled with fear
111 *steel* (of arms and armour)
112 *Whitebeards* old men
114 *speak big* imitate men's tones
    female womanish
115 *stiff unwieldy* (perhaps because new, or because the boys are not strong enough to wear it properly)
    arms armour
116 *beadsmen* almsmen, pensioners (with the duty of offering prayers or 'beads' on behalf of their benefactors)
117 *double-fatal yew* (fatal both because the tree's berries are poisonous and because its wood is used to make bows)

118 *distaff-women* women normally occupied in spinning
    manage wield
    bills bill-hooks, halberds. These are *rusty* from long disuse.
119 *seat* throne
122 *Where is Bagot?* He appears again in IV.1. It has been thought odd that Richard, at line 132, in referring to *Three Judases*, and again at line 141, when he names all but Bagot, should seem to know without being told that Bagot has survived. This may be the result of imperfect revision on Shakespeare's part. Ure comments: 'I suggest that Shakespeare, when he wrote l. 132, was already thinking ahead to ll. 141–2 and IV.1; he was planning to have one of the four

Where is the Earl of Wiltshire? Where is Bagot?
What is become of Bushy, where is Green,
That they have let the dangerous enemy
Measure our confines with such peaceful steps?
If we prevail, their heads shall pay for it.
I warrant they have made peace with Bolingbroke.

SCROOP

Peace have they made with him indeed, my lord.

KING RICHARD

O, villains, vipers, damned without redemption!
Dogs easily won to fawn on any man!   130
Snakes in my heart-blood warmed, that sting my heart;
Three Judases, each one thrice worse than Judas –
Would they make peace? Terrible hell

men alive for IV.I, but forgot that
Richard could not yet know, when
he breaks out at l. 132, what Shakespeare was arranging to have him
told at ll. 141–2: Shakespeare carelessly anticipated but did not grossly
resurrect.' He may, however, have
recalled that according to Holinshed
Bagot 'escaped into Ireland', which
probably means to join the King
there. See note to II.2.122.

125 *Measure* pass through
peaceful unopposed

128 *Peace have they made with him indeed.*
The quibble on 'making peace' is
not uncommon, and Scroop's line
should carry a sombre irony. Compare *Macbeth*, IV.3.178–9:

MACDUFF
The tyrant has not battered at their
peace?
ROSS
No. They were well at peace when I
did leave 'em.

129 *vipers, damned without redemption.* The
viper was traditionally treacherous.

Shakespeare may have been influenced by Matthew 23.33: 'Ye ser-
pents, ye generation of vipers, how
will ye escape the damnation of hell?'
(*without*, beyond hope of)

131 *Snakes in my heart-blood warmed, that
sting my heart.* The image was
common. Shakespeare uses it again
at V.3.57 (*A serpent that will sting thee
to the heart*), and in *2 Henry VI*,
III.1.343–4: 'I fear me you but
warmed the starved snake | Who,
cherished in your breasts, will sting
your hearts.' There was a well-
known fable about a farmer bitten
by a snake which he found nearly
dead from cold and warmed in his
breast.

132 *Judases.* Richard elsewhere (for example, IV.1.170) compares himself to
Christ; but Judas was a common
word for a traitor.

133 *Would they make peace? Terrible hell.*
The line is metrically short. This may
be intended to invite emphasis on
Richard's outburst. *They* is emphatic.
F reads:

Make war upon their spotted souls for this.

SCROOP

Sweet love, I see, changing his property,
Turns to the sourest and most deadly hate.
Again uncurse their souls. Their peace is made
With heads and not with hands. Those whom you curse
Have felt the worst of death's destroying wound,
And lie full low, graved in the hollow ground.

140

AUMERLE

Is Bushy, Green, and the Earl of Wiltshire dead?

SCROOP

Ay. All of them at Bristol lost their heads.

AUMERLE

Where is the Duke, my father, with his power?

KING RICHARD

No matter where. Of comfort no man speak.
Let's talk of graves, of worms, and epitaphs;
Make dust our paper, and with rainy eyes
Write sorrow on the bosom of the earth.
Let's choose executors and talk of wills –
And yet not so; for what can we bequeath

150

Save our deposèd bodies to the ground?
Our lands, our lives, and all are Bolingbroke's,
And nothing can we call our own but death

Would they make peace? terrible Hell
  make warre
Vpon their spotted Soules for this
  Offence.

This is probably an unauthentic
attempt to regularize the metre.
134 *spotted* stained, sinful. There may
also be a hint of the spotted skin of
the viper.
135 *his property* its distinctive quality
138 *hands* (for signing treaties, or shak-
ing in amity, or lifting in submission)

138–40 *Those . . . ground*. The inflated expression gives weight to the statement of a fact which has been in
suspense since line 122.
140 *graved* buried
141 Richard's failure – or inability – to
speak here may give a cue to the
actor. As often in Shakespeare, afflic-
tion does not find immediate
expression.
150 *deposèd*. Richard already sees himself
as deposed from the throne. The
word may also carry the sense of
'deposited'.

And that small model of the barren earth
Which serves as paste and cover to our bones.
For God's sake let us sit upon the ground
And tell sad stories of the death of kings –
How some have been deposed, some slain in war,
Some haunted by the ghosts they have deposed,
Some poisoned by their wives, some sleeping killed,
All murdered. For within the hollow crown   160
That rounds the mortal temples of a king
Keeps death his court; and there the antic sits,
Scoffing his state and grinning at his pomp,
Allowing him a breath, a little scene,
To monarchize, be feared, and kill with looks,
Infusing him with self and vain conceit,
As if this flesh which walls about our life

153–4 *that small model of the barren earth | Which serves as paste and cover to our bones*. Probably a reference to the flesh as microcosm, corresponding on a small scale to the earth. But *model* might also mean 'mould' or 'something that envelops closely'. According to this interpretation Richard says that all we finally possess is the earth that surrounds our body.

154 *paste* pastry (alluding to the pastry cover, sometimes called a coffin, in which meat was baked)

156 *stories of the death of kings*. The most famous collection of such stories was *A Mirror for Magistrates* (1559 etc.) but there were others. The lines that follow recall Shakespeare's *Richard III*, v.3, in which the ghosts of his dead enemies appear to Richard.

158 *ghosts they have deposed* ghosts of those whom they have deprived of life.

162 *antic* buffoon, jester. Dr Johnson commented 'Here is an allusion to the *antick* or *fool* of old farces, whose chief part is to deride and disturb the graver and more splendid personages'; the image is continued in *little scene* (line 164). Death was frequently portrayed as a skeleton grinning at the futile pretensions of mankind.

163 *Scoffing his state* scoffing at his (the king's) splendour

164 *scene*. The image of life as a play enacted upon the stage of the world was common; see Introduction, pages 37–8.

165 *monarchize* play a king's part. This is the first known use of the word.
kill with looks (an image of kingly power, able to order execution with a glance)

166 *self and vain conceit* vain conceit of himself. *Self* is adjectival.

167–8 *As if this flesh which walls about our life | Were brass impregnable*. This may be influenced by Job 6.12: 'Is my strength the strength of stones? or is my flesh of brass?' But brass was a common symbol of imperishability. In the story of Friar Bacon and Friar Bungay, well known to

Were brass impregnable; and humoured thus,
Comes at the last, and with a little pin
170   Bores through his castle wall, and – farewell, king!
Cover your heads, and mock not flesh and blood
With solemn reverence. Throw away respect,
Tradition, form, and ceremonious duty;
For you have but mistook me all this while.
I live with bread, like you; feel want,
Taste grief, need friends. Subjected thus,
How can you say to me I am a king?

BISHOP OF CARLISLE
My lord, wise men ne'er sit and wail their woes,
But presently prevent the ways to wail.
180   To fear the foe, since fear oppresseth strength,
Gives in your weakness strength unto your foe,
And so your follies fight against yourself.
Fear, and be slain. No worse can come to fight;
And fight and die is death destroying death,
Where fearing dying pays death servile breath.

Shakespeare and his audience through Robert Greene's play, one of Friar Bacon's aims is to surround Britain with a wall of brass; and Marlowe's Doctor Faustus says 'I'll have them wall all Germany with brass' (I.I).

168 *humoured thus*. Either 'death having thus amused himself'; or 'death having thus indulged the king'; or 'while the king is in this humour (mood)'. All three meanings may well be present.

169–70 *pin | Bores through his castle wall*. The image changes, and becomes that of an attack on a besieged castle.

171 *Cover your heads* replace your hats. Richard tells his subjects not to treat him with the reverence due to kingship. He is stressing his humanity.

175–6 The short lines invite the actor to use pauses for emphasis. There is no need to assume textual corruption.

176 *Subjected*. The King is a 'subject' – to human needs.

179 *presently* promptly
prevent the ways to wail. An odd expression: *prevent* is used in the now obsolete sense 'avoid by prompt action'; *the ways to wail* seems to mean 'paths to grief'. The desire for alliteration probably played its part in the choice of words.

183 *to fight* in fighting; if you fight

184–5 *fight and die is death destroying death, | Where fearing dying pays death servile breath* to die fighting is to destroy death's power by means of death, whereas to live in fear of death is to pay it undeserved homage

AUMERLE

    My father hath a power. Inquire of him,
    And learn to make a body of a limb.

KING RICHARD

    Thou chidest me well. Proud Bolingbroke, I come
    To change blows with thee for our day of doom.
    This ague-fit of fear is overblown.   190
    An easy task it is to win our own.
    Say, Scroop, where lies our uncle with his power?
    Speak sweetly, man, although thy looks be sour.

SCROOP

    Men judge by the complexion of the sky
        The state and inclination of the day.
    So may you by my dull and heavy eye
        My tongue hath but a heavier tale to say.
    I play the torturer, by small and small
    To lengthen out the worst that must be spoken.
    Your uncle York is joined with Bolingbroke,   200
    And all your northern castles yielded up,
    And all your southern gentlemen in arms
    Upon his party.

KING RICHARD   Thou hast said enough.

    (*To Aumerle*)

    Beshrew thee, cousin, which didst lead me forth

---

186 *of* from (or perhaps, since at line 192 Richard inquires about York's whereabouts, 'about')

187 *make a body of a limb* make a single troop as effective as an entire army

189 *change* exchange
    our day of doom day that decides our fate

190 *overblown* blown over, passed away

194 *complexion* general appearance

196–7 *eye* | *My* eye that my. Q has a colon following *eye*. An alternative reading is that line 196 is a separate sentence.

198 *by small and small* little by little

199 *To lengthen out the worst* lengthening, stretching out the worst news. The metaphor is of the rack.

202 *gentlemen* men of rank
    gentlemen in arms (perhaps both 'gentlemen-in-arms', that is 'gentlemen bearing coats-of-arms', and 'gentlemen are up in arms')

203 *Upon his party* on his side

204 *Beshrew* (a mild oath) confound

204–5 *forth* | *Of* out of, away from

Of that sweet way I was in to despair.
What say you now? What comfort have we now?
By heaven, I'll hate him everlastingly
That bids me be of comfort any more.
Go to Flint Castle. There I'll pine away.
210   A king, woe's slave, shall kingly woe obey.
That power I have, discharge, and let them go
To ear the land that hath some hope to grow;
For I have none. Let no man speak again
To alter this; for counsel is but vain.

AUMERLE
My liege, one word!

KING RICHARD   He does me double wrong
That wounds me with the flatteries of his tongue.
Discharge my followers. Let them hence away:
From Richard's night to Bolingbroke's fair day. *Exeunt*

III.3   *Enter with drum and colours Bolingbroke, York,*
           Northumberland, attendants, and soldiers

BOLINGBROKE
So that by this intelligence we learn

207–8 Dr Johnson comments 'This sentiment is drawn from nature. Nothing
is more offensive to a mind convinced that his distress is without a
remedy, and preparing to submit quietly to irresistible calamity, than these
petty and conjectured comforts
which unskilful officiousness thinks
it virtue to administer.'
212 *ear* plough, till
   the land (metaphorically for Bolingbroke's cause)
213 *none* no hope (of growing, or
   prospering)
214 *counsel is but vain* advice (to the contrary) will be ineffectual

215 *double wrong* (in thinking to deceive
   me and in increasing my grief by
   again leading me into false hope.
   The notion of the *double* or forked
   tongue of a snake may be present.)

III.3 This scene takes place outside the
walls of Flint Castle, on the estuary of
the River Dee. It is based on Holinshed,
though Shakespeare has omitted an episode in which King Richard, having arrived in Wales, is kidnapped and forcibly
taken to Flint.
   Staging: The staging of this scene
presents problems. The first episode
takes place outside the castle (lines 20,
26). Bolingbroke sends Northumberland

The Welshmen are dispersed, and Salisbury
Is gone to meet the King, who lately landed
With some few private friends upon this coast.

NORTHUMBERLAND
The news is very fair and good, my lord.
Richard not far from hence hath hid his head.

YORK
It would beseem the Lord Northumberland
To say 'King Richard'. Alack the heavy day
When such a sacred king should hide his head!

NORTHUMBERLAND
Your grace mistakes. Only to be brief   10
Left I his title out.

YORK   The time hath been,
Would you have been so brief with him, he would
Have been so brief with you to shorten you,
For taking so the head, your whole head's length.

BOLINGBROKE
Mistake not, uncle, further than you should.

YORK
Take not, good cousin, further than you should,
Lest you mistake the heavens are over our heads.

---

towards the castle in order to deliver his
message (line 32). In the meantime he
and those with him will *march | Upon
the grassy carpet of this plain* (lines 49–
50), and he gives the command to do so.
Some stylization of movement seems inevitable. Perhaps on the Elizabethan
stage Bolingbroke and his men would
have conversed at the front of one side
of the platform, and marched across to
the other. Richard's entry at line 61 must
be on an upper level and therefore at the
back of the stage. For the staging of the
rest of the scene, see notes to line 61,
stage direction, and line 183, stage
direction.

(stage direction) *colours* banners

1 *So that by this intelligence* . . . The scene
  begins in the middle of a conversation. Presumably Bolingbroke enters
  with a written message that he has
  been reading.
  intelligence information
6 *hid his head* taken shelter
6–11 On the significance of this quibbling, see Introduction, pages 17–18.
13 *so brief* . . . *to* so brief as to
14 *taking* . . . *the head* acting without restraint *and* omitting the title
15 *Mistake* misunderstand
17 *mistake the heavens are* 'fail to remember that the heavens are' or 'trans-

BOLINGBROKE

I know it, uncle, and oppose not myself
Against their will. But who comes here?

Enter Harry Percy

20   Welcome, Harry. What, will not this castle yield?

PERCY

The castle royally is manned, my lord,
Against thy entrance.

BOLINGBROKE

Royally?
Why, it contains no king.

PERCY   Yes, my good lord,

It doth contain a king. King Richard lies
Within the limits of yon lime and stone,
And with him are the Lord Aumerle, Lord Salisbury,
Sir Stephen Scroop, besides a clergyman
Of holy reverence; who, I cannot learn.

NORTHUMBERLAND

30   O, belike it is the Bishop of Carlisle.

BOLINGBROKE

Noble lord,
Go to the rude ribs of that ancient castle,
Through brazen trumpet send the breath of parley
Into his ruined ears, and thus deliver:

---

gress against the heavens which . . .'
(though this does not suit well with
Bolingbroke's response). Some editors break the sentence after *mistake*.
25 *lies* resides, dwells
31 *Noble lord* (probably Northumberland)
32 *rude ribs* rough walls
33 *breath of parley* call (of a trumpet)
inviting opponents to conference

34 *his* its. This is the normal form; but
the *ears* may be the King's as well as
the castle's. Coleridge commented: 'I
have no doubt that Shakespeare pur-
posely used the personal pronoun,
"his", to shew, that although Bolingbroke was only speaking of the
castle, his thoughts dwelt on the
king.'

Henry Bolingbroke
On both his knees doth kiss King Richard's hand,
And sends allegiance and true faith of heart
To his most royal person, hither come
Even at his feet to lay my arms and power,
Provided that my banishment repealed   40
And lands restored again be freely granted.
If not, I'll use the advantage of my power
And lay the summer's dust with showers of blood
Rained from the wounds of slaughtered Englishmen;
The which how far off from the mind of Bolingbroke
It is such crimson tempest should bedrench
The fresh green lap of fair King Richard's land
My stooping duty tenderly shall show.
Go signify as much while here we march
Upon the grassy carpet of this plain.   50
Let's march without the noise of threatening drum,
That from this castle's tattered battlements
Our fair appointments may be well perused.

35 *Henry Bolingbroke.* Coleridge commented: 'almost the only instance in
which a name forms the whole line;
Shakespeare meant it to convey Bolingbroke's opinion of his own
importance'.
40 *banishment repealed* the revoking of my
banishment
42 *advantage of my power* superiority of
my forces
43 *summer's dust.* Historically it was
August 1399.
45 Coleridge's comment may afford a
hint to the actor: 'At this point Bolingbroke seems to have been checked
by the eye of York ... He passes
suddenly from insolence to humility,
owing to the silent reproof he received from his uncle.' But Bolingbroke could be hypocritical rather

than humble. Coleridge suggests that
'York again checks him' at the end
of line 57.
46 *is such* is that such
48 *stooping duty* submissive kneeling
52 *tattered* 'having pointed projections'
or 'dilapidated' (in contrast with *Our
fair appointments*). The word does not
necessarily imply that the castle is
easily to be taken, though *ruined ears*
(line 34) might support such an
interpretation.
53–61 *fair appointments ... on the walls.*
Holinshed reports that Northumberland 'mustered his army before the
King's presence, which undoubtedly
made a passing fair show', and that
the King 'was walking aloft on the
brayes [outworks] of the walls to
behold the coming of the Duke afar

Methinks King Richard and myself should meet
With no less terror than the elements
Of fire and water when their thundering shock
At meeting tears the cloudy cheeks of heaven.
Be he the fire, I'll be the yielding water;
The rage be his, whilst on the earth I rain
60   My waters – on the earth, and not on him.
March on, and mark King Richard, how he looks.

off'. His companions here seem to derive from a later stage in Holinshed's account, corresponding to Shakespeare's line 176: 'The King accompanied with the Bishop of Carlisle, the Earl of Salisbury, and Sir Stephen Scroop, knight, who bare the sword before him, and a few other, came forth into the outer ward and sat down in a place prepared for him.'

53 *appointments may be well perused* equipment may be well observed. The silence of the drums will make this a peaceable show of strength.

56 *fire and water* (in the form of lightning and rain or cloud)

56-7 *shock | At meeting tears the cloudy cheeks of heaven*. Bolingbroke alludes to the belief that thunder was caused by a clash between the opposed elements of fire and water in the form of lightning and rain.

57 *cheeks of heaven*. This may allude to the puffing cheeks of cherubs often represented in maps.

58 *fire . . . yielding water*. In the traditional 'chain of being' fire was dominant among the elements, so water would 'yield' to it. Similarly Richard

is seen in line 63 as the sun, dominant among planets, in line 68 as the king, dominant among men, and in line 69 as the eagle, dominant among birds. Bolingbroke is not obviously yielding to Richard. He may be claiming that while Richard rages, Bolingbroke will drop tears of sorrow on the ground. There may also be the implication that this is the more fruitful thing to do.

59-60 *I rain | My waters – on the earth, and not on him*. This is a difficult passage. Q prints:

> I raigne.
> My water's on the earth, and not on
>   him.

If the second of these lines is intended to be a separate sentence, it may mean 'My (beneficent) water falls on the earth, not on Richard'. This would also mean that a strong pun would be felt in line 59 ('rain', 'reign'). On the other hand the full stop after 'raigne' in Q may be accidental – it comes at the end of a page. If so, Bolingbroke must mean 'Let him rage in anger while I scatter my blessings on the earth, though not on Richard.'

The trumpets sound parley without, and answer within; then a flourish. King Richard appeareth on the walls with the Bishop of Carlisle, Aumerle, Scroop, and Salisbury

BOLINGBROKE

See, see, King Richard doth himself appear,
As doth the blushing, discontented sun
From out the fiery portal of the east
When he perceives the envious clouds are bent
To dim his glory and to stain the track
Of his bright passage to the occident.

YORK

Yet looks he like a king. Behold, his eye,
As bright as is the eagle's, lightens forth
Controlling majesty. Alack, alack for woe   70
That any harm should stain so fair a show!

---

61 (stage direction) King Richard's appearance on the walls is an impressive moment. When he speaks, at line 72, he explains why he has not spoken before. This strongly suggests that his entry should be made in silence, to be commented on by Bolingbroke and York only when he has taken up his position. Formality of staging seems essential. Probably Northumberland and the other lords should be with the trumpeters, as Bolingbroke has instructed them to speak on his behalf, and King Richard's amazement (line 72) should be addressed directly to them. Bolingbroke and York should stand somewhat aside (line 91).

The trumpets sound parley without, and answer within.

This presumably means that the stage trumpets (those *without*) sound and are answered by the backstage ones (those *within*), imagined to be inside the castle.

the walls (the upper level of the stage)

63 *blushing, discontented sun.* This passage may be referring to the proverb 'A red morning foretells a stormy day'. The rising sun is *discontented* because the day is to be one of bad weather.

65 *he* (the sun)
envious. In Shakespeare's time this word had the stronger sense of 'hostile', 'harmful', rather than simply 'jealous'.

68 *Yet* 'still' as well as 'nevertheless'

68–9 *eye,* | *As bright as is the eagle's.* The eagle, king of birds, was believed to be able to look into the sun, chief of the heavenly bodies, without coming to harm.

69 *lightens forth* sends down as lightning, flashes out

71 *stain* (compare line 66)
show sight

KING RICHARD

We are amazed; and thus long have we stood
To watch the fearful bending of thy knee
Because we thought ourself thy lawful king.
And if we be, how dare thy joints forget
To pay their awful duty to our presence?
If we be not, show us the hand of God
That hath dismissed us from our stewardship;
For well we know no hand of blood and bone

80   Can grip the sacred handle of our sceptre
Unless he do profane, steal, or usurp.
And though you think that all, as you have done,
Have torn their souls by turning them from us,
And we are barren and bereft of friends,
Yet know, my master, God omnipotent,
Is mustering in his clouds on our behalf
Armies of pestilence; and they shall strike
Your children yet unborn and unbegot,
That lift your vassal hands against my head

90   And threat the glory of my precious crown.
Tell Bolingbroke – for yon methinks he stands –
That every stride he makes upon my land
Is dangerous treason. He is come to open
The purple testament of bleeding war;

72 ff. *We*. Richard repeatedly uses the royal plural.

72–3 *stood | To watch* stood in expectation of seeing

76 *awful duty* duty of showing awe or reverence

77 *hand* signature

79–81 *hand . . . he*. The hand is representative of the person.

81 *profane* commit sacrilege

83 *torn their souls* (sinned by turning their allegiance from Richard to Bolingbroke. The jingle with *turning* is deliberate.)

85 *my*. Here and later in the speech Rich-

ard lapses from the plural form as he speaks of himself as an individual rather than a king.

88–9 *Your children . . . | That lift your* the children . . . of you who lift your

89 *vassal* subject

91 *yon methinks he stands*. King Richard has not so far addressed Bolingbroke since he returned from exile, and now does not deign to address him directly.

93–4 *open | The purple testament* open the blood-coloured will (– in which war is bequeathed – preparatory to putting it into operation)

But ere the crown he looks for live in peace
Ten thousand bloody crowns of mothers' sons
Shall ill become the flower of England's face,
Change the complexion of her maid-pale peace
To scarlet indignation, and bedew
Her pastor's grass with faithful English blood.   100

NORTHUMBERLAND
The King of heaven forbid our lord the King
Should so with civil and uncivil arms
Be rushed upon. Thy thrice-noble cousin
Harry Bolingbroke doth humbly kiss thy hand;
And by the honourable tomb he swears
That stands upon your royal grandsire's bones,
And by the royalties of both your bloods,
Currents that spring from one most gracious head,
And by the buried hand of warlike Gaunt,
And by the worth and honour of himself,   110
Comprising all that may be sworn or said,
His coming hither hath no further scope
Than for his lineal royalties, and to beg
Enfranchisement immediate on his knees,
Which on thy royal party granted once
His glittering arms he will commend to rust,
His barbèd steeds to stables, and his heart

---

95 *ere the crown he looks for live in peace*
before the English crown, which Bolingbroke hopes for (or 'expects'),
may be worn in peace

95–6 *crown . . . crowns* crown (of kingship) . . . heads

97 *the flower of England's face*. Three
senses are felt. England is likened to
a flower; so is the human face; and
the flower suggests brave young men.

100 *pastor's* shepherd's (Richard's).
Many editors read 'pasture's' or
'pastures'.

102 *civil and uncivil arms. Civil*, used in
civil war; *uncivil*, barbarous.

103 *thrice-noble* (by descent from Edward
III; by descent from John of Gaunt;
and on his own account, as the following lines make plain)

106 *your royal grandsire* (King Edward
III)

108 *head* source (as of a spring)

112 *scope* aim

113 *lineal royalties* hereditary rights of
royalty

114 *Enfranchisement* freedom from banishment (and restoration of rights)

115 *thy royal party* your majesty's part

116 *commend* hand over

117 *barbèd* armoured with barbs

To faithful service of your majesty.
This swears he as he is a prince and just,
120   And as I am a gentleman I credit him.
KING RICHARD
Northumberland, say thus. The King returns
His noble cousin is right welcome hither,
And all the number of his fair demands
Shall be accomplished without contradiction.
With all the gracious utterance thou hast
Speak to his gentle hearing kind commends.
(*To Aumerle*)
We do debase ourselves, cousin, do we not,
To look so poorly and to speak so fair?
Shall we call back Northumberland and send
130   Defiance to the traitor, and so die?
AUMERLE
No, good my lord. Let's fight with gentle words
Till time lend friends, and friends their helpful swords.
KING RICHARD
O God, O God, that e'er this tongue of mine,
That laid the sentence of dread banishment
On yon proud man, should take it off again
With words of sooth! O that I were as great
As is my grief, or lesser than my name,
Or that I could forget what I have been,
Or not remember what I must be now!
140   Swellest thou, proud heart? I'll give thee scope to beat,
Since foes have scope to beat both thee and me.
AUMERLE
Northumberland comes back from Bolingbroke.

coverings for the breasts and flanks
of war-horses)
121–2 *returns | His* replies that his
128 *look so poorly* seem so abject
speak so fair speak so courteously
136 *sooth* blandishment, flattery
140 *Swellest thou, proud heart? I'll.* Q has
'Swellst thou (prowd heart) Ile'

which might suggest the meaning 'If
thou swellest, I'll . . .', but the inter-
rogative form seems more actable.
Presumably the King's excited state
of mind has a physical effect; the
actor would naturally put his hand
to his heart
140–41 *scope . . . scope* room, space . . .

KING RICHARD

What must the King do now? Must he submit?
The King shall do it. Must he be deposed?
The King shall be contented. Must he lose
The name of king? A God's name, let it go.
I'll give my jewels for a set of beads,
My gorgeous palace for a hermitage,
My gay apparel for an almsman's gown,
My figured goblets for a dish of wood,   150
My sceptre for a palmer's walking-staff,
My subjects for a pair of carvèd saints,
And my large kingdom for a little grave,
A little, little grave, an obscure grave;
Or I'll be buried in the King's highway,
Some way of common trade where subjects' feet
May hourly trample on their sovereign's head,
For on my heart they tread now whilst I live,

permission, opportunity (and compare line 112)

143–54 This passage may have been suggested by Hall's Chronicle, where it is said that Richard 'with a lamentable voice and a sorrowful countenance delivered his sceptre and crown to the Duke of Lancaster, requiring every person severally by their names to grant and assent that he might live a private and a solitary life, with the sweetness whereof he would be so well pleased that it should be a pain and punishment to him to go abroad'.

143 *the King . . . he*. Richard begins by referring to himself in the third person, as if conscious of the division between the man and the office.

146 *A* in

147 *a set of beads* a rosary

149 *gay apparel*. Richard was known for his extravagance in dress. Holinshed records that 'he was in his time exceeding sumptuous in apparel, insomuch as he had one coat which he caused to be made for him of gold and stone, valued at 30,000 marks'. See also note to II.1.21.

almsman (beggar who prayed for those who gave him alms). *Gown* suggests one who wore the uniform of a particular institution.

150 *figured* decorated
dish of wood (alms-dish)

151 *palmer* pilgrim

152 *carvèd saints* (wooden figures of saints such as might be in a monk's cell)

154 *obscure* (accented on the first syllable)

155 *I'll be buried in the King's highway*. There is obvious irony in the suggestion that the King will be buried, not in a sanctified place, but under his own highway.

156 *trade* traffic (quibbling with *tread*, in line 158)

And buried once, why not upon my head?
160   Aumerle, thou weepest, my tender-hearted cousin.
We'll make foul weather with despisèd tears.
Our sighs and they shall lodge the summer corn
And make a dearth in this revolting land.
Or shall we play the wantons with our woes,
And make some pretty match with shedding tears,
As thus to drop them still upon one place
Till they have fretted us a pair of graves
Within the earth, and therein laid there lies
Two kinsmen digged their graves with weeping eyes.
170   Would not this ill do well? Well, well, I see
I talk but idly, and you laugh at me.
Most mighty prince, my Lord Northumberland,
What says King Bolingbroke? Will his majesty
Give Richard leave to live till Richard die?
You make a leg, and Bolingbroke says 'Ay'.

NORTHUMBERLAND
My lord, in the base-court he doth attend
To speak with you, may it please you to come down.

KING RICHARD
Down, down I come like glistering Phaethon,

159 *buried once* once I am buried
162 *Our sighs and they* (like wind and rain)
lodge beat down
163 *revolting* rebelling
164 *play the wantons* play a game, amuse ourselves
165 *Make some pretty match* play a clever game
166 *still* continually
167 *fretted us* worn out for us
168–9 *there lies | Two kinsmen digged their graves with weeping eyes.* The rhyme helps to give this the quality of an imaginary epitaph
171 *idly* foolishly
173–4 *Will his majesty | Give Richard leave to live till Richard die?* (a

trick question, showing Richard's distrust)
175 *make a leg* an obeisance, a bend of the knee. Addressing Northumberland, Richard seems ironically to be saying that if Northumberland gives assent, Bolingbroke is sure to say yes.
176 *base-court* (lower or outer court of the castle, occupied by servants)
177 *may it please you to come down.* This may mean 'if it please you to come down', or may be an independent question.
178 *glistering Phaethon.* Phaethon (three syllables) was the mythical son of Apollo, the sun-god. He borrowed his father's sun-chariot but was too

Wanting the manage of unruly jades.
In the base-court – base-court, where kings grow base   180
To come at traitors' calls, and do them grace.
In the base-court. Come down – down court, down
      King,
For night-owls shriek where mounting larks should sing.

Exeunt from above

BOLINGBROKE
What says his majesty?

NORTHUMBERLAND   Sorrow and grief of heart
Makes him speak fondly, like a frantic man.
Yet he is come.

Enter King Richard attended, below

BOLINGBROKE
Stand all apart,
And show fair duty to his majesty.

He kneels down

weak to control it and drove dangerously close to the earth. Zeus prevented the destruction of the earth
by killing Phaethon with a thunderbolt. The story was a common image
of rash failure. It is especially appropriate to Richard in this play because
of his frequent association with the
sun (which was his own badge). 'Phaethon' is the Greek for 'shining' (or
'glistering').

179 *Wanting the manage of* lacking the
power to control. *Manage* was
a technical term in horsemanship.

  unruly jades (compared with the rebellious nobles. *Jades* is a contemptuous
term for horses.)

181 *do them grace* favour them

182 *base-court . . . court*. Richard plays on
the ideas of 'courtyard' and the
King's 'court', and also puns on
'base'.

183 *night-owls shriek where mounting larks
should sing* instead of the lark's song

we hear the cries of owls, foreboding
evil

(stage direction) Probably on the Elizabethan stage the King and his
followers left the upper stage and descended out of view of the audience.
On the modern stage a stairway is
sometimes used so that he is in view
throughout.

185 *fondly* foolishly

187 *Stand all apart*. Probably he instructs
his men to stand at a respectful distance from Richard.

188 (stage direction) *He kneels down*.
This is one of the rare directions for
action in Q.

188–207 *He kneels down . . . force will have
us do*. Holinshed has: 'Forthwith as
the Duke got sight of the King he
showed a reverend duty, as became
him in bowing his knee, and coming
forward did so likewise the second
and third time, till the King took
him by the hand and lift [sic] him
up, saying "Dear cousin, ye are

My gracious lord!

KING RICHARD

190   Fair cousin, you debase your princely knee
To make the base earth proud with kissing it.
Me rather had my heart might feel your love
Than my unpleased eye see your courtesy.
Up, cousin, up. Your heart is up, I know,
Thus high at least, although your knee be low.

BOLINGBROKE

My gracious lord, I come but for mine own.

KING RICHARD

Your own is yours, and I am yours and all.

BOLINGBROKE

So far be mine, my most redoubted lord,
As my true service shall deserve your love.

KING RICHARD

200   Well you deserve. They well deserve to have
That know the strongest and surest way to get.
(To York)
Uncle, give me your hands. Nay, dry your eyes.
Tears show their love, but want their remedies.
(To Bolingbroke)
Cousin, I am too young to be your father
Though you are old enough to be my heir.
What you will have, I'll give, and willing too;
For do we must what force will have us do.

---

welcome." The Duke humbly thank-
ing him said "My sovereign lord and
king, the cause of my coming at this
present is, your honour saved, to
have again restitution of my person,
my lands and heritage, through your
favourable licence." The King here-
unto answered "Dear cousin, I am
ready to accomplish your will, so
that ye may enjoy all that is yours
without exception." '

192 *Me rather had* I had rather
193 *courtesy* (combining the modern, gen-

eral meaning with the sense of an
obeisance)

195 *Thus high at least.* Richard touches
his head to indicate the crown.

202 *hands.* F's 'Hand' may well be
correct.

203 *want their remedies* lack the capacity
to cure the misfortunes with which
they show sympathy

204–5 *I am too young to be your father |
Though you are old enough to be my heir.*
Historically both Richard and Boling-
broke were thirty-three.

Set on towards London, cousin – is it so?

BOLINGBROKE
Yea, my good lord.

KING RICHARD Then I must not say no.

Flourish. Exeunt

Enter the Queen with two Ladies, her attendants   III.4

QUEEN ISABEL
What sport shall we devise here in this garden
To drive away the heavy thought of care?

FIRST LADY
Madam, we'll play at bowls.

QUEEN ISABEL
'Twill make me think the world is full of rubs
And that my fortune runs against the bias.

SECOND LADY
Madam, we'll dance.

QUEEN ISABEL
My legs can keep no measure in delight
When my poor heart no measure keeps in grief.
Therefore no dancing, girl. Some other sport.

III.4 This scene has no historical basis. It is apparently set in the Duke of York's garden (see II.2.116–17 and III.4.70). In Q the direction refers to the Queen 'with her attendants', who are not distinguished in the speech prefixes. F has 'and two Ladies'. Shakespeare may have thought of more than two ladies, one perhaps suggesting each type of diversion; but the Folio probably reflects the stage practice of Shakespeare's time. The division of speeches in the present edition is arbitrary, and may be varied at will by a producer. On the significance of the scene, see Introduction, pages 20–21.

1 *here in this garden*. This phrase sets the scene economically.

3 *bowls*. This was a common Elizabethan game. Bowling greens were often found in gardens.

4 *rubs*. A *rub* in bowls was a technical term for anything which impeded the course of the bowl. It was often used metaphorically of a difficulty – 'Ay, there's the rub' (*Hamlet*, III.1.65).

5 *runs against the bias*. In bowls, *bias* is a weight inserted in the side of the bowl to make it run in a certain way. The Queen feels that her fortune is going against its natural inclination.

7–8 *can keep no measure ... no measure keeps* cannot dance (*measure* dance step) ... knows no bounds

FIRST LADY

10   Madam, we'll tell tales.

QUEEN ISABEL

Of sorrow or of joy?

FIRST LADY   Of either, madam.

QUEEN ISABEL

Of neither, girl.

For if of joy, being altogether wanting,

It doth remember me the more of sorrow;

Or if of grief, being altogether had,

It adds more sorrow to my want of joy;

For what I have I need not to repeat,

And what I want it boots not to complain.

SECOND LADY

Madam, I'll sing.

QUEEN ISABEL   'Tis well that thou hast cause;

20   But thou shouldst please me better wouldst thou weep.

SECOND LADY

I could weep, madam, would it do you good.

QUEEN ISABEL

And I could sing would weeping do me good,

And never borrow any tear of thee.

Enter Gardeners, one the master, the other two his
*   men*

---

10 *tell tales*. See Introduction, pages 36–8.

13 *wanting* lacking, absent

14 *remember* remind

15 *being altogether had* since I possess it completely

18 *boots* helps

22–3 *And I could sing would weeping do me good,* | *And never borrow any tear of thee*. The Queen probably means that she herself has already wept so much that if this could have done her any good all would now be well, and she would feel like singing.

23 (stage direction) *Gardeners*. Q has 'Enter Gardeners', F 'Enter a Gar-

diner and two Seruants'. The Gardener's first speech makes it clear that there are two under-gardeners. The fact that the Gardener has two men under him may make it less surprising that he should speak as formally as he does. The gardens of great Elizabethan estates were internationally famous, and their Head Gardeners had heavy responsibility. Admittedly Shakespeare's Gardener is not a pure administrator – he is going to *root away* | *The noisome weeds* – but he is a man of authority. More to the purpose, dramatically he is a symbolic rather than naturalistic char-

But stay, here come the gardeners.
Let's step into the shadow of these trees.
My wretchedness unto a row of pins
They will talk of state; for everyone doth so
Against a change. Woe is forerun with woe.

The Queen and her Ladies stand apart

GARDENER (*to one man*)
Go, bind thou up young dangling apricocks
Which, like unruly children, make their sire   30
Stoop with oppression of their prodigal weight.
Give some supportance to the bending twigs.
(*To the other*)
Go thou, and like an executioner
Cut off the heads of too fast-growing sprays
That look too lofty in our commonwealth.
All must be even in our government.
You thus employed, I will go root away
The noisome weeds which without profit suck
The soil's fertility from wholesome flowers.

FIRST MAN
Why should we, in the compass of a pale,   40

acter, and it is more important for the actor to concentrate attention on what he says than to entertain by his manner of saying it. See Introduction, pages 20–21.

26 *My wretchedness unto a row of pins* I will wager my misery against something very trivial that . . .

27 *They will*. The metre seems to demand elision: 'They'll.'

28 *Against a change* when a change is about to happen

29 *young*. Q1 has 'yong'; Q2–5, 'yon'; F, 'yond'. Q1 has superior authority and this looks like a simple case of progressive textual corruption. A. W. Pollard comments: 'it is the word "yong" that suggested the comparison of the fruit to "vnruly children" in the next line' (*King Richard II: A*

New Quarto, 1916, page 56).

apricocks apricots

31 *Stoop* (punning on the bending of the boughs and of the back of an old man)

prodigal (punning on 'excessive' and 'prodigal' or 'unruly' children; *weight* thus has both literal and metaphorical force)

32 *bending* (with the weight of the fruit)

35 *lofty* 'tall' and 'overweening'

36 *even* equal

38 *noisome* harmful

40, 54 (*first part*), 67 (speech prefixes) Neither Q nor F differentiates between the two men. The present arrangement is arbitrary.

40 *compass of a pale* (small area – in contrast to the kingdom)

pale fence (and 'national boundary')

Keep law and form and due proportion,
Showing as in a model our firm estate,
When our sea-walled garden, the whole land,
Is full of weeds, her fairest flowers choked up,
Her fruit trees all unpruned, her hedges ruined,
Her knots disordered, and her wholesome herbs
Swarming with caterpillars?

GARDENER   Hold thy Peace.
He that hath suffered this disordered spring
Hath now himself met with the fall of leaf.
50   The weeds which his broad-spreading leaves did shelter,
That seemed in eating him to hold him up,
Are plucked up, root and all, by Bolingbroke –
I mean the Earl of Wiltshire, Bushy, Green.

SECOND MAN
What, are they dead?

GARDENER   They are; and Bolingbroke
Hath seized the wasteful King. O, what pity is it
That he had not so trimmed and dressed his land
As we this garden! We at time of year
Do wound the bark, the skin of our fruit trees,
Lest being overproud in sap and blood
60   With too much riches it confound itself.
Had he done so to great and growing men
They might have lived to bear, and he to taste
Their fruits of duty. Superfluous branches
We lop away that bearing boughs may live.
Had he done so, himself had borne the crown
Which waste of idle hours hath quite thrown down.

42 *firm* stable
43 *sea-walled*. Compare II.1.46–7.
46 *knots* (flower-beds laid out in intricate designs)
47 *caterpillars* (echoing Bolingbroke's word for the traitors, II.3.165)
48 *suffered* permitted
49 *fall of leaf* autumn
57 *at time of year* in season
58 *skin* (introduced to stress the metaphor)
59 *overproud in* excessively swollen with
65 *crown* (the king's, and the crown of a tree)

FIRST MAN

 What, think you the King shall be deposed?

GARDENER

 Depressed he is already, and deposed

 'Tis doubt he will be. Letters came last night

 To a dear friend of the good Duke of York's   70

 That tell black tidings.

QUEEN ISABEL

 O, I am pressed to death through want of speaking!

  She comes forward

 Thou, old Adam's likeness, set to dress this garden,

 How dares thy harsh rude tongue sound this unpleasing

  news?

 What Eve, what serpent hath suggested thee

 To make a second Fall of cursed man?

 Why dost thou say King Richard is deposed?

 Darest thou, thou little better thing than earth,

 Divine his downfall? Say, where, when, and how

 Camest thou by this ill tidings? Speak, thou wretch! 80

GARDENER

 Pardon me, madam. Little joy have I

 To breathe this news. Yet what I say is true.

 King Richard he is in the mighty hold

 Of Bolingbroke. Their fortunes both are weighed.

 In your lord's scale is nothing but himself

---

67 Editors have sometimes padded out the short line, but the rhythmical irregularity emphasizes the exclamation.

68 *Depressed* brought low

69 *'Tis doubt* there is a risk

72 *pressed to death*. An allusion to *la peine forte et dure*, a punishment of pressing to death inflicted by English law on those accused of felony or petty treason who refused to plead either guilty or not guilty: who, that is, like the Queen here, stood silent.

73 *old Adam's likeness*. Adam was the first gardener.

75 *suggested* tempted

79 *Divine* predict

82 *To breathe* in speaking

84–9 *Their fortunes both are weighted . . . King Richard down*. The Gardener's imagery anticipates the symbol of the buckets in IV.1.183–8.

84 *weighed* balanced against each other

And some few vanities that make him light.
But in the balance of great Bolingbroke
Besides himself are all the English peers,
And with that odds he weighs King Richard down.
90 Post you to London and you will find it so.
I speak no more than everyone doth know.

QUEEN ISABEL
Nimble mischance, that art so light of foot,
Doth not thy embassage belong to me,
And am I last that knows it? O, thou thinkest
To serve me last that I may longest keep
Thy sorrow in my breast. Come, ladies, go
To meet at London London's king in woe.
What was I born to this – that my sad look
Should grace the triumph of great Bolingbroke?
100 Gardener, for telling me these news of woe,
Pray God the plants thou graftest may never grow.

Exit Queen with her Ladies

GARDENER
Poor Queen, so that thy state might be no worse
I would my skill were subject to thy curse.
Here did she fall a tear. Here in this place
I'll set a bank of rue, sour herb of grace.
Rue even for ruth here shortly shall be seen
In the remembrance of a weeping Queen.   *Exeunt*

86 *vanities* 'follies'; or specifically, 'Richard's favourites' (opposed to the *peers* of line 88)
   light (in the balance, and also 'of little value')
89 *odds* advantage, superiority
90 *Post* hasten
93 *Doth not thy embassage belong to me* does your message not concern me
95 *serve me* serve (your message) on me
96 *Thy sorrow* the sorrow that you report
98 *What* (perhaps 'why' rather than an exclamation)
104 *fall* let fall
105 *rue, sour herb of grace*. The herb 'rue' was known as 'herb of grace' because 'rue' means 'repentance', which comes by the grace of God. Here it is associated especially with pity.
106 *for ruth* as a symbol of pity

Enter Bolingbroke with the Lords Aumerle, IV.I
Northumberland, Harry Percy, Fitzwater, Surrey, the
Bishop of Carlisle, the Abbot of Westminster, another
Lord, Herald, and officer, to Parliament

BOLINGBROKE

Call forth Bagot.

Enter Bagot with officers

Now, Bagot, freely speak thy mind
What thou dost know of noble Gloucester's death,

IV.I The place is Westminster Hall; Richard himself had caused it to be splendidly rebuilt. The material of the scene derives from Holinshed, but Shakespeare compresses the time-scheme and rearranges the order of events. He begins with accusations against Aumerle by Bagot, Fitzwater, and others. According to Holinshed Bagot made his accusation on Thursday, 16 October 1399, and Fitzwater two days later. Bolingbroke's proposal (line 87) that Mowbray be recalled from exile was made on 27 October. After Carlisle has reported Mowbray's death York enters with news of Richard's abdication. His brief speech reports the events of 30 September, when the commissioners who had witnessed the abdication reported to Parliament. Bolingbroke's acceptance of the throne is resisted by Carlisle, who speaks in defence of Richard. According to Holinshed the Bishop made such a speech on 22 October, and it was directed, not against the deposition, but against the proposal that Richard 'might have judgement decreed against him so as the realm were not troubled by him'. Shakespeare then turns to the account of the abdication, which happened in the Tower of London on 29 September. In Holinshed Richard signs an instrument of abdication, represented in the play by his great speech of renunciation (lines 200–221). The scene's closing episode shows the beginning of the Abbot of Westminster's plot against King Henry. In Holinshed this was planned at the Abbot's house some three months later.

(stage direction) *Fitzwater.* Walter, Baron Fitzwalter, 1368–1406 or 1407. *Fitzwater* is the form of the name in Holinshed, representing the old pronunciation.

Surrey. The son of Richard's half-brother, Sir Thomas Holland, he lived from 1374 to 1400, when he was executed. He is the Earl of Kent referred to in v.6.8, he and Aumerle both having been deprived of their dukedoms for their parts in the conspiracy against Bolingbroke – see note to v.2.41. See also the note on the Lord Marshal, 1.1, opening stage direction.

Abbot of Westminster. The Abbot at the time of the events shown in the play was William of Colchester. *to Parliament.* This (as in Q) and F's '*as to the Parliament*' suggest a processional entry.

2 *speak thy mind* (probably this is felt as a single, transitive verb – 'tell')

Who wrought it with the King, and who performed
The bloody office of his timeless end.

BAGOT

Then set before my face the Lord Aumerle.

BOLINGBROKE

Cousin, stand forth, and look upon that man.

BAGOT

My Lord Aumerle, I know your daring tongue
Scorns to unsay what once it hath delivered.
10 In that dead time when Gloucester's death was plotted
I heard you say 'Is not my arm of length,
That reacheth from the restful English court
As far as Calais to mine uncle's head?'
Amongst much other talk that very time
I heard you say that you had rather refuse
The offer of an hundred thousand crowns
Than Bolingbroke's return to England,
Adding withal how blest this land would be
In this your cousin's death.

AUMERLE   Princes and noble lords,
20 What answer shall I make to this base man?

---

4 *wrought it with the King* 'persuaded Richard to have Gloucester killed' or 'collaborated with him in the plan to
have him killed' (*wrought it*, 'worked'
it, brought it about)

5 *timeless* untimely

6 *Aumerle*. Holinshed has: 'there was no
man in the realm to whom King
Richard was so much beholden as to
the Duke of Aumerle; for he was the
man that, to fulfil his mind, had set
him in hand with all that was done
against the said duke'.

10–17 *In that dead time when Gloucester's
death was plotted . . . Than Bolingbroke's
return to England.* This is historically
inaccurate, as Gloucester was killed
before Bolingbroke's banishment.

10 *dead time* past (with all the overtones
of 'dead')

11 *Of length* long

12 *restful* quiet (untroubled by Gloucester's plots)

13 *Calais* (where Gloucester was killed)

15–19 *I heard . . . cousin's death*. Holinshed says that in Bagot's bill read to
the Parliament of 16 October 1399 it
was stated 'that Bagot had heard the
Duke of Aumerle say that he had
rather than twenty thousand pounds
that the Duke of Hereford were
dead, not for any fear he had of him,
but for the trouble and mischief that
he was like to procure within the
realm'.

17 *Than Bolingbroke's return* (that is, than
that Bolingbroke should return – an
elliptical construction)

18 *withal* as well

Shall I so much dishonour my fair stars
On equal terms to give him chastisement?
Either I must, or have mine honour soiled
With the attainder of his slanderous lips.

He throws down his gage

There is my gage, the manual seal of death,
That marks thee out for hell. I say thou liest,
And will maintain what thou hast said is false
In thy heart-blood, though being all too base
To stain the temper of my knightly sword.

BOLINGBROKE

Bagot, forbear. Thou shalt not take it up.   30

AUMERLE

Excepting one, I would he were the best
In all this presence that hath moved me so.

FITZWATER

If that thy valour stand on sympathy
There is my gage, Aumerle, in gage to thine.

---

21 *fair stars* noble birth. Dr Johnson comments: 'The *birth* is supposed to be influenced by the *stars,* therefore our author with his usual licence takes *stars* for *birth.*'

22 *On equal terms.* Aumerle, being of higher rank than Bagot, could refuse to fight him.

24 *attainder* accusation

25 *gage . . . manual seal.* See note to I.1.69. *manual seal* (or 'sign manual')

28 *being* it (the blood) is

29 *temper* quality (especially the bright surface of a well-tempered sword)

31–2 *Excepting one . . . moved me so.* Though he despises Bagot as his inferior, Aumerle has challenged him. Now he says that, for his own greater honour, he wishes his accuser were the noblest of all present except Bolingbroke, whom he would prefer to fight.

31 *best* highest in rank

32 *moved* angered

33–90 Holinshed's account of the examination of Bagot includes the statement that 'The Lord Fitzwater herewith rose up and said to the King that where the Duke of Aumerle excuseth himself of the Duke of Gloucester's death, "I say" quoth he "that he was the very cause of his death," and so he appealed him of treason, offering by throwing down his hood as a gage to prove it with his body. There were twenty other lords also that threw down their hoods as pledges to prove the like matter against the Duke of Aumerle.'

33 *thy valour* (possibly ironical: 'thy valorous self')
stand on insist on, raise difficulties about (as in 'stand on ceremony')
sympathy correspondence (in rank). Fitzwater sneeringly asserts his equality with Aumerle.

34 *in gage* in pledge

He throws down his gage
By that fair sun which shows me where thou standest
I heard thee say, and vauntingly thou spakest it,
That thou wert cause of noble Gloucester's death.
If thou deniest it twenty times, thou liest,
And I will turn thy falsehood to thy heart,
40   Where it was forgèd, with my rapier's point.

AUMERLE

Thou darest not, coward, live to see that day.

FITZWATER

Now by my soul, I would it were this hour.

AUMERLE

Fitzwater, thou art damned to hell for this.

PERCY

Aumerle, thou liest. His honour is as true
In this appeal as thou art all unjust;
And that thou art so there I throw my gage
To prove it on thee to the extremest point
Of mortal breathing.
        He throws down his gage
                Seize it if thou darest.

AUMERLE

And if I do not may my hands rot off,
50   And never brandish more revengeful steel
Over the glittering helmet of my foe.

ANOTHER LORD

I task the earth to the like, forsworn Aumerle,

---

40 *rapier*. This could be either a long or a short sword, used for thrusting. It was in use in Shakespeare's time, but not in Richard II's. Dr Johnson sternly commented: 'The edge of a sword had served his purpose as well as the point of a rapier, and he had then escaped the impropriety of giving the English nobles a weapon which was not seen in England till two centuries afterwards.'

45 *appeal* accusation

all entirely

47–8 *to the extremest point | Of mortal breathing* to the death

49 *And if* (perhaps *An if*, if)

50 *more* again

52–9 F omits these lines, perhaps simply to economize on actors, perhaps because the number of challenges seemed excessive. See Introduction, pages 21–2.

52 *task the earth to the like* charge the earth in similar fashion (perhaps by

And spur thee on with full as many lies
As may be hollowed in thy treacherous ear
From sun to sun.

> *He throws down his gage*

>   There is my honour's pawn.
Engage it to the trial if thou darest.

AUMERLE
Who sets me else? By heaven, I'll throw at all.
I have a thousand spirits in one breast
To answer twenty thousand such as you.

SURREY
My Lord Fitzwater, I do remember well   / 60
The very time Aumerle and you did talk.

FITZWATER
'Tis very true. You were in presence then,
And you can witness with me this is true.

SURREY
As false, by heaven, as heaven itself is true.

FITZWATER
Surrey, thou liest.

SURREY   Dishonourable boy,
That lie shall lie so heavy on my sword
That it shall render vengeance and revenge
Till thou, the lie-giver, and that lie do lie
In earth as quiet as thy father's skull.
In proof whereof, there is my honour's pawn.   70

---

throwing down another gage)
53 *lies* accusations of lying
54 *hollowed* shouted loudly, 'hollered'
55 *From sun to sun* from sunrise to sunset.
This was the prescribed time-limit
for single combat. Q reads 'sinne to
sinne', which could conceivably be
defended.
56 *Engage it* take up the gage, accept the
challenge
57 *Who sets me else?* who else challenges

me, puts up stakes against me? *Sets*
and *throw* are both dicing metaphors.
62 *in presence* present
65 *boy* (a strong insult here; the word
was used of a menial servant)
66 *That lie* (both the accusation of lying,
and the lie that the accusation is.
These lines are full of quibbles on
the word.)
67 *it shall render* my sword will give
back in return (for the accusation)

He throws down his gage
Engage it to the trial if thou darest.

FITZWATER

How fondly dost thou spur a forward horse!
If I dare eat, or drink, or breathe, or live,
I dare meet Surrey in a wilderness
And spit upon him whilst I say he lies,
And lies, and lies. There is my bond of faith
To tie thee to my strong correction.
As I intend to thrive in this new world
Aumerle is guilty of my true appeal.
80 Besides, I heard the banished Norfolk say
That thou, Aumerle, didst send two of thy men
To execute the noble Duke at Calais.

AUMERLE

Some honest Christian trust me with a gage.
He throws down a gage
That Norfolk lies here do I throw down this,
If he may be repealed to try his honour.

72 *How fondly dost thou spur a forward
horse* (related to the proverb 'Do not
spur a free horse')
fondly foolishly, unnecessarily
forward willing
74 *in a wilderness* (that is, even in a wilderness, where they would fight uninter-
rupted to the bitter end. Compare
1.1.64–6.)
76 *There is my bond of faith* there is my
gage (or *honour's pawn*, line 70).
Either he throws down a second
gage or points to the one he threw at
line 34.
77 *tie thee to my strong correction* engage
you to undergo severe punishment
at my hands
78 *in this new world* (under the new order,
with a new king)
79 *appeal* accusation
80 *Norfolk* (Mowbray)
83–4 *Some honest Christian trust me with a*

gage. | That Norfolk lies. Q and F
have a comma after *gage*. Aumerle is
asking to borrow a gage, either because he has thrown down both his
gloves (at lines 25 and 57) or because
Shakespeare is now thinking of the
gages as hoods not gloves (see Commentary to 1.1.69). It may be that he
asks specially to be trusted with a
gage with which to prove *That Norfolk lies.* If so he receives it after *lies.*
Otherwise he receives it after *gage*
and then says 'Now I throw down
this to prove that . . .'
85 *repealed* called back (from banishment)
to try his honour. This may modify
repealed ('called back in order to put
his honour to the test') or *throw* ('I
throw this down . . . as a test of his
honour').

BOLINGBROKE

These differences shall all rest under gage
Till Norfolk be repealed. Repealed he shall be,
And, though mine enemy, restored again
To all his lands and signories. When he is returned
Against Aumerle we will enforce his trial.   90

BISHOP OF CARLISLE

That honourable day shall never be seen.
Many a time hath banished Norfolk fought
For Jesu Christ in glorious Christian field,
Streaming the ensign of the Christian cross
Against black pagans, Turks, and Saracens,
And, toiled with works of war, retired himself
To Italy, and there at Venice gave
His body to that pleasant country's earth,
And his pure soul unto his captain, Christ,
Under whose colours he had fought so long.   100

BOLINGBROKE

Why, Bishop, is Norfolk dead?

BISHOP OF CARLISLE

As surely as I live, my lord.

BOLINGBROKE

Sweet peace conduct his sweet soul to the bosom
Of good old Abraham! Lords appellants,

86–9 *These differences . . . signories.* Holinshed: 'The King licensed the Duke
of Norfolk to return, that he might
arraign his appeal.' Holinshed also
reports that 'This year Thomas Mowbray, Duke of Norfolk, died in exile
at Venice, whose death might have
been worthily bewailed of all the
realm if he had not been consenting
to the death of the Duke of
Gloucester.'
86 *rest under gage* remain as challenges
89 *he is.* This is printed as 'he's' in F,
and elision seems necessary; but the
line is long in any case.

90 *we.* Bolingbroke begins to use the
royal plural.
his trial (either 'Aumerle's testing of
Mowbray's honour', or 'Mowbray's
proving of his honour in opposition
to Aumerle' – in either case, in trial
by combat)
91 *never.* So Q; 'ne're' F, which may
indicate the correct pronunciation.
93 *field* (of battle)
96 *toiled* exhausted
retired himself withdrew
103–4 *bosom | Of good old Abraham* (a
biblical – and proverbial – way of
saying 'heavenly rest')

Your differences shall all rest under gage
Till we assign you to your days of trial.
>   *Enter York*

YORK
Great Duke of Lancaster, I come to thee
From plume-plucked Richard, who with willing soul
Adopts thee heir, and his high sceptre yields
110 To the possession of thy royal hand.
Ascend his throne, descending now from him,
And long live Henry, fourth of that name!

BOLINGBROKE
In God's name I'll ascend the regal throne.

BISHOP OF CARLISLE
Marry, God forbid!
Worst in this royal presence may I speak,
Yet best beseeming me to speak the truth:
Would God that any in this noble presence
Were enough noble to be upright judge

---

108 *plume-plucked* humbled (possibly in reference to the fable attributed to Aesop about the crow that dressed itself in stolen feathers and was shamed when other birds took them away)

112 *fourth of that name.* The metre seems defective, and F's version − 'of that name, the fourth' − is attractive.

113–35 Holinshed reports that Carlisle 'boldly showed forth his opinion concerning that demand' (that Richard, having abdicated, should be tried), 'affirming that there was none amongst them worthy or meet to give judgement upon so noble a prince as King Richard was, whom they had taken for their sovereign and liege lord by the space of two-and-twenty years and more. "And I assure you," said he, "there is not so rank a traitor nor so arrant a thief nor yet so cruel a murderer appre-

hended or detained in prison for his offence but he shall be brought before the justice to hear his judgement; and will ye proceed to the judgement of an anointed king, hearing neither his answer nor excuse? I say that the Duke of Lancaster, whom ye call king, hath more trespassed to King Richard and his realm than King Richard hath done either to him or us.'

115–16 *Worst in this royal presence may I speak,* | *Yet best beseeming me to speak the truth* though in the presence of royalty it is as the lowest in rank that I speak, still it is fitting that I even more than anyone else should speak the truth (as I am a bishop). It is interesting that the Bishop modifies *royal* to *noble* two lines later, perhaps as he is about to deny Bolingbroke's regality.

Of noble Richard. Then true noblesse would
Learn him forbearance from so foul a wrong.   120
What subject can give sentence on his king? –
And who sits here that is not Richard's subject?
Thieves are not judged but they are by to hear
Although apparent guilt be seen in them;
And shall the figure of God's majesty,
His captain, steward, deputy elect,
Anointed, crownèd, planted many years,
Be judged by subject and inferior breath
And he himself not present? O, forfend it God
That in a Christian climate souls refined   130
Should show so heinous, black, obscene a deed!
I speak to subjects, and a subject speaks,
Stirred up by God thus boldly for his king.
My Lord of Hereford here, whom you call king,
Is a foul traitor to proud Hereford's King;
And if you crown him, let me prophesy
The blood of English shall manure the ground,
And future ages groan for this foul act.
Peace shall go sleep with Turks and infidels,
And in this seat of peace tumultuous wars   140
Shall kin with kin, and kind with kind, confound.

119 *noblesse* nobility
120 *Learn him forbearance* teach him to
refrain
foul a wrong (as presuming to sit in
judgement on his King)
123 *but* except when
124 *apparent* obvious
125 *figure* image
126 *elect* chosen
129 *forfend it God* may God forbid
130 *souls refined* civilized, or Christian-
ized, people
134 *My Lord of Hereford.* The Bishop
uses the least of Bolingbroke's titles.
136–49 *let me prophesy.* The Bishop's
prophecy recalls John of Gaunt's
(II.1.33–68), though this is spoken in
favour of Richard, whereas that criti-
cized him. The two thus reflect a
central problem of the play: that England, which has suffered under Richard's irresponsible reign, will suffer
too if his right to the crown is
usurped. Carlisle looks forward to
the state of affairs to be portrayed in
1 and *2 Henry IV.* His sentiments
reflect those of the 'Homily against
Disobedience and Wilful Rebellion',
which was familiar through being
regularly read aloud in church.
141 *kin with kin, and kind with kind, confound* destroy kinsmen and fellow-
countrymen by their own actions.
The killing of each other by members

Disorder, horror, fear, and mutiny
Shall here inhabit, and this land be called
The field of Golgotha and dead men's skulls.
O, if you raise this house against this house
It will the woefullest division prove
That ever fell upon this cursèd earth.
Prevent it; resist it; let it not be so,
Lest child, child's children, cry against you woe.

NORTHUMBERLAND

150   Well have you argued, sir; and for your pains
Of capital treason we arrest you here.
My Lord of Westminster, be it your charge
To keep him safely till his day of trial.
May it please you, lords, to grant the commons' suit?

BOLINGBROKE

Fetch hither Richard, that in common view
He may surrender. So we shall proceed

---

of the same family, and especially of son by father or father by son, is a common symbol in Shakespeare for the worst kind of disorder such as is brought about by civil war.

144 *field of Golgotha and dead men's skulls.* Golgotha, or Calvary, where Jesus Christ was crucified, means 'the place of skulls'. Carlisle anticipates Richard's comparisons of himself with Christ (lines 169–71, 238–41). In the Bishops' Bible Golgotha is called 'a place of a skull' (Mark 15.22, etc.), and the Prayer Book Gospel for Good Friday includes John 19.17: 'and went forth into a place which is called the place of dead men's skulls; but in Hebrew Golgotha'.

145 *this house against this house.* Carlisle foresees the Wars of the Roses, with an echo of biblical phraseology as in Mark 3.25: 'And if a house be divided against itself that house cannot continue.'

149 *cry against you woe* (*woe* probably has

adverbial rather than exclamatory force)

150–53 *Well. . .day of trial.* Holinshed: 'As soon as the Bishop had ended this tale he was attached by the Earl Marshal and committed to ward in the abbey of Saint Albans.'

151 *Of* on a charge of

154–319 This passage is not in Q1–3. See 'An Account of the Text', page 42, and Introduction, page 7.

154 *commons' suit.* Holinshed: 'On Wednesday [22 October 1399] following, request was made by the commons that sith King Richard had resigned and was lawfully deposed from his royal dignity, he might have judgement decreed against him, so as the realm were not troubled by him, and that the causes of his deposing might be published through the realm for satisfying of the people; which demand was granted.'

156 *surrender* (his throne); abdicate

Without suspicion.

YORK   I will be his conduct   *Exit*

BOLINGBROKE

Lords, you that here are under our arrest,
Procure your sureties for your days of answer.
Little are we beholding to your love,   160
And little looked for at your helping hands.
    Enter Richard and York

RICHARD

Alack, why am I sent for to a king
Before I have shook off the regal thoughts
Wherewith I reigned? I hardly yet have learned
To insinuate, flatter, bow, and bend my knee.
Give sorrow leave awhile to tutor me
To this submission. Yet I well remember
The favours of these men. Were they not mine?
Did they not sometime cry 'All hail!' to me?
So Judas did to Christ. But He in twelve   170
Found truth in all but one; I, in twelve thousand, none.
God save the King! Will no man say Amen?
Am I both priest and clerk? Well then, Amen.
God save the King, although I be not he;
And yet Amen if Heaven do think him me.

157 *conduct* escort
159 *sureties* men who will be responsible
for your appearance
    your days of answer the time when you
must appear to stand trial
161 *looked for* expected
(stage direction) From this point onwards F ceases to use 'King' for
Richard in speech prefixes and stage
directions. Q continues to do so till
the end of v.1.
163 *shook* shaken (a common Elizabethan form)
167 *Yet I well remember*. . .Holinshed:
'Which renunciation to the deposed
king was a redoubling of his grief,
insomuch as thereby it came to his

mind how in former times he was
acknowledged and taken for their
liege lord and sovereign, who now –
whether in contempt or in malice,
God knoweth – to his face forsware
him to be their king.'
168 *favours* 'faces' and 'friendly acts'
170 *Judas did to Christ.* Matthew 26.49:
'And forthwith when he came to
Jesus, he said "Hail, master"; and
kissed him.'
171 (an alexandrine)
173 *clerk* altar-server (who makes the
responses – *Amen* being the most
frequent – at the end of each prayer
read by the priest)

    To do what service am I sent for hither?

YORK

    To do that office of thine own good will

    Which tired majesty did make thee offer:

    The resignation of thy state and crown

    To Henry Bolingbroke.

180 RICHARD   Give me the crown.

    Here, cousin – seize the crown. Here, cousin –

    On this side, my hand; and on that side, thine.

    Now is this golden crown like a deep well

    That owes two buckets, filling one another,

    The emptier ever dancing in the air,

    The other down, unseen, and full of water.

    That bucket down and full of tears am I,

    Drinking my griefs whilst you mount up on high.

BOLINGBROKE

    I thought you had been willing to resign.

RICHARD

190   My crown I am; but still my griefs are mine.

    You may my glories and my state depose,

    But not my griefs. Still am I king of those.

BOLINGBROKE

    Part of your cares you give me with your crown.

RICHARD

    Your cares set up do not pluck my cares down.

---

176 *service* (punning on the ecclesiastical and the general sense)

180 *Give me the crown.* Presumably it has been carried in by Richard's attendants.

183 *Now is this golden crown like a deep well.* In stage practice it is most effective if the crown is held upside-down between Richard and Bolingbroke. The notion of Fortune's buckets is not uncommon in medieval and Elizabethan literature. There was a prover-bial expression 'Like two buckets of a well, if one go up the other must go down.'

184 *owes* owns, has

    filling one another (because when the full bucket is raised it causes the other to descend and be filled in turn)

194–6 *Your cares . . . new care won.* These lines include elaborate wordplay on *care.* First it means 'grief', then 're-sponsibility', then 'diligence', then

My care is loss of care by old care done;
Your care is gain of care by new care won.
The cares I give, I have, though given away.
They 'tend the crown, yet still with me they stay.

BOLINGBROKE

Are you contented to resign the crown?

RICHARD

Ay, no. No, ay; for I must nothing be.   200
Therefore no no, for I resign to thee.
Now mark me how I will undo myself
I give this heavy weight from off my head,
And this unwieldy sceptre from my hand,
The pride of kingly sway from out my heart.
With mine own tears I wash away my balm,
With mine own hands I give away my crown,
With mine own tongue deny my sacred state,
With mine own breath release all duteous oaths.
All pomp and majesty I do forswear.   210
My manors, rents, revenues I forgo.

'anxiety'. We may paraphrase: 'The cause of my grief is my loss of responsibility, brought about by my former lack of diligence; the cause of your trouble is the access of responsibility achieved by your recent pains.'

198 *'tend* are attendant upon

200 *Ay, no. No, ay.* Both 'Yes, no. No, yes' and 'I, no. No I'. M. M. Mahood comments: 'besides suggesting in one meaning (Aye, no; no, aye) his tormenting indecision, and in another (Aye – no; no I) the over-wrought mind that finds an outlet in punning, also represents in the meaning "I know no I" Richard's pathetic play-acting, his attempt to conjure with a magic he no longer believes. Can he exist if he no longer bears his right name of King? The mirror shows him the question is rhetorical but

he dashes it to the ground, only to have Bolingbroke expose the self-deception of this histrionic gesture: "The shadow ..."' (*Shakespeare's Wordplay*, page 87).

200 *nothing* (and *'no* thing')

201 *no no, for I resign to thee* (I cannot say 'no', because in fact I *do* resign in your favour)

202 *undo* ('undress', as he removes the emblems of kingship, 'unmake', and 'ruin')

203 *heavy weight* (the crown: *heavy* also meaning 'sad')

206 *balm* consecrated oil (with which he had been anointed at his coronation)

209 *release all duteous oaths* release my subjects from all the oaths of allegiance to me that they have sworn

211 *revenues* (accented on the second syllable)

My acts, decrees, and statutes I deny.
God pardon all oaths that are broke to me;
God keep all vows unbroke are made to thee;
Make me, that nothing have, with nothing grieved,
And thou with all pleased, that hast all achieved.
Long mayst thou live in Richard's seat to sit,
And soon lie Richard in an earthy pit.
'God save King Henry,' unkinged Richard says,
220   'And send him many years of sunshine days.'
What more remains?

NORTHUMBERLAND   No more but that you read
These accusations and these grievous crimes
Committed by your person and followers
Against the state and profit of this land,
That by confessing them the souls of men
May deem that you are worthily deposed.

RICHARD
Must I do so? And must I ravel out
My weaved-up follies? Gentle Northumberland,
If thy offences were upon record,
230   Would it not shame thee in so fair a troop
To read a lecture of them? If thou wouldst,
There shouldst thou find one heinous article,

214 *are made* (that) are made
215 *Make me* (God) make me
with nothing grieved. There is deliberate
paradox here. Richard asks to be
grieved by having nothing, but also
to be grieved by nothing. The ambi-
guity is highly expressive of the delicate balance of Richard's state of
mind, wishing to be relieved of his
care yet reluctant to give up his
crown.
221–2 *that you read* | *These accusations*. In
Holinshed Richard himself 'read the
scroll of resignation', though 'for the
articles which before ye have heard
were drawn and engrossed up . . .

the reading of those articles at that
season was deferred'. Shakespeare
chooses not to remind us of Richard's sins.
221 *read* (aloud, as an admission of guilt)
227 *ravel out* unravel; expose
229 *record* (accented on the second
syllable)
231 *read a lecture* (read aloud, as a
warning)
232 *heinous article*. Holinshed reports that
Parliament considered the thirty-
three articles 'heinous to the ears of
all men'.
article item

Containing the deposing of a king
And cracking the strong warrant of an oath,
Marked with a blot, damned in the book of heaven.
Nay, all of you that stand and look upon me,
Whilst that my wretchedness doth bait myself,
Though some of you – with Pilate – wash your hands,
Showing an outward pity, yet you Pilates
Have here delivered me to my sour cross,   240
And water cannot wash away your sin.

NORTHUMBERLAND

My lord, dispatch. Read o'er these articles.

RICHARD

Mine eyes are full of tears. I cannot see.
And yet salt water blinds them not so much
But they can see a sort of traitors here.
Nay, if I turn mine eyes upon myself
I find myself a traitor with the rest.
For I have given here my soul's consent
To'undeck the pompous body of a king;
Made glory base, and sovereignty a slave;   250
Proud majesty, a subject; state, a peasant.

NORTHUMBERLAND

My lord –

RICHARD

No lord of thine, thou haught, insulting man;

---

234 *oath* (Bolingbroke's oath of loyalty)
237 *bait* torment
238 *with* like
  with Pilate. Bolingbroke had implicitly compared himself to Pilate at
  III.1.5–6. The image occurs in Holinshed where, in the Flint Castle episode, the Archbishop of Canterbury
  promises that Richard shall not be
  hurt, 'but he prophesied not as a
  prelate, but as a Pilate'.
240 *delivered*. This may create a quibble
  on *Pilate* as 'pilot'. Christ was 'deliv-

ered' to Pilate and by him back to
the Jews.
  sour bitter
245 *sort* pack, gang (contemptuous). Perhaps there is a pun on *salt*.
248–9 *soul's . . . body*. In this antithesis,
  frequent in the play, Richard asserts
  his right to the crown while renouncing its attributes.
249 *pompous* magnificent, splendid
251 *state* stateliness
253 *haught* haughty

Nor no man's lord. I have no name, no title –
No, not that name was given me at the font –
But 'tis usurped. Alack the heavy day,
That I have worn so many winters out
And know not now what name to call myself!
O that I were a mockery king of snow,
260　　Standing before the sun of Bolingbroke,
To melt myself away in water-drops!
Good king; great king – and yet not greatly good –
An if my word be sterling yet in England
Let it command a mirror hither straight
That it may show me what a face I have
Since it is bankrupt of his majesty.

BOLINGBROKE
Go some of you, and fetch a looking-glass.

Exit attendant

NORTHUMBERLAND
Read o'er this paper while the glass doth come.

RICHARD
Fiend, thou torments me ere I come to hell.

BOLINGBROKE
270　　Urge it no more, my Lord Northumberland.

NORTHUMBERLAND
The commons will not then be satisfied.

RICHARD
They shall be satisfied. I'll read enough
When I do see the very book indeed

256 *'tis usurped* (possibly an allusion to the Lancastrian rumour that Richard was illegitimate. Or he may mean that now he is unkinged, he has no identity. Either he admits that he himself usurps a name to which he has no right, or he claims that others usurp his name from him.)

260 *sun of Bolingbroke.* Now the image of the sun is transferred from Richard to Bolingbroke.

261 *water-drops* tears
263 *An if* if
   sterling valid currency. The image is continued in *bankrupt* (line 266).
264 *straight* immediately
266 *his* its
267 *some* (could mean 'some one')
269 *torments* (a form of 'tormentest')

Where all my sins are writ; and that's myself.
    Enter attendant with a glass
Give me that glass, and therein will I read.
No deeper wrinkles yet? Hath sorrow struck
So many blows upon this face of mine
And made no deeper wounds? O, flattering glass,
Like to my followers in prosperity,
Thou dost beguile me. Was this face the face   280
That every day under his household roof
Did keep ten thousand men? Was this the face
That like the sun did make beholders wink?
Is this the face which faced so many follies,
That was at last outfaced by Bolingbroke?
A brittle glory shineth in this face.
As brittle as the glory is the face,
    (*he throws the glass down*)
For there it is, cracked in an hundred shivers.
Mark, silent King, the moral of this sport:
How soon my sorrow hath destroyed my face.   290

BOLINGBROKE
The shadow of your sorrow hath destroyed

280 *Was this face* . . . It is difficult not to associate these lines with Marlowe's *Doctor Faustus*, v.1.99: 'Was this the face that launched a thousand ships . . .', and Shakespeare's audience, too, may well have noticed the resemblance. Marlowe's play was written a few years before Shakespeare's.

281–2 *under his household roof | Did keep ten thousand men*. Holinshed, summarizing Richard's character, says that 'there resorted daily to his court above ten thousand persons that had meat and drink there allowed them'.

283 *wink* close their eyes

284 *Is this the face which*. This is the reading of F, the most authoritative text for this section of the play. But Q4 repeats 'Was . . . that', as in lines

280 and 282. We cannot say for certain which is right, and an actor would be justified in following Q4 if he preferred to do so.

284–5 *faced . . . outfaced* countenanced . . . discountenanced, superseded

285 *That*. Q4 has 'And'. The situation is the same as that referred to in the note to line 284. An actor might prefer 'And'.

288 *an*. Q4's reading, 'a', is also possible. See the note to line 284.

291–3 *shadow of your sorrow* . . . 'shadow of my sorrow'. Bolingbroke speaks contemptuously: 'the (mere) shadow cast by your sorrow', the action provoked by it, or *external manner of laments* (line 295) had destroyed the shadow of your face simply by passing across

The shadow of your face.

RICHARD   Say that again!
'The shadow of my sorrow' – ha, let's see.
'Tis very true. My grief lies all within,
And these external manner of laments
Are merely shadows to the unseen grief
That swells with silence in the tortured soul.
There lies the substance; and I thank thee, King,
For thy great bounty, that not only givest
300   Me cause to wail, but teachest me the way
How to lament the cause. I'll beg one boon,
And then be gone and trouble you no more.
Shall I obtain it?

BOLINGBROKE   Name it, fair cousin.

RICHARD
'Fair cousin'? I am greater than a king;
For when I was a king my flatterers
Were then but subjects; being now a subject
I have a king here to my flatterer.
Being so great, I have no need to beg.

BOLINGBROKE
Yet ask.

RICHARD
310   And shall I have?

BOLINGBROKE
You shall.

RICHARD
Then give me leave to go.

---

it, as one shadow obliterates another.
Richard takes up the phrase with a
suggestion of greater reality: 'the
shadowing forth, or embodiment, of
my sorrow'.

295 *these external manner* (an archaic construction   comparable   with   'all
manner of', or the modern colloquial
'these kind of . . .' Q4's 'manners',

followed by many editors, is probably a sophistication.)

296 *to* compared to

298 *substance* (opposed to *shadow*; compare II.2.14: *Each substance of a grief
hath twenty shadows*)

299 *thy . . . that* of you . . . who

307 *to* as

312 *Then give me leave to go.* Richard's

BOLINGBROKE

Whither?

RICHARD

Whither you will, so I were from your sights.

BOLINGBROKE

Go some of you, convey him to the Tower.

RICHARD

O, good, 'convey!' – Conveyors are you all,
That rise thus nimbly by a true king's fall.

BOLINGBROKE

On Wednesday next we solemnly proclaim
Our coronation. Lords, be ready, all.

Exeunt all except the Abbot of Westminster,
the Bishop of Carlisle, Aumerle

ABBOT OF WESTMINSTER

A woeful pageant have we here beheld.   320

BISHOP OF CARLISLE

The woe's to come. The children yet unborn
Shall feel this day as sharp to them as thorn.

AUMERLE

You holy clergymen, is there no plot
To rid the realm of this pernicious blot?

ABBOT OF WESTMINSTER

My lord,
Before I freely speak my mind herein
You shall not only take the Sacrament
To bury mine intents, but also to effect

request seems anticlimactic. It may represent a calculated deflation of Bolingbroke, Richard having led him to expect a more taxing request.

314 *sights* (the sight of each one of you)

316 *'convey'*. The word was slang for 'steal', and Richard picks it up in this sense.

317 *nimbly* (also associated with thieving. Compare *The Winter's Tale*, IV.4.667–8: 'a nimble hand is necessary for a cutpurse'.)

320 *pageant* spectacle. (The line would have been inappropriate when the deposition scene was omitted.)

321 *to end of scene* Holinshed reports on 'the conspiracy which was contrived by the Abbot of Westminster as chief instrument thereof'. The Abbot 'highly feasted these lords his special friends' and they devised the plot referred to at v.2.52, 96–9, and v.3.14–19.

328 *bury mine intents* conceal my plans

Whatever I shall happen to devise.
330   I see your brows are full of discontent,
Your hearts of sorrow, and your eyes of tears.
Come home with me to supper, I will lay
A plot shall show us all a merry day.   *Exeunt*

V.I   *Enter the Queen with her attendants*
QUEEN ISABEL
This way the King will come. This is the way
To Julius Caesar's ill-erected Tower,
To whose flint bosom my condemned lord
Is doomed a prisoner by proud Bolingbroke.
Here let us rest, if this rebellious earth
Have any resting for her true King's Queen.
                    Enter Richard and guard
But soft, but see, or rather do not see,
My fair rose wither. Yet look up, behold,
That you in pity may dissolve to dew
10   And wash him fresh again with true-love tears.
Ah, thou the model where old Troy did stand!

---

332 *supper*. The sentence is sometimes
made to end here, but probably *Come*
is subjunctive: 'If you will come . . .'

v.1 The material of this scene is not
derived from Holinshed (except for lines
51–2). In portraying a final meeting between Richard and his Queen Shakespeare may have been influenced by
Samuel Daniel's *Civil Wars*, though his
treatment is different; see note to lines
40–50, and Introduction, page 10.
(stage direction) *attendants* (presumably the Ladies of III.4)
2 *Julius Caesar's ill-erected Tower* (the
Tower of London. There was an old
tradition that it had originally been

built by Julius Caesar.)
ill-erected built for evil purposes or
with evil results. The Queen is thinking especially of its present use, for
imprisoning Richard.
3 *flint* flinty, merciless
6 (stage direction) *guard* (perhaps implying more than one man)
8 *rose*. In *1 Henry IV*, 1.3.173, Hotspur
calls Richard 'that sweet lovely rose'.
11 *the model where old Troy did stand*. She
addresses Richard, and finds that in
his present condition he is to his
former self as the ruins of Troy were
to the city in its greatness.
model ground plan

Thou map of honour, thou King Richard's tomb,
And not King Richard! Thou most beauteous inn,
Why should hard-favoured grief be lodged in thee
When triumph is become an alehouse guest?

RICHARD

Join not with grief, fair woman, do not so,
To make my end too sudden. Learn, good soul,
To think our former state a happy dream,
From which awaked the truth of what we are
Shows us but this. I am sworn brother, sweet,   20
To grim Necessity, and he and I
Will keep a league till death. Hie thee to France,
And cloister thee in some religious house.
Our holy lives must win a new world's crown
Which our profane hours here have thrown down.

QUEEN ISABEL

What, is my Richard both in shape and mind
Transformed and weakened? Hath Bolingbroke
Deposed thine intellect? Hath he been in thy heart?
The lion dying thrusteth forth his paw

old Troy. London was known as 'Troia novans', or 'new Troy', because of a legend that after the Trojan war Aeneas led a party of Trojans to Britain and that his great-grandson, Brut, founded London and called it Troia-Nova.

12 *map* image, outline of former glory

15 *triumph is become an alehouse guest*. Triumph is entertained in the *alehouse* Bolingbroke, opposed to the more beautiful and stately *inn*.

18 *state* stateliness, splendour

22 *Hie* go, hasten

24-5 *Our holy lives must win a new world's crown | Which our profane hours here have thrown down* by leading holy lives we must win in heaven the crown that our worldly lives here have cast away

25 *thrown* (probably to be pronounced 'throwen'. F's 'stricken' could be correct)

29-31 *The lion dying thrusteth forth his paw | And wounds the earth, if nothing else, with rage | To be o'erpowered.* The comparison between a monarch and lion is commonplace, but Shakespeare may have been influenced here by Marlowe's *Edward II,* V.I.11-15, where Edward says of himself:

But when the imperial lion's flesh is
    gored
He rends and tears it with his
    wrathful paw,
And, highly scorning that the lowly
    earth
Should drink his blood, mounts up
    to the air.

30   And wounds the earth, if nothing else, with rage
    To be o'erpowered. And wilt thou pupil-like
    Take the correction, mildly kiss the rod,
    And fawn on rage with base humility,
    Which art a lion and the king of beasts?

RICHARD

    A king of beasts indeed! If aught but beasts
    I had been still a happy king of men.
    Good sometimes queen, prepare thee hence for France.
    Think I am dead, and that even here thou takest
    As from my deathbed thy last living leave.
40   In winter's tedious nights sit by the fire
    With good old folks, and let them tell thee tales
    Of woeful ages long ago betid;
    And ere thou bid goodnight, to quite their griefs
    Tell thou the lamentable tale of me,
    And send the hearers weeping to their beds;

---

32 *correction, mildly kiss*. F has 'correction midly, kiss', which is as plausible a reading.

37 *sometimes* sometime, former

38 *even* (probably to be pronounced 'e'en')

40–50 *In winter's tedious nights . . . a rightful king*. These lines seem to show the verbal influence of Daniel's *Civil Wars*, III, stanza 65. Richard soliloquizes on the difference between himself in prison and a peasant:

Thou sitt'st at home safe by thy quiet fire,
And hearest of other's harms, but feelest none;
And there thou tellest of kings and who aspire,
Who fall, who rise, who triumphs, who do moan.
Perhaps thou talkest of me, and dost inquire

Of my restraint, why I live here alone.
O, know 'tis others' sin, not my desert,
And I could wish I were but as thou art.

41 *tales*. See Introduction, page 37.

42 *betid* past

43 *quite* (or 'quit') requite, cap

44 *lamentable tale of me*. The phrase resembles one used by Sidney in *Astrophil and Stella* (published in 1591), in which the lover complains that his beloved wept to hear a sad tale of love but does not pity his real plight. So he says:

Then think, my dear, that you in me do read
Of lover's suit some sad tragedy.
I am not I; pity the tale of me.

For why the senseless brands will sympathize
The heavy accent of thy moving tongue,
And in compassion weep the fire out;
And some will mourn in ashes, some coal-black,
For the deposing of a rightful king.   50
    Enter Northumberland

NORTHUMBERLAND
My lord, the mind of Bolingbroke is changed.
You must to Pomfret, not unto the Tower.
And, madam, there is order ta'en for you:
With all swift speed you must away to France.

RICHARD
Northumberland, thou ladder wherewithal
The mounting Bolingbroke ascends my throne,

46 *For why* because (that is, 'weeping because')
   senseless inanimate, without feeling
   sympathize respond to
48 *weep the fire out*. There is an allusion to the 'weeping' of resin from burning wood, as in *The Tempest*, III.I.18–19, when Miranda says to Ferdinand 'When this burns, | 'Twill weep for having wearied you.'
49 *some* (of the brands)
52 *Pomfret* (Pontefract, in Yorkshire. Holinshed: 'For shortly after his resignation he was conveyed to the castle of Leeds in Kent, and from thence to Pomfret.')
53 *there is order ta'en* arrangements have been made
55–9 *Northumberland, thou ladder . . . into corruption*. These lines are recalled by King Henry in 2 *Henry IV*, III.I.65–79:

    But which of you was by –:
  You, cousin Nevil, as I may
    remember –:

When Richard, with his eye brimful of tears,
Then checked and rated by Northumberland,
Did speak these words, now proved a prophecy?
'Northumberland, thou ladder by the which
My cousin Bolingbroke ascends my throne' –
Though then, God knows, I had no such intent
But that necessity so bowed the state
That I and greatness were compelled to kiss –
'The time shall come,' thus did he follow it,
'The time will come that foul sin, gathering head,
Shall break into corruption'; so went on,
Foretelling this same time's condition
And the division of our amity.

The time shall not be many hours of age
More than it is ere foul sin, gathering head,
Shall break into corruption. Thou shalt think,
60 Though he divide the realm and give thee half,
It is too little, helping him to all.
He shall think that thou, which knowest the way
To plant unrightful kings, wilt know again,
Being ne'er so little urged another way,
To pluck him headlong from the usurped throne.
The love of wicked men converts to fear,
That fear to hate, and hate turns one or both
To worthy danger and deserved death.

NORTHUMBERLAND
My guilt be on my head, and there an end.
70 Take leave and part, for you must part forthwith.

RICHARD
Doubly divorced! Bad men, you violate
A two-fold marriage – 'twixt my crown and me,
And then betwixt me and my married wife.
(*To Queen Isabel*)
Let me unkiss the oath 'twixt thee and me;
And yet not so; for with a kiss 'twas made.
– Part us, Northumberland: I towards the north,
Where shivering cold and sickness pines the clime;
My wife to France, from whence set forth in pomp
She came adorned hither like sweet May,

58–9 *foul sin, gathering head,* | *shall break into corruption* (like an ulcer or boil)
61 *helping him to all* as you have helped him to get it all
68 *worthy* deserved
69 *and there an end* (a common tag meaning 'and let that be the end of it')
70 *part . . . part* part (from your Queen) . . . depart
74 *unkiss the oath* (unseal with a kiss the marriage vow that had been ratified by a kiss)

75 *And yet not so* 'yet let us not kiss, since it was with a kiss that the vow was made', or 'yet the oath cannot be kissed away, as it was made with a kiss'
77 *pines the clime* afflicts the land
78 *pomp* splendour. Holinshed describes the great splendour of the wedding.
79 The scene moves into couplets for the grave, stylized parting of Richard and his Queen.

Sent back like Hallowmas or shortest of day.   80

QUEEN ISABEL

And must we be divided? Must we part?

RICHARD

Ay, hand from hand, my love, and heart from heart.

QUEEN ISABEL (*to Northumberland*)

Banish us both, and send the King with me.

RICHARD

That were some love, but little policy.

QUEEN ISABEL

Then whither he goes, thither let me go.

RICHARD

So two together weeping make one woe.

Weep thou for me in France, I for thee here.

Better far off than, near, be ne'er the nea'er.

Go count thy way with sighs, I mine with groans.

QUEEN ISABEL

So longest way shall have the longest moans.   90

RICHARD

Twice for one step I'll groan, the way being short,

And piece the way out with a heavy heart.

Come, come – in wooing sorrow let's be brief,

Since wedding it, there is such length in grief.

---

80 *Hallowmas*. All Saints' Day, 1 November; because of the change in calendar it corresponded in Shakespeare's time to our 12 November, so was closer to the shortest day.
shortest of day (the winter solstice)

84 *That were . . . policy*. F, followed by most editors, gives this line to Northumberland, but this breaks the rhythm of the speeches and has no special authority.
little policy hardly politic, poor statesmanship

86–96 These lines bring together many of the words in the play's vocabulary of grief – *weeping, woe, sighs, groans,*

moans, sorrow, and *grief.* See Introduction, pages 33–4.

86 *So* (tantamount to 'No; for if so . . .')

88 *Better far off than, near, be ne'er the nea'er* it is better to be far apart than, being near to each other, be no closer to being together. Dr Johnson comments: 'To be *never the nigher*, or as it is commonly spoken in the midland counties, *ne're the ne'er*, is *to make no advance towards the good desired.*' The final word is a comparative form which has become contracted.

92 *piece the way out* make the journey seem longer

One kiss shall stop our mouths, and dumbly part.
Thus give I mine, and thus take I thy heart.

    They kiss

QUEEN ISABEL

Give me mine own again. 'Twere no good part
To take on me to keep and kill thy heart.

    They kiss

So, now I have mine own again, be gone,
100   That I may strive to kill it with a groan.

RICHARD

We make woe wanton with this fond delay.
Once more, adieu. The rest let sorrow say.   *Exeunt*

V.2   *Enter Duke of York and the Duchess*

DUCHESS OF YORK

My lord, you told me you would tell the rest,
When weeping made you break the story off,
Of our two cousins' coming into London.

---

96 *mine* my heart. The conceit that lovers exchanged hearts was commonplace.

97 *Give me mine own again* (in a second kiss)

97–98 *'Twere no good part | To take on me to keep and kill thy heart* it would not be a good action for me to undertake to look after your heart and then to kill it (as my grief would kill me and therefore also it)

101 *make woe wanton* play verbal games with grief. The characters show consciousness of the dramatist's word-play, as Gaunt and Richard had at II.1.84–8.
fond loving yet also pointless

v.2 The first part (to line 40) is probably indebted to Daniel's *Civil Wars*, II, stanzas 66–70, which describe the triumphal

entry of Bolingbroke into London, with the humbled Richard behind him. Holinshed too has a description of Bolingbroke's triumphal progress and reception. The remainder of the scene is based on Holinshed (see notes to line 52 *to end*).

(stage direction) *the Duchess*. Historically, York's wife at this time was Aumerle's stepmother. Aumerle's mother, Isabella of Castile, had died in 1394. Shakespeare was mainly interested in providing a wife for York and a mother for Aumerle.

2 *story*. The Duchess's words recall Richard's prophecy that the Queen, by telling *the lamentable tale of me*, would *send the hearers weeping to their beds* (v.1.44–5).

3 *cousins* (Richard and Bolingbroke)

YORK
    Where did I leave?

DUCHESS OF YORK At that sad stop, my lord,
    Where rude misgoverned hands from windows' tops
    Threw dust and rubbish on King Richard's head.

YORK
    Then, as I said, the Duke, great Bolingbroke,
    Mounted upon a hot and fiery steed
    Which his aspiring rider seemed to know,
    With slow but stately pace kept on his course,   10
    Whilst all tongues cried 'God save thee, Bolingbroke!'
    You would have thought the very windows spake,
    So many greedy looks of young and old
    Through casements darted their desiring eyes
    Upon his visage, and that all the walls
    With painted imagery had said at once
    'Jesu preserve thee, welcome Bolingbroke',
    Whilst he, from the one side to the other turning,
    Bare-headed, lower than his proud steed's neck
    Bespake them thus: 'I thank you, countrymen.'   20
    And thus still doing, thus he passed along.

5–6 This episode is recalled by the Archbishop of York in *2 Henry IV*, 1.3.103–7, speaking of Richard:

> Thou that threwest dust upon his goodly head,
> When through proud London he came sighing on
> After the admired heels of Bolingbroke,
> Criest now 'O earth, yield us that king again,
> And take thou this!'

5 *rude* (stronger in Shakespeare's time than now: 'brutal')
  windows' tops upper windows

6 *King Richard*. The Duchess still refers to Richard as the King.

9 *his aspiring rider seemed to know* seemed to know how aspiring its rider was

15–16 *that all the walls | With painted imagery*. This refers to the painted cloths common in Elizabethan houses, on which figures were portrayed with sentences issuing from their mouths, as in a strip cartoon. York imagines that the walls were covered with such cloths.

16 *at once* all together

19 *lower* (bowing lower, deferentially addressing the crowd)

21 *still* continually, all the time

DUCHESS OF YORK

Alack, poor Richard! Where rode he the whilst?

YORK

As in a theatre the eyes of men,
After a well graced actor leaves the stage,
Are idly bent on him that enters next,
Thinking his prattle to be tedious:
Even so, or with much more contempt, men's eyes
Did scowl on gentle Richard. No man cried 'God save
    him!'
No joyful tongue gave him his welcome home;
30 But dust was thrown upon his sacred head,
Which with such gentle sorrow he shook off,
His face still combating with tears and smiles,
The badges of his grief and patience,
That had not God for some strong purpose steeled
The hearts of men, they must perforce have melted,
And barbarism itself have pitied him.
But heaven hath a hand in these events,
To whose high will we bound our calm contents.
To Bolingbroke are we sworn subjects now,
40 Whose state and honour I for aye allow.

Enter Aumerle

DUCHESS OF YORK

Here comes my son Aumerle.

YORK   Aumerle that was;

24 *well graced* 'graceful' and 'popular'
25 *idly* listlessly, indifferently
27 *Even* (probably to be pronounced 'e'en')
28 *gentle*. This word is omitted in F. Since it is extrametrical and comes again in line 31, its presence in Q may be accidental.
33 *badges* outward signs (*tears* of grief, *smiles* of patience)

36 *barbarism itself* even savages
38 *bound our calm contents* submit ourselves in calm content
41 *Aumerle that was*. Holinshed: 'it was finally enacted that such as were appellants in the last Parliament against the Duke of Gloucester and other, should in this wise following be ordered: the Dukes of Aumerle, Surrey, and Exeter there present were judged

But that is lost for being Richard's friend;
And, madam, you must call him Rutland now.
I am in Parliament pledge for his truth
And lasting fealty to the new-made King.

DUCHESS OF YORK

Welcome, my son! Who are the violets now
That strew the green lap of the new-come spring?

AUMERLE

Madam, I know not, nor I greatly care not.
God knows I had as lief be none as one.

YORK

Well, bear you well in this new spring of time,   50
Lest you be cropped before you come to prime.
What news from Oxford? Do these justs and triumphs
    hold?

to lose their names of Dukes, together with the honours, titles, and
dignities thereunto belonging.'
42 *that* (that title)
43 *Rutland.* Aumerle had been made Earl
of Rutland in 1390, and after the
Duke of Gloucester's arrest was
given the Dukedom of Aumerle.
44 *in Parliament.* See notes to line 52 *to
end.*
46–7 *the violets now | That strew the green
lap of the new-come spring* (those
who are in favour in the new court)
52 *to end of scene   What news from Oxford?
Do these justs and triumphs hold?* Holinshed reports that the Abbot of Westminster and his confederates 'devised
that they should take upon them a
solemn justs to be enterprised between him [the Earl of Huntingdon]
and twenty on his part, and the Earl
of Salisbury and twenty with him at
Oxford, to the which triumph King
Henry should be desired, and when
he should be most busily marking
the martial pastime he suddenly

should be slain and destroyed, and
so by that means King Richard, who
as yet lived, might be restored to
liberty and have his former estate
and dignity.' When Huntingdon arrived at Oxford 'he found all his
mates and confederates there, well
appointed for their purpose, except the Earl of Rutland, by whose
folly their practised conspiracy was
brought to light and disclosed to
King Henry. For this Earl of Rutland
departing before from Westminster
to see his father the Duke of York as
he sat at dinner had his counterpane
of the indenture of the confederacy
in his bosom.

'The father espying it would needs
see what it was; and though the son
humbly denied to show it, the father
being more earnest to see it by force
took it out of his bosom, and, perceiving the contents thereof, in a great
rage caused his horses to be saddled
out of hand and, spitefully reproving
his son of treason for whom he was

AUMERLE

For aught I know, my lord, they do.

YORK

You will be there, I know.

AUMERLE

If God prevent not, I purpose so.

YORK

What seal is that that hangs without thy bosom?
Yea, lookest thou pale? Let me see the writing.

AUMERLE

My lord, 'tis nothing.

YORK   No matter, then, who see it.

I will be satisfied. Let me see the writing.

AUMERLE

60   I do beseech your grace to pardon me.
It is a matter of small consequence
Which for some reasons I would not have seen.

YORK

Which for some reasons, sir, I mean to see.
I fear – I fear!

DUCHESS OF YORK

What should you fear?
'Tis nothing but some bond that he is entered into
For gay apparel 'gainst the triumph day.

become surety and mainpernor for his good a-bearing in open Parliament, he incontinently mounted on horseback to ride towards Windsor to the King to declare unto him the malicious intent of his complices.' (The remainder of the episode is represented in v.3.23 *to end.*)

52 *Do these justs and triumphs hold*? F reads 'Hold those jousts and triumphs?' This improves the metre; but the line may be deliberately irregular in preparation for the short ones that follow.
Do . . . hold will (they) be held
justs and triumphs tournaments and processional shows
55 *If God prevent not, I purpose so* (with sinister overtones)
56 *seal* (the wax seal, usually red, hanging from the document)
without outside
57 *lookest.* The metre demands elision.
66 *'gainst* in preparation for

YORK
    Bound to himself? What doth he with a bond
    That he is bound to? Wife, thou art a fool.
    Boy, let me see the writing.

AUMERLE
    I do beseech you, pardon me. I may not show it.   70

YORK
    I will be satisfied. Let me see it, I say.
      He plucks it out of his bosom, and reads it

YORK
    Treason! Foul treason! Villain! Traitor! Slave!

DUCHESS OF YORK
    What is the matter, my lord?

YORK
    Ho, who is within there? Saddle my horse.
    God for his mercy! What treachery is here!

DUCHESS OF YORK
    Why, what is it, my lord?

YORK
    Give me my boots, I say. Saddle my horse.
    Now, by mine honour, by my life, by my troth,
    I will appeach the villain.

DUCHESS OF YORK
    What is the matter?

YORK   Peace, foolish woman.   80

DUCHESS OF YORK
    I will not peace. What is the matter, Aumerle?

---

67 *Bound to himself?* York points out that if, as his wife suggests, Aumerle had borrowed money on a bond, the document would be in his creditor's possession, not his own.

74 Many editors add 'Enter a Servant' after *there*. This is unnecessary. York calls impatiently, and is not answered till line 84.

79 *I will appeach the villain* (appeach, inform against, denounce). York's vehemence against his son may be explained partly by the fact that he has entered into surety for Aumerle's loyalty (lines 44–5). Aumerle has thus let him down personally, as well as endangered him.

AUMERLE

  Good mother, be content. It is no more
  Than my poor life must answer.

DUCHESS OF YORK   Thy life answer?

YORK

  Bring me my boots. I will unto the King.

    His man enters with his boots

DUCHESS OF YORK

  Strike him, Aumerle! Poor boy, thou art amazed.

    (*To York's man*)

  Hence, villain! Never more come in my sight!

YORK

  Give me my boots, I say!

    York's man gives him the boots and goes out

DUCHESS OF YORK

  Why, York, what wilt thou do?
  Wilt thou not hide the trespass of thine own?
90 Have we more sons? Or are we like to have?
  Is not my teeming-date drunk up with time?
  And wilt thou pluck my fair son from mine age?
  And rob me of a happy mother's name?
  Is he not like thee? Is he not thine own?

YORK

  Thou fond, mad woman,
  Wilt thou conceal this dark conspiracy?
  A dozen of them here have ta'en the Sacrament

85–7 The reactions of the silent servant are a likely source of comedy in the staging of this episode.

85 *Strike him, Aumerle! Poor boy, thou art amazed.*
Presumably the Duchess instructs her son to strike the servant so as to obstruct York's preparations for departure. But he is too *amazed* ('bewildered') to do so.

87 (stage direction) The servant's exit is not marked in the early editions. He could remain on stage as a bewildered, perhaps amused, observer of the quarrel between his master and mistress.

90 *Have we more sons?* Historically the answer was yes; York had another son, Richard, who is the Earl of Cambridge in *Henry V*.

91 *my teeming-date* the time during which I may have children

95 *fond* foolish

And interchangeably set down their hands
To kill the King at Oxford.

DUCHESS OF YORK   He shall be none.

We'll keep him here. Then what is that to him?   100

YORK

Away, fond woman. Were he twenty times my son
I would appeach him.

DUCHESS OF YORK

Hadst thou groaned for him as I have done
Thou wouldst be more pitiful.
But now I know thy mind. Thou dost suspect
That I have been disloyal to thy bed,
And that he is a bastard, not thy son.
Sweet York, sweet husband, be not of that mind.
He is as like thee as a man may be;
Not like to me, or any of my kin,   110
And yet I love him.

YORK   Make way, unruly woman.   *Exit*

DUCHESS OF YORK

After, Aumerle. Mount thee upon his horse.
Spur, post, and get before him to the King,
And beg thy pardon ere he do accuse thee.
I'll not be long behind – though I be old,
I doubt not but to ride as fast as York;
And never will I rise up from the ground
Till Bolingbroke have pardoned thee. Away, be gone!

                                        Exeunt

98 *interchangeably set down their hands*
signed reciprocally (so that each had
a record of the other's oath)
99 *He shall be none* he shall not be one of
them
100 *that* what they do
103 *groaned* (in childbirth)
104 *Thou wouldst* (probably to be pronounced 'thou'dst')

113 Holinshed: 'Rutland, seeing in what
danger he stood, took his horse and
rode another way to Windsor in post,
so that he got thither before his father.'
post hasten
117–18 *never will I rise up from the ground
| Till Bolingbroke have pardoned thee.*
She fulfils this threat.

V.3   *Enter Bolingbroke, now King Henry, with Harry*
            Percy and other lords

KING HENRY

Can no man tell me of my unthrifty son?
'Tis full three months since I did see him last.
If any plague hang over us, 'tis he.
I would to God, my lords, he might be found.
Inquire at London 'mongst the taverns there;
For there, they say, he daily doth frequent
With unrestrainèd loose companions,
Even such, they say, as stand in narrow lanes
And beat our watch, and rob our passengers,
10   Which he – young wanton, and effeminate boy –
Takes on the point of honour to support
So dissolute a crew.

PERCY

My lord, some two days since I saw the Prince,
And told him of those triumphs held at Oxford.

KING HENRY

And what said the gallant?

PERCY

His answer was he would unto the stews,
And from the commonest creature pluck a glove,

---

v.3 The first part of the scene looks
forward to the plays about Prince Hal,
and may have been written for this purpose. Legends about the young prince's
dissolute behaviour were common. For
the remainder of the scene, see notes to
line 23 *to end.*

1 *unthrifty* prodigal, profligate
  son (Prince Hal, later Henry V; historically he was only twelve years old at
  this time)

3 *plague* calamity (as prophesied by Richard, III.3.85–90, and Carlisle, IV.1.-
  137–47)
  hang over (because plague was believed
  to come from the clouds)

9 *watch* night-watchmen, civic guard
  passengers wayfarers, travellers

10 *Which.* The construction seems
  clumsy. Many editors emend to
  'While'.
  wanton (probably the noun, meaning
  'spoiled child')

11 *Takes on the* takes as a

15 *gallant* (accented on the second syllable) fine young gentleman (ironically)

16 *would* would go
  stews 'brothels' or 'disreputable area'

And wear it as a favour; and with that
He would unhorse the lustiest challenger.

KING HENRY

As dissolute as desperate. Yet through both   20
I see some sparks of better hope, which elder years
May happily bring forth. But who comes here?
          Enter Aumerle, amazed

AUMERLE

Where is the King?

KING HENRY

What means our cousin, that he stares and looks so
          wildly?

AUMERLE

God save your grace. I do beseech your majesty
To have some conference with your grace alone.

KING HENRY

Withdraw yourselves, and leave us here alone.
          Exeunt Harry Percy and the other lords
What is the matter with our cousin now?

AUMERLE

For ever may my knees grow to the earth,

---

18 *with that* (with the glove as a favour)
20 *both* (both his *dissolute* and his *desperate* characteristics)
22 *happily* 'perhaps' and 'happily'
22 (stage direction) *amazed* (this is Q's word) distraught
23 *to end of scene*—Here Shakespeare resumes the episode begun at v.2.52 (see note). Holinshed's narration continues: 'The Earl of Rutland, seeing in what danger he stood, took his horse and rode another way to Windsor in post, so that he got thither before his father, and when he was alighted at the castle gate he caused the gates to be shut, saying that he must needs deliver the keys to the King. When he came before the King's presence he kneeled down on his knees, beseeching him of mercy

and forgiveness, and, declaring the whole matter unto him in order as everything had passed, obtained pardon. Therewith came his father, and, being let in, delivered the indenture which he had taken from his son unto the King, who, thereby perceiving his son's words to be true, changed his purpose for his going to Oxenford and dispatched messengers forth to signify unto the Earl of Northumberland his High Constable, and to the Earl of Westmorland his High Marshal, and to other his assured friends, of all the doubtful danger and perilous jeopardy.' The conspirators rose in open rebellion and were defeated at Cirencester.
25 *God save your grace.* Aumerle kneels,

30 My tongue cleave to my roof within my mouth,
Unless a pardon ere I rise or speak.

KING HENRY

Intended or committed was this fault?
If on the first, how heinous e'er it be
To win thy after-love I pardon thee.

AUMERLE

Then give me leave that I may turn the key
That no man enter till my tale be done.

KING HENRY

Have thy desire.

*Aumerle locks the door. The Duke of York knocks at
the door and crieth*

YORK (*within*)

My liege, beware, look to thyself,
Thou hast a traitor in thy presence there.

KING HENRY (*to Aumerle*)

40 Villain, I'll make thee safe!

AUMERLE

Stay thy revengeful hand, thou hast no cause to fear.

YORK

Open the door, secure foolhardy King.
Shall I for love speak treason to thy face?
Open the door, or I will break it open.

King Henry opens the door. Enter York

KING HENRY

What is the matter, uncle? Speak, recover breath,

---

probably here, and remains kneeling till line 37.

26 *To have* that I may have

30 *My tongue cleave to my roof within my mouth.* Compare Psalm 137.6: 'let my tongue cleave to the roof of my mouth'.

33 *on the first* (*Intended*, not *committed*)

34 *after-love* gratitude and future loyalty

35 *turn the key* (of one of the doors on the stage)

38–46 There are metrical irregularities in these lines – 41 and 45 are alexandrines, and 38, 40, and 46 are short lines – but this is not uncommon in the play.

40 *safe* harmless (probably he draws his sword)

42 *secure* over-confident

43 *Shall I for love speak treason to thy face?* must I because of my love and loyalty speak treason (call you foolhardy) to your face?

Tell us how near is danger,
That we may arm us to encounter it.

YORK

Peruse this writing here, and thou shalt know
The treason that my haste forbids me show.

AUMERLE

Remember, as thou readest, thy promise passed.   50
I do repent me. Read not my name there.
My heart is not confederate with my hand.

YORK

It was, villain, ere thy hand did set it down.
I tore it from the traitor's bosom, King.
Fear, and not love, begets his penitence.
Forget to pity him lest thy pity prove
A serpent that will sting thee to the heart.

KING HENRY

O, heinous, strong, and bold conspiracy!
O loyal father of a treacherous son,
Thou sheer immaculate and silver fountain   60
From whence this stream through muddy passages
Hath held his current and defiled himself —
Thy overflow of good converts to bad,
And thy abundant goodness shall excuse
This deadly blot in thy digressing son.

YORK

So shall my virtue be his vice's bawd
An he shall spend mine honour with his shame,

---

49 *my haste forbids me show* (through lack
of breath)
50 *thy promise passed* the promise you
have passed (or 'given')
52 *hand* handwriting
56 *Forget* forget your promise
60 *sheer* pure
63 *converts to bad* changes to bad (in
Aumerle)
65 *digressing* (continuing the metaphor of
the stream) transgressing

66 *be his vice's bawd* serve his wickedness
67 *An* if. Q2 and later editions, as well
as modern editors, read 'And'. But
Q1 is the authoritative text, 'and'
was in any case a common form of
'an' meaning 'if', and the sense is at
least as good if we read *An* – York
says 'if he consumes my honourable
reputation in his shameful one, then
my virtue . . .'

As thriftless sons their scraping fathers' gold.
Mine honour lives when his dishonour dies,
70   Or my shamed life in his dishonour lies.
Thou killest me in his life – giving him breath,
The traitor lives, the true man's put to death.

DUCHESS OF YORK (*within*)

What ho, my liege, for God's sake let me in!

KING HENRY

What shrill-voiced suppliant makes this eager cry?

DUCHESS OF YORK

A woman, and thy aunt, great King. 'Tis I.
Speak with me, pity me, open the door!
A beggar begs that never begged before.

KING HENRY

Our scene is altered from a serious thing,
And now changed to 'The Beggar and the King'.
80   My dangerous cousin, let your mother in.
I know she is come to pray for your foul sin.

    Aumerle admits the Duchess. She kneels

YORK

If thou do pardon, whosoever pray,
More sins for this forgiveness prosper may.
This festered joint cut off, the rest rest sound;
This let alone will all the rest confound.

DUCHESS OF YORK

O King, believe not this hard-hearted man.
Love loving not itself, none other can.

---

69 *his dishonour dies* (that is, he dies himself)

79 '*The Beggar and the King*' (a reference to the title of an old ballad about King Cophetua and a beggar-maid. King Henry suggests that the *scene* has changed from that of a serious play to a frivolity.)

84–5 *This festered joint cut off, the rest rest sound*; | *This let alone will all the rest*

confound if this diseased limb (Aumerle) is amputated, the others will remain healthy; otherwise it will contaminate and destroy all the others

87 *Love loving not itself, none other can.* Probably the Duchess means 'If York does not love himself (in his son), he can love no other', that is, his advice to Bolingbroke cannot be trusted.

YORK

> Thou frantic woman, what dost thou make here?
> Shall thy old dugs once more a traitor rear?

DUCHESS OF YORK

> Sweet York, be patient. Hear me, gentle liege.   90

KING HENRY

> Rise up, good aunt!

DUCHESS OF YORK   Not yet, I thee beseech.

> For ever will I walk upon my knees,
> And never see day that the happy sees
> Till thou give joy, until thou bid me joy
> By pardoning Rutland, my transgressing boy.

AUMERLE

> Unto my mother's prayers I bend my knee.
> > *He kneels*

YORK

> Against them both my true joints bended be.
> > *He kneels*
> Ill mayst thou thrive if thou grant any grace.

DUCHESS OF YORK

> Pleads he in earnest? Look upon his face.
> His eyes do drop no tears, his prayers are in jest;   100
> His words come from his mouth, ours from our breast.
> He prays but faintly, and would be denied;
> We pray with heart and soul, and all beside.
> His weary joints would gladly rise, I know;
> Our knees still kneel till to the ground they grow.
> His prayers are full of false hypocrisy,

But the line could be a more private plea, addressed either to York or uttered as a generalization: 'If York does not love his own son, who else can be expected to do so?'

88 *make* do

89 *Shall thy old dugs once more a traitor rear?* are you, old as you are, going to rear this traitor anew (by redeem-

ing him from death)?

92 *walk upon my knees* (a traditional form of penance)

96 *Unto* in support of

97 *true* loyal

101 *from our breast* (from the heart)

102 *would be denied* wishes to be refused

105 *still kneel* will kneel perpetually ('shall' in F and some editions)

Ours of true zeal and deep integrity.
Our prayers do outpray his: then let them have
That mercy which true prayer ought to have.

KING HENRY

110   Good aunt, stand up!

DUCHESS OF YORK   Nay, do not say 'Stand up!'
Say 'Pardon' first, and afterwards, 'Stand up!'
An if I were thy nurse thy tongue to teach,
'Pardon' should be the first word of thy speech.
I never longed to hear a word till now.
Say 'Pardon', King. Let pity teach thee how.
The word is short, but not so short as sweet.
No word like 'Pardon' for kings' mouths so meet.

YORK

Speak it in French, King: say 'Pardonne-moi.'

DUCHESS OF YORK

Dost thou teach pardon pardon to destroy?
120   Ah, my sour husband, my hard-hearted lord!
That sets the word itself against the word.
Speak 'Pardon' as 'tis current in our land;
The chopping French we do not understand.
Thine eye begins to speak. Set thy tongue there;
Or in thy piteous heart plant thou thine ear,
That hearing how our plaints and prayers do pierce,
Pity may move thee pardon to rehearse.

112 *An if* if, supposing that

116 *short as sweet*. The saying 'short and
sweet' was current in Shakespeare's
time.

118 *'Pardonne-moi'* excuse me; forgive me
for refusing you. *Moi* rhymes with
destroy.

121 *sets the word itself against the word*
makes the word contradict itself

123 *chopping* (a contemptuous word, perhaps meaning 'affected', or perhaps
'chopping and changing' with reference to the wordplay that has just

been heard)

124 *to speak. Set thy tongue there* to show
pity. Let your tongue express it.

125 *in thy piteous heart plant thou thine ear*
(an exceptionally strained image) let
there be no division between your
ear and your piteous heart

126 *pierce* (pronounced to rhyme with
rehearse, as in *Love's Labour's Lost*,
IV.2.79: 'Master Person – quasi
Pierce-one')

127 *rehearse* pronounce, repeat

KING HENRY

  Good aunt, stand up.

DUCHESS OF YORK   I do not sue to stand.

  Pardon is all the suit I have in hand.

KING HENRY

  I pardon him as God shall pardon me.   130

DUCHESS OF YORK

  O, happy vantage of a kneeling knee!

  Yet am I sick for fear. Speak it again.

  Twice saying pardon doth not pardon twain,

  But makes one pardon strong.

KING HENRY   With all my heart

  I pardon him.

DUCHESS OF YORK

          A god on earth thou art!

    York, Duchess of York, and Aumerle stand

KING HENRY

  But for our trusty brother-in-law and the Abbot,

  With all the rest of that consorted crew,

  Destruction straight shall dog them at the heels.

  Good uncle, help to order several powers

  To Oxford, or where'er these traitors are.   140

  They shall not live within this world, I swear,

---

129 *suit* (as in a card game – 'in hand' – as well as 'plea')

131 *happy vantage of* fortunate gain from

133 *Twice saying pardon doth not pardon twain.* Either the Duchess assures the King that to say 'pardon' again will not pardon someone else as well, or else *twain* means 'divide in two' in which case she must mean 'to say "pardon" again will not weaken the pardon (as a second negative weakens the first)'.

136 *But* but as for
  trusty (ironically)
  brother-in-law (John Holland, Duke of Exeter and Earl of Huntingdon,

Richard II's half-brother on his mother's side). He had married Bolingbroke's sister, Elizabeth, and was deprived of his dukedom at the same time as Aumerle (see note to v.2.41). He is referred to at II.1.281, but the reference here is not likely to mean much to the audience.
  the Abbot (of Westminster, who appears at the end of IV.1)

137 *consorted crew* conspiring gang (there were about a dozen altogether; see v.2.96–9)

138 *straight* immediately

139 *powers* forces

But I will have them if I once know where.
Uncle, farewell; and cousin, adieu.
Your mother well hath prayed; and prove you true.

DUCHESS OF YORK

Come, my old son. I pray God make thee new.   *Exeunt*

V.4   *Enter Sir Piers of Exton and a Man*

EXTON

Didst thou not mark the King, what words he spake?
'Have I no friend will rid me of this living fear?'
Was it not so?

MAN   These were his very words.

EXTON

'Have I no friend?' quoth he. He spake it twice,
And urged it twice together, did he not?

---

145 *old* unregenerate. She refers to his character thus far, which she wishes to be changed. In fact Aumerle did 'prove true'. He died heroically at the Battle of Agincourt. Shakespeare describes his death in *Henry V*, IV.6.3–32.

old . . . I pray God make thee new. The biblical 'Therefore if any man be in Christ he is a new creature; old things are passed away; behold, all things are become new' (2 Corinthians 5.17) had passed into proverbial use.

v.4 This scene is based on Holinshed: 'One writer which seemeth to have great knowledge of King Richard's doings saith that King Henry, sitting on a day at his table, sore sighing, said "Have I no faithful friend which will deliver me of him, whose life will be my death, and whose death will be the preservation of my life?" This saying was much noted of them which were present, and especially of one called Sir Piers of Exton.

This knight incontinently departed from the court with eight strong persons in his company, and came to Pomfret . . .' Shakespeare's indebtedness to this episode resumes at v.5.98.

(stage direction) Q has no scene divisions, and its direction here is 'Manet sir Pierce Exton, etc.' Exton may have been among the nobles on stage at the beginning of the previous scene, but it seems unlikely that he would remain throughout the interview with York and his family: see v.3.27: *Withdraw yourselves, and leave us here alone.*

Sir Piers of Exton. Nothing is known of him except that he is said to have been the murderer of King Richard.

Man servant (Q has '*Man*' as the speech prefix; F has '*Enter Exton and Servants*'. Only one servant is necessary, but there may be others.)

2 *will* who will

5 *urged it* insisted on it

MAN

  He did.

EXTON

  And speaking it, he wishtly looked on me,
  As who should say 'I would thou wert the man
  That would divorce this terror from my heart' —
  Meaning the King at Pomfret. Come, let's go.   10
  I am the King's friend, and will rid his foe.   *Exeunt*

                Enter Richard alone   V . 5

RICHARD

  I have been studying how I may compare
  This prison where I live unto the world;
  And for because the world is populous,
  And here is not a creature but myself,
  I cannot do it. Yet I'll hammer it out.
  My brain I'll prove the female to my soul,
  My soul the father, and these two beget
  A generation of still-breeding thoughts,
  And these same thoughts people this little world,
  In humours like the people of this world.   10
  For no thought is contented; the better sort,
  As thoughts of things divine, are intermixed
  With scruples, and do set the word itself

---

7 *wishtly.* The context makes it clear that this word means 'intently' or 'significantly', but the exact form and meaning of the word are doubtful. It may be a variant form of 'wistly' (as it is printed in Q 3–5 and F), meaning 'intently', or of 'whistly', meaning 'silently', or of the later dialectical 'wisht' meaning 'melancholy'.

11 *rid* get rid of

v.5 Most of the first part is invented. Later Shakespeare uses Holinshed; see note to line 98.

3 *for because* because

5 *hammer it out* puzzle it out

8 *generation* progeny, offspring
  still-breeding thoughts thoughts which will continually produce other thoughts

9 *this little world* (the prison; also perhaps his *little world* of man — itself a prison)

10 *In humours like the people of this world* in their temperaments like the people of this real world

13 *scruples* doubts

13–14 *do set the word itself | Against the*

Against the word; as thus: 'Come, little ones';
And then again,
'It is as hard to come as for a camel
To thread the postern of a small needle's eye.'
Thoughts tending to ambition, they do plot
Unlikely wonders – how these vain weak nails
20   May tear a passage through the flinty ribs
Of this hard world, my ragged prison walls,
And for they cannot, die in their own pride.
Thoughts tending to content flatter themselves
That they are not the first of Fortune's slaves,
Nor shall not be the last; like seely beggars,
Who, sitting in the stocks, refuge their shame
That many have, and others must sit there.
And in this thought they find a kind of ease,
Bearing their own misfortunes on the back
30   Of such as have before endured the like.
Thus play I in one person many people,
And none contented. Sometimes am I king.
Then treasons make me wish myself a beggar;
And so I am. Then crushing penury
Persuades me I was better when a king.
Then am I kinged again; and by and by
Think that I am unkinged by Bolingbroke,
And straight am nothing. But whate'er I be,
Nor I, nor any man that but man is,

---

word set one passage of Scripture against another, contradictory one (the expression is also used at V.3.121)

14–17 *'Come, little ones'; | And then again, | 'It is as hard to come as for a camel | To thread the postern of a small needle's eye.'* The texts referred to here come together in Matthew 19.14, 24, Mark 10.14, 25, and Luke 18.16, 25. The second presents difficulties of interpretation of which Shakespeare may have been aware.

Camel may mean 'cable-rope' rather than the animal; and *needle* the entrance for pedestrians in a large city-gate. Shakespeare's *thread* and *postern* seem to hint at both possibilities.

17 *needle* (pronounced 'neele' or 'neeld')

20 *ribs* (framework of the castle, as the ribs are of a man's chest)

21 *ragged* rugged

25 *seely* simple-minded

26–7 *refuge their shame | That* take shelter from their shame in the thought that

33 *treasons* (the thought of them)

With nothing shall be pleased till he be eased   40
With being nothing. (*The music plays*) Music do I hear.
Ha, ha; keep time! How sour sweet music is
When time is broke, and no proportion kept.
So is it in the music of men's lives;
And here have I the daintiness of ear
To check time broke in a disordered string,
But for the concord of my state and time,
Had not an ear to hear my true time broke.
I wasted time, and now doth time waste me;
For now hath time made me his numbering clock.   50
My thoughts are minutes, and with sighs they jar
Their watches on unto mine eyes, the outward watch
Whereto my finger, like a dial's point,
Is pointing still in cleansing them from tears.
Now, sir, the sound that tells what hour it is

40–41 *With nothing shall be pleased till he be eased | With being nothing.* The first *nothing* may be part of a double negative: 'shall be pleased by anything till he has been granted the "ease" of death'; or it may mean the opposite: 'shall be pleased by having nothing (or losing everything) till . . .'

41 *Music do I hear.* This may be either a statement or a question.

42 *Ha, ha* (an exclamation as he catches out the musician in a rhythmical error; not a laugh)

43 *time is broke, and no proportion kept* the rhythm is faulty, and the correct note values are not observed

46 *check* rebuke

46–8 *disordered string . . . true time broke.* E. W. Naylor (*Shakespeare and Music*, 1931, page 32) explains: 'The "disorder'd string" is himself, who has been playing his part "out of time" ("disorder'd" simply means "out of its place" – i.e. as we now say, "a bar wrong"), and this has resulted in breaking the "concord" – i.e. the

harmony of the various parts which compose the state.'

46 *string* stringed instrument

47 *my* (emphatic)

48 *my true time broke* the discord in my own affairs

49 *waste* (including the sense of 'cause to waste away')

50 *numbering clock* (one on which the hours are numbered, not an hourglass)

51–4 *My thoughts are minutes, and with sighs they jar | Their watches on unto mine eyes, the outward watch | Whereto my finger, like a dial's point, | Is pointing still in cleansing them from tears.* This is a difficult passage. It may be paraphrased: 'each of my sad thoughts is like a minute, and the sighs that they cause impel the intervals of time forward to my eyes, which are the point on the outer edge of the watch to which my finger, like a hand on a dial, continually points in wiping tears from them'.

Are clamorous groans which strike upon my heart,
Which is the bell. So sighs, and tears, and groans
Show minutes, times, and hours. But my time
Runs posting on in Bolingbroke's proud joy,
60   While I stand fooling here, his jack of the clock.
This music mads me. Let it sound no more;
For though it have holp madmen to their wits,
In me it seems it will make wise men mad.
Yet blessing on his heart that gives it me;
For 'tis a sign of love, and love to Richard
Is a strange brooch in this all-hating world.
            Enter a Groom of the stable

GROOM
Hail, royal prince!
RICHARD   Thanks, noble peer.
The cheapest of us is ten groats too dear.
What art thou, and how comest thou hither

58 *times* quarters and halves
59 *posting* hastening
60 *jack of the clock* (a small figure of a man which struck the bell of a clock every quarter or every hour). The general meaning is that for Bolingbroke time now passes with joyful rapidity, while Richard languishes in prison, counting the hours away.
62 *though it have holp madmen to their wits* (*have holp*, may have helped). The idea that music could help to restore sanity was accepted in Shakespeare's day. He makes notable use of it in *King Lear*, IV.7.25 ff.
66 *strange brooch* rare jewel
67–8 *royal ... noble ... groats*. These were all coins. A royal was ten shillings, a noble six-and-eightpence, and a groat fourpence. The difference between a royal and a noble was thus ten groats. Richard is *the cheapest* of those present; to call him royal is to price him ten groats too high. A

similar witticism is recorded of Queen Elizabeth. An eighteenth-century anecdote about a clergyman called John Blower runs: ''Tis said that he never preached but one sermon in his life, which was before Queen Elizabeth; and that as he was going about to caress the Queen, he first said 'My royal Queen', and a little after 'My noble Queen'. Upon which says the Queen 'What, am I ten groats worse than I was?' At which words being baulked (for he was a man of modesty) he could not be prevailed with to preach any more, but he said he would always read the Homilies for the future; which accordingly he did' (from Thomas Hearne's 'A letter containing an Account of some Antiquities between Windsor and Oxford' in his edition of *The Itinerary of John Leland the Antiquary*, 1711).
67 *peer* 'lord' and 'equal'

Where no man never comes but that sad dog   70
That brings me food to make misfortune live?

GROOM
I was a poor groom of thy stable, King,
When thou wert king; who travelling towards York
With much ado at length have gotten leave
To look upon my sometimes royal master's face.
O, how it earned my heart when I beheld
In London streets, that coronation day,
When Bolingbroke rode on roan Barbary,
That horse that thou so often hast bestrid,
That horse that I so carefully have dressed!   80

RICHARD
Rode he on Barbary? Tell me, gentle friend,
How went he under him?

GROOM
So proudly as if he disdained the ground.

RICHARD
So proud that Bolingbroke was on his back!
That jade hath eat bread from my royal hand;
This hand hath made him proud with clapping him.
Would he not stumble, would he not fall down –
Since pride must have a fall – and break the neck
Of that proud man that did usurp his back?
Forgiveness, horse! Why do I rail on thee,   90
Since thou, created to be awed by man,
Wast born to bear? I was not made a horse,
And yet I bear a burden like an ass,
Spurred, galled, and tired by jauncing Bolingbroke.

70 *sad dog* dismal fellow
75 *sometimes* once
76 *earned* grieved
78 *roan* of mixed colour
    Barbary (an exceptionally good breed
    of horse, here also used as the name
    of a particular one)
80 *dressed* tended, groomed
85 *jade* worthless horse

eat (pronounced 'et') eaten
86 *clapping* patting
88 *pride must have a fall.* The proverb is
    biblical (Proverbs 16.18: 'Pride goeth
    before destruction; and an high mind
    before the fall').
94 *galled* made sore
    jauncing moving up and down (with
    the horse's motion)

Enter Keeper to Richard with meat

KEEPER (*to Groom*)

Fellow, give place. Here is no longer stay.

RICHARD (*to Groom*)

If thou love me, 'tis time thou wert away.

GROOM

What my tongue dares not, that my heart shall say.

Exit

KEEPER

My lord, will't please you to fall to?

RICHARD

Taste of it first, as thou art wont to do.

(stage direction) *meat* food

95 The change to couplets heightens the tension.

98 Here Shakespeare resumes the episode from Holinshed quoted in the preliminary note to v.4 (page 208). Sir Piers, arrived at Pomfret, commanded 'the esquire that was accustomed to sew [serve] and take the assay before King Richard to do so no more, saying "Let him eat now, for he shall not long eat." King Richard sat down to dinner and was served without courtesy or assay; whereupon much marvelling at the sudden change he demanded of the esquire why he did not his duty. "Sir," said he, "I am otherwise commanded by Sir Piers of Exton, which is newly come from King Henry." When King Richard heard that word he took the carving knife in his hand and strake the esquire on the head, saying "The devil take Henry of Lancaster and thee together." And with that word Sir Piers entered the chamber, well armed, with eight tall men likewise armed, every of them having a bill in his hand.

'King Richard, perceiving this, put the table from him, and, stepping to the foremost man, wrung the bill out of his hands and so valiantly defended himself that he slew four of those that thus came to assail him. Sir Piers being half dismayed herewith leapt into the chair where King Richard was wont to sit, while the other four persons fought with him and chased him about the chamber. And in conclusion, as King Richard traversed his ground from one side of the chamber to another, and coming by the chair where Sir Piers stood he was felled with a stroke of a poleaxe which Sir Piers gave him upon the head, and therewith rid him out of life, without giving him respite once to call to God for mercy of his past offences. It is said that Sir Piers of Exton, after he had thus slain him, wept right bitterly as one stricken with the prick of a guilty conscience for murdering him whom he had so long time obeyed as king.'

99 *Taste of it first, as thou art wont to do.* It was a customary precaution for

KEEPER

My lord, I dare not. Sir Piers of Exton,   100
Who lately came from the King, commands the contrary.

RICHARD (*attacks the Keeper*)

The devil take Henry of Lancaster, and thee.
Patience is stale, and I am weary of it.

KEEPER

Help, help, help!

    The murderers, Exton and servants, rush in

RICHARD

How now! What means death in this rude assault?
Villain, thy own hand yields thy death's instrument.

    He snatches a weapon from a servant and kills him

Go thou, and fill another room in hell.

    He kills another servant. Here Exton strikes him
    down

RICHARD

That hand shall burn in never-quenching fire
That staggers thus my person. Exton, thy fierce hand
Hath with the King's blood stained the King's own land.   110
Mount, mount, my soul. Thy seat is up on high,
Whilst my gross flesh sinks downward here to die.

                He dies

---

the king's food to be tasted before he ate it.

105 *What means death in this rude assault?* This line has been variously explained. It may mean 'what does death mean by assaulting me so violently?' or *means* may be equivalent to 'meanest': 'What do you mean, death, by . . .?' or 'What – do you [the murderers] mean death . . .?' Or the line may be taken along with the next as an expression of the paradox that though death apparently means to kill him, yet he is able to wrest a weapon from one of his attackers and kill him with it.

107 *room* place

109 *staggers* causes to stagger
   my person (a last assertion of royalty)

111–12 C. E. Montague writes of F. R. Benson that, having uttered these lines 'much as any other man might utter them under the first shock of the imminence of death, he half rises from the ground with a brightened face and repeats the two last words with a sudden return of animation and interest, the eager spirit leaping up, with a last flicker before it goes quite out, to seize on this new "idea of" the death of the body'.

EXTON

As full of valour as of royal blood.
Both have I spilled. O, would the deed were good!
For now the devil, that told me I did well,
Says that this deed is chronicled in hell.
This dead King to the living King I'll bear.
Take hence the rest, and give them burial here.

Exeunt with the bodies

v.6   *Flourish. Enter King Henry with the Duke of York,*
             other lords, and attendants

KING HENRY

Kind uncle York, the latest news we hear
Is that the rebels have consumed with fire
Our town of Ciceter in Gloucestershire.
But whether they be ta'en or slain we hear not.
             Enter Northumberland
Welcome, my lord. What is the news?

NORTHUMBERLAND

First, to thy sacred state wish I all happiness.
The next news is, I have to London sent

v.6. The material of the final scene is compressed from Holinshed. See note to line 30.

3 *Ciceter.* The town now known as Cirencester, spelt here as in the early editions. The name is still often pronounced like this, or as 'Cicester'.

7–8 *The next news is, I have to London sent | The heads of Salisbury, Spencer, Blunt, and Kent.* The reason is given in Holinshed: 'the heads of the chief conspirators were set on poles over London Bridge, to the terror of others'. The baldness of the couplet

is not altogether happy. Dover Wilson says of it and the following one: 'Is not this the very accent of Quince himself? The immortal lines

The actors are at hand and by their
    show
You shall know all that you are like
    to know,

go on like rhyming stilts, and to the identical jog-trot in metre' (New Cambridge edition, Introduction, page lxx).

The heads of Salisbury, Spencer, Blunt, and Kent.
The manner of their taking may appear
At large discoursèd in this paper here.   10

KING HENRY

We thank thee, gentle Percy, for thy pains;
And to thy worth will add right worthy gains.

Enter Lord Fitzwater

FITZWATER

My lord, I have from Oxford sent to London
The heads of Brocas and Sir Bennet Seely,
Two of the dangerous consorted traitors
That sought at Oxford thy dire overthrow.

KING HENRY

Thy pains, Fitzwater, shall not be forgot.
Right noble is thy merit, well I wot.

*Enter Harry Percy with the Bishop of Carlisle,
guarded*

PERCY

The grand conspirator Abbot of Westminster
With clog of conscience and sour melancholy   20

---

8 *Salisbury, Spencer, Blunt.* Q has *Oxford, Salisbury, Blunt. Oxford* is historically wrong; he was not implicated in the plot against Henry. This may well have been Shakespeare's error, though it is sometimes blamed on the printer. But the fact that the statement is corrected in F, which may transmit an alteration made or approved by Shakespeare, justifies the emendation.

10 *At large discoursèd* related in full

14 *Brocas and Sir Bennet Seely.* This is based on Holinshed: 'Many other that were privy to this conspiracy were taken and put to death, some at Oxford, as Sir Thomas Blunt, Sir Bennet Cilie, knight . . . but Sir Leon-ard Brokas and [others] . . . were drawn, hanged, and beheaded at London.'

15 *consorted* conspiring

18 *wot* know

19–21 *The grand conspirator . . . to the grave.* Holinshed has: 'the Abbot of Westminster, in whose house the conspiracy was begun, as is said, going between his monastery and mansion, for thought fell into a sudden palsy, and shortly after, without speech, ended his life'.

20 *clog* burden
   sour bitter
   melancholy (thought of as a physical substance, black bile, causing disease when present in excess)

Hath yielded up his body to the grave;
But here is Carlisle living, to abide
Thy kingly doom and sentence of his pride.

KING HENRY

Carlisle, this is your doom:
Choose out some secret place, some reverent room
More than thou hast, and with it joy thy life.
So as thou livest in peace, die free from strife;
For though mine enemy thou hast ever been,
High sparks of honour in thee have I seen.

Enter Exton with the coffin

EXTON

30   Great King, within this coffin I present
Thy buried fear. Herein all breathless lies
The mightiest of thy greatest enemies,
Richard of Bordeaux, by me hither brought.

KING HENRY

Exton, I thank thee not; for thou hast wrought
A deed of slander with thy fatal hand

22–9 Holinshed has: 'The Bishop of Carlisle was impeached, and condemned
of the same conspiracy; but the King
of his merciful clemency pardoned
him of that offence, although he died
shortly after, more through fear than
force of sickness, as some have
written.'

23 *doom* judgement

25 *reverent room* place of religious retirement (*reverent*, worthy of respect)

26 *More than thou hast* (perhaps 'bigger
than you have', that is, your prison
cell)
joy 'enjoy', or 'add joy to'. Probably
Bolingbroke is (whether ironically or
not) proposing to Carlisle the pleasures of monastic retirement.

30 Shakespeare takes up again Holin-

shed's episode of the murder of Richard: 'After he was thus dead, his
body was embalmed and cered and
covered with lead, all save the face,
to the intent that all men might see
him and perceive that he was departed this life; for as the corpse was
conveyed from Pomfret to London,
in all the towns and places where
those that had the conveyance of it
did stay with it all night, they caused
dirge to be sung in the evening, and
mass of Requiem in the morning;
and as well after the one service as
the other, his face, discovered, was
showed to all that coveted to behold
it.' Holinshed records King Henry's
presence at the solemn obsequies at
Saint Paul's and Westminster.

Upon my head and all this famous land.

EXTON

From your own mouth, my lord, did I this deed.

KING HENRY

They love not poison that do poison need;
Nor do I thee. Though I did wish him dead,
I hate the murderer, love him murderèd.   40
The guilt of conscience take thou for thy labour,
But neither my good word nor princely favour.
With Cain go wander thorough shades of night,
And never show thy head by day nor light.

Exit Exton

Lords, I protest, my soul is full of woe
That blood should sprinkle me to make me grow.
Come mourn with me for what I do lament,
And put on sullen black incontinent.
I'll make a voyage to the Holy Land
To wash this blood off from my guilty hand.   50
March sadly after. Grace my mournings here
In weeping after this untimely bier.   *Exeunt*

---

38 *They love not poison that do poison need*
    (recalling the proverbial expression
    'A king loves the treason but hates
    the traitor')
43 *With Cain* like Cain (who killed his
    own brother. Compare 1.1.104.).
48 *incontinent* immediately

49 *I'll make a voyage to the Holy Land.*
    Henry's intention of undertaking a
    crusade in expiation of his sin is
    several times referred to in *1* and *2
    Henry IV*.
51 *Grace* honour with your presence

HENRY IV, PART ONE

Introduction

Towards the end of *The First Part of Henry IV*, Prince Hal stands over two bodies. One is his dead rival, Hotspur, and the other, Falstaff, who, having been attacked by Douglas, has fallen down 'as if he were dead'. It is for Hal a moment of triumph. He has shown himself superior in battle, made 'this northern youth exchange | His glorious deeds' for Hal's own indignities, and redeemed the promise made to his father in their scene of reconciliation.

This representation of the victorious Hal standing over the two prostrate bodies is emblematic of an important aspect of the play. To Elizabethan audiences, well aware of the myth of the regenerate Hal, it must have seemed an almost mystical moment. There was a long way to go before Agincourt, but, for an audience to whom the story was familiar, this was the moment when Hal could be seen to have triumphed not only over Hotspur but also over those characteristics of his own waywardness epitomized by the fallen Falstaff.

A lesser dramatist might have made this the last moment of the play, allowing it to linger in the memory as the audience drifted from the theatre. But this is not quite the end. Hal's two epitaphs are not fashioned to give an audience the thrill of victory.

> *No, Percy, thou art dust,*
> *And food for —*

'For worms,' adds Hal, as Percy dies before being able to complete his sentence.

When that this body did contain a spirit,
A kingdom for it was too small a bound.
But now two paces of the vilest earth
Is room enough . . .
But let my favours hide thy mangled face . . .

v.4.88—95

Hal speaks sadly, regretfully; there is no glorification of victory. But that is not all. Even before Falstaff undergoes his comic resuscitation we have speeches by Hal that subtly modify the moment of triumph. 'O, I should have a heavy miss of thee' (v.4.104), he says over Falstaff's 'dead' body. The pun is obvious and it recalls a line in the epitaph spoken over Hotspur, which might so easily have been comic if spoken over Falstaff:

This earth that bears thee dead
Bears not alive so stout a gentleman.

Hal, as he looks down on the two bodies, is a symbol of what he has striven for throughout the play – reformation that will glitter like bright metal on a sullen ground. He has found the mean between the two extremes that Aristotle described in the Nicomachean Ethics, that which results from excess and that which results from defect. His centrality is paramount, yet, curiously, not a single title-page of any of the early quartos, nor the title of the play in the Folio of 1623, so much as mentions Hal. Nominally the play concerns Henry IV, and it is in his reign that all the events occur, but the title-pages go to some trouble to publicize the names of Hotspur and Falstaff. Even the very first mention we have of the play, in the Stationers' Register, 25 February 1598, does exactly the same:

. . . *a booke intituled The historye of* HENRY *the 111]th with his battaile of Shrewsburye against* HENRY HOTTSPURRE *of the Northe with the conceipted mirthe of Sir* JOHN FFALSTOFF.

The battle is rightly and historically given as Henry IV's and it is language such as this which, with slight variations, is used on the title-pages of edition after edition. Shakespeare was almost certainly not responsible for the advertising matter that appeared on the title-pages of his plays. We cannot be at all sure that the description in the Stationers' Register stemmed from him. Nevertheless, in a play in which the central character is so clearly Prince Hal, it is, at first sight, a little surprising that his name should invariably be omitted.

If Hal is central to *1 Henry IV*, Falstaff is undoubtedly the play's most attractive character. He immediately became enormously popular and there have come down to us a large number of references to him and the play in the correspondence and literature of the time. One example will show how eagerly those first audiences hung on his words. In a commendatory poem by Sir Thomas Palmer, printed in the Folio edition of the works of Beaumont and Fletcher in 1647, there appeared these lines:

> *I could praise Heywood now; or tell how long*
> *Falstaff from cracking nuts hath kept the throng.*

During the Commonwealth, when the theatres were closed, at least one short farcical piece – a droll – was extracted from *1 Henry IV*. It was called *The Bouncing Knight, or, The Robbers Robbed* and later in the seventeenth century a second playlet was similarly extracted – *The Boaster: or, Bully-Huff catched in a trap*.

As the titles indicate, the subject of these adaptations is Falstaff. Just as the attention of audiences has been attracted to Falstaff, so has that of critics. Inevitably one is in danger of seeing the play as his, whereas it is undoubtedly the development of Hal's character which is the play's major concern.

Although Shakespeare did not write his history plays in chronological order, he did, so far as we can tell, dramatize the three successive reigns of Richard II, Henry IV, and Henry V in that order, and he probably wrote all four plays within a period of five or six years. We do not know whether, when writing

1 Henry IV, Shakespeare had a second part in mind. It is possible he intended to write only one play on this reign but found he had too much material for a single play and thus began to prepare for a second part by building up the character of Hal's brother, John of Lancaster, and suggesting, by means of the scene with the Archbishop of York (IV.4), that though Hotspur was to be beaten, further rebellion would follow.

Perhaps the success of Part One, and of Falstaff in particular, encouraged the businessman in Shakespeare to provide a second play. Certainly the pattern of scenes of each part is remarkably similar, as if a formula were being followed, and it is curious that Hal and his father should be as estranged in Part Two as ever they were in Part One. However, when Shakespeare wrote *1 Henry IV*, probably in 1596, he was an experienced man of the theatre and it is difficult to believe that by the time he was half-way through *1 Henry IV* he did not realize he had a success on his hands. Thus, if a second part was not planned from the beginning (which at least seems possible), it was probably projected when Shakespeare came near to the completion of *1 Henry IV*.

Whether the two parts were ever performed successively in the late 1590s we do not know. From the evidence we have of actual performances of plays in two parts (such as Marlowe's *Tamburlaine*), it is not unlikely. In Shakespeare's lifetime the two parts were rather roughly put together to make a single play and a manuscript of this, the Dering version, exists. A conflation of the two parts, at least as rough, was presented at the Edinburgh Festival in 1964. The practice of performing both parts in a single day, though still uncommon, was initiated in 1923 by Birmingham Repertory Theatre (the first company to play *1 Henry IV* in full, at least since Shakespeare's day).

There is no doubt at all – because we have the evidence of the plays themselves – that Shakespeare thought of these plays as a group. It is possible he had in mind the whole sequence of plays when he first set about writing *Richard II*. Though Shakespeare's style develops from one play to the

next, the continuity of theme is so strong, and the references
from one reign to another so frequent, that the four plays give
a strong sense of unity.

To what extent the differences in style are a result of the
development of Shakespeare's art, and to what extent they are a
result of his finding a medium for the particular events he
wished to dramatize, it is difficult to say. Certainly we seem to
move from a medieval world in *Richard II* – medieval in its
attitude to kingship, in its values, and in its style – to a world
that, if very different from ours, is nevertheless one with which
we seem to have much in common. It would not be possible to
imagine the Gardener of *Richard II* (III.4) speaking his symbolic
verse in the inn yard at Rochester. The Carriers who complain
of bots and peas and beans in II.1 would seem incongruous in
the earlier play. Yet the transition is nothing like as sudden as
these extremes might indicate. When Worcester offers to read
'matter deep and dangerous' we are very close to the world of
medieval romance:

> *As full of peril and adventurous spirit*
> *As to o'er-walk a current roaring loud*
> *On the unsteadfast footing of a spear.*

> 1.3.189–91

When Vernon describes those who follow Hal, 'Glittering in
golden coats like images', and tells how he saw young Harry
with his beaver on, we are not far from the chivalric tourney
that takes place in the third scene of *Richard II*:

> *His cuishes on his thighs, gallantly armed,*
> *Rise from the ground like feathered Mercury,*
> *And vaulted with such ease into his seat*
> *As if an angel dropped down from the clouds*
> *To turn and wind a fiery Pegasus,*
> *And witch the world with noble horsemanship.*

> IV.1.105–10

Yet here in *1 Henry IV*, and more obviously when Hotspur

speaks of his willingness 'To pluck bright honour from the pale-faced moon', we are aware that the world of Hal is not the world of Richard and Hotspur. Hotspur's eagerness is at once captivating and out-dated. If there is a touch of high romance in Worcester's description of the dangers he unfolds, there is not an atom of romance about the speaker. Glendower, recounting the names of devils who are his lackeys, telling of the dreamer Merlin and his prophecies, and conjuring music from the air, is a high-romance figure from an age that goes back even before the medieval period. Alas, the past that is recalled by Glendower is as out-dated as Hotspur's concept of honour. Shakespeare deliberately makes a gentlemanly, if comically irascible, figure of poetry and music out of the barbarian he found in Holinshed and the crafty dreamer described by Thomas Phaer in *A Mirror for Magistrates* (1559), but in the 'jolly jar | Between the king and Percy's worthy bloods' (as Phaer puts it), Glendower is disastrously ineffective. The worlds of chivalry and romance, though they are not lost entirely from sight, are already of another age.

The divinity that attended upon King Richard is also departed. Once effective usurpation of a monarch divinely appointed was seen to be possible, then clearly the concept of divinity could no longer be maintained. What matters in a secular authority is the quality of the man, and it is for this reason that Hal's evolution was so fascinating and so important a subject for Shakespeare and his audiences. Henry IV was tainted, for he had usurped the throne. Despite his desire to rule well, he is burdened by an intolerable burden of guilt, for he took not only Richard's throne but also his life. 'The hot vengeance and the rod of heaven' punish his 'mistreadings', he says (*1 Henry IV*, III.2.10–11). In the Second Part of the play he is more open:

> God knows, my son,
> By what by-paths and indirect crooked ways
> I met this crown . . .   2 Henry IV, IV.5.184–6

And Hal himself, when Henry V, can beg,

> *Not today, O Lord,*
> *O not today, think not upon the fault*
> *My father made in compassing the crown!*
>
> Henry V, IV.1.285–8

Henry's sin was something Shakespeare iterated at great length no fewer than four times in *1 Henry IV*. Twice Hotspur recounts the story of Henry's usurpation (1.3.158–84 and IV.3.54–92); once Henry himself tells the story (III.2.39–84); and finally Worcester, as guilty as Henry in the actual usurpation, gives his version (V.1.32–71). It is this burden of guilt that makes Henry IV seem so sick and aged in the plays of his name (though he was active enough at the end of *Richard II*) and it is partly for this reason that Shakespeare takes such care to dissociate Hal from his father (just as he dissociates Hotspur from the policy of his father and uncle). The taint of the tavern is to be preferred to that of the parent.

Shakespeare retells the fall of Richard for a purpose that was obvious to his audiences but is less apparent to us. We are inured to missing many of the puns and to being unable to follow some of the allusions in an Elizabethan play. A modern audience cannot be expected to know that there were two Edmund Mortimers alive at the same time, two kinds of Marcher Lords (Welsh and Scottish), and two Walter Blunts. As Shakespeare was confused over the Mortimers and the Earls of March, and did not bother to distinguish between the Blunts, we are in good company. Nor can we, unless we have specialized knowledge, readily see Poins's witticism at II.4.211 when Falstaff explains that the points of the swords of the nine men in buckram were broken. This kind of difficulty we expect and, although it is meat to annotators, it is usually of small account in performance.

A more serious difficulty is the difference between Elizabethan and modern conceptions of the use of history. To an Elizabethan, history was directly educative in a way which we should consider naïve. By holding up a mirror to the past it was thought possible to learn how to amend one's own life and how to anticipate events. Further, since the time when John Bale had written his play, *King John* (about 1534), drama had been a means by which subjects and their rulers might be instructed in their duties one to another.

The experience of the past made the Elizabethans fear rebellion and disorder so greatly that it was considered better to obey a tyrant than to foment civil war. It is probably this attitude rather than Shakespeare's specific political beliefs (whatever they may have been) that has led some critics to see Shakespeare's histories as politically conservative. It is as if, for many people, Shakespeare's attitude were like that of York in *Richard II* when, perhaps, they would wish it were like that of his son, Aumerle. There are two further difficulties that face us. First of all, before Shakespeare's play was performed, Hal was a legend; Falstaff — Shakespeare's Falstaff, at least — was totally unknown. Shakespeare would need to characterize Hal in such a way that the audience would accept him as the man they imagined him to be. In this apparent disadvantage, however, lay an asset that Shakespeare used in similar circumstances in other plays — in *Troilus and Cressida*, for example, in dramatizing Ajax, Achilles, and Cressida herself. In dramatizing Hal, Shakespeare could rely on the strength of the legend — Hal's 'given personality' — and might, simultaneously, gently reassess Hal in a way that would pass almost unnoticed except by the most thoughtful. It was an ideal technique for pleasing a large audience of widely differing intellectual standards.

We have no such 'received opinion' of Hal and as a result our view of Hal, taken simply from what Shakespeare has given us, may become distorted. It led George Bernard Shaw to call him 'an able young Philistine' who repeatedly made it clear that he would turn on his friends later on, and that 'his self-indulgent good-fellowship with them is consciously and deliberately treacherous'. Shaw may exaggerate a modern view of Hal, but it is a view that is not uncommon. Shakespeare is a little critical of Hal, but his criticism does not amount to condemnation. Hal, as Henry V, is to represent an ideal of kingship, in so far as it is possible for human beings to create such an ideal.

The final difficulty for us springs from dramatic and not national history. Before *1 Henry IV* there was a long history of Morality drama. In Shakespeare's day, though it was old-fashioned to the relatively sophisticated Globe audience, it was still performed in country districts and was often parodied in London (as it is in *1 Henry IV*). Besides referring to a place known for the stage-plays performed at its fairs, Manningtree, Shakespeare mentions on a number of occasions figures from Morality plays. The law is Father Antic (1.2.60), and Falstaff is 'that reverend Vice, that grey Iniquity, that Father Ruffian, that Vanity in years' (II.4.441–2). The whole world and meaning of Morality drama is assumed by Shakespeare to be within the knowledge of his audience. Not only are there references that are for us oblique and often obscure, but the implications of the deceptions of Falstaff as that 'villainous abominable mis-leader of youth' (II.4.449), and his relationship to Hal, stem from the Morality tradition. It is not that the relationship is identical; it is not as if Falstaff *were* The Vice, or Hal were Everyman, or Magnificence, or Temporal Justice, but that they exist, as dramatic characters, in a relationship which has grown out of a tradition familiar to the original audiences.

The traditional position of man in a Morality play was between his good and evil influences. Faustus, in Marlowe's play, is flanked by good and evil angels, but these angels are not wholly and unequivocally good or evil, as their names might suggest. Shakespeare, in dramatizing Hal, Hotspur, and Falstaff, seems to have had this kind of Morality pattern in the back of his mind, but the result is very much more complex. Within the play it is plain that Hal's father is anxious that he should imitate Hotspur.

> *O that it could be proved*
> *That some night-tripping fairy had exchanged*
> *In cradle-clothes our children where they lay,*
> *And called mine Percy, his Plantagenet!*
>
> I.I.85–8

To the King, Hotspur is the epitome of all that is brave and honourable, even though they are in conflict. It is noticeable that Henry here speaks in terms of out-dated romance; 'night-tripping fairies' might be expected to be in Glendower's retinue.

Simultaneously, Hal's tavern companions seek to make him completely one of them, so that he becomes 'sworn brother to a leash of drawers' (II.4.6–7). Falstaff, for his part, expects the land to be made safe for thieves when Hal is King (I.2.58–61). The faults of Hotspur and Falstaff are plain. Both are rebels, one against the King himself, denying him prisoners, maintaining that, as a usurper, he has no right to the throne but ought to surrender it to Mortimer. Falstaff, though professing loyalty to the King's person, rebels against all authority, lacking any sense of social responsibility.

The 'education' of Hal is not simply a matter of making a choice of one or other of these 'angels'. Instead, he must realize in himself what is good in each of them and ignore what will be harmful to him as a king. It is to this end that Hal is directing himself when, upbraided by the King, he says,

> *I shall hereafter, my thrice-gracious lord,*
> *Be more myself.*   III.2.92–3

Because Shakespeare's creation is capable of existing in its own right, we are able to follow and enjoy the play sufficiently even without being aware of the play's dramatic heritage, but the lack of such knowledge can lead to misunderstanding. Nowhere is this more obvious than in Hal's speech at the end of the second scene. It is this speech in particular that has given Hal a reputation for treachery and priggishness.

Writing of Henry V in *Ideas of Good and Evil* in 1903, W. B. Yeats said:

He has the gross vices, the coarse nerves of one who is to rule among violent people, and he is so little 'too friendly' with his friends that he bundles them out of doors when their time is over. He is as remorseless and undistinguished as some natural force ... His purposes are so intelligible to everybody that everybody talks of him as if he succeeded, although he fails in the end, as all men great and little fail in Shakespeare.

Yeats is writing of Shakespeare's complete dramatic creation but he expresses, better than Shaw, not merely opposition to Hal, but an understanding of why he is as he is. The situation demanded a ruler who would not be betrayed by human weakness – a ruler who could, despite the joys of good-fellowship, reject a Corinthian, a boon companion. But Shakespeare's presentation of Hal is much more subtle than Yeats allows and its subtlety in part depends upon the dramatic inheritance and the dramatic conventions which Shakespeare used.

Hal's speech has often been considered to be wholly in character, seeming to reveal cold, calculated treachery, but it is very much more probable that it ought to be seen as a speech of explanation, spoken by Hal, of course, but not as an expression of his character. It is as if Hal were a kind of Chorus. There is a difficulty in such an explanation. We expect a character speaking a soliloquy to say what he believes to be true and also to speak as himself. Can we be sure that the function of this speech is, as Dr Johnson said, 'to keep the prince from appearing vile in the opinion of the audience'?

Until recently, owing to the realistic dramatic inheritance of the nineteenth and twentieth centuries that separates us from the Elizabethan age more sharply than the years themselves, audiences have found it very difficult to accept breaks in the continuity of the conventional suspension of disbelief. For a character to be himself and something other than himself (common enough in music hall and television comedy) – to have two different relationships with his audience – has been out of the question.

In Shakespeare's day it was possible for an actor to move easily and rapidly from direct appeal to an audience to seeming unawareness of its presence. Thus, in *1 Henry IV*, Falstaff seems to step outside his part in telling the story of the fight at Gad's Hill. We can see something similar in Vernon's speech at IV.I.97–110, and possibly in Hotspur's at III.I.246 (see note). When Hal describes his plans at the end of I.2, he is offering his Elizabethan audience an assurance that he will not be led astray like the prodigal child in the Morality stories with which they were so familiar. It is very difficult to be sure when Shakespeare is bending the conventions, at least as we understand them, and it is partly this that makes particularly difficult a just assessment of Falstaff's part in IV.2 and V.4, and Hal's soliloquy in I.2.

It is one thing to offer an explanation, however; it is another to remove all prejudice. Ironically, it is the very assurance that Shakespeare sought to give his own audience which makes us so unsure. Even if we accept the need to renounce Falstaff, and Bardolph and Poins, as inevitably part of Hal's responsibilities of office, can we also stomach the latter part of the speech in which Hal designs to appear 'more goodly'? If we pause to consider the matter it is impossible, though in the theatre the moment passes quickly and we enter into Gad's Hill and the tavern in Eastcheap and the speech is forgotten. But once one *is* aware that cold calculation is implied, it is hard not to think ill of Hal. There is one way in which Hal may here prove acceptable to us. Furthermore, it avoids dependence on a tradition now largely lost.

Hal's speech can be taken in much the same way as we take Hotspur's speech on his quest for honour (I.3.199). Just as Hotspur is over-eager for honour, so is Hal over-anxious to pursue the course that will lead to his reformation, to being himself as he really is. Hal's pursuit of honour (for that is what it amounts to) is as youthfully naïve as Hotspur's. Both reveal, in these speeches, a certain selfishness, yet both show, as the play progresses, a more generous nature. It is mistaken to read, or perform, this speech as if Hal were a Machiavellian schemer like Shakespeare's Richard III. He is, as Hotspur is shown to be, young, inexperienced, but beginning to be aware of his responsibilities.

There were available to Shakespeare a number of accounts and legends of Hal's life, some not very reliable. His major source was the second edition of Holinshed's *Chronicles of England*, 1587. From this he obtained the basic details for his story of Hal, though he adapted them considerably to make the story more dramatic. He adjusted the ages of the principal characters (making Hal and Hotspur of the same age though Hotspur was two years older than Henry IV), brought forward Henry's reference to a crusade, anticipated Hal's reported attempt to depose his father, delayed Northumberland's sickness so that news of its occurrence arrived on the eve of the battle of Shrewsbury, and greatly enlarged the part played by Hal in the battle.

According to Holinshed, Hal 'that day helped his father like a lusty young gentleman'. He was hurt in the face by an arrow but refused to leave the field. Hotspur appears from Holinshed to have been killed in a mêlée, but though a careless reading might make it seem that Hal was involved, there is no historical justification (though ample dramatic justification) for a confrontation between the two men. Hal was barely sixteen at the time; his brother John was only thirteen and took no part in the battle. Shakespeare amplified the parts played by Blunt and Vernon, and virtually created Lady Mortimer and Lady Percy (christening her Kate – though Holinshed called her Eleanor, and her real name was Elizabeth).

Shakespeare also used Daniel's poem, *The First Four Books of the Civil Wars between the two houses of Lancaster and York* (1595), as he had when writing *Richard II*, and he followed it where dramatically convenient (as in its report that the Welsh failed to arrive at Shrewsbury). There is some evidence that there were earlier plays on Henry V, and there might even have been one on Hotspur. One such play survives and this, and perhaps Stowe's *The Chronicles of England* (1580) and *The Annals of England* (1592), may have provided supplementary material on Hal's madcap youth, though the legend of Hal's youth was very well known.

Hotspur is a figure cast in the old heroic mould. Like Hal's, his reputation was established before Shakespeare wrote *1 Henry IV*. If the names of those who have acted the parts of Hotspur and Hal are anything to go by, then there is no doubt which character has proved more attractive to actors. Hotspur has been played by Quin (who was later to play Falstaff) and Kemble in the eighteenth century; Macready and Phelps (who also went on to play Falstaff), Bourchier and Lewis Waller, in the nineteenth century; Matheson Lang, Gielgud, Olivier, and Redgrave, in this century. Hotspur's part allows for the legitimate display of the heroic, expressed in rhetoric that, although exaggerated, is nevertheless excellent to deliver. There is also a sense of doom about Hotspur, and he has a moving death-scene, both of which demand (but do not always receive) sensitive interpretation.

Although Falstaff offers to speak in King Cambyses's vein, it is Hotspur who comes very much closer to the kind of hyperbole associated with earlier dramatists. That Hotspur's speech on honour was taken to be a deliberate exaggeration in its own day is evident from its use in Beaumont's play *The Knight of the Burning Pestle*, when a character has to speak what is described there as 'a huffing part'. Hospur's pursuit of honour, his petulant reiteration of his complaint about his Scottish prisoners, and a lack of sensitivity towards others, can very easily lead to his being seen and presented as a boor. He will look even more ridiculous if he is made to speak ludicrously because of the too enthusiastic taking-up of a hint in the Second Part of the play about his manner of speech. Lady Percy says:

> *And speaking thick, which nature made his blemish,*
> *Became the accents of the valiant;*
> *For those that could speak low and tardily*
> *Would turn their own perfection to abuse*
> *To seem like him.*   *2 Henry IV*, 11.3.24–8

Lady Percy describes her now-dead husband as a man who was a pattern for all youth:

> *He was the mark and glass, copy and book,*
> *That fashioned others.*   11.3.31–2

She is not, of course, without prejudice, but in describing how even Hotspur's fault of speech was slavishly imitated, she suggests how greatly he was admired – a characteristic not always brought out in performance. The precise nature of Hotspur's defect of speech is puzzling. The word 'thick' can mean husky, hoarse, or rapid – and 'tardily' suggests the third of these. Certainly rapid speech suits a character of such impetuosity. In 1914, however, Sir Herbert Beerbohm Tree persuaded Matheson Lang to stammer, and this was enthusiastically followed by other actors. Olivier hesitated slightly before 'w' and Redgrave spoke with a thick 'r'. Unless, however, such a performance is most carefully controlled, it gives way to guying, and this is destructive of Shakespeare's creation. Hotspur ought, above all else, to be the kind of young man who sets alight admiration in everyone, young and old.

Harry Percy is, as his nickname indicates, headstrong and wilful and this is apparent from his behaviour, his flood of language, his exaggeration, and the reputation he has with others. His very name for impetuosity will serve, says Worcester, as 'an adopted name of privilege', preventing his being taken too seriously. He is 'A hare-brained Hotspur, governed by a spleen' (v.2.19). On the other hand, even if his kind of honour is self-indulgent, and though there is no place for it in the post-medieval world, his standards of integrity are far

removed from the shifting expediency of Henry and Worcester.
Nor is there anything morbid in his manner of facing death:

> *Come, let us take a muster speedily.*
> *Doomsday is near. Die all, die merrily.*
>
> IV.1.133–4

The contrast here with Glendower and Douglas is sharp. The
Welshman's promises come to nothing, and Douglas hardly
makes good the boast,

> *Talk not of dying, I am out of fear*
> *Of death or death's hand for this one half year.*
>
> IV.1.135–6

So precipitate is the flight of that 'ever valiant and approvèd
Scot' (I.1.54) that, when fleeing with the rest, he falls from a
hill and

> *was so bruised*
> *That the pursuers took him.*   V.5.21–2

The death of Enobarbus in a ditch, that 'master leaver' and
'fugitive' of *Antony and Cleopatra*, is much more honourable
than this.

It is incorrect to interpret Shakespeare's presentation of
honour in *1 Henry IV* as wholly satirical, much though that
may accord with current fashion. Hotspur, like Coriolanus, is
still adolescent in temperament, great though each is in courage
and physical might. His view of honour is partly selfish, it is
true – 'out upon this half-faced fellowship', he cries – but we
are not to assume, because neither Glendower nor Douglas
lives up to his words, nor because Henry and Worcester and
Northumberland are all treacherous, that honour is meaningless. Hotspur's attachment to an out-dated concept of honour,
and Falstaff's brilliant depreciation of what it signifies, are
traps that Hal avoids but into which we often nowadays tend
to fall. In the world of York and Lancaster, honour is urgently
needed, but it must be a new kind of honour, an integrity, a

selflessness, quite different from that chivalric honour the loss of whose titles Hotspur bemoans more than life itself.

In many ways Hotspur and Hal are closely akin. Their lack of self-management takes different forms, but it is apparent in each. Hotspur's frankness is one of his most engaging qualities; in Hal, in his speech at the end of 1.2, it is equally apparent, though many critics (if not audiences) are disturbed by it. Hal's aspirations may be veiled by 'base contagious clouds' but they are as strong as those more obviously displayed by Hotspur. It is in their humour, however, that Hal and Hotspur share a particularly interesting characteristic.

It has been customary to regard Hal as at least as witty a character as Falstaff. This is to do less than justice to Shakespeare's skill in distinguishing between alacrity of mind, with which he invests Falstaff, and the modest extent of Hal's inventive capacities – less remarkable than those of Poins. With much preparation Hal arranges a joke on Francis, the drawer. We probably do not have too much sympathy with Francis, but the repetition of the joke, and, compared with the fruitfulness of Poins's Gad's Hill plot, its lack of imagination, rightly lead Poins to ask, 'come, what's the issue?' And Hal's answer is as lame as it is when he is made to confess by Falstaff that he has picked the fat rogue's pocket (III.3.167). It is not merely that Hal's inventiveness is moderate, but that he takes such delight in the skill he has revealed. He cannot forbear to tease Francis again. 'What's o'clock, Francis?' he asks, having just said it is 'this present twelve o'clock at midnight', and he receives, once again, Francis's pitiful response, 'Anon, anon, sir.'

Hotspur is made to seem just as delighted with himself at his putting down of Glendower when Glendower tells him he can teach him to command the devil.

> *And I can teach thee, coz, to shame the devil*
> *By telling truth. Tell truth, and shame the devil.*

III.1.54–5

And then, a line or two later – almost, one imagines, hugging himself with delight at his clever turning of the phrase – he repeats:

> *O, while you live, tell truth and shame the devil!*

These examples reveal Hal and Hotspur at their lowest level of wit but both are given something more imaginative. In each instance the form of humour is parody. Hal's burlesque of Hotspur (II.4.100–107) is justifiably admired. Hotspur's imitation of his wife (III.1.241–50) is, appropriately, gentler and therefore less striking. More subtle, because it is a parody that informs his manner of expression rather than being directly imitative, is Hotspur's witty description of the 'certain lord' who came to him on the battlefield to demand his prisoners (I.3.30–63). Nowhere is Hal given a speech as delightful as this.

> *When I was dry with rage and extreme toil,*
> *Breathless and faint, leaning upon my sword . . .*
> *Out of my grief and my impatience*
> *Answered neglectingly, I know not what,*
> *He should, or he should not, for he made me mad*
> *To see him shine so brisk, and smell so sweet,*
> *And talk so like a waiting-gentlewoman*
> *Of guns, and drums, and wounds, God save the mark! . . .*

Hotspur's account, later in this scene, of Mortimer's fight with Glendower on 'gentle Severn's sedgy bank' is conscious, purple verse, appropriate to describe the single combat of medieval romance; but such poetry, from one who affects hostility to 'metre ballad-mongers', ironically suggests the quality, the *virtù*, of one too facilely interpreted as a barbarian. Such language is not to be dissociated from character in the way we separate Vernon's description of Hal and his followers in IV.1 from the speaker. Words tumble at all times too freely, too thickly, indeed, for this style to be anything but the man.

In one other respect Hotspur has the advantage of Hal. Lady Percy is Shakespeare's creation (though there was a real wife) and he gives her a name he seems to have liked, Kate. Hal's field of action is Gad's Hill; he is at home in a tavern. Action for Hotspur means Holmedon, and domesticity, Kate. The effect is obvious. Lady Percy's love for 'my heart's dear Harry', as she calls him in *2 Henry IV* (II.3.12), is transparently clear and in the banter they exchange one can detect his love for her.

It would be an absurd exaggeration to speak of the tragedy of Hotspur, but there is, nevertheless, a tragic aspect to his character. In Lady Percy's talk of his nightmares, and in his and her relationship with each other, it is possible to see that Hotspur is growing up. It is his misfortune to be killed before he has time to reach the maturity that might have forewarned him from Shrewsbury. It is this that must not happen to Hal.

The titles that Hal wins in overcoming Hotspur are not those that Hotspur was so anxious not to lose. Hal wins something less tangible. His victory marks a coming to one kind of maturity, an acceptance of princely responsibilities and a demonstration, in a world of violence, that he is stronger than those who would oppose him. But Hal has, of course, another kind of maturity to seek.

Hal's 'education in a tavern' has often been remarked upon. In a world in which hierarchical differences were even more marked than they are now, Hal's behaviour, Elizabethan though it may be rather than medieval, is particularly fascinating. A man who is to wield supreme authority is here seen in the most easy contact with ordinary men and women. It is this that will prepare him, and us, for that remarkable scene in *Henry V*, the dialogue with Bates and Williams.

Whilst a part of Hal's legend was his association with commoners of the lowest orders in a society we take to be rigidly structured, most of those we see Hal meeting are hardly ordinary men and women. Shakespeare goes so far as to draw our attention to their extraordinariness by dramatizing the world of the Carriers. This is shown to be quite different from the world of Gadshill and his new associates. We cannot possibly mistake the fleas, the jordan and the chamber-lye of Rochester for the sack and anchovies of Eastcheap. Furthermore, Falstaff, though he inhabits a tavern, is not ordinary in the hierarchical sense – he is a knight – and in the dramatic sense he is quite the most extraordinary comic character that any dramatist has created. Falstaff's success was instantaneous and he has stood the test of time with astonishing ease. He has attracted many great actors – not always with the happiest results. Perhaps one of Shaw's most cutting comments was directed at Beerbohm Tree's performance of Falstaff in 1906. 'Mr Tree only wants one thing to make an excellent Falstaff, and that is to get born over again as unlike himself as possible . . . The basket-work figure, the lifeless mask, the voice coarsened, vulgarized, and falsified, without being enriched and coloured – Mr Tree might as well try to play Juliet.'

It is very easy, in performance and criticism, to coarsen Falstaff, to make him appear even more bloated than he already is. Despite his undoubted girth, despite his habits, there is about Falstaff, paradoxically, a delicacy that demands to be realized.

Just as Falstaff has attracted actors (and audiences) so has he attracted scholars and critics. His ancestry, his characteristics, and what he stands for (as if he were an actual Morality figure), have been discussed for generations. We can be certain that the name originally given to this character was not Falstaff but Oldcastle, a knight of great courage who had been a companion of Henry V in his youth, but who later took part in a rebellion and, as a follower of Wycliffe, was burnt. Sir William Brooke, a descendant of Oldcastle's wife by a former marriage, was Lord Chamberlain for a short time until his death in 1597. It would seem that he, or his son, Sir Henry, objected to Oldcastle's being maligned. Certainly the name was changed and Sir Henry was mockingly referred to as Sir John Falstaff by his enemies. It is probably no coincidence that when the jealous

Ford in *The Merry Wives of Windsor* is given a false name it is 'Brook' – a name that also seems to have aroused hostility for it appears as 'Broome' in the Folio, making nonsense of one of the jokes.

Oldcastle himself was the subject of legends. He was damned as a heretic by the orthodox (the Roman Catholics in his time), and hailed as a hero and martyr by Protestants such as Bale and Foxe about 150 years later. His religious associations were well known and these are carried over into Shakespeare's Falstaff, who has a large store of Biblical knowledge, which he is adept at perverting.

Oldcastle also appears in a gallimaufry of a play called *The Famous Victories of Henry the Fifth*. It covers the ground of both parts of *Henry IV* and also *Henry V*, and throughout its course Hal is called Henry V, even though his father is alive. The version we have, which is very short and corrupt, was published in the same year as Shakespeare's play *1 Henry IV*, but it is likely that it is not the earliest or only version, for a play of this name is recorded in 1594, and it, or another, was performed a number of times in 1595 and 1596. Sir John Oldcastle's part is not large; one extract will suggest how abysmal is the non-Shakespearian play and how remarkable is the transformation made by Shakespeare.

The Famous Victories of Henry the Fifth describes an incident in detail that Shakespeare virtually ignores, Hal's reputed striking of the Lord Chief Justice. *In 1 Henry IV* we have only the indirect allusion, 'Thy place in Council thou hast rudely lost' (III.2.32), but the incident is dramatized in the non-Shakespearian play, then forms the subject of 'a play extempore', and, in Scene 6, it is recalled by the Prince.

HENRY V *But Ned, so soon as I am King, the first thing I will do shall be to put my Lord Chief Justice out of office, and thou shalt be my Lord Chief Justice of England.*

NED *Shall I be Lord Chief Justice? By gog's wounds, I'll be the bravest Lord Chief Justice that ever was in England.*

HENRY V *Then Ned, I'll turn all these prisons into fence schools, and I will endue thee with them, with lands to maintain them withal. Then I will have a bout with my Lord Chief Justice. Thou shalt hang none but pick-purses and horse-stealers, and such base-minded villains. But that fellow that will stand by the highway-side courageously, with his sword and buckler, and take a purse — that fellow, give him commendations. Beside that, send him to me and I will give him an annual pension out of my Exchequer to maintain him all the days of his life.*

SIR JOHN OLDCASTLE *Nobly spoken Harry! We shall never have a merry world till the old King be dead.*

In addition to an historic source, Shakespeare drew upon dramatic sources in creating Falstaff. He has been likened to the Vice of the old Moralities, and to a variety of other names associated with such drama. The references are direct in Shakespeare (11.4.441–2) and scholars have related him to Riot, the misleader of youth, to Misrule, Gluttony, and Monsieur Remorse (by which title he is called at 1.2.111–12). His relationship to court and stage fools has been examined; he has been compared to the *miles gloriosus* of Plautine comedy, to the braggart soldier of the Italian *commedia erudita*, and to the captains of Elizabeth's armies; he has been thought to have descended from the stage parasite of Latin comedy; to be a caricature of the Puritans; and even to represent 'the supernatural order of Charity'. Although the search for Falstaff's ancestry is occasionally perverse, so rich is Shakespeare's characterization, nearly all such associations have an element of conviction about them.

He was to Dryden 'the best of comical characters'; to Dr Johnson, 'unimitated, unimitable'; his 'alacrity of mind' appealed to the man who vigorously first defended Falstaff from the charge of cowardice in the eighteenth century, Maurice Morgann; to Tolstoy Falstaff seemed 'a natural and typical character', perhaps, perversely, 'the only natural and typical character portrayed by Shakespeare'. He has seemed to one psychoanalyst to be a 'depreciated father figure', and to another, 'the personification of the wholly self-centred pleasure-seeking principle'. His warmth, his wit, his clarity of vision, his comic insight, have all been justly admired. He has, it has been said, 'a set of spiritual conceptions at once simple enough to be popular and sufficiently profound to cover the wealth of human experience'. There is, it has been explained, a Falstaff in each of us and it is this that gives him an appeal that is so widespread, despite his manifold faults, his gluttony, his irresponsibility, and his selfishness.

An even tougher battle has been waged over the matter of Falstaff's cowardice than was fought between Hotspur and Hal at Shrewsbury. One is tempted, like Falstaff at Gad's Hill, to run away, roaring. Briefly, it might be said that Falstaff's cowardice was not in dispute until Maurice Morgann published a spirited defence of Falstaff in 1777. The early critics, and actors of all periods, have considered Falstaff to be cowardly. Later critics have seen him as wily; an experienced soldier, a realist; a Bluntschli with sack instead of chocolates in his holster. It has been pointed out that he does not lose his presence of mind at Shrewsbury, but he certainly roars heartily at Gad's Hill, and Poins's scheme depends for its success on the certainty that Falstaff will run away. The puzzle is that Falstaff's cowardice should have so disturbed the critics. Our admiration for the character is not dependent upon valour. He is no Hal; he is no Hotspur. No critic castigates Douglas because he flees twice (v.4.42, stage direction, and v.5.20). Indeed, Hal, when permitting Douglas to leave ransomless, actually says:

> *His valours shown upon our crests today*
> *Have taught us how to cherish such high deeds,*
> *Even in the bosom of our adversaries.*   v.5.29–31

Falstaff's quality is quality of the imagination. He is not a mere liar but a creative genius, or, as A. C. Bradley put it, 'The bliss of freedom gained in humour is the essence of Falstaff'.

But Falstaff is not the central figure, dominate the stage and our affections though he will. He stands to one side of Hal as Hotspur does the other. Both Falstaff and Hotspur, the former in his rejection, the latter in his death, have been seen as means, actual or symbolic, whereby Hal rids himself of his urge to depose his father. In *1 Henry IV*, however, Shakespeare has toned down Hal's opposition to his father, for it is only glanced at – 'Thou . . . art like enough . . .' says his father, 'To fight against me under Percy's pay' (III.2.124–6). Hal's aversion to his father is much stronger in *The Famous Victories of Henry the Fifth* and Holinshed reports an attempt by Hal to usurp the throne in 1412, nearly a decade after Shrewsbury.

Hal's rejection of Falstaff does not occur until the end of the Second Part of the play but it is foreshadowed in *1 Henry IV* (and sometimes overstressed in performance). Falstaff, I think, is shown to suspect what the eventual outcome of their relationship must be as early as II.4.476–8. Given that he is meant to be as shrewd as we all take him to be, it is hard to believe that he could not tell which way the wind would blow, however much he might hope otherwise. This, surely, is one of the main marks of difference between the extract from *The Famous Victories of Henry the Fifth* quoted earlier and the corresponding passage in *1 Henry IV*.

Though the comedy of the situations protects the character of Falstaff very considerably, the satire on pressing soldiers, and the ignominious stabbing of the valiant traitor, Hotspur, are not in accord with the spirit of comedy that pervades Gad's Hill and Eastcheap. This is no miscalculation on Shakespeare's part. Just as Hal must stand a little apart from the pitch with which he is associating (II.4.405), so must we, despite our delight in Falstaff, see the implications of such gay licence. In the theatre nowadays this does not always happen. We grasp too eagerly at the Falstaff who is the expression of our own repressed irresponsibilities. We delight too single-mindedly in his wit and his capacity to undercut pretension. It is one thing to point to the worthlessness of a certain kind of 'grinning honour as Sir Walter hath' and quite another to seek such honour by the means Falstaff employs. It is tempting to gloss over the implications of Falstaff's behaviour in IV.2 and V.4 as if it was but an extension of his attack on empty honour. Shakespeare dramatizes the need for trust and integrity as forcefully as he reveals how empty is the display of honour and its total abandonment.

This is not to say that Falstaff 'deserves' rejection. He deserves rejection no more than Hotspur deserves to be deceived by Worcester. What Shakespeare is dramatizing is the pain and sacrifice entailed in the 'education' of a successful and acceptable ruler. The price for public humanity is private humanity. The magnanimity Hal learns from Falstaff and his companions will make him a better ruler, but it requires also rejection of Falstaff. Hal has to learn when it is no longer possible that 'all the year' be 'playing holidays'. As for the rejection itself, it *ought* to be painful.

Hal's relationship to Falstaff and Hotspur, and his preparation for kingship, lead to the play's being set in a variety of contrasting spheres. We seem to inhabit at least three worlds. There is the world of the King, his court, and his camp at Shrewsbury. There is Hotspur's world – a difference in atmosphere as much as place – and thirdly there is Falstaff's world – Gad's Hill, Eastcheap, the road to Sutton Coldfield – and even his part of the battlefield. 'Place' as such is of little significance; what is telling is the atmosphere and tone of each of the worlds.

No single world can be assigned to Hal. He is physically present at Gad's Hill and Eastcheap; he comes to court and is spoken of in his absence; he is present in the King's camp and on the battlefield; he is in Percy's mouth before and at Shrewsbury; and in his challenge to Hotspur to single combat he even has about him a trace of the world of medieval romance. It has been suggested that the play is divided too sharply between

its various spheres of interest, and possibly this impression
has been accentuated by the alternation of comic and historic,
of prose and verse, and the absence of a unifying pattern
of images such as is found in *Antony and Cleopatra*. Only
the language of Falstaff is at all rich in imagery, the chief
sources being food (not surprisingly), the Bible, and other
literature.

Nevertheless, despite these accusations, the interaction of the
various parts of the play is very close. There was no formal
separation of Acts and scenes in Elizabethan productions and
we have experienced in recent years how exciting and rational
the fluid presentation of Shakespeare can be, one scene running
into the next without delay of curtain fall or lengthy change of
scenery. Sometimes Shakespeare contrasts one scene with the
next so that one comments on the other. After Hotspur has
made his plea at the end of 1.3:

> *O, let the hours be short,*
> *Till fields, and blows, and groans applaud our sport!*

we have, not a curtain, nor an empty page and the heading
ACT II, SCENE 1, but a great yawn, 'Heigh-ho!', from the
first Carrier. No sooner has Gadshill explained to the Chamberlain that his associates are no 'sixpenny strikers', no 'mad
mustachio purple-hued maltworms', but we have Falstaff be-
moaning his fate. At the end of III.2 the King is eager to be
off:

> *Our hands are full of business, let's away,*
> *Advantage feeds him fat while men delay.*

And we turn, at once, without intermission, to advantage in
the shape of Falstaff feeding himself fat, despite his complaint
that he is 'withered like an old apple-john'. Falstaff's and
Hotspur's reactions are similarly contrasted at the end of IV.2
and the beginning of IV.3; and at the end of V.1, as Falstaff
completes his catechism, 'Honour is a mere scutcheon', on
walks Worcester:

O no, my nephew must not know, Sir Richard,
The liberal and kind offer of the King.   v.2.1—2

There is another kind of relationship, so manifold, so inter-woven, that it forms almost the substance of the play itself. Time after time, events in one world are imitated in another. The most obvious example is the way in which Falstaff's description of honour echoes Hotspur's, but there are many of lesser magnitude.

Gadshill boasts of his confederates – Hotspur has confidence in his allies; Falstaff's bawling for his horse in II.2 is followed by Hotspur's shouting after his in the following scene. After Hotspur has fought at Holmedon, we see Hal involved in the farce of the battle of Gad's Hill; Hotspur's description of Mortimer's fight with Glendower is recounted in terms of high romance – Falstaff's fight with the men in buckram is altogether of another order; and Falstaff's ragamuffins are not in accord with the magnificent description of Hal's followers that is given by Vernon. There are many more examples, but these few may suffice to suggest that *1 Henry IV* is, in its own way, as formally patterned as *Richard II*.

A measure of Shakespeare's achievement in *1 Henry IV* is the extent to which his three principal characters seem to exist for us outside the confines of the printed page. Falstaff in particular has so seized men's imaginations that it is as if this character really lived in the very flesh about which we hear so much. Of all the legends that have come down to us about Shakespeare, none strikes us as more likely to be true than that which tells of Queen Elizabeth's demand for more of Sir John. Falstaff's zest for life is so abundant that it permeates the whole play. It is perhaps this, more than any other single quality, that has given *1 Henry IV* so wide an appeal for so long.

Further Reading

Editions, Editorial Problems, and Sources

Sir Walter Greg's facsimile of the first Quarto was reissued by
The Clarendon Press, Oxford, in 1966 with an additional
introduction by Charlton Hinman. The Folio version can conveniently be read in the reduced facsimile, *Mr William Shakespeare's Comedies, Histories, & Tragedies*, prepared by Helge
Kökeritz (not to the entire satisfaction of all critics), and
published by Oxford University Press in 1955. The principal
recent editions are those of G. L. Kittredge (1940, reissued in a
revised form by Irving Ribner, 1966, Blaisdell), John Dover
Wilson (New Cambridge Shakespeare, 1946) and A. R. Humphreys (new Arden Shakespeare 1960, revised 1965). My debt
to these editions is particularly heavy. The Norton Critical
Edition, edited by James L. Sanderson, includes a lengthy and
particularly well-chosen selection of essays on the play. *The
Famous Victories of Henry the Fifth* can conveniently be read in
the major collection of source material for *1 Henry IV*, Geoffrey
Bullough's *Narrative and Dramatic Sources of Shakespeare*, volume
IV (London, 1962). It is also to be found in the Signet edition
of *1 Henry IV* (1965), which contains a helpful introduction by
the editor, Maynard Mack.

A comprehensive survey of the text is to be found in the
New Variorum Edition, edited by S. B. Hemingway (Philadelphia, 1936). This has been admirably brought up to date by G.
Blakemore Evans in the summer issue of *Shakespeare Quarterly*,
1956. A brief but useful annotated list of some later criticism is
given by James Sanderson in his edition of the play.

The whole sequence of Shakespeare's history plays has been
considered in recent years by E. M. W. Tillyard (*Shakespeare's*

History Plays, 1944, reprinted by Penguin Books, 1962); Lily B. Campbell (*Shakespeare's 'Histories'*, San Marino, 1947); D. A. Traversi (*Shakespeare from Richard II to Henry V*, Hollis and Carter, 1957); and M. M. Reese (*The Cease of Majesty*, Arnold, 1961). Harold Jenkins surveyed work on the history plays between 1900 and 1951 in *Shakespeare Survey 6*, 1953, and *1 Henry IV* is selected for study by Cleanth Brooks and Robert B. Heilman in *Understanding Drama* (New York, 1948).

Criticism

Critical comment on Falstaff is as enormous in bulk as the character himself – and as varied. Quite the most useful summary is 'Gadshill Revisited' (*Shakespeare Quarterly*, IV, 1953, reprinted in the Norton edition) by Arthur C. Sprague, who is also the author of an excellent account of *1 Henry IV* on the stage in his *Shakespeare's Histories, Plays for the Stage* (Society for Theatre Research, London, 1964). The most influential studies of Falstaff have been those of Maurice Morgann (1777), available in *Eighteenth Century Essays on Shakespeare* (edited by D. Nichol Smith, Glasgow, 1903); A. C. Bradley ('The Rejection of Falstaff', in *Oxford Lectures on Poetry*, 1909); E. E. Stoll (in *Shakespeare Studies*, New York, 1927); and John Dover Wilson, whose book *The Fortunes of Falstaff* (Cambridge, 1943) deals with more than 'that reverend Vice'. Falstaff and Hotspur, as well as Hal, are discussed in the chapter 'Henry of Monmouth' in John Palmer's *Political Characters of Shakespeare* (Macmillan, 1945). An interesting and vigorously hostile view of Hal is expressed by John Masefield in his *William Shakespeare*, 1911.

The imagery of the play is examined by Caroline Spurgeon in *Shakespeare's Imagery and what it tells us* (Cambridge, 1935) and, more comprehensively, by Madeleine Doran in 'Imagery in *Richard II* and in *Henry IV*' (*Modern Language Review* XXXVII, 1942). The language of the play, and the ironic relationship of court, tavern, and rebel camp, are discussed by William Empson in *Some Versions of Pastoral* (1935). M. A.

Shaaber argues forcibly that the unity of the two parts of *Henry IV* is 'a theatrical impossibility' in 'The Unity of *Henry IV*' (*Joseph Quincy Adams Memorial Studies*, Washington, 1948) but Harold Jenkins, in *The Structural Problem in Shakespeare's 'Henry IV*' (Methuen, 1956), argues that the two parts are complementary yet also 'independent and even incompatible'. Professor Jenkins's study is reprinted in *Shakespeare's Histories: An Anthology of Modern Criticism*, edited by William A. Armstrong (Penguin Shakespeare Library, 1972), and in *Discussions of Shakespeare's Histories*, edited by R. J. Dorius (Boston, 1965), which also includes four essays on Falstaff and A. P. Rossiter's illuminating discussion of the juxtaposition of opposed value-judgements in *1 Henry IV* – 'Ambivalence: the Dialectic of the Histories', first published in *Angel with Horns* (London, 1961).

The play is interpreted as a satire on war and policy by L. C. Knights in 'Notes on Comedy', originally published in *Scrutiny* in 1933, and reprinted the following year in *Determinations* (edited by F. R. Leavis). Knights's interpretation is challenged by C. L. Barber as 'obviously an impossible, anachronistic view' in the essay 'From Ritual to Comedy: an examination of *Henry IV*', first published in *English Stage Comedy* (edited by W. K. Wimsatt, New York, 1955) and reproduced as chapter eight of his book *Shakespeare's Festive Comedy* (Princeton, 1959). In this study the play, and Falstaff in particular, are related to the saturnalian tradition. A more sombre view of the play is taken by J. F. Danby in *Shakespeare's Doctrine of Nature* (London, 1949). He argues that those who see the world of *Henry IV* 'as some vital, joyous Renaissance England must go behind the facts Shakespeare presents'.

There are two interesting psychological studies of the play to which reference is made in the Introduction: Franz Alexander's 'A Note on Falstaff' (*Psychoanalytic Quarterly*, 1933), and, in that same journal in 1948, Ernst Kris's 'Prince Hal's Conflict' (which is reprinted in *Approaches to Shakespeare*, edited by Norman Rabkin, New York, 1964). The merging of Falstaff's identity, for a few instants, 'with that of a typical vaudeville comedian' was suggested by A. J. A. Waldock in 'The Men in Buckram' (*Review of English Studies*, 1947).

A useful collection of essays is *King Henry IV Parts 1 and 2: A Casebook* (Macmillan, 1970), edited by G. K. Hunter, whose introductory essay is particularly helpful.

An Account of the Text

When we read a book in a certain edition we expect every copy of that edition to be identical. If a dozen people were each to use a copy of this edition of *1 Henry IV* for study or in preparing a production of the play, they would rightly expect the same words to appear in the same places in each person's copy. The content of books can change from edition to edition, and that of newspapers invariably does, but sometimes books will go through edition after edition without any changes being made, other than the date of the edition, repeating even errors that are obvious.

This edition of Shakespeare's play differs from versions prepared by other editors. The arrangement of the contents and the editorial comment will be expected to be different, but it may come as a surprise that the words of the play itself are sometimes different from those in other editions. The text given here is similar to that in the edition prepared by A. R. Humphreys in 1960, rather less like that published in 1946 by John Dover Wilson, and quite different from the version printed in the collected edition of Shakespeare's plays published nine years after his death. Some of the changes reflect different approaches to modernization. The 1598 edition prints *coarse* at IV.1.123 but the Arden editor spells this 'corse' whereas it is fully modernized to 'corpse' in this edition. Some changes are the result of different ways of adapting Elizabethan punctuation to modern needs. Only occasionally is meaning affected in *1 Henry IV*. All editors find it necessary to change the names of the speakers at II.4.168, 169, 171, and 175, from those given in 1598. Many editors consider that 'Oneyres' (II.1.77) needs amendment. This kind of variation is not the product of editorial pedantry. Each editor has tried to provide his readers with what Shakespeare intended to be his *First Part of King Henry the Fourth* in a way 'that will be comprehensible to them. But the editor has then to work out what Shakespeare did intend. *1 Henry IV*, like many plays of the period, was published in different versions that might or might not represent its author's intention and copies of the same edition read differently in places because in Shakespeare's time printing often began before proofs were read.

As our knowledge of Shakespeare's plays, and the ways in which they were printed, has grown, it has become possible, despite many frustrations and uncertainties, to present texts which are believed to be closer to what Shakespeare wrote than those published a decade or a century ago, or even than those published in his own lifetime. This is not as surprising as it might seem, for the texts of works by modern authors are not always printed as they have directed.

Obviously an editor's problem is more difficult when he cannot know at first hand what an author intended. Nowadays most authors have some say in the printing of their work. What they say may not be noted, or the author may have said different things on different occasions so that the resulting editions are not always readily reconcilable, or the author may not have noticed errors made in printing or reproduced from his original.

It cannot be taken for granted that an author saw his work through the press in Shakespeare's day and it has long been asserted that most dramatists, and Shakespeare especially, had little control over the printing of their work. So inaccurate are even the best early editions of some of Shakespeare's plays that scholars have felt reluctant to believe that such a genius could have been so careless of his reputation. One contemporary of Shakespeare, Thomas Heywood, in an epistle printed with his play *The English Traveller* in 1633, stated that actors were averse to the publication of those of his plays which were still in the repertoire because they 'think it against their peculiar profit to have them come into print'. In the prologue to his delightfully named play, *If You Know Not Me You Know Nobody*, in 1637, he maintained that a quarter of a century earlier this play had been pirated (published without authority): 'some by Stenography drew the plot: put it in print: (scarce one word true)'. Evidence of this kind, and our knowledge that the law of copyright did not then protect authors to the extent it does now, have given the impression that dramatists had little control over the publication of their plays.

On the other hand, Thomas Heywood also tells us, in an address to the reader published in 1608 with his play *The Rape of Lucrece*, that some playwrights sold their work twice, first to a company of actors and then to a printer. In recent years close examination of various kinds of evidence, including plays themselves, has shown that more dramatists than was once thought likely read proofs of their plays and sometimes even added material to them for the benefit of their readers. Thus, quite recently, it has been suggested that Shakespeare too might have been more active in the publication of his plays than was once thought.

It seems to me that the printer's copy used for the publication of *1 Henry IV* in 1598 was in Shakespeare's handwriting and that he may have slightly revised it for this purpose. There is no evidence that he did more than that.

The first complete version of *1 Henry IV* that has come down to us is the first Quarto, of 1598 (Q1). It is called a quarto because the individual sheets used to make up the book were each folded twice to give four leaves (eight pages). A century ago, in 1867, it was reported that a single sheet of a slightly earlier version had been found in the binding of an Italian grammar published over three hundred years earlier (though obviously bound later). This fragment is called Q0. From the similarity of type used it seems to have been printed by the same printer, Peter Short, as Q1. Q1 has one line more on each page than Q0 and these extra lines made it possible to print Q1 much more economically, saving not only two leaves required for these extra lines but also the paper for the blank leaves that would usually be used with these additional pages. For these and other reasons Q1 is thought to be a reprint of Q0.

Each of the succeeding five quartos was printed from its predecessor and one cannot take very seriously the claim on the title page of Q2 that it has been 'Newly corrected by *W. Shakespeare*'. Then, in 1623, Shakespeare's plays were gathered together and printed in what has come to be called the Folio. Later quartos introduced colloquial contractions, and the Folio introduces, among other things, Act divisions, the purging of oaths (in belated accordance with an Act of Parliament passed in 1606), and a very small number of interesting amendments. In addition, 'Bardolph' usually replaced 'Bardol'. The only other text of the period is a handwritten version, the Dering Manuscript, which is made up from both parts of *Henry IV*, evidently for a private performance.

It is known that some literary works were prepared by their authors in different versions on, or for, different occasions. We know that Thomas Middleton, a contemporary of Shakespeare, wrote different versions of his play *A Game at Chess*; these versions, in his own handwriting, have come down to us. Furthermore, these versions coexist – one does not replace the other.

It has recently been argued from evidence of this kind that different versions of words and lines in Shakespeare's plays may be Shakespearian – that though some variant forms result from the errors of scribes or the men who set the type, we ought to take into account the possibility that Shakespeare, like Middleton and others, may have produced more than one 'final' version of his work. If this argument is correct, then an editor has to choose between correct and incorrect readings and also between different authorial versions. When looked at in isolation the choice between these readings may be slight but cumulatively the effect can be significant. For example, the tone of *1 Henry IV* differs quite surprisingly if an editor (or producer) chooses colloquial instead of formal readings.

Some editors have considered that when the text for the Folio was prepared, Q5 (upon which it was certainly based) was corrected from the prompt book that had been used in the Globe Theatre. If this were so, it is very surprising that so *few* changes were made. Indeed, all the changes introduced could have been made without reference to any other manuscript. If the prompt-book had been used, we should expect amplified stage directions; the supply of those missing (rather than their *omission*); the correction of long-standing errors; and perhaps the restoration of *fat* at II.2.109, a word omitted in all editions after Q0. It has been argued that Shakespeare would naturally have written colloquially (especially in prose passages) and that a pedantic scribe or compositor was responsible for expanding many colloquialisms. But there is no necessity for even such a line as 'All is one for that' (II.4.150) to be made colloquial, for it is at least as dramatically effective in its context that *All* should be stressed as it is to say 'All's one for that'. If such pedantry were practised it is remarkable that so many colloquial contractions were allowed to stand and even in the Folio there are many places where contractions are not used. Furthermore, these colloquial contractions do not all appear for the first time in the Folio but are introduced gradually, quarto by quarto. It seems more likely that as compositors said lines over to themselves – carrying them in their heads as they set the type – they themselves colloquialized the lines. Contractions, incidentally, require less work to set, and speed is always an attraction to compositors.

As it stands, Q1 does not read like an acting script. It lacks, for example, certain entrances and exits; a few, if unimportant, speech prefixes are inexact; and there are references to non-existent characters. It is likely that from Shakespeare's manuscript he, or someone else, prepared a version for use as the theatrical prompt-book, tidying up details in order to make the

play suitable for performance. This copy would be sent to the
Master of the Revels, Edmund Tilney, who was required to
authorize plays for performance – that is, act as censor. Although the manuscript believed to have been used for the first
edition of the play was not entirely suitable for performance as
it stood, it was in very much better order than is usually the
case in copy of this kind – much better than that used for *2
Henry IV* for example.

We are here in the field of conjecture (as is everyone endeav-
ouring to solve this problem), but it may be helpful to imagine
what occurred when objections were raised to the use of the
name of Oldcastle in *1 Henry IV* (see Introduction, pages 242–3),
and perhaps also to the use of the names 'Harvey' and 'Russell'
which seem originally to have been used for 'Bardolph' and
'Peto'. ('Harvey' and 'Russell' survive in Q1 at 1.2.160.) There
existed a prompt-book manuscript and the manuscript on which
it was based. Changes had to be made in the prompt-book at
once and this task would, it seems to me, have been given to
the author, who might be expected to provide alternative
names and would be the person most familiar with the text,
and thus most able to make the necessary changes rapidly.
Later, when printing was proposed, a manuscript would have
to be provided. Even if the play was not then being performed,
it is unlikely that the prompt-book would be released, because
it would contain the precious authorization for performance;
and, in any case, the text we have is not prepared for performance. In order to avoid giving offence by the use of the name
'Oldcastle' it would be necessary to amend the earlier manuscript or to make a copy of either the manuscript or the
prompt-book. This work could have been done by a scribe or
by Shakespeare.

A scribe, one imagines, would need the prompt-book before
him to see what changes were necessary, and these would be
hard to miss if they stood out like the emendations in the
prompt-book of Massinger's *Believe as You List* (which has
come down to us). It is not unreasonable to suggest that if a

scribe had collated this manuscript with the prompt-book, though he would doubtless have made errors, he might have been expected to make a more thorough job of the entries and exits than is the case. I imagine, therefore, that Shakespeare himself made the emendations in his own manuscript and, simultaneously, tidied up most of the speech prefixes. That is, he changed chiefly what was obvious (for example, speech prefixes) but missed what wasn't, such as the prefix *Per. (Percy)* instead of *Hot. (Hotspur)* in IV.1, the reference to Harvey and Russell at 1.2.160, the three speeches attributed to Russell in II.4 and the entries and exits already lacking.

Thus I believe (for there is no certainty) that the manuscript used in 1598 by Peter Short, the printer, was in Shakespeare's handwriting and that there is a reasonable likelihood that he revised it slightly for publication; and, furthermore, that no later edition, nor the Dering Manuscript, has any authority, though these versions contain occasional acceptable guesses. It seems to me improbable that the existence of full and elided expressions represents alternative readings both having Shakespeare's authority.

How far can we rely upon Peter Short's workmanship? There are two emendations that appear in the Folio ('President' – for 'precedent' – at II.4.32 and 'cantle' at III.1.96) and one in the Dering Manuscript ('tristful' at II.4.386) that every editor is grateful for. Some editors make use of more readings from editions published after Q1 than do others, but on the whole Q1 gives the impression of being a very reliable edition. Its printer, Peter Short, was very respectable. He printed Foxe's *Acts and Monuments* for the Company of Stationers, and a number of works by St Augustine, Bede, and Thomas à Kempis; by Lodge, Drayton, and Garnier; music by Farnaby, Morley, and Dowland; Daniel's *Civil Wars* (a source of *1 Henry IV*); Meres's *Palladis Tamia* (which quotes a line from *1 Henry IV*, though they were published in the same year); as well as two plays with Shakespearian associations, *The Taming of a Shrew* (in two editions) and *The True Tragedy of Richard Duke of*

York; and editions of Shakespeare's *Venus and Adonis* and *The Rape of Lucrece*.

In the past decade or so editors have devoted particular attention to what went on in Elizabethan printing-houses. Efforts have been made by a variety of techniques to identify the work and habits of those who set type, the aim being to evolve techniques that are objective and demonstrable in order that the editor's subjective impressions shall not unduly influence his decisions. The application of such techniques to Q1 of *1 Henry IV* virtually proves what might be guessed from the publication of a second edition (Q1) within a few months of the first (Q0), and it also reveals an unusual printing procedure.

There are still words in English which may, allowably, be spelt in different ways. In consequence printing houses must decide whether, for example, they will favour endings in '-ise' or '-ize', and whether they will spell 'judgement' as 'judgment'. In Elizabethan times spelling was far more variable. In Q1 of *1 Henry IV* we have, for example, *tongue, toung*, and *tong*. It is sometimes possible to distinguish between the men who set type by examining the way they spelt. There are many difficulties; some compositors did not stick to preferred spellings; some altered spellings to make words fit the length of line required; sometimes they adopted spellings from the copy they were setting, especially in line-for-line reprints like Q1.

The problem is made difficult, wellnigh impossible indeed, in *1 Henry IV* because we have only eight pages of Q0 (too small a sample in this case to make precise discrimination possible) and Q1 reveals a bewildering variation of spellings. In the part we can check, we can see that whoever set Q1 changed *enough* in Q0 to *inough* on two occasions; changed *tongue* to *toung*, *all* to *al* – and *al* to *all*! Six times *-ie* endings were changed to *-y* endings – and six times exactly the opposite change was made. Either one or two men could have set Q1 so far as the evidence of spelling alone is concerned. What is clear is that though spellings were altered, Q1 follows Q0 remarkably faithfully by the standards of Elizabethan dramatic printing. A slight error is corrected (*my* is changed to *mine*) and one word, *fat* at II.2.109, is erroneously omitted.

Of the other editorial techniques applied, only one produced useful information. At the top of each page of Q1 of *1 Henry IV* the play's title is given in the form *The History* | *of Henry the fourth* (spelt in a variety of ways). It was customary for such 'running titles' to be transferred, after they had been used with one set of type, to another set of pages. Whereas the type for the text had to be broken up to be used again, the type for running titles could be kept standing. In Q1 of *1 Henry IV* four pages of type were printed simultaneously on *one side* of a large sheet of paper. This required four running titles – two for *The History* and two for *of Henry the fourth*. After the first four pages had been printed on one side of the large sheet, the four pages that backed on to them had to be printed on the other side. This, when folded twice, gave eight pages of text (four leaves). It was (and is) possible to use the same running titles for both sides of the sheet, but it seems likely that it was more economical of time to arrange two sets of four running titles, each set forming a 'skeleton'. Recent studies of printed books of the late Elizabethan period have indicated that normal practice was for these skeletons to be used alternately.

It so happens that in Q1 not only are the running titles spelt in different ways but some of the pieces of type can be individually identified and it is thus possible to demonstrate that Q1 uses eight titles, making two distinct skeletons. But, instead of being used alternately, one is used twice, then the other occurs twice, and so on. As the whole point of making up two skeletons is to use them alternately, why did Short's men do this?

In all the other plays Short printed before 1598, whether quartos or octavos, only one skeleton is used for each text. Though the evidence is slight, a single skeleton seems to have been used for the fragment we have of Q0. The effect of using two skeletons in this manner in QI is as if *two* compositors had set the type, each one using a single skeleton for the pages he set, and each man setting an alternate eight pages. What we normally expect when two men set type for a quarto is the use of four skeletons (as for *Hamlet* in 1604). The implications are modest but support an editor's reliance on Qo and QI.

It will be remembered that Qo and QI do not show as much colloquial elision as later quartos and the Folio and that it has been agreed by some editors the lack of colloquialism in QI was caused by a pedantic compositor. Certainly we can say that QI follows Qo exactly. Furthermore, lines where colloquial elision occurs in later quartos and the Folio, where past forms of verbs are wrongly left unelided, and lines in QI which might have been adapted to suit the metre, are evenly distributed between the two men conjectured to have set QI. We can reasonably assume that what we have in QI almost certainly represents the copy provided for these two compositors – that is, Qo. Unfortunately we cannot extract as much information as we should like about Qo from the fragment that has come down to us. We can but wonder if whoever set the type was as accurate as his colleagues who set QI, if, indeed, he was not one of them.

That Short took the, for him, unusual step of putting two men to set the type for QI confirms what we might guess: that there was a heavy demand for the play and he was anxious to publish it quickly. (It is the only play by Shakespeare of which two editions were published in the same year – and a third appeared in the following year.) Yet the evidence we have shows no sign of carelessness or undue haste on the part of the compositors. It would seem that Short's compositors were competent craftsmen who followed their copy with care – much more than can be said for the compositor who set the greater part of *1 Henry IV* in the Folio. Until further evidence comes to light we must put our trust in the 1598 editions of *1 Henry IV*, and we may do so, I believe, with some confidence.

COLLATIONS

The lists that follow are *selective*. Except where a passage has been relineated for the first time in this edition, relineation (usually of prose to verse) is not noted; nor are changes in punctuation, and minor variants that are undisputed. The long s used in printing the early texts (ʃ) is replaced here by modern s (except where long s affects the reading).

I

The first word or phrase is that given in this edition; the word or phrase after the square bracket is what is given by Q1, in its original spelling. Most of the changes are modern forms of archaic words.

I.I.	4	strands] stronds
	43	corpses] corpes
I.2.	33	moon. As for proof? Now,] moone, as for proofe. Now
	136	Who I? Rob? I a thief?] Who I rob, I a thiefe? (*Most editors read* Who, I rob? I a thief?)
I.3.	13	helped] holpe
	43	corpse] coarse (*and at* IV.I.123)
II.I.	18	Christian] christen
	56	Weald] wilde
	77	O-yeas] Oneyres (*see textual note*)
II.2.	0	Peto *omitted from this entry and added, with* Bardolph, *at line 46 stage direction* (*see textual note*)
II.3.	94	Kate?] Kate (*see textual note*)
III.2.	59	won] wan
III.3.	132	owed] ought
IV.2.	3	Sutton Coldfield] Sutton cop-hill

v.3.   42   Whose deaths . . . prithee] *taken as verse*; Lend me
follows preethe *in* Q1.

2

The following readings have been adopted from editions other
than Q0 and Q1. Only the more interesting changes, and any
that could be considered significant from the early quartos and
the Folio, are included. The first word or phrase is that given
in this text. It is followed by a square bracket and sometimes
the source of the emendation. Usually where no source is
named the emendation is the work of an eighteenth-century
editor, e.g. Capell, Theobald, Hanmer, or Steevens. The second
word or phrase quoted is the reading of Q1 unless a statement
to the contrary appears.

I.1.   0   *Sir Walter Blunt*] added from Dering Ms.

          30   Therefor] *A.R. Humphreys*; Therefore

          62   a dear] deere

      75–6   In faith, | It is] In faith it is. *spoken by King*

I.2.   79   similes] Q5; smiles

I.2.   80   sweet] sweer (*the error in* Q1 *not noted elsewhere*)

     160   Falstaff] Falstalffe (*and frequently*)
             Bardolph, Peto] Haruey Rossill (*see An Account of
the Text, pages 259–60*)

I.3.   95   tongue for] tongue: for

    199   HOTSPUR] Q5; *omitted from* Q0 *and* Q1

    260   granted. (*To Northumberland*) You my lord,]
             granted you my Lord.

II.2.   12   square] squire

    109   fat] *omitted from the Folio and from all early quartos
except* Q0

II.3.   50   thee] the

    72   A roan] Q3; Roane

II.4.   6   bass string] *G. L. Kittredge*; base string

II.4.	7	Christian] Q5; christen
	32	precedent] F (President); present
	168	PRINCE HAL] *Prince* F; *Gad.*
169, 171, 175		GADSHILL] *Gad.* F; *Ross. (see An Account of the Text, page 260]*
	240	elf-skin] Q3 (elfskin); elfskin Q1; *many editors emend the reading of* Q1 *to eel-skin – see textual note.*
	386	tristful] *Dering Ms.*; trustful
	394	yet] Q3; so
III.1.	96	cantle] F; scantle
III.3.	56	tithe] tight
IV.1.	20	I, my lord] I my mind
	55	is] F; tis
	108	dropped] Q2 (dropt); drop
	126	cannot] Q5; can
	127	yet] Q5; it
V.2.	3	undone] Q5; vnder one
V.3.	22	A fool] Ah foole
	36	ragamuffins] rag of Muffins
V.4.	67	Nor] F; Now
	91	thee] the
	164	nobleman] Q4; noble man

3

The short list that follows gives a few of the more interesting readings that have not been adopted in this edition. The textual notes to II.1.77 and II.4.240 might also be consulted in this connexion. The reading of the present text is given first.

I.1.	16	allies] all eyes Q4
I.3.	233	wasp-stung] waspe-tongue Q2
II.2.	34	my] Q0; mine Q1
II.4.	122	lime in it] in't *uncorrected Folio*; lime *corrected Folio. The Folio compositor missed out the word* lime *when he*

set this passage and the result was nonsense. To make sense (but not quite that of the original) without re-adjusting all the type that followed in order to take in an extra word, in't *was simply replaced by* lime.

333   O, Glendower] Q2; O Glendower Q1; Owen Glendower *Dering Ms.*

III.2.   156   intemperance] intemperature F

Genealogical Table

Claimants to the Throne of England after the deposition of Richard II

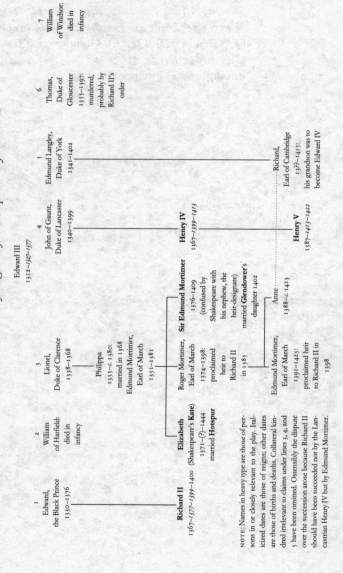

Edward III
1312–1327–1377

1
Edward,
the Black Prince
1330–1376

2
William
of Hatfield:
died in
infancy

3
Lionel,
Duke of Clarence
1338–1368

4
John of Gaunt,
Duke of Lancaster
1340–1399

5
Edmund Langley,
Duke of York
1341–1402

6
Thomas,
Duke of
Gloucester
1355–1397:
murdered,
probably by
Richard II's
order

7
William
of Windsor:
died in
infancy

Richard II
1367–1377–1399–1400

Philippa
1355–*c.* 1380:
married in 1368
Edmund Mortimer,
Earl of March
1351–1381

Elizabeth
1371–(?)–1444
(Shakespeare's **Kate**)
married **Hotspur**

Henry IV
1367–1399–1413

Richard,
Earl of Cambridge
1375?–1415:
his grandson was to
become Edward IV

Roger Mortimer,
Earl of March
1374–1398:
proclaimed
heir to
Richard II
in 1385

Sir Edmund Mortimer
1376–1409
(confused by
Shakespeare with
his nephew, the
heir-designate)
married **Glendower**'s
daughter 1402

Edmund Mortimer,
Earl of March
1391–1425:
proclaimed heir
to Richard II in
1398

Anne
1388–*c.* 1413

Henry V
1387–1413–1422

NOTE: Names in heavy type are those of persons in or closely relevant to the play. Italicized dates are those of reigns; other dates
are those of births and deaths. Collateral kindred irrelevant to claims under lines 3, 4, and
5 have been omitted. Ostensibly the dispute
over the succession arose because Richard II
should have been succeeded not by the Lancastrian Henry IV but by Edmund Mortimer.

THE FIRST PART OF
KING HENRY THE FOURTH
The Characters in the Play

The King's Party

KING HENRY IV, formerly Henry Bolingbroke, son of John
   of Gaunt

HENRY (or HAL), Prince of Wales, the King's eldest son

LORD JOHN OF LANCASTER, a younger son of King
   Henry IV

EARL OF WESTMORLAND, kinsman by law to Henry IV

SIR WALTER BLUNT

The Rebels

HENRY PERCY, Earl of Northumberland

HARRY HOTSPUR, his son

LADY PERCY (KATE), Hotspur's wife, sister of Mortimer

THOMAS PERCY, Earl of Worcester

EDMUND, LORD MORTIMER

LADY MORTIMER, Mortimer's wife, daughter of Glendower

OWEN GLENDOWER

EARL OF DOUGLAS

SIR RICHARD VERNON

RICHARD SCROOP, Archbishop of York

SIR MICHAEL, a member of the household of the Archbishop

Hal's Companions

SIR JOHN FALSTAFF

POINS

BARDOLPH

PETO

MISTRESS QUICKLY, hostess of the Tavern in Eastcheap

FRANCIS, a drawer
Vintner

At Rochester
GADSHILL
Two Carriers
Chamberlain

Sheriff and Officers
Ostler
Messengers
Travellers
Lords and Attendants
Soldiers

Enter the King, Lord John of Lancaster, Earl of
Westmorland, Sir Walter Blunt, with others

KING HENRY
  So shaken as we are, so wan with care,
  Find we a time for frighted peace to pant,
  And breathe short-winded accents of new broils
  To be commenced in strands afar remote.

References to plays by Shakespeare not yet available in the New Penguin Shakespeare are to Peter Alexander's edition of the *Complete Works*, London 1951.

I.I Shakespeare does not give locations for any of the scenes in *1 Henry IV* and the first Quarto (Q1) is not even divided into scenes and Acts. Such divisions, and insistence on places of action, impose a formal and rigid structure which the play does not have. The transition from scene to scene in Elizabethan drama was rapid and informal and many modern productions have, with advantage, adopted a similar method of presenting plays of this period. What we need to know about location in *1 Henry IV* is told us in the play itself, either by direct statement – thus we know the robbery takes place at Gad's Hill and that the character Gadshill 'lies tonight in Rochester' (1.2.127–8), indicating the location of II.1 – or, less precisely, by the style of the language. Thus we can gather as much as we need to know about the situation of the action from the play

itself. It has been customary in the past, particularly in the eighteenth century, for editors to obtain possible locations from external sources. Thus III.1 has sometimes been placed in the Archdeacon's House in Bangor, North Wales, because the historian Holinshed records that the 'tripartite indenture' was sealed there by the principal rebels. Such particularity is perhaps more distracting than helpful.

1 *we* (the nation and the King himself)

2 *frighted peace to pant.* Peace, like an animal terrified in the chase, needs to recover strength. The play concerning the deposition of Henry's predecessor, *Richard II*, concluded with the outbreak of civil strife and reports of the unruly behaviour of Henry's son, Prince Hal. These events are recalled in this opening scene.

3 *accents* words, discussion
  broils battles, warfare

4 *strands* shores, lands

No more the thirsty entrance of this soil
Shall daub her lips with her own children's blood,
No more shall trenching war channel her fields,
Nor bruise her flowerets with the armèd hoofs
Of hostile paces. Those opposèd eyes,
10   Which, like the meteors of a troubled heaven,
All of one nature, of one substance bred,
Did lately meet in the intestine shock

5-6 *No more the thirsty entrance of this soil | Shall daub her lips with her own children's blood*. The fratricidal strife following the deposition of Richard is foretold by Carlisle in *Richard II*, IV.I.II5-49, and by Richard himself, III.3.85-100. The King concludes his prophecy with a warning that seems from Henry's statement to have been fulfilled:

Ten thousand bloody crowns of mothers'
*   sons*
Shall . . . bedew
Her pastor's grass with faithful English
*   blood.*

The idea of the earth as a thirsty mouth may have been suggested to Shakespeare by Genesis 4.II, where the earth is said to have 'opened her mouth to receive thy brother's blood from thy hand'. (The quotation, in a modernized spelling, is taken from the Bishops' Bible, I568 – the version known to Shakespeare.)

6 *daub* paint, defile

7 *trenching* cutting, wounding

8 *flowerets*. It has been customary to indicate elisions by an apostrophe in texts of Shakespeare produced since the eighteenth century. Thus the 'flourets' of the first Quarto has been represented as 'flow'rets'. With the exception of 'e'er' and 'ne'er', which have established for themselves an existence of their own, at least in verse, this practice has not been fol-

lowed in this edition. A major virtue of the English language is its infinite variety of stress. It is possible to vary the number of syllables in the iambic pentameter (a line not originally designed for the English language) to give a wide range of effects. This Shakespeare knew and any competent actor can demonstrate. It has been thought more helpful to a modern reader to print the words fully and to rely upon actors and actresses to give the amount of stress and the degree of elision necessary to the line as required by the context. (See also note on v.2.32.)

9 *opposèd eyes* (the eyes of conflicting forces. These, after being likened to meteors, are not thought of simply as gazing at each other but actually meeting in the 'furious close of civil butchery'.)

10 *meteors of a troubled heaven*. Shakespeare frequently relates human action to cosmic harmony and disturbance. Meteors had for Elizabethans something of the mystery and variable properties that some people nowadays associate with unidentified flying objects of other kinds. They might be associated with rain, hail, snow, wind, thunder, or lightning, and they suggested the involvement of other worlds in human affairs. (See also the note on I.2.I95.)

12 *intestine* internal

And furious close of civil butchery,
Shall now, in mutual well-beseeming ranks,
March all one way, and be no more opposed
Against acquaintance, kindred, and allies.
The edge of war, like an ill-sheathed knife,
No more shall cut his master. Therefore friends,
As far as to the sepulchre of Christ –
Whose soldier now, under whose blessed cross   20
We are impressèd and engaged to fight –
Forthwith a power of English shall we levy,
Whose arms were moulded in their mother's womb
To chase these pagans in those holy fields
Over whose acres walked those blessèd feet,
Which fourteen hundred years ago were nailed
For our advantage on the bitter cross.
But this our purpose now is twelve month old,
And bootless 'tis to tell you we will go.
Therefor we meet not now. Then let me hear   30
Of you, my gentle cousin Westmorland,
What yesternight our Council did decree
In forwarding this dear expedience.

WESTMORLAND
My liege, this haste was hot in question,

13 *close* engagement
19 *As far as to the sepulchre of Christ.* At
the very end of *Richard II*, Henry
vows to 'make a voyage to the Holy
Land | To wash this blood off from
my guilty hand' for the part he
played in Richard's murder. Shakespeare here recalls that vow but in
doing so brings the proposed crusade
forward from the end of Henry's
reign, when plans were made for this
expedition, to the early months of
his reign. This strengthens the sense
of continuation from the end of Richard's reign, and as line 28 of this
scene reveals, Shakespeare seemed
anxious to avoid there seeming to be

too great a gap in time between the
two plays, presumably to be able to
stress the relationship, dramatic and
historic, of cause and effect
21 *impressèd* conscripted, bound (by his
vow)
28 *twelve month old.* Two years had, in
fact, elapsed between Richard's
murder in February 1400 and the
Battle of Holmedon.
29 *bootless* useless
30 *Therefor* for that purpose
31 *Of* from
33 *dear expedience* cherished and urgent
expedition
34 *hot in question* urgently before us,
actively debated

And many limits of the charge set down
But yesternight, when all athwart there came
A post from Wales, loaden with heavy news,
Whose worst was that the noble Mortimer –
Leading the men of Herefordshire to fight
40 Against the irregular and wild Glendower –
Was by the rude hands of that Welshman taken,
A thousand of his people butcherèd,
Upon whose dead corpses there was such misuse,
Such beastly shameless transformation
By those Welshwomen done, as may not be
Without much shame retold or spoken of.

KING HENRY

It seems then that the tidings of this broil
Brake off our business for the Holy Land.

WESTMORLAND

This matched with other did, my gracious lord,
50 For more uneven and unwelcome news
Came from the north, and thus it did import.
On Holy-rood day, the gallant Hotspur there,
Young Harry Percy, and brave Archibald,
That ever valiant and approvèd Scot,
At Holmedon met, where they did spend

35 *limits of the charge set down* many duties
and commands had been assigned
36 *all athwart* across (our purpose),
thwartingly
37 *post* messenger
38 *Mortimer.* There were two Edmund
Mortimers: one, Hotspur's brother-
in-law; the other, that Edmund's
nephew. These two men were confused by Shakespeare (and see also
the notes to 1.3.79, 83).
40 *irregular and wild Glendower.* The description hardly accords with the
man who, he tells us, 'was trained up
in the English court' and was capable
of framing 'to the harp | Many an

English ditty lovely well'!
irregular (as in guerrilla warfare, and
possibly also glancing at Glendower's conduct)
41 *rude* uncivilized
47 *broil* quarrel, strife
52 *Holy-rood day* Holy-cross day (14 September)
53 *Archibald.* Douglas's full title was
Archibald, 4th Earl of Douglas.
55 *Holmedon.* That is, Humbleton, Northumberland, though the battle is also
known as Homildon Hill. It took
place nearly three months after Mortimer's defeat but Shakespeare brings
the events together for dramatic

A sad and bloody hour –
As by discharge of their artillery,
And shape of likelihood, the news was told;
For he that brought them, in the very heat
And pride of their contention did take horse,   60
Uncertain of the issue any way.

KING HENRY

Here is a dear, a true industrious friend,
Sir Walter Blunt, new lighted from his horse,
Stained with the variation of each soil
Betwixt that Holmedon and this seat of ours,
And he hath brought us smooth and welcome news.
The Earl of Douglas is discomfited.
Ten thousand bold Scots, two-and-twenty knights,
Balked in their own blood, did Sir Walter see
On Holmedon's plains. Of prisoners Hotspur took   70
Mordake, Earl of Fife and eldest son
To beaten Douglas, and the Earl of Atholl,
Of Murray, Angus, and Menteith:
And is not this an honourable spoil?
A gallant prize? Ha, cousin, is it not?

---

effect. (Curiously the Scots were beaten at Nesbit on the day Mortimer lost to Glendower.)

57 *artillery*. This included catapults, slings, bows, and arrows, although at II.3.55 basilisks, cannon, and culverin are mentioned.

58 *shape of likelihood* the way events were shaping

63 *Sir Walter Blunt*. The news was brought by Nicholas Merbury, who received a grant of £40 a year for this service. By assuming Blunt to be the messenger (no name is given by Holinshed), Shakespeare is able to draw attention to the King's dependence on Blunt, which will be of some importance in IV.3 and V.3. (See also the note to IV.3.30.)

66 *smooth* pleasant

68 *two-and-twenty* (three-and-twenty according to Holinshed)

69 *Balked in their own blood*. A balk is the ridge left between two furrows in ploughing. The bodies fell in blood-stained rows. Compare the use of 'trenching war channel her fields' at line 7.

71 *Mordake*. Murdoch Stewart was the eldest son of Robert, Duke of Albany, Regent of Scotland. Shakespeare's error stems from a misplaced comma in his source, Holinshed.

73 *Menteith* (not a separate individual but one of Mordake's titles)

75 *A gallant prize*. As we are told that Blunt left the battle at its climax – the 'pride of their contention' – it is a little odd that he should know the final outcome in such detail. It is

WESTMORLAND   In faith,
  It is a conquest for a prince to boast of.
  KING HENRY
  Yea, there thou makest me sad, and makest me sin
  In envy that my Lord Northumberland
  Should be the father to so blest a son:
80 A son who is the theme of honour's tongue,
  Amongst a grove the very straightest plant,
  Who is sweet Fortune's minion and her pride –
  Whilst I by looking on the praise of him
  See riot and dishonour stain the brow
  Of my young Harry. O that it could be proved
  That some night-tripping fairy had exchanged
  In cradle-clothes our children where they lay,
  And called mine Percy, his Plantagenet!
  Then would I have his Harry, and he mine.
90 But let him from my thoughts. What think you, coz,
  Of this young Percy's pride? The prisoners

---

also a little strange that the King should have spoken of the urgent preparations for an expedition to the Holy Land, though it is now evident he knew of trouble in the North. At first sight this might seem like duplicity but, though Hotspur had refused to give up his prisoners, the King could hardly have expected that this would lead to civil war. It is the tidings from Wales, which the King did not know, which cause him to break off the crusade (as is precisely stated in lines 47–8). This victory is, then, a gallant prize, securing rather than threatening the safety of the country (that is, England, not Great Britain). By lines 99–101 Percy has become an excuse for delay.

82 *minion* darling

86–7 exchanged | *In cradle-clothes our children*. Shakespeare frequently makes radical changes in the ages of his characters. At this time, Hotspur was thirty-eight, Henry, three years younger, and Hal, only fifteen. What is of greater interest than these minor distortions of fact is the way in which Shakespeare uses age. He not only makes comparison frequently between youth and age, but will make some characters seem to age more rapidly than others. Richard II was only three months older than Henry IV, yet the former ages much more rapidly than the latter in *Richard II*, and Henry seems to age quickly in the year or two separating that play and *1 Henry IV*.

90 *coz* cousin (though often used loosely, as here).

91 *The prisoners*. Hotspur was entitled to retain all prisoners except those of the blood royal and it was, therefore, only Mordake who had to be surrendered.

Which he in this adventure hath surprised
To his own use he keeps, and sends me word
I shall have none but Mordake, Earl of Fife.

WESTMORLAND

This is his uncle's teaching. This is Worcester,
Malevolent to you in all aspects,
Which makes him prune himself, and bristle up
The crest of youth against your dignity.

KING HENRY

But I have sent for him to answer this,
And for this cause awhile we must neglect   100
Our holy purpose to Jerusalem.
Cousin, on Wednesday next our Council we
Will hold at Windsor, so inform the lords.
But come yourself with speed to us again,
For more is to be said and to be done
Than out of anger can be utterèd.

WESTMORLAND

I will, my liege   *Exeunt*

Enter Prince of Wales and Sir John Falstaff   I.2
FALSTAFF Now Hal, what time of day is it lad?
PRINCE HAL Thou art so fat-witted with drinking of old

---

97 *prune* preen (a term from falconry)
99 *I have sent for him to answer this.* According to Holinshed, Hotspur and his father came of their own accord to Windsor to outface the King. Shakespeare makes Henry seem to have the power to command their presence.
106 *out of anger can be utterèd* can be said in public in anger

I.2 Shakespeare does not state a location for this scene and it has at various times since the eighteenth century been placed in an apartment of the Prince's, in the palace, in a room in a tavern, before a tavern, and in the street. It has also been suggested that Hal should engage in some silent stage-business as he 'discovers' Falstaff asleep within the inner stage – a curtained-off recess. What is much more important than location is that Hal and Falstaff should be seen and heard together, without the intervention of their cronies, so that the audience can gauge the nature of Hal's association with Falstaff.
2 *fat-witted* thick-witted

sack, and unbuttoning thee after supper, and sleeping upon benches after noon, that thou hast forgotten to demand that truly which thou wouldst truly know. What a devil hast thou to do with the time of the day? Unless hours were cups of sack, and minutes capons, and clocks the tongues of bawds, and dials the signs of leaping-houses, and the blessed sun himself a fair hot wench in flame-coloured taffeta, I see no reason why thou shouldst be so superfluous to demand the time of the day.

FALSTAFF Indeed, you come near me now Hal, for we that take purses go by the moon and the seven stars, and not 'by Phoebus, he, that wandering knight so fair'. And I prithee sweet wag, when thou art King, as God save thy grace – majesty I should say, for grace thou wilt have none –

PRINCE HAL What, none?

FALSTAFF No, by my troth, not so much as will serve to be prologue to an egg and butter.

---

3 *sack*. The precise nature of Falstaff's wine is a matter of dispute. It was probably a generic term for sweet white wines such as sherry and canary (which are confused in response to a cry for sack in a play by Thomas Heywood and William Rowley called *Fortune by Land and Sea*).

4–5 *thou hast forgotten to demand that truly which thou wouldst truly know*. Time for Falstaff is measured by sack and capons and as time is thus meaningless to him, he has not asked about what really concerns him.

6 *What a devil hast thou to do with the time of the day?* Night is Falstaff's time, not day.

9 *leaping-houses* brothels

10 *flame-coloured taffeta*. Prostitutes were traditionally dressed in red taffeta.

11 *superfluous* needlessly concerned (with quibble on the meaning 'self-indulgent')

14 *go by* 'travel by' and 'tell time by' *the seven stars* the Pleiades (and possibly an inn sign)

15 *'by Phoebus, he, that wandering knight so fair'* (possibly a line from a ballad of the time)

17 *grace*. Three meanings are suggested here: refinement; the favour of God – divine grace; majesty. It is given a fourth meaning when Falstaff says, in lines 20–1, that Hal will not have sufficient grace (before food) as would precede so simple a meal as 'an egg and butter'.

PRINCE HAL Well, how then? Come, roundly, roundly.

FALSTAFF Marry then, sweet wag, when thou art King let
not us that are squires of the night's body be called
thieves of the day's beauty. Let us be Diana's foresters,
gentlemen of the shade, minions of the moon. And let
men say we be men of good government, being governed
as the sea is, by our noble and chaste mistress the moon,
under whose countenance we steal.

PRINCE HAL Thou sayest well, and it holds well too, for   30
the fortune of us that are the moon's men doth ebb and
flow like the sea, being governed as the sea is, by the
moon. As for proof? Now, a purse of gold most res-
olutely snatched on Monday night, and most dissolutely
spent on Tuesday morning, got with swearing 'Lay by!',
and spent with crying 'Bring in!', now in as low an ebb

22 *roundly* plainly (and perhaps referring
to Falstaff's girth)

23 *Marry*. This was a very mild oath
derived from the name of Christ's
mother, Mary; it was of such mild-
ness that when oaths were expunged
from the Folio edition, *Marry* was
unaffected. Its force is no more than
the exclamatory use of 'why'.

24 *squires of the night's body* nobleman's
attendants (with a quibble on *night* to
give the meaning 'knight', and *body*,
'bawdy')

25 *thieves of the day's beauty*. The general
sense is clear here, but the precise
sense is a little awkward. Those who
work, or rob, at night waste (rather
than steal) the day. Perhaps they may
be said to rob the day of its beauty
and what it has to offer – its 'booty'.
Diana's foresters. Diana was goddess
of chastity, the moon, and hunting.
Falstaff's concern is not with chastity, needless to say, but with hunting

by moonlight, robbery.

26 *gentlemen of the shade* (an ironic description like that used for a pirate – a
gentleman of fortune – derived perhaps from an honourable title such
as Gentlemen of the Chamber or
Gentlemen-at-Arms)
minions favourites

27 *of good government* orderly, and serving
a good ruler

29 *countenance* (with a quibble on 'face'
and 'patronage') *steal* (both 'rob' and
'go stealthily')

30 *it holds well* the simile is apt

31 *the moon's men*. It has been suggested
that as Queen Elizabeth was frequently described as Diana, this reference might be to her favourites –
whose fortunes certainly ebbed and
flowed.

35 '*Lay by!*' (a robber's or highwayman's
command)

36 '*Bring in!*' (a demand for food and
drink)

as the foot of the ladder, and by and by in as high a flow
as the ridge of the gallows.

FALSTAFF By the Lord thou sayest true lad – and is not
40   my Hostess of the tavern a most sweet wench?

PRINCE HAL As the honey of Hybla, my old lad of the
castle. And is not a buff jerkin a most sweet robe of
durance?

FALSTAFF How now, how now, mad wag? What, in thy
quips and thy quiddities? What a plague have I to do
with a buff jerkin?

PRINCE HAL Why, what a pox have I to do with my
Hostess of the tavern?

FALSTAFF Well, thou hast called her to a reckoning many
50   a time and oft.

36–7 *as low an ebb as the foot of the ladder*.
For the robber, the ebb and flow of
fortune is likened to the low point of
his end, the foot of the ladder leading
up to the gallows, and the high point
of his end, the 'ridge', or crossbar,
from which the hangman will launch
him into eternity.

41 *Hybla*. Hybla Major, near the modern
town of Melilli in Sicily, was famous
for its honey in classical times.

41–2 *old lad of the castle*. This is surely a
pun on Falstaff's original name, Oldcastle (see Introduction, page 242),
and a famous brothel of the time
called The Castle.

42–3 *is not a buff jerkin a most sweet robe
of durance*. A *buff jerkin* was a close-
fitting, leather jacket worn by soldiers; *durance* means long-wearing.
Durance can also mean imprisonment and it is the idea that he might
end up in prison that makes Falstaff
react as he does. In relating the buff
jerkin and durance to the Hostess
and Hyblaean honey in this way, Hal

is being ironically critical of Falstaff's
attitudes. Subtly, here and elsewhere,
Shakespeare distinguishes the natures
of the two characters one from another, making it clear that the Prince
is not wholly involved in the ways
of the world he has temporarily
adopted.

44 *wag* habitual joker. The word is repeated in line 58 and this leads in to
Falstaff's request regarding hanging.
There is possibly a suggestion here
of 'waghalter' – one destined to
hang.

45 *quiddities* quibbles

47 *what a pox*. The exclamation is given
a particular point by its venereal association with the 'Hostess of the
tavern'. The prince's exclamation
echoes Falstaff's 'What a plague' in
the preceding line.

49 *called her to a reckoning* 'asked for the
bill', and also, 'demanded that she
give an account of herself' (with
sexual implications)

PRINCE HAL Did I ever call for thee to pay thy part?

FALSTAFF No, I'll give thee thy due, thou hast paid all there.

PRINCE HAL Yea, and elsewhere, so far as my coin would stretch, and where it would not I have used my credit.

FALSTAFF Yea, and so used it that were it not here apparent that thou art heir apparent – but I prithee sweet wag, shall there be gallows standing in England when thou art King? And resolution thus fubbed as it is with the rusty curb of old Father Antic the law? Do not thou   60
when thou art King hang a thief.

PRINCE HAL No, thou shalt.

FALSTAFF Shall I? O rare! By the Lord, I'll be a brave judge!

PRINCE HAL Thou judgest false already! I mean thou shalt have the hanging of the thieves, and so become a rare hangman.

FALSTAFF Well, Hal, well! And in some sort it jumps with my humour – as well as waiting in the court, I can tell you.   70

PRINCE HAL For obtaining of suits?

FALSTAFF Yea, for obtaining of suits, whereof the hangman hath no lean wardrobe. 'Sblood, I am as melancholy as a gib cat, or a lugged bear.

---

59 *resolution* enterprise
   fubbed fobbed off, cheated
60 *old Father Antic the law*. An Antic was, in Tudor drama, a clown, and thus Falstaff makes himself ridiculous by speaking of the law in terms which describe himself.
63 *brave* fine
65–6 *thou shalt have the hanging of the thieves*. Falstaff takes this to mean that he will be made hangman but Hal presumably also implies that Falstaff shall suffer the fate of all thieves

in those days, hanging.
68 *jumps* agrees
69 *court* (1) king's court (as a courtier); (2) courts of justice
71 *suits* preferment at court
72 *suits* the condemned man's clothing (to which the executioner was entitled)
73 *no lean wardrobe* (because there are plenty of hangings)
   'Sblood God's blood (an oath)
74 *gib cat* castrated male cat
   lugged baited

PRINCE HAL Or an old lion, or a lover's lute.

FALSTAFF Yea, or the drone of a Lincolnshire bagpipe.

PRINCE HAL What sayest thou to a hare, or the melancholy of Moorditch?

FALSTAFF Thou hast the most unsavoury similes, and art
80   indeed the most comparative rascalliest sweet young
prince. But Hal, I prithee trouble me no more with
vanity. I would to God thou and I knew where a commodity of good names were to be bought. An old lord of
the Council rated me the other day in the street about
you, sir, but I marked him not, and yet he talked very
wisely, but I regarded him not, and yet he talked wisely
– and in the street too.

PRINCE HAL Thou didst well, for wisdom cries out in the
streets and no man regards it.

76 *drone of a Lincolnshire bagpipe.* This is
a very puzzling reference. It is possible that Shakespeare is referring to
the sound of frogs or bitterns, but
the word *drone* is particularly inexact
for their croaking and booming.
There was probably no such instrument as a Lincolnshire bagpipe,
though bagpipes seem to have been
played on festive occasions in Lincolnshire and Lancashire and we
have references to this practice in
Shakespeare's time (one by the man
who probably played Touchstone,
Feste and Lear's Fool – Robert Armin).
The only known bagpipe associated
with an English county is the Northumbrian bagpipe, but this seems to have
been developed a little later. Further,
it is hardly melancholy and does not
have an obtrusive drone. And had
Shakespeare heard of this bagpipe he
would surely have related it to Hotspur. A final possibility is that Shakespeare had in mind the drone of a
long-winded speaker. 'Bagpipe' is recorded as being used with this meaning in 1603 (compare 'windbag').

77 *hare.* The hare was traditionally melancholic, but *hare* here also meant
'whore'.

78 *Moorditch* (a filthy channel between
Bishopsgate and Cripplegate, traditionally associated with melancholy
– and with, probably, a suggestion
of venereal disease)

80 *comparative* abusive (one who compares adversely – see also III.2.67)

82 *vanity* worldly things (see note on
V.3.33)

82–87 *I would to God . . . and in the street
too.* Shakespeare has Falstaff imitate a
Puritan divine.

82–3 *commodity* supply (literally, a means
of raising money)

84 *rated* scolded, rebuked

88–9 *for wisdom cries out in the streets and
no man regards it.* Proverbs 1.20:
'Wisdom crieth without, and putteth
forth her voice in the streets'; and
verse 24: 'Because I have called, and
ye refused, I have stretched out my
hand, and no man regarded.'

FALSTAFF O, thou hast damnable iteration, and art   90
indeed able to corrupt a saint. Thou hast done much
harm upon me, Hal, God forgive thee for it. Before I
knew thee Hal, I knew nothing, and now am I, if a man
should speak truly, little better than one of the wicked.
I must give over this life, and I will give it over. By the
Lord, an I do not I am a villain. I'll be damned for
never a king's son in Christendom.

PRINCE HAL Where shall we take a purse tomorrow,
Jack?

FALSTAFF Zounds, where thou wilt lad, I'll make one; an   100
I do not, call me a villain and baffle me.

PRINCE HAL I see a good amendment of life in thee, from
praying to purse-taking.

FALSTAFF Why Hal, 'tis my vocation, Hal. 'Tis no sin
for a man to labour in his vocation.

    Enter Poins
Poins! Now shall we know if Gadshill have set a

90 *damnable iteration* (the devil's capacity
to quote the Scriptures)
94 *the wicked* (again in imitation of the
current Puritan jargon)
95 *I must give over this life*. Oldcastle
(Falstaff's original name – see Introduction, page 242) was a Lollard
(follower of John Wycliffe) and thus
a heretic. It is possible that there is
an allusion here to the original Oldcastle. It might have been humour of
this kind, as much as the name itself,
to which Oldcastle's descendants
objected.
100 *Zounds* God's wounds (an oath)
    an if
101 *baffle*. A knight who perjured himself was baffled, that is, degraded by
being hanged upside down. An
effigy, or the knight's shield, might
be used in place of the knight

himself.
104–5 *'Tis no sin for a man to labour in his
vocation*. This text, much favoured by
Elizabethan divines, was one which
secular writers took much delight in
perverting.
106 *Gadshill*. In *The Famous Victories of
Henry the Fifth* (see Introduction,
pages 243–4) the thief is hailed by
Derrick in the second scene as 'Gads
Hill': 'Whoop hollo! Now Gads Hill,
knowest thou me?' When he is tried
in the fourth scene 'for setting upon
a poor Carrier upon Gads Hill in
Kent, and having beaten and
wounded the said Carrier, and taken
his goods from him', he is called
Cutbert Cutter. Shakespeare takes as
a proper name the nickname used in
the second scene.
106–7 *set a match* planned a robbery

match! O, if men were to be saved by merit, what
hole in hell were hot enough for him? This is the most
omnipotent villain that ever cried 'Stand!' to a true man.

110   PRINCE HAL Good morrow, Ned.

POINS Good morrow, sweet Hal. What says Monsieur
Remorse? What says Sir John Sack – and Sugar? Jack!
How agrees the devil and thee about thy soul, that thou
soldest him on Good Friday last, for a cup of Madeira
and a cold capon's leg?

PRINCE HAL Sir John stands to his word, the devil shall
have his bargain, for he was never yet a breaker of
proverbs. He will give the devil his due.

POINS Then art thou damned for keeping thy word with
120   the devil.

PRINCE HAL Else he had been damned for cozening the
devil.

POINS But my lads, my lads, tomorrow morning, by four
o'clock early at Gad's Hill, there are pilgrims going to
Canterbury with rich offerings and traders riding to
London with fat purses. I have vizards for you all – you
have horses for yourselves. Gadshill lies tonight in
Rochester. I have bespoke supper tomorrow night in
Eastcheap. We may do it as secure as sleep. If you will

---

107 *merit* personal quality or good
works (more frequently the latter)
which entitle one to reward from
God. In *Love's Labour's Lost* the Princess maintains that her beauty 'will
be saved by merit' (IV.1.201).

109 *a true* an honest

112 *Sack – and Sugar*. To further sweeten
sack (see note to line 3) was regarded
as a sign of advancing years.

118 *He will give the devil his due*. The
devil's due will be Falstaff himself –
and in this way Falstaff will break no
proverb.

121 *cozening* cheating

124 *Gad's Hill*. This was a place notori-

ous for robberies, two miles from
Rochester in Kent. It is after this
place, where he practised his vocation,
that the character Gadshill is named.

126 *vizards* masks

129 *Eastcheap*. This is the scene for II.4.
A tavern in Eastcheap is referred to
in *The Famous Victories of Henry the
Fifth* but it is never named by Shakespeare. The traditional name, the
Boar's Head, is, however, suggested
in *2 Henry IV* when Hal asks after
Falstaff: *Doth the old boar feed in the
old frank?*, and Bardolph replies: *At
the old place, my lord, in Eastcheap*
(II.2.141).

go, I will stuff your purses full of crowns. If you will   130
not, tarry at home and be hanged.

FALSTAFF Hear ye, Yedward, if I tarry at home and go
not, I'll hang you for going.

POINS You will, chops?

FALSTAFF Hal, wilt thou make one?

PRINCE HAL Who I? Rob? I a thief? Not I, by my faith.

FALSTAFF There's neither honesty, manhood, nor good
fellowship in thee, nor thou camest not of the blood
royal, if thou darest not stand for ten shillings.

PRINCE HAL Well then, once in my days I'll be a mad-   140
cap.

FALSTAFF Why, that's well said.

PRINCE HAL Well, come what will, I'll tarry at home.

FALSTAFF By the Lord, I'll be a traitor then, when thou
art King.

PRINCE HAL I care not.

POINS Sir John, I prithee leave the Prince and me alone.
I will lay him down such reasons for this adventure that
he shall go.

FALSTAFF Well, God give thee the spirit of persuasion,   150
and him the ears of profiting, that what thou speakest
may move, and what he hears may be believed, that the
true prince may – for recreation sake – prove a false
thief, for the poor abuses of the time want countenance.

---

132 *Yedward* Edward
134 *chops* fat cheeks
139 *royal* (with a quibble on the meaning
    'a coin worth ten shillings')
    stand for (1) be worth; (2) make a
    fight for
150–54 *God give thee the spirit of persuasion
    . . . want countenance* (further imitation
    of Puritan pulpit oratory)
153 *for recreation sake* for amusement
154 *the poor abuses of the time want coun-
    tenance.* Some *abuses of the time* were
    certainly given countenance by Puri-

tans at this time but they were not
those which Falstaff, or Shakespeare,
had in mind as needing attention.
Philip Stubbes's *The Anatomy of
Abuses* (1583) was a violent attack
upon the stage. The players were,
said Stubbes, 'painted sepulchres'
and the plays they presented, did
they not 'maintain bawdry, infinite
foolery, and renew the remembrance
of heathen idolatry?' and did. they
not 'induce whoredom and unclean-
ness?'

Farewell, you shall find me in Eastcheap.

PRINCE HAL Farewell, the latter spring! Farewell, All-
hallow summer!   *Exit Falstaff*

POINS Now my good sweet honey lord, ride with us
tomorrow. I have a jest to execute that I cannot manage
alone. Falstaff, Bardolph, Peto, and Gadshill shall rob
those men that we have already waylaid – yourself and I
will not be there. And when they have the booty, if you
and I do not rob them – cut this head off from my
shoulders.

PRINCE HAL How shall we part with them in setting
forth?

POINS Why, we will set forth before or after them, and
appoint them a place of meeting – wherein it is at our
pleasure to fail – and then will they adventure upon
the exploit themselves, which they shall have no sooner
achieved but we'll set upon them.

PRINCE HAL Yea, but 'tis like that they will know us by
our horses, by our habits, and by every other appointment to be ourselves.

POINS Tut, our horses they shall not see, I'll tie them in
the wood. Our vizards we will change after we leave
them. And, sirrah, I have cases of buckram for the nonce,
to immask our noted outward garments.

PRINCE HAL Yea, but I doubt they will be too hard for
us.

POINS Well, for two of them, I know them to be as true-

---

156 *the latter spring* youthful old age

156–7 *All-hallow summer* fine weather
about All Saints' Day (1 November)

173 *habits* clothing

173–4 *appointment* accoutrement

177 *sirrah*. Here *sirrah* is used as a
familiar form of 'sir'. It can be used
to imply 'villain', as it is at 1.3.116.
cases of buckram 'rough cloth suits',

or perhaps 'overalls'. Buckram could
be stiffened with glue and *case* suggests that this was so here.
nonce occasion

178 *immask* hide (a word peculiar to
Shakespeare)
noted well-known

179 *hard* strong

bred cowards as ever turned back, and for the third, if
he fight longer than he sees reason, I'll forswear arms.
The virtue of this jest will be the incomprehensible lies
that this same fat rogue will tell us when we meet at
supper. How thirty at least he fought with, what wards,
what blows, what extremities he endured, and in the
reproof of this lives the jest.

PRINCE HAL Well, I'll go with thee. Provide us all things
necessary and meet me tomorrow night in Eastcheap.   190
There I'll sup. Farewell.

POINS Farewell, my lord.   *Exit*

PRINCE HAL
I know you all, and will awhile uphold
The unyoked humour of your idleness.
Yet herein will I imitate the sun,
Who doth permit the base contagious clouds
To smother up his beauty from the world,
That when he please again to be himself,

---

184 *incomprehensible* infinite, beyond com-
prehension
186 *wards* postures of defence (a fencing
term)
188 *reproof* disproof
190 *tomorrow night*. The meeting at Gad's
Hill is to be the following morning;
it is at the tavern in Eastcheap that
they will all meet on the next
evening.
193–215 *I know you all . . . Redeeming time
when men think least I will*. This speech
is considered in detail in the Introduction, pages 233–5.
194 *unyoked humour* unbridled inclination
195 *the sun*. Like the eagle and the lion
(see III.3.147), the sun was a traditional symbol of royalty. When Richard is forced to obey Henry IV when
the latter is still Henry Bolingbroke,
this image, as 'glistering Phaethon',

is brilliantly combined with the physical descent of the king from the
battlements of the castle, where he
stands, to the 'base' court:

*Down, down I come like glistering
Phaethon,*
Wanting the manage of unruly jades.
*In the base-court – base court, where
kings grow base*
*To come at traitors' calls, and do them
grace.*
*In the base court. Come down – down
court, down King,*
*For night-owls shriek where mounting
larks should sing.*
    Richard II, III.3.178–83

It is noticeable that here Hal is only
imitating the sun: he is not actually
King yet.

Being wanted, he may be more wondered at
200   By breaking through the foul and ugly mists
Of vapours that did seem to strangle him.
If all the year were playing holidays,
To sport would be as tedious as to work;
But when they seldom come, they wished-for come,
And nothing pleaseth but rare accidents.
So when this loose behaviour I throw off,
And pay the debt I never promisèd,
By how much better than my word I am,
By so much shall I falsify men's hopes.
210   And like bright metal on a sullen ground,
My reformation, glittering o'er my fault,
Shall show more goodly, and attract more eyes
Than that which hath no foil to set it off.
I'll so offend, to make offence a skill,
Redeeming time when men think least I will.

Exit

I.3   *Enter the King, Northumberland, Worcester, Hot-*
           spur, Sir Walter Blunt, with others

KING HENRY
My blood hath been too cold and temperate,
Unapt to stir at these indignities,
And you have found me – for accordingly
You tread upon my patience. But be sure
I will from henceforth rather be myself,

---

201 *strangle* stifle
205 *accidents* incidental occasions
210 *sullen ground* dull background
215 *Redeeming time* making amends for
     wasted time (perhaps suggested by
     Ephesians 5.16, 'Redeeming the time,
     because the days are evil')

I.3 This scene is presumably the meeting

of the Council ordered at 1.1.102–3, and
in this it accords with Shakespeare's
source, Holinshed.
3 *found me* found me so
5 *be myself.* The precise nature of kingship is frequently discussed in drama
   of the Elizabethan and Jacobean
   period. A king had two selves: one
   was human, one royal (and perhaps

Mighty, and to be feared, than my condition,
Which hath been smooth as oil, soft as young down,
And therefore lost that title of respect
Which the proud soul ne'er pays but to the proud.

WORCESTER
Our house, my sovereign liege, little deserves   10
The scourge of greatness to be used on it,
And that same greatness too which our own hands
Have helped to make so portly.

NORTHUMBERLAND   My lord —

KING HENRY
Worcester, get thee gone, for I do see
Danger and disobedience in thine eye.
O sir, your presence is too bold and peremptory,
And majesty might never yet endure
The moody frontier of a servant brow.
You have good leave to leave us. When we need
Your use and counsel we shall send for you.   20

                              Exit Worcester

(*To Northumberland*) You were about to speak.

NORTHUMBERLAND   Yea, my good lord.
Those prisoners in your highness' name demanded,

---

divine). Separating these two selves is dramatized in *Richard II* (and was enacted before an even larger audience at the execution of Charles I). Henry is now resorting to his regal self, 'Mighty, and to be feared', abandoning his humane self, 'soft as young down'. The regal Richard is strikingly contrasted with the human being in the opening scenes of *Richard II*.

6 *condition* natural disposition

12–13 *that same greatness too which our own hands | Have helped to make so portly*. The Percies (of which the Earl of Worcester was one) had been largely instrumental in enabling Henry, as Bolingbroke, to regain his lands, and had then supported his usurpation of the throne. In all this, it is Northumberland who plays the major role in *Richard II*. Worcester does not appear (although he is mentioned) and Hotspur's part is small, though he recalls his first meeting with Henry later in this scene (lines 239–50).

13 *portly* stately

18 *moody frontier of a servant brow* angry defiance of a subject's frown

Which Harry Percy here at Holmedon took,
Were, as he says, not with such strength denied
As is delivered to your majesty.
Either envy therefore, or misprision,
Is guilty of this fault, and not my son.

HOTSPUR

My liege, I did deny no prisoners.
But I remember when the fight was done,
When I was dry with rage and extreme toil,
Breathless and faint, leaning upon my sword,
Came there a certain lord, neat and trimly dressed,
Fresh as a bridegroom, and his chin new reaped
Showed like a stubble-land at harvest-home.
He was perfumèd like a milliner,
And 'twixt his finger and his thumb he held
A pouncet-box, which ever and anon
He gave his nose, and took it away again –
Who therewith angry, when it next came there,
Took it in snuff. And still he smiled and talked.
And as the soldiers bore dead bodies by,

30

40

---

25 *delivered* reported
26 *envy* malice
  misprision misunderstanding
28–68 *My liege, I did deny no prisoners . . .*
  Betwixt my love and your high majesty.
  The rhythm of Hotspur's speech is
  particularly varied. The first line has
  been made a flatter denial than the
  punctuation of Q1 might suggest.
  Q1 concludes the line with a comma
  but the nature of Hotspur's statement
  demands a stop here. The division of
  lines 31–3 is almost imitative of the
  breathlessness of which Hotspur
  speaks but this gives way to lines
  which run on into those that follow.
  Then, from line 48, the rhythm suggests Hotspur's short-temperedness.

The three lines beginning with 'And
(54, 56, 58) give vent to the force of
Hotspur's feelings; there is no pausing as he hastens on from indignity
to absurdity. Hotspur's rhetoric is
more fully examined in the Introduction, pages 236–41.
33 *new reaped* freshly barbered
34 *stubble-land at harvest-home.* His beard
  was closely clipped; not 'unkempt',
  of course.
37 *pouncet-box.* This was a word of Shakespeare's own for a small box with a
  perforated lid. It held snuff, made
  possibly of powdered tobacco or,
  more probably, aromatic herbs.
40 *Took it in snuff* (1) was angry; (2)
  snuffed it up

He called them untaught knaves, unmannerly,
To bring a slovenly unhandsome corpse
Betwixt the wind and his nobility.
With many holiday and lady terms
He questioned me, amongst the rest demanded
My prisoners in your majesty's behalf.
I then, all smarting with my wounds being cold,
To be so pestered with a popinjay,
Out of my grief and my impatience   50
Answered neglectingly, I know not what,
He should, or he should not, for he made me mad
To see him shine so brisk, and smell so sweet,
And talk so like a waiting-gentlewoman
Of guns, and drums, and wounds, God save the mark!
And telling me the sovereignest thing on earth
Was parmacity for an inward bruise,
And that it was great pity, so it was,
This villainous saltpetre should be digged
Out of the bowels of the harmless earth,   60
Which many a good tall fellow had destroyed
So cowardly, and but for these vile guns
He would himself have been a soldier.
This bald unjointed chat of his, my lord,
I answered indirectly, as I said,
And I beseech you, let not his report
Come current for an accusation
Betwixt my love and your high majesty.

45 *holiday* not everyday
    lady lady-like
46 *questioned me* conversed with me
49 *popinjay* parrot, prattler
50 *grief* pain
55 *God save the mark!* God avert evil!
    The meaning of *the mark* is uncertain;
    it may be the sign of the cross.
57 *parmacity* (a corruption of spermaceti
    – a fatty substance derived from the

head of the sperm whale – by association with 'Parma city')
59 *saltpetre* (used in the manufacture of
    gunpowder)
61 *tall* valiant
65 *indirectly* without paying him full
    attention
67 *Come current* be accepted at its face
    value

BLUNT
    The circumstance considered, good my lord,
70   Whate'er Lord Harry Percy then had said
    To such a person, and in such a place,
    At such a time, with all the rest retold,
    May reasonably die, and never rise
    To do him wrong, or any way impeach
    What then he said, so he unsay it now.

KING HENRY
    Why, yet he doth deny his prisoners,
    But with proviso and exception,
    That we at our own charge shall ransom straight
    His brother-in-law, the foolish Mortimer,
80   Who, on my soul, hath wilfully betrayed
    The lives of those that he did lead to fight
    Against that great magician, damned Glendower,
    Whose daughter, as we hear, that Earl of March
    Hath lately married. Shall our coffers then
    Be emptied to redeem a traitor home?
    Shall we buy treason, and indent with fears
    When they have lost and forfeited themselves?
    No, on the barren mountains let him starve.
    For I shall never hold that man my friend

---

74 *wrong* injury
   impeach discredit
76 *yet* (emphasized – 'despite all this')
79 *brother-in-law*. As noted at 1.1.38, there were two Edmund Mortimers and these Holinshed and Shakespeare confused. Glendower's daughter was married to Sir Edmund Mortimer (1376–1409), brother of Roger Mortimer, already dead at this time, and Elizabeth, whom Hotspur married (though Shakespeare calls her Kate – and Holinshed Eleanor). See also the note below to line 83.
83 *that Earl of March*. This is the reading of the first two quartos. The later

quartos and the Folio read 'the' but 'that' makes the relationship to Mortimer more obvious. As mentioned in the preceding note, Shakespeare was confused over the relationship of the Mortimers. The Earl of March, alive at the time of the play, was the son of Roger Mortimer (Hotspur's brother-in-law) but he had the same name, Edmund, as his uncle (another brother-in-law to Hotspur). This Earl of March was *not* married to Glendower's daughter.
86 *indent* bargain
   fears 'things feared', and also, 'cowards'

Whose tongue shall ask me for one penny cost   90
To ransom home revolted Mortimer.

HOTSPUR

Revolted Mortimer!
He never did fall off, my sovereign liege,
But by the chance of war. To prove that true
Needs no more but one tongue for all those wounds,
Those mouthèd wounds, which valiantly he took,
When on the gentle Severn's sedgy bank,
In single opposition hand to hand,
He did confound the best part of an hour
In changing hardiment with great Glendower.   100
Three times they breathed, and three times did they
     drink
Upon agreement of swift Severn's flood,
Who then affrighted with their bloody looks
Ran fearfully among the trembling reeds,
And hid his crisp head in the hollow bank,
Bloodstained with these valiant combatants.
Never did bare and rotten policy
Colour her working with such deadly wounds,
Nor never could the noble Mortimer
Receive so many, and all willingly.   110
Then let not him be slandered with revolt.

KING HENRY

Thou dost belie him, Percy, thou dost belie him,
He never did encounter with Glendower.
I tell thee, he durst as well have met the devil alone
As Owen Glendower for an enemy.

---

91 *revolted* rebellious
96 *mouthèd wounds*. Compare 1.1.5: 'the
    thirsty entrance of this soil' and the
    note thereon.
97 *sedgy* bordered with reeds and rushes
99 *confound* spend, consume
100 *changing hardiment* each displaying his
    valour to the other
105 *crisp* (1) curled; (2) rippled
    head (1) surface; (2) pressure of water
    (a head of water)
107 *bare* beggarly (and perhaps 'bare-
    faced')
    policy expediency
112 *belie* slander

Art thou not ashamed? But sirrah, henceforth
Let me not hear you speak of Mortimer.
Send me your prisoners with the speediest means –
Or you shall hear in such a kind from me
120 As will displease you. My Lord Northumberland:
We license your departure with your son.
Send us your prisoners, or you will hear of it.

Exit the King with Blunt and train

HOTSPUR
And if the devil come and roar for them
I will not send them. I will after straight
And tell him so, for I will ease my heart,
Albeit I make a hazard of my head.

NORTHUMBERLAND
What? Drunk with choler? Stay, and pause awhile,
Here comes your uncle.

Enter Worcester

HOTSPUR   Speak of Mortimer?
Zounds, I will speak of him, and let my soul
130 Want mercy if I do not join with him.
Yea, on his part I'll empty all these veins
And shed my dear blood, drop by drop in the dust,
But I will lift the down-trod Mortimer
As high in the air as this unthankful King,
As this ingrate and cankered Bolingbroke.

NORTHUMBERLAND
Brother, the King hath made your nephew mad.

---

116 *sirrah* (used scornfully; compare the usage at 1.2.177)
119 *kind* manner
123 *if the devil come and roar for them.* This line has been likened to the 'roaring devil' of the old Morality plays, but it is no more than the extravagant reaction we might expect to what Hotspur doubtless considers to be the King's 'bald unjointed chat'.
124 *I will after straight* I'll immediately chase after him
130 *Want mercy* be damned
135 *cankered* rotten to the core
Bolingbroke (Henry IV's name – as used in *Richard II*)
136 *Brother, the King hath made your nephew mad* (ironic understatement)

WORCESTER

Who struck this heat up after I was gone?

HOTSPUR

He will forsooth have all my prisoners,
And when I urged the ransom once again
Of my wife's brother, then his cheek looked pale,   140
And on my face he turned an eye of death,
Trembling even at the name of Mortimer.

WORCESTER

I cannot blame him. Was not he proclaimed,
By Richard that dead is, the next of blood?

NORTHUMBERLAND

He was, I heard the proclamation.
And then it was, when the unhappy King –
Whose wrongs in us God pardon! – did set forth
Upon his Irish expedition;
From whence he, intercepted, did return
To be deposed, and shortly murderèd.   150

WORCESTER

And for whose death we in the world's wide mouth

---

140 *brother* (see the notes to lines 83 and 154)

141 *an eye of death.* The meaning is not quite certain. It could mean 'an eye threatening death' but it more probably means 'an eye of mortal fear'.

144 *next of blood* heir to the throne

147 *in us* done by us

148 *Irish expedition.* Henry IV (when still Bolingbroke) returned to England from his banishment whilst Richard was engaged in suppressing a rebellion in Ireland.

149–50 *From whence he, intercepted, did return | To be deposed, and shortly murderèd.* Northumberland's summary gives little indication of the part he played in Richard's deposition, particularly the treacherous interception of Richard in which he was involved. An Elizabethan audience hearing these words would not, however, be unmindful of the part he had played and the way that Shakespeare had dramatized him in *Richard II.* The audience's sympathies would not easily be aroused for the Percies, and this must particularly reflect upon the way in which Hotspur would be seen, even though his part in the deposition of Richard was so small.

151–2 *we in the world's wide mouth | Live scandalized.* Worcester seems to imply that public opinion misjudges the Percies. This is only true to the extent that Henry must share the blame, but Shakespeare, in this play, is subtly insulating Henry from his share in Richard's deposition (see especially his description of his and Richard's behaviour in III.2.50–73).

Live scandalized and foully spoken of.

HOTSPUR

But soft, I pray you, did King Richard then
Proclaim my brother Edmund Mortimer
Heir to the crown?

NORTHUMBERLAND He did, myself did hear it.

HOTSPUR

Nay then, I cannot blame his cousin King
That wished him on the barren mountains starve.
But shall it be that you that set the crown
Upon the head of this forgetful man,
160   And for his sake wear the detested blot
Of murderous subornation – shall it be
That you a world of curses undergo,
Being the agents, or base second means,
The cords, the ladder, or the hangman rather?
O pardon me, that I descend so low,
To show the line and the predicament
Wherein you range under this subtle King!
Shall it for shame be spoken in these days,
Or fill up chronicles in time to come,
170   That men of your nobility and power
Did gage them both in an unjust behalf –
As both of you, God pardon it, have done –
To put down Richard, that sweet lovely rose,

---

154 *Proclaim my brother*. The heirs proclaimed by Richard II were the Earls
of March (Roger, then Edmund). By
confusing the two Edmunds, Shakespeare took Glendower's prisoner to
be Earl of March and rightful heir to
the throne. (The true Earl of March
was, in fact, loyal to Henry IV and
Henry V.) See also note to line 83.

161 *murderous subornation* aiding and abet-
ting murder

164 *The cords, the ladder, or the hangman
rather?* The imagery used here first
suggests means of ascent (*cords,*

ladder) and from this it is an easy leap
to *hangman*.

165 *I descend so low*. Carrying on the hanging image, Hotspur 'drops' his tone.

166 *line* degree (and continuing the sense
of 'cords' in line 164)
predicament (1) category; (2) the
danger in which they find themselves

167 *range* are classified (according to
'line' – degree – and 'predicament' –
category)

171 *gage them both* pledge both (the 'nobility and power' of the preceding line)

And plant this thorn, this canker Bolingbroke?
And shall it in more shame be further spoken,
That you are fooled, discarded, and shook off
By him for whom these shames ye underwent?
No, yet time serves wherein you may redeem
Your banished honours, and restore yourselves
Into the good thoughts of the world again: 180
Revenge the jeering and disdained contempt
Of this proud King, who studies day and night
To answer all the debt he owes to you,
Even with the bloody payment of your deaths.
Therefore, I say –

WORCESTER   Peace, cousin, say no more.
And now I will unclasp a secret book,
And to your quick-conceiving discontents
I'll read you matter deep and dangerous,
As full of peril and adventurous spirit
As to o'er-walk a current roaring loud   190
On the unsteadfast footing of a spear.

HOTSPUR
If he fall in, good night, or sink, or swim!
Send danger from the east unto the west,
So honour cross it from the north to south,
And let them grapple. O, the blood more stirs
To rouse a lion than to start a hare!

NORTHUMBERLAND
Imagination of some great exploit

---

174 *canker* the wild- or dog-rose (contrasted with Richard, the 'sweet
lovely [garden] rose', line 173); and
also, both 'canker-worm' (which infects the rose) and 'ulcer'
181 *disdained* disdainful
187 *quick-conceiving discontents* discontented minds ready to catch the
meaning
190–91 *As to o'er-walk a current roaring*

*loud | On the unsteadfast footing of
a spear.* A reference to a typical peril
of medieval romances in which the
knight crosses a perilous bridge.
192 *If he fall in, good night, or sink, or
swim* (a knight falling from such a
bridge is doomed, whether he sink
or swim)
194 *So* provided that
196 *rouse ... start* (from cover)

Drives him beyond the bounds of patience.

HOTSPUR

By heaven, methinks it were an easy leap

200   To pluck bright honour from the pale-faced moon,
Or dive into the bottom of the deep,
Where fathom-line could never touch the ground,
And pluck up drownèd honour by the locks,
So he that doth redeem her thence might wear
Without corrival all her dignities.
But out upon this half-faced fellowship!

WORCESTER

He apprehends a world of figures here,
But not the form of what he should attend.
Good cousin, give me audience for a while.

HOTSPUR

I cry you mercy.

210   WORCESTER   Those same noble Scots
That are your prisoners –

HOTSPUR   I'll keep them all!
By God he shall not have a Scot of them,
No, if a scot would save his soul he shall not.
I'll keep them, by this hand!

WORCESTER   You start away,

200 *bright honour*. The equation of Hotspur with honour is belied by the
language in which he expresses himself. His extravagance and his use of
clichés (particularly diving to an un-
fathomed depth) make him appear
ridiculous. Similarly, his frequent
return to the subject of his prisoners,
and the way in which his uncle reacts
to him (lines 231–2), and his father's
impatience (lines 233–5), clearly reveal
his immaturity. His undoubted valour
sorts incongruously with his boyish
petulance and we cannot take his
adoration of honour at its face value.

203 *locks* hair (but honour with flowing
locks is ridiculous)

205 *corrival* equal
206 *half-faced fellowship*. Hotspur is self-
ishly concerned with monopolizing
honour – he has no wish to share it.
Unless he has it all (both sides of the
coin) it will be incomplete so far as
he is concerned.

207 *apprehends* snatches at
figures figures of speech, and also,
vain imaginings

208 *form* true meaning

213 *if a scot* if a small amount (a 'scot'
was a small payment)

214 *You start away*. It is small animals
that start – the hare, not the royal
lion; the distinction has been made
at line 196.

And lend no ear unto my purposes.
Those prisoners you shall keep –

HOTSPUR   Nay, I will. That's flat!
He said he would not ransom Mortimer,
Forbade my tongue to speak of Mortimer,
But I will find him when he lies asleep,
And in his ear I'll holla 'Mortimer!'   220
Nay, I'll have a starling shall be taught to speak
Nothing but 'Mortimer', and give it him
To keep his anger still in motion.

WORCESTER
Hear you, cousin, a word.

HOTSPUR
All studies here I solemnly defy,
Save how to gall and pinch this Bolingbroke.
And that same sword-and-buckler Prince of Wales –
But that I think his father loves him not
And would be glad he met with some mischance –
I would have him poisoned with a pot of ale.   230

WORCESTER
Farewell, kinsman. I'll talk to you
When you are better tempered to attend.

NORTHUMBERLAND
Why, what a wasp-stung and impatient fool
Art thou to break into this woman's mood,
Tying thine ear to no tongue but thine own!

HOTSPUR
Why, look you, I am whipped and scourged with rods,

223 *still* continually
225 *studies* pursuits
    defy renounce
227 *sword-and-buckler*. A *buckler* was a
    small round shield. Hotspur's implica-
    tion is that Hal's tastes are plebeian.
    In Shakespeare's day (though not in
    the time of Henry IV) the sword and
    buckler were no longer used by
    gentlemen, having been replaced by

the rapier and dagger.
230 *pot of ale*. This is another reference
    to the lowliness of Hal's tastes; in
    theory at least, Elizabethan gentle-
    men drank wine.
234 *to break into this woman's mood*. This
    accusation is ironic in view of Hot-
    spur's objection to the 'certain lord'
    who talked 'so like a waiting-gentle-
    woman' (line 54).

Nettled, and stung with pismires, when I hear
Of this vile politician Bolingbroke.
In Richard's time – what do you call the place?
240 A plague upon it, it is in Gloucestershire.
'Twas where the madcap Duke his uncle kept –
His uncle York – where I first bowed my knee
Unto this king of smiles, this Bolingbroke –
'Sblood, when you and he came back from Ravens-
        purgh –

NORTHUMBERLAND
At Berkeley Castle.

HOTSPUR
You say true.
Why, what a candy deal of courtesy
This fawning greyhound then did proffer me!
'Look when his infant fortune came to age',
250 And 'gentle Harry Percy', and 'kind cousin'.
O, the devil take such cozeners – God forgive me!
Good uncle, tell your tale. I have done.

WORCESTER
Nay, if you have not, to it again,

---

237 *pismires* ants
239–46 *In Richard's time...You say true.*
The colloquial urgency of Hotspur's
search for the name of the place
where he first met Bolingbroke
breaks down the metre of the lines
without their completely losing their
shape. Hotspur's animation is skilfully, and attractively, conveyed.
241 *madcap Duke.* The historian Holinshed describes the Duke of York's
love of pleasure rather than business,
but this aspect is not dramatized by
Shakespeare in *Richard II.* Hal says
he will be a *madcap* at 1.2.140–41 and
he is called *madcap* at IV.1.95.
   kept lived, kept up
244 *Ravenspurgh* (near Spurn Head, York-

shire, where Bolingbroke landed;
now covered by the sea)
247 *candy deal* sugary amount
248 *fawning greyhound.* Sweetmeats and
treacherous dogs are frequently associated by Shakespeare – for example,
in *Antony and Cleopatra*:

The hearts
That spanielled me at heels, to whom I
        gave
Their wishes, do discandy, melt their
        sweets
On blossoming Caesar.
IV.12.20–23

251 *cozeners* deceivers (with a quibble on
'coz', cousin)

We will stay your leisure.

HOTSPUR   I have done, i'faith.

WORCESTER
Then once more to your Scottish prisoners.
Deliver them up without their ransom straight,
And make the Douglas' son your only mean
For powers in Scotland, which, for divers reasons
Which I shall send you written, be assured
Will easily be granted. (*To Northumberland*) You my   260
      lord,
Your son in Scotland being thus employed,
Shall secretly into the bosom creep
Of that same noble prelate well-beloved,
The Archbishop.

HOTSPUR   Of York, is it not?

WORCESTER   True, who bears hard
His brother's death at Bristol, the Lord Scroop.
I speak not this in estimation,
As what I think might be, but what I know
Is ruminated, plotted, and set down,
And only stays but to behold the face
Of that occasion that shall bring it on.   270

HOTSPUR
I smell it! Upon my life it will do well!

---

254 *stay* await
257 *the Douglas' son* (the Earl of Fife,
     mistakenly said to be Douglas's son
     – see note to 1.1.71)
259 *Which I shall send you written.* In this
     way Shakespeare avoids giving de-
     tails tedious to relate and unnecessary
     to his major concerns.
262 *secretly into the bosom creep* win the
     confidence
264 *True.* Hotspur's interjection, 'Of
     York, is it not', and the breaking of
     the line into three parts, may suggest
     urgency, but the effect can also be

comic. Worcester's *True* can reveal
pained resignation.
     bears hard takes ill
265 *brother's death.* The William Scrope,
     Earl of Wiltshire, who was executed
     at Bristol by Bolingbroke in *Richard
     II* was a cousin of the Archbishop.
     The Earl's death is reported by his
     brother Sir Stephen Scroop at III.2.
     142 of that play. The error is
     Holinshed's. There is a reference to
     another member of the family in *1
     Henry IV* at IV.4.3.
266 *estimation* conjecture

NORTHUMBERLAND
Before the game is afoot thou still lettest slip.

HOTSPUR
Why, it cannot choose but be a noble plot;
And then the power of Scotland, and of York,
To join with Mortimer, ha?

WORCESTER   And so they shall.

HOTSPUR
In faith it is exceedingly well aimed.

WORCESTER
And 'tis no little reason bids us speed,
To save our heads by raising of a head.
For, bear ourselves as even as we can,
The King will always think him in our debt,
And think we think ourselves unsatisfied,
Till he hath found a time to pay us home.
And see already how he doth begin
To make us strangers to his looks of love.

HOTSPUR
He does, he does, we'll be revenged on him.

WORCESTER
Cousin, farewell. No further go in this
Than I by letters shall direct your course.
When time is ripe, which will be suddenly,
I'll steal to Glendower, and Lord Mortimer,
Where you, and Douglas, and our powers at once,
As I will fashion it, shall happily meet
To bear our fortunes in our own strong arms,
Which now we hold at much uncertainty.

NORTHUMBERLAND
Farewell, good brother. We shall thrive, I trust.

---

272 *thou still lettest slip.* Once again
  Northumberland rebukes his son for
  his childish impetuosity.
274 *power* army
278 *head* army
279 *even* carefully

282 *pay us home* 'pay us out', and perhaps
  also, 'send us to eternity'
288 *suddenly* at once
290 *at once* altogether
294 *thrive* be successful

HOTSPUR

Uncle, adieu. O, let the hours be short,
Till fields, and blows, and groans applaud our sport!

Exeunt

Enter a Carrier with a lantern in his hand II.I

FIRST CARRIER Heigh-ho! An it be not four by the day
I'll be hanged. Charles's Wain is over the new chimney,
and yet our horse not packed. What, Ostler!

OSTLER (*within*) Anon, anon.

FIRST CARRIER I prithee, Tom, beat Cut's saddle, put a
few flocks in the point; poor jade is wrung in the withers
out of all cess.

Enter another Carrier

SECOND CARRIER Peas and beans are as dank here as a
dog, and that is the next way to give poor jades the bots.
This house is turned upside down since Robin Ostler 10
died.

---

296 *fields* battlefields. But if Act II runs
straight on, it is not this applause
that Hotspur's plea receives, but a
mighty yawn from the First
Carrier!

II.I This scene is laid in Rochester,
Kent, early in the morning. The language of the scene depicts remarkably
vividly the uncomfortable, rough world
of ordinary men and women. It presents
the other side of the merry, irresponsible
world of the Tavern in Eastcheap.
1 *by the day* in the morning
2 *Charles's Wain* (the Plough or Great
Bear)
3 *horse* (plural here)

packed loaded with goods (they are
pack-horses)
5 *beat* (to soften)
Cut (a work-horse)
5–6 *put a few flocks in the point* stuff wool
into the saddle-bow (for comfort)
6 *jade* a worn-out horse
wrung in the withers rubbed or bruised
along the ridge between the
shoulder-blades
7 *out of all cess* excessively
8 *Peas and beans* (horse-feed)
dank damp (making an alliterative
jingle with 'dog')
9 *next* quickest
bots stomach worms
10 *house* inn

FIRST CARRIER   Poor fellow never joyed since the price of
oats rose, it was the death of him.

SECOND CARRIER   I think this be the most villainous
house in all London road for fleas, I am stung like a
tench.

FIRST CARRIER   Like a tench! By the mass, there is ne'er
a king Christian could be better bit than I have been
since the first cock.

20   SECOND CARRIER   Why, they will allow us ne'er a
jordan, and then we leak in your chimney, and your
chamber-lye breeds fleas like a loach.

FIRST CARRIER   What, Ostler! Come away, and be
hanged, come away!

SECOND CARRIER   I have a gammon of bacon, and two
razes of ginger, to be delivered as far as Charing Cross.

FIRST CARRIER   God's body! The turkeys in my pannier

12-13 *since the price of oats rose.* There were too many poor harvests in the 1590s, resulting in higher prices, for this to be a specific topical allusion, although the price of oats was particularly high in 1596. It is such a passing reference as this that helps suggest another kind of low life than that shown in the Tavern in Eastcheap.

15-16 *stung like a tench* (stung, as by its markings the tench appears to have been, or because it was thought to breed parasites)

17 *By the mass* (a mild oath, but not sufficiently so to save its being expunged from the Folio – see An Account of the Text)

17-18 *there is ne'er a king Christian could be better bit* there is no Christian king (who might be expected to have the best of things) who could receive more bites

19 *first cock.* By convention, the first cock-crow occurred at midnight; the second at 3 a.m.; and the third, an hour before dawn.

21 *jordan* chamber-pot
leak urinate
chimney fire-place

22 *chamber-lye* urine. The practice described must have been common for it was specifically condemned by a Tudor physician, Andrew Boorde, as early as 1542.
loach. The loach, a small, fresh-water fish, was thought to breed parasites. The word was also a slang term for a simpleton and this meaning may also be implied.

23 *Come away* come along!

26 *razes* roots
Charing Cross. Charing Cross was not at this time a district of London but a village lying between the city and Westminster.

27 *God's body* (another oath omitted from the Folio)

are quite starved. What, Ostler! A plague on thee, hast
thou never an eye in thy head? Canst not hear? An
'twere not as good deed as drink to break the pate on   30
thee, I am a very villain. Come, and be hanged! Hast no
faith in thee?

    Enter Gadshill

GADSHILL Good morrow, carriers, what's o'clock?

FIRST CARRIER I think it be two o'clock.

GADSHILL I prithee lend me thy lantern, to see my
gelding in the stable.

FIRST CARRIER Nay, by God, soft! I know a trick worth
two of that, i'faith.

GADSHILL I pray thee lend me thine.

SECOND CARRIER Ay, when? Canst tell? Lend me thy   40
lantern, quoth he! Marry I'll see thee hanged first.

GADSHILL Sirrah carrier, what time do you mean to come
to London?

SECOND CARRIER Time enough to go to bed with a
candle, I warrant thee! Come, neighbour Mugs, we'll

28–9 *What Ostler! . . . Canst not hear?* It
was the ostler's responsibility to prepare the horses for travellers and to
help them on their way. Evidently
Robin the Ostler was very much better
at this than his successor.

30 *as good deed as drink.* Falstaff uses this
proverbial saying in the next scene
(II.2.21–2). It is a little clearer as
used in *Twelfth Night*:
    SIR ANDREW *'Twere as good a deed as
    to drink when a man's a-hungry, to chal-
    lenge him the field and then to break
    promise with him and make a fool of
    him.*   II.3.122–4

30–31 *the pate on thee* your head

31 *very* true

31–2 *Hast no faith in thee?* can't you be
relied upon?

34 *two o'clock.* That it is four o'clock
was established in the very first line

of the scene. But this is no oversight
on Shakespeare's part. From the first
the Carriers are mistrustful of Gadshill. They are not prepared to give
him the time of the day, never mind
trust him with a lantern. This is an
effective, and very economical, juxtaposition of the workaday world of
the Carriers and that of Gadshill (and
Falstaff).

37 *soft* gently, go easy

40 *Ay, when? Canst tell?* Oh yes, sure.
But *when* do you think you'll get it?
(The statement is tantamount to a
refusal.)

44–5 *Time enough to go to bed with a candle.*
The journey from Rochester to Charing Cross – about 30 miles – would
be a long day's ride with a pack-
horse, but the Carrier is being evasive, again, rather than informative.

call up the gentlemen, they will along with company, for
they have great charge.   *Exeunt Carriers*

GADSHILL   What ho! Chamberlain!

Enter Chamberlain

CHAMBERLAIN   'At hand, quoth pick-purse.'

50   GADSHILL   That's even as fair as 'At hand, quoth the
chamberlain', for thou variest no more from picking of
purses than giving direction doth from labouring. Thou
layest the plot how.

CHAMBERLAIN   Good morrow, Master Gadshill. It holds
current that I told you yesternight. There's a franklin in
the Weald of Kent hath brought three hundred marks
with him in gold – I heard him tell it to one of his
company last night at supper, a kind of auditor, one that
hath abundance of charge too, God knows what. They

60   are up already, and call for eggs and butter. They will
away presently.

GADSHILL   Sirrah, if they meet not with Saint Nicholas'

46   *along with company* travel in a group
(for safety's sake)

47   *great charge* much money (or bag-
gage)

48   *Chamberlain* (servant in charge of
guests' rooms)

49   *'At hand, quoth pick-purse'* 'Ready, said
the pickpocket' (a popular catch-
phrase of the time)

52   *giving direction* 'supervising (the servants' work)', and also, 'planning a
robbery'
labouring (the work of the servants,
and also, that of the robbers)

52–3   *Thou layest the plot how*. The double
meaning here is precisely the same as
for 'giving direction' (line 52). Inn-
servants at the time were frequently
accused of providing robbers with
information about those who stayed
at their inns, giving details of what
they had that was worth stealing, and
whither they were bound and when.

54–5   *It holds current* it's still true

55   *that* what
franklin rich freeholder

56   *Weald of Kent* (the land lying between
the North and South Downs.) The
spelling of Q1 is 'wilde of Kent' but
the spelling of the origin of the word
(Anglo-Saxon *weald*, a forest) is the
same as the modern spelling and it
has been adopted here; 'wilde' gives
a false impression of the sense.
three hundred marks (£200; a mark was
an amount, not a coin – like
a guinea)

58   *auditor* (an official of the Exchequer)

61   *presently* immediately

62–3   *Saint Nicholas' clerks*. This was a
slang expression meaning 'highway-
men'. Saint Nicholas was the patron
saint of, among others, children,
scholars (clerks), and travellers, and
the latter came to include robbers as
well as those upon whom they

clerks, I'll give thee this neck.

CHAMBERLAIN No, I'll none of it, I pray thee keep that
for the hangman, for I know thou worshippest Saint
Nicholas, as truly as a man of falsehood may.

GADSHILL What talkest thou to me of the hangman? If I
hang, I'll make a fat pair of gallows. For if I hang, old
Sir John hangs with me, and thou knowest he is no
starveling. Tut, there are other Troyans that thou   70
dreamest not of, the which for sport sake are content to
do the profession some grace, that would, if matters
should be looked into, for their own credit sake make all
whole. I am joined with no foot-landrakers, no long-
staff sixpenny strikers, none of these mad mustachio
purple-hued maltworms, but with nobility and tranquillity, Burgomasters and great O-yeas, such as can

---

preyed. The saint was depicted as
holding three balls or purses of gold
and it has been suggested that it was
these that made him appear to be a
patron appropriate to robbers. Various puns explaining the association
have also been suggested. Nick can
refer to Old Nick (the devil) or, as a
verb, to cheating and defrauding.
Nicholas also sounds like 'necklace'
– the halter destined for robbers who
were caught.

63 *I'll give thee this neck* you can hang me
68 *fat* full-bodied
70 *Troyans* roisterers, good companions
(like the 'Corinthian' of II.4.11)
72 *the profession* (of highwayman)
74 *foot-landrakers* vagabond footpads
74–5 *long-staff* quarterstaff
75 *sixpenny strikers* footpads who would
hold up a man for sixpence
75–6 *mad mustachio purple-hued maltworms*
roaring, bewhiskered, purple-faced,
drinkers (compare Falstaff's description of Bardolph, III.3.29–47)
77 *great O-yeas*. The word given for *O-
yeas* in Qo and Q1 is 'Oneyres'; the

later quartos and the Folio print
'Oneyers'. Many attempts have been
made to explain this word – to suggest either what it means as it stands
or what it ought to be. The simplest
interpretation has been 'one-ers'
(used by Dickens and still heard colloquially); the most ingenious, that it
comes from an obscure Exchequer
term, 'to ony', meaning to mark the
abbreviation o. ni. (*oneratur, nisi habeat
sufficientem exonerationem*) against a
sheriff's name to show he was responsible for certain moneys. Emendations suggested have included
'Seigniors', 'Moneyers', 'Wan-dyers',
'one-eyers', 'owners', 'mynheers',
'meyers', and, for the whole expression, 'great ones; – yes'. Though the
simple 'one-ers', seems possible, it is
a thin expression in such a rich flow
of language.

It is argued in An Account of the
Text that the men who set the type
of Q1 were skilled craftsmen who
followed their copy. 'Oneyres' must
have seemed to them the word

hold in, such as will strike sooner than speak, and speak
sooner than drink, and drink sooner than pray. And yet,
80   zounds, I lie, for they pray continually to their saint the
commonwealth, or rather not pray to her, but prey on
her, for they ride up and down on her, and make her
their boots.

CHAMBERLAIN What, the commonwealth their boots?
Will she hold out water in foul way?

GADSHILL She will, she will, justice hath liquored her.

intended (which supports 'one-ers')
but it does not guarantee that they
understood the word they set. We
can be fairly certain that 'Oneyres'
closely represents what the word
looked like in the manuscript and
this excludes words of quite different
outline like 'Moneyers'. The likely
word must have been related to 'Burgomasters' in the same line (cf. the
preceding 'nobility and tranquillity'),
it must be capable of being used
ironically, and ideally should fit the
pattern of word-play that follows. It
ought also to be a word Shakespeare
might have used, although he did
create words for a single occasion
(so 'ony-ers' is possible) and he was
not always consistent in his wordplay.

The word that fits these stringent re-
quirements is *O-yeas*. It might well
have been spelt by Shakespeare as it
was sounded – 'Owyres'; 'w', of all
letters in Elizabethan handwriting, is
easily misread as two letters and quite
easily as 'ne'. *O-yeas* imitates the
'Oyez!' of the Town Crier (for whom
it stands), an office that goes well
with that of Burgomaster (the 'o' of
which it incidentally echoes). Shakespeare uses 'oyes' in *The Merry Wives
of Windsor* (v.5.47, rhyming with
'toys') and *Troilus and Cressida* ('On
whose bright crest Fame with her
loud'st oyes | Cries, "This is he!"',

IV.5.142–3) and the expression 'great
O' (= capital O) is also Shakespearian (*cf. Twelfth Night*, II.5.87–8: 'and
thus makes she her great P's'). The
'great O' is surely Falstaff (a 'capital'
crier if ever there was one). The *great
O* of Falstaff (his girth – *such as can
hold in*) is as a cipher, signifying nothing (cf. *King Lear*, 1.4.214). The puns
on 'strike' and 'speak' are given just
the right comic tone and point when
related to Falstaff and there is an
individuality about *O-yeas* which is
lacking in 'one-ers'; and it would
have had a more obvious, and more
direct appeal, than the obscure *ony-
ers*.

78 *hold in.* This is a multiple pun: (1)
keep counsel; (2) stick together; (3)
hold fast to the quarry (a hunting
term); (4) be held within Falstaff's
great girth.

strike rob

speak (second time) (1) swear; (2) rob

83 *boots* booty

85 *hold out water in foul way* remain water-
proof (that is, protect you in
difficulty)

86 *justice hath liquored her.* The general
sense is clear and the pun on *liquored*
is plain enough – 'greased' (as were
boots in order to keep out water),
'bribed', and 'made drunk'. Gadshill
means that he and his companions
will be protected from the full rigour

We steal as in a castle, cock-sure. We have the receipt
of fern-seed, we walk invisible.

CHAMBERLAIN Nay, by my faith, I think you are more
beholding to the night than to fern-seed for your   90
walking invisible.

GADSHILL Give me thy hand, thou shalt have a share in
our purchase, as I am a true man.

CHAMBERLAIN Nay, rather let me have it as you are a
false thief.

GADSHILL Go to, *homo* is a common name to all men.
Bid the ostler bring my gelding out of the stable.
Farewell, you muddy knave.   *Exeunt*

Enter Prince and Poins   II.2
POINS Come, shelter, shelter! I have removed Falstaff's

---

of the law – 'the commonwealth',
line 84 – but *justice* ought to be
equated with 'commonwealth' and
although, in the event, Hal inter-
venes, he is hardly *justice*.

87 *as in a castle* in complete security
(with, perhaps, a reference in the
unrevised version to Oldcastle)
receipt recipe

88 *fern-seed*. Fern-seed was thought to
be visible only on St John's Eve
(Midsummer's Night). If gathered
then it was thought to confer invis-
ibility on whoever carried it.

93 *our purchase* what we obtain by
robbery

93, 95 *true, false* (a repetition of the fairly
simple kind of word-play used by
the Chamberlain in line 66)

96 homo *is a common name to all men.*
Gadshill is prepared to give his word
simply as a man ('*homo*'), for, whether
true or false, all are men. The definition is derived from a Latin grammar
by William Lily and John Colet,
Grammatices Rudimenta, known usu-

ally as *Lily's Latin Grammar* or *The
Accidence*. It was the grammar that
Shakespeare learned from and it is
possible that it is referred to in *The
Merry Wives of Windsor*; Sir Hugh
Evans, at Mistress Page's request,
asks William 'some questions in his
accidence' (IV.1.18).

98 *muddy* dull-witted

II.2 (stage direction) *Enter Prince and
Poins.* Qo has here: *Enter Prince,
Poines, and Peto, &c.* A separate entry
is given for Falstaff (as here) after
Stand Close! The *&c* would imply
Bardolph, but if Peto and Bardolph
were to enter here it would mean
that these two were a party to Poins's
plot for, presumably, they would
hear him tell the Prince that Falstaff's
horse had been removed (line 1, and
Falstaff at lines 11–12) and they
would have to be restrained from
answering Falstaff when he called
them at line 20. Whilst, doubtless,
they would be willing parties to such

horse, and he frets like a gummed velvet.

PRINCE HAL Stand close!

They hide
Enter Falstaff

FALSTAFF Poins! Poins, and be hanged! Poins!

PRINCE HAL (*coming forward*) Peace, ye fat-kidneyed
rascal, what a bawling dost thou keep!

FALSTAFF Where's Poins, Hal?

PRINCE HAL He is walked up to the top of the hill. I'll
go seek him.

He steps to one side

10 FALSTAFF I am accursed to rob in that thief's company.
The rascal hath removed my horse and tied him I know
not where. If I travel but four foot by the square further
afoot, I shall break my wind. Well, I doubt not but to
die a fair death for all this, if I scape hanging for killing
that rogue. I have forsworn his company hourly any
time this two-and-twenty years, and yet I am bewitched
with the rogue's company. If the rascal have not given
me medicines to make me love him, I'll be hanged. It
could not be else. I have drunk medicines. Poins! Hal!
20 A plague upon you both! Bardolph! Peto! I'll starve ere

a deception, it would rather spoil the
private nature of the joke being practised on Falstaff. Furthermore, in II.4
they seem unaware of what the
Prince and Poins have done and their
ignorance is essential to the carrying
out of the deception. It has sometimes been suggested that 'Bardolph'
in line 49 is a speech prefix and that
the speech given him beginning in
line 51 ought to be Gadshill's. This
is an attractive emendation from Qo,
but the case for the change is not
strong enough to justify alteration of
the quarto. The stage direction at
the beginning of the scene, as it is
printed in Qo, ought, perhaps, to be
taken as a general call for those involved in all the to-ing and fro-ing

that this scene demands, much of
which is not indicated in the original
stage directions.

2 *frets like a gummed velvet.* Just as unpiled
fabric could be treated with glue (as
noted at 1.2.177) so could velvet. As
a result it was more inclined to wear
quickly — to *fret* (here also meaning
'be vexed').

3 *Stand close!* hide!

12 *square* (a measuring instrument)

13 *break my wind* pant breathlessly (with
an obscene quibble)

13–14 *to die a fair death for all this* to
make a good end as a result of so
much suffering

18 *medicines* love potions

20 *starve* die

I'll rob a foot further – an 'twere not as good a deed as
drink to turn true man, and to leave these rogues, I am
the veriest varlet that ever chewed with a tooth. Eight
yards of uneven ground is threescore-and-ten miles
afoot with me, and the stony-hearted villains know it
well enough. A plague upon it when thieves cannot be
true one to another!

They whistle

Whew! A plague upon you all. Give me my horse you
rogues, give me my horse and be hanged!

PRINCE HAL (*coming forward*) Peace, ye fat-guts, lie   30
down, lay thine ear close to the ground and list if thou
canst hear the tread of travellers.

FALSTAFF Have you any levers to lift me up again, being
down? 'SBlood, I'll not bear my own flesh so far afoot
again for all the coin in thy father's exchequer. What a
plague mean ye to colt me thus?

PRINCE HAL Thou liest, thou art not colted, thou art
uncolted.

FALSTAFF I prithee good Prince Hal, help me to my
horse, good king's son.   40

PRINCE HAL Out, ye rogue, shall I be your ostler?

FALSTAFF Hang thyself in thine own heir-apparent
garters! If I be taken, I'll peach for this. An I have not

21–22 *as good a deed as drink* (see note to
II.1.30)
22 *true* honest
28 *Whew!* This may represent Falstaff's
breathlessness, but there is comic
business to be derived from his attempting vainly (because out of
breath) to respond to the whistling
of the Prince and Poins.
33 *Have you any levers to lift me up again.*
Although Falstaff is unaware of the
trick about to be played on him, his
capacity to make a joke of his own
size here suggests to the audience
that he too is sharing in the joke.
This has the effect of stressing the

playfulness of the action, robbing it
of any pain (or inhibiting sympathy),
so that an audience can enjoy the
sport to the full.
34 *bear my own flesh* carry my own
weight
afoot on foot
36 *colt* trick
42–3 *Hang thyself in thine own heir-apparent
garters!* The heir apparent was a
Knight of the Garter and Falstaff
has adapted this honour to the popular riposte: 'He may hang himself in
his own garters.'
43 *peach* inform against you (thus saving
himself)

ballads made on you all, and sung to filthy tunes, let a
cup of sack be my poison. When a jest is so forward –
and afoot too – I hate it!

Enter Gadshill, Bardolph, and Peto

GADSHILL Stand!

FALSTAFF So I do, against my will.

POINS O, 'tis our setter, I know his voice. Bardolph, what
news?

BARDOLPH Case ye, case ye, on with your vizards, there's
money of the King's coming down the hill. 'Tis going
to the King's exchequer.

FALSTAFF You lie, ye rogue, 'tis going to the King's
tavern.

GADSHILL There's enough to make us all –

FALSTAFF To be hanged.

PRINCE HAL Sirs, you four shall front them in the narrow
lane. Ned Poins and I will walk lower – if they scape
from your encounter, then they light on us.

PETO How many be there of them?

GADSHILL Some eight or ten.

FALSTAFF Zounds, will they not rob us?

PRINCE HAL What, a coward, Sir John Paunch?

---

44 *ballads.* The ballads to which Falstaff refers are those which were composed to mark special occasions (a victory, a murder, an execution) or to libel enemies. They were printed on broadsides (single sheets of paper) and sold in the street. Music was rarely printed with the ballad but an indication was given of a popular tune appropriate (in terms of its measure and rhythm if not its association) to the words of the new ballad. Such ballads were enormously popular and the practice flourished until late in the nineteenth century – until, that is, the rise of popular, cheap newspapers. Some ballads in the nineteenth century sold between two and three million copies. Figures for Shakespeare's time are not available, but from the number of references to such street ballads it is clear that they were comparably popular. A possible source of the pound of flesh story, used by Shakespeare in *The Merchant of Venice*, is 'The Ballad of the Cruelty of Gernutus', although the story appeared elsewhere. Cleopatra fears that 'scald rimers [will] Ballad us out o'tune' (*Antony and Cleopatra*, v.2.214–15).

45 *is so forward* goes so far

49 *setter* informant

51 *Case ye* disguise yourselves

58 *front* confront

59 *lower* lower down

FALSTAFF Indeed, I am not John of Gaunt your grandfather, but yet no coward, Hal.

PRINCE HAL Well, we leave that to the proof.

POINS Sirrah Jack, thy horse stands behind the hedge.
When thou needest him, there thou shalt find him. Farewell, and stand fast!   70

FALSTAFF Now cannot I strike him, if I should be hanged.

PRINCE HAL (*aside to Poins*) Ned, where are our disguises?

POINS Here, hard by, stand close. *Exeunt Prince and Poins*

FALSTAFF Now, my masters, happy man be his dole, say
I. Every man to his business.

     Enter the Travellers

FIRST TRAVELLER Come, neighbour, the boy shall lead
our horses down the hill. We'll walk afoot awhile and
ease our legs.

THIEVES Stand!   80

SECOND TRAVELLER Jesus bless us!

FALSTAFF Strike, down with them, cut the villains'
throats! Ah, whoreson caterpillars, bacon-fed knaves,
they hate us youth! Down with them, fleece them!

FIRST TRAVELLER O, we are undone, both we and ours
for ever!

---

65 *John of Gaunt*. Falstaff is, of course,
very fat; Hal, according to contemporary descriptions, was tall and thin,
as the descriptions of him at
11.4.240–43 indicate. In *Richard II*,
11.1.74, Hal's grandfather, John of
Gaunt, plays on his name – 'Old
Gaunt indeed, and gaunt in being old'
– and this is probably recalled here.

75 *happy man be his dole* may each man's
lot be one of happiness (a proverbial
expression)

76 *Every man to his business*. This is another proverbial expression, calling
to mind Falstaff's assertion ''Tis no
sin for a man to labour in his vocation' (1.2.104–5).

83 *caterpillars*. These parasites are twice
referred to in *Richard II*. It is the
'caterpillars of the commonwealth'
(11.3.166) who, according to the Gardener, swarm on England's 'wholesome herbs' (111.4.46). It has been
pointed out that Falstaff's abuse is
all applicable to himself.
bacon-fed knaves. Andrew Boorde, the
Tudor physician who condemned
'pissing in chimneys' (see notes to
11.1.22), considered bacon to be good
for carters and ploughmen, 'the
which be ever labouring in the earth
or dung'.

85 *undone* ruined

FALSTAFF Hang ye, gorbellied knaves, are ye undone?
No, ye fat chuffs, I would your store were here! On,
bacons, on! What, ye knaves, young men must live!
90   You are grandjurors, are ye? We'll jure ye, faith.

Here they rob them and bind them

Exeunt

Enter the Prince and Poins, disguised

PRINCE HAL The thieves have bound the true men.
Now, could thou and I rob the thieves, and go merrily to
London, it would be argument for a week, laughter for a
month, and a good jest for ever.

POINS Stand close, I hear them coming.

They hide

Enter the thieves again

FALSTAFF Come my masters, let us share, and then to
horse before day. An the Prince and Poins be not two
arrant cowards there's no equity stirring. There's no
more valour in that Poins than in a wild duck.

*As they are sharing the Prince and Poins set upon
them*

100   PRINCE HAL Your money!

POINS Villains!

*They all run away, and Falstaff after a blow or two
runs away too, leaving the booty behind them*

PRINCE HAL
Got with much ease. Now merrily to horse.

---

87 *gorbellied* pot-bellied
88 *chuffs* (a term of contempt for rich,
and perhaps miserly, men)
your store were here your property were
in your bellies
89 *bacons* fat men (compare 'porkers')
90 *grandjurors* (men of substance who
served on grand juries)
We'll jure ye when we've finished
with you, we shall have given you
reason to serve on a jury. This literary device is still common. Another
good example of its use by Shake-

speare occurs in *Coriolanus*. Referring
to the defeat of Aufidius by Coriolanus, Menenius says: 'I would not
have been so fidiused for all the
chests in Corioles' (II.1.125-6).
91 *true* honest
93 *argument* subject for discussion
97 *An* if
98 *there's no equity stirring* there's no justice in the world
102-8 *Got with much ease ... I should pity
him*. This passage, like a number of
others in the play, is printed as prose

The thieves are all scattered and possessed with fear
So strongly that they dare not meet each other.
Each takes his fellow for an officer!
Away, good Ned! Falstaff sweats to death,
And lards the lean earth as he walks along.
Were it not for laughing I should pity him.
POINS How the fat rogue roared!   *Exeunt*

           Enter Hotspur alone, reading a letter   II.3
HOTSPUR *But for mine own part, my lord, I could be well*
contented to be there, in respect of the love I bear your
house.

---

in Q1. Alexander Pope first arranged
this passage as verse in the eighteenth
century and most editors have followed his practice. It is not always
possible to be sure that such relineation is correct – the passage at
v.3.42–3 is usually regarded as prose
though printed in verse in this edition – and this is particularly true of
very short passages. The problem
arises partly from the state of the
original copy, where lines might be
run one into another, giving rise to
uncertainty in the printing-house,
and partly because a passage of plain
blank verse can read like prose, the
rhythm of such verse not being
unlike rather formal English speech.
In the case of one dramatist of the
period, Philip Massinger, it is not
only possible to read much of his
verse as if it were prose, but it has
been shown to be possible to print
certain known prose (the preliminar-
ies to a play) as blank verse.
105 *an officer* a constable
106 *Away, good Ned! Falstaff sweats to*
death. This line reads awkwardly as
verse (see the note to lines 102–8),

although one should not expect the
metre to be rigidly exact. It has been
pointed out, however, that the line
would read normally if the name here
were 'Oldcastle' for *Falstaff* (see Introduction, page 242).
107 *lards* drips fat in the form of sweat,
bastes

II.3 Shakespeare gives no location for
this scene, and Warkworth Castle in
Northumberland has been proposed.
Various authors have been suggested as
the letter-writer, the likeliest being
George Dunbar, third Earl of March
(the Scottish, not the Marches of Wales
with which Mortimer is associated).
Dunbar, though a Scot, fought against
his own people at Holmedon, and then
informed on the Percies and fought for
Henry IV at Shrewsbury against Hotspur and Douglas (see lines 31–2). He
changed sides again some years later,
becoming reconciled with Douglas, and
returned to Scotland. What matters in
the play, of course, is Hotspur's reaction
to the letter, not its author. An
eighteenth-century critic remarked that
'did not Sir John need breathing-space'
this scene 'might well be spared'.
3 *house* family

He could be contented! Why is he not then? In respect
of the love he bears our house? He shows in this he
loves his own barn better than he loves our house. Let
me see some more.
The purpose you undertake is dangerous,
Why, that's certain. 'Tis dangerous to take a cold, to
sleep, to drink. But I tell you, my lord fool, out of this
nettle, danger, we pluck this flower, safety.
*The purpose you undertake is dangerous, the friends you
have named uncertain, the time itself unsorted, and your
whole plot too light, for the counterpoise of so great an
opposition.*
Say you so, say you so? I say unto you again, you are a
shallow cowardly hind, and you lie. What a lack-brain is
this! By the Lord, our plot is a good plot, as ever was
laid, our friends true and constant. A good plot, good
friends, and full of expectation. An excellent plot, very
good friends. What a frosty-spirited rogue is this! Why,
my Lord of York commends the plot, and the general
course of the action. Zounds, an I were now by this
rascal I could brain him with his lady's fan. Is there not
my father, my uncle, and myself? Lord Edmund
Mortimer, my Lord of York, and Owen Glendower? Is
there not besides the Douglas? Have I not all their
letters to meet me in arms by the ninth of the next
month, and are they not some of them set forward
already? What a pagan rascal is this, an infidel! Ha!
You shall see now in very sincerity of fear and cold heart
will he to the King, and lay open all our proceedings!
O, I could divide myself, and go to buffets, for moving

---

6 *barn* (contemptuously for the writer's
  residence)
13 *unsorted* unsuitable
14 *for the counterpoise of* to weigh against
17 *hind* peasant
22 *Lord of York* (the Archbishop of

York)
30 *pagan* lacking faith
33 *I could divide myself, and go to buffets* I
   could split myself into two parts and
   fall to blows with myself

such a dish of skim milk with so honourable an action!
Hang him, let him tell the King, we are prepared. I will
set forward tonight.

    Enter his lady

How now, Kate? I must leave you within these two
hours.

LADY PERCY

O my good lord, why are you thus alone?
For what offence have I this fortnight been   40
A banished woman from my Harry's bed?
Tell me, sweet lord, what is it that takes from thee
Thy stomach, pleasure, and thy golden sleep?
Why dost thou bend thine eyes upon the earth,
And start so often when thou sittest alone?
Why hast thou lost the fresh blood in thy cheeks,
And given my treasures and my rights of thee
To thick-eyed musing, and curst melancholy?
In thy faint slumbers I by thee have watched
And heard thee murmur tales of iron wars,   50
Speak terms of manage to thy bounding steed,
Cry 'Courage! To the field!' And thou hast talked
Of sallies, and retires, of trenches, tents,

---

37 *Kate*. Hotspur's wife was called Elizabeth, and Holinshed mistakenly
called her Eleanor (the name of the
loyal Edmund Mortimer's sister —
see note to 1.3.83). The change of
name is presumably deliberate and
Kate certainly seems to have been a
favourite name of Shakespeare's.
39–66 *O my good lord . . . else he loves me
not*. This speech, and the discussion
that follows, have often been compared with the scene between Brutus
and Portia in *Julius Caesar* (II.1.233–
309). The similarity of situation, and
Shakespeare's capacity to handle his

material differently, have been noted.
What is so characteristic of this scene
is the juxtaposition of playful banter
and Lady Percy's deep concern.
These qualities are beautifully
brought together in lines 88–103.

43 *stomach* appetite
45 *when thou sittest alone* (a sign of melancholy)
47 *given* given away
48 *thick-eyed* dull-sighted *curst* ill-
tempered
51 *manage* manège, horsemanship
53 *retires* retreats

Of palisadoes, frontiers, parapets,
Of basilisks, of cannon, culverin,
Of prisoners' ransom, and of soldiers slain,
And all the currents of a heady fight.
Thy spirit within thee hath been so at war,
And thus hath so bestirred thee in thy sleep,
60 That beads of sweat have stood upon thy brow
Like bubbles in a late-disturbed stream,
And in thy face strange motions have appeared,
Such as we see when men restrain their breath
On some great sudden hest. O, what portents are these?
Some heavy business hath my lord in hand,
And I must know it, else he loves me not.

HOTSPUR
What ho!
            Enter a Servant
            Is Gilliams with the packet gone?
SERVANT He is, my lord, an hour ago.
HOTSPUR Hath Butler brought those horses from the
70 sheriff?
SERVANT One horse, my lord, he brought even now.
HOTSPUR What horse? A roan, a crop-ear is it not?
SERVANT
It is, my lord.

---

54 *palisadoes* (a defensive point con-
structed from iron-tipped stakes)
frontiers outworks (of a fortified
position)
55 *basilisks*. This was the largest size of
cannon, named after a fabulous snake
hatched by a reptile from a cock's
egg (hence its alternative name,
'cockatrice'); its breath, or a look
from it, were said to be fatal. The
cannon's shot weighed about 200 lb.
cannon (here a cannon of medium
size)

culverin. This was the smallest size of
cannon, named after the French word
for an adder. A number of cannons
of the Elizabethan period that have
come down to us have reptiles sculp-
tured on them and it is possible that
this is the source of their names.
57 *currents* eddies, movements
heady impetuous, headstrong
62 *motions* (1) emotions; (2) workings
(of the features)
64 *hest* behest, command
65 *heavy* weighty

HOTSPUR That roan shall be my throne.
    Well, I will back him straight. O Esperance!
    Bid Butler lead him forth into the park.

Exit Servant

LADY PERCY But hear you, my lord.
HOTSPUR What sayest thou, my lady?
LADY PERCY What is it carries you away?
HOTSPUR Why, my horse, my love, my horse.
LADY PERCY
    Out, you mad-headed ape!   80
    A weasel hath not such a deal of spleen
    As you are tossed with. In faith,
    I'll know your business, Harry, that I will.
    I fear my brother Mortimer doth stir
    About his title, and hath sent for you
    To line his enterprise. But if you go –
HOTSPUR
    So far afoot I shall be weary, love.
LADY PERCY
    Come, come, you paraquito, answer me
    Directly unto this question that I ask.
    In faith, I'll break thy little finger, Harry   90
    An if thou wilt not tell me all things true.

---

74 *Esperance. Esperance* alone, or as '*Esperance ma comforte*', was the Percy motto. It means 'Hope is my reliance'. *Esperance* is used by Hotspur as a battle-cry at v.2.96.

78 *carries you away* (1) takes you away; (2) excites, 'transports' you

81 *A weasel hath not such a deal of spleen.* The *weasel* was thought to be particularly quarrelsome and the *spleen* was thought to be the organ of the body which excited sudden emotion or action and thus irritability and ill-humour.

82 *tossed* tossed about

84 *my brother Mortimer*. For this relationship, see the notes to 1.3.79, 83, and 154.

85 *his title* (Mortimer's supposed claim to the throne – see 1.3.143–4 and the notes to 1.3.83 and 154)

86 *line* strengthen (as with a lining to a garment)

88 *paraquito* parrot

90 *break thy little finger* (a lovers' endearment)

91 *An if* if

HOTSPUR

Away,
Away, you trifler! Love! I love thee not,
I care not for thee, Kate? This is no world
To play with mammets, and to tilt with lips.
We must have bloody noses, and cracked crowns,
And pass them current too. God's me! My horse!
What sayst thou, Kate? What wouldst thou have with
        me?

LADY PERCY

Do you not love me? Do you not indeed?
100   Well, do not then, for since you love me not
I will not love myself. Do you not love me?
Nay, tell me if you speak in jest or no?

HOTSPUR

Come, wilt thou see me ride?
And when I am a-horseback I will swear
I love thee infinitely. But hark you, Kate,
I must not have you henceforth question me

93–4 *I love thee not,* | *I care not for thee,*
Kate? The question mark has been
added in this edition. Hotspur is
more troubled here, about his enterprise, and about his wife, than his
childishness in 1.3 suggests. Lady
Percy's vivid account of his nightmares and his melancholy suggests a
character rather different from that
described by Hal in the next scene:
'he that kills me some six or seven
dozen of Scots at a breakfast, washes
his hands, and says to his wife, "Fie
upon this quiet life, I want work"'
(II.4.101–103). Shakespeare's depic-
tion of this side of Hotspur, so close
to Hal's comment, is for a good
dramatic purpose. Thus, this is no
bold statement of fact to be denied a
moment later (as at lines 102–3). It is
the kind of self-questioning that suggests that Hotspur is beginning to
be aware of the implications of rebellion. The way in which Kate and
Hotspur exchange banter here implies that neither can quite face what
they feel will be the outcome of this
revolt. This momentary sign of maturity in Hotspur needs to be set
against what often seems to be an
unthinking brashness in him.

95 *mammets* dolls
tilt with lips kiss (*tilt* has the implication of 'tourney')

97 *pass them current.* Cracked crowns
(five-shilling pieces) were not legal
tender ('current coinage').
God's me! God save me. This was an
oath which escaped the purging carried out when the Folio was printed
– see An Account of the Text.

Whither I go, nor reason whereabout.
Whither I must, I must. And, to conclude,
This evening must I leave you, gentle Kate.
I know you wise, but yet no farther wise   110
Than Harry Percy's wife. Constant you are,
But yet a woman. And for secrecy,
No lady closer, for I well believe
Thou wilt not utter – what thou dost not know.
And so far will I trust thee, gentle Kate.

LADY PERCY
How? So far?

HOTSPUR
Not an inch further. But hark you, Kate,
Whither I go, thither shall you go too.
Today will I set forth, tomorrow you.
Will this content you, Kate?

LADY PERCY   It must, of force.   *Exeunt*   120

Enter Prince and Poins   II.4

PRINCE HAL Ned, prithee come out of that fat room,
and lend me thy hand to laugh a little.

POINS Where hast been, Hal?

PRINCE HAL With three or four loggerheads, amongst
three or fourscore hogsheads. I have sounded the very
bass string of humility. Sirrah, I am sworn brother to a

107 *whereabout* on what business
114 *Thou wilt not utter – what thou dost not know* (an ancient witticism that goes back to the Elder Seneca and was popular in Shakespeare's time)
118 *Whither I go, thither shall you go too.* This echoes closely Ruth's famous promise to Naomi ('whither thou goest, I will go also', Ruth 1.16). It is indicative of a much more serious Hotspur than was revealed in 1.3, and it must modify our view of him when he is described by Hal in II.4. Kate, incidentally, has the answer to her question.

120 *of force* of necessity

II.4 This is the meeting planned at 1.2.128–9 and traditionally the scene is set at the Boar's Head, Eastcheap (but see the note to 1.2.129).

1 *fat* 'vat', or, 'stuffy' (though a pun seems unlikely)
4 *loggerheads* blockheads
4–5 *amongst three or fourscore hogsheads.* Favoured customers might be invited to drink in the cellar amidst the casks.

leash of drawers, and can call them all by their Christian
names, as Tom, Dick, and Francis. They take it already
upon their salvation that though I be but Prince of
Wales yet I am the king of courtesy, and tell me flatly I
am no proud Jack like Falstaff, but a Corinthian, a lad of
mettle, a good boy – by the Lord, so they call me! – and
when I am King of England I shall command all the
good lads in Eastcheap. They call drinking deep
'dyeing scarlet', and when you breathe in your watering
they cry 'Hem!' and bid you 'Play it off!' To conclude,
I am so good a proficient in one quarter of an hour that I
can drink with any tinker in his own language during my
life. I tell thee, Ned, thou hast lost much honour that
thou wert not with me in this action. But, sweet Ned –
to sweeten which name of Ned I give thee this pennyworth of sugar, clapped even now into my hand by an
underskinker, one that never spake other English in his

---

7 *leash* trio
11 *Jack* ill-mannered fellow
   Corinthian drinking companion (as
   'Troyans', II.1.70)
15 *'dyeing scarlet'*. The obvious meaning
   here is that regular drinking results
   in a red complexion – Bardolph is
   'the Knight of the Burning Lamp'
   (III.3.26–7). There may also be a reference to the Elizabethan use of urine
   as lye in textile processing, to assist
   in washing wool, for example, and
   particularly to assist in fixing the
   colour, to prevent undue running.
   breathe in your watering. Recently this
   passage has been interpreted to mean
   'pause in the middle of drinking', at
   which there was a cry of 'Hem!',
   signifying that the throat should be
   cleared, and the drink polished off
   ('Play it off!', line 16). Eighteenth-
   century editors offered an interpretation which Boswell castigated as
   'filthy', but which is surely nearer

the truth. It is difficult to believe
that *watering* could be applied to the
drinking of sack. Although there are
plenty of references to the iniquity of
those who need to take breath when
they drink, none of these uses 'water'
as a synonym for beer or wine. *Watering*
is surely 'urinating' (carrying on the
implication of 'dyeing scarlet', same
line) and such breathing that evokes
the responses 'Hem!' and 'Play it off!'
is 'breaking wind'.
18 *drink with any tinker in his own language.*
   Tinkers had the reputation of being
   great drinkers and they had their
   own slang.
20 *action* encounter
21–2 *pennyworth of sugar.* Dekker, in *The
   Gull's Horn-book* (1609), refers to the
   practice of sweetening wine 'in two
   pitiful papers of sugar'. Sugar for
   this purpose was sold by tapsters.
23 *underskinker* under wine-waiter (to
   skink is to draw wine)

life than 'Eight shillings and sixpence', and 'You are welcome', with this shrill addition, 'Anon, anon, sir! Score a pint of bastard in the Half-moon!', or so. But Ned, to drive away the time till Falstaff come – I prithee do thou stand in some by-room while I question my puny drawer to what end he gave me the sugar. And do thou never leave calling 'Francis!', that his tale to me may be nothing but 'Anon'. Step aside, and I'll show thee a precedent.   *Exit Poins*

30

POINS (*within*) Francis!
PRINCE HAL Thou art perfect.
POINS (*within*) Francis!
         Enter Francis, a Drawer
FRANCIS Anon, anon, sir. Look down into the Pomgarnet, Ralph!
PRINCE HAL Come hither, Francis.
FRANCIS My lord?
PRINCE HAL How long hast thou to serve, Francis?   40
FRANCIS Forsooth, five years, and as much as to –
POINS (*within*) Francis!
FRANCIS Anon, anon, sir.
PRINCE HAL Five year! By'r lady, a long lease for the

---

25 *Anon, anon, sir!* coming, sir!
26 *Score* chalk up
   bastard (sweet Spanish wine)
   Half-moon (a fancy name for an inn-room)
29 *puny* inexperienced (a term applied to Oxford freshmen and new students at the Inns of Court, at one time)
32 *a precedent* an example (worth imitating). Q1 has 'present' here but this was changed in F to 'President' (the Elizabethan spelling for 'precedent'). This has been thought by some editors to suggest that another manuscript written by Shakespeare (or copied from such a manuscript) was

available and was used in the course of printing F. This change could, however, have been fairly readily made without the aid of another manuscript and the word is used here because it is a sound guess, not because it is supposed to have any special authority. (See also An Account of the Text.)
36 *Pomgarnet* Pomegranate (another fancy name for an inn-room)
40 *to serve* (as an apprentice)
41 *five years* (the full term was seven years; Francis will be fourteen to sixteen years of age)

clinking of pewter. But Francis, darest thou be so valiant as to play the coward with thy indenture, and show it a fair pair of heels, and run from it?

FRANCIS O Lord, sir, I'll be sworn upon all the books in England, I could find in my heart –

50 POINS (*within*) Francis!

FRANCIS Anon, sir.

PRINCE HAL How old art thou, Francis?

FRANCIS Let me see, about Michaelmas next I shall be –

POINS (*within*) Francis!

FRANCIS Anon, sir – pray stay a little, my lord.

PRINCE HAL Nay but hark you, Francis, for the sugar thou gavest me, 'twas a pennyworth, was it not?

FRANCIS O Lord, I would it had been two!

PRINCE HAL I will give thee for it a thousand pound –
60 ask me when thou wilt, and thou shalt have it.

POINS (*within*) Francis!

FRANCIS Anon, anon.

PRINCE HAL Anon, Francis? No, Francis, but tomorrow, Francis. Or Francis, a-Thursday. Or indeed Francis, when thou wilt. But Francis!

FRANCIS My lord?

PRINCE HAL Wilt thou rob this leathern-jerkin, crystal-button, not-pated, agate-ring, puke-stocking, caddis-

---

46 *indenture* articles of apprenticeship

48 *books* Bibles

49 *I could find in my heart* –. John Dover Wilson has pointed out that the humour of this exchange lies in Francis's hopes of an appointment in the Prince's household – but the frequent interruptions dash these hopes. The interlude also delays Falstaff's entrance and builds up tension in the audience, eager to know what he will say and how he will behave.

67 *rob* (the Vintner by breaking his indenture)

67–9 *leather-jerkin . . . Spanish pouch*. This catalogue describes the Vintner's dress, presumably, but it is reeled off in such a way as to confuse poor Francis, and his wits are further muddled by Hal's next speech.

68 *not-pated* crop-headed. 'Not' is not the common adverb of negation but a word meaning 'crop-headed' even without the addition of 'pated'. Although now a dialect word, 'not' still can be used for a 'hornless sheep'.
agate-ring (wearing a seal ring with a carved agate mounted thereon)

garter, smooth-tongue Spanish pouch?

FRANCIS O Lord, sir, who do you mean?   70

PRINCE HAL Why then your brown bastard is your only
drink. For look you, Francis, your white canvas doublet
will sully. In Barbary, sir, it cannot come to so much.

FRANCIS What, sir?

POINS (*within*) Francis!

PRINCE HAL Away, you rogue, dost thou not hear them
call?

Here they both call him; the Drawer stands amazed,
not knowing which way to go
Enter Vintner

VINTNER What, standest thou still and hearest such a
calling? Look to the guests within.   *Exit Francis*
My lord, old Sir John with half-a-dozen more are at the   80
door. Shall I let them in?

PRINCE HAL Let them alone awhile, and then open the
door.   *Exit Vintner*
Poins!

Enter Poins

POINS Anon, anon, sir.

PRINCE HAL Sirrah, Falstaff and the rest of the thieves
are at the door. Shall we be merry?

puke-stocking (dark-coloured woollen stockings)

68–9 *caddis-garter* (coloured tape used for garters by those who could not afford, or would not pay the price of, silk)

69 *Spanish pouch* (Spanish-leather wallet)

71–3 *Why then your brown bastard . . . it cannot come to so much.* This is nonsense uttered in order to mystify Francis even further. The wretched apprentice hardly seems game worthy of Hal.

71 *brown bastard* (a particularly sweet Spanish wine)

72–3 *your white canvas doublet will sully.* The implication is, perhaps, stick to your apprenticeship and, in the modern colloquial expression, 'keep your nose clean'.

73 *In Barbary, sir, it cannot come to so much.* If Francis runs away, even to such a far-off place as Barbary, it (his white doublet) will not count for much. It was from Barbary (North Africa) that sugar was imported into England.

POINS As merry as crickets, my lad. But hark ye, what
cunning match have you made with this jest of the
90   drawer? Come, what's the issue?

PRINCE HAL I am now of all humours that have showed
themselves humours since the old days of goodman
Adam to the pupil age of this present twelve o'clock at
midnight.

Enter Francis

What's o'clock, Francis?

FRANCIS Anon, anon, sir.   *Exit*

PRINCE HAL That ever this fellow should have fewer
words than a parrot, and yet the son of a woman! His
industry is up-stairs and down-stairs, his eloquence the
100   parcel of a reckoning. I am not yet of Percy's mind, the
Hotspur of the north, he that kills me some six or seven

88–90 *what cunning match ... what's the
issue?* Poins, whose trick with Falstaff
is more ingenious and more fruitful
of humour than Hal's with Francis,
might well ask, *what's the issue?* One
result has been to put Hal in an
excellent humour. Hal's relish at his
joke is not unlike Hotspur's enjoyment of his turn of words at
III.1.54–8. One rather doubts if Poins
will find it a 'precedent' (line 32) so
much worth the repetition.

91–94 *I am now of all humours ... at
midnight* I am now in the mood to
enjoy any jest, any fancy, that man
has enjoyed since time began

95 *What's o'clock, Francis?* Hal has just
said 'this present twelve o'clock at
midnight' (the repetition being designed to ensure that the audience is
aware of the time) and thus his request to Francis is simply a prolonga-
tion of his 'precedent' – his joke
with Francis.

100 *parcel of a reckoning* items making up
a bill

I am not yet of Percy's mind. It has been
suggested that it is the feverish activity of Francis that calls Hotspur to
Hal's mind, or that Hal contrasts his
delight in 'all humours' (line 91) with
what he takes to be the single
humour of Percy – bloodshed –
which he proceeds to satirize. *I am
not yet of Percy's mind* has more than
one meaning. Hal means he is not as
is Hotspur (as Hal's father wishes his
son were); that he has not reached
the stage of delighting in bloodshed
that Hotspur has; and also, unwittingly, 'I am not fully aware of all
that is in Hotspur's mind' – as can
be seen by comparing Hal's satire
with the perturbation dramatized in
II.3. (See note to II.3.93–4.)

101–107 *he that kills me ... 'a trifle, a
trifle'.* Although it does not quite
accord with the Hotspur we have

dozen of Scots at a breakfast, washes his hands, and says to his wife, 'Fie upon this quiet life, I want work.' 'O my sweet Harry,' says she, 'how many hast thou killed today?' 'Give my roan horse a drench,' says he, and answers, 'Some fourteen,' an hour after, 'a trifle, a trifle'. I prithee call in Falstaff. I'll play Percy, and that damned brawn shall play Dame Mortimer his wife. 'Rivo!' says the drunkard. Call in Ribs, call in Tallow!

> *Enter Falstaff, Gadshill, Bardolph, and Peto; followed by Francis, with wine*

POINS Welcome, Jack, where hast thou been?   110

FALSTAFF A plague of all cowards, I say, and a vengeance too, marry and amen! Give me a cup of sack, boy. Ere I lead this life long, I'll sew nether-stocks, and mend them and foot them too. A plague of all cowards! Give me a cup of sack, rogue. Is there no virtue extant?

> *He drinks*

PRINCE HAL Didst thou never see Titan kiss a dish of butter – pitiful-hearted Titan! – that melted at the sweet tale of the sun's? If thou didst, then behold that compound.

just seen, Hal's satire is superb. It has just the right degree of exaggeration, just the right touches of incongruity such as the killing of six or seven dozen Scots before breakfast, and the excellent take-off of Hotspur's trick of delaying an answer (compare how II.3.93 reverts to Lady Percy's words at line 66; and also at IV.I.13). Although we do not have the play of Hotspur and Lady Percy which Hal suggests at lines 108–9, this brief satire is not at all a bad substitute.

109 *Rivo!* So far, *Rivo* has not been satisfactorily explained. It presumably

means 'More wine!' A recent suggestion, that it is derived from the Italian 'riviva', meaning 'Another toast!', is attractive.

113 *nether-stocks* stockings

116 *Titan* (the sun – Falstaff's red cheek sunk into his cup of sack)

117 *pitiful-hearted Titan.* The repetition of *Titan* has troubled many editors and it has been suggested that the compositor should have set 'butter' for *Titan*. Although butter melts easily in the sun, *pitiful-hearted* makes a much less satisfactory epithet for 'butter' than it does for *Titan*.

120   FALSTAFF You rogue, here's lime in this sack too. There
       is nothing but roguery to be found in villainous man, yet
       a coward is worse than a cup of sack with lime in it. A
       villainous coward! Go thy ways, old Jack, die when thou
       wilt. If manhood, good manhood, be not forgot upon
       the face of the earth, then am I a shotten herring. There
       lives not three good men unhanged in England, and one
       of them is fat, and grows old. God help the while, a bad
       world I say. I would I were a weaver: I could sing
       psalms – or anything. A plague of all cowards, I say still.

130   PRINCE HAL How now, woolsack, what mutter you?

       FALSTAFF A king's son! If I do not beat thee out of thy
       kingdom with a dagger of lath, and drive all thy subjects
       afore thee like a flock of wild geese, I'll never wear hair
       on my face more. You, Prince of Wales!

       PRINCE HAL Why, you whoreson round man, what's the
       matter?

       FALSTAFF Are not you a coward? Answer me to that –
       and Poins there?

120 *lime* (added to wine to improve its sparkle)

125 *a shotten herring* (as thin as) a herring that has shot its roe (yet another food image associated with Falstaff)

127 *God help the while* God help these times

128–9 *I would I were a weaver: I could sing psalms.* Weavers had a reputation for singing at their work and, as many were Puritans, they sang psalms. In *Twelfth Night* Sir Toby asks, 'Shall we rouse the night-owl in a catch that will draw three souls out of one weaver?' (II.3.55–7).

131–2 *beat thee out of thy kingdom with a dagger of lath.* A feature of the old Morality plays was the Vice, who, equipped with a dagger of lath, or wooden sword, belaboured the devil or fought his associates. Falstaff's likening himself to the Vice is particularly interesting. It suggests the awareness of a character within a play of the part he is playing. An Elizabethan audience would be aware that the end for the Vice was to be beaten away and, occasionally, executed. It is not possible to know whether Shakespeare had this in mind for Falstaff when he wrote *1 Henry IV* (but see 1.2.193–215); Falstaff is certainly turned away in the second part of the play, however (and in *Henry V* Bardolph will be hanged).

POINS Zounds, ye fat paunch, an ye call me coward by
the Lord I'll stab thee.   140

FALSTAFF I call thee coward? I'll see thee damned ere I
call thee coward, but I would give a thousand pound I
could run as fast as thou canst. You are straight enough
in the shoulders, you care not who sees your back. Call
you that backing of your friends? A plague upon such
backing, give me them that will face me! Give me a cup
of sack! I am a rogue if I drunk today.

PRINCE HAL O villain! Thy lips are scarce wiped since
thou drunkest last.

FALSTAFF All is one for that. (*He drinks*) A plague of all   150
cowards, still say I.

PRINCE HAL What's the matter?

FALSTAFF What's the matter? There be four of us here
have taken a thousand pound this day morning.

PRINCE HAL Where is it, Jack, where is it?

FALSTAFF Where is it? Taken from us it is. A hundred
upon poor four of us.

PRINCE HAL What, a hundred, man?

FALSTAFF I am a rogue if I were not at half-sword with a
dozen of them two hours together. I have scaped by   160
miracle. I am eight times thrust through the doublet,
four through the hose, my buckler cut through and
through, my sword hacked like a handsaw – *ecce
signum*! I never dealt better since I was a man. All would

---

139 *an* if
145 *backing* supporting
154 *a thousand pound.* At II.1.56 and
II.4.505 the amount is stated to be
300 marks – £200. This is probably
just Falstaff's exaggeration, but, in
his defence, it could be said that at

II.1.58–9 the Chamberlain says the
auditor is one 'that hath abundance
of charge too'.
159 *half-sword* shortened swords (as used
at close quarters)
162–3 *buckler . . . sword* (see note to
1.3.227)

not do. A plague of all cowards! Let them speak. If they
speak more or less than truth, they are villains and the
sons of darkness.

PRINCE HAL Speak, sirs, how was it?

GADSHILL We four set upon some dozen —

170 FALSTAFF Sixteen at least, my lord.

GADSHILL And bound them.

PETO No, no, they were not bound.

FALSTAFF You rogue, they were bound, every man of
them, or I am a Jew else: an Ebrew Jew.

GADSHILL As we were sharing, some six or seven fresh
men set upon us —

FALSTAFF And unbound the rest, and then come in the
other.

PRINCE HAL What, fought you with them all?

180 FALSTAFF All? I know not what you call all, but if I
fought not with fifty of them I am a bunch of radish. If
there were not two or three and fifty upon poor old
Jack, then am I no two-legg'd creature.

PRINCE HAL Pray God you have not murdered some of
them.

FALSTAFF Nay, that's past praying for, I have peppered
two of them. Two I am sure I have paid, two rogues in

163–4 *ecce signum* behold the evidence (a
popular tag of the time)

165 *of* on

167 *sons of darkness*. This may have been
suggested by I Thessalonians 5.5: 'Ye
are all the children of light . . . we
are not of the night, neither of
darkness'.

168 PRINCE HAL. This speech is given
to Gadshill in Q1 and the speeches
at lines 169, 171, and 175 to *Ross*.
(presumably the Russell who has
been expunged from the play and
replaced by Peto, as discussed in An

Account of the Text). It has been
suggested that when it became necessary to remove *Ross.*, the prefix for
Gadshill was written in once, adjacent to that for the Prince, and that
in this way Gadshill was given the
Prince's line (and he ought to be
forward in asking this question here)
while the lines below remained attributed to Russell. (See An Account of
the Text.)

174 *an Ebrew Jew* a Jew of Jews, a very
Jew

187 *paid* settled, killed

buckram suits. I tell thee what, Hal, if I tell thee a lie, spit in my face, call me horse. Thou knowest my old ward – here I lay, and thus I bore my point. Four rogues in buckram let drive at me – 190

PRINCE HAL What, four? Thou saidst but two even now.

FALSTAFF Four, Hal, I told thee four.

POINS Ay, ay, he said four.

FALSTAFF These four came all afront, and mainly thrust at me. I made me no more ado, but took all their seven points in my target, thus!

PRINCE HAL Seven? Why, there were but four even now.

FALSTAFF In buckram? 200

POINS Ay, four, in buckram suits.

FALSTAFF Seven, by these hilts, or I am a villain else.

PRINCE HAL Prithee let him alone, we shall have more anon.

FALSTAFF Dost thou hear me, Hal?

PRINCE HAL Ay, and mark thee too, Jack.

FALSTAFF Do so, for it is worth the listening to. These nine in buckram that I told thee of –

PRINCE HAL So, two more already.

FALSTAFF Their points being broken – 210

POINS Down fell their hose.

FALSTAFF – began to give me ground. But I followed me

189 *horse* (taken to be stupid, like the ass or donkey)
190 *ward* posture of defence
192 *even* just
195 *afront* abreast
   mainly with might and main
196 *I made me* (an archaic dative construction; 'me' is not now required)
197 *target* shield (larger than the buckler with which Falstaff was equipped)
202 *these hilts*. The hilt was in three

parts, so the word could be used in the plural.
210-11 *Their points being broken – | Down fell their hose.* The joke is lost on a modern audience. *Points* are not only the sharp ends of swords but were also the laces which fastened stockings (*hose*) to doublet.
212 *I followed me* (see the note to line 196)

close, came in, foot and hand, and, with a thought, seven of the eleven I paid.

PRINCE HAL O monstrous! Eleven buckram men grown out of two!

FALSTAFF But as the devil would have it, three misbegotten knaves in Kendal green came at my back and let drive at me, for it was so dark, Hal, that thou couldst
220   not see thy hand.

PRINCE HAL These lies are like their father that begets them, gross as a mountain, open, palpable. Why, thou clay-brained guts, thou knotty-pated fool, thou whoreson obscene greasy tallow-catch —

FALSTAFF What, art thou mad? Art thou mad? Is not the truth the truth?

PRINCE HAL Why, how couldst thou know these men in Kendal green when it was so dark thou couldst not see thy hand? Come, tell us your reason. What sayest thou
230   to this?

POINS Come, your reason, Jack, your reason!

FALSTAFF What, upon compulsion? Zounds, an I were at the strappado, or all the racks in the world, I would

---

213 *with a thought* quick as thought

218 *Kendal green*. This was a cloth of green, associated with Kendal in Westmorland, worn by foresters, servants, and country people. Robin Hood's men were said to wear Kendal green, and Robert Armin, who probably played Touchstone in the first productions of *As You Like It*, wrote in his *A Nest of Ninnies*: 'Truth, in plain attire, is the easier known: let fiction mask in Kendal green', suggesting that it was also a garb worn by thieves.

223 *knotty-pated* block-headed (compare note on line 68)

224 *tallow-catch*. This may be a dripping-pan to catch the fat from meat being roasted, or 'keech' (rolled fat used by candle-makers) may be intended by *catch*.

225-6 *Is not the truth the truth?* (a proverbial saying)

233 *strappado* (a torture or punishment in which the victim was strung up by the arms and then dropped suddenly, so jerking the arms from their sockets)
racks (an instrument of torture by which the victim was slowly stretched)

not tell you on compulsion. Give you a reason on compulsion? If reasons were as plentiful as blackberries, I would give no man a reason upon compulsion, I.

PRINCE HAL I'll be no longer guilty of this sin. This sanguine coward, this bed-presser, this horse-back-breaker, this huge hill of flesh —

FALSTAFF 'Sblood, you starveling, you elf-skin, you dried   240
neat's-tongue, you bull's-pizzle, you stock-fish! O for breath to utter what is like thee! You tailor's-yard, you sheath, you bow-case, you vile standing tuck!

PRINCE HAL Well, breathe awhile, and then to it again,

235 *reasons* (puns on 'raisins')

238 *sanguine coward*. Cowards were proverbially pale — lily-livered — and thus *sanguine coward* is a comic contradiction in terms. *Sanguine* describes Falstaff's drink-flushed complexion.

240 *starveling* thin, lanky person
elf-skin mere nothing. Q1 reads *elf-skin*. Q3, Q4, Q5, and F, have *elf-skin*, with or without a hyphen, but many editors have thought the word should be 'eel-skin', a word that accords with the ensuing descriptions and was used elsewhere by Shakespeare. It has excellent support, therefore. It has also been suggested that the word 'elshin' is intended. An 'elsin' is a northern dialect word for a shoemaker's awl — an appropriate description of Hal, but a very obscure word.

There is one curiosity about the way that this word is printed in Q1 that has led to the reading *elf-skin* being chosen here. Almost invariably when a double s was required for Q1 a ligatured long s ($\int\int$) was used. The difference between $\int$ and f was minute and mistakes sometimes occurred.

Setting the two letters, and s, required the compositor to make two deliberate choices from his type case. Thus, if *eel-skin* was intended, he has not mistaken a single letter only, but has made a rather complex sequence of errors — a mistaken letter and a reversal of letters. On the other hand, if *elf-skin* was intended, a very simple and likely error has occurred — $\int$ has been set instead of f. This was probably the result of faulty distribution: that is, $\int$ could have been put into the compartment reserved for f in the compositor's case when type previously used was being distributed.

The choice is not an easy one, but as the meaning is sound, it is felt that the implications of the setting of $\int$ and s should here be taken into account and *elf-skin* selected.

241 *neat's tongue* ox-tongue *bull's-pizzle* bull's penis (which when dried was used as a whip)
stock-fish dried cod

243 *standing tuck* (a small rapier standing on its end. A rapier was also said to stand when the blade was no longer resilient.)

and when thou hast tired thyself in base comparisons
hear me speak but this.

POINS Mark, Jack!

PRINCE HAL We two saw you four set on four, and bound
them and were masters of their wealth – mark now how a
250   plain tale shall put you down. Then did we two set on
you four, and, with a word, out-faced you from your
prize, and have it, yea, and can show it you here in the
house. And Falstaff, you carried your guts away as
nimbly, with as quick dexterity, and roared for mercy,
and still run and roared, as ever I heard bull-calf. What
a slave art thou to hack thy sword as thou hast done, and
then say it was in fight! What trick, what device, what
starting-hole canst thou now find out, to hide thee from
this open and apparent shame?

260   POINS Come, let's hear Jack, what trick hast thou now?

251   *with a word* in brief
258   *starting-hole* bolt-hole
259   *apparent* manifest
260   *what trick hast thou now?* The problem
here, for critics and performers, is,
who is tricking whom? The 'fourth-
wall convention', which still consti-
tutes a very large part of our theatrical experience (in which the audience
'overhears' what is going on on the
stage, as if the fourth wall of the
room had been removed), was not
known to the Elizabethans. We
know that the Elizabethan comedians
directed their attentions directly to
the audience, conversed with members of the audience, and even moved
among them. The relationship of performers (especially clowns) to audience was similar to that of music-hall
performers to audience, and this may,
to some extent, have been so for
serious scenes also (as at 1.2.193–215
in this play. See also the Introduction, pages 233–4).

Whilst this scene could be played as

if the audience 'overheard' what was
going on, and the actors assumed
that the audience was not there, it
has been more recently felt either
that the Prince and Poins share the
joke with the audience, or that Falstaff does. Falstaff is certainly in a
corner when Poins poses this question at line 260 – but the scene can
be played so that it is he who has led
the Prince and Poins into a verbal
ambush (just as they ambushed him
physically in 11.2). Falstaff is enjoying
the situation as much as the Prince
and Poins – and the audience.

It is a commonplace of duo acts of
this kind in the nineteenth and twentieth centuries (and their type can be
seen in Shakespeare's own plays) that
both parties appeal directly to the audience. Thus, after the quite magical
pause that should follow Poins's question, we with the Prince and Poins
are put down, yet, because of our
association with Falstaff also, we delight in our discomfiture. The perfec-

FALSTAFF By the Lord, I knew ye as well as he that made
ye. Why, hear you, my masters, was it for me to kill the
heir apparent? Should I turn upon the true prince?
Why, thou knowest I am as valiant as Hercules. But
beware instinct. The lion will not touch the true prince.
Instinct is a great matter. I was now a coward on
instinct. I shall think the better of myself, and thee,
during my life – I for a valiant lion, and thou for a true
prince. But by the Lord lads, I am glad you have the
money! Hostess, clap to the doors! Watch tonight, pray   270
tomorrow! Gallants, lads, boys, hearts of gold, all the
titles of good fellowship come to you! What, shall we be
merry? Shall we have a play extempore?

PRINCE HAL Content, and the argument shall be thy
running away.

FALSTAFF Ah, no more of that Hal, an thou lovest me.

    Enter Hostess

HOSTESS O Jesu, my lord the Prince!

PRINCE HAL How now, my lady the Hostess, what
sayest thou to me?

HOSTESS Marry my lord, there is a nobleman of the court   280
at door would speak with you. He says he comes from
your father.

tion of such a joke as this depends
not on wit, but upon the relationships established between performers
and audience, and it is these relationships, if re-created by the actors, that
make this moment supremely comic
time after time. As at II.2.33, Falstaff's enjoyment of the joke is vital
(see note to that line), but line 276
shows he is also hurt.

265 *The lion will not touch the true prince* (a
belief traceable back to Pliny)

268–9 *thou for a true prince.* That Falstaff,
the lion, would not touch Hal proves
his legitimacy – and see 1.2.138–9,
152–54.

270–71 *Watch tonight, pray tomorrow!*
'Watch' means both to keep watch
and to revel or carouse. Once again,
Falstaff echoes a Biblical text –
'Watch, and pray, that ye enter not
into temptation', Matthew 26.41 –
and once again Falstaff perverts the
meaning. The joke would have been
more obvious, to an Elizabethan audience, if Falstaff was called after the
Lollard, Oldcastle.

274 *argument* plot (some plays were preceded in printed editions with an
outline of the plot and this was called
The Argument)

276 *no more of that* (the joke is now over)

PRINCE HAL Give him as much as will make him a royal
man and send him back again to my mother.

FALSTAFF What manner of man is he?

HOSTESS An old man.

FALSTAFF What doth gravity out of his bed at midnight?
Shall I give him his answer?

PRINCE HAL Prithee do, Jack.

290 FALSTAFF Faith, and I'll send him packing.   *Exit*

PRINCE HAL Now, sirs, by'r lady, you fought fair, so did
you, Peto, so did you, Bardolph. You are lions too, you
ran away upon instinct, you will not touch the true
prince, no, fie!

BARDOLPH Faith, I ran when I saw others run.

PRINCE HAL Faith, tell me now in earnest, how came
Falstaff's sword so hacked?

PETO Why, he hacked it with his dagger, and said he
would swear truth out of England but he would make
300 you believe it was done in fight, and persuaded us to do
the like.

BARDOLPH Yea, and to tickle our noses with spear-grass,
to make them bleed, and then to beslubber our garments
with it, and swear it was the blood of true men. I did
that I did not this seven year before: I blushed to hear
his monstrous devices.

PRINCE HAL O villain, thou stolest a cup of sack eighteen

283–4 *royal man.* A noble ('nobleman',
line 280) was worth 6s. 8d., and a
royal, ten shillings.

287 *What doth gravity out of his bed at
midnight?* This is a question, in so far
as gravity implied old age, that Falstaff might have asked of himself.

299 *swear truth out of England* swear so
fully and so falsely that there would
be no place left for truth in England

302 *tickle our noses with spear-grass.* The
nose could be made to bleed easily,
and fairly painlessly, by irritating the

inside of the nostril with one of a
variety of grasses. It was done by
beggars at one time; it is still done
by children. Derrick, in *The Famous
Victories of Henry the Fifth* tells how
he did this when a soldier:

Every day when I went into the field,
I would take a straw and thrust it into
        my nose
And make my nose bleed.

305 *that* something

years ago, and wert taken with the manner, and ever
since thou hast blushed extempore. Thou hadst fire and
sword on thy side, and yet thou rannest away. What   310
instinct hadst thou for it?

BARDOLPH My lord, do you see these meteors? Do you
behold these exhalations?

PRINCE HAL I do.

BARDOLPH What think you they portend?

PRINCE HAL Hot livers, and cold purses.

BARDOLPH Choler, my lord, if rightly taken.

PRINCE HAL No, if rightly taken, halter.

Enter Falstaff

Here comes lean Jack, here comes bare-bone. How now
my sweet creature of bombast, how long is't ago, Jack,   320
since thou sawest thine own knee?

FALSTAFF My own knee? When I was about thy years,
Hal, I was not an eagle's talon in the waist — I could have
crept into any alderman's thumb-ring. A plague of
sighing and grief, it blows a man up like a bladder.
There's villainous news abroad. Here was Sir John
Bracy from your father. You must to the court in the
morning. That same mad fellow of the north, Percy,
and he of Wales that gave Amamon the bastinado, and
made Lucifer cuckold, and swore the devil his true   330
liegeman upon the cross of a Welsh hook — what a
plague call you him?

308 *taken with the manner* caught in the
act (a legal expression)

309 *fire* (referring to Bardolph's complexion – as does Falstaff, III.3.26–7)

313 *exhalations* fiery meteors

316 *Hot livers, and cold purses* liverishness
and an empty purse (because got
with drinking)

317 *Choler.* Bardolph maintains he is not
to be trifled with.

318 *rightly taken* (1) properly understood; (2) justly arrested
halter (destined for hanging)

320 *bombast* (1) cotton or wool used for
padding (2) high-flown language

324 *thumb-ring* (used in sealing documents)

329 *Amamon* (a devil)
bastinado beating on the soles of the
feet

330 *made Lucifer cuckold* was the reason
why horns grew on Lucifer's head

331 *liegeman* subject
Welsh hook (pike or bill – having no
hilt, forming a cross, it could not be
sworn on. See note to II.4.202.)

POINS O, Glendower.

FALSTAFF Owen, Owen, the same. And his son-in-law Mortimer, and old Northumberland, and that sprightly Scot of Scots, Douglas, that runs a-horseback up a hill perpendicular –

PRINCE HAL He that rides at high speed, and with his pistol kills a sparrow flying.

340 FALSTAFF You have hit it.

PRINCE HAL So did he never the sparrow.

FALSTAFF Well, that rascal hath good mettle in him, he will not run.

PRINCE HAL Why, what a rascal art thou then, to praise him so for running!

FALSTAFF A-horseback, ye cuckoo, but afoot he will not budge a foot.

PRINCE HAL Yes, Jack, upon instinct.

FALSTAFF I grant ye, upon instinct. Well, he is there too, 350 and one Mordake, and a thousand blue-caps more. Worcester is stolen away tonight. Thy father's beard is turned white with the news. You may buy land now as cheap as stinking mackerel.

PRINCE HAL Why then, it is like if there come a hot June, and this civil buffeting hold, we shall buy maidenheads as they buy hob-nails, by the hundreds.

FALSTAFF By the mass, lad, thou sayest true, it is like we shall have good trading that way. But tell me, Hal, art not thou horrible afeard? Thou being heir apparent, 360 could the world pick thee out three such enemies again,

---

341 *So did he never the sparrow.* Hal's wit is, at times, very like Hotspur's – compare this with the latter's response to Glendower's claim that he 'can call spirits from the vasty deep'. 'But will they come,' says Hotspur, 'when you do call for them?' (III.1.50–52).

342 *good mettle* (1) a good spirit (and so no coward); (2) good metal (which does not run)

346 *cuckoo* (to cuckoo is to repeat incessantly)

350 *blue-caps* Scots (in blue bonnets)

as that fiend Douglas, that spirit Percy, and that devil
Glendower? Art thou not horribly afraid? Doth not thy
blood thrill at it?

PRINCE HAL Not a whit, i'faith, I lack some of thy
instinct.

FALSTAFF Well, thou wilt be horribly chid tomorrow
when thou comest to thy father. If thou love me,
practise an answer.

PRINCE HAL Do thou stand for my father and examine
me upon the particulars of my life.   370

FALSTAFF Shall I? Content! This chair shall be my state,
this dagger my sceptre, and this cushion my crown.

PRINCE HAL Thy state is taken for a joint-stool, thy
golden sceptre for a leaden dagger, and thy precious rich
crown for a pitiful bald crown.

FALSTAFF Well, an the fire of grace be not quite out of
thee, now shalt thou be moved. Give me a cup of sack to
make my eyes look red, that it may be thought I have
wept, for I must speak in passion, and I will do it in
King Cambyses' vein.   380

PRINCE HAL Well, here is my leg.

361 *spirit* 'spirited', and perhaps, 'devil'
368 *practise an answer.* This is the play
extempore suggested by Falstaff at
line 273, but the subject is of Falstaff's choosing. A play is also given
in *The Famous Victories of Henry the
Fifth* in which John Cobbler plays
the Lord Chief Justice and Derrick
the young Prince.
371 *state* chair of state
374 *leaden* (and so, useless)
376–7 *an the fire of grace be not quite out of
thee.* At 1.2.17–18 Falstaff maintains
the Prince has none.
379 *in passion* with deep emotion
379–80 *in King Cambyses' vein* after the
style of *Cambyses*, Thomas Preston's
extravagant but primitive tragedy

(1569). Dr Johnson thought Shakespeare may not have known the play
at first hand (though he seems to
parody its title in *A Midsummer
Night's Dream*). Certainly Shakespeare does not imitate its rhymed
fourteeners. Falstaff begins in an exaggerated style (lines 384 and 386–
7), but with his 'Peace, good pint-
pot' he quickly relapses into a form
of humour more suitable for him. It
is doubtful if an extended parody of
Preston's play was ever intended.
Lyly is a more likely object of parody
and Kyd has been suggested for lines
386–7.
381 *my leg* my bow (to introduce myself)

FALSTAFF And here is my speech. Stand aside, nobility.

HOSTESS O Jesu, this is excellent sport, i'faith.

FALSTAFF

Weep not, sweet Queen, for trickling tears are vain.

HOSTESS O the Father, how he holds his countenance!

FALSTAFF

For God's sake, lords, convey my tristful Queen,

For tears do stop the floodgates of her eyes.

HOSTESS O Jesu, he doth it as like one of these harlotry
players as ever I see!

390 FALSTAFF Peace, good pint-pot, peace, good tickle-
brain.

(*as* KING)

Harry, I do not only marvel where thou spendest thy time,
but also how thou art accompanied. For though the camomile, the more it is trodden on the faster it grows, yet youth,
the more it is wasted the sooner it wears. That thou art my
son I have partly thy mother's word, partly my own opinion,
but chiefly a villainous trick of thine eye, and a foolish hanging of thy nether lip, that doth warrant me. If then thou be son
to me — here lies the point — why, being son to me, art thou
400 so pointed at? Shall the blessed sun of heaven prove a micher,

384 *Weep not.* Preston's *Cambyses* has a
stage direction instructing the queen
to weep. The Hostess's tears are of
laughter, of course.

385 *holds his countenance* keeps a straight
face

386 *tristful.* The reading of all the quartos and the Folio is 'trustful'. This
emendation comes from the Dering
manuscript (see An Account of the
Text) but that does not mean the
reading has special authority: it is
simply an excellent conjecture which
later editors have been glad to accept.

388 *harlotry* (used affectionately, not
abusively)

390–91 *tickle-brain* (a cant name at the
time for a strong drink)

393–4 *camomile.* The camomile proverbially grew faster the more it was trodden on. The style parodies Lyly's
Euphues.

397 *trick* characteristic
foolish wanton, roguish

398 *nether* lower
warrant indicate

400 *pointed at* (contemptuously)

400–401 *prove a micher, and eat blackberries.* To mitch or mooch was to play
truant, especially to gather blackberries. This passage has also been said
to be imitative of Lyly.

and eat blackberries? A question not to be asked. Shall
the son of England prove a thief, and take purses? A question
to be asked. There is a thing, Harry, which thou hast
often heard of, and it is known to many in our land by the
name of pitch. This pitch – as ancient writers do report –
doth defile, so doth the company thou keepest. For, Harry,
now I do not speak to thee in drink, but in tears; not in
pleasure, but in passion; not in words only, but in woes also.
And yet there is a virtuous man whom I have often noted in
thy company, but I know not his name.   410

PRINCE HAL (*as himself*)
What manner of man, an it like your Majesty?

FALSTAFF (*as* KING)
A goodly portly man, i'faith, and a corpulent; of a cheerful
look, a pleasing eye, and a most noble carriage; and, as I
think, his age some fifty, or by'r lady inclining to threescore.
And now I remember me, his name is Falstaff. If that man
should be lewdly given, he deceiveth me, for, Harry, I see
virtue in his looks. If then the tree may be known by the fruit,
as the fruit by the tree, then peremptorily I speak it, there
is virtue in that Falstaff. Him keep with, the rest banish.
And tell me now, thou naughty varlet, tell me where hast   420
thou been this month?

PRINCE HAL Dost thou speak like a king? Do thou stand
for me, and I'll play my father.

FALSTAFF Depose me? If thou dost it half so gravely, so
majestically, both in word and matter, hang me up by the

---

402 *son* (a quibble on 'sun', the symbol
of royalty; see note to 1.2.195)

405 *ancient writers*. One ancient writer
who stated that 'Who so toucheth
pitch, shall be defiled withal' was the
author of Ecclesiasticus (13.1) and
another, less ancient, was Lyly. The
joke lies in giving ancient authority
for the most common expression.

408 *in passion* with emotion

412 *portly* stately
corpulent well-made

416 *lewdly* wickedly

417–18 *If then the tree may be known . . . as
the fruit by the tree*. This was a popular
saying. It occurs in Matthew 12.33
and Luke 6.44.

418 *peremptorily* decisively

heals for a rabbit-sucker, or a poulter's hare.

PRINCE HAL　Well, here I am set.

FALSTAFF　And here I stand. Judge, my masters.

PRINCE HAL (*as* KING)

　　Now, Harry, whence come you?

FALSTAFF (*as* HAL)

430　　My noble lord, from Eastcheap.

PRINCE HAL (*as* KING)

　　The complaints I hear of thee are grievous.

FALSTAFF (*as* HAL)

　　'Sblood, my lord, they are false!

　　Nay, I'll tickle ye for a young prince, i'faith.

PRINCE HAL (*as* KING)

　　Swearest thou, ungracious boy? Henceforth ne'er look on me.
　　Thou art violently carried away from grace. There is a devil
　　haunts thee in the likeness of an old fat man, a tun of man is
　　thy companion. Why dost thou converse with that trunk of
　　humours, that bolting-hutch of beastliness, that swollen
　　parcel of dropsies, that huge bombard of sack, that stuffed
440　　cloak-bag of guts, that roasted Manningtree ox with the
　　pudding in his belly, that reverend Vice, that grey Iniquity,

426　*for a rabbit-sucker, or a poulter's hare*
for (something as slight as) a baby
rabbit or a hare hanging in a poul-
terer's shop

427　*set* seated

434　*ungracious* graceless

436　*tun* 'large barrel' (with a quibble on
'ton weight')

438　*humours* secretions (with the implication of 'diseases')
　bolting-hutch sifting-bin

439　*bombard* large leather wine-vessel

440　*cloak-bag* portmanteau
　Manningtree ox. East Anglia was well-
known for its cattle but not Manningtree specifically. Thomas Heywood, however, in his *An Apology
for Actors* (1612) states that 'to this
day, in divers places in England,

there be towns that hold the privilege
of their fairs, and other charters by
yearly stage-plays, as at Manningtree
in Suffolk, and Kendal in the North,
and others'. The reference to fairs
suggests that such festivities included
the roasting of a whole ox − something that might well have had pleasant associations for actors concerned
with the plays − and a sequence of
morality terms occurs in the next
two lines.

441　*pudding* stuffing

441−2　*Vice . . . Iniquity . . . Ruffian . . .
Vanity.* These are all names of characters in Morality plays. A *ruffian* (or
ruffin) was a devil. For the Vice, see
note to lines 131−2.

that Father Ruffian, that Vanity in years? Wherein is he
good, but to taste sack and drink it? Wherein neat and
cleanly, but to carve a capon and eat it? Wherein cunning,
but in craft? Wherein crafty, but in villainy? Wherein
villainous, but in all things? Wherein worthy, but in nothing?

FALSTAFF (*as* HAL)
I would your grace would take me with you. Whom means
your grace?

PRINCE HAL (*as* KING)
That villainous abominable misleader of youth, Falstaff,
that old white-bearded Satan.   450

FALSTAFF (*as* HAL)
My lord, the man I know.

PRINCE HAL (*as* KING)
I know thou dost.

FALSTAFF (*as* HAL)
But to say I know more harm in him than in myself were to
say more than I know. That he is old, the more the pity, his
white hairs do witness it, but that he is, saving your reverence, a whoremaster, that I utterly deny. If sack and sugar
be a fault, God help the wicked! If to be old and merry be a
sin, then many an old host that I know is damned. If to be
fat be to be hated, then Pharaoh's lean kine are to be loved.
No, my good lord! Banish Peto, banish Bardolph, banish   460
Poins — but for sweet Jack Falstaff, kind Jack Falstaff, true
Jack Falstaff, valiant Jack Falstaff — and therefore more
valiant, being as he is old Jack Falstaff — banish not him thy

444 *cleanly* deft
     cunning skilful
447 *take me with you* let me know your
     meaning
455-6 *saving your reverence* (a formula ex-
     cusing possible offence)
459 *Pharaoh's lean kine* (Genesis 41)
465 *Banish plump Jack, and banish all the
     world.* As Falstaff ends this speech,
     the mood of comedy gives way to

sentiment — indeed to sentimentality
on his part. Perhaps he senses that so
far as Hal is concerned, he is expend-
able. The knocking at the door
comes at just the right moment to
ensure that an even keel is restored,
for as Falstaff angrily says in his next
speech, 'I have much to say in the
behalf of that Falstaff.'

Harry's company, banish not him thy Harry's company.
Banish plump Jack, and banish all the world.

PRINCE HAL (*as* KING)

I do, I will.

A knocking heard

Exeunt Hostess, Francis and Bardolph

Enter Bardolph, running

BARDOLPH　O my lord, my lord, the sheriff with a most
monstrous watch is at the door.

FALSTAFF　Out, ye rogue! Play out the play! I have much
470　to say in the behalf of that Falstaff.

Enter the Hostess

HOSTESS　O Jesu, my lord, my lord!

PRINCE HAL　Heigh, heigh, the devil rides upon a fiddle-
stick. What's the matter?

HOSTESS　The sheriff and all the watch are at the door.
They are come to search the house. Shall I let them in?

FALSTAFF　Dost thou hear, Hal? Never call a true piece of

---

468 *watch* watchmen, officers to maintain order

472–3 *the devil rides upon a fiddle-stick*
what the devil's all the fuss (a proverbial expression)

476 *Dost thou hear, Hal?* This first sentence of a puzzling speech can refer
to two things: Falstaff's wish to say
what he has to say 'in the behalf of
that Falstaff' (his situation being very
like that of Francis at the beginning
of the scene when Poins kept inter-
rupting – see note to line 49); and
Falstaff's attempt to get Hal to take
the arrival of this 'most monstrous
watch' seriously. As Falstaff tries to
get rid of Bardolph and his unwelcome news (lines 469–70), it is more
likely that he is trying, with some
desperation, to hold Hal's attention
for just a moment longer. If this is
so, it suggests the meaning underlying the obscure lines that follow.

476–8 *Never call a true piece of gold a
counterfeit. Thou art essentially made
without seeming so.* Many interpretations have been offered of these lines.
One possibility, quite different from
that suggested here, is that Falstaff is
begging not to be given away. Some
editors have suggested amending
made to 'mad'.

The first sentence clearly means do
not mistake the genuine for the false.
The key word in the second sentence
(addressed to Hal) is *essentially*. This
occurs in *Hamlet*, III.4.187, being opposed to 'craft' (a word associated
with *counterfeit*): 'I essentially am not
in madness, | But mad in craft.' The
opposition in this second line is,
again, between the genuine and the
false. The whole passage may be explained, however, from within *1
Henry IV*, as a whole, and from this
scene in particular. Frequently in the

gold a counterfeit. Thou art essentially made without
seeming so.

PRINCE HAL And thou a natural coward without in-
stinct.   480

FALSTAFF I deny your major. If you will deny the sheriff,
so; if not, let him enter. If I become not a cart as well as
another man, a plague on my bringing up! I hope I shall
as soon be strangled with a halter as another.

PRINCE HAL Go hide thee behind the arras. The rest,
walk up above. Now, my masters, for a true face, and
good conscience.

FALSTAFF Both which I have had, but their date is out,
and therefore I'll hide me.

Exeunt all but the Prince and Peto

play the word 'true' occurs. In this
scene it is used by Falstaff of Hal
and of himself. At lines 263–9 we
have the business of the lion recognizing a 'true prince' – and this Hal is,
with some emphasis, recognized as
being. At lines 460–65 Falstaff makes
his appeal – not comic, but deeply
felt – that 'true Jack Falstaff' (with
many other qualities besides) should
not be banished.

It is in these lines that we have the
essence of Falstaff's plea. He begs
that he will not be regarded as anything but true: and as Hal is a true
prince (which, however he behaves,
essentially he is), he will not neglect
(banish) a comrade, for to do so
would be the reverse of being true.

This interpretation is in accord
with the play as a whole. Hal is seeking his true self and his awareness of
this, and ours, is made clear in
1.2.193–215, where he compares himself, amongst other things, to 'bright
metal on a sullen ground' (line 210).
As 'bright metal' he is *essentially made*
even if, because his (the sun's) beauty
has been smothered from the world,

he is *essentially made without seeming so.*
(And if the metaphors appear to be
mixed in this explication, it might be
claimed that gold was thought to be
a product of the sun.) See also Hal's
answer at III.2.92–3.

481 *I deny your major. If you will deny the
sheriff* . . . Falstaff has failed to get
his message through to Hal – he has
been dismissed as 'a natural coward
without instinct'. He resorts to an
involved pun (on *major* and 'mayor'
– the sheriff being his officer) and
attempts to use syllogistic logic to
answer Hal – he denies his major
premiss. But more important than
this involved quibbling is the anticipation this moment has of Falstaff's
rejection in *2 Henry IV*. Faced with
the possibility of arrest Falstaff retains a certain dignity (which he will
soon lose): 'If you will deny the sheriff, so; if not, let him enter.'

483 *bringing up* (1) upbringing, (2) being
summonsed

485 *arras* (here, the curtain closing off
the inner stage from the main playing
area)

490   PRINCE HAL Call in the Sheriff.
      Enter Sheriff and the Carrier
   Now, master Sheriff, what is your will with me?

SHERIFF
   First, pardon me, my lord. A hue and cry
   Hath followed certain men unto this house.

PRINCE HAL
   What men?

SHERIFF
   One of them is well known my gracious lord,
   A gross fat man.

CARRIER   As fat as butter.

PRINCE HAL
   The man I do assure you is not here,
   For I myself at this time have employed him.
   And Sheriff, I will engage my word to thee,
500   That I will by tomorrow dinner-time
   Send him to answer thee, or any man,
   For anything he shall be charged withal.
   And so let me entreat you leave the house.

SHERIFF
   I will, my lord. There are two gentlemen
   Have in this robbery lost three hundred marks.

PRINCE HAL
   It may be so. If he have robbed these men
   He shall be answerable. And so, farewell.

SHERIFF
   Good night, my noble lord.

PRINCE HAL
   I think it is good morrow, is it not?

SHERIFF
510   Indeed, my lord, I think it be two o'clock.

                           Exit with Carrier

---

492 *hue and cry* general pursuit
497 *not here*. This is not strictly 'true'.
    Falstaff is not in the room because
    he has hidden behind the arras.

500 *dinner-time*. Dinner was served some
    time before noon and could last two
    or three hours.
502 *withal* in addition

PRINCE HAL This oily rascal is known as well as Paul's.
Go call him forth.

PETO Falstaff! Fast asleep behind the arras, and snorting
like a horse.

PRINCE HAL Hark how hard he fetches breath. Search
his pockets.

     Peto searcheth his pockets, and findeth certain papers

What hast thou found?

PETO Nothing but papers, my lord.

PRINCE HAL Let's see what they be, read them.

PETO *Item a capon* *2s. 2d.*   520
    Item sauce .   .   .   .   .   .   *4d.*
    Item sack two gallons   .   .   .   *5s. 8d.*
    Item anchovies and sack after supper   .   *2s. 6d.*
    Item bread   .   .   .   .   .   *ob.*

PRINCE HAL O monstrous! But one halfpennyworth of
bread to this intolerable deal of sack? What there is else
keep close, we'll read it at more advantage. There let him
sleep till day. I'll to the court in the morning. We must
all to the wars, and thy place shall be honourable. I'll
procure this fat rogue a charge of foot, and I know his   530
death will be a march of twelve score. The money shall
be paid back again with advantage. Be with me betimes
in the morning, and so, good morrow, Peto.

PETO Good morrow, good my lord.   *Exeunt*

---

511 *Paul's* (St Paul's Cathedral)
524 *ob.* obolus, halfpenny (sometimes modernized in performance)
526 *intolerable* exceedingly great
527 *close* safely, secretly

at more advantage at a more convenient time
530 *a charge of foot* an infantry company
531 *twelve score* (paces)
532 *advantage* interest

III.I   *Enter Hotspur, Worcester, Lord Mortimer, Owen,*
               Glendower

MORTIMER

    These promises are fair, the parties sure,
    And our induction full of prosperous hope.

HOTSPUR

    Lord Mortimer, and cousin Glendower, will you sit
        down?
    And uncle Worcester. A plague upon it!
    I have forgot the map.

GLENDOWER   No, here it is.
    Sit, cousin Percy, sit – good cousin Hotspur –
    For by that name as oft as Lancaster doth speak of you
    His cheek looks pale, and with a rising sigh
    He wisheth you in heaven.

HOTSPUR   And you in hell,
10   As oft as he hears Owen Glendower spoke of.

GLENDOWER

    I cannot blame him. At my nativity
    The front of heaven was full of fiery shapes,
    Of burning cressets, and at my birth
    The frame and huge foundation of the earth
    Shaked like a coward.

HOTSPUR   Why, so it would have done
    At the same season if your mother's cat

III.1 Shakespeare gives no location but
an eighteenth-century editor suggested
the Archdeacon's house in Bangor, North
Wales, where, according to the historian
Holinshed, such a meeting took place.
2 *induction* opening scene (of a play)
   prosperous hope hopes of success
11 *my nativity*. These portents may have
   been suggested by those that are reported by Holinshed to have occurred at Mortimer's birth. Holinshed also mentions a blazing star
   which was seen in 1402 and was said

to foretell Glendower's success in
battle against Lord Grey; this may
have suggested to Shakespeare the
idea of associating portents with
Glendower's birth.
13 *cressets*. A cresset was a metal basket,
   suspended or carried on a pole, into
   which were put combustible materials, the result, when set alight, being
   like a blazing torch. The word here
   suggests 'blazing stars', perhaps from
   the star observed in 1402 (see note
   on line 11).

Had but kittened, though yourself had never been born.
GLENDOWER
I say the earth did shake when I was born.
HOTSPUR
And I say the earth was not of my mind,
If you suppose as fearing you it shook.   20
GLENDOWER
The heavens were all on fire, the earth did tremble –
HOTSPUR
O, then the earth shook to see the heavens on fire,
And not in fear of your nativity.
Diseasèd nature oftentimes breaks forth
In strange eruptions, oft the teeming earth
Is with a kind of colic pinched and vexed
By the imprisoning of unruly wind
Within her womb, which for enlargement striving
Shakes the old beldam earth, and topples down
Steeples and moss-grown towers. At your birth   30
Our grandam earth, having this distemperature,
In passion shook.
GLENDOWER   Cousin, of many men
I do not bear these crossings. Give me leave
To tell you once again that at my birth
The front of heaven was full of fiery shapes,
The goats ran from the mountains, and the herds
Were strangely clamorous to the frighted fields.
These signs have marked me extraordinary,
And all the courses of my life do show
I am not in the roll of common men.   40

25 *eruptions* outbreaks (as in the eruption
   of spots in the course of a disease)
25–30 *oft the teeming earth | Is with a kind
   of colic pinched . . . and topples down |
   Steeples and moss-grown towers.* This explanation of earthquakes goes back
   to classical times. It is mentioned by
   Aristotle and Pliny.
25 *teeming* pregnant, over-full

29 *beldam* grandmother (with a suggestion of witchcraft from the second
   meaning of *beldam*: hag or witch)
31 *distemperature* disorder
32 *passion* agony
   of from
33 *crossings* contradictions
35 *front of heaven* sky

Where is he living, clipped in with the sea
That chides the banks of England, Scotland, Wales,
Which calls me pupil or hath read to me?
And bring him out that is but woman's son
Can trace me in the tedious ways of art,
And hold me pace in deep experiments.

HOTSPUR

I think there's no man speaks better Welsh.
I'll to dinner.

MORTIMER

Peace, cousin Percy, you will make him mad.

GLENDOWER

50   I can call spirits from the vasty deep.

HOTSPUR

Why, so can I, or so can any man:
But will they come when you do call for them?

GLENDOWER

Why, I can teach you, cousin, to command the devil.

HOTSPUR

And I can teach thee, coz, to shame the devil
By telling truth. Tell truth, and shame the devil.
If thou have power to raise him, bring him hither,
And I'll be sworn I have power to shame him hence.
O, while you live, tell truth, and shame the devil!

MORTIMER

Come, come, no more of this unprofitable chat.

GLENDOWER

60   Three times hath Henry Bolingbroke made head

41 *clipped* bound
42 *chides* contends with, beats against
43 *read to* lectured
45 *trace* follow
46 *hold me pace* keep up with me
   deep experiments investigations into
   the depths – the occult
47 *speak better Welsh*. The surface meaning is obvious but beneath the compliment is a double insult. To 'speak
   Welsh' was to speak double-Dutch –

nonsense; it was also to brag.
55 *Tell truth, and shame the devil*. Hotspur's delight in his use of this proverbial saying is very clear and rather
   childlike. His humour in these exchanges is not unlike Hal's in his
   little game with Francis (II.4).
60 *Three times* (1400, 1402, and, ante-
   dated here, 1405)
   made head raised an army

Against my power, thrice from the banks of Wye
And sandy-bottomed Severn have I sent him
Bootless home, and weather-beaten back.

HOTSPUR

Home without boots, and in foul weather too!
How scapes he agues, in the devil's name?

GLENDOWER

Come, here is the map, shall we divide our right
According to our threefold order taken?

MORTIMER

The Archdeacon hath divided it
Into three limits very equally.
England, from Trent and Severn hitherto,   70
By south and east is to my part assigned.
All westward, Wales beyond the Severn shore,
And all the fertile land within that bound,
To Owen Glendower. And, dear coz, to you
The remnant northward lying off from Trent.
And our indentures tripartite are drawn,
Which being sealed interchangeably –
A business that this night may execute –
Tomorrow, cousin Percy, you and I
And my good Lord of Worcester will set forth   80
To meet your father and the Scottish power,
As is appointed us, at Shrewsbury.
My father Glendower is not ready yet,
Nor shall we need his help these fourteen days.
(*To Glendower*) Within that space you may have drawn
          together

---

63 *Bootless* unsuccessful
    weather-beaten (according to Holin-
    shed, 'by mists and tempests sent')
65 *scapes* escapes
66 *right* rights, what we claim
67 *threefold order taken* triple entente
70 *hitherto* to this point
76 *indentures tripartite* triple agreement
    drawn drawn up

77 *sealed interchangeably* (so that each
    party to the agreement has a copy
    signed by the other two)
78 *this night may execute* may be done this
    evening
83 *father* father-in-law

Your tenants, friends, and neighbouring gentlemen.

GLENDOWER

A shorter time shall send me to you, lords,
And in my conduct shall your ladies come,
From whom you now must steal and take no leave,
For there will be a world of water shed
Upon the parting of your wives and you.

HOTSPUR

Methinks my moiety, north from Burton here,
In quantity equals not one of yours.
See how this river comes me cranking in,
And cuts me from the best of all my land
A huge half-moon, a monstrous cantle out.
I'll have the current in this place dammed up,
And here the smug and silver Trent shall run
In a new channel fair and evenly.
It shall not wind with such a deep indent,
To rob me of so rich a bottom here.

GLENDOWER

Not wind? It shall, it must – you see it doth.

MORTIMER

Yea,
But mark how he bears his course, and runs me up
With like advantage on the other side,
Gelding the opposèd continent as much
As on the other side it takes from you.

WORCESTER

Yea, but a little charge will trench him here,

90

100

88 *in my conduct* escorted by me, in my
    care
92 *Methinks my moiety*. When Hal imi-
    tated Hotspur he parodied this habit
    his rival had of delaying his response
    (II.4.106–7).
    moiety share (not necessarily a half)
    Burton (on the river Trent)
94 *cranking* winding
96 *cantle*. All the quartos print 'scantle',
    which means a small portion. The

Folio has 'cantle', a segment. The
Folio's emendation has generally
been accepted. 'Scantle' may have
been the result of the final letter of
'monstrous' being attracted to
'cantle' as the compositor said the
line to himself as he set it in type.
98 *smug* smooth
101 *bottom* valley
106 *Gelding* cutting
    continent bank (that which contains)

And on this north side win this cape of land,
And then he runs straight and even.   110

HOTSPUR
I'll have it so, a little charge will do it.

GLENDOWER
I'll not have it altered.

HOTSPUR   Will not you?

GLENDOWER
No, nor you shall not.

HOTSPUR   Who shall say me nay?

GLENDOWER
Why, that will I.

HOTSPUR
Let me not understand you then, speak it in Welsh.

GLENDOWER
I can speak English, lord, as well as you,
For I was trained up in the English court,
Where being but young I framèd to the harp
Many an English ditty lovely well,
And gave the tongue a helpful ornament –   120
A virtue that was never seen in you.

HOTSPUR
Marry and I am glad of it with all my heart!
I had rather be a kitten and cry 'mew'
Than one of these same metre ballad-mongers
I had rather hear a brazen canstick turned,
Or a dry wheel grate on the axle-tree,
And that would set my teeth nothing on edge,
Nothing so much as mincing poetry.
'Tis like the forced gait of a shuffling nag.

---

111 *charge* expenditure
120 *gave the tongue a helpful ornament*. Glen-
     dower quibbles. When he sang 'an
     English ditty', he graced it with a
     delightful accent (a defence of his
     Welsh), set it to music ('framed to
     the harp'), and gave to the English

language (*tongue*) something of literary worth (*a helpful ornament*) –
achievements Hotspur could not
claim.
124 *metre* metrical, doggerel
125 *canstick* candlestick
128 *mincing* affected (poetic) feet

GLENDOWER

130 Come, you shall have Trent turned.

HOTSPUR

I do not care, I'll give thrice so much land
To any well-deserving friend.
But in the way of bargain, mark ye me,
I'll cavil on the ninth part of a hair.
Are the indentures drawn? Shall we be gone?

GLENDOWER

The moon shines fair, you may away by night.
I'll haste the writer, and withal
Break with your wives of your departure hence.
I am afraid my daughter will run mad,
140 So much she doteth on her Mortimer.   *Exit*

MORTIMER

Fie, cousin Percy, how you cross my father!

HOTSPUR

I cannot choose. Sometime he angers me
With telling me of the moldwarp and the ant,
Of the dreamer Merlin and his prophecies,
And of a dragon and a finless fish,
A clip-winged griffin and a moulten raven,
A couching lion and a ramping cat,
And such a deal of skimble-skamble stuff

---

131 *I do not care*. Hotspur may seem capricious, but his attitudes, though they change rapidly, are not unbecoming to him by Elizabethan standards. He is at one and the same time quixotically generous and determined to maintain his rights (as he understands them).

138 *Break with* break the news to

142–3 *Sometime he angers me | With telling me*. It is a trifle ironic that Hotspur, so free with his views, should complain of Glendower's capacity for talking. As events prove, however, Hotspur's talking is supported by his actions whereas Glendower is 'o'erruled by prophecies' (IV.4.18). It is noteworthy that Hotspur, on hearing the news that Glendower has failed them, wastes no breath in bemoaning his absence (IV.1.130–34).

143 *moldwarp* mole

144 *Merlin* (wizard or prophet at King Arthur's court)

147 *couching, ramping* (parodic forms of heraldic terms: couchant – lying; rampant – rearing)

148 *skimble-skamble* nonsense (a word coined by Shakespeare)

As puts me from my faith. I tell you what –
He held me last night at least nine hours   150
In reckoning up the several devils' names
That were his lackeys. I cried 'Hum', and 'Well, go to!'
But marked him not a word. O, he is as tedious
As a tired horse, a railing wife,
Worse than a smoky house. I had rather live
With cheese and garlic in a windmill, far,
Than feed on cates and have him talk to me
In any summer house in Christendom.

MORTIMER
In faith, he is a worthy gentleman,
Exceedingly well read, and profited   160
In strange concealments, valiant as a lion,
And wondrous affable, and as bountiful
As mines of India. Shall I tell you, cousin?
He holds your temper in a high respect
And curbs himself even of his natural scope
When you come 'cross his humour, faith he does.
I warrant you that man is not alive
Might so have tempted him as you have done
Without the taste of danger and reproof.
But do not use it oft, let me entreat you.   170

WORCESTER
In faith, my lord, you are too wilful-blame,
And since your coming hither have done enough
To put him quite besides his patience.
You must needs learn, lord, to amend this fault.
Though sometimes it show greatness, courage, blood –

---

149 *faith* (in Christ)
152 *'Hum', and 'Well, go to'* (simulating
   interest when bored)
156 *windmill* (because noisy and
   unsteady)
157 *cates* delicacies

160–1 *profited* | *In strange concealments* pro-
   ficient in secret arts (compare line
   46)
171 *wilful-blame* wilfully blameworthy
175 *blood* spirit

And that's the dearest grace it renders you –
Yet oftentimes it doth present harsh rage,
Defect of manners, want of government,
Pride, haughtiness, opinion, and disdain,
180   The least of which haunting a nobleman
Loseth men's hearts and leaves behind a stain
Upon the beauty of all parts besides,
Beguiling them of commendation.

HOTSPUR
Well, I am schooled – good manners be your speed!
Here come our wives, and let us take our leave.
          Enter Glendower with the ladies

MORTIMER
This is the deadly spite that angers me,
My wife can speak no English, I no Welsh.

GLENDOWER
My daughter weeps, she'll not part with you,
She'll be a soldier too, she'll to the wars.

MORTIMER
190   Good father, tell her that she and my aunt Percy
Shall follow in your conduct speedily.
          *Glendower speaks to her in Welsh, and she answers him
          in the same*

---

176 *dearest* noblest
     grace credit
177 *present* show
178 *want of government* lack of self-
     control
179 *opinion* conceit
183 *Beguiling* cheating, defrauding
184 *good manners be your speed* may it be
     good manners that gives you success
     (in battle). In view of the way in
     which Worcester beguiles Hotspur
     by not revealing 'The liberal and
     kind offer of the King' (v.2.2), this
     is rather an ironic exchange.
185 *and.* In Elizabethan English *and*
     could connect an affirmation and a

command. Another instance occurs
at v.4.33.
190 *my aunt Percy.* The Mortimer who
     was Glendower's son-in-law was
     Lady Percy's brother; the Mortimer
     who was proclaimed heir to the
     throne was Lady Percy's nephew –
     but he did not marry Glendower's
     daughter. The family relationship is
     described in notes to 1.3.79 and
     83.
191 (stage direction) *Glendower speaks to
     her in Welsh.* It has been suggested
     that when the play was first per-
     formed, a Welsh singing boy was
     available to Shakespeare's company.

GLENDOWER She is desperate here, a peevish, self-willed
harlotry, one that no persuasion can do good upon.

The lady speaks in Welsh

MORTIMER

I understand thy looks, that pretty Welsh
Which thou pourest down from these swelling heavens
I am too perfect in, and but for shame
In such a parley should I answer thee.

The lady speaks again in Welsh

I understand thy kisses, and thou mine,
And that's a feeling disputation,
But I will never be a truant, love,   200
Till I have learnt thy language, for thy tongue
Makes Welsh as sweet as ditties highly penned,
Sung by a fair queen in a summer's bower
With ravishing division to her lute.

GLENDOWER

Nay, if you melt, then will she run mad.

The lady speaks again in Welsh

MORTIMER

O, I am ignorance itself in this!

GLENDOWER

She bids you on the wanton rushes lay you down,
And rest your gentle head upon her lap,
And she will sing the song that pleaseth you,
And on your eyelids crown the god of sleep,   210
Charming your blood with pleasing heaviness,

---

193 *harlotry*. As at II.4.388, *harlotry* is
not used here to imply prostitution.
It is intended affectionately, if
slightly deprecatingly, as if to say
Glendower's daughter is a silly little
wretch, a misery.

195 *swelling heavens* eyes filled with tears

196 *I am too perfect in* I understand only
too well

197 *should I answer thee* (by weeping also
– were it not shameful)

199 *feeling disputation* dialogue of feelings
(not speech)

202 *highly penned* high flown

204 *division* (a rapid passage of short
notes based on a simple theme)

207 *wanton rushes*. Rushes covered the
floor (and also the stage in all probability), and these have been spread
wantonly – without restraint.

210 *crown* give absolute power to

Making such difference 'twixt wake and sleep
As is the difference betwixt day and night,
The hour before the heavenly-harnessed team
Begins his golden progress in the east.

MORTIMER

With all my heart I'll sit and hear her sing,
By that time will our book I think be drawn.

GLENDOWER

Do so, and those musicians that shall play to you
Hang in the air a thousand leagues from hence,
220 And straight they shall be here. Sit, and attend.

HOTSPUR

Come, Kate, thou art perfect in lying down.
Come, quick, quick, that I may lay my head in thy lap.

LADY PERCY   Go, ye giddy goose.

The music plays

HOTSPUR

Now I perceive the devil understands Welsh,
And 'tis no marvel he is so humorous,
By'r lady, he is a good musician.

214 *heavenly-harnessed team* sun (from the
     team of horses driven by Helios, the
     sun god)
217 *book* indentures tripartite (men-
     tioned in line 76)
218–19 *those musicians that shall play to
     you | Hang in the air a thousand
     leagues from hence.* The musicians
     who are to provide the music are
     spirits, like those which Prospero re-
     quires to give *Some heavenly music* (*The
     Tempest*, v.1.52).
221 *thou art perfect in lying down* (with
     sexual innuendo)
225 *he is so humorous.* The punctuation of
     Q1 at the end of lines 224 and 225
     (given in this text) does not make it
     clear whether the devil (*he*) is humor-
     ous because he speaks Welsh (a comi-

cal language to learn in Hotspur's
opinion), or because of the association of humour and music with the
devil (compare II.4.472–3 – 'the devil
rides upon a fiddle-stick'). Q6 (1622)
made the matter clear by punctuating
with a full stop after 'Welsh' (line
224). This is attractive (though that
quarto has no special authority) as
an emendation, but it has not been
used here because, whether intended
or not, the punctuation given us in
Q1 suggests the way Hotspur's mind
moves from one association to another. Lady Percy, it will be noted,
takes up the association of *humorous*
and 'musician', punning on the first
word to give 'humours' – whims
(see note to IV.1.31).

LADY PERCY
   Then should you be nothing but musical,
   For you are altogether governed by humours.
   Lie still, ye thief, and hear the lady sing in Welsh.

HOTSPUR I had rather hear Lady my brach howl in Irish.   230

LADY PERCY Wouldst thou have thy head broken?

HOTSPUR No.

LADY PERCY Then be still.

HOTSPUR Neither, 'tis a woman's fault.

LADY PERCY Now, God help thee!

HOTSPUR To the Welsh lady's bed.

LADY PERCY What's that?

HOTSPUR Peace, she sings.

       Here the lady sings a Welsh song
   Come, Kate, I'll have your song too.

LADY PERCY Not mine, in good sooth.   240

HOTSPUR Not yours, in good sooth! Heart, you swear like
   a comfit-maker's wife – 'Not you, in good sooth!' and
   'As true as I live!', and 'As God shall mend me!', and
   'As sure as day!' –
   And givest such sarcenet surety for thy oaths
   As if thou never walkest further than Finsbury.

---

229 *Lie still, ye thief, and hear the lady sing in Welsh.* This banter delightfully expresses Lady Percy's love for her husband (see also the note to II.3.93–4).

230 *brach.* Properly, this is a hound that hunts by scent; loosely it means a 'bitch', and is used as a term of abuse. Hotspur is surely using a word that has all the appearances of being Welsh (though it is not) as a kind of joke – a rather more subtle one than he usually makes. The phrase 'Lady the brach' occurs in *King Lear* (I.4.111), and 'brach' within a list of dogs at III.6.68 in that same play.

233 *still* silent

234 *'tis a woman's fault* (to be unable to remain quiet or still)

241–2 *you swear like a comfit-maker's wife.* Just as Hal parodied Hotspur in II.4, so now Hotspur mimics his wife. The relationship of the humour used by Hal and Hotspur is discussed in the Introduction. 'Comfits' were sugar-plums – crystallized fruits.

243 *mend* amend

245 *sarcenet* (light as) silk

246 *Finsbury.* In Shakespeare's day, a favourite walk and place of recreation was Finsbury Fields. It was the sort of entertainment enjoyed by sober citizens – or so it is implied. The joke is not so much at Lady Percy's expense (though it fits the context

Swear me, Kate, like a lady as thou art,
A good mouth-filling oath, and leave 'In sooth',
And such protest of pepper-gingerbread,
250   To velvet-guards, and Sunday citizens.
Come, sing.

LADY PERCY I will not sing.

HOTSPUR 'Tis the next way to turn tailor, or be redbreast
teacher. An the indentures be drawn I'll away within
these two hours. And so, come in when ye will.   *Exit*

GLENDOWER
Come, come, Lord Mortimer, you are as slow
As hot Lord Percy is on fire to go.
By this our book is drawn – we'll but seal,
And then to horse immediately.

MORTIMER   With all my heart.

                                        Exeunt

III.2   *Enter the King, Prince of Wales, and others*

KING HENRY
Lords, give us leave. The Prince of Wales and I

well enough if one allows for the anachronism), as an allusion for the enjoyment of the audience for whom it would be local and topical. This is an example of a character stepping out of his role, though not to the same extent as Falstaff does in recounting the events at Gad's Hill (see the note to II.4.260).

247 *a lady* an aristocrat (a plebeian concept, surely, and hardly appropriate to Hotspur)

249 *protest* protestation
pepper-gingerbread. The precise meaning is not clear – perhaps 'mealy-mouthed' with a touch of pepper, a touch of 'acid', is the nearest equivalent. Whatever the exact meaning,

Hotspur's protest comes across vividly.

250 *velvet-guards* velvet trimmings (that is, those who wear them – citizens in their finery)

253-4 *'Tis the next way to turn tailor, or be redbreast teacher.* Hotspur offers mock encouragement, realizing Lady Percy will not sing: 'It's the best way to fit yourself to be a tailor, or to become a teacher of robins'. Tailors, like weavers (see II.4.128-9) and robins, were held to be good singers.

258 *By this* (time)
book agreement
but just

III.2.1 *give us leave* (to be alone)

Must have some private conference – but be near at
    hand,
For we shall presently have need of you.   *Exeunt Lords*
I know not whether God will have it so
For some displeasing service I have done,
That in his secret doom out of my blood
He'll breed revengement and a scourge for me.
But thou dost in thy passages of life
Make me believe that thou art only marked
For the hot vengeance and the rod of heaven,   10
To punish my mistreadings. Tell me else,
Could such inordinate and low desires,
Such poor, such bare, such lewd, such mean attempts,
Such barren pleasures, rude society,
As thou art matched withal, and grafted to,
Accompany the greatness of thy blood
And hold their level with thy princely heart?

PRINCE HAL
So please your majesty, I would I could
Quit all offences with as clear excuse
As well as I am doubtless I can purge   20
Myself of many I am charged withal.
Yet such extenuation let me beg
As, in reproof of many tales devised,
Which oft the ear of greatness needs must hear,

6 *doom* judgement
8 *Passages* events, incidents
9–11 *thou art only marked . . . To punish my mistreadings.* The meaning here is ambiguous. The passage can mean that Hal will suffer for Henry's sins (Richard's deposition) or that Henry is already being punished for his sins by the manner of Hal's behaviour. The second meaning is probably intended. There seems no justification on this occasion for arguing that both meanings are meant.
12 *inordinate* (1) immoderate; (2) out of order (unworthy of your high rank)
13 *bare* wretched
   lewd base
   attempts exploits
14 *rude* uncivilized
15 *withal* with (and at line 21)
17 *hold their level with* put themselves on a level with
19 *Quit* acquit myself of
20 *doubtless* certain
22 *extenuation* mitigation
23 *many tales devised* much malicious gossip

By smiling pickthanks, and base newsmongers,
I may for some things true, wherein my youth
Hath faulty wandered and irregular,
Find pardon on my true submission.

KING HENRY

God pardon thee! Yet let me wonder, Harry,
30   At thy affections, which do hold a wing
Quite from the flight of all thy ancestors.
Thy place in Council thou hast rudely lost,
Which by thy younger brother is supplied,
And art almost an alien to the hearts
Of all the court and princes of my blood.
The hope and expectation of thy time
Is ruined, and the soul of every man
Prophetically do forethink thy fall.
Had I so lavish of my presence been,
40   So common-hackneyed in the eyes of men,
So stale and cheap to vulgar company,
Opinion, that did help me to the crown,
Had still kept loyal to possession,

25 *pickthanks* talebearers (the word is derived from Holinshed)
28 *Find pardon on my true submission.* Hal asks forgiveness for what he has truly done especially as he is guiltless of many things said against him.
30 *affections* inclinations
    hold a wing take a course (a term from falconry)
31 *from* away from
32 *rudely lost.* Shakespeare omits the reason here, although it is mentioned in all the sources, including *The Famous Victories of Henry the Fifth*, and by Falstaff in *2 Henry IV*, when he says to the Lord Chief Justice, 'For the box o' the ear that the prince gave you, he gave it like a rude Prince, and you took it like a sensible

lord' (1.2.182–3). It is noticeable that 'rude' (uncivilized) is used on each occasion.
39 *Had I so lavish of my presence been.* It was not thought proper for a king to show himself over-frequently to his people.
40 *common-hackneyed.* One part of this word duplicates the other; in combination the result is forceful and individual. Henry's account of his behaviour does not tally with that given by Richard in *Richard II* where, with a variety of detail, he is said to court the common people, seeming 'to dive into their hearts | With humble and familiar courtesy' (1.4.25–6).
43 *possession* the possessor (King Richard)

And left me in reputeless banishment,
A fellow of no mark nor likelihood.
By being seldom seen, I could not stir
But like a comet I was wondered at,
That men would tell their children, 'This is he!'
Others would say, 'Where, which is Bolingbroke?'
And then I stole all courtesy from heaven,   50
And dressed myself in such humility
That I did pluck allegiance from men's hearts,
Loud shouts and salutations from their mouths,
Even in the presence of the crownèd King.
Thus did I keep my person fresh and new,
My presence, like a robe pontifical,
Ne'er seen but wondered at, and so my state,
Seldom, but sumptuous, showed like a feast,
And won by rareness such solemnity.
The skipping King, he ambled up and down,   60
With shallow jesters, and rash bavin wits,
Soon kindled and soon burnt, carded his state,

45 *likelihood* (of having a future)
50 *I stole all courtesy from heaven* I assumed
    a divine graciousness. The word *stole*
    is not without significance. Although
    Henry is being shown in a favourable
    light here, he did steal Richard's
    throne.
54 *Even in the presence of the crownèd King.*
    The allusion is probably to the entry
    of Bolingbroke (Henry) and Richard
    into London, described in *Richard II*,
    v.2, by York.
56 *pontifical* (as worn by a Pope or
    bishop)
60 *skipping* frivolous. Richard's faults
    are, not surprisingly, exaggerated by
    Henry.
61 *rash* quickly lighted
    bavin faggot used for kindling (and
    soon burnt out)
62 *carded his state*. To 'card' wool is to
    tease out impurities and to straighten

the fibres by means of a comb-like
device. It is not, as has sometimes
been suggested, a process in which
various qualities of fibre are mixed
(hence implying that the King debased himself by associating with in-
feriors), but essentially a cleansing
and straightening process. Carding
of the mixing kind was used for
shuffling cards, but as this fault is
described in the line that follows
('Mingled his royalty with capering
fools'), there is no need to repeat it.
The word *carded* here means, surely,
'tortured' – tore at, or scratched, his
state – a form of torture practised in
the period. The textile association of
carded presumably led Shakespeare to
think of mingling. Another textile
processing term is used at III.2.137 –
'scour'.

Mingled his royalty with capering fools,
Had his great name profaned with their scorns,
And gave his countenance against his name
To laugh at gibing boys, and stand the push
Of every beardless vain comparative,
Grew a companion to the common streets,
Enfeoffed himself to popularity,
70   That, being daily swallowed by men's eyes,
They surfeited with honey, and began
To loathe the taste of sweetness, whereof a little
More than a little is by much too much.
So, when he had occasion to be seen,
He was but as the cuckoo is in June,
Heard, not regarded; seen, but with such eyes
As, sick and blunted with community,
Afford no extraordinary gaze,
Such as is bent on sun-like majesty
80   When it shines seldom in admiring eyes,
But rather drowsed and hung their eyelids down,
Slept in his face, and rendered such aspect
As cloudy men use to their adversaries,
Being with his presence glutted, gorged, and full.
And in that very line, Harry, standest thou,
For thou hast lost thy princely privilege
With vile participation. Not an eye
But is a-weary of thy common sight,
Save mine, which hath desired to see thee more,

65 *countenance* authority
    against his name to the detriment of
    his reputation
66 *push* pushing and shoving
67 *comparative* dealer in insults (see also
    1.2.80)
69 *Enfeoffed* surrendered
    popularity the common people
77 *community* familiarity

79 *sun-like majesty.* The sun is a traditional symbol of royalty (see note to
1.2.195). Its association here with
'cloudy men' (line 83), hostile to the
sun, is similar to the association of
the sun with 'the base contagious
clouds' in 1.2.195–6.
87 *vile participation* (low companions)

Which now doth that I would not have it do,   90
Make blind itself with foolish tenderness.

PRINCE HAL
  I shall hereafter, my thrice-gracious lord,
  Be more myself.

KING HENRY   For all the world
  As thou art to this hour was Richard then
  When I from France set foot at Ravenspurgh,
  And even as I was then is Percy now.
  Now by my sceptre, and my soul to boot,
  He hath more worthy interest to the state
  Than thou the shadow of succession.
  For of no right, nor colour like to right,   100
  He doth fill fields with harness in the realm,
  Turns head against the lion's armèd jaws,
  And being no more in debt to years than thou
  Leads ancient lords and reverend bishops on
  To bloody battles, and to bruising arms.
  What never-dying honour hath he got
  Against renownèd Douglas! Whose high deeds,
  Whose hot incursions and great name in arms,
  Holds from all soldiers chief majority
  And military title capital   110
  Through all the kingdoms that acknowledge Christ.

91 *foolish tenderness* tears
94 *As thou art to this hour was Richard.*
The likeness of Hal to Richard may
not seem obvious, but it evidently
struck Shakespeare. In *Richard II*,
when Henry anxiously asked after
Hal he described him as a 'young
wanton and effeminate boy' (v.3.10).
In one of Shakespeare's sources for
that play, and this one, Samuel
Daniel's *The First Four Books of the
Civil Wars Between the Two Houses of
Lancaster and York* (1595), Richard II

is called 'This wanton young effeminate'.
97 *to boot* as well
98 *worthy interest* right by worth
100 *colour* semblance
101 *harness* armed men
102 *Turns head* (1) turns his eyes; (2)
turns the army he has raised
103 *And being no more in debt to years than
thou.* Hotspur was actually older than
Henry IV, Hal's father (see note to
1.1.86–7).
109 *chief majority* pre-eminence

Thrice hath this Hotspur, Mars in swaddling clothes,
This infant warrior, in his enterprises
Discomfited great Douglas, taken him once,
Enlargèd him, and made a friend of him,
To fill the mouth of deep defiance up,
And shake the peace and safety of our throne.
And what say you to this? Percy, Northumberland,
The Archbishop's Grace of York, Douglas, Mortimer,
120   Capitulate against us and are up.
But wherefore do I tell these news to thee?
Why, Harry, do I tell thee of my foes,
Which art my nearest and dearest enemy?
Thou that art like enough, through vassal fear,
Base inclination, and the start of spleen,
To fight against me under Percy's pay,
To dog his heels, and curtsy at his frowns,
To show how much thou art degenerate.

PRINCE HAL

Do not think so, you shall not find it so;
130   And God forgive them that so much have swayed
Your majesty's good thoughts away from me!
I will redeem all this on Percy's head,
And in the closing of some glorious day

---

112 *Thrice.* The battles were Otterburn (at which the English were defeated and Hotspur was captured; Hal was then aged one), Nesbit (see note to 1.1.55), and Holmedon. Douglas's father was killed by Hotspur at Otterburn.

116 *To fill . . . up* to increase, to enlarge

120 *Capitulate* sign agreements
    are up (in arms)

123 *dearest.* The first meaning is 'most precious' but there is also a pun on *dearest*: 'direst'.

124 *vassal* base, abject

125 *start of spleen* fit of pique

126 *To fight against me under Percy's pay.* This very serious charge had no foun-

dation at the time but it is possible that Shakespeare had in mind a reported usurpation of the crown by Hal in 1412, a decade later. There is a dramatic moment in *2 Henry IV* when Hal, believing his father to be dead, puts the crown on his head, only to be bitterly rebuked by Henry:

I stay too long by thee, I weary thee.
Dost thou so hunger for my empty chair
That thou wilt needs invest thee with
    mine honours
Before thy hour be ripe?   IV.5.92–5

See also v.4.50–56 of this play.

Be bold to tell you that I am your son,
When I will wear a garment all of blood,
And stain my favours in a bloody mask,
Which, washed away, shall scour my shame with it.
And that shall be the day, whene'er it lights,
That this same child of honour and renown,
This gallant Hotspur, this all-praisèd knight,   140
And your unthought-of Harry chance to meet.
For every honour sitting on his helm,
Would they were multitudes, and on my head
My shames redoubled. For the time will come
That I shall make this northern youth exchange
His glorious deeds for my indignities.
Percy is but my factor, good my lord,
To engross up glorious deeds on my behalf,
And I will call him to so strict account
That he shall render every glory up,   150
Yea, even the slightest worship of his time,
Or I will tear the reckoning from his heart.
This in the name of God I promise here,
The which if He be pleased I shall perform,
I do beseech your majesty may salve
The long-grown wounds of my intemperance.
If not, the end of life cancels all bonds,
And I will die a hundred thousand deaths
Ere break the smallest parcel of this vow.

KING HENRY

A hundred thousand rebels die in this.   160
Thou shalt have charge and sovereign trust herein.

---

136 *favours* features
141 *unthought-of* poorly thought-of, despised
147 *factor* agent
151 *worship of his time* honour of his lifetime
156 *intemperance* wild behaviour. F substitutes 'intemperature', which is an attractive reading (for it means both

'licentiousness' and 'distempered condition') but, as is argued in An Account of the Text, has no authority.
159 *parcel* portion
161 *charge* a command
sovereign trust (1) a most important command; (2) the King's wholehearted trust

Enter Blunt

How now, good Blunt? Thy looks are full of speed.

BLUNT

So hath the business that I come to speak of.
Lord Mortimer of Scotland hath sent word
That Douglas and the English rebels met
The eleventh of this month at Shrewsbury.
A mighty and a fearful head they are,
If promises be kept on every hand,
As ever offered foul play in a state.

KING HENRY

170   The Earl of Westmorland set forth today,
With him my son, Lord John of Lancaster,
For this advertisement is five days old.
On Wednesday next, Harry, you shall set forward.
On Thursday we ourselves will march.
Our meeting is Bridgnorth, and, Harry, you
Shall march through Gloucestershire, by which account,
Our business valued, some twelve days hence
Our general forces at Bridgnorth shall meet.
Our hands are full of business, let's away,
180   Advantage feeds him fat while men delay.   *Exeunt*

III.3   *Enter Falstaff and Bardolph*

FALSTAFF   Bardolph, am I not fallen away vilely since this

---

164 *Lord Mortimer of Scotland.* This is
yet another, but a different, confusion concerning the Mortimers,
who were Lords of the Welsh
Marches (or Borders). George Dunbar was Earl of the Scottish Marches
(see note introducing II.3).
167 *head* army
172 *advertisement* news
175–6 *Harry, you | Shall march through
Gloucestershire.* This would require a

journey by a secondary route. Shakespeare, or Hal, forgets this plan, for
Hal meets Falstaff in IV.2 near Coventry on the main Shrewsbury road.
177 *Our business valued* our affairs put in
order
180 *him* himself

III.3 As the Hostess enters after line 50,
we are evidently in the tavern in
Eastcheap.

last action? Do I not bate? Do I not dwindle? Why, my
skin hangs about me like an old lady's loose gown. I am
withered like an old apple-john. Well, I'll repent, and
that suddenly, while I am in some liking. I shall be out
of heart shortly, and then I shall have no strength to
repent. An I have not forgotten what the inside of a
church is made of, I am a peppercorn, a brewer's horse.
The inside of a church! Company, villainous company,
hath been the spoil of me.   10

BARDOLPH Sir John, you are so fretful you cannot live
long.

FALSTAFF Why, there is it. Come, sing me a bawdy song,
make me merry. I was as virtuously given as a gentleman need to be. Virtuous enough. Swore little. Diced
not above seven times a week. Went to a bawdy-house
not above once in a quarter — of an hour. Paid money
that I borrowed — three or four times. Lived well, and in
good compass: and now I live out of all order, out of all
compass.   20

BARDOLPH Why, you are so fat, Sir John, that you must
needs be out of all compass, out of all reasonable compass, Sir John.

FALSTAFF Do thou amend thy face, and I'll amend my
life. Thou art our admiral, thou bearest the lantern in
the poop, but 'tis in the nose of thee. Thou art the

2 *last action* (at Gad's Hill, or possibly
the engagement with Hal in II.4)
bate lose weight
4 *old apple-john* (an apple noted for its
long-keeping qualities. Although
the flesh remained sound, the skin
shrivelled.)
5 *suddenly* at once
am in some liking (1) feel like doing so;
(2) still have some flesh on me
5–6 *out of heart* (1) dispirited; (2) in poor
condition

6 *no strength* (of body, and, of purpose)
7 *An* if
8 *peppercorn* mere nothing (as in 'a peppercorn rent')
brewer's horse (notoriously worn out)
11 *fretful* (1) anxious; (2) fretted (worn)
13 *there is it* there it is
18–19 *in good compass* within bounds
19–20 *out of all compass* (with a glance at
his girth)
25 *admiral* flagship

Knight of the Burning Lamp.

BARDOLPH Why, Sir John, my face does you no harm.

FALSTAFF No, I'll be sworn, I make as good use of it as
many a man doth of a death's-head, or a *memento mori*.
I never see thy face but I think upon hell-fire, and Dives
that lived in purple: for there he is in his robes, burning,
burning. If thou wert any way given to virtue, I would
swear by thy face. My oath should be 'By this fire, that's
God's angel!' But thou art altogether given over, and
wert indeed, but for the light in thy face, the son of
utter darkness. When thou rannest up Gad's Hill in the
night to catch my horse, if I did not think thou hadst
been an *ignis fatuus*, or a ball of wildfire, there's no
purchase in money. O, thou art a perpetual triumph, an
everlasting bonfire-light! Thou hast saved me a thousand
marks in links and torches, walking with thee in the
night betwixt tavern and tavern. But the sack that thou
hast drunk me would have bought me lights as good
cheap at the dearest chandler's in Europe. I have
maintained that salamander of yours with fire any time
this two-and-thirty years, God reward me for it!

27 *Knight of the Burning Lamp* (a parody
of Amadis, Knight of the Burning
Sword, a chivalric figure. Beaumont
parodies him in his *The Knight of the
Burning Pestle*.)

29–30 *as good use of it as many a man doth
of a death's-head.* This seems to be
ambiguous, perhaps deliberately so.
Rings were engraved with a skull
and these served as a reminder of
death ('*memento mori*'). But they were
regularly worn by prostitutes, of
which many a man makes use.

31 *Dives* (the rich man who feasted
whilst Lazarus starved – Luke 16;
see also IV.2.24)

35 *God's angel.* The allusion is probably

to the story of Moses and the Burning Bush in which, it is said, 'the
angel of the Lord appeared unto him
in a flame of fire' (Exodus 3.2).
given over (to Satan)

39 *ignis fatuus* fool's fire, will o'the wisp
ball of wildfire firework (and possibly,
erysipelas – a skin disease)

40 *purchase* value
triumph illumination for a festival

42 *links* small flaming torches

44 *drunk me* (an archaic construction;
modern English does not require
'me')

44–5 *good cheap* cheaply

46 *salamander* (fabulous lizard that lives
in and on fire)

BARDOLPH 'Sblood, I would my face were in your belly!

FALSTAFF God-a-mercy! So should I be sure to be heart-
burnt.   50

  Enter Hostess

How now, dame Partlet the hen, have you enquired yet
who picked my pocket?

HOSTESS Why, Sir John, what do you think, Sir John, do
you think I keep thieves in my house? I have searched, I
have enquired, so has my husband, man by man, boy by
boy, servant by servant – the tithe of a hair was never
lost in my house before.

FALSTAFF Ye lie, hostess. Bardolph was shaved and lost
many a hair, and I'll be sworn my pocket was picked.
Go to, you are a woman, go!   60

HOSTESS Who, I? No, I defy thee! God's light, I was
never called so in mine own house before.

FALSTAFF Go to, I know you well enough.

HOSTESS No, Sir John, you do not know me, Sir John, I
know you, Sir John, you owe me money, Sir John, and
now you pick a quarrel to beguile me of it. I bought you
a dozen of shirts to your back.

FALSTAFF Dowlas, filthy dowlas. I have given them away
to bakers' wives. They have made bolters of them.

HOSTESS Now as I am a true woman, holland of eight   70
shillings an ell! You owe money here besides, Sir John,
for your diet, and by-drinkings, and money lent you,
four-and-twenty pound.

---

48 *I would my face were in your belly* (proverbial retort)

51 *dame Partlet* (a traditional name for a
hen, and so a fussy woman. 'Perte-
lote' is the name of the hen in Chaucer's *Nun's Priest's Tale*.)

58 *shaved*. In addition to its usual meaning, 'shaved' could mean 'cheated'
and 'to have caught syphilis' (which
was believed to lead to baldness).

60 *you are a woman* (and thus unreliable if
not untrustworthy)

68 *Dowlas* (cheap linen from Doulas in
Brittany)

69 *bolters* (cloths used for sieving)

70 *holland* (fine linen, and rather over-
priced at eight shillings an ell)

71 *ell* (in England, 45 inches)

72 *by-drinkings* drinks between meals

FALSTAFF He had his part of it, let him pay.

HOSTESS He? Alas, he is poor, he hath nothing.

FALSTAFF How? Poor? Look upon his face. What call
you rich? Let them coin his nose, let them coin his
cheeks, I'll not pay a denier. What, will you make a
younker of me? Shall I not take mine ease in mine inn
80   but I shall have my pocket picked? I have lost a seal-
ring of my grandfather's worth forty mark.

HOSTESS O Jesu, I have heard the Prince tell him I know
not how oft, that that ring was copper.

FALSTAFF How? The Prince is a Jack, a sneak-up.
'Sblood, an he were here I would cudgel him like a dog
if he would say so.

> *Enter the Prince marching, with Peto, and Falstaff
> meets him, playing upon his truncheon like a fife*

How now, lad? Is the wind in that door, i'faith, must
we all march?

BARDOLPH Yea, two and two, Newgate fashion.

90   HOSTESS My lord, I pray you hear me.

PRINCE HAL What sayest thou, Mistress Quickly? How
doth thy husband? I love him well, he is an honest man.

HOSTESS Good my lord, hear me.

FALSTAFF Prithee let her alone, and list to me.

PRINCE HAL What sayest thou, Jack?

FALSTAFF The other night I fell asleep here, behind the
arras, and had my pocket picked. This house is turned
bawdy-house, they pick pockets.

PRINCE HAL What didst thou lose, Jack?

100   FALSTAFF Wilt thou believe me, Hal, three or four bonds

---

78 *denier* (one-tenth of a penny)

79 *younker*. An alternative name for the
prodigal in the parable of the prodigal son was 'the younger'.

81 *mark* (13s. 4d.)

84 *Jack* knave

86 (stage direction) *playing upon his truncheon like a fife*. Presumably when

Falstaff says in line 85 that he would
cudgel Hal, he imitates the action.
When Hal enters Falstaff rapidly and
comically changes his 'business' to
meet the new situation.

87 *door* quarter

89 *Newgate fashion* two by two (as
prisoners)

of forty pound apiece, and a seal-ring of my grandfather's.

PRINCE HAL A trifle, some eightpenny matter.

HOSTESS So I told him, my lord, and I said I heard your
grace say so. And, my lord, he speaks most vilely of you,
like a foul-mouthed man as he is, and said he would
cudgel you.

PRINCE HAL What! He did not?

HOSTESS There's neither faith, truth, nor womanhood in
me else.   110

FALSTAFF There's no more faith in thee than in a stewed
prune, nor no more truth in thee than in a drawn fox –
and for womanhood, Maid Marian may be the deputy's
wife of the ward to thee. Go, you thing, go!

HOSTESS Say, what thing, what thing?

FALSTAFF What thing? Why, a thing to thank God on.

HOSTESS I am no thing to thank God on, I would thou
shouldst know it, I am an honest man's wife, and setting
thy knighthood aside, thou art a knave to call me so.

FALSTAFF Setting thy womanhood aside, thou art a beast   120
to say otherwise.

HOSTESS Say, what beast, thou knave, thou?

FALSTAFF What beast? Why – an otter.

PRINCE HAL An otter, Sir John? Why an otter?

FALSTAFF Why? She's neither fish nor flesh, a man knows
not where to have her.

111–12 *stewed prune* prostitute

112 *drawn fox*. The meaning is not clear;
perhaps the joke has been lost to us.
It has been explained as a fox drawn
from cover and so relying upon cunning for its life; a disembowelled
fox; a dead fox used to give a false
trail; and a drawn sword (so named
because of the figure of a wolf engraved on the blade which was mistaken for a fox).

113–14 *Maid Marian may be the deputy's*

wife of the ward to thee. The deputy of
a ward was a highly respectable citizen, and his wife was expected to be
so also. Maid Marian's reputation
was very low, however, and thus
Falstaff says that compared to the
Hostess, Maid Marian was a highly
respectable woman.

116 *What thing* (a sexual quibble)

117 *no thing* (another sexual quibble)

126 *where to have her* (with sexual
quibble)

HOSTESS Thou art an unjust man in saying so, thou or
any man knows where to have me, thou knave, thou.

PRINCE HAL Thou sayest true, Hostess, and he slanders
130 thee most grossly.

HOSTESS So he doth you, my lord, and said this other day
you owed him a thousand pound.

PRINCE HAL Sirrah, do I owe you a thousand pound?

FALSTAFF A thousand pound, Hal? A million, thy love is
worth a million, thou owest me thy love.

HOSTESS Nay my lord, he called you Jack, and said he
would cudgel you.

FALSTAFF Did I, Bardolph?

BARDOLPH Indeed, Sir John, you said so.

140 FALSTAFF Yea, if he said my ring was copper.

PRINCE HAL I say 'tis copper, darest thou be as good as
thy word now?

FALSTAFF Why Hal, thou knowest as thou art but man I
dare, but as thou art prince, I fear thee as I fear the
roaring of the lion's whelp.

PRINCE HAL And why not as the lion?

FALSTAFF The King himself is to be feared as the lion.
Dost thou think I'll fear thee as I fear thy father? Nay,
an I do, I pray God my girdle break.

150 PRINCE HAL O, if it should, how would thy guts fall
about thy knees! But sirrah, there's no room for faith,
truth, nor honesty in this bosom of thine. It is all filled
up with guts and midriff. Charge an honest woman with
picking thy pocket? Why, thou whoreson impudent
embossed rascal, if there were anything in thy pocket
but tavern reckonings, memorandums of bawdy-
houses, and one poor pennyworth of sugar-candy to

---

147 *The King himself is to be feared as the
lion.* The lion, like the sun, was a
symbol of royalty (see note to 1.2.195).

149 *I pray God my girdle break* (a proverbial saying)

155 *embossed rascal.* There are probably

puns on both words. *Embossed* can
mean (1) swollen; (2) slavering like a
hunted deer; *rascal* is (1) a knave; (2)
a lean, inferior deer.

157–8 *sugar-candy to make thee long-winded.*
Even in Shakespeare's day sugar was

make thee long-winded, if thy pocket were enriched
with any other injuries but these, I am a villain. And yet
you will stand to it, you will not pocket up wrong! Art   160
thou not ashamed?

FALSTAFF Dost thou hear, Hal? Thou knowest in the
state of innocency Adam fell, and what should poor
Jack Falstaff do in the days of villainy? Thou seest I
have more flesh than another man, and therefore more
frailty. You confess then, you picked my pocket?

PRINCE HAL It appears so by the story.

FALSTAFF Hostess, I forgive thee, go make ready
breakfast, love thy husband, look to thy servants,
cherish thy guests, thou shalt find me tractable to any   170
honest reason, thou seest I am pacified still — nay
prithee be gone.   *Exit Hostess*
Now, Hal, to the news at court: for the robbery, lad,
how is that answered?

PRINCE HAL O my sweet beef, I must still be good angel
to thee — the money is paid back again.

FALSTAFF O, I do not like that paying back, 'tis a double
labour.

PRINCE HAL I am good friends with my father and may
do anything.   180

FALSTAFF Rob me the exchequer the first thing thou
dost, and do it with unwashed hands too.

BARDOLPH Do, my lord.

PRINCE HAL I have procured thee, Jack, a charge of foot.

---

prescribed to aid stamina — particularly that of fighting cocks!

159 *injuries* (things whose loss you complain of as injuries. The use of *injuries*
with this meaning makes possible a
pun on 'wrong' in line 160.)

167 *by* according to

168 *Hostess, I forgive thee.* Doubtless
Dame Partlet will be so flustered by

now that she will feel gratified at being
forgiven for what is Falstaff's fault.

171 *still* now

177–8 *double labour* (taking it and returning it)

182 *with unwashed hands* without wasting
any time

184 *charge of foot* company of infantry
(see II.4.530)

FALSTAFF   I would it had been of horse. Where shall I
find one that can steal well? O for a fine thief of the age
of two-and-twenty or thereabouts! I am heinously unprovided. Well, God be thanked for these rebels, they
offend none but the virtuous. I laud them, I praise them.

190   PRINCE HAL   Bardolph!

BARDOLPH   My lord?

PRINCE HAL

Go bear this letter to Lord John of Lancaster,
To my brother John, this to my Lord of Westmorland.
                                        Exit Bardolph

Go, Peto, to horse, to horse, for thou and I
Have thirty miles to ride yet ere dinner-time.   *Exit Peto*
Jack, meet me tomorrow in the Temple hall
At two o'clock in the afternoon.
There shalt thou know thy charge, and there receive
Money and order for their furniture.

200   The land is burning, Percy stands on high,
And either we or they must lower lie.   *Exit*

FALSTAFF

Rare words! Brave world! Hostess, my breakfast, come!
O, I could wish this tavern were my drum.   *Exit*

---

196   *the Temple hall* Inner Temple Hall (a
popular meeting-place)

199   *furniture* furnishing, equipment

203   *I could wish this tavern were my drum*.
This has not been wholly satisfactorily explained. It has been suggested
that there is a pun on *tavern* and
'taborn', a kind of drum; or that
Falstaff wishes the tavern were the
only drum he must follow, which, as
it stands, is not very close although
the sense is reasonable.

There seem to be two other possibilities. A *drum* was at this time a
small party of soldiers sent, with a
drummer, to discuss terms with an
enemy. Falstaff might feel that any
military party discussing terms might
for preference meet at a tavern. Sec-
ondly, Falstaff says *my drum* – Jack's
Drum. Jack Drum's Entertainment
was a rowdy reception – a fair description of a battle, and of the behaviour of Falstaff and company in the
tavern (as, for example, when the
Sheriff arrives in 11.4). Shakespeare
uses the expression John Drum's entertainment in *All's Well that Ends
Well* (111.6.33) and Marston wrote a
play called *Jack Drum's Entertainment*,
published in 1600.

Enter Hotspur, Worcester, and Douglas   IV.1

HOTSPUR

Well said, my noble Scot! If speaking truth
In this fine age were not thought flattery,
Such attribution should the Douglas have
As not a soldier of this season's stamp
Should go as general current through the world.
By God, I cannot flatter, I do defy
The tongues of soothers, but a braver place
In my heart's love hath no man than yourself.
Nay, task me to my word, approve me, lord.

DOUGLAS

Thou art the king of honour.   10
No man so potent breathes upon the ground
But I will beard him.

HOTSPUR   Do so, and 'tis well.

Enter one with letters

What letters hast thou there? – I can but thank you.

MESSENGER

These letters come from your father.

HOTSPUR

Letters from him? Why comes he not himself?

MESSENGER

He cannot come, my lord, he is grievous sick.

IV.1 The scene is set in the camp of the
rebels at Shrewsbury.

2 *fine* refined

3 *attribution* (of praise)

4 *stamp* stamping, coinage

5 *general current* widely accepted (and see
the note on the use of *current* at
II.3.97)

6 *defy* distrust

7 *soothers* flatterers
braver finer

9 *task* test
approve me put me to the proof

11 *ground* earth

12 *beard* come face to face (literally, 'pull
by the beard', and particularly 'beard
the lion')

13 *I can but thank you.* Hotspur's reply is
delayed – a trick imitated by Hal (see
note to II.4.101–107) – but here with
some reason as he responds naturally
to the Messenger's entry.

16 *he is grievous sick.* Northumberland's
illness occurred earlier. It is mentioned by Holinshed immediately
after his account of how Worcester,
'that had the government of the
Prince of Wales' conveyed himself

HOTSPUR

Zounds, how has he the leisure to be sick
In such a justling time? Who leads his power?
Under whose government come they along?

MESSENGER

His letters bear his mind, not I, my lord.

WORCESTER

I prithee tell me, doth he keep his bed?

MESSENGER

He did, my lord, four days ere I set forth,
And at the time of my departure thence
He was much feared by his physicians.

WORCESTER

I would the state of time had first been whole
Ere he by sickness had been visited.
His health was never better worth than now.

HOTSPUR

Sick now? Droop now? This sickness doth infect
The very life-blood of our enterprise.
'Tis catching hither, even to our camp.

'in secret manner' out of the Prince's house. Shakespeare brings news of Northumberland's illness to light just before the battle of Shrewsbury, so bringing out his son's impetuosity and courage, and perhaps suggesting that the father was as devious as the son was outspoken. His reasons for not sending a force to support his son (lines 32–8) are not very convincing. Whereas Shakespeare refashions history for dramatic effect in this instance, he makes no use of the fact, available in the same section of the same source, that Worcester 'had the government' of Hal – except possibly to pick up the word 'government' (command) for line 19.

20 *His letters bear his mind, not I, my lord.* This reply, what Touchstone might have called 'the Retort Courteous' (*As You Like It*, v.4.70), is not as deferential in tone as one would expect from a mere messenger – especially the carrier of bad tidings. The Messenger ought, perhaps, to be a member of the Percy household, a squire. In the quartos and the Folio, *bear* is given as 'bears'. Though a plural subject sometimes did have a verb in the singular in Elizabethan English, this has been emended here.

24 *feared* feared for

30 *'Tis catching hither* it will infect us here

He writes me here that inward sickness –
And that his friends by deputation could not
So soon be drawn, nor did he think it meet
To lay so dangerous and dear a trust
On any soul removed but on his own.
Yet doth he give us bold advertisement
That with our small conjunction we should on,
To see how fortune is disposed to us.
For, as he writes, there is no quailing now,
Because the King is certainly possessed   40
Of all our purposes. What say you to it?

WORCESTER
Your father's sickness is a maim to us.

HOTSPUR
A perilous gash, a very limb lopped off –
And yet, in faith, it is not! His present want
Seems more than we shall find it. Were it good
To set the exact wealth of all our states
All at one cast? To set so rich a main
On the nice hazard of one doubtful hour?
It were not good, for therein should we read
The very bottom and the soul of hope,   50

---

31 *inward sickness* –. The quartos merely
have a comma after *sickness*. Clearly
the sense cannot run on to the next
line. It is conceivable that a line has
been lost, but the text as we have it
is more likely a representation of the
way in which Hotspur's thoughts run
ahead of what he says (see also the
note to III.1.225).

32 *deputation* others acting as his deputy

33 *drawn* drawn in, involved
   meet appropriate

35 *removed* not closely connected

36 *bold advertisement* (either 'confident
   advice', or 'instruction to be
   resolute')

37 *conjunction* forces so far joined

together
on go on

44 *present want* absence now

45 *more* greater
   find it (to be)

47 *main* (quibbling on 'stake' in a game
   of chance, and 'army')

48 *nice* delicate

50 *very bottom* whole extent
   soul essence (possibly with quibble
   on 'sole', the 'bottom' of the shoe,
   and the 'singleness' of such hope –
   but such is Shakespeare's potentiality
   for quibbling that we are inclined to
   see puns where none were intended
   and where they may be inappropriate)

The very list, the very utmost bound
Of all our fortunes.

DOUGLAS

Faith, and so we should, where now remains
A sweet reversion – we may boldly spend
Upon the hope of what is to come in.
A comfort of retirement lives in this.

HOTSPUR

A rendezvous, a home to fly unto,
If that the devil and mischance look big
Upon the maidenhead of our affairs.

WORCESTER

60   But yet I would your father had been here.
The quality and hair of our attempt
Brooks no division. It will be thought,
By some that know not why he is away,
That wisdom, loyalty, and mere dislike
Of our proceedings kept the Earl from hence.
And think how such an apprehension
May turn the tide of fearful faction,
And breed a kind of question in our cause.
For well you know we of the offering side
70   Must keep aloof from strict arbitrement,
And stop all sight-holes, every loop from whence
The eye of reason may pry in upon us.
This absence of your father's draws a curtain

51 *very list* extreme limit
54 *reversion* inheritance (prospect) to
    look forward to
56 *of retirement* into which to retreat
58–9 *look big | Upon* threaten
59 *maidenhead* first trial
61 *hair* appearance
62 *Brooks* permits
64 *mere* downright
66 *apprehension* idea, belief
67 *fearful* timorous
69 *offering side* side offering a challenge.

'Offering' is spelt 'offring' in Q1 to
make it, strictly, a two-syllable word.
It has been spelt in full here, the
speaker being expected to adjust the
stress to suit his own style of speech
(see also the note to 1.1.8).

70 *strict arbitrement* impartial adjudica-
    tion. Worcester's behaviour at the
    opening of v.2 accords with the opin-
    ion expressed here.

71 *loop* loop-hole
73 *draws* draws aside

That shows the ignorant a kind of fear
Before not dreamt of.

HOTSPUR   You strain too far.
I rather of his absence make this use.
It lends a lustre and more great opinion,
A larger dare to our great enterprise,
Than if the Earl were here. For men must think
If we without his help can make a head   80
To push against a kingdom, with his help
We shall o'erturn it topsy-turvy down.
Yet all goes well, yet all our joints are whole.

DOUGLAS
As heart can think. There is not such a word
Spoke of in Scotland as this term of fear.

            Enter Sir Richard Vernon

HOTSPUR
My cousin Vernon! Welcome, by my soul!

VERNON
Pray God my news be worth a welcome, lord.
The Earl of Westmorland seven thousand strong
Is marching hitherwards, with him Prince John.

HOTSPUR
No harm, what more?

VERNON   And further, I have learned,
The King himself in person is set forth,   90
Or hitherwards intended speedily,
With strong and mighty preparation.

HOTSPUR
He shall be welcome too. Where is his son,
The nimble-footed madcap Prince of Wales,

74 *a kind of fear* (in us)
75 *strain too far* exaggerate
77 *opinion* repute
78 *dare* risk
80 *make a head* raise (such) a force
83 *joints* limbs

92 *intended* on the point of setting out
95 *nimble-footed*. Hal was reported in the
     histories to be particularly fleet of
     foot.
     madcap (see 1.2.140–41)

> And his comrades that daffed the world aside
> And bid it pass?
>   VERNON   All furnished, all in arms,
> All plumed like estridges that with the wind
> Bated, like eagles having lately bathed,
> Glittering in golden coats like images,
> As full of spirit as the month of May,
> And gorgeous as the sun at midsummer,

100

96 *daffed* tossed aside (compare 'doffed')

98-9 *All plumed like estridges that with the wind | Bated, like eagles having lately bathed.* These lines introduce a passage rich in images. Vernon's speech is no more representative of character than the Queen's speech in *Hamlet* that begins 'There is a willow grows aslant a brook' (IV.7.167). Vernon's words evoke that spirit of pride, honour, royalty, and ceremony, which is appropriate to this occasion. The moment here is one of chivalric challenge. It will be contrasted by Shakespeare with its opposite, Falstaff's consideration of honour, his 'killing' of the dead Hotspur, and his comment on the 'grinning honour as Sir Walter hath' (V.3.59) (see also the Introduction). These two lines of Vernon's speech have been called the 'chief crux of the text' by John Dover Wilson and a number of emendations have been proposed. Two of the most interesting are the substitution of 'wing' for *with* and a much more radical rearrangement involving the omission of *estridges*, which, it is suggested, Shakespeare had failed to cancel clearly during revision. This would give the single line, 'All plumed like eagles having lately bathed', instead of the two lines printed in this edition (and QI). The first proposal is helpful, but not essential; the second, though attractive, requires the omission of a particularly appropriate and colourful image, the Prince of Wales's plumes (ostrich feathers) ruffled (*Bated*) in the breeze. *Bated* can mean refreshed (exactly as in the dialect noun, 'bait', for food between main meals) but it is applied to food, not the refreshment that comes from bathing. *Estridges* could be goshawks, though this seems unlikely here. The passage may have been inspired by descriptions in Thomas Nashe's *The Unfortunate Traveller*, Spenser's *Faerie Queene* (I.XI.33-4), and most interestingly George Chapman's *De Guiana Carmen Epicum* (1596) where the following lines occur as Raleigh is about to leave on his second expedition to Guiana:

>   *where round about*
> *His bating colours English valour*
>   *swarms . . .*
> *And now a wind as forward as their*
>   *spirits,*
> *Sets their glad feet on smooth* Guiana's
>   *breast . . .*
> *And there doth plenty crown their wealthy*
>   *fields,*
> *There Learning eats no more his thriftless*
>   *books,*
> *Nor Valour estridge-like his iron arms.*

100 *coats* surcoats (worn over the armour and usually having the knight's arms depicted thereon)
images effigies (of saints or warriors)

Wanton as youthful goats, wild as young bulls.
I saw young Harry with his beaver on,
His cuishes on his thighs, gallantly armed,
Rise from the ground like feathered Mercury,
And vaulted with such ease into his seat
As if an angel dropped down from the clouds
To turn and wind a fiery Pegasus,
And witch the world with noble horsemanship.   110

HOTSPUR

No more, no more! Worse than the sun in March,
This praise doth nourish agues. Let them come!
They come like sacrifices in their trim,
And to the fire-eyed maid of smoky war
All hot and bleeding will we offer them.
The mailèd Mars shall on his altar sit
Up to the ears in blood. I am on fire
To hear this rich reprisal is so nigh,

104 *beaver* (part of a helmet protecting the lower jaw)
105 *cuishes* cuisses, thigh-armour
107 *vaulted with such ease.* To jump, fully armoured, into the saddle was a feat requiring great strength and agility.
109 *turn and wind* turn and wheel-about (terms in horsemanship)
110 *witch* bewitch
111–12 *Worse than the sun in March, | This praise doth nourish agues.* The sun in March was thought to be strong enough to assist in the breeding of fevers without dispelling them. Some contemporary references relate to this action of the sun on the bodily humours, but the expression may also be related to the effect of the sun on marshland, for there, sun of this strength would encourage the marsh vapours to rise and propagate but would not be strong enough to dry up the marsh. (Compare *King*

Lear: 'You fen-sucked fogs, drawn by the powerful sun', II.4.169.)
113 *like sacrifices in their trim.* Decked like this, they are as beasts for sacrifice.
114 *fire-eyed maid of smoky war* (Bellona, goddess of war. Macbeth was described by Shakespeare as 'Bellona's bridegroom' (*Macbeth*, I.2.56))
116 *Mars* (Roman god of war)
118 *this rich reprisal.* 'Reprisal' means 'prize'. The phrase is also appropriate to describe the style of Hotspur's rhetoric in reply to Vernon's description of Hal's chivalric company. The language in this speech is of blood, mail, smoke, and sacrifice. The images in Vernon's speech are altogether different; indeed, they are '*full of spirit as the month of May*' (line 101) as opposed to Hotspur's '*Worse than the sun in March*' (line 111).

And yet not ours! Come, let me taste my horse,
120   Who is to bear me like a thunderbolt
Against the bosom of the Prince of Wales.
Harry to Harry shall, hot horse to horse,
Meet and ne'er part till one drop down a corpse.
O that Glendower were come!

VERNON   There is more news.
I learned in Worcester as I rode along
He cannot draw his power this fourteen days.

DOUGLAS
That's the worst tidings that I hear of yet.

WORCESTER
Ay, by my faith, that bears a frosty sound.

HOTSPUR
What may the King's whole battle reach unto?

VERNON
To thirty thousand.

130   HOTSPUR   Forty let it be.
My father and Glendower being both away,
The powers of us may serve so great a day.

---

123 *corpse*. In Q1 the spelling 'coarse' is used (for 'corse'), indicative of the Elizabethan pronunciation of this word.

126 *He cannot draw his power this fourteen days* he cannot collect his army together for a fortnight. Hotspur is now let down again, yet there is no outburst from him as there is when he describes the tedium of Glendower's conversation (III.1.142–58). In Holinshed's chronicle, the Welsh are said to be present at the battle, but in Daniel's poem on the civil war (see note to III.2.94) it is said that 'The swift approach and unexpected speed' of Henry's advance did not give time for the Welsh forces to reach Shrewsbury. Shakespeare evidently follows Daniel's account at this point and the reason is plain – Hotspur is further isolated.

129 *battle* battle array

130 *thirty thousand*. It is not possible to take too certainly estimates of numbers involved in medieval battles. Hotspur was said by Holinshed to have had 14,000 men, but his chronicle does not give a number for the King's army; another chronicle does give a figure of 30,000, and Hall gives a figure of 40,000 for those engaged on both sides.

132 *powers of us* forces we have
serve suffice

Come, let us take a muster speedily.
Doomsday is near. Die all, die merrily.

DOUGLAS
Talk not of dying, I am out of fear
Of death or death's hand for this one half year.   *Exeunt*

Enter Falstaff and Bardolph   IV.2

FALSTAFF Bardolph, get thee before to Coventry. Fill me
a bottle of sack. Our soldiers shall march through. We'll
to Sutton Coldfield tonight.

BARDOLPH Will you give me money, captain?

FALSTAFF Lay out, lay out.

BARDOLPH This bottle makes an angel.

FALSTAFF And if it do, take it for thy labour – and if it
make twenty, take them all, I'll answer the coinage. Bid
my lieutenant Peto meet me at town's end.

BARDOLPH I will, captain. Farewell.   *Exit*   10

FALSTAFF If I be not ashamed of my soldiers, I am a
soused gurnet. I have misused the King's press damnably. I have got in exchange of a hundred and fifty

---

134 *Die all, die merrily* if die we must, let
it be cheerfully
135 *out of* free from

IV.2.3 *Sutton Coldfield* (to the north-east
of Birmingham, well off the
Coventry-Shrewsbury route)
5 *Lay out* use your own money
6 *an angel*. An *angel* was a coin with the
Archangel Michael stamped on it and
worth between 6s. 8d. and ten shillings – eleven or twelve shillings
being a journeyman's weekly wage
at the time.
8 *answer the coinage* be answerable for
making money that way ('coining'
money on bottles)

9 *Peto*. At III.3.195 Hal tells Peto they
have thirty miles to ride together. It
may seem (as it did to Dr Johnson)
that as Peto is with Falstaff here,
some other name (such as Poins's)
should be substituted at III.3.195. As,
however, Hal was to travel through
Gloucestershire (III.2.175–6) but appears in this scene, it is clear that the
plans have been changed, wittingly
or not, by Shakespeare.
12 *soused gurnet* preserved gurnet (a small
fish with a big head)
misused the King's press misapplied the
commission to draft men (compare
the expression 'press-gang')

soldiers three hundred and odd pounds. I press me
none but good householders, yeomen's sons, enquire
me out contracted bachelors, such as had been asked
twice on the banns, such a commodity of warm slaves as
had as lief hear the devil as a drum, such as fear the
report of a caliver worse than a struck fowl or a hurt wild
20 duck. I pressed me none but such toasts-and-butter,
with hearts in their bellies no bigger than pins' heads,
and they have bought out their services. And now my
whole charge consists of ancients, corporals, lieutenants,
gentlemen of companies – slaves as ragged as Lazarus in
the painted cloth, where the glutton's dogs licked his
sores. And such as indeed were never soldiers, but dis-

14–15 *I press me none but good householders.*
Falstaff's description of his technique
is amusing roguery, but it must have
struck audiences of the time as not
wholly comic. The satire on the practice of pressing men (very common
in the 1590s) might have been taken
as an 'act', a turn, in its own right and
accepted as comic social comment.
Such turns were not uncommon in
Elizabethan drama (for example,
Launcelot Gobbo's monologue in
The Merchant of Venice, II.2) but
Shakespeare, unlike many of his colleagues, very soon begins to integrate
these in his plays (as is evident in the
example from *The Merchant of Venice*).
If, however, we are to see this
account of pressing as integrated
wholly within the play, and thus
being an outcome of Falstaff's character (rather than a comic vehicle for
the comedian), then it must reflect
on the character himself and this
seems to be happening here. Here
we have a characteristic of Falstaff
which an audience aware of the implications of pressing would not find

wholly to its liking. The process
begun at II.4.476–8 (and see note
thereon) is now put into effect,
subtly but distinctly. (See also Introduction, pages 246–7.)

15 *good* substantial (with money to buy
themselves out)

17 *commodity.* Falstaff speaks of his men
as merchandise which he can trade in
order to make a profit.
warm well-to-do
slaves (contemptuous for 'subjects')

19 *caliver* light musket

20 *toasts-and-butter milksops*

23 *ancients* ensigns (of which the word is
a corruption)

24 *gentlemen of companies* (gentlemen vol-
unteers who held no formal rank –
and see note to I.2.26.)

24–5 *Lazarus in the painted cloth.* Falstaff
has already referred to the parable of
Dives and Lazarus (III.3.31) and it is,
once again, an instance of Falstaff's
store of Biblical knowledge. 'Painted
cloth' was a very inferior form of
tapestry. (See note to line 33,
below.)

carded unjust serving-men, younger sons to younger
brothers, revolted tapsters, and ostlers trade-fallen, the
cankers of a calm world and a long peace, ten times more
dishonourable-ragged than an old fazed ancient. And   30
such have I to fill up the rooms of them as have bought
out their services, that you would think that I had a
hundred and fifty tattered prodigals lately come from
swine-keeping, from eating draff and husks. A mad
fellow met me on the way, and told me I had unloaded
all the gibbets and pressed the dead bodies. No eye hath
seen such scarecrows. I'll not march through Coventry
with them, that's flat. Nay, and the villains march wide
betwixt the legs as if they had gyves on, for indeed I had
the most of them out of prison. There's not a shirt and a   40
half in all my company, and the half shirt is two napkins
tacked together and thrown over the shoulders like a
herald's coat without sleeves. And the shirt to say the
truth stolen from my host at Saint Albans, or the red-
nose innkeeper of Daventry. But that's all one, they'll
find linen enough on every hedge.

Enter the Prince and the Lord of Westmorland

27 *unjust* dishonest

27-8 *younger sons to younger brothers* (having no prospect of inheritance)

28 *revolted* runaway (see II.4.45-7)
trade-fallen out of work

29 *cankers* parasites
long peace (considered to be unhealthy
— as if the state needed its blood let
in accordance with the current medical practice)

30 *fazed* frayed

33 *prodigals.* Another Biblical reference
from Falstaff, this time to the best
known of all parables. The prodigal
son, when he had spent all his
money, was reduced to eating the
food he had to serve the pigs. Shakespeare uses the word 'husks'. This is
found in the Geneva Bible, not the

Bishops' Bible (where 'cedes' is
used), which he seems to have been
most familiar with (and from which
Biblical quotations in this Commentary are taken). Falstaff also refers to
the parable of the prodigal son in
2 Henry IV, II.1.140.

34 *draff* pig swill

40 *out of prison.* The practice of releasing
prisoners to serve in the armed forces
still occurs in some countries. It had
been permitted in London in 1596,
just before *1 Henry IV* was first performed, to provide men for the expedition to Cadiz.

46 *find linen . . . on every hedge.* Linen was
put out to dry by draping it over
hedges (a practice still employed by
gipsies).

PRINCE HAL How now, blown Jack? How now, quilt?

FALSTAFF What, Hal! How now, mad wag? What a devil
dost thou in Warwickshire? My good Lord of Westmorland, I cry you mercy, I thought your honour had
already been at Shrewsbury.

WESTMORLAND Faith, Sir John, 'tis more than time that
I were there, and you too, but my powers are there
already. The King I can tell you looks for us all, we must
away all night.

FALSTAFF Tut, never fear me, I am as vigilant as a cat to
steal cream.

PRINCE HAL I think, to steal cream indeed, for thy theft
hath already made thee butter. But tell me, Jack, whose
fellows are these that come after?

FALSTAFF Mine, Hal, mine.

PRINCE HAL I did never see such pitiful rascals.

FALSTAFF Tut, tut, good enough to toss, food for powder, food for powder, they'll fill a pit as well as better.
Tush, man, mortal men, mortal men.

WESTMORLAND Ay, but Sir John, methinks they are

47 *blown* (1) short-winded; (2) swollen
Jack (besides Falstaff's name, a contemptuous word for 'fellow' and also
the name for a soldier's quilted
jacket)

48–9 *What a devil dost thou in Warwickshire?* Falstaff quickly asks Hal (perhaps bearing in mind the original
arrangement – III.2.175–6 – though
Falstaff was not present on the occasion that this was revealed to the
audience), before Hal can ask him
what he's up to.

58 *steal cream*. A pun on 'stale cream'
has been suggested here.

61 *Mine, Hal, mine*. The absence of any
shame here (despite his earlier assertion that he will not march through
Coventry with such a rabble), indeed,

the positive pride, is quite
outrageous.

63 *to toss* (on pikes, as in 3 *Henry VI*,
I.1.244: 'The soldiers should have
tossed me on their pikes')

63–4 *food for powder*. Falstaff's lack of
concern for his men is surely more
than a reflection of the attitude of
captains to their men in Elizabethan
times – a greater concern for their
men's pay than their lives. This is no
comic turn in isolation (see the note
on lines 14–15, above) but an attitude
that draws a little sympathy away
from Falstaff. Were he not a comic
figure he could not but appear despic-
able here; the dramatic conventions
of comedy protect him from the full
implications of what he says.

exceeding poor and bare, too beggarly.

FALSTAFF Faith, for their poverty I know not where they
had that. And for their bareness I am sure they never
learned that of me.   70

PRINCE HAL No, I'll be sworn, unless you call three
fingers in the ribs bare. But sirrah, make haste. Percy is
already in the field.   *Exit*

FALSTAFF What, is the King encamped?

WESTMORLAND He is, Sir John, I fear we shall stay too
long.   *Exit*

FALSTAFF Well,
To the latter end of a fray, and the beginning of a feast
Fits a dull fighter and a keen guest.   *Exit*

Enter Hotspur, Worcester, Douglas, Vernon   IV.3

HOTSPUR We'll fight with him tonight.

WORCESTER   It may not be.

DOUGLAS
You give him then advantage.

VERNON   Not a whit.

HOTSPUR
Why say you so, looks he not for supply?

VERNON
So do we.

HOTSPUR His is certain, ours is doubtful.

WORCESTER
Good cousin, be advised, stir not tonight.

71–2 *three fingers in the ribs.* A finger
measured three-quarters of an inch
and thus Falstaff's ribs are well covered with flesh. In *The Merchant of
Venice* there is a contrary use of the
relationship of ribs and fingers.
Launcelot refers to his being badly
fed by saying, 'you may tell every

finger I have with my ribs' (II.2.99),
and traditionally he makes his blind
father feel his fingers spread over his
chest.

IV.3 The scene is set in Hotspur's camp
at Shrewsbury.

3 *supply* reinforcements

VERNON
  Do not, my lord.
DOUGLAS   You do not counsel well.
  You speak it out of fear and cold heart.
VERNON
  Do me no slander, Douglas. By my life,
  And I dare well maintain it with my life,
10 If well-respected honour bid me on,
  I hold as little counsel with weak fear
  As you, my lord, or any Scot that this day lives.
  Let it be seen tomorrow in the battle
  Which of us fears.
DOUGLAS   Yea, or tonight.
VERNON   Content.
HOTSPUR
  Tonight, say I.
VERNON
  Come, come, it may not be. I wonder much,
  Being men of such great leading as you are,
  That you foresee not what impediments
  Drag back our expedition. Certain horse
20 Of my cousin Vernon's are not yet come up,
  Your uncle Worcester's horse came but today,
  And now their pride and mettle is asleep,
  Their courage with hard labour tame and dull,
  That not a horse is half the half himself.
HOTSPUR
  So are the horses of the enemy
  In general journey-bated and brought low.
  The better part of ours are full of rest.
WORCESTER
  The number of the King exceedeth ours.

10 *well-respected* well-considered   22 *pride and mettle* spirit
17 *of such great leading* who are such expe-   26 *journey-bated* weakened by travel
    rienced generals

For God's sake, cousin, stay till all come in.
> *The trumpet sounds a parley*
> *Enter Sir Walter Blunt*

BLUNT

I come with gracious offers from the King,   30
If you vouchsafe me hearing and respect.

HOTSPUR

Welcome, Sir Walter Blunt: and would to God
You were of our determination!
Some of us love you well, and even those some
Envy your great deservings and good name,
Because you are not of our quality,
But stand against us like an enemy.

BLUNT

And God defend but still I should stand so,
So long as out of limit and true rule
You stand against anointed majesty.   40
But to my charge. The King hath sent to know
The nature of your griefs, and whereupon
You conjure from the breast of civil peace
Such bold hostility, teaching his duteous land
Audacious cruelty. If that the King
Have any way your good deserts forgot,
Which he confesseth to be manifold,
He bids you name your griefs, and with all speed
You shall have your desires with interest

---

29 *stay* wait
30 *I come with gracious offers from the King.* The King's ambassador was the Abbot of Shrewsbury but, as in the first scene of the play, Blunt's role is enlarged (see note to 1.1.63). From Hotspur's response, Blunt is clearly regarded highly by the rebels as well as by Henry. Thus his death, and Falstaff's reaction to it (see v.3.58–9), are built up to be more

than incidental.
31 *respect* attention
36 *quality* party (with no reference to 'worth')
38 *defend* forbid
    still always
39 *limit* bounds of allegiance
41 *charge* official duty
42 *griefs* injuries
    whereupon wherefore
43 *conjure* call up

50   And pardon absolute for yourself, and these
      Herein misled by your suggestion.

HOTSPUR
      The King is kind, and well we know the King
      Knows at what time to promise, when to pay.
      My father, and my uncle, and myself
      Did give him that same royalty he wears,
      And when he was not six-and-twenty strong,
      Sick in the world's regard, wretched and low,
      A poor unminded outlaw sneaking home,
      My father gave him welcome to the shore.
60   And when he heard him swear and vow to God
      He came but to be Duke of Lancaster,
      To sue his livery, and beg his peace
      With tears of innocency and terms of zeal,
      My father, in kind heart and pity moved,
      Swore him assistance, and performed it too.
      Now when the lords and barons of the realm
      Perceived Northumberland did lean to him,
      The more and less came in with cap and knee,
      Met him in boroughs, cities, villages,
70   Attended him on bridges, stood in lanes,
      Laid gifts before him, proffered him their oaths,
      Gave him their heirs as pages, followed him

51 *suggestion* temptation (*suggestion* being
a more sinister word than it now is)
52–3 *The King is kind . . . When to pay.*
These lines are neatly phrased by
Hotspur to give just the right satiric
impression. Whether the injuries Hotspur feels he has suffered are sufficient to justify rebellion or not, he
here makes, very coolly and satirically, an exposé of Henry's usurpation of Richard's throne. Blunt's
response – 'Tut, I came not to hear
this' – could be as much embarrass-
ment as awareness that this was not
the reason for Hotspur's present feelings of injury.
62 *sue his livery* beg for his inheritance
following his father's death. ('As I
was banished, I was banished Here-
ford; | But as I come, I come for
Lancaster', *Richard II*, II.3.113–14).
beg his peace (from Richard)
64 *in kind heart and pity moved.* Northumberland's heart was moved solely by
self-interest.
68 *more and less* high and low
with cap and knee cap in hand and on
bended knee
70 *Attended* waited for

Even at the heels in golden multitudes.
He presently, as greatness knows itself,
Steps me a little higher than his vow
Made to my father while his blood was poor
Upon the naked shore at Ravenspurgh;
And now forsooth takes on him to reform
Some certain edicts and some strait decrees
That lie too heavy on the commonwealth,   80
Cries out upon abuses, seems to weep
Over his country's wrongs – and by this face,
This seeming brow of justice, did he win
The hearts of all that he did angle for.
Proceeded further – cut me off the heads
Of all the favourites that the absent King
In deputation left behind him here,
When he was personal in the Irish war.

BLUNT

Tut, I came not to hear this.

HOTSPUR   Then to the point.
In short time after he deposed the King,   90
Soon after that deprived him of his life,
And in the neck of that tasked the whole state.
To make that worse, suffered his kinsman March –
Who is, if every owner were well placed,

---

73 *golden* richly dressed
75 *Steps me* (an archaic construction;
'me' is no longer required)
his vow (to seek no more than the
inheritance to which he was entitled)
79 *strait* overstrict
82 *face* appearance assumed for the
occasion
83 *seeming brow* front, semblance
85–6 *cut me off the heads | Of all the
favourites.* This refers to the execution of Bushy, Green, and Wiltshire
in *Richard II* (the two first-named in

III.1). Bolingbroke had no right to
order these executions; he was already assuming Richard's preroga-
tive. The word *me* would be omitted
in modern English; it does not imply
that the heads were cut off to please
Hotspur.
87 *In deputation* as his deputies
88 *personal* personally engaged
92 *in the neck of* immediately after
tasked taxed (a technical term for a
tax of one-fifteenth)
93 *his kinsman March.* See note to 1.3.83.

Indeed his King – to be engaged in Wales,
There without ransom to lie forfeited.
Disgraced me in my happy victories,
Sought to entrap me by intelligence,
Rated mine uncle from the Council-board,
100   In rage dismissed my father from the court,
Broke oath on oath, committed wrong on wrong,
And in conclusion drove us to seek out
This head of safety, and withal to pry
Into his title, the which we find
Too indirect for long continuance.

BLUNT

Shall I return this answer to the King?

HOTSPUR

Not so, Sir Walter. We'll withdraw awhile.
Go to the King, and let there be impawned
Some surety for a safe return again,
110   And in the morning early shall mine uncle
Bring him our purposes – and so, farewell.

BLUNT

I would you would accept of grace and love.

HOTSPUR

And may be so we shall.

BLUNT   Pray God you do.   *Exeunt*

---

95 *engaged* held hostage

98 *intelligence* use of spies

99 *Rated* berated, dismissed with abuse. This refers to the dismissal of Worcester, 1.3.14–20. Hal, of course, had also been 'rated' – III.2.32–3.

100 *In rage dismissed my father from the court.* The King's words at 1.3.120–22 are hardly in rage.

103 *head of safety* army with which to protect ourselves
withal in addition

105 *indirect* 'not of the true line of descent', and also 'morally crooked'

108 *impawned* pledged (by exchange of hostages)

111 *purposes* proposals

113 *And may be so we shall.* Hotspur's conciliatory tone is surprising. Although it accords with Holinshed, that is not the reason for Shakespeare's use of it. Henry is not without fault (as he himself knows, III.2.4–11). His deception in the course of usurping Richard's throne is recounted not only here but also in *2 Henry IV* – 'God knows, my son, | By what by-paths and indirect

Enter the Archbishop of York and Sir Michael   IV.4

ARCHBISHOP

Hie, good Sir Michael, bear this sealèd brief
With wingèd haste to the Lord Marshal,
This to my cousin Scroop, and all the rest
To whom they are directed. If you knew
How much they do import you would make haste.

SIR MICHAEL

My good lord,
I guess their tenor.

ARCHBISHOP   Like enough you do.
Tomorrow, good Sir Michael, is a day
Wherein the fortune of ten thousand men
Must bide the touch. For, sir, at Shrewsbury,   10
As I am truly given to understand,

crooked ways | I met this crown' (iv.5.184–6) – and even by Hal himself in *Henry V*: 'Not today, O Lord, | O not today, think not upon the fault | My father made in compassing the crown!' (iv.1.285–7). This is not just the opposition of right and wrong. Henry's faults were very serious and the implications of his usurpation of Richard's throne were well known in Shakespeare's day. It still left the problem unresolved as to whether it was permissible to rebel against a sovereign, as Hotspur is doing. Shakespeare, however, in addition to making clear Henry's guilt, also brings out two elements from the chronicles that favour the character of Hotspur. First, his willingness to reflect (here), and secondly, Worcester's deception of Hotspur (v.2).

iv.4 The scene is presumably set in York. Sir Michael (Mighell in Q1) is not known to history. 'Sir' was a courtesy title for priests, and a priest might well be the Archbishop's messenger, or Sir Michael might be a knight. The scene serves to heighten the desperate state in which Hotspur finds himself. There would not, of course, have been any point in Shakespeare keeping secret the outcome of the battle: an Elizabethan audience would know only too well who had won.

1 *brief* letter

2 *Lord Marshal* (Thomas Mowbray, Duke of Norfolk)

3 *my cousin Scroop*. It is uncertain to which of several Scroops this refers. The Sir Stephen Scrope (members of the family spelt their name differently) who tells Richard II of his younger brother's execution by Bolingbroke at Bristol (referred to at 1.3.265) seems likely. It could, however, be Sir Henry Scroop, executed as a traitor in *Henry V*, ii.2.

7 *tenor* purport

10 *bide the touch* be put to the test

The King with mighty and quick-raisèd power
Meets with Lord Harry, and I fear, Sir Michael,
What with the sickness of Northumberland,
Whose power was in the first proportion,
And what with Owen Glendower's absence thence,
Who with them was a rated sinew too,
And comes not in, o'er-ruled by prophecies,
I fear the power of Percy is too weak

20   To wage an instant trial with the King.

SIR MICHAEL

Why, my good lord, you need not fear,
There is Douglas, and Lord Mortimer.

ARCHBISHOP

No, Mortimer is not there.

SIR MICHAEL

But there is Mordake, Vernon, Lord Harry Percy,
And there is my Lord of Worcester, and a head
Of gallant warriors, noble gentlemen.

ARCHBISHOP

And so there is. But yet the King hath drawn
The special head of all the land together.
The Prince of Wales, Lord John of Lancaster,

30   The noble Westmorland, and warlike Blunt,
And many more corrivals and dear men
Of estimation and command in arms.

SIR MICHAEL

Doubt not, my lord, they shall be well opposed.

ARCHBISHOP

I hope no less, yet needful 'tis to fear,
And to prevent the worst, Sir Michael, speed.
For if Lord Percy thrive not, ere the King

---

15 *first proportion* greatest magnitude
17 *rated sinew* valued source of strength
18 *o'er-ruled by prophecies.* Shakespeare here maligns Glendower. According to Holinshed, the Welsh were at Shrewsbury, but, as mentioned in the note on IV.1.126, Daniel states they did not reach Shrewsbury in time owing to the King's rapid advance.
20 *instant* immediate
31 *corrivals* associates
dear noble (as at I.1.62)
35 *prevent* forestall

Dismiss his power he means to visit us,
For he hath heard of our confederacy,
And 'tis but wisdom to make strong against him.
Therefore make haste – I must go write again   40
To other friends. And so, farewell, Sir Michael.

Exeunt

Enter the King, Prince of Wales, Lord John of   V.I
Lancaster, Sir Walter Blunt, Falstaff

KING HENRY
How bloodily the sun begins to peer
Above yon bulky hill! The day looks pale
At his distemperature.

PRINCE HAL   The southern wind
Doth play the trumpet to his purposes,
And by his hollow whistling in the leaves
Foretells a tempest and a blustering day.

KING HENRY
Then with the losers let it sympathize,
For nothing can seem foul to those that win.

The trumpet sounds
Enter Worcester and Vernon

How now, my Lord of Worcester! 'Tis not well
That you and I should meet upon such terms   10
As now we meet. You have deceived our trust,
And made us doff our easy robes of peace
To crush our old limbs in ungentle steel.

---

38 *our confederacy* our united opposition

v.i The scene is the King's Camp at
Shrewsbury.
3 *distemperature* cosmic disorder
4 *his* (the sun's)

6 *Foretells a tempest and a blustering day.*
The relation of cosmic to human
affairs was frequently observed by
the Elizabethans and occurs often in
Shakespeare.
13 *our old limbs.* Henry was younger than
Hotspur (see note to 1.1.86–7).

This is not well, my lord, this is not well.
What say you to it? Will you again unknit
The churlish knot of all-abhorrèd war,
And move in that obedient orb again
Where you did give a fair and natural light,
And be no more an exhaled meteor,
20   A prodigy of fear, and a portent
Of broachèd mischief to the unborn times?

WORCESTER
Hear me, my liege.
For mine own part I could be well content
To entertain the lag end of my life
With quiet hours. For I protest
I have not sought the day of this dislike.

KING HENRY
You have not sought it? How comes it, then?

FALSTAFF Rebellion lay in his way, and he found it.

PRINCE HAL Peace, chewet, peace!

WORCESTER
30   It pleased your majesty to turn your looks
Of favour from myself, and all our house,
And yet I must remember you, my lord,
We were the first and dearest of your friends.
For you my staff of office did I break

---

17 *obedient orb* sphere of loyal obedience (the idea being that the planet circles the earth, which most people in Shakespeare's day believed to be fixed)

19 *exhaled* dragged from rightful course

20 *prodigy of fear* fearful omen

26 *dislike* discord

28 *Rebellion lay in his way, and he found it.* Falstaff's witticism puts Worcester's 'protest' (line 25) perfectly in its place, as Hal's affectionate 'chewet' indicates.

29 *chewet* (1) jackdaw (a chatterer); (2) minced meat dressed with butter (both applicable to Falstaff)

32 *remember* remind

34–5 *For you my staff of office did I break | In Richard's time.* This event is recorded by Holinshed and, though Worcester does not himself appear, it is mentioned twice in *Richard II* (II.2.58–9 and II.3.26–7). The Percies' case has already been presented in detail by Hotspur in IV.3 and described in I.3.146–74. That it is now described a third time suggests the importance attached by Shakespeare

In Richard's time, and posted day and night
To meet you on the way, and kiss your hand,
When yet you were in place and in account
Nothing so strong and fortunate as I.
It was myself, my brother, and his son,
That brought you home, and boldly did outdare   40
The dangers of the time. You swore to us,
And you did swear that oath at Doncaster,
That you did nothing purpose 'gainst the state,
Nor claim no further than your new-fallen right,
The seat of Gaunt, dukedom of Lancaster.
To this we swore our aid. But in short space
It rained down fortune showering on your head,
And such a flood of greatness fell on you,
What with our help, what with the absent King,
What with the injuries of a wanton time,   50
The seeming sufferances that you had borne,
And the contrarious winds that held the King
So long in his unlucky Irish wars
That all in England did repute him dead.
And from this swarm of fair advantages
You took occasion to be quickly wooed
To gripe the general sway into your hand,
Forget your oath to us at Doncaster,
And being fed by us, you used us so
As that ungentle gull the cuckoo's bird   60
Useth the sparrow – did oppress our nest,
Grew by our feeding to so great a bulk
That even our love durst not come near your sight
For fear of swallowing. But with nimble wing

to Henry's mode of accession. Lines
41–5 are particularly noteworthy, repeating what Hotspur said at
IV.3.60–63. Worcester's interest was
no more selfless than was Northumberland's, needless to say.

44 *new-fallen* newly fallen due to you
50 *injuries* abuses
   wanton time period of misgovernment
57 *gripe* seize
   sway rule (of the whole country)
60 *gull, bird* nestling

We were enforced for safety sake to fly
Out of your sight, and raise this present head,
Whereby we stand opposèd by such means
As you yourself have forged against yourself,
By unkind usage, dangerous countenance,
70   And violation of all faith and troth
Sworn to us in your younger enterprise.

KING HENRY
These things indeed you have articulate,
Proclaimed at market crosses, read in churches,
To face the garment of rebellion
With some fine colour that may please the eye
Of fickle changelings and poor discontents,
Which gape and rub the elbow at the news
Of hurlyburly innovation.
And never yet did insurrection want
80   Such water-colours to impaint his cause,
Nor moody beggars starving for a time
Of pell-mell havoc and confusion.

PRINCE HAL
In both your armies there is many a soul
Shall pay full dearly for this encounter
If once they join in trial. Tell your nephew,
The Prince of Wales doth join with all the world
In praise of Henry Percy. By my hopes,

69 *dangerous countenance* threatening looks
71 *younger enterprise* earlier undertaking
(his claim to his inheritance)
72 *articulate* formulated item by item
74 *face.* The meaning here seems to be
to cover (as with one fabric by another) – to put a different face on
things, rather than simply to adorn.
75 *colour* (the colour of the facing, with
also the metaphorical implication of
misrepresentation)
77 *rub the elbow* hug themselves with
pleasure, arms crossed. Joy was be-

lieved to make the elbows itch.
78 *innovation* revolution
80 *water-colours.* Painting in water-
colours was not considered permanent – they might easily be washed
off. 'Impaint', in this same line, is the
first recorded use of this word. The
effect of 'Such water-colours to impaint his cause' must have been striking when used here.
his its
81 *moody* sullen

This present enterprise set off his head,
I do not think a braver gentleman,
More active-valiant or more valiant-young,   90
More daring or more bold, is now alive
To grace this latter age with noble deeds.
For my part, I may speak it to my shame,
I have a truant been to chivalry,
And so I hear he doth account me too.
Yet this before my father's majesty –
I am content that he shall take the odds
Of his great name and estimation,
And will, to save the blood on either side,
Try fortune with him in a single fight.   100

KING HENRY

And, Prince of Wales, so dare we venture thee,
Albeit considerations infinite
Do make against it. No, good Worcester, no,
We love our people well, even those we love
That are misled upon your cousin's part,
And will they take the offer of our grace,
Both he, and they, and you, yea, every man
Shall be my friend again, and I'll be his.
So tell your cousin, and bring me word
What he will do. But if he will not yield,   110
Rebuke and dread correction wait on us,
And they shall do their office. So, be gone.
We will not now be troubled with reply.
We offer fair, take it advisedly.

Exeunt Worcester and Vernon

---

88 *set off his head* removed from his account, not counted against him
89 *braver* finer
100 *in a single fight*. There is no reference in any source to such a challenge but it accords with the chivalric tone that Shakespeare is setting here and in Vernon's description of Hal (IV.1.97–110).
105 *cousin's*. 'Cousin' did not in Shakespeare's time necessarily imply the precise family relationship which the word denotes to us (and see note to 1.1.90).
106 *grace* pardon
111 *wait on us* are at hand
114 *We offer fair*. As Holinshed says: 'the king had condescended unto all

PRINCE HAL

It will not be accepted, on my life.
The Douglas and the Hotspur both together
Are confident against the world in arms.

KING HENRY

Hence, therefore, every leader to his charge,
For on their answer will we set on them,
And God befriend us as our cause is just!

Exeunt all but the Prince and Falstaff

FALSTAFF Hal, if thou see me down in the battle and
bestride me, so. 'Tis a point of friendship.

PRINCE HAL Nothing but a Colossus can do thee that
friendship. Say thy prayers, and farewell.

FALSTAFF I would 'twere bed-time, Hal, and all well.

PRINCE HAL Why, thou owest God a death. *Exit*

FALSTAFF 'Tis not due yet – I would be loath to pay him
before his day. What need I be so forward with him that
calls not on me? Well, 'tis no matter, honour pricks
me on. Yea, but how if honour prick me off when I
come on, how then? Can honour set to a leg? No. Or
an arm? No. Or take away the grief of a wound? No.
Honour hath no skill in surgery then? No. What is

120

130

---

that was reasonable at his hands to be
required, and seemed to humble himself more than was meet for his
estate'.

122 *bestride me* (stand over Falstaff to
protect him)

123 *a Colossus*. A colossus is a statue
considerably larger than life size and
there were a number in the ancient
world. *The* Colossus, however, was
that of Helios at Rhodes, which was
over 100 feet high. It was destroyed
by an earthquake after standing for
fifty-six years, about 224 B.C., but
many Elizabethans believed that its
legs still stood over the entrance to
the harbour.

124 *Say thy prayers, and farewell.* Hal's
abruptness is understandable in the
circumstances, but its degree is, perhaps, a little surprising.

125 *I would 'twere bed-time, Hal, and all
well.* One of the most human touches
in all Shakespeare. The Prince in his
reply takes the sense of *bed-time* to be
debt-time (a similar quibble occurs at
1.3.183–4).

129 *pricks* spurs

130 *prick me off* select me for death
(compare, select by picking with a
pin)

131 *set to a leg* set a broken leg

132 *grief* pain

honour? A word. What is in that word honour? What is
that honour? Air. A trim reckoning! Who hath it? He
that died a'Wednesday. Doth he feel it? No. Doth he
hear it? No. 'Tis insensible, then? Yea, to the dead.
But will it not live with the living? No. Why? Detraction will not suffer it. Therefore I'll none of it. Honour
is a mere scutcheon – and so ends my catechism.   *Exit*   140

Enter Worcester and Sir Richard Vernon   V.2

WORCESTER
O no, my nephew must not know, Sir Richard,
The liberal and kind offer of the King.

VERNON
'Twere best he did.

WORCESTER   Then are we all undone.
It is not possible, it cannot be,
The King should keep his word in loving us.
He will suspect us still, and find a time
To punish this offence in other faults.
Supposition all our lives shall be stuck full of eyes,
For treason is but trusted like the fox,
Who, never so tame, so cherished and locked up,   10
Will have a wild trick of his ancestors.
Look how we can or sad or merrily,
Interpretation will misquote our looks,

---

137 *insensible* not perceptible to the
senses
138–9 *Detraction* slander
139 *suffer* allow
140 *scutcheon* funeral hatchment (a square
or lozenge-shaped tablet)
catechism. This describes the question
and answer technique which Falstaff
has just used. Falstaff's 'theory of
honour' is now, rather ironically,
shown in practice. (See also the Intro-

duction, pages 237–9.)

v.2 The scene is the rebels' camp at
Shrewsbury.
1 *my nephew must not know.* Worcester's
deception of Hotspur is recounted
by Holinshed. Honour is, indeed, 'a
mere scutcheon'!
6 *still* always
11 *trick* trait
12 *or ... or* either ... or

And we shall feed like oxen at a stall,
The better cherished still the nearer death.
My nephew's trespass may be well forgot,
It hath the excuse of youth and heat of blood,
And an adopted name of privilege –
A hare-brained Hotspur, governed by a spleen.
20   All his offences live upon my head
And on his father's. We did train him on,
And, his corruption being taken from us,
We as the spring of all shall pay for all.
Therefore, good cousin, let not Harry know
In any case the offer of the King.

VERNON

Deliver what you will; I'll say 'tis so.
Here comes your cousin.

Enter Hotspur and Douglas

HOTSPUR   My uncle is returned;
Deliver up my Lord of Westmorland.
Uncle, what news?

WORCESTER

30   The King will bid you battle presently.

DOUGLAS

Defy him by the Lord of Westmorland.

HOTSPUR

Lord Douglas, go you and tell him so.

---

18 *an adopted name of privilege* a nickname
licensing him (to be rash)
19 *a spleen* an impulse
20 *live* are active
22 *taken* caught (as in 'take cold')
28 *Deliver up my Lord of Westmorland.*
Westmorland was evidently the
'surety for a safe return' of Worcester
and Vernon (IV.3.109). He is now to
be released. It has been suggested, as
we are not told that Westmorland is
to be held hostage, that a passage
has been omitted, by accident or

through revision. It is at least as
possible that Shakespeare is using a
short-cut to avoid cluttering the
action with unimportant details. (See
note to I.3.259.)

32 *Douglas.* Strictly speaking, line 32
has only nine syllables, but, if it
were desired that the iambic metre
be preserved exactly, *Douglas* could
be pronounced as three syllables.
The situation is the reverse of that
discussed at I.1.8. Rhythm in Shakespeare, and indeed in much English

DOUGLAS

   Marry, and shall, and very willingly.   *Exit*

WORCESTER

   There is no seeming mercy in the King.

HOTSPUR

   Did you beg any? God forbid!

WORCESTER

   I told him gently of our grievances,
   Of his oath-breaking – which he mended thus,
   By now forswearing that he is forsworn.
   He calls us rebels, traitors, and will scourge
   With haughty arms this hateful name in us.   40

      Enter Douglas

DOUGLAS

   Arm, gentlemen, to arms! For I have thrown
   A brave defiance in King Henry's teeth,
   And Westmorland that was engaged did bear it,
   Which cannot choose but bring him quickly on.

WORCESTER

   The Prince of Wales stepped forth before the King,
   And, nephew, challenged you to single fight.

HOTSPUR

   O, would the quarrel lay upon our heads,
   And that no man might draw short breath today
   But I and Harry Monmouth! Tell me, tell me,
   How showed his tasking? Seemed it in contempt?   50

VERNON

   No, by my soul, I never in my life
   Did hear a challenge urged more modestly,
   Unless a brother should a brother dare

---

verse, is more subtle than counting
syllables will allow.
34 *seeming* semblance of
38 *forswearing* denying by a false oath
43 *engaged* held as a hostage (as Mortimer
   at IV.3.95)
48 *draw short breath* become short-

winded (by exertion in battle). Short
of breath to the point of death is also
implied.
50 *showed his tasking* offered he the
challenge
52 *urged* proposed

To gentle exercise and proof of arms.
He gave you all the duties of a man,
Trimmed up your praises with a princely tongue,
Spoke your deserving like a chronicle,
Making you ever better than his praise
By still dispraising praise valued with you,
And, which became him like a prince indeed,
He made a blushing cital of himself,
And chid his truant youth with such a grace
As if he mastered there a double spirit
Of teaching and of learning instantly.
There did he pause. But let me tell the world —
If he outlive the envy of this day,
England did never owe so sweet a hope
So much misconstrued in his wantonness.

HOTSPUR

Cousin, I think thou art enamourèd
On his follies! Never did I hear
Of any prince so wild a liberty.
But be he as he will, yet once ere night
I will embrace him with a soldier's arm,
That he shall shrink under my courtesy.
Arm, arm with speed! And fellows, soldiers, friends,
Better consider what you have to do

54 *proof* trial
55 *duties of a man* praises due a man
59 *dispraising praise valued with you* disparaging praise itself as compared to
   you yourself, the object of praise
61 *blushing cital of himself*. Either, he gave
   a modest recital of his own merits,
   or, in his recital of his own merits he
   blushingly called himself to account.
64 *instantly* simultaneously
66 *envy* ill-will
67 *owe* own
71 *liberty* reckless freedom
74 *That* so that

76–8 *Better consider what you have to do |
   Than I that have not well the gift of
   tongue | Can lift your blood up with
   persuasion* you are better able to consider for yourselves what you have
   to do than I am able, by gifts of
   oratory, to inspire you. The tortuous
   expression of Hotspur's meaning
   here might suggest he did lack *the
   gift of tongue* were it not that elsewhere he hardly strikes one as being
   tongue-tied. The highly compressed
   style here may occur by chance, or it
   might, perhaps, be intended as a hu-

Than I that have not well the gift of tongue
Can lift your blood up with persuasion.

    Enter a Messenger

FIRST MESSENGER My lord, here are letters for you.

HOTSPUR I cannot read them now.   80

    O gentlemen, the time of life is short!
    To spend that shortness basely were too long
    If life did ride upon a dial's point,
    Still ending at the arrival of an hour.
    And if we live, we live to tread on kings,
    If die, brave death when princes die with us!
    Now, for our consciences, the arms are fair
    When the intent of bearing them is just.

    Enter another Messenger

SECOND MESSENGER
    My lord, prepare, the King comes on apace.

HOTSPUR
    I thank him that he cuts me from my tale,   90
    For I profess not talking. Only this –
    Let each man do his best. And here draw I
    A sword whose temper I intend to stain
    With the best blood that I can meet withal
    In the adventure of this perilous day.
    Now, Esperance! Percy! and set on!
    Sound all the lofty instruments of war,
    And by that music let us all embrace,

---

morous touch. He does, nevertheless, make a modest address to his followers in lines 90–100. This has a half-comic beginning which supports the suggestion of humour in these three lines.

82–4 *To spend that shortness basely were too long . . . ending at the arrival of an hour* if life lasted but an hour, it would be too long if it were spent basely

83 *dial's point* finger of a clock

90 *cuts me from my tale* stops me talking

91 *I profess not talking* talking is not my profession

91–2 *Only this – | Let each man do his best.* The effect of bathos here is at once comic and touching.

94 *withal* with

96 *Esperance!* This was the Percy battle-cry (see also the note to II.3.74).

For, heaven to earth, some of us never shall
100   A second time do such a courtesy.
       Here they embrace, the trumpets sound   *Exeunt*

V.3   *The King enters with his power. Alarum to the battle.*
          Then enter Douglas, and Sir Walter Blunt, disguised
          as the King

BLUNT

   What is thy name that in the battle thus
   Thou crossest me? What honour dost thou seek
   Upon my head?

DOUGLAS   Know then my name is Douglas,

   And I do haunt thee in the battle thus
   Because some tell me that thou art a king.

BLUNT

   They tell thee true.

DOUGLAS

   The Lord of Stafford dear today hath bought
   Thy likeness, for instead of thee, King Harry,
   This sword hath ended him: so shall it thee
10   Unless thou yield thee as my prisoner.

BLUNT

   I was not born a yielder, thou proud Scot,
   And thou shalt find a king that will revenge
   Lord Stafford's death.
       They fight; Douglas kills Blunt
       Then enter Hotspur

HOTSPUR

   O Douglas, hadst thou fought at Holmedon thus
   I never had triumphed upon a Scot.

---

99 *heaven to earth* odds of infinity to
   nothing

v.3 Although the rest of the play is divided into three scenes, the place and
time are not differentiated. What is said
in the opening comment to 1.1 applies
here with particular force.

DOUGLAS
All's done, all's won. Here breathless lies the King.
HOTSPUR Where?
DOUGLAS Here.
HOTSPUR
This, Douglas? No, I know this face full well.
A gallant knight he was, his name was Blunt,   20
Semblably furnished like the King himself.
DOUGLAS
A fool go with thy soul, whither it goes!
A borrowed title hast thou bought too dear.
Why didst thou tell me that thou wert a king?
HOTSPUR The King hath many marching in his coats.
DOUGLAS
Now, by my sword, I will kill all his coats!
I'll murder all his wardrobe, piece by piece,
Until I meet the King.
HOTSPUR   Up and away!
Our soldiers stand full fairly for the day.   *Exeunt*
        Alarum. Enter Falstaff alone
FALSTAFF Though I could scape shot-free at London, I   30
fear the shot here, here's no scoring but upon the pate.
Soft! Who are you? Sir Walter Blunt – there's honour
for you! Here's no vanity! I am as hot as molten lead,
and as heavy too. God keep lead out of me, I need no
more weight than mine own bowels. I have led my
ragamuffins where they are peppered. There's not three

21 *Semblably furnished* seemingly armed
22 *A fool go with thy soul.* Q1 has 'Ah foole, goe with thy soule', but the emended form, proposed in the eighteenth century, seems to give what was intended, as this makes a popular colloquial formula – 'the name of fool go with you'.
25 *coats* surcoats (see note to IV.1.100)
29 *stand full fairly for the day* are a fair way to victory

30 *shot-free* (1) unwounded; (2) without paying the bill
31 *scoring* (1) charging to an account; (2) cutting (wounding)
33 *Here's no vanity.* All (in life) is vanity, but here in death there is no vanity. Another Biblical reference by Falstaff (to Ecclesiastes 12.8).
35 *led* (but not necessarily from the front – 'I have led them to a place where they might be peppered')

of my hundred-and-fifty left alive — and they are for the town's end, to beg during life. But who comes here?

Enter the Prince

PRINCE HAL

What, standest thou idle here? Lend me thy sword.
40 Many a nobleman lies stark and stiff
Under the hoofs of vaunting enemies,
Whose deaths are yet unrevenged. I prithee
Lend me thy sword.

FALSTAFF O Hal, I prithee give me leave to breathe awhile. Turk Gregory never did such deeds in arms as I have done this day. I have paid Percy, I have made him sure.

PRINCE HAL

He is indeed, and living to kill thee.
I prithee lend me thy sword.

50 FALSTAFF Nay, before God, Hal, if Percy be alive thou gets not my sword, but take my pistol if thou wilt.

PRINCE HAL Give it me. What, is it in the case?

FALSTAFF Ay, Hal, 'tis hot, 'tis hot. There's that will sack a city.

The Prince draws it out, and finds it to be a bottle of sack

37–8 *the town's end* (to beg near the town gates)

39 *What* why (exclamation)

43 *Lend me thy sword.* In Q1, 'thy sword' is printed as prose in the same line as 'Whose deaths are yet unrevenged. I prethee.' The sudden shift to a line of prose is awkward, though most editors accept it — it is not, of course, exceptional. The arrangement in this edition makes a slightly smoother transition to Falstaff's prose, but the result cannot be called remarkable poetry. (See also the note to 11.2.102–108.)

45 *Turk Gregory.* The Turks had a reputation for ferocity. Two popes have

been suggested as the Gregory referred to, Gregory VII, who reigned in the eleventh century, and, much more convincingly, Gregory XIII, 1572–85, who not only was credited with encouraging the Massacre of St Bartholomew and plots to murder Elizabeth I, but, with Nero and the Grand Turk, appeared in a coloured print called *The Three Tyrants of the World*, being sold in the streets of London in Shakespeare's time.

46 *paid* killed

52 *is it in the case?* (instead of primed, ready for use)

53 *'tis hot* (with great use)

PRINCE HAL

What, is it a time to jest and dally now?

> *He throws the bottle at him*   *Exit*

FALSTAFF Well, if Percy be alive, I'll pierce him. If he do
come in my way, so. If he do not, if I come in his
willingly, let him make a carbonado of me. I like not
such grinning honour as Sir Walter hath. Give me life,
which if I can save, so. If not, honour comes unlooked   60
for, and there's an end.   *Exit*

> *Alarum. Excursions. Enter the King, the Prince,*   V.4
> *Lord John of Lancaster, Earl of Westmorland*

KING HENRY

I prithee, Harry, withdraw thyself, thou bleedest too
   much.

Lord John of Lancaster, go you with him.

LANCASTER

Not I, my lord, unless I did bleed too.

PRINCE HAL

I beseech your majesty, make up,

Lest your retirement do amaze your friends.

KING HENRY

I will do so. My Lord of Westmorland,

Lead him to his tent.

WESTMORLAND

Come, my lord, I'll lead you to your tent.

PRINCE HAL

Lead me, my lord? I do not need your help,

And God forbid a shallow scratch should drive   10

The Prince of Wales from such a field as this,

---

56 *pierce* (pronounced 'perce')
58 *carbonado* (rasher for grilling)
59 *such grinning honour.* See note to
   IV.3.30.
61 *there's an end* (of life, or, the subject)

v.4.4 *make up* go to the front
5 *retirement* retreat
   amaze dismay

Where stained nobility lies trodden on,
And rebels' arms triumph in massacres!

LANCASTER
We breathe too long: come, cousin Westmorland,
Our duty this way lies: for God's sake, come.

Exeunt Lancaster and Westmorland

PRINCE HAL
By God, thou hast deceived me, Lancaster,
I did not think thee lord of such a spirit:
Before, I loved thee as a brother, John,
But now I do respect thee as my soul.

KING HENRY
20
I saw him hold Lord Percy at the point
With lustier maintenance than I did look for
Of such an ungrown warrior.

PRINCE HAL   O, this boy
Lends mettle to us all!   *Exit*
        Enter Douglas

DOUGLAS
Another king! They grow like Hydra's heads.
I am the Douglas, fatal to all those
That wear those colours on them. What art thou
That counterfeitest the person of a king?

KING HENRY
The King himself, who, Douglas, grieves at heart
So many of his shadows thou hast met,
30
And not the very King. I have two boys
Seek Percy and thyself about the field,
But seeing thou fallest on me so luckily
I will assay thee, and defend thyself.

---

12 *stained* (1) blood-stained; (2) disgraced (by defeat)
23 *mettle* spirit
24 *Hydra's heads.* The Hydra was a
many-headed monster, eventually
killed by Hercules, which grew two

heads for each one cut off.
26 *those colours* (the King's)
29 *shadows* imitations
30 *very* true
33 *assay* try

DOUGLAS
  I fear thou art another counterfeit,
  And yet, in faith, thou bearest thee like a king –
  But mine I am sure thou art, whoe'er thou be,
  And thus I win thee.
      They fight, the King being in danger; enter
      Prince of Wales

PRINCE HAL
  Hold up thy head, vile Scot, or thou art like
  Never to hold it up again! The spirits
  Of valiant Shirley, Stafford, Blunt are in my arms.   40
  It is the Prince of Wales that threatens thee,
  Who never promiseth but he means to pay.
      They fight; Douglas flees
  Cheerly, my lord, how fares your grace?
  Sir Nicholas Gawsey hath for succour sent,
  And so hath Clifton – I'll to Clifton straight.

KING HENRY
  Stay and breathe a while.
  Thou hast redeemed thy lost opinion,
  And showed thou makest some tender of my life
  In this fair rescue thou hast brought to me.

PRINCE HAL
  O God, they did me too much injury   50
  That ever said I hearkened for your death.
  If it were so, I might have let alone
  The insulting hand of Douglas over you,

41 *It is the Prince of Wales that threatens thee*. Hal's part in the battle was small, though he seems to have been wounded and refused to leave the field (see lines 10–11).

42 *Who never promiseth but he means to pay*. This is surely an echo of 1.2.206–8, especially the second line: 'And pay the debt I never promised'.

47 *opinion* reputation

48 *makest some tender of* hast some regard for

50–51 *they did me too much injury | That ever said I hearkened for your death*. There was no ground for such accusations at this time – but see note to III.2.126.

51 *hearkened for* desired

53 *insulting* contemptuous, exultant

Which would have been as speedy in your end
As all the poisonous potions in the world,
And saved the treacherous labour of your son.

KING HENRY

Make up to Clifton, I'll to Sir Nicholas Gawsey.   *Exit*
        Enter Hotspur

HOTSPUR

If I mistake not, thou art Harry Monmouth.

PRINCE HAL

Thou speakest as if I would deny my name.

HOTSPUR

My name is Harry Percy.

60   PRINCE HAL   Why then I see
A very valiant rebel of the name.
I am the Prince of Wales, and think not, Percy,
To share with me in glory any more.
Two stars keep not their motion in one sphere,
Nor can one England brook a double reign
Of Harry Percy and the Prince of Wales.

HOTSPUR

Nor shall it, Harry, for the hour is come
To end the one of us; and would to God
Thy name in arms were now as great as mine.

PRINCE HAL

70   I'll make it greater ere I part from thee,
And all the budding honours on thy crest
I'll crop to make a garland for my head.

---

57 *Make up* advance
64 *Two stars keep not their motion in one sphere*. According to Ptolemaic astronomy, each star had its own course.
65 *brook* endure
68–9 *would to God | Thy name in arms were now as great as mine*. It was a principle of chivalric combat that a knight only fought another of equal rank.

Hal's rank is above Percy's, but not the honour he has won. Hotspur's statement is not as self-regarding as it sounds to us. In *Richard II* Aumerle makes much the same point when insulted by Bagot:

Shall I so much dishonour my fair stars
On equal terms to give him chastisement?

                                    IV.1.21—2

HOTSPUR
    I can no longer brook thy vanities.
        They fight
        Enter Falstaff
FALSTAFF Well said, Hal! To it, Hal! Nay, you shall find
    no boy's play here, I can tell you.
        Enter Douglas; he fighteth with Falstaff; who falls
        down as if he were dead

                                    Exit Douglas

        The Prince mortally wounds Hotspur
HOTSPUR
    O Harry, thou hast robbed me of my youth!
    I better brook the loss of brittle life
    Than those proud titles thou hast won of me.
    They wound my thoughts worse than thy sword my
        flesh.
    But thoughts, the slaves of life, and life, time's fool,   80
    And time, that takes survey of all the world,
    Must have a stop. O, I could prophesy,
    But that the earthy and cold hand of death
    Lies on my tongue. No, Percy, thou art dust,
    And food for –   *He dies*
PRINCE HAL
    For worms, brave Percy. Fare thee well, great heart!
    Ill-weaved ambition, how much art thou shrunk.
    When that this body did contain a spirit,
    A Kingdom for it was too small a bound.
    But now two paces of the vilest earth   90

---

74 *Well said* well done!
75 *boy's* child's
80–82 *But thoughts, the slaves of life, and
    life, time's fool, | And time, that takes
    survey of all the world, | Must have a
    stop* (thoughts, life, and eventually,
    time itself, must all end)

82 *I could prophesy.* Prophecy was associ-
    ated with dying men. Gaunt, in *Rich-
    ard II*, thought himself 'a prophet
    new inspired' (II.1.31).
87 *Ill-weaved ambition.* Poorly woven
    cloth shrank easily.
89 *bound* boundary

Is room enough. This earth that bears thee dead
Bears not alive so stout a gentleman.
If thou wert sensible of courtesy
I should not make so dear a show of zeal,
But let my favours hide thy mangled face,
And even in thy behalf I'll thank myself
For doing these fair rites of tenderness.
Adieu, and take thy praise with thee to heaven!
Thy ignominy sleep with thee in the grave,
100   But not remembered in thy epitaph.

He spieth Falstaff on the ground

What, old acquaintance, could not all this flesh
Keep in a little life? Poor Jack, farewell!
I could have better spared a better man.
O, I should have a heavy miss of thee
If I were much in love with vanity.
Death hath not struck so fat a deer today,
Though many dearer, in this bloody fray.

---

92 *stout* valiant
93 *sensible of* able to respond to
94 *dear a show* warm a display
95 *favours*. In Hal's case these would seem to be the plumes from his helmet, which were mentioned by Vernon at IV.1.98 (see note). In a tournament a favour was usually a scarf or glove, worn by a knight as a sign of a lady's favour. It has been argued that such a favour is intended here, on the grounds that Hal's badge, the three ostrich feathers, was not well known in Shakespeare's time.
104 *heavy* (a pun – Falstaff's flesh is compared with Hotspur's *stout* spirit, line 92)
107 *dearer*. The pun here is obvious – 'more loved' and 'more noble' – and it is clear that there are many who

have fallen (Sir Walter Blunt, for example) who are more noble than Falstaff. But do we expect any of them, even Sir Walter, to be more loved by Hal? The ironical banter of the opening of the speech (so similar in tone to that exchanged by Hotspur and Lady Percy) is certainly affectionate and the implication of 'I could have better spared a better man' perfectly sums up Hal's affection for Falstaff and his realization of Falstaff's shortcomings. Possibly, as Dr Johnson complained, a pun was irresistible to Shakespeare and we ought not to attach too great significance to this apparent lowering of Falstaff in Hal's affections. (See also the note to IV.2.14–15, and Introduction, pages 246–7.)

Embowelled will I see thee by and by,
Till then in blood by noble Percy lie.   *Exit*
     Falstaff riseth up

FALSTAFF Embowelled? If thou embowel me today, I'll   110
give you leave to powder me and eat me too tomorrow.
'Sblood, 'twas time to counterfeit, or that hot termagant
Scot had paid me, scot and lot too. Counterfeit? I lie,
I am no counterfeit. To die is to be a counterfeit, for he
is but the counterfeit of a man who hath not the life of
a man. But to counterfeit dying, when a man thereby
liveth, is to be no counterfeit, but the true and perfect
image of life indeed. The better part of valour is discretion, in the which better part I have saved my life.
Zounds, I am afraid of this gunpowder Percy, though he   120
be dead. How if he should counterfeit too and rise? By
my faith, I am afraid he would prove the better counterfeit. Therefore I'll make him sure, yea, and I'll swear I
killed him. Why may not he rise as well as I? Nothing

108 *Embowelled* disembowelled (for em-
balming). A sequence of puns involving hunting terms begin here. Falstaff has just been called 'a deer' (line
106), and deer, on being killed, were
disembowelled. When Hal leaves Falstaff to lie 'in blood' he means, in his
own blood, but he uses a term which,
in hunting, meant 'in full vigour' –
and as Falstaff is feigning, this happens to be true. The expression 'to
powder' (line 111) meant 'to pickle'
and refers to the deer's flesh.

109 (stage direction) *Falstaff riseth up.*
Hal's speech over Falstaff is sufficiently serious and deeply-felt to suggest that Falstaff might have seemed
to be truly dead to an audience as
well as to Hal. The stage direction
after line 75 is ambiguous: *he fighteth
with Falstaff, who falls down as if he
were dead.* Falstaff's rising up here

should not follow immediately on
Hal's exit. There ought to be a pause
because, whether a modern audience
believes him to be dead or not (and
many members of a modern audience
will know he is feigning), his coming
to life is a moment of comedy of
which an actor can make much. It is
comparable to the situation in
II.4.261 when, even if we know what
Falstaff's answer is to be, we await it
with anxiety and receive it with
delight.

112–3 *that hot termagant Scot* (Douglas)

113 *scot and lot* in full (with a pun on
'Scot')

119 *part* quality (not 'portion')

124–5 *Nothing confutes me but eyes* no one
can prove me wrong but an eye-
witness (and there is none here,
except the audience who Falstaff
assumes will take his part)

confutes me but eyes, and nobody sees me. Therefore,
sirrah (*stabbing him*), with a new wound in your thigh,
come you along with me.
        He takes up Hotspur on his back
        Enter Prince and John of Lancaster

PRINCE HAL
    Come, brother John, full bravely hast thou fleshed
    Thy maiden sword.

LANCASTER   But soft, whom have we here?
130   Did you not tell me this fat man was dead?

PRINCE HAL
    I did, I saw him dead,
    Breathless and bleeding on the ground. Art thou alive?
    Or is it fantasy that plays upon our eyesight?
    I prithee speak, we will not trust our eyes
    Without our ears. Thou art not what thou seemest.

FALSTAFF No, that's certain, I am not a double-man. But
    if I be not Jack Falstaff, then am I a Jack. There is
    Percy!

126 *thigh*. Why Falstaff should choose
the thigh as a place to wound Hotspur is puzzling. The thighs would
be covered with 'cuishes' (Hal's are
referred to at IV.1.105), and, indeed,
at the time of Shrewsbury all the
front of a man in armour was fully
protected. Whilst Shakespeare could
hardly be expected to know the details of the armour used two centuries before he wrote *1 Henry IV*, the
armour he could have seen would, if
anything, have been even more elaborate. Hotspur's 'mangled face' is up-
permost (line 95) and thus it would
seem that the action required – and
presumably carried out in the original production in Shakespeare's own
time – would be for Falstaff to turn
the body over and stab it in the only
unprotected place – the top of the
thigh, the bottom – 'protected' by
being sat on when the knight was on

horseback. If the actor deliberated
over speaking the word *thigh* as he
stabbed, the effect would be grue-
somely comic and it might thus
remove, through the convention of
comedy, the full implications of Falstaff's dishonourable act. What follows is certainly in the vein of
comedy. (See also the notes to
IV.2.14–15 and IV.2.63–4, and that to
line 150, below.)

128 *fleshed* used for the first time. John
of Lancaster was then only 13. The
attention given him at the end of *1
Henry IV* has been thought by some
critics to be a preparation for his
part, as Bedford, in *2 Henry IV*. If
that is so it is one piece of evidence
to indicate that Shakespeare had a
second part of *Henry IV* in mind
when writing this part (but see Introduction, pages 225–6).

137 *Jack* knave

>   *He throws the body down*

If your father will do me any honour, so. If not, let him
kill the next Percy himself. I look to be either earl or   140
duke, I can assure you.

PRINCE HAL Why, Percy I killed myself, and saw thee
dead.

FALSTAFF Didst thou? Lord, Lord, how this world is
given to lying! I grant you I was down, and out of
breath, and so was he, but we rose both at an instant,
and fought a long hour by Shrewsbury clock. If I may
be believed, so. If not, let them that should reward
valour bear the sin upon their own heads. I'll take it
upon my death, I gave him this wound in the thigh. If   150
the man were alive, and would deny it, zounds, I would
make him eat a piece of my sword.

LANCASTER This is the strangest tale that ever I heard.

PRINCE HAL This is the strangest fellow, brother John.
Come, bring your luggage nobly on your back.
(*Aside to Falstaff*) For my part, if a lie may do thee
>   grace,
I'll gild it with the happiest terms I have.

>   *A retreat is sounded*

The trumpet sounds retreat, the day is ours.
Come, brother, let us to the highest of the field,
To see what friends are living, who are dead.   160

>   *Exeunt Prince of Wales and Lancaster*

FALSTAFF I'll follow, as they say, for reward. He that

149-50 *I'll take it upon my death* (an oath
  of particular solemnity)
150 *thigh*. Falstaff repeats the place of
  wounding and, if the argument on
  its meaning in line 126 is correct,
  this would again be comic – more
  comic than before, indeed, for the
  unlikely case of killing a man by
  stabbing in such a place would be
  very obvious.

156 *a lie* (of yours)
157 *happiest terms* most favourable expressions of support
159 *highest* (part of the ground)
161 *I'll follow, as they say, for reward*. This
  is another quibble based on hunting.
  The hounds are said to *follow* and
  they are given as *reward* portions of
  the deer that has been brought
  down.

rewards me, God reward him! If I do grow great, I'll
grow less, for I'll purge, and leave sack, and live
cleanly as a nobleman should do.

Exit, bearing off the body

v.5   *The trumpets sound. Enter the King, Prince of Wales,*
             Lord John of Lancaster, Earl of Westmorland, with
             Worcester and Vernon prisoners

KING HENRY

Thus ever did rebellion find rebuke.
Ill-spirited Worcester, did not we send grace,
Pardon, and terms of love to all of you?
And wouldst thou turn our offers contrary?
Misuse the tenor of thy kinsman's trust?
Three knights upon our party slain today,
A noble earl, and many a creature else
Had been alive this hour
If like a Christian thou hadst truly borne
10   Betwixt our armies true intelligence.

WORCESTER

What I have done my safety urged me to,
And I embrace this fortune patiently,
Since not to be avoided it falls on me.

KING HENRY

Bear Worcester to the death, and Vernon too.
Other offenders we will pause upon.

Exeunt Worcester and Vernon

How goes the field?

PRINCE HAL

The noble Scot, Lord Douglas, when he saw

---

163 *purge* (1) repent; (2) take laxatives

v.5.1 *rebuke* violent check
2 *Ill-spirited* evil-minded
   did not we send grace. Compare 'will

they take the offer of our grace' –
pardon – at v.1.106.

6 *Three knights* (ten, in Holinshed)

15 *pause upon* postpone taking a decision

The fortune of the day quite turned from him,
The noble Percy slain, and all his men
Upon the foot of fear, fled with the rest,   20
And falling from a hill he was so bruised
That the pursuers took him. At my tent
The Douglas is – and I beseech your grace
I may dispose of him.

KING HENRY   With all my heart.

PRINCE HAL

Then, brother John of Lancaster, to you
This honourable bounty shall belong.
Go to the Douglas and deliver him
Up to his pleasure, ransomless and free.
His valours shown upon our crests today
Have taught us how to cherish such high deeds,   30
Even in the bosom of our adversaries.

LANCASTER

I thank your grace for this high courtesy,
Which I shall give away immediately.

KING HENRY

Then this remains, that we divide our power.
You, son John, and my cousin Westmorland,
Towards York shall bend you with your dearest speed
To meet Northumberland and the prelate Scroop,
Who, as we hear, are busily in arms.
Myself and you, son Harry, will towards Wales,
To fight with Glendower and the Earl of March.   40
Rebellion in this land shall lose his sway,
Meeting the check of such another day,
And since this business so fair is done,
Let us not leave till all our own be won.   *Exeunt*

---

20 *Upon the foot of fear* with the speed of
panic
36 *bend you* you direct your course
dearest best
41 *his* its
43–4 *And since this business so fair is done* | 43 *fair* successfully

Let us not leave till all our own be won.
This does not read like the end of
Henry IV as Shakespeare conceived
it: it almost invites our attention to a
second part.

HENRY IV, PART TWO

Introduction

The Second Part of *Henry IV* is the third in a series of four plays by Shakespeare which dramatize the reigns of Richard II, Henry IV, and Henry V. They are closely related, and the plays of the reigns of Henry IV and V refer frequently to events dramatized in the first play of the series, *Richard II*. Nevertheless, the most important point to grasp in an understanding of *2 Henry IV* is that it is a play in its own right, a play of its own kind, and especially that it is very different from *1 Henry IV*. Though, like the other plays of the tetralogy, it is concerned with historical events, it is quite unlike them in its style, its mood, and its tone. Since they were first produced, the First Part of *Henry IV* has been more popular than the Second. *2 Henry IV* has been interpreted and produced in the light – in the shadow – of *1 Henry IV*. This is damaging to the play itself, obscuring its particular qualities, and harmful to the contribution it makes to the tetralogy of which it forms a part.

The circumstances in which plays were published in the early seventeenth century are often unknown, and it may be that the appearance of only one edition of *2 Henry IV* (in 1600), as compared to seven of *1 Henry IV*, prior to the publication of Shakespeare's works in 1623, was due to factors other than the demand for the play. Nevertheless, though the proportion of one to seven exaggerates the difference in popularity of the two parts, it shows how, from the very beginning, *2 Henry IV* has proved the less popular of the two plays. Despite this, I would argue that *2 Henry IV* is the more interesting and, in some ways, the greater play. But it will never have the popular appeal of the First Part. *1 Henry IV* has a natural exuberance that is instantly attractive; and, even though Hotspur fails and dies, it epitomizes a sense of 'life to be grasped' that makes it, essentially, a great comic drama. Such drama is not solely concerned with being funny (though there is much to laugh at in *1 Henry IV*). It is much more concerned with rejoicing in life in a way that seems to overcome death. We should, if Hotspur's character is well and sympathetically realized, feel the poignancy of his death just as the putting out of a very bright light makes us not only more conscious of the darkness but, from the illusion of light retained by the eye, aware also of what has been extinguished.

There is no death in *2 Henry IV* that we feel as sharply as Hotspur's in the First Part, and the comedy in Gloucestershire can provide as much laughter as anything in *1 Henry IV*; yet *2 Henry IV* is not in any sense that comedy which celebrates 'life to be grasped'. Despite its wonderfully humorous scenes, it is, for much of its length, closer in mood to *All's Well That Ends Well* than to *1 Henry IV*. Prince Henry's weariness of spirit in Act II, scene 2 (and elsewhere), anticipates Bertram's disillusion in Act II, scenes 3 and 5, of *All's Well That Ends Well*. Popularity is not readily achieved by plays in this mood, especially when such a play invites comparison with another which is a comic masterpiece.

A second reason for the play's lesser popularity stems from the first reason. It has been persistently interpreted as the sequel to the First Part, an understandable enough error, but an error nevertheless if the interpretation tries to find in the Second Part the mood of the First. Some adaptations, such as that of 1719, go so far as to refer to this part as 'The Sequel to Henry the Fourth'. Producers and critics have been far too ready to see the play as a pale imitation of the First Part; and Shakespeare himself, though perhaps unwittingly, nudges us into doing just that. Two plays with the same nominal subject and sharing several characters, one of whom is the greatest of all comic creations, Falstaff, must invite that interpretation. Then, the themes and structures of the two plays have much in

common. Each play begins with the heir to the throne in
disfavour and each ends with the reprobate regenerate. The
planning of the scenes has many parallels – the juxtaposition of
historical event and comic action; the confrontation of Prince
Henry and Falstaff in Act II, scene 4, of each play; Falstaff's
recruiting and his diversions at Sutton Coldfield in *1 Henry IV*
and in Gloucestershire in *2 Henry IV*, on his way to Shrewsbury
and Gaultree Forest respectively; and a whole host of major
and minor connexions to which scholars have pointed. The
result has been that readers, critics, and especially producers
have tried to reproduce the mood and tone of *1 Henry IV* in
this 'sequel'. Thus *2 Henry IV* has been assessed in terms of
expectations of *1 Henry IV*, and, not surprisingly, has proved
disappointing. *2 Henry IV* is *not* a sequel to *1 Henry IV*; nor is
it a pot-boiler, cashing in on the success of its First Part; still
less is it a 'ramshackle rag-bag of a piece' (as Richard David
described it in *Shakespeare Survey* 6 (1953), page 137).

If a simple term were needed to describe the Second Part in
relation to the First it would be not 'sequel' but 'obverse'. The
two plays show these similarities because each presents opposite
sides of the same coin. Shakespeare may very well have started
out on *2 Henry IV* because he realized, perhaps even before
completing the First Part, that he had a successful play on his
hands; but the greatest artists are not simply repetitive. If any
truism about Shakespeare holds, it is that his work shows
infinite variety. On the only occasion when he seemed in
danger of repeating himself, he appears to have left one of the
plays concerned, *Timon of Athens*, uncompleted. What is remarkable about *2 Henry IV* is its distinctiveness from *1 Henry IV*.
Falstaff's role is large in both plays, but differs in style and
tone. This is not just because the story requires that he be
rejected, nor even because he is kept apart from Prince Henry
for most of the Second Part; it lies in the differences in his use
of language and his ability to dominate a scene. How different
are the confrontations of Falstaff and the Prince (Act II, scene
4, of each play)! And in *Part Two*, with the exception of 133

lines of this scene (of which only some seventy involve the
Prince and Falstaff in the same conversation), the two characters
never meet before the rejection scene. Falstaff, as will be shown
later, here lacks much of that imaginative faculty which makes
him so much a master of his scenes in *1 Henry IV*. Even when
the Prince and Poins, by a complicated stratagem, gain a
technical victory after Gad's Hill, it is Falstaff who, paradoxically, takes the moral triumph. In *2 Henry IV* Falstaff has two
victories, one, a little surprisingly, over the sturdy Colevile,
and the other an empty victory over Shallow. In all else he
loses. Even a fairly cursory study of Falstaff suggests that
Shakespeare is not repeating what he did in *1 Henry IV*, and
the minor scenes which, over the centuries, adapters have not
hesitated to cut show quite strikingly that Shakespeare is
working a different vein of drama here. Thus, one of the most
wonderful sixteenth-century dramatizations of 'real life' (three-
and-a-half centuries before realism was conceived as a dramatic
mode) occurs in *1 Henry IV* when Shakespeare presents the
early-morning awakening of the Carriers in the inn yard at
Rochester:

FIRST CARRIER *I prithee, Tom, beat Cut's saddle, put a few
flocks in the point; poor jade is wrung in the withers out of all cess.*
SECOND CARRIER *Peas and beans are as dank here as a dog, and
that is the next way to give poor jades the bots. This house is turned
upside down since Robin Ostler died.*

1 Henry IV, II.1.5–11

This is not a pretty picture of rural life, nor is it intended to be.
It offers an insight into the other side of life in a tavern from
that enjoyed by Hal and Falstaff. Compare it, however, with
the little scene in Act v of *2 Henry IV* in which the Hostess and
Doll are dragged to prison. This is 'real' enough, but its
function is not simply to represent *actualité*, but to remind us of
a whole world which the Prince must reject. The provision of
this scene is one way of solving a structural problem created by
the need to allow dramatic time for Falstaff and Shallow to

travel from Gloucestershire, where they hear the news of
Henry V's accession (v.3), to London, where the coronation
takes place (v.5). It is not essential to dramatize the ending of
the play in this way; it is quite simple to arrange the events so
that Act v, scene 4, is unnecessary. Thus, Charles Kemble's
coronation production of 1821 (which was based on J. P.
Kemble's text for the 1804 production) begins the fifth act by
combining Shakespeare's scenes 1 and 3, so that the announce-
ment of Henry V's accession is made before we see Henry as
king. The second scene is a much cut version of Shakespeare's
Act v, scene 2, as far as line 62, presenting the King in 'This
new and gorgeous garment, majesty'. Then the nineteenth-
century versions omit Act v, scene 4 (the arrests), and the
Grooms' strewing of rushes, and jump to Shakespeare's Act v,
scene 5, from line 5 to line 93 (much cut), and follow that with
the reconciliation of King and Lord Chief Justice (v.2.67–145,
again cut). Thus the reconciliation occurs after the rejection,
and Doll and the Hostess are not hauled away to prison before
our eyes.

What the Kembles did to *2 Henry IV* gives a clue to what
Shakespeare may have intended in his arrangement of the
ending. It will be clear that their version is perfectly feasible in
terms of story-telling, and indeed has the merit of greater
simplicity. It is so obvious a way of concluding the story that it
can hardly have escaped Shakespeare's attention. Apart from its
greater simplicity, the Kembles' ending is also happier than
that provided by Shakespeare. Their version ends on a note of
reconciliation, whereas Shakespeare not only does not soften
the rejection in this way but actually rubs it in. Of his own
accord he has Falstaff and Shallow and their companions
imprisoned (v.5.94–5), a detail not in any of the sources, and
omitted by the Kembles; and he concludes with the uncharming
John of Lancaster in congratulatory mood, also omitted by the
Kembles. The difference between the endings of Shakespeare
and the Kembles is not unlike that which distinguishes those of
George Bernard Shaw's *Pygmalion* and Lerner and Loewe's *My*

Fair Lady, in that case the difference between human self-realization and sentimentality.

From the very first scene in which Falstaff appears in 1 *Henry IV* it is apparent that his chance of gaining high office under Henry V is limited. He refers to the law as 'Father Antic', and shortly afterwards Hal tells him 'Thou judgest false already' (1.2.60–65). From then on there are indications which point clearly to Falstaff's eventual rejection, and an Elizabethan audience would, I do not doubt, perceive this. However, actors and producers, dazzled by Falstaff's theatrical brilliance, are as easily deceived by him as is Shallow, and they are understandably reluctant to let go a character who wins such applause and affection. The text the Kembles used is never so revealing as in the way it attempts to soften the impact of the rejection; and although modern productions do not usually rewrite the endings of Shakespeare's plays as Lerner and Loewe altered the end of *Pygmalion*, not all capture successfully the tone and mood of 2 *Henry IV* as Shakespeare wrote it.

If Shakespeare had no need to include a scene at Act v, scene 4, he also had no need, if such a scene were to be included, to write one in the style he chose. In *As You Like It*, for example, when dramatic time is needed between scenes 2 and 4 of Act v to indicate the passing of a day (for Rosalind insists that all will be resolved 'tomorrow'), Shakespeare writes the delightful 'It was a lover and his lass', and provides two Pages to sing it and to cheek Touchstone: a pleasant interlude of some forty-five lines. The scene provided in 2 *Henry IV* is also brief (about thirty lines), but there is nothing pleasant about it. The long-suffering Hostess and the foul-tongued Doll are dragged away, protesting loudly, by beadles, one of whom was probably played originally by John Sincklo (see the note to the opening stage direction of v.4), who must have looked the personification of death. This short and brutish scene, coupled with Henry's rejection of Falstaff, the committal to prison of Falstaff and his followers, and Lancaster's expression of satisfaction, makes the end of 2 *Henry IV* anything but comfortable. It is stark, cold, almost puritanical. It is not the stuff of easy popularity – no Eliza marries a Higgins in *this* atmosphere – but, interpreted well, it is strong drama, capable of moving any audience not exclusively addicted to sentimentality.

There are three plays by Shakespeare which feature Falstaff, and they seem to have been written in the years 1596, 1597, and 1598 in the order *1 Henry IV*, *The Merry Wives of Windsor*, and *2 Henry IV*, though the last two may have overlapped. *2 Henry IV* was first published in 1600 (two years after the First Part). The title-page of this Quarto edition makes plain the relationship of the play to the First Part, though it must be remembered that Elizabethan title-pages formed a kind of advertisement which, like modern paperback covers, sometimes promised more than the text fulfilled. The body of the title-page reads: 'The Second Part of Henry the Fourth, continuing to his death, and coronation of Henry the Fifth. With the humours of Sir John Falstaff, and swaggering Pistol. As it hath been sundry times publicly acted by the right honourable the Lord Chamberlain his servants. Written by William Shakespeare'. The year 1600 also saw the publication of the play *Sir John Oldcastle*, which seems to have been commissioned to put the record straight on the public stage following the ridicule the Brooke family felt it had suffered in providing the original for Sir John Falstaff (see page 445). *2 Henry IV* was not reprinted until the Folio edition of 1623 (see the Account of the Text, page 459). The title and 'introductory description' in the Folio is briefer than on the title-page of the Quarto: 'The Second Part of Henry the Fourth, containing his death, and the coronation of King Henry the Fifth'. 'Continuing' in the Quarto seems to have become 'containing' in the Folio. No satisfactory reason has been given for the absence of a Quarto reprint. Censorship has been suggested, but this did not prevent the reprinting of *Richard II*, a much more dangerous play, for it dealt with the deposition of a monarch, and what is more the later reprints included the deposition scene itself, which had at first been omitted. It has been thought possible that a very large number of copies of the first edition was printed because of the phenomenal success of the First Part. It is a fact that, whereas only thirteen copies and an eight-page fragment survive of the first three editions of *1 Henry IV*, twenty-one copies have survived of the 1600 edition of *2 Henry IV*. However, it was illegal to publish more than 1,500 copies of a book from the same setting of type at this period without a special licence, and though we cannot be sure that the law was obeyed in the printing of *2 Henry IV* there is certainly no evidence that it was broken. It is at least as likely that Falstaff's humours and the swaggering of Pistol advertised on the title-page did not provide that neverending source of amusement which Falstaff's 'humorous conceits' did in the First Part.

There is no reason to doubt that *2 Henry IV* was presented at the Globe shortly after the First Part had been performed. We know from the diary of Philip Henslowe, a theatrical entrepreneur, that one of the rival theatre companies, the Admiral's Men, frequently (though not invariably) presented plays in two parts at successive performances in 1594, 1595, and 1596. It is not unlikely that this practice was adopted for *1* and *2 Henry IV*, especially if Shakespeare's company was anxious to demonstrate how far its treatment of the story of Prince Hal was superior to the Admiral's play, *The Famous Victories of Henry the Fifth*, which was published in 1598 (the same year as *1 Henry IV*) but seems to be referred to as early as 1594. *The Famous Victories* gives in one play what Shakespeare dramatizes in both parts of *Henry IV* and *Henry V*. Even before Shakespeare's death, the two parts of *Henry IV* were being combined into a single play, and since then several adapters have made free with Shakespeare, either to present an even meatier part for the actor playing Falstaff or to grind a particular political axe.

The principal source upon which Shakespeare relied for the details of Henry IV's reign and Henry V's accession was Raphael Holinshed's *Chronicles of England*, probably the second edition of 1587 (which was certainly used for *1 Henry IV*).

Though he departed from this at times, particularly in his account of the principal personalities involved on the King's side at Gaultree Forest, and also in the arrest of Sir John after his rejection, the main outline, and some of the specific detail, comes from Holinshed. It is possible without too much imagination to see Shakespeare discarding from Holinshed as well as selecting. Thus the names Umfrevile, Fauconbridge, and Kent, all in Holinshed, appear vestigially in *2 Henry IV* (see the Account of the Text, page 460). Holinshed's title for this section of his chronicle may have proved more influential than the facts themselves in suggesting the tone of *2 Henry IV*: 'King Henry's Unquiet Reign'. This title comes from an earlier history, Edward Hall's *The Union of the Two Noble and Illustre Families of Lancaster and York* (1548), which has the title 'The Unquiet Time of King Henry the Fourth', a phrase which Shakespeare echoes at 1.2.152. It has not been possible to demonstrate that Shakespeare made direct use of Hall (much of which is repeated in Holinshed), but a reading of Hall suggests to me that Shakespeare was greatly influenced by the dramatic nature of Hall's account and by Hall's sense of history, rather than Holinshed's recounting of events.

These were by no means Shakespeare's only sources. There was current in his time a lively tradition of legend about Hal's life, so that an audience would come to these plays at least as well informed (and perhaps as prejudiced) as a modern audience at a play about Vietnam or Northern Ireland or racial violence. Shakespeare had to dramatize the story of Henry V's reformation against a background of adulation for the victor of Agincourt, a leader who had triumphed against all odds and who had, through his years of 'wanton' living (as Henry IV puts it in *Richard II*, v.3.6–12), experienced raw life and come to know ordinary and extraordinary people. To an Elizabethan audience the remarkable scene in *Henry V* in which this great military leader spends the night before the battle justifying his actions to three ordinary soldiers (which even today would be unlikely) seemed a natural outcome of Henry's riotous early life.

Henry's behaviour before Agincourt may well have epitomized the ideal of kingship as the Elizabethans would have
liked to believe it.

A lesser dramatist than Shakespeare, such as the unknown
author of *The Famous Victories of Henry the Fifth*, would simply
go along with the legend. Shakespeare, however, never seems
completely at ease with it. Trying to detect from his dramatization of the source material what Shakespeare himself thought
about kingship and politics is a dangerous form of fictional
biography, but there are moments in *1 Henry IV* (such as
1.2.193–215) when he seems able to rely on the adulation for
Prince Henry to permit him to make a cooler assessment of the
Prince's intentions. In *2 Henry IV*, whether intuitively or
consciously, he plays down Prince Henry (even to call him
'Hal' any longer sounds impertinent), associates him with the
cold deception of his brother, and has him inherit that touch of
expediency that was associated with Henry IV (and the Tudors),
for example, in acceding to his father's suggestion that the best
way to distract minds from troubles at home is by waging war
abroad (see IV.5.213–15 and V.5.108–11). We, without the
legend of Hal's regeneration as part of our everyday literary
and historical experience, may tend to overstress the critical
aspects of Shakespeare's dramatization; and, in evaluating what
happens in *2 Henry IV*, it is important to bear in mind the
influence of the legend and the extent to which Henry's behaviour accorded with the very real ideal of kingship which
Erasmus and others defined in the sixteenth century.

Shakespeare also had available (as he did for *Richard II* and
1 Henry IV) Samuel Daniel's long poem, *The First Four Books of
the Civil Wars between the Two Houses of Lancaster and York*
(1595), which concentrates much of its attention on Henry's
anxiety about his usurpation of the throne:

> *And lying on his last afflicted bed,*
> *Where death and conscience both before him stand,*
> *Th'one holding out a book wherein he read*

In bloody lines the deeds of his own hand;
The other shows a glass, which figurèd
An ugly form of foul corrupted sand;
Both bringing horror in the highest degree
With what he was, and what he straight should be.

III.118

The Second Part of *Henry IV* pays considerable attention to another legend, the story of the Prince having struck the Lord Chief Justice, even though that incident was not dramatized in the First Part. The earliest account of this occurrence was published in 1531, when it appeared in Sir Thomas Elyot's *The Book Named the Governor*, and it is featured several times in *The Famous Victories of Henry the Fifth* (see the Introduction to *1 Henry IV*, pages 243–4). The Page in *2 Henry IV* refers to the incident at 1.2.54, and Falstaff mentions it, with an undercutting comic aside, at 1.2.195–9. It becomes a matter of some moment when in Act v the new king's quality is immediately tested as he meets the Lord Chief Justice for the first time after his accession. His confirmation of the Lord Chief Justice in his office (v.2.103) bodes ill for Falstaff's cry at the end of the next scene, 'woe to my Lord Chief Justice!'

Shakespeare gives less weight than *The Famous Victories* to the discreditable aspects of Prince Henry's life as they affect the King and the law. The earlier play, as well as dramatizing the striking of the Lord Chief Justice, shows Hal entering his father's chamber with a dagger and being rebuked by Henry IV for intending his death. Shakespeare ignores the second of these incidents (except for a possible fleeting reference at IV.5.107; see the textual note), and in the story of the striking of the Lord Chief Justice he concentrates, so far as the Prince is concerned, on his submission. Indeed the contrast in *2 Henry IV* between Falstaff's and Prince Henry's attitudes to this incident is indicative of the gulf that separates them. That the incident of the striking of the Lord Chief Justice was performed in some play on the life of Henry V (though not necessarily

The Famous Victories) seems very likely from a story in an anonymous book called *Tarlton's Jests*. The earliest version of this book that has survived is dated 1608 and Tarlton died in 1588. We cannot be certain whether the story is apocryphal or not, but it is probably not untypical of conditions in the theatre a few years before *2 Henry IV* was performed, when clowns took full advantage of opportunities to speak more than was set down for them, 'though in the meantime some necessary question of the play be then to be considered', as Hamlet complains.

At the Bull at Bishopsgate was a play of Henry the Fifth, *wherein the judge was to take a box on the ear; and because he was absent that should take the blow, Tarlton himself, ever forward to please, took upon him to play the same judge, besides his own part of the clown. And Knell, then playing Henry V, hit Tarlton a sound box indeed, which made the people laugh the more because it was he. But anon the judge goes in, and immediately Tarlton in his clown's clothes comes out and asks the actors 'What news?' 'O,' saith one, 'hadst thou been here thou shouldst have seen Prince Henry hit the judge a terrible box on the ear!' 'What, man,' said Tarlton, 'strike a judge?' 'It is true, i' faith,' said the other. 'No other like,' said Tarlton, 'and it could not be but terrible to the judge, when the report so terrifies me that methinks the blow remains still on my cheek that it burns again.' The people laughed at this mightily.*

Shakespeare seems also to have been acquainted with either one or both of John Stow's *The Chronicles of England* (1580) and *The Annals of England* (1592; see the note to IV.4.20–48); a collection of verse stories called *A Mirror for Magistrates* (1559); and John Eliot's *Orthoepia Gallica* (1593), which probably suggested Pistol's language (see the Commentary to II.4.152–5). Yet, despite such a variety of sources, and even taking into account the legends and the plays which held the stage before 1596, it is impossible to be sure that we have recovered all the works upon which Shakespeare drew directly or, more importantly, those which influenced his approach to his subject. It is

one thing to identify with some confidence the source of
Pistol's rant or the men who might have suggested the names
of Wart, Visor, and Perkes (see the notes to III.2.135 and
v.1.33–4), but it is quite another to be at all sure why Shakespeare introduced Pistol or Shallow or Silence or the county of
Gloucestershire.

Even when evidence for the use of a source or the identification of a character with a real person can be asserted, we may
be puzzled as to why Shakespeare has used his reading and his
experience in the way he has. Thus, though in *2 Henry IV*
Shallow and Silence seem particularly at home in Gloucestershire, Gloucestershire may be no more than an afterthought.
Falstaff would have to make a wide detour to travel to Yorkshire via Gloucestershire, yet he manages to arrive at Gaultree
Forest on time. When he first visits Shallow there is no
mention of Gloucestershire or of any place in that area. A more
likely county would have been either Huntingdon, Rutland, or
Lincolnshire, all on the direct route north and making more
logical Shallow's inquiry about prices at Stamford fair (III.2.37).
In Act IV, scene 3, however, Gloucestershire is mentioned for
the first time (lines 80–81 and 125); Act v establishes a setting
there, and Shakespeare seems to have known the area well (see
the note to v.1.33–4). How was it that he came to settle upon
Gloucestershire, apparently after having another locality in
mind in Act III? Does the countryside of Gloucestershire give
an atmosphere, a quality of life, which make a particular
contribution to the play? At the end of his life he chose to
return home to live at Stratford in a neighbouring county, so
one can presume he had some affection for the area where he
originated; and his knowledge of Gloucestershire has been
proved from a precise reference to one part of the county in
Richard II (II.3.53). He is certainly making a strong contrast
between the virtues of the country life and the coldness and
expediency of that other world he depicts in *2 Henry IV*.
Shallow may be silly – and he can, though rather perversely, be
interpreted as venal (see the note to v.1.46) – but his kindness,

his hospitality, and his naturalness impress us quite as much as his simplicity. This is particularly apparent at the opening of Act v. In the fourth act we have the treachery at Gaultree, the symbolic usurpation of the crown, sickness, and impending death. The very first line of Act v sets a totally different tone:

By cock and pie, sir, you shall not away tonight.

First, the country-sounding oath, naïve and euphemistic, conscious of the sensibilities of others in its simple avoidance of profanity; then, the insistence on hospitality. When Davy enters he has an easy association with Shallow, and the latter's natural peremptoriness is refreshing after the formal relationships of the preceding act, which are at best cold, at worst malignant. The delight in giving, rather than taking; the order to 'Use his men well'; Davy's expectation that even an arrant knave shall have a fair hearing; and the many references to the ordinary events of daily country life, all suggest a world of a different kind from that which has been presented earlier in the play. Above all we have the dramatization of good fellowship and generosity, which seem to epitomize the goodness and beneficence of the country in sharp and pleasant contrast to the worlds of court and city.

It has already been suggested that the way Shakespeare uses the story of the striking of the Lord Chief Justice enables him to dramatize the widening of a gulf between the Prince and Falstaff, and that Shakespeare's ignoring of the story of the dagger avoids the direct imputation of treason to the Prince. These characteristics seem to determine the way that he uses the other material at his disposal. Falstaff's response to the hospitality shown him in Gloucestershire is to become increasingly covetous. Laughter at Shallow's folly, his delight in youthful memories, his ineptness, should not blind us to the fact that he is a kind and gracious host in an age when to be such was greatly esteemed. Shakespeare is adept at showing the apparent defeat of good intentions by politic cunning and yet enabling us to understand that such victories are hollow and even self-defeating. Nowhere is this more skilfully done than in *As You Like It*, written in the same period as *2 Henry IV* (see the note to v.1.58). Producers and audiences must exercise some discernment here. The 'Old Iniquity', the element of the Vice that Falstaff has inherited from the earlier Tudor drama, is strong in Shakespeare's characterization of him in *2 Henry IV*. Thus, although Shallow will receive due reward for his folly, a modern audience must realize that Falstaff, in *2 Henry IV*, is much more seriously at fault than is Shallow and will be judged much more severely. He is not merely a jolly, comfortable practical joker. At the time when Prince Henry is ordering his life more in accord with what is proper to an heir to the throne – someone who must assume authority – Falstaff's behaviour becomes more self-indulgent than ever, and his belief that 'the laws of England are at my commandment' (v.3.134–5) recklessly threatens the society of the play. In order to show how separate are Falstaff and the Prince, Shakespeare does not rely solely on dramatizing his story in such a way that they scarcely meet; he shows how, when apart, they develop in opposite directions in their attitudes to law and the society of which they form a part. Gloucestershire, as much as the tavern world, skilfully indicates the different qualities in that society and the nature of the choices open to Falstaff and to the Prince.

One of the most subtle and economical ways in which Shakespeare dramatizes the character of the Prince is by simultaneously detaching him from acts which are treasonable (such as the striking of the Lord Chief Justice and the threat to his father's life) or dishonourable (Falstaff's incursion into Gloucestershire) and yet showing him as one of a family which reached its position by usurpation and maintains it by duplicity. Whatever Henry IV's rationalizations, he is a usurper (see the Commentary to IV.5.185) and Prince Henry is the successor to a usurper. Henry IV's advice to his son that he should make war abroad when he is king (IV.5.213–15) is quickly followed (v.5.108–11 and the play of *Henry V*). More subtly, Shakespeare alters the account in his sources. He adds the imprisonment of

Falstaff and his friends by the Lord Chief Justice, and has Prince John, not Westmorland, trick the rebels at Gaultree Forest. There is no doubt that Prince John's behaviour was acceptable according to the standards of Shakespeare's time: there was no need to keep faith with rebels or heretics (see the note to IV.2.54–65). Nevertheless there is nothing noble or courageous, nothing inspiring about such conduct. It is of a piece with the coldness and the unattractiveness of Prince John himself. The way Shakespeare presents Prince John and his device never tempts us to applaud. Falstaff has no love for Prince John (see IV.3.85–93), and in the scale of values which Shakespeare seems to imply (it is no stronger), Prince John falls below Falstaff, having his cunning but lacking his warmth. John is not Henry, but the heir to the throne is not only his father's son but his brother's brother, and we cannot avoid being aware that Prince Henry stands in close relationship to men of a cold and calculating nature. At times Shakespeare lets us see such calculation rising to the surface. When Prince Henry protests to his father that he meant no ill in taking the crown, he bursts out:

> If I do feign,
> O, let me in my present wildness die,
> And never live to show th'incredulous world
> The noble change that I have purposed!

IV.5.152–5

Does one 'purpose' a 'noble change'? At IV.4.74–5 Warwick reports that the Prince will, 'in the perfectness of time, | Cast off his followers'. Is there not a slightly awkward association of the 'perfectness' of time and the idea of 'casting off' followers? Delicately Shakespeare uses his source materials to present in a complex way a man's struggle to realize his own personality and yet come to terms with the burden of authority he must assume. Shakespeare's presentation of Prince Henry's dilemma is as far from the adulation of the Tudor ballad writer as it is from the easy condemnation of the twentieth-century critic.

The imprisonment of Falstaff and the trick at Gaultree Forest are only two of the incidents which help give the play a tone very different from that of *1 Henry IV*. We are never in doubt that the Gad's Hill robbery is at the level of game. Hal's willingness to return the money stolen, and 'with advantage' (*1 Henry IV*, II.4.532), comes a little too pat and does not quite absolve him from his promise a few lines earlier that if Falstaff has robbed the Carriers he shall be made answerable (lines 506–7). Even Hal's plan to gain experience by associating with people whom later he will discard (1.2.193–215) can be seen, if in character, as the result of youthful inexperience, or as being choric and not even to be regarded as 'in character' (any more than is Gertrude's description of the drowning of Ophelia, which, if realistically in character, would demand the question 'Why did you not try to save her?', a question which the choric nature of the speech does not prompt). Throughout *1 Henry IV* there is that sense of *joie de vivre* that seems to make the life lived in the play worth living and to elicit from us a similar response.

The difference in tone, at least in so far as it affects the Prince, is effectively epitomized by his first appearance in each play. In *1 Henry IV* Hal appears in the second scene with Falstaff in the role of boon companion. Falstaff begins in terms of complete familiarity: 'Now, Hal, what time of day is it, lad!', and Hal's reply is in kind:

Thou art so fat-witted with drinking of old sack, and unbuttoning thee after supper, and sleeping upon benches after noon, that thou hast forgotten to demand that truly which thou wouldst truly know. What a devil hast thou to do with the time of the day?

1.2.2–6

Hal's humour never has a genuinely light touch (see the Introduction to *1 Henry IV*, pages 239–40), but here he summons up a gusto typical of his character in the First Part. In the Second Part, however, there is rarely, if ever, the sense that this is the Hal of the First Part. We are more conscious that the character before us is Prince Henry, heir to the throne. The exuberance of the First Part has quite gone. The Prince does not appear until the second scene of the second act, and his first line might be spoken by another of Shakespeare's princes, Hamlet: 'Before God, I am exceeding weary'. The speeches that follow are full of distaste and self-disgust. The complexion of his greatness is discoloured (lines 4–5); he is out of love with his own greatness (line 12); it is a disgrace to him to remember Poins's name (lines 12–13); his heart bleeds inwardly that his father is so sick (line 45), but it is not appropriate that he should show his sadness (lines 37–8).

Prince Henry's part in the prank played on Falstaff, when he and Poins listen to what the old man says whilst they are disguised as drawers, is of the lowest kind of invention. This is not to criticize Shakespeare's inventive talent: it would have been the simplest matter to devise, or even filch, something more novel. It is as if Shakespeare were in this way dramatizing the Prince's lack of interest in such escapades. On the only occasion when Falstaff and the Prince meet before the rejection, a device as unmemorable as this is made to serve as the excuse for their coming together. When Peto enters with news the Prince stays no longer than to hear it and speak five lines of self-criticism, with a sixth to demand his sword and cloak and bid Falstaff the briefest of good-nights (II.4.356–61).

Prince Henry makes only one other appearance in the Second Part before becoming king. This is his last meeting with his father (IV.5). When he enters, his speech seems inapt and less than sympathetic: 'How now, rain within doors, and none abroad?' (lines 10–11). As he watches over the King, something akin to remorse comes over him:

> Thy due from me
> Is tears and heavy sorrows of the blood,
> Which nature, love, and filial tenderness
> Shall, O dear father, pay thee plenteously.

IV.5.38–41

Then, believing his father dead, he takes the crown and puts it on his head. This assumption of the symbol of sovereignty whilst the King still lives offends the canons of propriety and merits the King's outburst that follows. The action almost obscures the words which the Prince utters as he takes, indeed seizes, the crown (as his father had done from Richard II):

> *My due from thee is this imperial crown,*
> *Which, as immediate from thy place and blood,*
> *Derives itself to me.*   IV.5.42–4

What the Prince sees as his due, deriving itself to him, jars with the remorse he has belatedly just expressed. Not so very deep in our memories are two lines from Act II, scene 2, which follow the Prince's assertion that keeping vile company has prevented him from showing sorrow for his father's illness (though why that should inevitably follow is difficult to understand). The Prince asked 'What wouldst thou think of me if I should weep?', and Poins replied 'I would think thee a most princely hypocrite'. What saves the Prince in our esteem, but by the narrowest of margins, is his reply to Poins: 'It would be every man's thought'. The Prince's realization that it would be natural for everyone to think him a hypocrite probably saves him from actually being a hypocrite at his father's deathbed. This does not make him in *2 Henry IV* an immediately attractive personality, but it does show that a new man has evolved, one who might be capable of fulfilling the office he inherits. It is only when he has actually put on the 'new and gorgeous garment, majesty', that he shows really attractive characteristics in *2 Henry IV*. He speaks his brothers fair and seems to mean what he says; he confirms the Lord Chief Justice in his appointment, an action which history does not record (see the note to I.2.52); and, though he rejects Falstaff, he assures him of the 'competence of life' (V.5.69). He is also curiously diffident about the use of the royal plural (unlike his father; see the note to V.2.134).

In presenting such a change of character Shakespeare had to

solve a problem of considerable difficulty. There is nothing worse in drama than a dominant character who betrays all the virtues – indeed, *betraying* the virtues is almost invariably what happens. When Shakespeare presents characters of pure goodness, such as Cordelia, he ensures that their appearances are infrequent and, in the case of Cordelia, that the first impression she makes on us involves an element of doubt ('Why cannot she simply *say* she loves the old man?'). He adopts much the same policy with Prince Henry. We see him disillusioned in Act II, scene 2, acting out a second-rate trick in Act II, scene 4, remorseful but anxious for the crown in Act IV, scene 5, and then behaving with dignity and propriety, and making a difficult decision, in Act V, scenes 2 and 5. In the whole play he has just over three hundred lines to speak, only a little over half the number he has in *1 Henry IV*, where he appears in twice as many scenes as he does in *2 Henry IV*. It has sometimes been commented upon that Henry IV plays only a minor role in the two plays which bear his name, but this obscures the fact that he has only eighteen lines fewer than his son in *2 Henry IV* (and his part in *1 Henry IV* is some twenty lines longer than his son's part in *2 Henry IV*). Naturally, when they do appear, King and Prince attract our attention, and both have long and important speeches; but their roles in *2 Henry IV* are relatively small in terms of lines spoken.

In tone and extent, then, Prince Henry's role in *2 Henry IV* is subdued and sometimes a trifle sour. The part he must play is defined by others as much as – indeed, more than – by what he does and says. One of the more remarkable features of *2 Henry IV* is the way in which our attitude to Prince Henry and his father, the two characters about whom the play revolves, is conditioned by others, some of whom are only on the fringes of the main areas of activity.

Falstaff's nature and origin have been a subject of wide-ranging interest to scholars and critics. Some account of the explanations offered for him is given in the Introduction to *1 Henry IV* (pages 242–7). The rejection of Falstaff is there to

some extent described in terms of its necessity as a part of the
Prince's education. It will perhaps be convenient if one or two
aspects of that account are repeated here, as an understanding
of them is essential to appreciating his role in *2 Henry IV*.

It is certain that Falstaff was called Oldcastle in Shakespeare's
draft of *1 Henry IV*. Oldcastle was a real person, a knight who
served Henry V but was martyred as a Lollard. By using his
name Shakespeare offended the Brooke family, which was
descended from Oldcastle's wife (and Brooke's name turns up
in *The Merry Wives of Windsor* but that too is changed, to
Broome). A speech prefix for Oldcastle survives in the Quarto
text of *2 Henry IV* (1.2.121), even though the name had been
changed to Falstaff before *1 Henry IV* was entered in the
Stationers' Register on 25 February 1598; so it looks as if
Shakespeare continued to have that name in the back of his
mind. Falstaff, like the original Oldcastle, is well acquainted
with religion, though he practises it less assiduously than the
Lollard martyr. Falstaff has been likened to the old Vice of the
Morality plays, and Shakespeare makes direct allusions to that
relationship in *1 Henry IV* (1.2.111–12 and 11.4.441–2). He has
also been said to derive from the *miles gloriosus* of Plautine
comedy and the braggart soldier of the Italian *commedia erudita*
(though in *2 Henry IV* it is Pistol who most obviously has these
characteristics), and he has been likened, among many other
things, to the venal captains of Elizabethan armies who made
handsome profits from their modes of recruiting and the deaths
of those they enlisted. In both parts of *Henry IV* Falstaff is
shown in that unsavoury light, easily recognizable to an Elizabethan audience.

Two of these sources are of particular importance for an
understanding of the Falstaff of *2 Henry IV*. The first is the
invariable tradition in earlier drama in which a Vice figure is
ejected from the play, sometimes being physically beaten off
the stage; the second is the obloquy attaching to captains who
abused the King's press (which offence Falstaff admits in *1
Henry IV*, 1v.2.12–13). Whatever else happened in these two

plays, it would be reasonable to argue that an Elizabethan audience would expect a Vice-like figure such as Falstaff to be past redemption (to be a tempter himself), and that not even the protection which the world of comedy affords would enable that audience to regard Falstaff's recruiting with much sympathy.

The manifold interpretations of Falstaff point, if to nothing else, to the richness of Shakespeare's creation. No character in all drama has seemed so much a creature of real flesh and blood as this figment of a man's imagination. It is for this reason that his rejection is so painful. There are, I believe, characters who are more comic than Falstaff, several of them created by Shakespeare; but if a Dogberry or a Doolittle were turned away we should not be affected as we are by Falstaff's rejection. Furthermore, if we interpret the play with the imagination of dramatic history, or even if we respond only to the signals Shakespeare posts so frequently in both parts of the play, we shall always be aware that the rejection must and will come: Hal tells Falstaff he will banish him as early as *1 Henry IV*, II.4.466, and Falstaff's claim at v.3.134–5, 'the laws of England are at my commandment', only eighty lines before the moment of rejection, would leave an Elizabethan audience in no doubt of the issues involved (see the note to v.3.134–6), miss them though we may. What hurts is that we witness the rejection of living humanity, not mere cardboard fiction. By succeeding so triumphantly in creating not simply a comic character but the very semblance of true flesh and blood, Shakespeare makes us participate in Hal's anguish in having to reject Falstaff. He knows what must be and he knows the pain it will cause; we should understand even more clearly than Prince Henry what will be the outcome of this relationship (for we have dramatic and historical precedents to go on as well as the particular circumstances), but we have been so attracted by Falstaff that we share in the pain of this rejection.

But does it work *quite* like this? In practice, no; at least, not for a modern audience. A. C. Bradley argued that the rejection of Falstaff was unaesthetic. Shakespeare, he said, failed in his intention of manoeuvring Falstaff into a sufficiently unsympathetic light. Of the many explanations as to why this scene does not quite convince us – leaves us not only regretful but a trifle dissatisfied – this comes nearest. On the other hand, if it is considered that Falstaff *is* shown sufficiently unsympathetically according to Elizabethan social conditions and dramatic conventions, it could be that we find difficulty in responding to that tradition. This difficulty is accentuated if the Falstaff of *2 Henry IV* is presented very much in the style of the Falstaff of *1 Henry IV*. (It is, unfortunately, a commonplace of criticism that, whereas the Falstaff of *The Merry Wives of Windsor* has nothing in common with the Falstaff of *1* and *2 Henry IV*, the Falstaffs of the two *Henry IV* plays are one and the same.) Thus, even if Falstaff's position is theoretically untenable, modern audiences and modern productions may not see it in this light.

The presentation of the other party to this rejection, Henry, also offers problems. The tone of his rejection of his former companion has been described as 'priggish', 'a drastic narrowing of awareness'. Such interpretations miss the formal quality of Henry's speech, or fail to take account of the reasons for its style. Henry speaks as he does in part to hide his troubled feelings, in part because he acts as tutored by the Lord Chief Justice, as he himself puts it: 'My voice shall sound as you do prompt mine ear' (v.2.119). If an actor comes to the rejection speech fully alerted to the King's dilemma, his dependence on the Lord Chief Justice, and the lack of assurance that he feels in his new role (the fact that this new garment of majesty 'Sits not so easy' on him as we may think – v.2.45), the priggishness can be avoided; a sensitive actor can make this moment painful for *both* characters (and not solely for Falstaff) and can demand for Henry as well as Falstaff the involvement of the audience in the anguish he experiences. Much depends upon the tone with which the actor speaks v.5.45–6, 'My Lord Chief Justice, speak to that vain man', and the degree of hesitation he gives to line

50, 'I know thee not, old man'. A bold address will ruin this moment; a touch of uncertainty about the new role Henry is called upon to play can invest him with humanity. He can then begin to fall back on a defensive formality (but see the note to v.5.56–8).

Not everything can be left to the moment of rejection if the right effect is to be created. The Prince's disgust must be made very clear from the moment he first appears. His weariness with tavern life and his desire to give vent to the sorrow he feels for his father in his last illness – remorse if not sorrow – indicate that he can no longer play the role in which others now cast him and his awareness that another end awaits him: 'thou thinkest me as far in the devil's book as thou and Falstaff, for obduracy and persistency. Let the end try the man' (II.2.42–4). Henry's self-conscious awareness that he is playing a role which no longer suits him is a sign of his increasing maturity; but such self-consciousness must be disquieting for him, for he cannot but know that it will lead to the rejection of Falstaff. This an audience must be made to understand.

We can so concentrate on Falstaff's suffering at the moment of rejection that we may not notice how Shakespeare indicates the Prince's sensitivity. It is possible that Shakespeare is being too complex, too demanding of his actors and his audiences. He expects us to respond to the Prince's disquiet and to be aware of his defensiveness when he rejects Falstaff, and yet, simultaneously, he expects us to be a trifle detached from this offspring of a usurper, yearning for a crown he takes to be his right, the member of a calculating and dissimulating family. Perhaps Shakespeare does not quite succeed, but we shall get nearer to the human complexities involved if the Prince is played or read for his sensitive awareness of the pain of rejection (rather than interpreting his behaviour as priggishly high-handed) and if we concentrate our doubts of the humanity of the house of Lancaster on Henry IV and Prince John.

Probably enough has been suggested to indicate how Falstaff's role in the Second Part of *Henry IV* is to be seen quite differently from that he played in the First Part. Two more aspects require mention.

It has been noted by many commentators that the vivacity of Falstaff's wit shows a decline in *2 Henry IV* as compared to the First Part. Though he tends to be played as the principal comic character, this role is no longer without challenge in the Second Part. Anyone who has seen a really good actor make the most of Shallow will know how readily the Gloucestershire Justice can steal the play, and even Pistol, very small though his part is, proves a rival to Falstaff's pre-eminence in terms of comic lead. But Falstaff's dominance is challenged in more subtle ways than simply in the number of his comic lines. He is too often on the defensive, with the Lord Chief Justice, for example, and even with the Hostess. He can still put a servant down (1.2.72–89) but the Lord Chief Justice's man insists on coming back for more. No longer can he take the audience with him, turning the tables on those who have endeavoured to outwit him, and putting on an air of outraged innocence that is utterly convincing (as in his defence of his actions at Gad's Hill in *1 Henry IV*). Thus when in *2 Henry IV* the Hostess accuses Falstaff of infidelity (II.1), though he cleverly manages to take evasive action with his assertion that the Hostess 'says up and down the town that her eldest son is like' the Lord Chief Justice (lines 102–3), he is put in his place by the Lord Chief Justice and can offer no reply; when ordered to make amends, he has to bluster, attempting to stand upon his dignity, without much success. He tries to regain something of his lost position at the end of the scene by inviting Gower to dinner, but he is rebuffed, courteously by Gower but sharply by the Lord Chief Justice. When he meets Prince Henry and Poins (II.4), though he immediately sees through their disguise, he is far from his wittiest in the exchanges with the Prince, particularly in his repetition of 'No abuse' (lines 308–19).

Falstaff has one final characteristic which requires comment – one that he shares with a number of the characters. He is old. It is not extraordinary to have old men in plays, especially history plays which demand large casts. *Richard II* has Gaunt and York, both of whom have significant if small roles, and also the aged Duchesses of Gloucester and York. In *1 Henry IV* the King himself, Northumberland, and Falstaff are all old; and presumably Glendower, though vigorous, is past the prime of youth. But the old people of *2 Henry IV* are many; they are often prominent, and several are sick. Even those, such as the Hostess and Northumberland, who appear in both parts of the play seem much older than the difference in time would allow. The Hostess draws attention to her age by her reference to having known Falstaff 'these twenty-nine years, come peascod-time' (and 'In Peascod-time' was a popular tune to which 'The Lamentable Ballad of the Lady's Fall' was sung; see the Commentary to II.4.378). Northumberland at the beginning of the play is 'crafty-sick' and is dressed as becomes an ill man. The King is weak and ill and dies during the play. The Lord Chief Justice is elderly, and Falstaff draws attention to his age, also maintaining (perhaps falsely) that he has been ill (1.2.94–100). Shallow and Silence are obviously old and spend much time recalling a far distant past. Falstaff himself is not only an old man but much concerned about the state of his urine (1.2.1). There are also minor characters who are old, such as Lady Northumberland and the Archbishop of York.

This accumulation of aged persons would be less significant were it not that time itself plays such an important role in the play. Not only is there the frequent appeal to the past, whether the joys of student days at Clement's Inn or the way Henry IV came by the throne; the word 'time' occurs unusually often in both parts of the play. (One commentator, Paul Jorgensen (see page 457), has counted thirty-four references to time in *2 Henry IV* and forty-one in *1 Henry IV*, and sixty-four references in the two parts of the play to units of time.) This awareness of time and its effects on human beings, the sense of mutability, and the belief in a judgement when time is no more, all contribute to the disquiet of the play. We are always being made conscious of lost opportunities. It is this that is Lady

Percy's particular contribution to the play in the little scene which so many adapters cut (II.3). She has less than fifty lines to speak, but they serve to bring home to us all that was lost when Hotspur died. (How it is possible to present him, as is sometimes done, as a loutish, huffing boor is astonishing in the light of her description, prejudiced though she is.) There is no need for Lady Percy to appear; she does not assist in telling the story of this part of *Henry IV*, and it is certainly not essential to have her present as a device for getting her father-in-law away to Scotland. She is there simply to remind us of what has been lost, as Doll and the Hostess are arrested (V.4) to show us what must be lost, to underline what time can never redeem.

Prince Henry's weariness, Falstaff's response to the hospitality of Shallow, King Henry's rationalization of his usurpation, Prince John's duplicity, Northumberland's desertion, Falstaff's rejection and imprisonment, the reminder of the loss of Hotspur, and the inexorableness of time, all go to make a play very different in tone from *1 Henry IV*. The result is a mood of weariness and a sense of disgust which are at times markedly sour. Neither is offset by our awareness of the virtues which the new king is attempting to master; these are underplayed in *2 Henry IV* so that they may the more dramatically come to fruition in *Henry V*. Only one element can make any counterbalance to this rather bitter mood: the scenes set in Gloucestershire, where, even if Shallow and Silence do not reassure us, the quality of country life does.

It has been well asked where our sympathies are meant to lie in *2 Henry IV*. There are no characters with whom we can readily and wholly feel in accord, no actions we can unreservedly admire, unless it be the preparations in Gloucestershire to receive guests. None of the major figures in the play strives for our acclaim and certainly none of them wins it. Those we can best applaud are Colevile of the Dale, Shallow, Pistol, Davy, and, surprisingly, that noble tailor, Feeble, who disdains to bear a base mind (III.2.229). But one cannot centre a play on such minor characters as these when its major concerns are all elsewhere. If there is to be a centre of concern in this play it will be provided not by a character but by England itself, realized indirectly through what motivates the actions of Henry IV and the rebels, and, more directly, through the portrayal of Gloucestershire and the constant reference to places and people English. It is as if, through the medium of proper names, rusticisms, and colloquialisms, Shakespeare were attempting to particularize his main 'character': England. The myth of an England of another sort is recalled by the ballad of Robin Hood, Scarlet, and John (v.3.103), and perhaps by the references to Scoggin (iii.2.29) and 'Sir Dagonet in Arthur's show' (iii.2.271-2). Two country fairs are mentioned, those at Stamford and Hinckley, and the London fair of St Bartholomew is implied. London place-names – Mile End Green, Turnbull Street, St George's Field, Eastcheap, Pie Corner, and Smithfield – are set against names of counties, a country district, and country towns – Staffordshire, Yorkshire, and Gloucestershire; the Cotswolds; Basingstoke, Windsor, St Albans, Oxford, and Tewkesbury. But it is not just place-names that occur; there is the relationship of people to places: William Visor of Woncot; Clement Perkes o'th'Hill; goodman Puff of Barson; and, linking countryside with London, the names of those who went up to study law at Clement's Inn – John Doit, George Barnes, Francis Pickbone, and Will Squele – or to fight Samson Stockfish, as Shallow did, behind Gray's Inn. So many names may seem at first sight to provide no more than a backcloth against which the King's party and the rebels fight out their story, but Shakespeare gives such prominence to names of people and places, especially in the scenes set in Gloucestershire, that they insistently claim our attention. In this England there is only one casualty, Colevile of the Dale, and he, significantly, has been misled by his 'betters', who have failed to heed him.

These ever-present reminders of an everyday England, of a delight in pippins and small beer and ordinary conversation, over-ride Henry IV's shifty rationalization. They make Necessity England's, not Henry's or Northumberland's (see the note to III.1.69), and they give point to Prince Henry's endeavour to rule with justice and mercy, whatever the cost to Falstaff and to himself. Humanity is *not* rejected with Falstaff. Only the most narrow concept of humanity can allow such an interpretation. Humanity resides elsewhere than in Falstaff, especially the Falstaff of the latter part of *2 Henry IV*; it is to be found in all the people and all the places which underlie the story that is being dramatized but which give it purpose and meaning.

The range of attitudes and emotions in *2 Henry IV* is wider and much more complex than in *1 Henry IV*. To present or read the Second Part in a way that brings out all its subtleties is a formidable task. It is not exaggerating to assert that *2 Henry IV* presents more problems for the producer and the reader than any other of Shakespeare's history plays. It will not respond to simple and single-minded approaches; but, given a sympathetic understanding, it can offer a deeply rewarding experience. It is, indeed, the play which is at the heart of the tetralogy of which it forms a part, for it brings together its author's concern with the predicament posed by the interaction of authority and humanity at a moment when that problem is fully realized (as it is not in *Richard II* and *1 Henry IV*) but not resolved, one way or the other, for better or ill (as it is in *Henry V*).

Further Reading

Texts, Editorial Problems, and Sources

There is as yet no Quarto facsimile of *2 Henry IV* in the series being issued by the Clarendon Press, and the 1600 edition must be consulted in the original or by means of a photocopy or microfilm. The copies chiefly used in the preparation of this edition were those in the British Library, which holds copies of both the four-leaf and six-leaf issues of gathering E (see the Account of the Text, page 461). The Folio version can most conveniently and reliably be read in *The Norton Facsimile. The First Folio of Shakespeare* (New York, 1968), prepared by Charlton Hinman. This is made up from clear and, where possible, final proof-corrected sheets of many copies of the first Folio. It should be consulted in conjunction with Professor Hinman's study, *The Printing and Proofreading of the First Folio of Shakespeare* (2 vols., Oxford, 1963). An edition of Charles Kemble's Coronation production of 1821 (see the Introduction, pages 429–30) with the text and full details of the staging has been published by the Cornmarket Press (London, 1971); the same publisher has issued several other adaptations of *2 Henry IV* in the two series, 'Acting Versions of Shakespeare'. *Tarlton's Jests* (referred to on pages 435–6 of the Introduction) is available in *Kemp's Nine Days Wonder and Tarlton's Jests* (Johnson Reprint Corporation, New York, 1972). Of great interest, but little textual relevance to *2 Henry IV*, is a facsimile of *The History of King Henry the Fourth, as revised by Sir Edward Dering, Bart.* (prepared by G. W. Williams and G. B. Evans and published by the University Press of Virginia, Charlottesville, 1974, for the Folger Shakespeare Library). This is the only surviving manuscript of a play (or rather plays) by Shakespeare from the reign of James I; it conflates both parts of *Henry IV* into a single play.

The most helpful editions of the play are the New Variorum (Philadelphia, 1940), edited by Matthias A. Shaaber; the New Cambridge (Cambridge 1946), edited by J. Dover Wilson; and the new Arden (London, 1966), edited by A. R. Humphreys. This edition is deeply indebted to them. There are many studies of the text and, as the Account of the Text shows, they are far from being in agreement. I suggest for further reading Professor Shaaber's discussion in the New Variorum edition and in *Shakespeare Quarterly* 6 (1955); Alice Walker's counter-arguments in the *Review of English Studies*, new series II (1951), and *The Library*, 5th series VI (1951); J. K. Walton's *The Quarto Copy for the First Folio of Shakespeare* (Dublin, 1971), which contains much that is relevant to the problem (but see the review by Albert Smith, *The Library*, 5th series XXVII, 1972); and Alan E. Craven's study of the work of Compositor A who set the Quarto of *2 Henry IV*, *Studies in Bibliography* XXVI, 1973.

Useful summaries of the sources are given in the New Variorum and the new Arden editions; the fullest collection is in Geoffrey Bullough's *Narrative and Dramatic Sources of Shakespeare*, volume IV (London, 1962), which includes *The Famous Victories of Henry the Fifth*.

Background and Criticism

Several books on the background to the history plays or considering the history plays as a whole are relevant for *Henry IV*. These include E. M. W. Tillyard, *Shakespeare's History Plays* (London, 1944, reprinted by Penguin Books, 1962); Lily B. Campbell, *Shakespeare's 'Histories': Mirrors of Elizabethan Policy* (San Marino, California, 1947); Paul A. Jorgensen, *Shakespeare's Military World* (Berkeley, California, 1956); D. A. Traversi, *Shakespeare: from 'Richard II' to 'Henry V'* (London, 1957); M. M. Reese, *The Cease of Majesty* (London, 1961); S. C. Sen Gupta, *Shakespeare's Historical Plays* (London, 1964); Gareth

Lloyd Evans, *Shakespeare II* (Edinburgh, 1969) in the series 'Writers and Critics'; and Robert Ornstein, *A Kingdom for a Stage* (Cambridge, Mass., 1972). *Shakespeare Survey 6* (Cambridge, 1953) includes a survey by Harold Jenkins of work on the history plays between 1900 and 1951; and in *Shakespeare: Select Bibliographical Guides* (Oxford, 1973), edited by Stanley Wells, A. R. Humphreys provides a useful bibliographical guide to the histories as a whole, with particular attention to the *Henry IV* plays.

Many of the critical studies referred to in the list of Further Reading for *1 Henry IV* are also relevant to *2 Henry IV*, and this applies especially to Falstaff. A particularly useful survey is Arthur C. Sprague's 'Gadshill Revisited', *Shakespeare Quarterly* 4 (1953), which is reprinted in the Norton Critical Edition of *1 Henry IV* (New York, 1962), edited by James L. Sanderson. Maurice Morgann's study of Falstaff (1777) is published in *Eighteenth Century Essays on Shakespeare*, edited by D. Nichol Smith (Glasgow, 1903), and in other collections (see below). Dr Johnson's comments are also frequently reprinted, as are A. C. Bradley, 'The Rejection of Falstaff', in his *Oxford Lectures on Poetry* (London, 1909); E. E. Stoll, from his *Shakespeare Studies* (New York, 1927), and J. Dover Wilson, *The Fortunes of Falstaff* (Cambridge, 1943). To the studies mentioned in *1 Henry IV* might be added William Empson, 'Falstaff and Mr Dover Wilson', *Kenyon Review* xv (1953), and Walter Kaiser, *Praisers of Folly: Erasmus, Rabelais, Shakespeare* (London, 1964). Other studies of the plays which are relevant are Caroline Spurgeon, *Shakespeare's Imagery and what it tells us* (Cambridge, 1935); on the relationship of the two parts of the play, M. A. Shaaber, 'The Unity of *Henry IV*', in *Joseph Quincy Adams Memorial Studies*, edited by J. G. McManaway, G. E. Dawson, and E. E. Willoughby (Washington, D.C., 1948), and Harold Jenkins, *The Structural Problem in Shakespeare's 'Henry the Fourth'* (London, 1956); A. P. Rossiter's essay, 'Ambivalence: the Dialectic of the Histories', in his *Angel with Horns* (London, 1961); and C. L. Barber, 'The Trial of Carnival in *Part*

Two', in his *Shakespeare's Festive Comedy* (Princeton, N.J., 1959).

Two useful collections of essays are available. G. K. Hunter has edited *King Henry IV Parts 1 and 2: A Casebook* (London, 1970). Professor Hunter's introduction is particularly valuable, and the volume includes comments by Johnson, some of the essays noted above (Morgann, Bradley, Dover Wilson, Tillyard, and Empson), and H. B. Charlton (extracts from his *Shakespeare, Politics and Politicians*, 1929), J. I. M. Stewart, 'The Birth and Death of Falstaff' (from his *Character and Motive in Shakespeare*, 1949), W. H. Auden, 'The Prince's Dog' (first printed in *Encounter* 13, 1959, as 'The Fallen City'; reprinted with the new title in his *The Dyer's Hand*, 1962), and Paul A. Jorgensen ('Redeeming Time in Shakespeare's *Henry IV*', *Tennessee Studies in Literature*, 1960).

The second collection is *Twentieth Century Interpretations of Henry IV, Part Two*, edited by David P. Young (Englewood Cliffs, N.J., 1968), with a useful introduction. Inevitably the two anthologies overlap to some extent. Among the contributions are L. C. Knights, 'Time's Subjects: The Sonnets and *King Henry IV, Part 2*', from his *Some Shakespearean Themes* (1959); Clifford Leech, 'The Unity of *2 Henry IV*' (from *Shakespeare Survey 6*, 1953); Harold E. Toliver, 'Falstaff, the Prince, and the History Play' (from *Shakespeare Quarterly* 16, 1965); and a previously unpublished essay by Robert B. Pierce, 'The Generations in *2 Henry IV*'. Barber, Traversi, Bradley, Dover Wilson, Tillyard, Jenkins, Rossiter, R. J. Dorius ('A Little More than a Little', *Shakespeare Quarterly* 11, 1960), and an extract from A. R. Humphreys's introduction to the new Arden edition are also included.

There is a very detailed study of Falstaff's language in Chapter 4 of Brian Vickers's *The Artistry of Shakespeare's Prose* (London, 1968). Vickers argues that in the prose, and therefore in the comedy, of *1 Henry IV*, 'Falstaff is the central figure and Hal is his Good Angel, while the unholy combination of Falstaff's Appetite, Reason and Conscience ... represents the devil', an arrangement quite different from the usual Morality pattern associated with that play, and different also from its modification proposed in my introduction to *1 Henry IV* (pages 231–2). This means, says Vickers, that 'when Hal has left Falstaff alone' (as happens in *2 Henry IV*), 'Sir John sells his soul to the devil for a few syllogisms and half-a-dozen puns'.

An Account of the Text

The Second Part of *Henry IV* presents an editor with difficult textual problems, and it would be foolish to pretend that they can be answered with certainty. One might well remember the words of Sir Francis Bacon in *The Advancement of Learning* (1605): 'If a man will begin with certainties, he shall end in doubts; but if he will be content to begin with doubts, he shall end in certainties'. Alas, the problems posed by *2 Henry IV* are such that, though an editor must begin with many doubts, he will feel fortunate if he ends by resolving any of them.

Modern editors of Elizabethan plays try to get as near as they can to what the author would have authorized as the fair copy of the finished work. This presents a number of difficulties. Authorial fair copies are few and far between (and there are none in Shakespeare's hand), so there is little to guide us in deciding what one of Shakespeare's 'authorized fair copies' looked like. Often we cannot be sure what kind of manuscript the printer used when setting an edition in type – it could vary from an unrevised rough draft to a presentation scribal copy of a manuscript modified from the stage version used in the author's lifetime – and we may doubt the accuracy with which the compositor set his manuscript in type.

For *2 Henry IV* we have two printed editions, the Quarto printed by Valentine Simmes in 1600 ('quarto' describes a book where the sheets of paper are each printed on both sides and folded twice to produce eight pages per 'gathering' or quire) and the text published in 1623 in the first Folio (in a folio text the sheet of paper is folded only once). The Folio contains thirty-six of Shakespeare's plays and seems to have been a project initiated by John Heminges and Henry Condell, two members of Shakespeare's company.

An editor must ask three questions of these two texts. What was the copy from which they were set? What is their relationship one to the other? And to what extent do they represent Shakespeare's intentions? In trying to answer these questions we must try to find out all we can of what happened in the printing-houses where the Quarto and Folio versions were set.

The Quarto seems to be derived from what editors call 'foul papers', a term used in Shakespeare's day by the dramatist Daborne to describe the rough draft or drafts which preceded the fair copy. The Quarto text, though almost complete, lacks eight passages (see collations list 1 below); some of these are inessential, but some make the action clear. It has been suggested that four of these passages may have been excised from the Quarto because they included references to the deposition of Richard II, a dangerous subject in the last years of the sixteenth century. The stage directions of the Quarto are often vague and frequently inadequate for performance, some of the characters are not consistently designated, and at one point (V.4.0) an actor, John Sincklo, is referred to by his own name instead of that of his role. There are also references to several mutes (characters who have nothing to say and no clear part in the play): Sir John Umfrevile (see the note to 1.1.161), Fauconbridge (see the headnote to 1.3), Sir John Russell (see the headnote to II.2), and Kent (see the headnote to IV.4). Presumably during the course of revision these names were dropped, for they do not appear in the Folio. Two characters, Sir John Blunt and the Earl of Surrey, also have no lines to speak; the Folio retains them where they are called for (Surrey's entry at III.1.31 and Blunt's escorting of Sir John Colevile at IV.3.74) but omits the other entries for Blunt given in the Quarto (III.1.31 and V.2.42), presumably because no action is demanded of him and he is not addressed by name in those scenes. Even Falstaff's original name, Oldcastle (see the Introduction, pages 445), makes a fleeting appearance in the Quarto as a speech prefix at 1.2.121 (and see the note to Epilogue 30). There is little doubt that what the compositor had before him in 1600 was a version of the play written before a fair copy had been produced.

The Quarto is unusual in that it exists in two versions. One gathering, E, has four leaves in some copies and six in others. It seems that, when the play was being set into type, III.1 was missed out, probably by mistake, and some copies of the play were made up and distributed before the omission was made good. In adding the scene to the remaining copies, the printer had to reset parts of II.4 and III.2, and, although the same man seems to have done the work, he did not follow exactly what he had set the first time. There are differences of spelling and occasionally of words: for example, he omitted 'good' in III.2.58, but added it in line 73. From this and other evidence of this man's work (he is identified as Simmes's Compositor 'A') it is possible to list the kind of changes and mistakes he makes – and they are many and varied.

2 Henry IV, unlike its First Part, was not reprinted until it appeared in the Folio in 1623. The publication of the Folio was a highly speculative venture (this was only the second time that an English dramatist's plays had been collected together: Jonson's *Works* had appeared in 1616, the year Shakespeare died), and it presented the printer with many problems. The printing of the Histories section clearly ran into all sorts of difficulties. By identifying the appearance and reappearance of individual pieces of type, it has been shown that the histories were not printed in the order in which they appear in the Folio. Thus *1* and *2 Henry IV* were printed later than *Henry V*, *1* and *2 Henry VI*, and part of *3 Henry VI*. The printing of *2 Henry IV* may have been delayed because of difficulties in obtaining permission to print *1 Henry IV*, the publisher not wanting to print the Second Part if the First was to be refused him by the owners of its copyright. The delay could also have been caused because the copy for *2 Henry IV* was not ready. Meanwhile space had to be left for *1* and *2 Henry IV*, and it was miscalculated. In 2 *Henry IV* there is also a curious error in the page numbering, and, quite exceptionally in the printing of the Folio (which is based on six-leaf quires – three sheets being folded together once to produce twelve pages), an eight-leaf quire had to be used. Furthermore the type for this quire was set in a strange order not found elsewhere in the Folio. The play is one of only seven in the Folio to be provided with a list of 'The Actors Names'; and the Epilogue is given a page to itself and printed in a larger type than usual. In a short account of the text it is not possible to go into every possibility that might explain these circumstances; what follows is a description of the basis on which this edition has been prepared. It must be stressed that it can only be conjectural – informed guesswork.

The texts of the Quarto and the Folio differ considerably. Although the Quarto omits eight passages, it contains many lines and part-lines that do not appear in the Folio. The Folio drops the names of characters in the Quarto who are not required by the action; and a few speeches are reallocated. The Folio has some additional stage directions but omits many that are given in the Quarto, and even when all the stage directions of the Quarto and Folio are assembled they are still short of what is needed to make the play actable. The Folio offers a much more literary text, removing colloquialisms, rusticisms, archaisms, and profanities (though occasionally a colloquialism is added).

Many editors have argued that the Folio shows some signs of stage practice – for example, the reallocation of speeches at the beginning of II.2 and possibly at III.2.54, and the entry of the prospective recruits at the beginning of III.2 (see the textual notes at each point, especially the headnote to III.2) – and that it must therefore be based either on a copy of the Quarto annotated by reference to a manuscript which had been used in the theatre, or on a new transcript of the prompt-book itself. Both theories have provoked much dispute and neither seems to me tenable. The crux of the problem is the excision, wholly or in part, of some twenty-five Quarto stage directions that are superior to those remaining in the Folio. Annotation of the Quarto would not necessarily have caused these to be obscured (to check that possibility I, like some other editors, have marked a photocopy of the Quarto to bring it into line with the Folio text); and a transcript based on the prompt-book, far from losing so many essential stage directions, would be expected to supplement them with others necessary for a production. The absence of so many essential entries and exits and of several of the Quarto's directions for sound effects does anything but suggest that the Folio was based on a manuscript that had been prepared for use in the theatre. Furthermore, all the directions added in the Folio are ones that a reasonably intelligent scribe could have supplied (many are final exeunts). The Folio also omits the first coronation procession (see the headnote to v.5) and three inessential but telling phrases: in the Quarto Rumour is described as 'painted full of tongues', the Page is said to bear Falstaff's sword and buckler at the beginning of 1.2, and Henry IV to enter in his nightgown in III.1. Were there no Quarto, editors could be excused for imagining that the Folio was based on a transcript of the author's foul papers, styled in a literary manner by a pedantic but rather careless scribe.

How can one explain the absence from the Folio of stage directions available in the Quarto, the tidying up of the Quarto's text (for example, the omission of mutes), the inclusion of eight passages not in the Quarto but the absence of many short passages, the literary style and omission of profanities, and the divergences of action and dialogue that might reflect stage practice? (There are other problems, particularly associated with the printing of the Folio, the use of capitals, the miscalculation of space for *2 Henry IV*, and the need for an eight-leaf gathering; these are more readily explicable, but as they are specialized and have little bearing on the edition printed here, they will not be discussed.)

Recently it has been suggested that some Folio texts were based on fair copies which scribes made from Shakespeare's foul papers before the production of a prompt-book. This seems to me unlikely in this case. The absence of important stage directions which appear in the text being copied is at least as odd in a fair copy as it is in a prompt-book, though oddness is not the same as impossibility, of course. It would not be beyond a scribe making a fair copy, especially if he was experienced (as some scribes were) in copying play documents, to provide exeunts that had been missed from what he was copying, to remove mutes, and simultaneously to omit one or two lines or phrases in error. He might also rearrange some prose as verse and some verse as prose. But the Folio text of *2 Henry IV* does not give the impression that it is based on a fair copy. There are changes which seem to be outside the jurisdiction of a scribe: for instance, the reduction in the numbers of Grooms (see the note to v.5.3–4) and of Drawers, with a reallocation of the Drawers' speeches that is no improvement on the Quarto (see the note to II.4.1–21), and the omission of the first coronation procession. Of course, the scribe might have been instructed to make such changes, but if fair copy *is* involved, then these changes cannot be among those which, as some scholars have thought, reflect stage practice. Indications of stage practice would be expected to originate from the prompt-book, as originally prepared or as amended. We know of fair copies that became prompt-books, but that cannot have happened in this case because the basic stage directions are so inadequate. It is hardly possible that the same manuscript could simultaneously be a fair copy inadequate for performance and a manuscript reflecting stage practice.

A scribal fair copy of *2 Henry IV* made before its first performance would be very unlikely to reveal censorship of the profanities found in the Quarto, since this practice was not legally required until 1606. Nor would one expect a fair copy to be so literary and so to reduce the colloquialisms which are a feature of the play. Again, it is possible that a fair copy made before the end of the sixteenth century was later amended to accord with the Act of 1606 (although strictly speaking that did not apply to the written word) and to remove colloquialisms and the like. But that still would not explain the absence of stage directions found in the Quarto.

If neither the prompt-book nor a fair copy was the basis for the Folio text, what was used? It seems likely to have been a transcript of something, since it is consistent in style, for instance in the frequent use of capital letters, which demonstrably originates from the copy, not from compositorial practice, since it occurs throughout and we know that the play was set by more than one compositor. It seems to reflect some stage practice, though we cannot be certain of that, and whatever theory is proposed must take account of the absence of some important stage directions. Finally, in the opinion of many scholars (particularly those who argue that the copy for the Folio was an annotated version of the Quarto) it should be possible for the theory proposed to allow for the influence of the Quarto on the Folio text. How influential the Quarto was is a matter of dispute, but the two opposing theories would be reconciled if what is proposed now enabled a transcript to form the basis of the Folio and yet allowed the influence of the Quarto to show through. As there was already a fairly good Quarto available, the material used for making a transcript must have *seemed* to the publishers of the Folio capable of providing a better text than was obtainable from the Quarto – otherwise they might have simply reprinted the Quarto, tidying up as common sense dictated (for example, omitting mutes and providing some exeunts) – and it must have been produced without recourse to the prompt-book, because if the prompt-book was available it would be far simpler to print from that, or, if it could not be released to the printer to make a transcript of it. It is possible that the prompt-book was unobtainable, for we know from a slip of paper surviving from about 1620 that *2 Henry IV* had not been performed in the preceding seven years.

Although the proposition is unorthodox, it seems to me worth considering whether, in the peculiar case of *2 Henry IV*, in order to produce what was thought to be a more reliable text a transcript was made with the aid of actors' parts, despite the trouble and expense this would mean. The objection to such a guess (it can be no more) is not so much its inherent improbability – for we have an improbable situation to contend with – as the practical difficulties that scholars have always assumed would obstruct the process of reconstructing the relationship of isolated lines from different parts, especially in scenes with several speakers. The one Elizabethan example we have of an actor's part shows that cues were brief and the name of the speaker of the cue was not given. It has also been assumed that the loss of a prompt-book would mean the loss of the actors' parts too. It might be difficult to relate lines from parts, especially if they had been modified in performance (and the opening of 11.4 might demonstrate that difficulty), but it is not impossible; and there is no certainty at all that the loss of a prompt-book *must* mean the loss of the parts, even though they were probably intended to be kept together. Indeed one of the greatest authorities on the Elizabethan theatre, Sir Edmund Chambers, though arguing against assembling a text in this manner (and his authority is often quoted by others in deciding the issue), also said 'I do not think assembling is inconceivable, as a last resort for recovering a text, when no original or foul papers or transcript was available. But surely it would be a very laborious and difficult business' (*William Shakespeare*, 1930, 1, 155). We may continue to wonder why a new text was desired though the Quarto was available; but desired – and produced – it was. With the Quarto at hand, an excellent guide to the order of speeches was available. If a scribe were writing up a manuscript from actors' parts with the aid of the Quarto, it would be fairly easy for him to miss entries that were in the Quarto if, in the main, he were using the Quarto only as a guide to the order of speeches; and it would be particularly easy for him to miss the instructions for sound effects given in the Quarto, especially if these did not appear in the actors' parts (as presumably they would not). It is noticeable that the only sound effect that the

Folio indicates is the trumpets at the second coronation procession (the only procession it gives). The Quarto, however, has
an indication for shouting at IV.2.86, for alarum and excursions
at IV.3.0, and for a retreat to be sounded after IV.3.23; it
indicates trumpets for the first procession but not the second,
which is not so much a procession as a straightforward entry of
the King and his train.

Were a scribe working from parts, this might also explain
the number of composite entries in the Folio. Thus at IV.1.0 it
indicates that Westmorland and Colevile enter at the beginning
of the scene, but the former is not required until line 24 (where
the Folio has a second direction that he should enter) and
Colevile does not appear until IV.3. At V.1.0 the Folio provides
an entry for Silence (who does not appear in this scene),
caused, perhaps, by an automatic association of Silence with
Shallow, and brings on Davy a few lines too early. In V.3 the
Folio brings on Pistol at the beginning of the scene as well as
at line 82 but omits to include an entry for Davy. The differences at the beginning of III.2 (where the Quarto brings on
only Shallow and Silence – presumably indicating that the
prospective recruits enter separately as their names are called –
and the Folio brings them all on at once; see the headnote)
may, as has been suggested, reflect stage practice; alternatively
there might have been some grouping by whoever prepared
the manuscript for the Folio. This was not complete, however,
since the entries for 'Bardolph and one with him' (III.2.53) and
Falstaff (III.2.80) were not gathered in.

The use of actors' parts might also explain the inclusion in
the Folio of certain phrases, not in the Quarto, that might be
actors' interpolations: for example, at IV.5.50, and the two half-
lines referred to in the note to IV.5.178 (though not that
discussed in the note to IV.5.76–7). The Folio's version of
II.1.71–2, expanding 'it is for all I have' to 'it is for all: all I
have', also has the ring of an actor's rhetorical embellishment,
as has the Folio's addition of 'Fy' a few lines later. There are
further suspicious intensificatives in the Folio which could

conceivably reflect either a scribe or performance: for example, 'good' is unnecessarily added at II.1.166, II.2.88 and 93, II.4.286, and III.2.192; 'new' is added at II.2.78; 'even' at II.4.286; 'but a very' at V.1.43; and 'your worship' (instead of 'you'), duplicating the same words in the previous sentence, at V.1.45. (For other cases where the influence of actors' parts is at least a possibility, see the notes to I.1.161 and II.2.103; and see the notes to III.2.54 and 148 and V.5.15, 17, 19 for possible applications of the theory.)

Editors have usually relied on the Quarto for their texts of 2 *Henry IV* but have often used the Folio very freely as a source of readings and for the arrangement of III.2. In the light of what I take to be the way the Folio text was produced, I have tended to base my text much more on the Quarto than has been customary. Though the Quarto is not based on a fair copy, it does seem to have been set from a manuscript in Shakespeare's hand (see the notes to III.2.87, IV.2.8, and IV.5.33); and many of its faults (such as mutes and lack of exeunts) can be put right by the common sense that the scribe who wrote out the copy for the Folio applied intermittently. In making amendments I have used Alan E. Craven's study of the work of the compositor who set the Quarto (*Studies in Bibliography* XXVI, 1973), and this, though not wholly reliable, has suggested some errors which that compositor might have made (see the notes to I.1.41, II.4.47 and 330, but compare IV.5.204). In adopting readings from the Folio I have tried to avoid those that seem more likely to derive from an actor than from Shakespeare. The literary language of the Folio has not been used, but the Folio has, of course, been the source of the passages not printed in the Quarto. As well as omitting what I take to be actors' interpolations (see the notes to I.1.96 and IV.5.50 and 178), I have in three places omitted passages which may represent Shakespeare's first thoughts. These are discussed (and the passages given) in the notes to III.1.53, IV.1.92–4, and IV.5.76–7.

Trying to restore the author's intention in a text with so

complex a history is fraught with difficulties and uncertainties. Many scholars have worked on these problems, and though at times I differ from them I am deeply in their debt. No edition of this play can hope to be definitive. Mine is no more than a fresh attempt to reproduce in modern spelling and punctuation what Shakespeare's fair copy of *2 Henry IV* might have been like had he himself seen it through the press.

COLLATIONS

The following lists are *selective*; the differences between the Quarto, the Folio, and the many later editions are manifold, and minor variants have been excluded here. List 1 shows the more important readings adopted for this edition from the Folio ('F'), with the rejected Quarto ('Q') readings. List 2 is a selection of the more important readings adopted from Q, with the rejected F readings. List 3 shows the major emendations incorporated in this edition. Stage directions are treated in list 4. List 5 notes some of the emendations suggested elsewhere but not adopted here. List 6 refers to textual notes about textual matters not included in the collation lists. Many of the readings in the other lists are also discussed in the textual notes and in the Account of the Text.

Readings of this edition are printed to the left of the square brackets. Quotations from Q and F are given in their original spelling, except that 'long s' (ʃ) has been replaced by 's'.

I

Readings adopted from F, with the rejected Q readings. F's readings (as given in this edition) are printed first, followed, to the right of the square bracket, by what appears in Q. The list is selective, and cases where the text is differently arranged as verse or prose in Q and F are not included.

THE CHARACTERS IN THE PLAY] *not in* Q (*see textual note*)
Induction

	36	Where] When
I.1.	28	whom] who
	41	ill] bad
	164	Lean on your] Leaue on you
	166–79	You cast . . . to be?] *not in* Q
	186	forth, body] forth body
	189–200	The gentle . . . follow him.] *not in* Q
I.2.	35	rascally yea-forsooth] rascall yea forsooth
	47	Where's Bardolph] (*follows* 'it' *in line 45 in* Q)
	86	me so?] me, so
	97	age] an ague
	98	time] time in you
	144	slenderer] slender
	172	and] and hath
	174	this] his
		them, are] the one
	205	and Prince Harry] *not in* Q
I.3.	21–4	Till we . . . admitted.] *not in* Q
	36–55	Yes . . . or else] *not in* Q
	58	one] on
	71	Are] And
	78	be] to be
	79–80	He . . . Baying] French and Welch he leaues his back vnarmde, they baying
	85–108	ARCHBISHOP Let us . . . worst.] *not in* Q
	109	MOWBRAY] *Bish.*
II.1.	21	vice] view
	25	continuantly] continually
	102	mad] made
	168	Basingstoke] Billingsgate
II.2.	15	viz.] with
	21	thy] the
	21–2	made a shift to] *not in* Q
	81	rabbit] rabble

	90	be] *not in* Q
	126	*familiars*] family
II.3.	11	endeared] endeere
	23–45	He had . . . grave.] *not in* Q
II.4.	42–3	them; I] I
	169	Die . . . crowns] Men like dogges giue crownes
	249	the] *not in* Q
III.1.	18	mast] masse *in corrected* Q (*the whole of* III.1 *was initially omitted from* Q; *see page 461*)
	22	billows] pillowes *in some copies of corrected* Q
	26	thy] them *in corrected* Q
	30	happy low, lie] (happy) low lie *in corrected* Q
	36	letters] letter *in corrected* Q
	53	liquors! 'Tis not ten years gone |] liquors! O, if this were seene, | The happiest youth viewing his progresse through, | What perills past, what crosses to ensue? | Would shut the booke and sit him downe and die: | Tis not ten yeeres gone, | *in corrected* Q
III.2.	37	Stamford] Samforth
	54	SHALLOW] *not in corrected* Q *as originally printed, nor as reset; Bardolfe. in uncorrected* Q
	65	accommodated] accommodate
	86	Surecard] Soccard
	110	FALSTAFF Prick him.] *Iohn prickes him.*
	120–21	see. Simon] see Simon
	142	for his] for
	285	my house] our house
	290	On] *Shal.* On
	304	ever] ouer
	320	him. Let] (F, Q *uncorrected*); him, till *in corrected* Q
IV.1.	55–79	And with . . . wrong.] *not in* Q
	92	divine? |] (F,Q *corrected*); divine, | And consecrate commotions bitter edge. | *in uncorrected* Q
	93	commonwealth, |] (F, Q *corrected — the latter*

omitting the comma); commonwealth | To brother borne an houshold cruelty, | *in uncorrected* Q

IV.I.	101–37	O, my . . . the King.] *not in* Q
	173	to our] our
	224	armies?] armies.
IV.2.	8	Than] That
		man] man talking
	26	taken] ta'en
	48	this] his
	69	HASTINGS] *Prince*
	117	and such acts as yours] *not in* Q
	122	these traitors] this traitour
IV.4.	32	melting] meeting
	52	Canst thou tell that?] *not in* Q
	94	heaven] heauens
	120	and will break out] *not in* Q
	132	Softly, pray.] *not in* Q
IV.5.	77	thighs] thigh,
	108	Which] Whom
	178	put it] put
V.I.	21	Hinckley] Hunkly
	41	if] *not in* Q
	51	all] *not in* Q
V.2.	46	mix] mixt
V.3.	5	here a] here
	6	and a] and
	124	knighthood] Knight
V.5.	15	SHALLOW] *Pist.*
	24	FALSTAFF] *not in* Q
	28	all] *not in* Q
	99	*spero me*] spero

2

Readings adopted from Q, with the rejected F readings (many of which are accepted in other modern editions: see page 468). Q's readings (as given in this edition) are printed first, followed, to the right of the square bracket, by what appears in F. The list is selective: there are many further minor differences, and the profanities and colloquialisms omitted or amended in F are not included (unless the reading is listed for other reasons).

I.I.	44	armèd] able
	96	slain —] slaine, say so:
	103	tolling] knolling
	126	So] Too
	161	LORD BARDOLPH This . . . lord.] (*Vmfr*. This . . . lord. Q); *not in* F
I.2.	28	Dommelton] *Dombledon*
	36–7	smoothy-pates] smooth-pates
	43	Well] Well,
	48	in] into
	171	times] *not in* F
	185	your chin double,] *not in* F
	188–9	about . . . afternoon,] *not in* F
	216–22	but . . . motion] *not in* F
I.3.	26	cause] case
	28	and] on
	66	so,] a
II.I	14	most beastly, in good faith] and that most beastly
	43	I] Sir *Iohn*, I
	46–7	in the channel] there
	54	or two] *not in* F
	66	thou upon] vpon
	71	all] all: all
	78	What] Fy, what a
	88	liking his father] lik'ning him

112   You . . . me,] I know you ha'
114–15   and . . . person] *not in* F
120   with her] her
150   dost . . . me? Come,] *not in* F
165   better] bitter
166   lord] good Lord
II.2.   16   once] ones
22–6   And God . . . strengthened.] *not in* F
30   at this time] *not in* F
71   virtuous] pernitious
78   petticoat] new Petticoat
88   blossom] good Blossome
93   lord] good Lord
128   POINS] *not in* F
168–9   descension] declension
II.4   1,10   FRANCIS] 1. *Drawer.*
4   DRAWER] 2. *Draw.*
13–14   DRAWER . . . Dispatch! . . . straight.] *not in* F
53   DOLL Hang . . . yourself!] *not in* F
132–3   FALSTAFF No . . . Pistol.] *not in* F
144–6   word as . . . sorted] word Captaine odious
155   faitours] Fates
162   Troyant] Troian
176   *contento*] *contente*
279   Poins his] *Poines,* his
286   grace] good Grace
290   light – flesh] (light, flesh, Q); light Flesh,
296   now] euen now
310   chipper] chopper
315   thee] him
383–4   Come! . . . Doll?] *not in* F
III.1.   24   deafing] deaff'ning
27   sea-son] (season Q); Sea-Boy
77   natures] nature
81   beginning] beginnings
III.2.   19   Barnes] *Bare*

	36	as the Psalmist saith] *not in* F
	69	ever were] euery where
	77–8	'a may be] he
	130	much] not
	172	prick] pricke me
	192	Master Shallow] good Master *Shallow*: No more of that
	253	Here's Wart;] Where's *Wart*?
	264	Thas! Thas! Thas!] thus, thus, thus.
	287	'Fore God, would you would.] I would you would, Master *Shallow*.
	303–4	yet . . . mandrake] *not in* F
	305–8	and sung . . . good-nights] *not in* F
	314	thrust] truss'd
IV.2.	24	Imply] Employ
	28	His] Heauens
IV.3.	2	place?] place, I pray?
	82	lord] Lord, 'pray,
	85	had the] had but the
	120	human] *not in* F
IV.4.	33	he is] hee's
	39	time] Line
	104	wet] write
		terms] Letters
IV.5.	50	majesty?] Maiestie? how fares your Grace?
	55	He . . . here.] *not in* F
	72	pillèd] (pilld Q); pyl'd
	76	tolling] culling
		flower,] flower | The vertuous sweetes, (*the lineation differs by approximately half a line in each line to 80*)
	161	worse than] worst of
	178	God] O my Sonne! | Heauen
	220	You] My gracious Liege: | You
V.1.	8	Davy! Let me see, Davy] *not in* F
	9	yea, marry] *not in* F
	12	hade land] head-land

	21	lost] lost the other day
	24	tiny] tine
	29	backbitten] bitten
	43	little] but a very litle
	45	you] your Worship
	48	Come, come, come,] Come,
	60	him] of him
	74	without] with
v.2.	36	impartial] Imperiall
v.3.	25	Give Master Bardolph] Good M. *Bardolfe*:
	29	must] *not in* F
	56	tiny] tyne
v.4.	5	whipping-cheer] Whipping cheere enough
	6	two] two (lately)
	9	I go] I now go
	11	I] hee
	29	atomy] Anatomy
v.5.	4	Dispatch, dispatch!] *not in* F
	5	Shallow] *Robert Shallow*
	99	*tormenta, spero*] *tormento, spera*
		contenta] *contento*

Epilogue

15–16	And so . . . Queen] (*after line 32 in* F, *and omitting* 'I']
23	seen] *seene before*

3

Emendations incorporated in this edition (not including stage directions and minor emendations, such as changes of punctuation that do not affect sense and the correction of obvious misprints). Emendations that were first made (unauthoritatively) in the second Folio (1632) are marked 'F2' ('F1' in these cases refers to the first Folio). Most of the other emendations were first made by eighteenth-century editors such as Rowe, Pope, Theobald, and Capell. Readings suggested by modern scholars are here attributed by name.

Induction

	35	hold] hole Q, F
I.I.	161	LORD BARDOLPH] *Vmfr.* (Q; *not in* F)
	162–3	MORTON Sweet ... honour;	The] (*J. Dover Wilson, 1946*); *Bard.* Sweet ... honour,	*Mour.* The Q (F: ... honor. | ...)
	178	brought] (F2); bring (F1; *not in* Q)
	192	My lord, your son] (*this edition*); My Lord (your Sonne) (F; *not in* Q)
	201–2	religion; ... thoughts,] Religion, ... Thoughts: (F; *not in* Q)
II.2.	109	borrower's] borowed Q, F
	119	PRINCE HENRY] *not in* Q, F
II.4.	15	WILL] (*this edition*); *Francis* Q; *2. Draw.* F
	19	FRANCIS] (*this edition*); *Dra.* Q; *1. Draw.* F
	21	DRAWER] *Francis* Q; *2. Draw.* F
	47	Yea, Mary's joys] (*this edition*); Yea ioy Q; I marry F
	82	swagger, 'a] (*F. C. Maxwell, 1947*); swaggrer Q; Swaggerer F
	330	devil binds] (*this edition*); diuel blinds Q; Deuill outbids F
IV.I.	36	appeared] appeare Q, F
	114	force perforce] forc'd, perforce (F; *not in* Q)
	137	indeed] and did (F; *not in* Q)
	183	not that.] (not that, F2); not, that (Q, F1)
IV.2.	0	*New scene not marked in Q or F*
	19	imagined] imagine Q, F
IV.3.	0	*New scene not marked in Q or F*
	41	Rome, three words] (*A. R. Humphreys, 1966*); Rome, there cosin Q; Rome, F
IV.5.	0	*New scene not marked in Q or F*
	82	have] (*M. R. Ridley, 1934*); hands Q; hath F
	204	my] thy Q, F
V.3.	46	thee,] (*J. Dover Wilson, 1946*); the Q, F

4

Stage directions (not including minor editorial adjustments such as the provision of obvious exits and the addition of '*aside*' and indications of the person addressed).

Induction

	0	*painted full of tongues*] Q; *not in* F
I.I	0	*Enter the Lord Bardolph at one door*] Q; *Enter Lord Bardolfe, and the Porter.* F
	I	*Enter the Porter*] F (*in opening stage direction*); *not in* Q
	6	*Exit Porter*] *not in* Q, F
I.2.	0	*Enter Sir John Falstaff, followed by his Page bearing his sword and buckler*] *Enter sir Iohn alone, with his page bearing his sword and buckler* Q; *Enter Falstaffe, and Page.* F
	52	*and his Servant*] F (*and Servant.*); *not in* Q
	229	*Exeunt Lord Chief Justice and Servant*] *not in* Q, F
I.3.	0	*Enter the Archbishop of York, Thomas Mowbray the Earl Marshal, Lord Hastings, and Lord Bardolph*] *Enter th'Archbishop, Thomas Mowbray (Earle Marshall) the Lord Hastings, Fauconbridge, and Bardolfe.* Q; *Enter Archbishop, Hastings, Mowbray, and Lord Bardolfe,* F
II.I.	0	*with two officers, Fang and Snare*] F; *and an Officer or two.* Q
	7	*from behind them*] *not in* Q, F
	36	*and the Page*] Q (*and the boy.*); *not in* F
	58	*and his men*] Q; *not in* F
	131	*He takes her aside*] *not in* Q, F
		Gower] F; *a messenger* Q
	134	*He gives him a letter*] *not in* Q, F
	164	*Exeunt Hostess, Fang, Snare, Bardolph, and Page*] *exit hostesse and sergeant.* Q; *not in* F
II.2.	0	*Enter Prince Henry and Poins*] *Enter the Prince,*

Poynes, sir Iohn Russel, with other. Q; *Enter Prince
Henry, Pointz, Bardolfe, and Page.* F

65 *Enter Bardolph and the Page*] Q; *Enter Bardolfe.* F
(*after line 68*)

103 *reading the letter*] F (*Letter.*); *not in* Q

159 *Exeunt Bardolph and Page*] *not in* Q, F

II.4. 0 *Enter Francis and another Drawer*] *Enter a Drawer
or two.* Q; *Enter two Drawers.* F

13 *preparing to leave*] *not in* Q, F

14 *Enter Will*] Q (*after line 18*); *not in* F

21 *Exeunt Francis and Drawer*] *Exit.* Q, F

31 *singing*] *not in* Q, F

33 *Exit Will*] *not in* Q, F

105 *Bardolph, and the Page*] *and Bardolfes boy.* Q; *and
Bardolph and his Boy.* F

155 *He brandishes his sword*] *not in* Q, F

178 *He lays down his sword*] *not in* Q, F

191 *He snatches up his sword*] *not in* Q, F

198 *drawing*] *not in* Q, F

200 *Falstaff thrusts at Pistol*] *not in* Q, F

202 *Exit Bardolph, driving Pistol out*] *not in* Q, F

206 *Enter Bardolph*] *not in* Q, F

222 *Music*] *not in* Q, F

228 *behind*] *not in* Q, F

disguised as drawers] F (*disguis'd*); *not in* Q

276 *coming forward*] *not in* Q, F

290–91 *laying his hand upon Doll*] *not in* Q, F

315 *turning to Prince Henry*] *not in* Q, F

346 *Peto knocks at door*] Q; *not in* F

348 *Enter Peto*] F; *not in* Q

363 *Knocking within . . . Exit Bardolph*] *not in* Q, F

364 *Enter Bardolph*] *not in* Q, F

376 *with Bardolph, Peto, Page, and musicians*] *not in*
Q, F

380 *at the door*] *not in* Q, F

III.1. 0 *in his nightgown*] Q *corrected; not in* F

   followed by a page] F (*with a Page.*); *alone* Q *corrected*

  3 *Exit page*] F (*Exit.*); *not in* Q

  31 *Enter Warwick and Surrey*] F; *Enter Warwike, Surry, and sir Iohn Blunt.* Q *corrected*

III.2. 0 *Enter Justice Shallow and Justice Silence*] Q *Enter Shallow and Silence; with Mouldie, Shadow, Wart, Feeble, Bull-calfe.* F.

  53 *Enter Bardolph and one with him*] Q; *Enter Bardolph and his Boy.* F (*after line* 51)

  100 *Enter Mouldy*] *not in* Q, F

  121 *Enter Shadow*] *not in* Q, F

  135 *Enter Wart*] *not in* Q, F

  146 *Enter Feeble*] *not in* Q, F

  169 *Enter Bullcalf*] *not in* Q, F

  214 *Exeunt Falstaff, Shallow, and Silence*] *exeunt.* Q; *not in* F

  234 *Enter Falstaff and the Justices*] Q; *not in* F

  290 *Exeunt Bardolph and the recruits*] *not in* Q, F

IV.1. 0 *Enter the Archbishop, Mowbray, and Hastings, with their forces, within the Forest of Gaultree*] *Enter the Archbishop, Mowbray, Bardolfe, Hastings, within the forrest of Gaultree.* Q; *Enter the Arch-bishop, Mowbray, Hastings, Westmerland, Coleuile.* F

  24 *Enter Westmorland*] Q (*after line* 25), F

  180 *Exit Westmorland*] Q (*after* 'decide it.'); *not in* F

  226 *They go forward*] *not in* Q, F

IV.2. 0 *Enter Prince John of Lancaster and his army*] Q (*after* IV.1.224); *Enter Prince Iohn.* F

  71 *Exit a captain*] F (*Exit.*); *not in* Q

  86 *Shouts within*] *shout.* Q; *not in* F

  92 *Exit Westmorland*] F (*Exit.*) *not in* Q

  96 *Exit Hastings*] F (*Exit.*); *not in* Q

IV.3. 0 *Alarum. Excursions. Enter Falstaff and Sir John Colevile*] *Alarum Enter Falstaffe excursions* Q; *Enter Falstaffe and Colleuile.* F

17 *He kneels*] *not in* Q, F

23 *Retreat sounded*] *Retraite* Q; *not in* F
*Enter Prince John, Westmorland, and Blunt, with
soldiers*] *Enter Iohn Westmerland, and the rest.*
Q; *Enter Prince Iohn, and Westmerland.* F

74 *Exit Blunt with Colevile*] F (*Exit with Colleuile.*);
not in Q

84 *Exeunt all but Falstaff*] F (*Exit.*); *not in* Q

IV.4. o *Enter the King, carried in a chair, Warwick,
Thomas Duke of Clarence, Humphrey Duke of
Gloucester, and attendant lords*] *Enter the King,
Warwike, Kent, Thomas duke of Clarence,
Humphrey of Gloucester.* Q; *Enter King, Warwicke,
Clarence, Gloucester.* F

IV.5. o *They take up the King and lay him on a bed*] *not in*
Q, F

21 *Exeunt all but Prince Henry*] *not in* Q, F

44 *He puts the crown on his head*] *not in* Q, F

49 *and attendant lords*] *not in* Q, F

139 *kneels*] *not in* Q, F

223 *Enter Prince John of Lancaster, Warwick, and
attendant lords*] *enter Lancaster.* Q; *Enter Lord
Iohn of Lancaster, and Warwicke.* F

V.1. o *Enter Shallow, Falstaff, Bardolph, and the Page*]
Enter Shallow, Falstaffe, and Bardolfe Q; *Enter
Shallow, Silence, Falstaffe, Bardolfe, Page, and
Dauie.* F

6 *Enter Davy*] *not in* Q, F

47 *Exit Davy*] *not in* Q, F

54 *Exit Shallow*] *not in* Q, F

55 *Exeunt Bardolph and Page*] *not in* Q, F

79 *within*] *not in* Q, F

V.2. o *Enter Warwick and the Lord Chief Justice*] *Enter
Warwike, duke Humphrey, L. chiefe Iustice, Thomas
Clarence, Prince Iohn, Westmerland.* Q; *Enter the
Earle of Warwicke, and the Lord Chiefe Iustice.* F

13   *and attendant lords*] *not in* Q, F
42   *Enter King Henry V, attended by Blunt and others*]
      Enter the Prince and Blunt Q; *Enter Prince Henrie.* F

v.3.   0   *Enter Falstaff, Shallow, Silence, Davy, Bardolph,
      and the Page*] Q; *Enter Falstaffe, Shallow,
      Silence, Bardolfe, Page, and Pistoll.* F
17   *sings*] *not in* Q, F
29   *Exit*] *not in* Q, F
32   *sings*] *not in* Q, F
39   *Enter Davy*] Q; *not in* F
45,52   *sings*] *not in* Q, F
69   *One knocks at door*] Q; *not in* F
70   *Exit Davy*] *not in* Q, F
71   *to Silence, seeing him drink*] *not in* Q, F
73   *sings*] *not in* Q, F
79   *Enter Davy*] *not in* Q, F
103   *sings*] *not in* Q, F

v.4.   0   *Enter Beadles dragging in Hostess Quickly and Doll
      Tearsheet*] *Enter Sincklo and three or foure officers.*
      Q; *Enter Hostesse Quickly, Dol Tearesheete, and
      Beadles.* F

v.5.   0   *Enter three Grooms, strewers of rushes*] *Enter strewers
      of rushes.* Q; *Enter two Groomes.* F
4   *Exeunt*] F; *not in* Q
      *Trumpets sound, and the King and his train pass over
      the stage. After them enter Falstaff, Shallow, Pistol,
      Bardolfe, and the Page.*] Q (. . . *and the Boy*); *Enter
      Falstaffe, Shallow, Pistoll, Bardolfe, and Page.* F
39   *The trumpets sound*] F (*after line* 40); *not in* Q
40   *Enter the King and his train, the Lord Chief Justice
      among them*] *Enter the King and his traine.* Q; *The
      Trumpets sound. Enter King Henrie the Fift, Brothers,
      Lord Chiefe Iustice.* F
75   *Exeunt King and his train*] *not in* Q; *Exit King.* F
93   *Enter the Lord Chief Justice and Prince John, with
      officers*] *Enter Iustice and prince Iohn* Q; *not in* F

99   *Exeunt all but Prince John and the Lord Chief Justice*]
      exeunt. Q (*after line* 98); *Exit. Manet Lancaster
      and Chiefe Iustice.* F

5

Rejected Emendations

A list of some of the more interesting emendations suggested
by other editors but not adopted in this edition.

I.I.   161   LORD BARDOLPH] TRAVERS
         183   ventured . . . proposed,] ventured . . . proposed
I.3.   36–9   (*see textual note*)
          47   least] last
          66   so,] so a
II.2.   71   POINS (*to Bardolph*)] BARDOLPH (*to the Page*)
         102–3 writes – POINS (*reading the letter*) *John Falstaff,*
                knight – every] writes – (*reads*) *John Falstaff, knight.*
                POINS Every
II.4.   330   devil binds] devil attends; devil bloats; devil's
                behind
III.I.   51   chance's mocks] chances mock
III.2.   148   SHALLOW] FALSTAFF
          302   invincible] invisible
IV.I.   34   rage] rags
           71   there] sphere; shore; flow
          178   At] And
IV.3.   60–61 Is . . . lord] *as a verse line*
           62   A . . . Colevile] *as a verse line*
IV.4.   10–17 (*see textual note*)
V.2.   102   right justice] right, justice
V.5.   17, 19 PISTOL] SHALLOW

6

Commentary on textual matters not included in the above lists
will be found in the following textual notes.

The Songs

1. 'When Arthur first in court' (II.4.32, 34). Falstaff sings a garbled version of the ballad *Sir Launcelot du Lake*, which in Shakespeare's time was sung to the tune 'Chevy Chase' (also known as 'Flying Fame'). The best surviving version, given below, is found eight times in Thomas D'Urfey's *Pills to Purge Melancholy* (1719–20), and is close to a Scottish manuscript version of about 1650–75.

2. 'Do me right' (V.3.73–5; see also the note to V.3.17–22). This is from the drinking song *Monsieur Mingo*, which, with music by Orlando di Lasso, was published first in Paris in 1570 and in London in the same year by a Huguenot refugee, Thomas Vautrollier, with a partially expurgated text. The music reproduced here is based on the edition of M. Henri Expert, *Les Maîtres musiciens de la renaissance française* (Paris, 1894), pages 72–5. English words (which are not a translation of the French) are first found in a seventeenth-century manuscript in the Bodleian Library (MS. Mus. f. 17–19). They are reproduced here from the text appended to an article on the

song in *Shakespeare Quarterly* 9 (1958), pages 105–16, by Dr F. W. Sternfeld, whose further assistance is gratefully acknowledged.

Mon-sieur Min-go For quaff-ing doth pass In cup, cruse, can, or glass; In cell-ar ne-ver was his fell-ow found To drink pro-found, By task and turn so round To quaff, ca-rouse so sound, And yet bear so fresh a brain, Fresh a brain, Sans taint or stain; Or foil, re-coil, or quar-rel, But to the beer and bar-rel, Where he works to win his name, Where he works to win his name; And stout doth stand, In Bac-chus' band, With pot in hand, To pur-chase fame; For he calls with cup and can: Come try my cour-age, man to man, And let him con-quer me that can, And spare not, I care not, While hands can heave the pot, No fear falls to my lot; God Bac-chus do me right, And dub me knight, Do-min-go.

THE SECOND PART OF
KING HENRY THE FOURTH
The Characters in the Play

RUMOUR, the presenter

KING HENRY IV
PRINCE HENRY, afterwards crowned King Henry V
PRINCE JOHN OF LANCASTER ⎫
Humphrey DUKE OF GLOUCESTER ⎬ sons of Henry IV and brothers of Henry V
Thomas DUKE OF CLARENCE ⎭

Of the King's Party
EARL OF WARWICK
EARL OF WESTMORLAND
Earl of Surrey
Sir John Blunt
GOWER
HARCOURT
The LORD CHIEF JUSTICE
A SERVANT of the Lord Chief Justice

Opposed to the King
EARL OF NORTHUMBERLAND
The ARCHBISHOP OF YORK
LORD MOWBRAY
LORD HASTINGS

'Q' here refers to the Quarto edition of the play (1600), 'F' to the first folio (1623). All references to *1 Henry IV* are to the edition printed in this volume. Biblical quotations are modernized from the Bishops' Bible (1568 etc.), the version that was probably best known to Shakespeare.

The Characters in the Play This arrangement is based on the grouping of the list headed 'The Actors Names' at the end of the F version of the play, except that the names of the King's party have here been placed before those of the rebels. Some of the headings, descriptions, and names are added or modified from those in F's list, though the curious description 'Irregular Humorists' and the order of those so described are as in F.

LORD BARDOLPH
TRAVERS
MORTON
SIR JOHN COLEVILE

LADY NORTHUMBERLAND, Northumberland's wife
LADY PERCY, Percy's widow

'Irregular Humorists'
POINS
SIR JOHN FALSTAFF
BARDOLPH
PISTOL
PETO
Falstaff's PAGE

HOSTESS Quickly
DOLL TEARSHEET

Robert SHALLOW }
SILENCE   } country justices
DAVY, Shallow's servant

Ralph MOULDY   ⎫
Simon SHADOW   ⎪
Thomas WART   ⎬ country soldiers
Francis FEEBLE ⎪
Peter BULLCALF ⎭

FANG } sergeants
SNARE }
FRANCIS, WILL, and another DRAWER
FIRST BEADLE
Three GROOMS

A PORTER
A MESSENGER

Speaker of the EPILOGUE

Officers, musicians, a page, soldiers, a captain, lords, beadles

INDUCTION

Enter Rumour, painted full of tongues

RUMOUR

Open your ears, for which of you will stop
The vent of hearing when loud Rumour speaks?

Act and scene divisions F divides the play into acts and scenes and names the Induction as such; Q makes no divisions at all. F's divisions are followed in this edition except in Act IV: see the headnotes to IV.2, 3, and 5.

Locations In only one stage direction in *2 Henry IV* does Shakespeare name the place where the scene is set: the Q opening direction to IV.1 locates it *'within the forrest of Gaultree'*. It has been common since the eighteenth century for editors to specify locations, but it is doubtful whether much is gained; when Shakespeare is concerned that we should be aware of the place of action he tells us by way of the dialogue (even in IV.1 he mentions Gaultree Forest in the first two lines of the scene). No other locations are provided in this edition. Too rigorous an insistence on place can imply for a present-day audience a realism – a relatively modern concept – that works against the understanding of Elizabethan drama.

Induction Many editors specify a location for Rumour based on the reference in lines 35–7 to the castle where Northumberland *Lies crafty-sick*. But Rumour is symbolic, not a particularized character like, say, Falstaff. No editor proposes a location for the speaker of the Epilogue,

and it is just as inappropriate to do so for Rumour.

Dr Johnson regarded Rumour's speech as 'wholly useless, since we are told nothing which the first scene does not clearly and naturally discover' (though he conceded that it was 'not inelegant or unpoetical'). This implicitly emphasizes the recounting of facts with economy, and Johnson fails to allow for the atmosphere that Rumour evokes. There is, moreover, some virtue in laying a clear foundation for a situation, even if that means giving facts more than once. Rumour serves this function, telling us where we are in the well-known story of Henry IV and Henry V; he also warns the discerning that this will not be a play to make *smooth comforts false, worse than true wrongs* (line 40). There is an element in *2 Henry IV* that is distinctly uncomfortable.

(stage direction) *painted full of tongues*. This is part of a long-standing description of Rumour and the associated figure of Fame, common in the sixteenth century but going back to Virgil and Ovid. In 1553 the Revels Office paid for a coat and cap to be painted for Fame with eyes, tongues, and ears.

I, from the orient to the drooping west,
Making the wind my post-horse, still unfold
The acts commenced on this ball of earth.
Upon my tongues continual slanders ride,
The which in every language I pronounce,
Stuffing the ears of men with false reports.
I speak of peace while covert enmity,
Under the smile of safety, wounds the world;
And who but Rumour, who but only I,
Make fearful musters, and prepared defence,
Whiles the big year, swollen with some other grief,
Is thought with child by the stern tyrant War,
And no such matter? Rumour is a pipe
Blown by surmises, jealousies, conjectures,
And of so easy and so plain a stop
That the blunt monster with uncounted heads,

10

3 *drooping* (where the sun declines)

4 *post-horse* (horse kept at an inn or staging point for use by those carrying post (or other travellers). The idea that rumours ride the wind has become a commonplace.)

4,19 *still* continually, always

6 *slanders.* Rumour's speech is full of images of incertitude and deception; *false reports, the smile of safety, surmises, jealousies, conjectures,* and *Rumour* itself all occur in nine lines. The sense of unease and doubt is also suggested by such epithets as *covert, uncounted,* and *still-discordant wavering,* which are summed up in the last sentence of the speech.

10 *safety.* This may mean here more than a sense of physical security. 'Safety' could imply the salvation of the soul. See the note to 1.2.43.

12 *Make* cause to be made
fearful musters frightening enrolments of troops. This line probably evoked for Shakespeare's audience the preparations made towards the end of 1596

and throughout much of 1597 against an expected Spanish invasion. Such preparations were again being made in 1599, though that would be rather too late a date for *2 Henry IV*. At a time when these preparations were common, a dramatist could easily conjure up such apprehensions, and specific dates may not be reliably determined.

13 *big* pregnant, full (of events)

15 *And no such matter* though there is no substance in such fears

16 *jealousies* suspicious apprehensions of evil

17 *so plain a stop* so easily played upon. The 'stops' of a recorder (the *pipe* of line 15) are the holes that are covered or uncovered to produce different notes. A similar image is used, though in a slightly different way, in *Hamlet*, III.2.68–9.

18 *the blunt monster with uncounted heads* (the people, seen as a mob, insensitive (*blunt*) and uncountable because so numerous)

The still-discordant wavering multitude,
Can play upon it. But what need I thus   20
My well-known body to anatomize
Among my household? Why is Rumour here?
I run before King Harry's victory,
Who in a bloody field by Shrewsbury
Hath beaten down young Hotspur and his troops,
Quenching the flame of bold rebellion
Even with the rebels' blood. But what mean I
To speak so true at first? My office is . . .
To noise abroad that Harry Monmouth fell
Under the wrath of noble Hotspur's sword,   30
And that the King before the Douglas' rage
Stooped his anointed head as low as death.
This have I rumoured through the peasant towns
Between that royal field of Shrewsbury
And this worm-eaten hold of ragg├¿d stone,
Where Hotspur's father, old Northumberland
Lies crafty-sick. The posts come tiring on,

19 *wavering* vacillating
21 *anatomize* analyse, dissect
22 *my household* those I influence (and, by implication, the audience)
23 *King Harry's victory*. This is the Battle of Shrewsbury, which Shakespeare dramatizes towards the end of *1 Henry IV*.
29 *Harry Monmouth*. Prince Hal, son of Henry IV, was born at Monmouth.
31-2 *the King . . . death*. In *1 Henry IV*, v.4.37, the King is attacked by Douglas, and, when in danger, is rescued by Hal.
33 *peasant* country
35 *hold* castle. Q and F both print 'hole', which makes a sort of sense. However, in Elizabethan ('secretary') handwriting 'd' is easily misread as 'e', and it is likely that Shakespeare wrote (or intended) 'hold'. *ragg├¿d*. There are two possibilities here. Combined with *worm-eaten*, *ragg├¿d* suggests

a broken-down castle, and those who support this interpretation argue that castles were falling into disarray in the later Tudor period. On the other hand *ragg├¿d* could refer to the castellations and projecting stonework of Northumberland's *hold*, and *worm-eaten* might refer to the holes seemingly eaten into the walls to make arrow-slits. In *Richard II*, when Richard is brought to ruin at Flint Castle, Bolingbroke speaks of the castle's 'ruined ears' and later of its 'tattered battlements' (III.3.34 and 52). 'Tattered' can imply 'broken-down', but it too can suggest castellation (and indeed it has a particular architectural meaning, 'denticulated'). In both cases Shakespeare combines a description of a castle with a suggestion of ruin and disorder.
37 *crafty-sick*. In *Richard II* and in both parts of *Henry IV* Northumberland

And not a man of them brings other news
Than they have learnt of me. From Rumour's tongues
40   They bring smooth comforts false, worse than true
wrongs.   *Exit*

I.I   *Enter the Lord Bardolph at one door*

LORD BARDOLPH
   Who keeps the gate here, ho?
           Enter the Porter

                                   Where is the Earl?

PORTER
   What shall I say you are?

is made to seem the cunning politician. His absence from Shrewsbury,
which contributed to the death of
his son and the defeat of his cause, is
ascribed to craft by Shakespeare, not
by the historians.
posts couriers
tiring exhaustedly
39–40 *From Rumour's tongues . . . wrongs.*
Rumour's final comment is applicable to more than the immediate situation – the arrival of news about the
Battle of Shrewsbury. It is easy to find
smooth comforts false in the play as a
whole, and it is important for the
audience to realize that upon the
tongue of Rumour, the presenter of
the story, *continual slanders ride.*

I.I The opening of this scene has attracted much attention, for it seems to
provide evidence that three places of
entry at stage level were available to the
Elizabethan dramatist. In Q no entry is
given for the Porter but the direction
for Lord Bardolph specifies that he
enters *'at one door'*, and his first line
implies that the Porter is somewhere
else. Some scholars have suggested that

the Porter enters on the upper stage, but
that involves a certain awkwardness
unless Lord Bardolph can appear from a
different direction and then Northumberland from a third.
   A more interesting problem is the
appearance in the play of two characters
with the same name, though this is not
unique in Shakespeare (there are, for
example, two characters called Jaques in
As You Like It). The duplication here is
particularly strange in that Bardolph was
probably originally called 'Harvey' in *1
Henry IV* (see page 259), but, as with the
original name for Falstaff, 'Oldcastle'
(see the note to 1.2.121), it seems that
pressure was brought to have the name
changed. Shakespeare apparently then
chose 'Bardolph' (a name which appears
among a list of recusants that includes
Shakespeare's father), not anticipating
that in a second part to *Henry IV* this
would present difficulties. It is possible
that Lord Bardolph was originally called
'Umfrevile', since the abbreviation
'*Vmfr.*' appears in Q as the speech prefix
at line 161, and Sir John Umfrevile is
referred to in line 34. Lord *Robert* Umfrevile was present at Gaultree Forest but

LORD BARDOLPH   Tell thou the Earl
That the Lord Bardolph doth attend him here.

PORTER

His lordship is walked forth into the orchard.
Please it your honour knock but at the gate,
And he himself will answer.
            Enter Northumberland
LORD BARDOLPH   Here comes the Earl.
                                          Exit Porter

NORTHUMBERLAND

What news, Lord Bardolph? Every minute now
Should be the father of some stratagem.
The times are wild; contention, like a horse
Full of high feeding, madly hath broke loose   10
And bears down all before him.

LORD BARDOLPH   Noble Earl,
I bring you certain news from Shrewsbury,

NORTHUMBERLAND

Good, an God will!

LORD BARDOLPH   As good as heart can wish.
The King is almost wounded to the death,
And, in the fortune of my lord your son,
Prince Harry slain outright; and both the Blunts

---

as a supporter of the King. The original
Lord Bardolph was a rebel and died of
wounds in 1408, after the Battle of Bramham Moor. The cursory reference to his
death at IV.4.97–9 makes it seem coincident with the events at Gaultree Forest
of 1405. Perhaps Shakespeare started by
giving Lord Bardolph his proper name,
toyed with changing the name, chose
Umfrevile, then, realizing that it was the
name of one of Bardolph's opponents,
made do with the original and historically
correct name. Something similar may be
involved in the cases of Fauconbridge and
Kent (see the headnotes to I.3 and IV.4).
1 *keeps* guards

3 *attend* await
8 *stratagem* (not 'plot' but 'violent and
bloody act', a usage found elsewhere
in Shakespeare's plays)
10 *high* too rich
12 *certain* reliable
13 *an* if
15 *in the fortune of* as for what has befallen
16 *the Blunts.* At the Battle of Shrewsbury several knights were disguised
as King Henry IV. One of these was
Sir Walter Blunt, who was killed by
Douglas (see the beginning of V.3 in
I Henry IV). There was no second
Blunt at Shrewsbury so far as historical records show; but Samuel Daniel

Killed by the hand of Douglas; young Prince John
And Westmorland and Stafford fled the field;
And Harry Monmouth's brawn, the hulk Sir John,
20   Is prisoner to your son. O, such a day,
So fought, so followed, and so fairly won,
Came not till now to dignify the times
Since Caesar's fortunes!

NORTHUMBERLAND   How is this derived?
Saw you the field? Came you from Shrewsbury?

LORD BARDOLPH
I spake with one, my lord, that came from thence,
A gentleman well bred, and of good name,
That freely rendered me these news for true.

Enter Travers

NORTHUMBERLAND
Here comes my servant Travers, whom I sent
On Tuesday last to listen after news.

LORD BARDOLPH
30   My lord, I over-rode him on the way,
And he is furnished with no certainties
More than he haply may retail from me.

(in his long poem *The First Four Books of the Civil Wars between the Two Houses of Lancaster and York* (1595), which Shakespeare knew) mentions the death of 'another Blunt' at Shrewsbury, and Holinshed tells of a Sir John Blunt who fought the French with distinction in 1412. *2 Henry IV* includes a non-speaking character called Blunt (see the note to the stage direction at III.1.31); editors usually call him Sir John Blunt, Sir Walter's son.

18 *Stafford*. The Earl of Stafford was one of those disguised as Henry IV; Douglas killed him as well as Blunt (*1 Henry IV*, v.3.7–9).

19 *brawn* (boar fattened for the table)
hulk (usually used of a ship) large unwieldy person

21 *So fought, so followed, and so fairly won.* This is reminiscent of the most famous of all rhetorical figures, Julius Caesar's *Veni, vidi, vici*, 'I came, I saw, I overcame' (quoted by Falstaff at IV.3.41). Caesar is, appropriately, referred to in line 23.

23 *fortunes* good fortune, success

27 *freely* openly
these news. In Elizabethan usage, 'news' could be singular or plural.

(stage direction) *Travers* (a character of Shakespeare's creation)

30 *over-rode* out-rode

NORTHUMBERLAND
> Now, Travers, what good tidings comes with you?

TRAVERS
> My lord, Sir John Umfrevile turned me back
> With joyful tidings, and, being better horsed,
> Out-rode me. After him came spurring hard
> A gentleman almost forspent with speed,
> That stopped by me to breathe his bloodied horse.
> He asked the way to Chester, and of him
> I did demand what news from Shrewsbury.   40
> He told me that rebellion had ill luck,
> And that young Harry Percy's spur was cold.
> With that he gave his able horse the head,
> And bending forward struck his armed heels
> Against the panting sides of his poor jade
> Up to the rowel-head; and starting so
> He seemed in running to devour the way,
> Staying no longer question.

> NORTHUMBERLAND   Ha? Again!
> Said he young Harry Percy's spur was cold?
> Of Hotspur, Coldspur? That rebellion   50
> Had met ill luck?

LORD BARDOLPH   My lord, I'll tell you what.
> If my young lord your son have not the day,
> Upon mine honour, for a silken point
> I'll give my barony – never talk of it.

---

33 *comes*. Like 'news', 'tidings' could be singular or plural.
34 *Sir John Umfrevile*. See the headnote to this scene, and the note to line 161.
37 *forspent* exhausted
38 *breathe* rest, allow to breathe
41 *ill*. This is F's reading. Q has 'bad', which makes good sense but could be a compositor's error unconsciously suggested by the previous word, *had*. There is evidence that the compositor who set Q was particularly prone to changing words under the influence of similar shapes or sounds. Northumberland repeats *ill* at line 51.

42 *spur . . . cold*. Hotspur (Harry Percy) is now cold in death. His father plays on his name and this news at line 50.
45 *jade* worn-out hack. (Compare 'jaded'.)
46 *starting* leaping forward
48 *Staying* waiting for
52 *have not the day* has not won the battle
53 *point* (lace for tying a garment)

NORTHUMBERLAND
Why should that gentleman that rode by Travers
Give then such instances of loss?

LORD BARDOLPH   Who, he?
He was some hilding fellow that had stolen
The horse he rode on, and, upon my life,
Spoke at a venture. Look, here comes more news.
        Enter Morton

NORTHUMBERLAND
60   Yea, this man's brow, like to a title-leaf,
Foretells the nature of a tragic volume.
So looks the strand whereon the imperious flood
Hath left a witnessed usurpation.
Say, Morton, didst thou come from Shrewsbury?

MORTON
I ran from Shrewsbury, my noble lord,
Where hateful death put on his ugliest mask
To fright our party.

NORTHUMBERLAND How doth my son, and brother?
Thou tremblest, and the whiteness in thy cheek
Is apter than thy tongue to tell thy errand.
70   Even such a man, so faint, so spiritless,
So dull, so dead in look, so woe-begone,
Drew Priam's curtain in the dead of night
And would have told him half his Troy was burnt;
But Priam found the fire ere he his tongue,
And I my Percy's death ere thou reportest it.
This thou wouldst say, 'Your son did thus and thus;
Your brother thus; so fought the noble Douglas',

---

55 *by* past
57 *hilding* contemptible
59 *at a venture* recklessly
(stage direction) *Morton* (a character cre-
    ated by Shakespeare)
60 *like to a title-leaf.* Title-pages of Eliza-
    bethan books served as an advertise-
    ment for the contents.
63 *a witnessed usurpation* evidence of en-

croachment (that is, the lines or wrinkles left in sand by the retreating tide)
72–3 *Drew Priam's curtain . . . burnt.* No
such instance is mentioned in the
Iliad, but in the *Aeneid* Aeneas is
warned of danger in a dream and
wakes to find Troy ablaze.
74 *found . . . tongue* discovered the fire
before the man could speak

Stopping my greedy ear with their bold deeds.
But in the end, to stop my ear indeed,
Thou hast a sigh to blow away this praise,   80
Ending with 'Brother, son, and all are dead'.

MORTON

Douglas is living, and your brother, yet;
But, for my lord your son —

NORTHUMBERLAND   Why, he is dead!
See what a ready tongue suspicion hath!
He that but fears the thing he would not know
Hath by instinct knowledge from others' eyes
That what he feared is chanced. Yet speak, Morton;
Tell thou an earl his divination lies,
And I will take it as a sweet disgrace
And make thee rich for doing me such wrong.   90

MORTON

You are too great to be by me gainsaid;
Your spirit is too true, your fears too certain.

NORTHUMBERLAND

Yet, for all this, say not that Percy's dead.
I see a strange confession in thine eye.
Thou shakest thy head, and holdest it fear or sin
To speak a truth. If he be slain —
The tongue offends not that reports his death;
And he doth sin that doth belie the dead,
Not he which says the dead is not alive.
Yet the first bringer of unwelcome news   100
Hath but a losing office, and his tongue

---

78 *Stopping* filling
79 *Stop my ear indeed* prevent my ever
   hearing again
87 *is chanced* has happened
88 *his divination lies* his conjecture is false
92 *spirit* (here not the soul or character
   but the powers of perception)
94 *strange* reluctant
95 *Thou shakest thy head.* This seems to
   imply a denial of Percy's death. Some
   commentators suggest that Morton's

action is to incline his head in silent
agreement; but it may be that he
does shake his head slowly from side
to side, not as a denial but in a
gesture of sorrow.

96 *slain.* F reads 'slaine, say so:', which
fills out the line to the correct
number of syllables. But it may be
an actor's or scribe's interpolation,
for Q's shorter line allows for a
dramatic pause.

Sounds ever after as a sullen bell
Remembered tolling a departing friend.

LORD BARDOLPH

I cannot think, my lord, your son is dead.

MORTON

I am sorry I should force you to believe
That which I would to God I had not seen;
But these mine eyes saw him in bloody state,
Rendering faint quittance, wearied and out-breathed,
To Harry Monmouth, whose swift wrath beat down
110 The never-daunted Percy to the earth,
From whence with life he never more sprung up.
In few, his death, whose spirit lent a fire
Even to the dullest peasant in his camp,
Being bruited once, took fire and heat away
From the best-tempered courage in his troops;
For from his metal was his party steeled,
Which once in him abated, all the rest
Turned on themselves, like dull and heavy lead;
And as the thing that's heavy in itself
120 Upon enforcement flies with greatest speed,
So did our men, heavy in Hotspur's loss,
Lend to this weight such lightness with their fear
That arrows fled not swifter toward their aim

102 *sullen* (funeral)
108 *faint quittance* weak resistance
109 *Harry Monmouth.* In this reference to
Hal as the slayer of Hotspur, Shakespeare follows his own alteration of
history in *1 Henry IV* (see page
235). The dramatic value of a confrontation between them is obvious.
112 *In few* in few words, in short
his death, whose the death of him
whose
114 *Being bruited once* as soon as it was
noised abroad
115 *best-tempered* of the finest temper (as
metal)
116 *metal.* F spells the word 'Mettle',

and Shakespeare is playing on the
two meanings. The imagery of this
passage (particularly lines 114–25)
has often attracted the attention of
critics. There are not only the obvious contrasts of well-tempered steel
and dull and heavy lead, but, more
subtly, the way in which the despond-
ency of the troops is expressed in
contrasting images which lead swiftly
to their flight from the battlefield.
117 *abated* blunted
123 *fled.* This unusual past form of 'fly'
vividly suggests those fleeing from
the battlefield as well as the arrows.

Than did our soldiers, aiming at their safety,
Fly from the field. Then was that noble Worcester
So soon ta'en prisoner, and that furious Scot,
The bloody Douglas, whose well-labouring sword
Had three times slain th'appearance of the King,
Gan vail his stomach, and did grace the shame
Of those that turned their backs, and in his flight,   130
Stumbling in fear, was took. The sum of all
Is that the King hath won, and hath sent out
A speedy power to encounter you, my lord,
Under the conduct of young Lancaster
And Westmorland. This is the news at full.

NORTHUMBERLAND

For this I shall have time enough to mourn.
In poison there is physic, and these news,
Having been well, that would have made me sick,
Being sick, have in some measure made me well.

---

128 *three times . . . the King.* In *1 Henry IV* the death of Blunt in the guise of the King is dramatized and the death of Stafford is referred to (see the notes to lines 16 and 18 above). Shakespeare may have had Shirley in mind as the third victim; Hal challenges Douglas with the words 'The spirits | Of valiant Shirley, Stafford, Blunt are in my arms' (*1 Henry IV*, v.4.39–40).

129–31 *Gan vail . . . took.* Holinshed, describing how Henry's enemies were put to flight, says that Douglas, 'for haste', fell from a crag, was taken, but 'for his valiantness' was released. Shakespeare stresses Douglas's flight and fear rather than his valour. Twice in *1 Henry IV* he has Douglas flee, at v.4.42 in a stage direction and v.5.20, where it is said he 'fled with the rest' on seeing his men 'Upon the foot of fear'. Here he is said to stumble with fear; the *bloody* Douglas's flight is contrasted with

his heroic pretensions, and might be compared with another doughty warrior's flight – Falstaff's from Gad's Hill.

129 *Gan* began to
vail his stomach fail in courage
grace excuse

133 *power* armed force

135 *at full* in full

137–9 *In poison . . . well.* Paradoxically, poisonous drugs, used in appropriate quantities, may be curative; thus, what would have made Northumberland ill were he well may cure him now he is sick. Such bitter news might renew his strength so much that he can fight back and revenge his son's death. As Shakespeare dramatizes the events, this does not happen; Northumberland again lets his colleagues down by not arriving with his forces at Gaultree Forest, and his death at the Battle of Bramham Moor is only glanced at (IV.4.97–9).

140 And as the wretch whose fever-weakened joints,
Like strengthless hinges, buckle under life,
Impatient of his fit, breaks like a fire
Out of his keeper's arms, even so my limbs,
Weakened with grief, being now enraged with grief,
Are thrice themselves. Hence, therefore, thou nice crutch!
A scaly gauntlet now with joints of steel
Must glove this hand. And hence, thou sickly coif!
Thou art a guard too wanton for the head
Which princes, fleshed with conquest, aim to hit.
150 Now bind my brows with iron, and approach
The raggèd'st hour that time and spite dare bring
To frown upon th'enraged Northumberland!
Let heaven kiss earth! Now let not Nature's hand
Keep the wild flood confined! Let order die!
And let this world no longer be a stage
To feed contention in a lingering act;

141 *under life* under the weight of the living man
142 *fit* seizure. There is a slight (though effective) confusion here between the weakness caused by fever and the paroxysm of a fit.
143 *keeper* nurse
144 *grief . . . grief* bodily pain . . . sorrow
145 *nice.* There may be a pun here on the very specific use of 'nice' to mean 'slender' or 'thin' (as in *Othello*, III.3.15, where policy is said to feed on 'such nice and waterish diet') and on the meaning 'unmanly'. Wordplay on such an occasion as this is typically Shakespearian. Compare the note to line 42.
146 *scaly* (made of overlapping plates of armour)
147 *coif* nightcap
148 *wanton* effeminate
149 *fleshed* initiated in bloodshed (as animals are for hunting)
151 *raggèd'st* roughest
154 *Let order die!* A serious, indeed a

shocking, plea in Elizabethan times, comparable with Falstaff's *woe to my Lord Chief Justice!* (v.3.136). Northumberland's passionate speech is reminiscent in style of his son's outbursts in *1 Henry IV*, and it also recalls the moment in *Richard II*, 1.4.31–3, when Bolingbroke (as Henry IV was then called) reverses order by doffing his bonnet to an oyster-wench and bending his knee to a brace of draymen. Here, Northumberland's cry is reinforced by a plea that all natural restraints be overturned and Cain's spirit reign in all men's hearts. One cannot know the precise effect on an Elizabethan audience, but this may be a good example of Shakespeare's skill in enabling his listeners to respond to the speaker's emotion whilst remaining detached from the plea itself.
156 *feed contention in a lingering act* foster dispute in a long-drawn-out action

But let one spirit of the first-born Cain
Reign in all bosoms, that, each heart being set
On bloody courses, the rude scene may end,
And darkness be the burier of the dead!   160

LORD BARDOLPH

This strainèd passion doth you wrong, my lord.

MORTON

Sweet Earl, divorce not wisdom from your honour;
The lives of all your loving complices
Lean on your health, the which, if you give o'er
To stormy passion, must perforce decay.
You cast th'event of war, my noble lord,
And summed the account of chance before you said
'Let us make head'. It was your presurmise
That in the dole of blows your son might drop.
You knew he walked o'er perils, on an edge,   170
More likely to fall in than to get o'er.

---

157 *Cain*. Traditionally Cain committed the first murder.

158 *that* so that

159 *rude* (1) discordant (of the action dramatized); (2) lacking polish (of the dramatist's art)

161 LORD BARDOLPH. Q's speech prefix for this line is '*Vmfr.*' – presumably the Sir John Umfrevile of line 34 (see the headnote to this scene). The F editor or compositor, perhaps puzzled, left the line out; if the conjecture that actors' parts underlie the F text is correct (see the Account of the Text, pages 465–8), it could be that the line was not retained when a part for Umfrevile was abandoned. The line is sometimes given to Travers, but a comment on the Earl's behaviour comes more appropriately from a lord than from a servant.

162 MORTON. Both Q and F give this line to Lord Bardolph, beginning Morton's speech at line 163. But this may be an error caused by the Q compositor's misreading a manuscript correction of the speech prefix for line 161. Line 162 seems to form a natural part of Morton's speech, and Q has a comma at the end of the line.

166 *cast th'event* calculated (cast up) the outcome

168 *make head* raise an army

169 *dole* distribution (perhaps with a pun on the meaning 'sorrow')

170 *edge* perilous path along a narrow ridge

171 *More likely to fall in than to get o'er.* In *1 Henry IV*, 1.3.190–92, Worcester proposes a dangerous policy which he likens to walking over 'a current roaring loud | On the unsteadfast footing of a spear'. Hotspur replies 'If he fall in, good night, or sink, or swim!' Shakespeare seems to be recalling that conversation here; the repetition of *fall in* is striking, since 'falling off' a narrow path would seem more logical. 'Edge' could mean a cutting

You were advised his flesh was capable
Of wounds and scars, and that his forward spirit
Would lift him where most trade of danger ranged.
Yet did you say 'Go forth'; and none of this,
Though strongly apprehended, could restrain
The stiff-borne action. What hath then befallen,
Or what hath this bold enterprise brought forth,
More than that being which was like to be?

LORD BARDOLPH

180 We all that are engagèd to this loss
Knew that we ventured on such dangerous seas
That if we wrought out life 'twas ten to one;
And yet we ventured for the gain proposed,
Choked the respect of likely peril feared,
And since we are o'erset, venture again.
Come, we will all put forth, body and goods.

MORTON

'Tis more than time. And, my most noble lord,
I hear for certain, and dare speak the truth,
The gentle Archbishop of York is up
190 With well-appointed powers. He is a man
Who with a double surety binds his followers.

weapon (as in *Coriolanus*, v.6.113), so
Shakespeare might well have associated *an edge* (path) with the spear
which, as in medieval romances, was
to provide the path across the 'current roaring loud'.
172 *advised* warned, apprised
172–3 *capable | Of* susceptible to
173 *forward* eager
174 *trade* interchange
177 *stiff-borne* obstinately pursued
180 *engagèd to* concerned with, involved
in
182 *wrought out life* won through alive
184 *respect* consideration
185 *o'erset* overthrown
186 *put forth* (1) put to sea; (2) stake

189 *gentle* well-born (as gentleman)
Archbishop of York Richard Scroop,
who is variously described as the
brother, cousin, or godson of William Scrope, Earl of Wiltshire, who
was executed at Bristol by order of
Bolingbroke (*Richard II*, III.2.141–2).
In *1 Henry IV*, 1.3.264–5, Worcester
tells Hotspur that the Archbishop
'bears hard | His brother's death'.
There were many Scroops (or
Scropes), and their relationships are
complicated and easily misunderstood.
up in arms
191 *a double surety* (bodily and spiritual
allegiance)

My lord, your son had only but the corpse,
But shadows and the shows of men, to fight;
For that same word 'rebellion' did divide
The action of their bodies from their souls.
And they did fight with queasiness, constrained,
As men drink potions, that their weapons only
Seemed on our side; but, for their spirits and souls,
This word – 'rebellion' – it had froze them up
As fish are in a pond. But now the Bishop   200
Turns insurrection to religion
Supposed sincere and holy in his thoughts,
He's followed both with body and with mind,
And doth enlarge his rising with the blood
Of fair King Richard, scraped from Pomfret stones;
Derives from heaven his quarrel and his cause;
Tells them he doth bestride a bleeding land,
Gasping for life under great Bolingbroke;
And more and less do flock to follow him.

NORTHUMBERLAND
    I knew of this before, but, to speak truth,   210

192 *My lord, your son.* F's reading (Q
omits lines 189–209) is 'My Lord
(your Sonne)', indicating that Hotspur is *My lord* (as at line 83). The
brackets may be Shakespeare's, but
they could have been introduced by
a scribe (or the compositor), and it
seems possible that *My lord* refers
to Northumberland, continuing Morton's note of cautious deference in
my most noble lord (line 187).
    only but only
    the corpse the bodies of men (whose
    souls (or hearts) were not in what
    they did). 'Corpse' could be either
    singular or plural.
193 *to fight* (as his soldiers)
197 *potions* medicine, poison
201 *Turns insurrection to religion* makes rebellion a sacred duty. In the sixteenth
and seventeenth centuries, rebellion

was not merely a civil offence; an
attack on the sovereign was an attack
on God's deputy on earth. It was,
therefore, particularly serious if rebellion was supported by the religious,
for it gave a seeming sanctity to what
otherwise was regarded as sacrileg-
ious. See the second note to 1.2.34.
202 *Supposed* believed to be. The word
does not imply doubt of the Archbishop's sincerity.
204 *enlarge* enhance
205 *Pomfret* (the castle where Richard II
was murdered)
206 *Derives from heaven his quarrel and his
cause* claims divine approval for the
arguments for his course of action
209 *more and less* all classes of people
210 *I knew of this before* (a typical example
of a character being told what he

This present grief had wiped it from my mind.
Go in with me, and counsel every man
The aptest way for safety and revenge.
Get posts and letters, and make friends with speed –
Never so few, and never yet more need.   *Exeunt*

I.2   *Enter Sir John Falstaff, followed by his Page bearing
his sword and buckler*

FALSTAFF Sirrah, you giant, what says the doctor to my
water?

PAGE He said, sir, the water itself was a good healthy
water; but, for the party that owed it, he might have
more diseases than he knew for.

FALSTAFF Men of all sorts take a pride to gird at me. The
brain of this foolish-compounded clay, man, is not able
to invent anything that intends to laughter more than I
invent, or is invented on me; I am not only witty in
myself, but the cause that wit is in other men. I do here
walk before thee like a sow that hath overwhelmed all
her litter but one. If the Prince put thee into my service
for any other reason than to set me off, why then I have
no judgement. Thou whoreson mandrake, thou art

10

already knows for the audience's
benefit, though Northumberland's
next line gives a sort of reason for
his forgetfulness)

214 *posts* couriers
make collect

I.2 (stage direction) In Q Sir John is
said to enter '*alone, with his page bearing
his sword and buckler*'; F has '*Enter
Falstaffe, and Page*'. '*Alone*' probably
implies that Falstaff enters in advance
of the Page, who follows at a respectful distance; it is used in a similar
way in Q's opening direction to III.1.
The sword and buckler, carried as if
in formal procession, represent Falstaff ironically as the hero of Shrews-

bury, where he 'killed' the dead Hotspur (see *1 Henry IV*, v.4.126). J.
Dover Wilson proposed that Falstaff
should hobble in with a stick, because of his sore toe (see line 247),
so that his entry is a ludicrous imitation of Northumberland's with his
nice crutch (I.1.45).
buckler shield
1 *giant* (ironically: the Page is very
small)
2 *water* urine
4 *owed* owned
6 *gird* gibe, jeer
7 *foolish-compounded* compounded of folly
8 *intends* inclines, tends
14 *whoreson* abominable (but sometimes,

fitter to be worn in my cap than to wait at my heels. I
was never manned with an agate till now, but I will inset
you neither in gold nor silver, but in vile apparel, and
send you back again to your master for a jewel – the
juvenal the Prince your master, whose chin is not yet
fledge. I will sooner have a beard grow in the palm of   20
my hand than he shall get one off his cheek; and yet he
will not stick to say his face is a face-royal. God may
finish it when He will, 'tis not a hair amiss yet. He may
keep it still at a face-royal, for a barber shall never earn
sixpence out of it. And yet he'll be crowing as if he had
writ man ever since his father was a bachelor. He may
keep his own grace, but he's almost out of mine, I can
assure him. What said Master Dommelton about the
satin for my short cloak and my slops?

PAGE He said, sir, you should procure him better assur-   30
ance than Bardolph. He would not take his bond and
yours; he liked not the security.

FALSTAFF Let him be damned like the glutton! Pray

---

as here, used with humorous familiarity)
mandrake. The Page, being small, is
likened to the plant with a tap root
subdivided so that it was said to
look like a man.
14–15 *thou art fitter to be worn in my cap*.
The Page is so small he might more
appropriately be worn as a brooch in
a man's cap than follow in his
footsteps.
16 *manned with* attended by
agate (small person, like the tiny figures that were carved on agates used
as jewellery or for seals)
19 *juvenal* young man (perhaps intended
as a play on the sound of *jewel*)
20 *fledge* covered with down
22 *stick* hesitate
a face-royal. The meaning is simply 'a
first-class face', but the implication
may be that it cannot be touched (by

a razor), as a stag-royal might not be
hunted by any but the king. There is
also a play on 'royal', a coin worth
10s., and the 'face' of that coin. This
meaning is taken up in lines 24–5
23 *a hair* (1) a hair of the beard; (2) one
iota
26 *writ* called himself
27 *grace* (1) title (as 'Your grace'); (2)
favour
28 *Dommelton*. F spells this '*Dombledon*';
the meaning of the word in its various forms in different dialects is
'blockhead'.
29 *short cloak* (probably a garment fashionable in Tudor, not Henrician,
times)
slops (wide knee-length breeches)
33 *the glutton*. Falstaff refers to the parable of Dives and Lazarus (Luke 16),
which clearly made a deep impression
on him, for he refers to it twice in

God his tongue be hotter! A whoreson Achitophel! A
rascally yea-forsooth knave, to bear a gentleman in hand,
and then stand upon security! The whoreson smoothy-
pates do now wear nothing but high shoes and bunches
of keys at their girdles; and if a man is through with

1 Henry IV (III.3.31 and IV.2.24). His
awareness of the Scriptures is strong.
He refers to the Prodigal Son at
II.1.143–4 in this play and at IV.2.33
of *1 Henry IV*; and in *The Merry
Wives of Windsor*, IV.5.7, his chamber
is said to be painted 'fresh and new'
with the story of the Prodigal. In
view of his behaviour, his regard for
these parables is ironic, but in view
of his association with the Morality
tradition (see the Introduction, pages
439 and 445–6), the relationship is
appropriate.

34 *his tongue be hotter*. Dives, when in
hell, begged Lazarus to dip the tip of
his finger in water and cool his
tongue (Luke 16.24). Falstaff obviously knows the details of the parable, not merely its general outline.
Achitophel. Achitophel sided with Absalom in his conspiracy against
David, but his advice was rejected in
favour of Hushai's and he hanged
himself (2 Samuel 16.20–17.22). The
story was well-known in the sixteenth century. Achitophel is dramatized briefly in George Peele's play
*The Love of King David and Fair
Bethsabe* (printed in 1599), but he
plays a large part in the Latin drama
Absalom written by Thomas Watson
some fifty or sixty years before
Peele's play. Watson's dramatization
was probably unknown to Shakespeare, but it well represents Tudor
attitudes as propounded by the
preachers of the time, with which he
would have been familiar. Achitophel is described as a perfidious

adviser to David, but his dilemma is
well dramatized and much is made
of his anguish when rejected. There
is not only dramatic irony in Falstaff's mentioning Achitophel, whose
rejection and broken heart anticipate
his own; the biblical account indicates that the peculiar wickedness of
Achitophel's treachery was that 'the
counsel of Achitophel which he coun-
selled in those days was as a man had
asked counsel at the oracle of God:
even so was all the counsel of Achitophel, both with David and with
Absalom' (2 Samuel 16.23). Support
for rebellion from men of God was
as heinous in David's time as in the
Tudor period (see the note to
I.I.201).

35 *yea-forsooth knave* (a tradesman who
could manage no more than the mild-
est of oaths in making his protesta-
tions)
bear . . . in hand encourage with false
expectations

36 *stand upon* insist on

36–7 *smoothy-pates*. Puritan tradesmen
(the same who were given to mild
oaths) cropped their hair short in a
style later associated with the Round-
heads. Many editors choose the F
reading, 'smooth-pates', but Q's version seems more appropriately to express Falstaff's contempt.

37 *high shoes* built-up shoes (appropriate
for upstarts)

37–8 *bunches of keys* (symbols of (false)
importance)

38 *is through* has agreed

them in honest taking up, then they must stand upon 40
security. I had as lief they would put ratsbane in my
mouth as offer to stop it with security. I looked 'a should
have sent me two-and-twenty yards of satin, as I am a
true knight, and he sends me 'security'! Well he may
sleep in security, for he hath the horn of abundance, and
the lightness of his wife shines through it − and yet
cannot he see, though he have his own lanthorn to light
him. Where's Bardolph?

PAGE He's gone in Smithfield to buy your worship a
horse.

FALSTAFF I bought him in Paul's, and he'll buy me a 50
horse in Smithfield. An I could get me but a wife in the
stews, I were manned, horsed, and wived.

Enter the Lord Chief Justice and his Servant

39 *taking up* agreement, bargain
40 *had as lief* would as willingly
ratsbane poison
41 *looked* expected
'a he
43 *security.* 'Security' (of mind) usually
meant 'false security', 'complacency',
with an element of culpable negligence, especially in religious matters.
44 *horn of abundance* (1) cornucopia (in
his trading); (2) cuckold's horn (citizens' wives were said to be particularly unfaithful)
45 *lightness* infidelity
45–7 *yet cannot he see, though he have his
own lanthorn to light him.* The tradesman cannot see his wife's infidelity
either by the light of his own cuckold's horn or by his wife's *lightness* −
and his security is false.
46 *lanthorn* (the old form of 'lantern',
preserved here for the sake of the
pun)
48 *in Smithfield.* 'In' was commonly used
for 'into' in the sixteenth century
(and later). F and many editors print
'into'. Live animals were sold at

Smithfield (originally a 'smooth
field') from well before the Tudor
period until 1855. The horses sold
there had a poor reputation.
50 *Paul's.* The nave of St Paul's Cathedral was used as a place where servants might find new masters.
51 *An* if
51–2 *a wife in the stews.* Reference to a
wife now completes a trio found in a
popular saying of the time that a
man must not choose a wife in Westminster, a horse in Smithfield, or a
servant in Paul's, 'lest he choose a
quean, a jade, or a knave'. A 'quean'
is a prostitute; hence Falstaff's reference to the *stews* (brothels).
52 (stage direction) *Lord Chief Justice.*
Sir William Gascoigne, appointed
Lord Chief Justice in 1401, was a
man of independence. He refused to
sentence the Archbishop of York to
death, and, traditionally at least, he
was responsible for committing
Prince Hal to the King's Bench
prison, though this distinction has
been claimed for two other judges

PAGE Sir, here comes the nobleman that committed the
Prince for striking him about Bardolph.

FALSTAFF Wait close; I will not see him.

LORD CHIEF JUSTICE What's he that goes there?

SERVANT Falstaff, an't please your lordship.

LORD CHIEF JUSTICE He that was in question for the
robbery?

60 SERVANT He, my lord – but he hath since done good
service at Shrewsbury, and, as I hear, is now going with
some charge to the Lord John of Lancaster.

LORD CHIEF JUSTICE What, to York? Call him back
again.

SERVANT Sir John Falstaff!

FALSTAFF Boy, tell him I am deaf.

PAGE You must speak louder; my master is deaf.

LORD CHIEF JUSTICE I am sure he is, to the hearing of
anything good. Go pluck him by the elbow; I must
70 speak with him.

SERVANT Sir John!

FALSTAFF What! A young knave, and begging! Is there
not wars? Is there not employment? Doth not the King
lack subjects? Do not the rebels need soldiers? Though

(one being Gascoigne's successor, Sir William Hankford). Gascoigne's reappointment by Hal (v.2) is contrary to fact. He was summoned to the first parliament of Henry V's reign but he either was dismissed, resigned, or died before that parliament met on 15 May 1413; Hankford was appointed from 29 March of that year according to the patent of his office, though 1414 is given by one authority. Three dates have been put forward for Gascoigne's death, 1412, 1413, and 1419. There was nothing remarkable in a Lord Chief Justice's being concerned with such a relatively trivial matter as that dramatized here.

Servant (tipstaff)

54 *for striking him.* The first known refer-

ence to this incident is no earlier than Sir Thomas Elyot's *The Book Named the Governor* (1531). It is also dramatized in *The Famous Victories of Henry the Fifth*, which was performed a few years before *2 Henry IV*. In Elyot's account Hal only threatens the Lord Chief Justice, but in the anonymous play there is a stage direction '*He giveth him a box on the ear*'. See the Introduction, page 435.

55 *close* concealed

58 *in question* examined judicially

72–100 Shakespeare employs here the comic device (still in use) where a comedian bullies a weak character and then is obsequious to a stronger one.

72–3 *Is . . . wars.* The singular form of

it be a shame to be on any side but one, it is worse shame
to beg than to be on the worst side, were it worse than
the name of rebellion can tell how to make it.

SERVANT You mistake me, sir.

FALSTAFF Why, sir, did I say you were an honest man?
Setting my knighthood and my soldiership aside, I had   80
lied in my throat if I had said so.

SERVANT I pray you, sir, then set your knighthood and
your soldiership aside, and give me leave to tell you you
lie in your throat if you say I am any other than an
honest man.

FALSTAFF I give thee leave to tell me so? I lay aside that
which grows to me? If thou gettest any leave of me,
hang me. If thou takest leave, thou wert better be
hanged. You hunt counter. Hence! Avaunt!

SERVANT Sir, my lord would speak with you.   90

LORD CHIEF JUSTICE Sir John Falstaff, a word with
you.

FALSTAFF My good lord! God give your lordship good
time of day. I am glad to see your lordship abroad; I
heard say your lordship was sick. I hope your lordship
goes abroad by advice. Your lordship, though not clean
past your youth, have yet some smack of age in you,

---

the verb with a plural subject was
acceptable in Elizabethan grammar.

80 *Setting my knighthood and my soldiership
aside*. Knighthood was, properly, too
honourable an estate to admit of
lying, and the soldier was supposed
to be too brave to descend to deceit-
fulness. Thus theoretically Falstaff is
doubly protected against accusations
of lying, but for the sake of the
point he will doff both these
honours.

81 *in my throat* outrageously

87 *grows to* is integral to

89 *hunt counter* follow the wrong scent,
are completely mistaken. There is a
pun on 'Counter' as the name of a

debtors' prison, or, more generally, a
petty legal officer who arrested for
debt and served writs.

97 *age*. This is F's reading; Q has 'an
ague', which is possible, since it relates to the Lord Chief Justice's sickness (line 95), but it may be a compositor's error. To say an old man
had 'yet some smack of youth' would
suggest that, despite his years, he
had retained a spirit of youthfulness
and could be a compliment. Falstaff's
suggestion that the Lord Chief Justice has *some smack of age* implies that
he is prematurely old; and this is
reiterated in the following phrase –
that the Lord Chief Justice has *some*

some relish of the saltness of time; and I most humbly
beseech your lordship to have a reverend care of your
health.

100

LORD CHIEF JUSTICE Sir John, I sent for you – before
your expedition to Shrewsbury.

FALSTAFF An't please your lordship, I hear his majesty
is returned with some discomfort from Wales.

LORD CHIEF JUSTICE I talk not of his majesty. You
would not come when I sent for you.

FALSTAFF And I hear, moreover, his highness is fallen
into this same whoreson apoplexy.

LORD CHIEF JUSTICE Well, God mend him! I pray you

110

let me speak with you.

FALSTAFF This apoplexy, as I take it, is a kind of
lethargy, an't please your lordship, a kind of sleeping in
the blood, a whoreson tingling.

LORD CHIEF JUSTICE What tell you me of it? Be it as
it is.

FALSTAFF It hath it original from much grief, from study,
and perturbation of the brain. I have read the cause of
his effects in Galen; it is a kind of deafness.

---

relish ... of time. Falstaff is super-
ficially solicitous for the health of
the Lord Chief Justice, but simultaneously continues to insult him by harp-
ing on the degree to which he has
aged. It is just possible that a particularly weak pun is intended on *age/*
'ague'; compare *gravity/gravy* (lines
163–4).

98 *saltness.* This could mean youthfulness or maturity and is appropriately
ambiguous, Falstaff meaning one
thing but being able, if challenged,
to claim he intends the opposite.

108 *apoplexy* paralysis. Falstaff's account
of the symptoms in the lines that
follow is correct. Henry IV did
suffer from 'apoplexy' but not as

early as this; see the headnote to
IV.4.

114 *What* for what, why

116, 118 *it ... his* its ... its. These
forms of neuter possessive pronoun
were being replaced by 'its' in Shakespeare's lifetime. In the first Folio
'its' appears ten times, on eight occasions in very late plays.

116 *original* origins
grief anxiety

118 *Galen* (Greek physician of the
second century A.D., still highly regarded in the seventeenth century).
Falstaff may be showing off, but, as
with the Bible (see the note to line
33), his knowledge is more than
merely superficial.

LORD CHIEF JUSTICE I think you are fallen into the
disease, for you hear not what I say to you.   120

FALSTAFF Very well, my lord, very well. Rather, an't
please you, it is the disease of not listening, the malady
of not marking, that I am troubled withal.

LORD CHIEF JUSTICE To punish you by the heels
would amend the attention of your ears, and I care not
if I do become your physician.

FALSTAFF I am as poor as Job, my lord, but not so
patient. Your lordship may minister the potion of
imprisonment to me in respect of poverty; but how I
should be your patient to follow your prescriptions, the   130
wise may make some dram of a scruple, or indeed a
scruple itself.

LORD CHIEF JUSTICE I sent for you, when there were
matters against you for your life, to come speak with me.

FALSTAFF As I was then advised by my learned counsel
in the laws of this land-service, I did not come.

LORD CHIEF JUSTICE Well, the truth is, Sir John, you
live in great infamy.

FALSTAFF He that buckles himself in my belt cannot live
in less.   140

LORD CHIEF JUSTICE Your means are very slender, and
your waste is great.

---

121 FALSTAFF. Q's speech prefix here
is 'Old.', which abbreviates Falstaff's
original name, Oldcastle. See the Introduction, page 445, and the
Account of the Text, page 460.
124 *punish you by the heels* put you in the
stocks (or in prison)
129 *in respect of poverty* (because he is too
poor to pay a fine)
131 *make some dram of a scruple* feel a
particle of doubt.
   Dram and *scruple* are quantities for
measuring potions (line 128).
134 *for your life* of a capital nature (that

is, in which his life might be forfeit)
135–6 *advised . . . land-service*. This is a
cunning quibble.
   Land-service was military service, and
whilst engaged in the campaign cul-
minating at Shrewsbury Falstaff was
immune from arrest. But *land-service*
might well refer to the service he
had attempted at Gad's Hill, robbery,
and he was advised not to risk facing
a charge on that account.
138 *infamy* (deliberately misunderstood
by Falstaff, who treats it as if it were
a fabric)

FALSTAFF I would it were otherwise; I would my means were greater and my waist slenderer.

LORD CHIEF JUSTICE You have misled the youthful Prince.

FALSTAFF The young Prince hath misled me. I am the fellow with the great belly, and he my dog.

LORD CHIEF JUSTICE Well, I am loath to gall a new
150   healed wound. Your day's service at Shrewsbury hath a little gilded over your night's exploit on Gad's Hill. You may thank th'unquiet time for your quiet o'erposting that action.

FALSTAFF My lord!

LORD CHIEF JUSTICE But since all is well, keep it so. Wake not a sleeping wolf.

FALSTAFF To wake a wolf is as bad as smell a fox.

LORD CHIEF JUSTICE What! You are as a candle, the better part burnt out.

---

147 *misled*. This may be simply a repetition of *misled* in line 145, but (especially with the puzzling sentence that follows – see the next note) it could be the dialect form 'mizzled', meaning 'confused' or 'mystified'. This word was in use in Shakespeare's day, and could be spelt 'misled'.

147–8 *I am ... my dog*. Dr Johnson, in his edition of Shakespeare, bluntly commented 'I do not understand this joke', and no one since has offered a satisfactory interpretation. It is possible that a topical character is referred to. The Prince returns the compliment at II.2.100–101: *I do allow this wen to be as familiar with me as my dog*.

151 *exploit on Gad's Hill*. See *1 Henry IV*, II.2.

152 *th'unquiet time* (a phrase used by the historians Hall and Holinshed in the titles of their accounts of the reign of Henry IV; see the Introduction, page 433)

152–3 *your quiet o'erposting that action* having your offence quietly passed over

157–9 *To wake ... burnt out*. Falstaff responds to the Lord Chief Justice's proverb (a version of 'let sleeping dogs lie') by comparing it with a tag meaning 'to have one's suspicions aroused'. The comparison seems a little forced, but Falstaff may be extending the expression to mean 'to sense trouble': to arouse a sleeping dog, as to have one's suspicions aroused, promises trouble. The Lord Chief Justice's response seems both a rebuke and a warning: the candle of Falstaff's life is more than half over, and what has been used up (which would hardly have the Lord Chief Justice's approval) was the *better part*; what is to come can surely only bring Falstaff more trouble. The relationship of these expressions is difficult to pin down precisely, but the general sense seems clear.

FALSTAFF A wassail candle, my lord, all tallow — if I did   160
say of wax, my growth would approve the truth.

LORD CHIEF JUSTICE There is not a white hair in your
face but should have his effect of gravity.

FALSTAFF His effect of gravy, gravy, gravy.

LORD CHIEF JUSTICE You follow the young Prince up
and down, like his ill angel.

FALSTAFF Not so, my lord; your ill angel is light, but I
hope he that looks upon me will take me without
weighing. And yet in some respects, I grant, I cannot
go — I cannot tell. Virtue is of so little regard in these   170
costermongers' times that true valour is turned bear-

160 *wassail candle* (large candle used at
feasts and designed to last the whole
night)
  tallow (made from animal fat, which
Falstaff presumably considers more
appropriate for him than wax, which
is secreted by bees)
161 *wax, my growth* (punning on 'wax'
meaning 'to grow')
  approve prove
163, 164 *gravity . . . gravy*. If the two first
syllables are pronounced alike (as
there is some evidence they were in
Shakespeare's time) a kind of pun is
obtained. The humour is not original
to Shakespeare; John Lyly, in his
play *Endymion* (published in 1591),
puns on 'grave' and 'gravity'.
164 *of gravy* (loosely, 'of being bathed in
sweat')
166 *ill angel*. Each man and woman was
said to be attended by a good and an
evil angel, and these were dramatized
in earlier drama, one warning and
one tempting. Shakespeare bur-
lesques their advice in Launcelot's
monologue in *The Merchant of Venice*,
11.2.1–28. Here Falstaff's association
with the Moralities is lightly touched
on (see the Introduction, page 445).
See also 11.4.330.

167 *your ill angel is light*. An angel was a
coin worth a third of £1; when
clipped it was said to be 'light' (of
some of its metal). There may be an
allusion to Satan's power to transform himself into 'an angel of light'
(2 Corinthians 11.14); if so Shakespeare may have expected his audience to remember the adjacent
verses, which speak of false apostles
and deceitful workers (13) and of
those 'whose end shall be according
to their works' (15), the fate in store
for Falstaff.
168 *take* accept
170 *go* (1) walk; (2) pass as good
money
  cannot tell (1) don't know; (2) cannot
count (as good money)
170–71 *these costermongers' times*. A costermonger was originally a man who
sold apples ('costards') from a
barrow. The costermonger lived by
his wits (so Falstaff's contempt may
rebound on him), but the implication
of the phrase is that life is reduced to
the lowest kind of buying and
selling.
171–2 *bearherd*. The man who looked
after bears used for bear-dancing or
bear-baiting was poorly regarded.

herd; pregnancy is made a tapster, and his quick wit
wasted in giving reckonings; all the other gifts appertinent to man, as the malice of this age shapes them, are
not worth a gooseberry. You that are old consider not
the capacities of us that are young; you do measure the
heat of our livers with the bitterness of your galls; and
we that are in the vaward of our youth, I must confess,
are wags too.

180 LORD CHIEF JUSTICE Do you set down your name in
the scroll of youth, that are written down old with all
the characters of age? Have you not a moist eye, a dry
hand, a yellow cheek, a white beard, a decreasing leg,
an increasing belly? Is not your voice broken, your wind
short, your chin double, your wit single, and every part
about you blasted with antiquity? And will you yet call
yourself young? Fie, fie, fie, Sir John!

FALSTAFF My lord, I was born about three of the clock
in the afternoon, with a white head, and something a

The spelling in Q, 'Berod', probably
indicates the pronunciation.

172 *pregnancy* quick-wittedness

172–3 *tapster ... giving reckonings.* The
intellectual ability of a tapster is to
be found only in his capacity to
deliver a bill for what has been
drunk.

173–4 *appertinent* belonging

177 *livers.* The liver was thought to be
the seat of violent passions.
galls bile

178 *in the vaward of our youth.* Falstaff
repeats his claim to be young, but
presumably those in the forefront or
vanguard (*vaward*) of youth are the
most advanced in years and so approaching middle age.

179 *wags too* (1) waggish as well as youthful; (2) waggish just as are young
people

182 *characters* (1) characteristics; (2)
letters

moist watery

182–3 *a dry hand* (said to be a sign of old
age)

183 *a decreasing leg.* Shakespeare may be
using *decreasing* to mean 'weakening'
or 'shrinking' (in the hams), but he
may be suggesting that, as Falstaff's
girth increases, so his legs seem to
diminish in length and to be less
fitted to support his weight.

185 *single* feeble

188–9 *I was born ... afternoon.* Falstaff
probably means he was born mature,
but as a nineteenth-century editor
(R. G. White) suggested, it might
also be implied that Falstaff, as a
dramatic creation, was born at the
time of the theatre performance
(which, in the public theatres of
Shakespeare's day, was in the afternoon).

189 *something a* a somewhat

round belly. For my voice, I have lost it with hallooing,   190
and singing of anthems. To approve my youth further,
I will not. The truth is, I am only old in judgement and
understanding; and he that will caper with me for a
thousand marks, let him lend me the money, and have
at him! For the box of the ear that the Prince gave you,
he gave it like a rude prince, and you took it like a
sensible lord. I have checked him for it, and the young
lion repents – (*aside*) marry, not in ashes and sackcloth,
but in new silk and old sack.

LORD CHIEF JUSTICE Well, God send the Prince a   200
better companion!

FALSTAFF God send the companion a better prince! I
cannot rid my hands of him.

LORD CHIEF JUSTICE Well, the King hath severed you
and Prince Harry. I hear you are going with Lord John
of Lancaster against the Archbishop and the Earl of
Northumberland.

FALSTAFF Yea, I thank your pretty sweet wit for it. But
look you pray, all you that kiss my lady Peace at home,
that our armies join not in a hot day; for, by the Lord,   210
I take but two shirts out with me, and I mean not to

190 *hallooing* shouting (when following hounds or on the battlefield)
191 *singing of anthems*. In *1 Henry IV*, II.4.128–9, Falstaff wishes he were a weaver so that he might sing at his work, as weavers (many of whom were puritans) were noted for doing: 'I could sing psalms – or anything'. See also the note to line 33 above.
193 *caper with me* challenge me to a dancing contest
193–4 *a thousand marks* £666. The mark was the value of two thirds of £1.
194–5 *have at him!* I'll be at him!
197 *sensible* (1) reasonable; (2) capable of feeling the pain of the blow
checked rebuked

198 *marry* (a corruption of 'Mary' (the Virgin), commonly used as a mild oath)
198–9 *ashes and sackcloth . . . sack*. This modification of the biblical mourning to that of much less deep regret (based on the proverbial 'to mourn in sack and claret') is an example of the turn of wit that seemed second nature to Falstaff in *1 Henry IV* but is much less apparent in this play.
199 *old sack*. The precise nature of the wine Falstaff drank is not known. 'Sack' may have been a general term for sweet white wine of the sherry and canary varieties. Old sack was preferred to new.
209 *look you* take care to

sweat extraordinarily. If it be a hot day, and I brandish anything but a bottle – I would I might never spit white again. There is not a dangerous action can peep out his head but I am thrust upon it. Well, I cannot last ever – but it was alway yet the trick of our English nation, if they have a good thing, to make it too common. If ye will needs say I am an old man, you should give me rest. I would to God my name were not so terrible to the enemy as it is. I were better to be eaten to death with a rust than to be scoured to nothing with perpetual motion.

LORD CHIEF JUSTICE Well, be honest, be honest, and God bless your expedition!

FALSTAFF Will your lordship lend me a thousand pound to furnish me forth?

LORD CHIEF JUSTICE Not a penny, not a penny! You are too impatient to bear crosses. Fare you well. Commend me to my cousin Westmorland.

Exeunt Lord Chief Justice and Servant

FALSTAFF If I do, fillip me with a three-man beetle. A man can no more separate age and covetousness than 'a can part young limbs and lechery; but the gout galls the one, and the pox pinches the other; and so both the degrees prevent my curses. Boy!

PAGE Sir?

212–3 *I brandish anything but a bottle*. In *1 Henry IV*, v.3.55, Hal, much to his annoyance, finds sack instead of a pistol in Falstaff's holster.

213 *spit white*. It is not clear what is meant here. Editors since the eighteenth century have attempted to pin the meaning down by reference to a variety of Tudor sources. The most likely meaning is probably 'to spit clean', that is, healthily. As one Tudor authority puts it, 'the white spittle, not knotty, signifieth health'.

221–2 *perpetual motion*. The idea of per-

petual motion, although not new, attracted some attention in Elizabeth's reign.

228 *crosses*. This is yet another money pun: (1) coins with a cross on one side; (2) afflictions.

230 *fillip* strike smartly
three-man beetle (ram or sledgehammer so large that three men are needed to use it)

233 *pinches* torments

233–4 *both the degrees prevent my curses* both age and youth have their own curses which anticipate mine

FALSTAFF What money is in my purse?

PAGE Seven groats and two pence.

FALSTAFF I can get no remedy against this consumption
of the purse; borrowing only lingers and lingers it out,
but the disease is incurable. Go bear this letter to my   240
lord of Lancaster; this to the Prince; this to the Earl
of Westmorland – and this to old mistress Ursula, whom
I have weekly sworn to marry since I perceived the first
white hair of my chin. About it! You know where to
find me.   *Exit Page*

A pox of this gout! Or a gout of this pox! For the one
or the other plays the rogue with my great toe. 'Tis no
matter if I do halt; I have the wars for my colour, and
my pension shall seem the more reasonable. A good wit
will make use of anything; I will turn diseases to com-   250
modity.   *Exit*

Enter the Archbishop of York, Thomas Mowbray the   1.3
Earl Marshal, Lord Hastings, and Lord Bardolph

ARCHBISHOP
Thus have you heard our cause and known our means,

236 *What ... purse?* Pages carried the
master's purse and made payments
on his behalf (as at II.4.368).

237 *groats* (4d. pieces)

241 *this to the Prince* (the letter that Bardolph delivers at II.2.94)

242–3 *Ursula, whom I have weekly sworn to
marry.* At II.1.84–90 Mistress Quickly
asserts that Falstaff once swore to
marry her. Whether she is Ursula or
whether Falstaff has been swearing
to marry another is not clear. In
Henry V Mistress Quickly is given
the first name Nell.

248 *halt* limp
colour pretext

250–51 *commodity* self-interest

1.3 Q here includes an entry for Fauconbridge, but there is no part for him to
play and he does not appear in F. Holinshed mentions him as one of the rebels,
and it is presumably from that source
that Shakespeare took the name. See also
the headnote to IV.4 and the Account of
the Text, page 460. The other rebels mentioned by Holinshed all enter here.

(stage direction) *Mowbray* (son of the
Mowbray banished for life in *Richard
II*)
Hastings (historically not a lord but a
knight, Sir Ralph Hastings)

1 *Thus have you heard ...* The Archbishop's first line, like Falstaff's in
1.2 and the Hostess's in II.1, refers to

And, my most noble friends, I pray you all
Speak plainly your opinions of our hopes.
And first, Lord Marshal, what say you to it?

MOWBRAY

I well allow the occasion of our arms,
But gladly would be better satisfied
How in our means we should advance ourselves
To look with forehead bold and big enough
Upon the power and puissance of the King.

HASTINGS

10   Our present musters grow upon the file
To five-and-twenty thousand men of choice;
And our supplies live largely in the hope
Of great Northumberland, whose bosom burns,
With an incensed fire of injuries.

LORD BARDOLPH

The question then, Lord Hastings, standeth thus —
Whether our present five-and-twenty thousand
May hold up head without Northumberland.

HASTINGS

With him we may.

LORD BARDOLPH   Yea, marry, there's the point;
But if without him we be thought too feeble,
20   My judgement is, we should not step too far

---

an action or conversation already
completed. This simple dramatic
device enables the new scenes to
move with pace from the beginning
and it helps to avoid any slackening
of momentum as the various actions
of the play are introduced. It is now
necessary, of course, for Shakespeare
leagues' reactions to the plan.
cause matter in dispute
to indicate what is proposed, and so
the Archbishop asks for his col-

4 *Lord Marshal* (only a courtesy title; the
Mowbrays claimed to be Earl Mar-
shals of England, but the office had
been given to Westmorland)
5 *allow* grant
7 *in* within
9,77 *puissance* strength
10 *file* roll
11 *men of choice* picked men
12 *supplies* reinforcements
largely abundantly

Till we had his assistance by the hand;
For in a theme so bloody-faced as this,
Conjecture, expectation, and surmise
Of aids incertain should not be admitted.

ARCHBISHOP

'Tis very true, Lord Bardolph, for indeed
It was young Hotspur's cause at Shrewsbury.

LORD BARDOLPH

It was, my lord; who lined himself with hope,
Eating the air and promise of supply,
Flattering himself in project of a power
Much smaller than the smallest of his thoughts,   30
And so, with great imagination
Proper to madmen, led his powers to death,
And winking leaped into destruction.

HASTINGS

But, by your leave, it never yet did hurt
To lay down likelihoods and forms of hope.

LORD BARDOLPH

Yes, if this present quality of war,

26 *cause* matter of concern. This is the
reading in Q; F prints 'case'. 'Cause'
with this meaning occurs elsewhere
in Shakespeare's works.

27 *who* (Hotspur)
lined fortified

28 *air and promise*. F has 'on' for *and*,
which makes easy sense. But the Q
reading has been described as a 'particularly forceful hendiadys' (a complex idea expressed by two words
joined by 'and'). It is possible that
the F reading represents a weakening
by someone copying Shakespeare's
text without fully understanding
it. The *air* on which Hotspur had
to live was, of course, his father's
promise to send reinforcements (in *1*

Henry IV).

29 *project* anticipation

33 *winking* shutting his eyes (to the
facts)

36–55 *Yes ... or else*. These lines are
omitted from Q, perhaps because of
the complexity of the opening lines
(36–9) and because the lengthy version of the parable is covered ad-
equately, so far as the play's action is
concerned, by lines 58–62.

36–9 *Yes ... th'appearing buds*. This difficult passage has often been emended.
This edition follows F except that a
comma has been added after *Indeed*; a
comma is used instead of a colon
after *action*; a dash is used in place of
a colon after *hope*; and a comma is

Indeed, the instant action, a cause on foot,
Lives so in hope – as in an early spring
We see th'appearing buds; which to prove fruit
40   Hope gives not so much warrant, as despair
That frosts will bite them. When we mean to build,
We first survey the plot, then draw the model,
And when we see the figure of the house,
Then must we rate the cost of the erection,
Which if we find outweighs ability,
What do we then but draw anew the model
In fewer offices, or at least desist
To build at all? Much more, in this great work –
Which is almost to pluck a kingdom down
50   And set another up – should we survey
The plot of situation and the model,
Consent upon a sure foundation,
Question surveyors, know our own estate,
How able such a work to undergo,
To weigh against his opposite; or else
We fortify in paper and in figures,
Using the names of men instead of men,
Like one that draws the model of an house
Beyond his power to build it, who, half-through,
60   Gives o'er, and leaves his part-created cost

omitted after *spring*. The passage can
be interpreted: 'Yes, *if* the present
occasion for war, the action now
imminent – the cause already afoot –
does live so in hope (just as do the buds
which appear in an early spring)'.

41–62 *When we ... tyranny* (a lengthy
version of the parable of the builder,
Luke 14.28–30: 'For which of you,
disposed to build a tower, sitteth not
down before and counteth the cost,
whether he have sufficient to perform it? Lest at any time after he
hath laid the foundation and is not
able to perform it, all that behold it

begin to mock him, saying, "This
man began to build, and was not
able to make an end"')
42 *model* architectural plan
43 *figure* design
44 *rate* calculate
45 *ability* (to pay)
47 *offices* rooms
52 *Consent* agree
55 *his opposite* its contrary (that is, all
that stands against the success of our
building plan, and, by implication,
our political plot)
60 *his part-created cost* the half-built
object of his expenditure

A naked subject to the weeping clouds,
And waste for churlish winter's tyranny.

HASTINGS
Grant that our hopes, yet likely of fair birth,
Should be still-born, and that we now possessed
The utmost man of expectation,
I think we are so, body strong enough,
Even as we are, to equal with the King.

LORD BARDOLPH
What, is the King but five-and-twenty thousand?

HASTINGS
To us no more, nay, not so much, Lord Bardolph;
For his divisions, as the times do brawl,   70
Are in three heads: one power against the French;
And one against Glendower; perforce a third
Must take up us. So is the unfirm King
In three divided, and his coffers sound
With hollow poverty and emptiness.

ARCHBISHOP
That he should draw his several strengths together
And come against us in full puissance
Need not be dreaded.

HASTINGS   If he should do so,
He leaves his back unarmed, the French and Welsh
Baying him at the heels; never fear that.   80

LORD BARDOLPH
Who is it like should lead his forces hither?

HASTINGS
The Duke of Lancaster, and Westmorland;

---

62 *waste* wasteland (with the implication
of the wasteful use of effort and
resources)
65 *The utmost man of expectation* every
man that we could possibly expect
70 *as the times do brawl* in these discordant times
74 *sound* ring (as does an empty metal
vessel)
76 *several* various

81 *is it like should* is likely to. (At
1.1.134–5 it was stated in Lord Bardolph's presence that the forces were
led by Lancaster and Westmorland.)
82 *Duke of Lancaster.* This title actually
belonged to Prince Henry. Prince
John was born at Lancaster and is
called John of Lancaster by Holinshed. See also the note to IV.1.129.

Against the Welsh, himself and Harry Monmouth;
But who is substituted 'gainst the French
I have no certain notice.

ARCHBISHOP   Let us on,
And publish the occasion of our arms.
The commonwealth is sick of their own choice;
Their over-greedy love hath surfeited.
An habitation giddy and unsure
90   Hath he that buildeth on the vulgar heart.
O thou fond many, with what loud applause
Didst thou beat heaven with blessing Bolingbroke,
Before he was what thou wouldst have him be!
And being now trimmed in thine own desires,
Thou, beastly feeder, art so full of him
That thou provokest thyself to cast him up.
So, so, thou common dog, didst thou disgorge
Thy glutton bosom of the royal Richard –
And now thou wouldst eat thy dead vomit up,
100   And howlest to find it. What trust is in these times?
They that, when Richard lived, would have him die
Are now become enamoured on his grave.
Thou that threwest dust upon his goodly head,

84 *substituted* delegated
85 *notice* information
89–90 *An habitation . . . heart* (an echo of
    Luke 6.49: 'But he that heareth and
    doeth it not is like a man that with-
    out foundation built an house upon
    the earth; against which the flood
    did beat vehemently, and it fell
    immediately')
91 *fond* foolish
    many multitude
94 *trimmed* dressed, tricked out
99 *now thou wouldst eat thy dead vomit up.*
    The dog that returns to its vomit
    was proverbial in Shakespeare's day
    and is found in the Old and New
    Testaments (Proverbs 26.11 and 2

Peter 2.22, the latter referring to the
expression as 'a true proverb').
100 *What trust is in these times?* Shake-
    speare has just had Falstaff inveigh
    against *these costermongers' times* (1.2.
    170–71). Northumberland, by sup-
    porting Bolingbroke against Rich-
    ard, had a large part in creating *these
    times.* The rebels, like Falstaff, must
    stand partly self-convicted by their
    condemnation of others.
103–5 *Thou that . . . Bolingbroke.* These
    lines recall York's description of the
    entry into London of Richard and
    Bolingbroke, one disgraced, one tri-
    umphant (*Richard II.* v.2.1–40; the
    throwing of dust occurs in line 6).

When through proud London he came sighing on
After th'admirèd heels of Bolingbroke,
Cryest now 'O earth, yield us that king again,
And take thou this!' O thoughts of men accursed!
Past and to come seems best; things present, worst.

MOWBRAY
Shall we go draw our numbers and set on?

HASTINGS
We are time's subjects, and time bids be gone.   110

Exeunt

Enter the Hostess of the tavern with two officers, Fang   II.I
and Snare

HOSTESS Master Fang, have you entered the action?

FANG It is entered.

HOSTESS Where's your yeoman? Is't a lusty yeoman?
Will 'a stand to't?

FANG Sirrah – where's Snare?

HOSTESS O Lord, ay! Good Master Snare.

---

108 *seems* (the singular form for the plural; see the note to 1.2.72–3)

109 *draw our numbers* assemble our army

II.I (stage direction) *the Hostess* (Mistress Quickly)

1,6 *Master*. Fang and Snare would not be entitled to be called *Master* (they are, respectively, a sergeant and his yeoman), but the Hostess often elevates the rank of those she addresses. Pistol is to her a *Captain* (II.4.134), and in lines 67–8 of this scene the Lord Chief Justice is called *your grace*, the form of address reserved for royalty, dukes, and archbishops.

1 *entered the action* begun the lawsuit (on the Hostess's behalf)

5 *Sirrah*. It has been suggested that Fang should be attended by a boy to whom *Sirrah* is addressed, but it is at least as likely that, as 'sirrah' could be used for either sex, he is speaking to the Hostess, or else that he is addressing Snare (and then notices his seeming absence): as this line follows the Hostess's questions about Snare, Fang might be calling him up to display his lustiness to her.

SNARE (*from behind them*) Here, here!

FANG Snare, we must arrest Sir John Falstaff.

HOSTESS Yea, good Master Snare, I have entered him and
all.

SNARE It may chance cost some of us our lives, for he will
stab.

HOSTESS Alas the day, take heed of him – he stabbed me
in mine own house, most beastly, in good faith. 'A cares
not what mischief he does, if his weapon be out. He
will foin like any devil; he will spare neither man,
woman, nor child.

FANG If I can close with him, I care not for his thrust.

HOSTESS No, nor I neither; I'll be at your elbow.

FANG An I but fist him once, an 'a come but within my
vice –

HOSTESS I am undone by his going, I warrant you, he's an
infinitive thing upon my score. Good Master Fang,
hold him sure; good Master Snare, let him not 'scape.
'A comes continuantly to Pie Corner – saving your

---

7 (stage direction) *from behind them*. This
is an editorial addition based on the
assumption that Snare follows so
closely on his master's heels that
Fang does not see him – an obvious
opportunity for comic business. It
has been suggested that, since the
company had an exceptionally thin
actor for the part of the First Beadle
(see the note to the opening stage
direction of v.4), he may also have
played Snare. The seeming absence
of a thin Snare could easily be made
visually comic.

13 *he stabbed me*. The Hostess, like so
many characters of this kind in the
plays of the period (for example, the
vintner's wife, Mistress Mulligrub,
in John Marston's *The Dutch Courtesan*, published in 1605), speaks a
double language. Her simple protesta-
tions are full of words that need no

stretch of imagination to take on
sexual meanings: *stabbed, weapon, foin,
thrust, undone,* and so on.

16 *foin* (technically, to thrust with a
pointed weapon; but see the previous
note)

21 *vice*. Q reads 'view', but that may be
a misreading of the manuscript caused
by the printer's inclining unwittingly
to an easier meaning. F's *vice* means
'grip', appropriate for Fang.

23 *infinitive* infinite. The Hostess has a
love of fine words (for all her impreci-
sion about their meanings and
forms); perhaps she picks them up
from her customers – that is the
source of Mistress Mulligrub's el-
evated vocabulary (*The Dutch Courtesan*, III.4.8–10).

upon my score in my accounts ('on the
slate')

25 *continuantly* (for 'incontinently') imme-

manhoods – to buy a saddle, and he is indited to dinner
to the Lubber's Head in Lumbert Street to Master
Smooth's the silkman. I pray you, since my exion is
entered, and my case so openly known to the world, let
him be brought in to his answer. A hundred mark is a long   30
one for a poor lone woman to bear, and I have borne,
and borne, and borne, and have been fubbed off, and
fubbed off, and fubbed off, from this day to that day,
that it is a shame to be thought on. There is no honesty
in such dealing, unless a woman should be made an ass,
and a beast, to bear every knave's wrong.

Enter Falstaff, Bardolph, and the Page

diately. Q prints 'continually', but,
as A. R. Humphreys puts it, 'F's fine
word is surely Shakespeare's'. Q's
reading is probably a mistaken attempt to 'correct' the Hostess's gran-
diose error; scribes and compositors,
because they are trained to produce a
correct text, are naturally reluctant
to copy a word they assume to be
accidentally wrong.

25–6 *Pie Corner – saving your manhoods.*
Pie Corner, the south-western corner
of Smithfield, where it is joined by
Giltspur Street, was noted for its
cook-shops, at which pigs were
dressed during Bartholomew fair. It
has been suggested that the Hostess's
apology (*saving your manhoods*) is for
mentioning a place redolent of killing
and cooking pigs. But would Fang
and Snare be so sensitive? It may be
that Pie Corner sold other flesh than
that of the pig. In Ben Jonson's play
Bartholomew Fair (1614), which shows
respectable women being corrupted
in the fair and becoming 'mistresses
o' the game', a distinction is drawn
between eating pig 'I'the heart o'the
fair; not at Pie Corner' (1.5.152). This
may simply refer to the greater attractions of the fair itself, but there might
also be an allusion to other noted
attributes of Pie Corner. *Wit's Recrea-*

tions (1640) uses the phrase 'cornered
π' in a sense that seems clearly
sexual, with the Greek letter ('pi') as
a visual symbol. See also the notes to
lines 26 and 68.

26 *buy a saddle.* There were many sad-
dlers near Smithfield. But as the Hostess is inclined to sexual innuendo
saddle may also imply that which is
mounted – a prostitute.
indited (for 'invited')

27 *Lubber's* (for 'Libbard's', that is,
'Leopard's')
Lumbert Lombard

28 *exion* (for 'action')

29 *case.* Again there is a sexual meaning
(the female genitals), illustrated by
the discussion of the 'genitive' case
in *The Merry Wives of Windsor*,
IV.1.53–64; the example given,
'*horum, harum, horum*', is taken to
refer to 'whore' by Mistress
Quickly, who cries 'Vengeance of
Jenny's case'.

31 *one* (reckoning)

36 (stage direction) *Bardolph.* A Bardolph appears in a list of recusants
which also includes Shakespeare's
father; and the names Bardolph and
Pistol appear in muster rolls of artil-
lerymen of 1435. See also the headnote to I.1.

Yonder he comes, and that arrant malmsey-nose knave
Bardolph with him. Do your offices, do your offices,
Master Fang and Master Snare, do me, do me, do me
40   your offices.

FALSTAFF How now, whose mare's dead? What's the
matter?

FANG I arrest you at the suit of Mistress Quickly.

FALSTAFF Away, varlets! Draw, Bardolph! Cut me off
the villain's head! Throw the quean in the channel!

HOSTESS Throw me in the channel? I'll throw thee in
the channel! Wilt thou, wilt thou, thou bastardly rogue?
Murder! Murder! Ah, thou honeysuckle villain, wilt
thou kill God's officers and the King's? Ah, thou
50   honeyseed rogue! Thou art a honeyseed, a man-queller
– and a woman-queller.

FALSTAFF Keep them off, Bardolph!

FANG A rescue! A rescue!

HOSTESS Good people, bring a rescue or two. Thou wot,
wot thou, thou wot, wot ta? Do, do, thou rogue! Do,
thou hempseed!

PAGE Away, you scullion! You rampallian! You fustilar-

---

37 *malmsey-nose.* Malmsey was a sweet
red wine, and the colour has spread
to Bardolph's nose.

39–40 *do me . . . your offices.* The *me* is an
'ethic dative', implying 'for me', as
in *Cut me* (line 44). Here there is also
a sexual pun in *do me*.

41 *whose mare's dead?* what's the fuss?
(Compare Prince Henry at IV.5.10–
11.)

45 *quean* prostitute
channel gutter

48, 50 *honeysuckle . . . honeyseed* (for 'homi-
cidal' and 'homicide')

49 *God's officers and the King's.* The officers execute the law on behalf of the
King's courts, and, as the King is
God's deputy, the officers are, indirectly, God's officers.

50 *queller* destroyer

53 *A rescue!* This is, curiously, an ambiguous expression, its meaning depending upon who shouts it. Here it
means that a rescue is being attempted and help is needed by the
officers of the law; but it was also
the cry of those who sought to rescue
someone being arrested.

54 *bring a rescue* (a recognized idiom, not
the Hostess's mistake)
wot (dialectal) wilt

55 *ta* (dialectal) thou

56 *hempseed.* The Hostess continues her
variations on 'homicide', but this one
is appropriate, since *hemp*, used to
make rope, was already associated
with hanging (for instance in the
word 'hempstring' for someone who
deserved hanging).

57 *rampallian* ruffian

ian! I'll tickle your catastrophe!

Enter the Lord Chief Justice and his men

LORD CHIEF JUSTICE What is the matter? Keep the
peace here, ho!   60

HOSTESS Good my lord, be good to me; I beseech you,
stand to me.

LORD CHIEF JUSTICE

How now, Sir John? What are you brawling here?

Doth this become your place, your time, and business?

You should have been well on your way to York.

Stand from him, fellow; wherefore hangest thou upon
          him?

HOSTESS O my most worshipful lord, an't please your
grace, I am a poor widow of Eastcheap, and he is
arrested at my suit.

LORD CHIEF JUSTICE For what sum?   70

HOSTESS It is more than for some, my lord, it is for all I
have. He hath eaten me out of house and home; he hath
put all my substance into that fat belly of his – but I
will have some of it out again, or I will ride thee a-nights
like the mare.

FALSTAFF I think I am as like to ride the mare if I have
any vantage of ground to get up.

57–8 *fustilarian*. This is a nonce word
(the Page seems to have caught the
Hostess's word disease). It may be derived from 'fusty', or 'fustian' (that is,
someone wearing such fabric); it is associated tentatively in the *O.E.D.* with
'fustilugs', a fat, frowzy woman.

58 *I'll tickle your catastrophe!* (a catch-
phrase of the period)

62 *stand to* stand by

63 *What* why

67–8 *your grace*. See the note to lines 1, 6.

68 *Eastcheap*. Like Pie Corner (see the
note to lines 25–6), Eastcheap was a
centre for cook-shops and butchers,
and it is described by Stow in his
Survey of London (1598) as 'a flesh

market'. This has been taken as an
appropriate setting for the glutton-
ous Falstaff, but as a market of flesh
in the sexual sense (see the note to
11.4.339) it would be appropriate for
the Hostess.

74–5 *ride thee a-nights like the mare* haunt
your sleep with nightmares

76 *ride the mare* (sexual, of course, but it
links with Falstaff's greeting at line
41 (*whose mare's dead?*) and the Hostess's complaint at lines 31–2 that she
has *borne, and borne, and borne*)

77 *vantage of ground to get up* superior
position to get astride the mare (a
military expression (compare 11.3.53),
with a sexual innuendo here)

LORD CHIEF JUSTICE How comes this, Sir John? What
man of good temper would endure this tempest of
exclamation? Are you not ashamed to enforce a poor
widow to so rough a course to come by her own?

FALSTAFF What is the gross sum that I owe thee?

HOSTESS Marry, if thou wert an honest man, thyself and
the money too. Thou didst swear to me upon a parcel-
gilt goblet, sitting in my Dolphin chamber, at the
round table, by a sea-coal fire, upon Wednesday in
Wheeson week, when the Prince broke thy head for
liking his father to a singing-man of Windsor, thou
didst swear to me then, as I was washing thy wound,
to marry me, and make me my lady thy wife. Canst
thou deny it? Did not goodwife Keech the butcher's
wife come in then and call me gossip Quickly? – coming

79 *temper* disposition
84–5 *parcel-gilt* partially gilded (usually
on the inner surface)
85 *Dolphin chamber*. Rooms in public
houses were each given names to
distinguish them.
86 *sea-coal* (mineral coal, brought by sea
from Newcastle to London, as distinct from charcoal)
87 *Wheeson* (dialectal) Whitsun
88 *liking his father*. This is Q's reading;
F has 'lik'ning him'. The Q compositor might have misread 'lik'ning' in
his copy as 'liking', but as 'like' was
an accepted form of 'liken' it might
simply represent his 'preferred spelling' (what he took to be the proper
form of the word). On the other
hand the scribe who prepared the
manuscript for F might have written
'lik'ning' as *his* preferred spelling.
There is no sure explanation for the
change from *his father* to 'him'. Possibly whoever prepared the F manuscript thought it was the Prince who
was being compared to the *singing-
man*; that might suggest that any allu-

sion to a pretender (see the next
note) was lost on him.
a singing-man of Windsor. Singing-men
were professional musicians of cathe-
drals and royal and university
chapels; in general they were well
regarded, though about this time
they were subject to some criticism,
by puritans and others, as fulfilling
no useful role and being given to
drink. But that would not be ground
for the Prince's objection to Falstaff's comparison. It may be that a
particular singing-man was or had
been a pretender to the throne, and
in view of the way Henry IV *came by
the crown* this would be a serious and
very dangerous allusion. A tenuous
link has been suggested with John
Magdalen, a priest who was involved
in the plot against Henry IV by 'The
grand conspirator Abbot of Westminster', which Shakespeare touches on
at the end of *Richard II* (v.6.21–3).
91 *Keech* (rolled-up animal fat)
92 *gossip* neighbour (as a familiar term
of address)

in to borrow a mess of vinegar, telling us she had a good
dish of prawns, whereby thou didst desire to eat some,
whereby I told thee they were ill for a green wound?
And didst thou not, when she was gone downstairs,
desire me to be no more so familiarity with such poor
people, saying that ere long they should call me madam?
And didst thou not kiss me, and bid me fetch thee thirty
shillings? I put thee now to thy book oath. Deny it if   100
thou canst.

FALSTAFF My lord, this is a poor mad soul, and she says
up and down the town that her eldest son is like you.
She hath been in good case, and the truth is, poverty
hath distracted her. But, for these foolish officers, I
beseech you I may have redress against them.

LORD CHIEF JUSTICE Sir John, Sir John, I am well
acquainted with your manner of wrenching the true
cause the false way. It is not a confident brow, nor the
throng of words that come with such more than   110
impudent sauciness from you, can thrust me from a
level consideration. You have, as it appears to me,
practised upon the easy-yielding spirit of this woman,
and made her serve your uses both in purse and in
person.

HOSTESS Yea, in truth, my lord.

LORD CHIEF JUSTICE Pray thee, peace. Pay her the
debt you owe her, and unpay the villainy you have done

---

93 *mess* small amount

95 *green* unhealed

97 *familiarity* (for 'familiar')

98 *madam*. A knight's wife was entitled
to be called 'madam'.

99–100 *didst thou . . . thirty shillings?* There
is a touching simplicity as well as
something comic in the Hostess's running on from the avowal of love to
the request for money.

100 *book oath* oath taken on the Bible

103 *her eldest son is like you*. This is a

skilful piece of impertinence, implying not only that the Hostess is unreliable but that the Lord Chief Justice
may have erred in times past. But
Falstaff's attempt to direct attention
away from his own villainy fails. See
the Introduction, page 449.

104 *in good case* well-off (but see the note
to line 29)

105 *distracted her* driven her mad
for as for

with her; the one you may do with sterling money and
120 the other with current repentance.

FALSTAFF My lord, I will not undergo this sneap without
reply. You call honourable boldness impudent sauciness; if a man will make curtsy and say nothing, he is
virtuous. No, my lord, my humble duty remembered,
I will not be your suitor. I say to you I do desire
deliverance from these officers, being upon hasty
employment in the King's affairs.

LORD CHIEF JUSTICE You speak as having power to do
wrong; but answer in the effect of your reputation, and
130 satisfy the poor woman.

FALSTAFF Come hither, hostess.

> *He takes her aside*
> *Enter Gower*

LORD CHIEF JUSTICE Now, Master Gower, what news?

GOWER
The King, my lord, and Harry Prince of Wales
Are near at hand; the rest the paper tells.

> *He gives him a letter*

FALSTAFF As I am a gentleman!

HOSTESS Faith, you said so before.

FALSTAFF As I am a gentleman! Come, no more words
of it.

HOSTESS By this heavenly ground I tread on, I must be
140 fain to pawn both my plate and the tapestry of my
dining-chambers.

FALSTAFF Glasses, glasses, is the only drinking; and for

---

120 *current* genuine (as 'current coin', reflecting *sterling money*).

121 *sneap* rebuke

123 *curtsy* bow (used for either sex)

128–9 *You speak . . . wrong.* See the note to v.3.134–6.

128 *having power* being empowered

129 *in the effect of your reputation* in accord with that reputation which you claim is yours

139 *By this heavenly ground.* The Hostess confuses the expressions 'by heaven' and 'by this ground', producing an effective paradox.

140 *fain* content

142 *Glasses.* Glasses were replacing metal drinking cups at this time; by pawning her plate the Hostess can become fashionable.
the only the best, the only acceptable

thy walls, a pretty slight drollery, or the story of the
Prodigal, or the German hunting, in waterwork, is
worth a thousand of these bed-hangers and these fly-
bitten tapestries. Let it be ten pound if thou canst.
Come, an 'twere not for thy humours, there's not a
better wench in England! Go, wash thy face, and draw
the action. Come, thou must not be in this humour with
me; dost not know me? Come, come, I know thou wast   150
set on to this.

HOSTESS Pray thee, Sir John, let it be but twenty nobles;
i'faith, I am loath to pawn my plate, so God save me,
la!

FALSTAFF Let it alone; I'll make other shift – you'll be a
fool still.

HOSTESS Well, you shall have it, though I pawn my
gown. I hope you'll come to supper. You'll pay me all
together?

FALSTAFF Will I live? (*To Bardolph*) Go, with her, with   160
her! Hook on, hook on!

HOSTESS Will you have Doll Tearsheet meet you at
supper?

drinking. The action is made to represent the vessel itself – a usage of
this word not recorded in the *O.E.D.*
It is possible that Shakespeare had in
mind the Tudor meaning of a 'drinking' as a convivial revel; but the
precise meaning is strained.

143 *drollery* comic picture, caricature

143–4 *the story . . . waterwork*. That is,
paintings on cloth of two of the
most popular subjects of the time, in
water-colour or distemper, imitative
of tapestry. There were complaints
throughout the sixteenth century of
such work from Germany and the
Netherlands (hence the reference to a
German hunting scene), so depriving
Englishmen of work.

145 *worth . . . bed-hangers*. Falstaff implies

that such tapestries as the Hostess
owns are fit only for bed-hangings
(of a four-poster).

147 *humours* moods

148 *wash thy face*. Presumably the Hostess has been crying.
    draw withdraw

152 *nobles*. The noble was a coin worth
one third of £1.

160 *Will I live?* as sure as I live!

161 *Hook on* follow, stick close

162 *Doll Tearsheet*. 'Doll' was commonly
used as a name for a prostitute. Coleridge suggested that the surname
should be 'Tearstreet', which would
fit not only her occupation but the
line *This Doll Tearsheet should be some
road* (II.2.160). But *Tearsheet* is not
inappropriate; in John Fletcher's

FALSTAFF No more words; let's have her.

      Exeunt Hostess, Fang, Snare, Bardolph, and Page

LORD CHIEF JUSTICE I have heard better news.

FALSTAFF What's the news, my lord?

LORD CHIEF JUSTICE Where lay the King tonight?

GOWER At Basingstoke, my lord.

FALSTAFF I hope, my lord, all's well. What is the news,
170   my lord?

LORD CHIEF JUSTICE Come all his forces back?

GOWER

    No, fifteen hundred foot, five hundred horse
    Are marched up to my lord of Lancaster
    Against Northumberland and the Archbishop.

FALSTAFF Comes the King back from Wales, my noble
    lord?

LORD CHIEF JUSTICE

    You shall have letters of me presently.
    Come, go along with me, good Master Gower.

FALSTAFF My lord!

180 LORD CHIEF JUSTICE What's the matter?

FALSTAFF Master Gower, shall I entreat you with me to
    dinner?

GOWER I must wait upon my good lord here, I thank you,
    good Sir John.

LORD CHIEF JUSTICE Sir John, you loiter here too long,
    being you are to take soldiers up in counties as you go.

FALSTAFF Will you sup with me, Master Gower?

LORD CHIEF JUSTICE What foolish master taught you
    these manners, Sir John?

Valentinian (c. 1614), III.1, a whore is
defined as 'a kind of kicker out of
sheets'.

168 *Basingstoke.* There is no reference in
Holinshed or Hall to Henry's staying
at Basingstoke at this time. Q reads
'Billingsgate', presumably the compositor's mistake.

177 *presently* immediately

181–2 *shall I . . . dinner?* Falstaff's invita-
tion is singularly inappropriate. It is
as if he were, rather feebly, trying to
gain the others' attention by any
means in order to become the centre
of the action. See the Introduction,
page 449.

186 *take . . . up* recruit

FALSTAFF Master Gower, if they become me not, he was   190
a fool that taught them me. This is the right fencing
grace, my lord: tap for tap, and so part fair.
LORD CHIEF JUSTICE Now the Lord lighten thee, thou
art a great fool   *Exeunt*

Enter Prince Henry and Poins   II.2
PRINCE HENRY Before God, I am exceeding weary.
POINS Is't come to that? I had thought weariness durst

192 *grace*. The meaning seems to be between 'propriety' and 'ornament'
(usages common by Shakespeare's
time); the word may here have the
specific sense 'procedure' (which Falstaff goes on to illustrate: *tap for tap*
. . .), though the O.E.D.'s earliest example of this is from 1607.
193 *lighten* enlighten

II.2 Prince Henry as dramatized at his
first appearance in the Second Part of
Henry IV is in sharp contrast to the
devil-may-care Hal of the tavern scenes
of the First Part and the bold and successful soldier to which he had matured at
the end of the earlier play. There is a
strong feeling of ennui and self-disgust.
It is with some force that he denies that
he is *as far in the devil's book* as Poins and
Falstaff (lines 42–3). In the jape on Falstaff that he devises with Poins (lines
163–70) Shakespeare dramatizes the
Prince's growing weariness with his
tavern life. The limitations of Hal's wit
have been pointed out in the Introduction to *1 Henry IV* (pages 239–40); the
trick planned here is no more imaginative than his joke on Francis in *Part One*
(II.4), and when it is carried out (II.4) he
shows little of the enthusiasm with

which he played the earlier game. (See
the Introduction, pages 443–4.)
    In Q an entry is also given here for
Sir John Russell (and an unnamed
'*other*'). This was the name originally
used for Peto in *Part One* (see the
Account of the Text of that play, page
259, and the headnote to 1.1 above).
Only Prince Henry and Poins are required, and the two extra characters,
given in F as Bardolph and the Page, are
not needed until line 65. Presumably
Shakespeare had the character Bardolph
in mind, though he used one of the
three names originally intended for *1
Henry IV* (Oldcastle for Falstaff, Harvey
for Bardolph, and Russell for Peto).
(stage direction) *Prince Henry*. In accord
    with the rather different role he per-
    forms in this play, he is referred to
    in this edition as Prince Henry in-
    stead of Prince Hal, which was used
    for *1 Henry IV*.
Poins. There is no historic source for
    Poins, though there was a Poyntz
    family in Gloucestershire, the county
    where Falstaff's recruiting scene is
    set. F frequently uses the spelling
    'Pointz', but no connexion with the
    family has been proved.

not have attached one of so high blood.

PRINCE HENRY Faith, it does me, though it discolours the complexion of my greatness to acknowledge it. Doth it not show vilely in me to desire small beer?

POINS Why, a prince should not be so loosely studied as to remember so weak a composition.

PRINCE HENRY Belike then my appetite was not princely
10   got, for, by my troth, I do now remember the poor creature small beer. But indeed, these humble consider-ations make me out of love with my greatness. What a disgrace is it to me to remember thy name! Or to know thy face tomorrow! Or to take note how many pair of silk stockings thou hast – viz. these, and those that were thy peach-coloured once! Or to bear the inventory of thy shirts, as, one for superfluity, and another for use! But that the tennis-court keeper knows better than I, for it is a low ebb of linen with thee when thou keepest
20   not racket there – as thou hast not done a great while,

---

3 *attached* laid hold of

4–5 *discolours the complexion of my greatness*
(1) makes me pale (with *weariness*);
(2) tarnishes my princely reputation

6 *show* look, appear
small beer beer thinned with water (served to children). Prince Henry's point is not that it is undignified for him to drink such beer but that what he enjoys is inferior in quality. His tone could be mildly ironic, but the domi-nant mood is one of self-disgust.

7 *loosely studied* negligent in what should concern him

11 *creature* food (after 1 Timothy 4.4: 'every creature of God is good, and nothing to be refused if it be received with thanksgiving')

12–13 *What . . . thy name!* That the new-made man soon forgets the names of his former associates was a common theme in the drama of the day. The Prince says it is shameful in him to remember Poins's name, but later in

the play he will be ready to banish the memory of the friends of his youth.

15,16 *viz . . . once*. Q reads 'with' for *viz.*, and F has 'ones' for *once*. Both readings may have been caused by mistaking the letters of the hand in which the copy was written, but the reading of 'once' as 'ones' may have been due to the word's being heard wrongly by the compositor as he said the words he was setting (aloud, or to himself), or it may be that the spellings were not automatically asso-ciated with the separate meanings now given to the two words. In this edition it has been assumed in both cases that the word of 'easier' mean-ing is erroneous.

16 *bear* bear in mind

17 *for superfluity* as a change of wear

19–20 *it is . . . racket there*. If Poins has a shirt to his back he will be found playing tennis, *racket* meaning (1) the tennis-racket; (2) an uproar.

because the rest of thy low countries have made a shift
to eat up thy holland. And God knows whether those
that bawl out the ruins of thy linen shall inherit His
kingdom – but the midwives say the children are not in
the fault. Whereupon the world increases, and kindreds
are mightily strengthened.

POINS How ill it follows, after you have laboured so hard,
you should talk so idly! Tell me, how many good young
princes would do so, their fathers being so sick as yours
at this time is?   30

PRINCE HENRY Shall I tell thee one thing, Poins?

POINS Yes, faith, and let it be an excellent good thing.

PRINCE HENRY It shall serve, among wits of no higher
breeding than thine.

POINS Go to, I stand the push of your one thing that you
will tell.

PRINCE HENRY Marry, I tell thee it is not meet that I
should be sad now my father is sick. Albeit I could tell
to thee, as to one it pleases me for fault of a better to
call my friend, I could be sad, and sad indeed too.   40

21–2 *low countries ... holland.* As elsewhere in Shakespeare, *low countries*
means the sexual parts of the body,
and, by extension, brothels. *Shift*
means (1) scheme; (2) shirt; (3)
change of clothing. *Holland* means
the country of that name in the Low
Countries and a fine linen. Poins has
been so busy begetting bastards (lines
23–4) that his linen has been spoiled
(by dirt or disease?); or pawned (to
pay for his low pleasures); or used
for baby clothes (lines 23–4), so that
he lacks a superfluity of shirts and
cannot now play tennis. However,
so many puns and combinations of
meaning are possible in these and
the following lines that the permuta-
tions are almost endless.

22–6 *And God ... strengthened.* This passage was omitted from F, perhaps, it

has been suggested, on the grounds
of taste or because it was thought
profane; but it might have been excised because it was too complex to
make its point clearly enough.

22–3 *those that ... linen* those babies that
cry from out of the remnants of your
shirts (in which they are swaddled)

23–4 *inherit His kingdom* (echoing Matthew 25.34) go to heaven

24–5 *not in the fault* not to be blamed
(for being illegitimate)

25–6 *Whereupon ... strengthened.* The air
of disillusionment about the conclusion of Prince Henry's description of
the way the peoples of the earth are
replenished accords with the mood
of lines 5–6.

28 *idly* carelessly

35 *stand the push* can stand up to

POINS Very hardly, upon such a subject.

PRINCE HENRY By this hand, thou thinkest me as far in the devil's book as thou and Falstaff, for obduracy and persistency. Let the end try the man. But I tell thee, my heart bleeds inwardly that my father is so sick; and keeping such vile company as thou art hath in reason taken from me all ostentation of sorrow.

POINS The reason?

PRINCE HENRY What wouldst thou think of me if I should weep?

POINS I would think thee a most princely hypocrite.

PRINCE HENRY It would be every man's thought, and thou art a blessed fellow, to think as every man thinks. Never a man's thought in the world keeps the roadway better than thine. Every man would think me an hypocrite indeed. And what accites your most worshipful thought to think so?

POINS Why, because you have been so lewd, and so much engraffed to Falstaff.

PRINCE HENRY And to thee.

POINS By this light, I am well spoke on; I can hear it with mine own ears. The worst that they can say of me is that I am a second brother, and that I am a proper fellow of my hands, and those two things I confess I cannot help. By the mass, here comes Bardolph.

Enter Bardolph and the Page

PRINCE HENRY And the boy that I gave Falstaff – 'a had

---

44 *Let the end try the man* (proverbial). This recalls Prince Henry's speech in *1 Henry IV*, 1.2.193–215, describing how he will surprise men by his reformation.

47 *ostentation* show (with no suggestion of boastfulness)

54 *keeps the roadway* holds to the common way (of thinking)

56 *accites* induces (and possibly 'summons' – a legal usage; hence *your most worshipful*)

58 *lewd* debased (rather than 'licentious')

59 *engraffed* attached

63 *second brother* younger brother (who, having no inheritance, must make his own way in the world)

63–4 *a proper fellow of my hands* good with my fists, a fine, bold fellow

him from me Christian, and look if the fat villain have
not transformed him ape.

BARDOLPH God save your grace!

PRINCE HENRY And yours, most noble Bardolph!   70

POINS (*to Bardolph*) Come, you virtuous ass, you bashful
fool, must you be blushing? Wherefore blush you now?
What a maidenly man-at-arms are you become! Is't
such a matter to get a pottle-pot's maidenhead?

PAGE 'A calls me e'en now, my lord, through a red lattice,
and I could discern no part of his face from the window.
At last I spied his eyes, and methought he had made
two holes in the ale-wife's petticoat, and so peeped
through.

PRINCE HENRY Has not the boy profited?   80

BARDOLPH Away, you whoreson upright rabbit, away!

PAGE Away, you rascally Althaea's dream, away!

PRINCE HENRY Instruct us, boy! What dream, boy?

PAGE Marry, my lord, Althaea dreamt she was delivered
of a firebrand; and therefore I call him her dream.

PRINCE HENRY A crown's-worth of good interpretation!
There 'tis, boy.

68 *transformed him ape.* The Page may be
cheekily 'aping' Bardolph by imitating his walk or gestures, but it would
be in accord with the play (and particularly with the Prince's disgust for
vanity and the emptiness of life) if
the Page had been tricked out in a
ridiculous livery. That which was
Christian has been transformed to
beastliness and, specifically, a devil
(see the second note to II.4.330).

71 *virtuous.* F reads 'pernitious', which
at first sight seems more appropriate;
but the unusualness of Q's *virtuous*
provides a phrase that has individuality (which is to be expected of Shakespeare). It is also a subtle joke:
virtue's colour was proverbially that
of blushing – red – and red is the

colour of Bardolph's drunken face.

74 *get a pottle-pot's maidenhead* knock off
a two-quart pot of ale

75 *e'en now* just now, a moment ago.
(For Q's idiomatic 'calls' F has
'call'd'.)
red lattice. Alehouses had red lattice
windows.

82 *Althaea's dream.* Dr Johnson pointed
out that Shakespeare was mistaken
in his mythology, for he confounded
Althaea's firebrand with Hecuba's:
'The firebrand of Althea was real:
but Hecuba, when she was big with
Paris, dreamed that she was delivered
of a firebrand and that consumed the
kingdom'. However, there are references in *2 Henry VI*, I.1.229, and
Troilus and Cressida, II.2.110, which

POINS O that this blossom could be kept from cankers! Well, there is sixpence to preserve thee.

90 BARDOLPH An you do not make him be hanged among you, the gallows shall have wrong.

PRINCE HENRY And how doth thy master, Bardolph?

BARDOLPH Well, my lord. He heard of your grace's coming to town. There's a letter for you.

POINS Delivered with good respect. And how doth the martlemas your master?

BARDOLPH In bodily health, sir.

POINS Marry, the immortal part needs a physician, but that moves not him. Though that be sick, it dies not.

100 PRINCE HENRY I do allow this wen to be as familiar with me as my dog, and he holds his place, for look you how he writes —

POINS (*reading the letter*) *John Falstaff, knight* — every

---

show that Shakespeare — if he wrote the line in the former, and by the time he wrote the latter — knew both dreams; so it may be the Page, not Shakespeare, who is mistaken.

88 *cankers*. This image appears many times in the literature of the period and especially in Shakespeare. A canker-worm was a caterpillar, or any insect larva which infected and destroyed from within the buds and fruit of plants. It was most frequently associated with the rose.

89 *sixpence to preserve thee*. The Elizabethan 6d. piece was decorated with a cross, and that (not the coin itself) is to preserve the Page as a Christian (line 67).

94 *a letter*. See 1.2.240.

96 *martlemas*. 'Martlemas' is a corruption of 'Martinmas', the Feast of St Martin (11 November), which was associated with plenty, especially of meat, since cattle that could not be fed through the winter were slaughtered about this time and their meat

preserved. In *1 Henry IV*, 1.2.156–7, Hal likens Falstaff to 'the latter spring' and 'All-hallown summer' (fine weather associated with All Saints' Day, 1 November). The implication of all three descriptions is the fullness of Falstaff's body, vigour, and years. For his age he is in fine fettle (and a St Martin's summer, like an All-hallown summer, is fine weather late in the year), but this spell of 'late spring' immediately precedes winter and the death of nature.

100–101 *I do allow ... dog*. At 1.2.148 Falstaff spoke of the Prince as his dog; here the roles are reversed.

100 *wen* tumour, swelling (hence, in Dr Johnson's words, 'a swollen excrescence of a man')

103 *John Falstaff, knight*. Q and F both give these words to Poins, but some editors, logically enough, transfer them to the Prince. However, if actors' parts underlie F (see pages 465–8), its reading would strongly support Q in giving the words to

man must know that as oft as he has occasion to name
himself, even like those that are kin to the king, for
they never prick their finger but they say 'There's some
of the King's blood spilt.' 'How comes that?' says he
that takes upon him not to conceive. The answer is as
ready as a borrower's cap: 'I am the King's poor
cousin, sir.'   110

PRINCE HENRY Nay, they will be kin to us, or they will
fetch it from Japhet. But the letter: *Sir John Falstaff,
knight, to the son of the King nearest his father, Harry
Prince of Wales, greeting.*

POINS Why, this is a certificate!

PRINCE HENRY Peace! *I will imitate the honourable Romans
in brevity.*

POINS He sure means brevity in breath, short-winded.

PRINCE HENRY *I commend me to thee, I commend thee, and
I leave thee. Be not too familiar with Poins, for he*   120
*misuses thy favours so much that he swears thou art to
marry his sister Nell. Repent at idle times as thou mayst,
and so farewell.*

> *Thine by yea and no – which is as much as to
> say, as thou usest him – Jack Falstaff with*

Poins; and if we suppose that he
looks at the letter (as suggested in
the stage direction supplied in this
edition), the arrangement of Q and F
can be maintained quite naturally.

108 *takes upon him not to conceive* pretends
not to understand

109 *borrower's*. Q and F both read
'borowed', and some sort of strained
sense can be taken from this. But a
misreading of manuscript, which
would probably have lacked the apostrophe in *borrower's*, would easily explain the error. A man bent on borrowing is only too willing to ingrati-
ate himself, doffing his cap, which
'Plays in the right hand, thus' (*Timon
of Athens*, II.1.19).

112 *fetch it from Japhet* prove it by tra-
cing their ancestry back to Japhet
(Noah's third son, who was said to
be the ancestor of all Europeans)

112–14 *Sir John . . . Prince of Wales.* Falstaff has inverted the correct order
by naming the sender first instead of
last. The whole letter is pompous
and presumptuous.

115 *certificate* formal document, patent

119–20 *I commend me . . . leave thee.* This,
presumably, is Falstaff's idea of
Roman *brevity*.

122 *at idle times* when you have nothing
better to do

124 *by yea and no* (a mild puritan oath;
see also 1.2.35)

> *my familiars, John with my brothers and*
> *sisters, and Sir John with all Europe.*

POINS My lord, I'll steep this letter in sack and make
him eat it.

130 PRINCE HENRY That's to make him eat twenty of his
words. But do you use me thus, Ned? Must I marry
your sister?

POINS God send the wench no worse fortune! But I never
said so.

PRINCE HENRY Well, thus we play the fools with the
time, and the spirits of the wise sit in the clouds and
mock us. – Is your master here in London?

BARDOLPH Yea, my lord.

PRINCE HENRY Where sups he? Doth the old boar feed
140 in the old frank?

BARDOLPH At the old place, my lord, in Eastcheap.

PRINCE HENRY What company?

PAGE Ephesians, my lord, of the old church.

PRINCE HENRY Sup any women with him?

PAGE None, my lord, but old Mistress Quickly, and
Mistress Doll Tearsheet.

PRINCE HENRY What pagan may that be?

PAGE A proper gentlewoman, sir, and a kinswoman of my
master's.

150 PRINCE HENRY Even such kin as the parish heifers are
to the town bull. Shall we steal upon them, Ned, at
supper?

POINS I am your shadow, my lord; I'll follow you.

---

139 *old boar.* At 1.1.19 Falstaff is called
brawn.

140 *frank* pig-sty

141 *the old place.* There was a Boar's
Head tavern in Eastcheap in the early
Tudor period. It is never named by
Shakespeare, but the inference that it
is the tavern at which Falstaff sups is
drawn from lines 139–41.

143 *Ephesians* good drinking companions. The relevance of the name is
pointed out here by the phrase *of the
old church*; St Paul's Epistle to
the Ephesians (5.18) warned them
against excess, particularly of wine.

147 *pagan* prostitute

151 *the town bull* (which was made available to all the farmers of the district)

PRINCE HENRY Sirrah, you boy, and Bardolph, no word
to your master that I am yet come to town. There's for
your silence.

BARDOLPH I have no tongue, sir.

PAGE And for mine, sir, I will govern it.

PRINCE HENRY Fare you well; go.

> *Exeunt Bardolph and Page*

This Doll Tearsheet should be some road.   160

POINS I warrant you, as common as the way between
Saint Albans and London.

PRINCE HENRY How might we see Falstaff bestow
himself tonight in his true colours, and not ourselves
be seen?

POINS Put on two leathern jerkins and aprons, and wait
upon him at his table as drawers.

PRINCE HENRY From a god to a bull? A heavy descension! It was Jove's case. From a prince to a prentice?
A low transformation, that shall be mine; for in every-   170
thing the purpose must weigh with the folly. Follow
me, Ned.   *Exeunt*

> *Enter Northumberland, Lady Northumberland, and* II.3
> *Lady Percy*

NORTHUMBERLAND

I pray thee, loving wife, and gentle daughter,
Give even way unto my rough affairs;

160 *should be* is likely to be
   some road as much frequented as a
   highway (from a proverbial saying)
161–2 *the way between Saint Albans and
   London* (a much used thoroughfare)
163–4 *bestow himself* behave
167 *drawers* drawers of beer, tavern
   waiters
168 *From a god to a bull.* Jupiter (*Jove*)
transformed himself into a bull for
love of Europa.
168–9 *heavy descension* great fall
171 *weigh with* counterbalance

II.3.1 *daughter* daughter-in-law
2 *Give even way unto my rough affairs* protest no more about my harsh course
   of action

Put not you on the visage of the times
And be like them to Percy troublesome.

LADY NORTHUMBERLAND
I have given over; I will speak no more.
Do what you will; your wisdom be your guide.

NORTHUMBERLAND
Alas, sweet wife, my honour is at pawn,
And but my going, nothing can redeem it.

LADY PERCY
O, yet, for God's sake, go not to these wars!
10 The time was, father, that you broke your word
When you were more endeared to it than now,
When your own Percy, when my heart's dear Harry,
Threw many a northward look to see his father
Bring up his powers. But he did long in vain.
Who then persuaded you to stay at home?
There were two honours lost, yours and your son's.
For yours, the God of heaven brighten it!
For his, it stuck upon him as the sun
In the grey vault of heaven, and by his light
20 Did all the chivalry of England move
To do brave acts. He was indeed the glass
Wherein the noble youth did dress themselves.
He had no legs that practised not his gait;
And speaking thick, which nature made his blemish,

---

3 *Put not you on the visage of the times* do
not look as bleak as are the times
11 *endeared* bound by affection
18 *stuck* (a particular use of the word to
express the fixity and lustre of a heavenly body in its sphere)
19 *the grey vault of heaven.* This may mean
lowering grey skies (against which the
sun stands out the more brightly); but
'grey' was used for 'blue' (as in *Titus
Andronicus*, II.2.1, 'The hunt is up, the
morn is bright and grey').
21, 31 *glass* mirror, ideal example
23 *He . . . his gait* any man who did not
emulate Hotspur's style of walking

might as well have had no legs
24 *speaking thick.* The precise nature of
Hotspur's defect (or peculiarity) of
speech is not clear. 'Thick' could
mean 'huskily' or 'rapidly' when applied to speech, and the second meaning may be implied if those who
normally spoke *tardily* (line 26) affected Hotspur's manner. Rapid
speech would be appropriate for an
impetuous character such as Hotspur
(see the Introduction to *1 Henry IV*,
page 237). The characteristic seems
to be Shakespeare's invention.

Became the accents of the valiant;
For those that could speak low and tardily
Would turn their own perfection to abuse,
To seem like him. So that in speech, in gait,
In diet, in affections of delight,
In military rules, humours of blood,   30
He was the mark and glass, copy and book,
That fashioned others. And him – O wondrous him!
O miracle of men! – him did you leave,
Second to none, unseconded by you,
To look upon the hideous god of war
In disadvantage, to abide a field
Where nothing but the sound of Hotspur's name
Did seem defensible. So you left him.
Never, O never, do his ghost the wrong
To hold your honour more precise and nice   40
With others than with him! Let them alone.
The Marshal and the Archbishop are strong;
Had my sweet Harry had but half their numbers,
Today might I, hanging on Hotspur's neck,
Have talked of Monmouth's grave.

NORTHUMBERLAND   Beshrew your heart,
Fair daughter, you do draw my spirits from me
With new lamenting ancient oversights.
But I must go and meet with danger there,
Or it will seek me in another place
And find me worse provided.

LADY NORTHUMBERLAND   O, fly to Scotland,   50
Till that the nobles and the armèd commons

---

29 *affections of delight* tastes for pleasure
30 *humours of blood* moods
31 *mark* guiding object
34 *unseconded* unsupported
36 *abide a field* face a battle
38 *defensible* able to provide means of
defence

40 *precise and nice* precisely and meticu-
lously. The words are almost synonymous here, and their rhyme suggests
a caustic note in Lady Percy's voice.
45 *Monmouth* (Prince Henry)
Beshrew your heart (a mild expression
of reproach)

Have of their puissance made a little taste.

LADY PERCY

If they get ground and vantage of the King,
Then join you with them like a rib of steel,
To make strength stronger; but, for all our loves,
First let them try themselves. So did your son;
He was so suffered; so came I a widow,
And never shall have length of life enough
To rain upon remembrance with mine eyes,
60   That it may grow and sprout as high as heaven
For recordation to my noble husband.

NORTHUMBERLAND

Come, come, go in with me. 'Tis with my mind
As with the tide swelled up unto his height,
That makes a still-stand, running neither way.
Fain would I go to meet the Archbishop,
But many thousand reasons hold me back.
I will resolve for Scotland. There am I,
Till time and vantage crave my company.   *Exeunt*

II.4   *Enter Francis and another Drawer*

FRANCIS   What the devil hast thou brought there – apple-
johns? Thou knowest Sir John cannot endure an apple-
john.

---

52   *taste* trial
53   *get ground* gain mastery
57   *suffered* allowed
59   *rain upon remembrance with mine eyes*
water the plant of remembrance (rose-
mary) with the water of my tears
61   *recordation* remembrance
64   *still-stand* stand-still, point of balance
67   *I will resolve for Scotland*. As usual,
Shakespeare chooses to blacken
Northumberland's character. Historically, although the outcome was no
different, Northumberland left for
Scotland only when he saw that the

Archbishop had moved too hastily.
He makes no further appearance in
the play, but his death (at the Battle
of Bramham Moor in 1408, three
years after Gaultree Forest) is indirectly mentioned at IV.4.94–101.

II.4 This scene makes an illuminating
comparison with II.4 of *1 Henry IV*.
Apart from the rejection, it is the only
time that Prince Henry and Falstaff meet
in this play, and the scene lacks the
panache and exuberance that spill over

DRAWER Mass, thou sayst true. The Prince once set a
dish of apple-johns before him, and told him there were
five more Sir Johns, and, putting off his hat, said 'I will
now take my leave of these six dry, round, old, withered
knights.' It angered him to the heart. But he hath forgot
that.

FRANCIS Why then, cover, and set them down, and see   10
if thou canst find out Sneak's noise. Mistress Tearsheet
would fain hear some music.

DRAWER (*preparing to leave*) Dispatch! The room where
they supped is too hot; they'll come in straight.

    Enter Will

WILL Sirrah, here will be the Prince and Master Poins
anon, and they will put on two of our jerkins and aprons,
and Sir John must not know of it. Bardolph hath
brought word.

---

in II.4 of *Part One*. The style of this
scene is set by the mood of II.2 (see the
headnote), and, most graphically, by Falstaff's instruction (line 33) to empty the
chamber-pot, given between two lines
of a drinking song. John Masefield described this as the 'finest tavern scene
ever written'; but it could be argued that
II.1 and II.4 of *1 Henry IV* are even more
effective, the first for its realism, the
second as an epitome of good fellowship.
(See the Introduction, pages 428, 442
and 449.)

1–21 The distribution of speech headings at the opening of the scene differs in Q and F, and neither is adequate. The first seven speeches are
allocated in Q to Francis, Drawer,
Francis, Drawer, Francis (then an
entry is given after line 18 for Will),
Drawer, Francis, then an exit is
marked. This edition brings Will on
earlier, allocates to him lines 15–18
(in Q he has nothing to say), and,

since he is the last of the drawers to
enter, retains him until line 33 to
carry away the jordan, a task given
to Francis by many editors (there is
no direction at that point in Q or F).
In F the opening stage direction is
'*Enter two Drawers*', and Francis is
not named; the speeches are allocated
alternately between First and Second
Drawer; lines 13–14 are omitted; and
there is no entry for Will. See the
Account of the Text, page 464.

1–2 *apple-johns* (long-keeping apples, at
their best when shrivelled)

6 *putting off his hat* (standing bare-headed
in mock respect)

10 *cover* lay the cloth (playing on *putting
off* in line 6)

11 *noise* band of musicians. In Marston's
The Dutch Courtesan, II.3.112–13, the
tavern has available 'Mr Creake's
noise', referred to as fiddlers.

14 *straight* very soon

FRANCIS By the mass, here will be old utis. It will be an
20   excellent stratagem.
DRAWER I'll see if I can find out Sneak.

Exeunt Francis and Drawer
Enter Hostess and Doll Tearsheet

HOSTESS I'faith, sweetheart, methinks now you are in an
excellent good temperality. Your pulsidge beats as
extraordinarily as heart would desire, and your colour,
I warrant you, is as red as any rose, in good truth, la!
But, i'faith, you have drunk too much canaries, and
that's a marvellous searching wine, and it perfumes the
blood ere one can say 'What's this?' How do you now?
DOLL Better than I was – hem!
30   HOSTESS Why, that's well said – a good heart's worth
gold. Lo, here comes Sir John.

Enter Falstaff, singing

FALSTAFF
          When Arthur first in court –
       empty the jordan –   *Exit Will*
          And was a worthy king –
       how now, Mistress Doll?
HOSTESS Sick of a calm, yea, good faith.

---

19 *old utis* a high old time. *Utis* may be a
Warwickshire or Worcestershire dialect word for 'noise', 'confusion', and
it may also mean a period of festivity
– strictly, the 'octave', that is the
eighth day, or period of eight days,
of a festival.

23 *temperality* (the Hostess's own compound of 'temper' (temperament,
physical condition) and 'quality')
pulsidge (not simply one pulse beating
well, but all the pulses of the body;
again a word of the Hostess's
own)

26 *canaries* (a light, sweet wine from the
Canary Islands)

27 *searching* discovering the weak spots
of the body (with the implication –
exemplified by Doll's being *sick of a
calm* – that it disturbs the bowels)
perfumes (for 'perfuses')

29 *hem!* (a hiccough)

32,34 *When Arthur . . . worthy king*. This
is a garbled version of the ballad *Sir
Launcelot du Lake*, which was sung in
Shakespeare's time to the tune
'Chevy Chase' (reprinted on page
485).

33 *jordan* chamber-pot
(stage direction) *Exit Will*. See the
note to lines 1–21.

FALSTAFF So is all her sect; an they be once in a calm
they are sick.

DOLL A pox damn you, you muddy rascal, is that all the
comfort you give me?   40

FALSTAFF You make fat rascals, Mistress Doll.

DOLL I make them? Gluttony and diseases make them;
I make them not.

FALSTAFF If the cook help to make the gluttony, you
help to make the diseases, Doll. We catch of you, Doll,
we catch of you. Grant that, my poor virtue, grant that.

DOLL Yea, Mary's joys, our chains and our jewels –

---

36 *calm* (for 'qualm')

37 *sect*. This stands for 'sex' and for
Doll's profession. The *sect* referred
to is the Family of Love, a genuine
religious sect, whose name was much
used by Elizbethan dramatists (such
as Marston and Middleton) for
prostitutes.

39 *muddy rascal*. A *rascal* was a young
deer, said to be *muddy* when out of
season and sluggish.

47 *Yea, Mary's joys*. Q reads 'Yea ioy'.
Shakespeare uses 'joy' elsewhere as a
term of endearment; in *Antony and
Cleopatra*, 1.5.57–8, it is used by Cleopatra of herself, but with a slight
suggestion that 'mistress' is implied
(Antony's 'remembrance lay | In
Egypt with his joy'). But as a term
of affection, it makes poor sense in
the context of what is being said
here and in the tone of this exchange
between Falstaff and Doll. F's reading is 'I marry' ('I' commonly represents 'Ay' in texts of this time),
which makes sense but does not explain how the Q reading came to be
as it is. The expression 'a maiden of
joy' (equivalent to the French *fille de
joie*) was used in 1585, and that sense
might be implied in some way in the
'joy' of the text, though not in the

form in which we have it. Editors
have suspected that 'Yea ioy' may
misrepresent some profanity which F
modified (as it did systematically
throughout the play; see the Account
of the Text, pages 462–5); 'Iesu' has
been suggested for 'ioy', though even
then the sense runs on awkwardly
from Falstaff's preceding speech.

There is one possible clue. In this
line Doll mentions two gifts, implying that prostitutes do no more than
give men the diseases they receive
from them, and Falstaff picks on this
and adds three more 'jewels'. From
the eighteenth century editors have
marked Falstaff's additions as if they came from
a song. This is an imaginative suggestion, but the song has not been identified. But the five precious jewels,
connected with the word 'joy', are
intriguing. In the Middle Ages Mary,
mother of Jesus, was said to have
five Joys, her son's Annunciation,
Nativity, Epiphany, and Resurrec-
tion, and her Assumption. There
was, of course, another Mary, Mary
Magdalen, and it is possible that Doll
suggests that what is granted the
prostitute is a perversion of the Joys

FALSTAFF – your brooches, pearls, and ouches – for to
serve bravely is to come halting off, you know; to come
50   off the breach, with his pike bent bravely; and to
surgery bravely; to venture upon the charged chambers
bravely –

DOLL Hang yourself, you muddy conger, hang yourself!

HOSTESS By my troth, this is the old fashion; you two
never meet but you fall to some discord. You are both,
i'good truth, as rheumatic as two dry toasts; you cannot
one bear with another's confirmities. What the goodyear! One must bear, and that (*to Doll*) must be you;

of Mary, mother of Jesus, as those
appropriate to a pre-penitent Mary
Magdalen. The *jewels* might all stand
for venereal sores, as *ouches* certainly
could. The F reading could easily
have been produced by a scribe or
compositor of the period without any
prompting, but it could equally have
been suggested by the appearance of
'Mary' in the manuscript underlying
F. This would certainly have been
modified in the process of reducing
profanity, and 'I marry' would be a
likely substitute.

    Any emendation can only be a
guess, but the Q text as it stands is
distinctly awkward in tone and in
the progression of speeches; and an
accidental omission of 'Mary's' seems
possible, since the compositor who
set Q was one of the two who omitted words in some twenty-seven
places in setting the second Quarto
of *Richard II*. The reading *Yea,
Mary's joys* offers one way of overcoming the problem posed by Q and
explaining the change made in F.

48 *ouches* (1) gems, brooches; (2) carbun-
cles, sores. See the previous note.

48–51 *to serve ... chambers* (military
phrases, all used with sexual innuendo)

53 DOLL *Hang ... yourself!* F omits this
line, probably in error.

54 *the old fashion* like the old days
conger (a term of abuse. The *conger* is
the sea eel; a sexual innuendo is
implied.)

56 *as rheumatic as two dry toasts*. The temperament was thought to be controlled by the balance (or imbalance) of
the four humours. By *rheumatic* the
Hostess presumably means 'choleric'.
Like *toast* Falstaff and Doll are hot
and dry, and, as Dr Johnson put it,
they 'cannot meet but they grate one
another'.

57 *confirmities* (for 'infirmities'; the *con-*
prefix suggests the coming together,
the grating, of Doll and Falstaff)

57–8 *What the goodyear!* The derivation
of this exclamation is far from clear.
It is possibly a dialect form of 'What
the devil!'; it may be derived from a
Dutch expression meaning 'As I
hope for a good year'; or, with much
less certainty though some plausibil-
ity, it might (as Sir Thomas Hanmer,
one of the earliest editors of Shakespeare, suggested) be derived from a
French word, *gouje*, a prostitute.

58 *bear* (1) put up with afflictions; (2)
support a man's weight (as in line
61); (3) give birth to children

you are the weaker vessel, as they say, the emptier
vessel.   60

DOLL Can a weak empty vessel bear such a huge full
hogshead? There's a whole merchant's venture of
Bordeaux stuff in him. You have not seen a hulk better
stuffed in the hold. Come, I'll be friends with thee,
Jack; thou art going to the wars, and whether I shall
ever see thee again or no there is nobody cares.

   Enter the Drawer

DRAWER Sir, Ancient Pistol's below, and would speak
with you.

DOLL Hang him, swaggering rascal. Let him not come
hither. It is the foul-mouthed'st rogue in England.   70

HOSTESS If he swagger, let him not come here. No, by
my faith! I must live among my neighbours; I'll no
swaggerers. I am in good name and fame with the very
best. Shut the door. There comes no swaggerers here. I
have not lived all this while to have swaggering now.
Shut the door, I pray you.

FALSTAFF Dost thou hear, hostess?

HOSTESS Pray ye, pacify yourself, Sir John; there comes

59 *the weaker vessel.* That woman is the
weaker of the sexes is an ancient
fallacy, and the expression *the
weaker vessel* is biblical (1 Peter 3.7).
It is given a sexual turn in lines
61–2.

62 *hogshead* large cask
venture cargo

63 *Bordeaux stuff* wine of Bordeaux.
(*Stuff* and the echo of 'boarding' may
be sexual innuendoes.)

67 *Ancient Pistol.* An 'ancient' was an
ensign or standard bearer. Falstaff is
the captain, Peto the lieutenant,
Pistol the ensign, and Bardolph the
corporal. The name Pistol is particularly suggestive. A Pistol and a Bardolph appear in muster rolls of artil-

lerymen of 1435. Shakespeare may
have known the Italian word *pistolfo*,
which John Florio (whom it is
thought Shakespeare knew) translated in 1611 as 'a roguing beggar, a
cantler, an upright man that liveth
by cozenage'. There is also in the
ancient's name a suggestion of
'pizzle' (see the notes to lines 112,
124, and 156); and the Tudor pistol
was a fearsome, erratic weapon,
likely to go off with a roar at half-
cock, very much as is the character
Pistol.

69 *swaggering* (then a new word) hector-
ing, blustering

72 *I'll* I'll have

78 *pacify yourself* keep yourself quiet (or,

no swaggerers here.

80   FALSTAFF Dost thou hear? It is mine ancient.

HOSTESS Tilly-fally, Sir John, ne'er tell me; an your ancient swagger, 'a comes not in my doors. I was before Master Tisick the debuty t'other day, and, as he said to me – 'twas no longer ago than Wednesday last, i'good faith – 'Neighbour Quickly,' says he – Master Dumb our minister was by then – 'Neighbour Quickly,' says he, 'receive those that are civil, for,' said he, 'you are in an ill name' – now 'a said so, I can tell whereupon. 'For,' says he, 'you are an honest woman, and well
90   thought on; therefore take heed what guests you receive; receive,' says he, 'no swaggering companions.' There comes none here. You would bless you to hear what he said. No, I'll no swaggerers.

FALSTAFF He's no swaggerer, hostess, a tame cheater, i'faith. You may stroke him as gently as a puppy grey-

---

if *pacify* is a mistake for 'satisfy', 'be you assured')

comes (the singular form for the plural)

81   *Tilly-fally* fiddlesticks

83   *Tisick* (for 'phthisic', a consumptive cough)

debuty (a corrupted form of 'deputy', used by others besides the Hostess, for a deputy alderman, or the citizen charged with keeping order in a ward or district)

85   *Master Dumb*. Clergy who merely read out others' sermons instead of preaching their own were called 'dumb dogs', not being able to bark (from Isaiah 56.10).

86   *by* nearby

87   *civil* well-behaved

87–88   *are in an ill name* have gained a bad reputation

88   *I can tell whereupon* I now understand why (for admitting such as Pistol)

94   *tame cheater*. This seems to be a particular usage of these words created by Shakespeare, and it is one which later authors (including Sir Walter Scott) took up. 'Cheater' originally meant one who looked after the royal escheats (that is, land which reverted to the king), but in Shakespeare's day it was coming to mean such a person who operated dishonestly. It is the *honest* escheator that the Hostess has in mind at line 100. 'Cheater' was applied to gamesters, presumably alluding to those who resorted to sharp practice, and the *tame cheater* is thought to have been the decoy who lured the innocent card-player into a game in which he could be fleeced. Thus in *The Fair Maid of the Inn* (1625) by John Fletcher (and probably others) a tame cheater is described as a 'decoy duck'. The implication is that Pistol is the last man

hound. He'll not swagger with a Barbary hen, if her feathers turn back in any show of resistance. Call him up, drawer.   *Exit Drawer*

HOSTESS Cheater, call you him? I will bar no honest man my house, nor no cheater, but I do not love swaggering; by my troth, I am the worse when one says 'swagger'. Feel, masters, how I shake, look you, I warrant you.   100

DOLL So you do, hostess.

HOSTESS Do I? Yea, in very truth, do I, an 'twere an aspen leaf. I cannot abide swaggerers.

Enter Ancient Pistol, Bardolph, and the Page

PISTOL God save you, Sir John!

FALSTAFF Welcome, Ancient Pistol! Here, Pistol, I charge you with a cup of sack – do you discharge upon mine hostess.

PISTOL I will discharge upon her, Sir John, with two bullets.   110

FALSTAFF She is pistol-proof, sir; you shall not hardly offend her.

HOSTESS Come, I'll drink no proofs, nor no bullets. I'll drink no more than will do me good, for no man's pleasure, I.

PISTOL Then to you, Mistress Dorothy! I will charge you.

DOLL Charge me? I scorn you, scurvy companion. What,

---

to frighten anyone; after all, as Thomas Dekker explained in *The Bellman of London* (1608), cheaters seldom swear or swagger, for fear of frightening off their prey.

96 *Barbary hen* guinea fowl (used to mean 'slut' or 'prostitute')

108 *charge . . . discharge* drink a toast (with a sexual innuendo and playing on the military meanings – loading and firing a pistol)

111 *bullets* (testes)

112 *She is pistol-proof* (1) she will not succumb to you; (2) she is past child-bearing (taking up the meaning of 'pistol' as a discharging weapon, and punning on 'pizzle')

not hardly scarcely (a colloquialism; the *not* is redundant)

114 *proofs . . . bullets*. The Hostess sees no hidden meanings – she is simply confused – in contrast to Doll, who immediately realizes what *charge* means (lines 119–22).

120   you poor, base, rascally, cheating, lack-linen mate!
Away, you mouldy rogue, away! I am meat for your
master.

PISTOL I know you, Mistress Dorothy.

DOLL Away, you cutpurse rascal, you filthy bung, away!
By this wine, I'll thrust my knife in your mouldy chaps
an you play the saucy cuttle with me. Away, you bottle-ale
rascal, you basket-hilt stale juggler, you! Since when,
I pray you, sir? God's light, with two points on your
shoulder? Much!

130   PISTOL God let me not live but I will murder your ruff
for this.

FALSTAFF No more, Pistol! I would not have you go off
here. Discharge yourself of our company, Pistol.

HOSTESS No, good Captain Pistol, not here, sweet captain!

DOLL Captain! Thou abominable damned cheater, art
thou not ashamed to be called captain? An captains

120 *mate* companion, fellow
121-2 *I am meat for your master* (a proverbial expression, here with a sexual
innuendo. There may be wordplay
on *meat* and *mate*).
124 *bung* (1) pickpocket ('bung' was a
cant word for purse); (2) pizzle (the
other meaning of 'bung' – something
that fills a hole)
125 *chaps* cheeks
126 *play the saucy cuttle*. The precise meaning of this delightfully evocative expression is not clear, but its implication is obvious. A 'cuttle' was the
knife used for cutting purses, and it
seems that Doll is warning Pistol not
to try any tricks with her.
127 *basket-hilt* (an expression of contempt for a swordsman; literally, a
sword hilt with steel basketwork to
protect the hand)

Since when since when were you a true
soldier?
128 *points* laces (here those used for securing armour). Doll implies that
Pistol is dressed more impressively
than he behaves.
129 *Much!* (an expression of scornful
disbelief)
130 *murder* destroy
132-3 FALSTAFF *No more ... Pistol.* F
omits these lines. Some editors at-
tribute this to their indecency, but
on that basis most of the scene up to
this point might also have been excised. It is more likely that the compositor's eye accidentally slipped
from Falstaff's *No* to the Hostess's
(line 134).
134 *Captain.* The Hostess's rapid promotion of Pistol may indicate her desire
to pacify him.

were of my mind, they would truncheon you out, for
taking their names upon you before you have earned
them. You a captain? You slave! For what? For tearing   140
a poor whore's ruff in a bawdy-house? He a captain!
Hang him, rogue, he lives upon mouldy stewed prunes
and dried cakes. A captain? God's light, these villains
will make the word as odious as the word 'occupy',
which was an excellent good word before it was ill-
sorted. Therefore captains had need look to't.

BARDOLPH Pray thee go down, good ancient.

FALSTAFF Hark thee hither, Mistress Doll.

PISTOL Not I; I tell thee what, Corporal Bardolph, I
could tear her! I'll be revenged of her.   150

PAGE Pray thee go down.

PISTOL I'll see her damned first! To Pluto's damnèd

---

142 *stewed prunes*. Pistol lives on what
others leave, not only in the sense of
food, but also as a pimp. Prunes
were thought to be a cure for venereal disease, and 'stews' were brothels. Pistol lives off the takings of
mouldy prostitutes.

144-6 *word as odious . . . ill-sorted*. For
these lines F has only 'word Captaine
odious', a weak modification which
avoids the 'odious' meaning of *occupy*:
'fornicate'. Here (in contrast to lines
132-3) the change seems deliberate,
because of the new sense that is produced; but in comparison with what
has gone before these lines are hardly
odious enough to be censored (and
the word is so used elsewhere in the
period). It is just possible that the
alteration was made to avoid the implication of some topical allusion,
now irrecoverable.

145-6 *ill-sorted* in bad company

152-5 *To Pluto's . . . here*? As in his development of Falstaff (and Shylock)
from characteristics inherited from

the earlier drama, with Pistol Shakespeare goes far beyond the braggart
soldier, the *miles gloriosus*, from whom
he stems. Falstaff and Shylock tran-
scend the stock dramatic elements of
their origin because Shakespeare creates a kind of humanity for them.
Pistol's development is different.
Shakespeare takes a dramatic stereo-
type and gives him a passion, a
passion for a kind of literary rant
that might appeal to such a braggart
soldier were he a real person. Shakespeare's peculiar genius appears in
his skilful control over this creation.
Shylock and more especially Falstaff
are inclined to take over their plays.
This problem does not arise with
Pistol, yet he is invested with a
colour and an imagination that make
him seem, like Falstaff and Shylock,
a world away from the ordinariness
of his origins.

Much of what Pistol says is drawn
from, or imitative of, the rant of
drama, and, as J. W. Lever showed

lake, by this hand, to th'infernal deep, with Erebus and
tortures vile also! Hold hook and line, say I! Down,
down, dogs! Down, faitours! Have we not Hiren here?

He brandishes his sword

HOSTESS Good Captain Peesel, be quiet; 'tis very late,
i'faith. I beseek you now, aggravate your choler.

PISTOL

These be good humours indeed! Shall pack-horses,
And hollow pampered jades of Asia,
160   Which cannot go but thirty mile a day,
Compare with Caesars and with Cannibals,
And Troyant Greeks? Nay, rather damn them with
King Cerberus, and let the welkin roar!
Shall we fall foul for toys?

HOSTESS By my troth, captain, these are very bitter
words.

---

in *Shakespeare Survey 6* (1953), pages
79–90, his classical learning seems
to be derived from a passage in
John Eliot's *Ortho-epia Gallica* (1593)
where a braggart is portrayed. In
this speech Pistol seems to be indebted to Eliot and to the dramatists
Peele, Greene, and Kyd.

152–3 *Pluto's damnèd lake* (probably a
confusion for the River Lethe or Styx
of Hades, which Pluto ruled)

153 *Erebus* (the son of Chaos and Night;
also a name for the underworld
itself)

155 *faitours*. The word is akin to 'factor',
but in Shakespeare's time it meant
an impostor or cheat. It seems to
have puzzled those involved in producing F, because they replaced it
with 'Fates'.
Hiren (probably a confusion of 'iron'
(that is, Pistol's sword) and 'Irene'
from a lost play by George Peele,
*The Turkish Mahomet and Hyrin the
Fair Greek*, written some five years
before *2 Henry IV*)

156 *Peesel*. The spelling indicates the pun

implicit in 'Pistol'/'pizzle'. See the
notes to lines 67 and 114.

157 *beseek* (either a blunder or a dialect
form) beseech
aggravate (another malapropism)

158 *good humours* fine goings-on

158–62 *Shall pack-horses ... Greeks.*
Pistol borrows from Marlowe for
lines 158–60 (2 *Tamburlaine*, IV.3.1–2:
'Holla, ye pampered jades of Asia!
What, can ye draw but twenty miles
a day') and from Eliot's *Ortho-epia
Gallica* for the next two lines.

161 *Cannibals*. This is not an error for
'Hannibals' (as might be expected
were the Hostess speaking); it is
drawn from Pistol's source, Eliot: 'I
fear not to fight with a whole army
if it be not of these miscreant Tartar-
ians, Cannibals, Indians, and Musco-
vites.'

162 *Troyant* Trojan

163 *Cerberus* (the three-headed dog that
guarded the underworld, here made
a king)

164 *fall foul for toys* fall out over trifles

BARDOLPH Be gone, good ancient; this will grow to a
brawl anon.

PISTOL Die men like dogs! Give crowns like pins! Have
we not Hiren here?   170

HOSTESS O' my word, captain, there's none such here.
What the goodyear, do you think I would deny her?
For God's sake, be quiet.

PISTOL
Then feed and be fat, my fair Calipolis!
Come, give's some sack.
Si fortune me tormente sperato me contento.
Fear we broadsides? No, let the fiend give fire!
Give me some sack. And, sweetheart, lie thou there!
      (*He lays down his sword*)
Come we to full points here? And are etceteras noth-
ings?

FALSTAFF Pistol, I would be quiet.   180

PISTOL Sweet knight, I kiss thy neaf. What! We have
seen the seven stars!

---

169 *Give crowns like pins!* Tamburlaine
gave his followers kingdoms.
172 *What the goodyear.* See the note to
lines 57–8.
174 *feed and be fat, my fair Calipolis!* (a
paraphrase of lines from Peele's play
The Battle of Alcazar, where Muly
Mahamet offers his starving mother
lion's flesh saying 'Feed then and
faint not, my fair Calipolis . . . Feed
and be fat that we may meet the foe'.
This, like Pistol's other allusions to
plays, would have been familiar to
Elizabethan audiences.)
175 *give's* give us
176 *Si fortune me tormente sperato me contento.* Which language Pistol thinks
he is speaking is uncertain. It is clos-
est to Italian, though, if Pistol's
sword is Spanish and the motto is
inscribed on it (as was common),

Spanish would be expected. He
means 'If fortune torments me, hope
contents me'. Later he offers a
slightly different version of his tag
(v.5.99).
177 *give fire* shoot
178 *sweetheart* (Pistol's sword)
179 *full points* full stops
etceteras nothings. Both words carry
the same innuendo: the female sexual
orifice.
181 *neaf* hand. Pistol's substitution of a
dialect word (meaning 'fist') for
'hand' makes a ridiculous end for his
high-flown phrase.
182 *seen the seven stars* enjoyed companion-
ship at night. The *seven stars* have
been identified as the Pleiades and as
Ursa Major, the latter being the more
arithmetically precise. Falstaff has a
similar phrase at III.2.209.

DOLL For God's sake, thrust him downstairs; I cannot endure such a fustian rascal.

PISTOL Thrust him downstairs? Know we not Galloway nags?

FALSTAFF Quoit him down, Bardolph, like a shove-groat shilling. Nay, an 'a do nothing but speak nothing, 'a shall be nothing here.

190 BARDOLPH Come, get you downstairs.

PISTOL

What! Shall we have incision? Shall we imbrue?
(*He snatches up his sword*)
Then death rock me asleep, abridge my doleful days!
Why then, let grievous, ghastly, gaping wounds
Untwind the Sisters Three! Come, Atropos, I say!

HOSTESS Here's goodly stuff toward!

FALSTAFF Give me my rapier, boy.

DOLL I pray thee, Jack, I pray thee do not draw.

FALSTAFF (*drawing*) Get you downstairs.

HOSTESS Here's a goodly tumult! I'll forswear keeping
200 house afore I'll be in these tirrits and frights! So!

---

184 *fustian* ranting
185 *Know* (1) recognize; (2) have intercourse with
185–6 *Galloway nags* prostitutes (lively as Galloway nags but which any man might ride)
187 *Quoit him* chuck him (like a quoit)
187–8 *shove-groat shilling*. In the game of *shove-groat* (the ancestor of shove-ha'penny), Edward VI shillings were popular as the coins to be pushed up the board. The implication is that Pistol should be given the push in the same way as the coins were.
191 *Shall we have incision? Shall we imbrue?* Both questions mean 'Shall I let blood?' The terms are from surgery.

We is the royal plural.
192 *death rock me asleep*. Either Anne Boleyn or her brother George wrote a lyric beginning 'O Death, rock me on sleep' as they both awaited execution in 1536.
194 *Untwind* untwine
   the Sisters Three (the three Fates. Clotho held the spindle of life's thread; it was drawn by Lachesis and cut by Atropos.)
195 *toward* forthcoming
200 *tirrits* (a word of the Hostess's own, combining 'terror' and 'fits'. It may have been suggested to Shakespeare by the spelling 'tirets' (for 'terrets', a harness ring) in Holinshed's account of Henry IV's reign.)

(Falstaff thrusts at Pistol)

Murder, I warrant now! Alas, alas, put up your naked weapons, put up your naked weapons.

Exit Bardolph, driving Pistol out

DOLL I pray thee, Jack, be quiet; the rascal's gone. Ah, you whoreson little valiant villain, you!

HOSTESS Are you not hurt i'th'groin? Methought 'a made a shrewd thrust at your belly.

Enter Bardolph

FALSTAFF Have you turned him out o'doors?

BARDOLPH Yea, sir, the rascal's drunk. You have hurt him, sir, i'th'shoulder.

FALSTAFF A rascal, to brave me!   210

DOLL Ah, you sweet little rogue, you! Alas, poor ape, how thou sweatest! Come, let me wipe thy face. Come on, you whoreson chops! Ah, rogue, i'faith, I love thee. Thou art as valorous as Hector of Troy, worth five of Agamemnon, and ten times better than the Nine Worthies. Ah, villain!

FALSTAFF A rascally slave! I will toss the rogue in a blanket.

DOLL Do, an thou darest for thy heart. An thou dost, I'll canvass thee between a pair of sheets.   220

---

204 *Whoreson . . . villain.* Doll uses these as terms of endearment. Falstaff's gratified response to the attentions he receives and his repeated recall of his ability in standing up to a mere swaggerer such as Pistol illustrate his decline.

206 *shrewd* vicious

211 *ape* fool (used affectionately)

214 *Hector* (leader of the Trojan forces during the siege of Troy)

218 *Agamemnon* (leader of the Greek forces besieging Troy)

215–16 *the Nine Worthies.* These were: three pagans, Hector, Alexander, and Julius Caesar; three Jews, Joshua, David, and Judas Maccabeus; and three Christians, King Arthur, Charlemagne, and Godfrey of Bouillon (who led the First Crusade).

220 *canvass* (an expression from hawking, meaning 'catch in a net'; here with a sexual innuendo, of course)

Enter musicians

PAGE The music is come, sir.

FALSTAFF Let them play. Play, sirs!

(*Music*)

Sit on my knee, Doll. A rascal bragging slave! The
rogue fled from me like quicksilver.

DOLL I'faith, and thou followed'st him like a church.
Thou whoreson little tidy Bartholomew boar-pig, when
wilt thou leave fighting a-days, and foining a-nights,
and begin to patch up thine old body for heaven?

*Enter, behind, the Prince and Poins disguised as
drawers*

FALSTAFF Peace, good Doll, do not speak like a death's-
230 head; do not bid me remember mine end.

DOLL Sirrah, what humour's the Prince of?

FALSTAFF A good shallow young fellow. 'A would have
made a good pantler; 'a would ha' chipped bread well.

DOLL They say Poins has a good wit.

FALSTAFF He a good wit? Hang him, baboon! His wit's
as thick as Tewkesbury mustard. There's no more con-

---

225 *thou followed'st him like a church.* As
churches are immobile (*the* Church,
indeed, being founded on a rock),
this presumably implies that Falstaff
did not move an inch.

226 *tidy* tender and fat
Bartholomew boar-pig. See the note to
II.1.25–6.

227 *foining* sword-thrusting (with an innuendo, as at II.1.16)

229–30 *a death's-head* a skull, used as a
memento mori. A real skull might serve
as a constant reminder of death as it
stood on a man's desk, and the
design of a skull was used on jewellery. Prostitutes wore rings so engraved; in *The Dutch Courtesan*,
1.2.48–9, they are said to have 'their
wickedness . . . always before their

eyes, and a death's-head most commonly on their middle finger'.

231 *what humour's* what mood is

233 *pantler* pantryman
chipped bread cut off the crusts of
loaves

235–6 *His wit's as thick as Tewkesbury
mustard.* Falstaff's analogy does not
work as he intends. Tewkesbury's
famous mustard was noted for its
sharpness, not its thickness, so the
reference to it would compliment
Poins rather than disparage him. It
seems unlikely that the confusion is
on Shakespeare's part, and it must
be that Falstaff's wit is solidifying,
not Poins's.

236–7 *conceit* wit, imagination

ceit in him than is in a mallet.

DOLL Why does the Prince love him so, then?

FALSTAFF Because their legs are both of a bigness, and 'a
plays at quoits well, and eats conger and fennel, and   240
drinks off candles' ends for flap-dragons, and rides the
wild mare with the boys, and jumps upon joint-stools,
and swears with a good grace, and wears his boots very
smooth like unto the sign of the leg, and breeds no bate
with telling of discreet stories, and such other gambol
faculties 'a has that show a weak mind and an able
body, for the which the Prince admits him. For the
Prince himself is such another – the weight of a hair
will turn the scales between their avoirdupois.

PRINCE HENRY Would not this nave of a wheel have his   250
ears cut off?

237 *mallet* wooden hammer (proverbial
for dullness)
239 *of a bigness* of equal size. (A well-
formed leg was important for a man
of fashion.)
240 *conger*. The conger eel was considered a heavy food and likely to dull
the wits.
fennel (a herb used to flavour fish; it
is supposedly good for the digestion,
hence its association with eel)
241 *flap-dragons*. In the game of flap-
dragons – an exercise in foolish
bravado – small objects (the *flap-
dragons*: sometimes raisins, or, as here,
candles) were floated in liquor. Then
either the liquor had to be drunk
with the objects alight, or the objects
were to be snatched into the mouth
from the burning liquor.
241–2 *rides the wild mare*. This probably
refers to a schoolboy game, still
played, which has many different
names. The 'mare' is formed by some
eight boys bending down one behind
the other, the first propped against a
wall; other boys then run up one

after another and jump astride the
mare with the object of seeing how
many boys it takes to make the mare
collapse.
242 *joint-stools* (stools with well-joinered
legs; jumping over them was another
high-spirited game)
244 *the sign of the leg*. Elizabethan shops
indicated what they sold by displaying an object representing it. Falstaff
means that Poins wears boots as
well-fitting as those of the boot-
maker's advertisement.
244–5 *breeds no bate with telling of discreet
stories*. This means either that Poins
causes no strife (*bate*) with his stories,
because they are discreet; or (more
likely) that he does not commit the
offence of restricting himself to stories that are discreet (that is, he
amuses the Prince with indiscreet
gossip).
245 *gambol* playful
250 *nave* hub (with a pun on 'knave',
Falstaff being as round as a wheel)
250–51 *have his ears cut off* (the penalty
for defaming royalty)

POINS Let's beat him before his whore.

PRINCE HENRY Look whe'er the withered elder hath not
his poll clawed like a parrot.

POINS Is it not strange that desire should so many years
outlive performance?

FALSTAFF Kiss me, Doll.

PRINCE HENRY Saturn and Venus this year in conjunction! What says th'almanac to that?

260 POINS And look whether the fiery trigon his man be not
lisping to his master's old tables, his note-book, his
counsel-keeper.

FALSTAFF Thou dost give me flattering busses.

DOLL By my troth, I kiss thee with a most constant heart.

FALSTAFF I am old, I am old.

DOLL I love thee better than I love e'er a scurvy young
boy of them all.

FALSTAFF What stuff wilt have a kirtle of? I shall receive
money a-Thursday; shalt have a cap tomorrow. A
270 merry song! Come, it grows late; we'll to bed. Thou'lt
forget me when I am gone.

DOLL By my troth, thou'lt set me a-weeping an thou
sayst so. Prove that ever I dress myself handsome till

---

253 *elder* (1) elder-tree; (2) old man

254 *his poll clawed like a parrot.* The precise meaning is not clear. Falstaff's
hair seems to have been ruffled so
that he looks like a parrot – presumably because Doll has been running
her hand through his hair. But par-
rots do not normally look particularly ruffled, though in excitement
their feathers can be disturbed. Some
verbal link may be intended between
'poll' (parrot) and 'Doll'.

258–9 *Saturn and Venus . . . conjunction.*
Saturn, representing old age, and
Venus, representing love, were
thought to be unlikely partners, and

astrologers believed (erroneously)
that the two planets were never *in
conjunction* (in apparent proximity).

260 *fiery trigon.* The twelve signs of the
zodiac were grouped into four tri-
gons (triangles), one of which con-
tained the three fiery signs, Aries,
Leo, and Sagittarius.

his man (Bardolph, with the fiery
countenance)

261 *lisping* speaking lovingly

tables (literally, a notebook for assig-
nations; here used to mean 'whore' –
the Hostess)

263 *busses* kisses

268 *kirtle* dress

thy return. Well, hearken a'th'end.

FALSTAFF Some sack, Francis.

PRINCE HENRY *and* POINS (*coming forward*) Anon, anon,
sir.

FALSTAFF Ha! A bastard son of the King's? And art not
thou Poins his brother?

PRINCE HENRY Why, thou globe of sinful continents,   280
what a life dost thou lead!

FALSTAFF A better than thou – I am a gentleman; thou
art a drawer.

PRINCE HENRY Very true, sir, and I come to draw you
out by the ears.

HOSTESS O, the Lord preserve thy grace! By my troth,
welcome to London! Now the Lord bless that sweet
face of thine! O Jesu, are you come from Wales?

FALSTAFF Thou whoreson mad compound of majesty,
by this light – flesh and corrupt blood (*laying his hand*   290
upon Doll), thou art welcome.

DOLL How! You fat fool, I scorn you.

POINS My lord, he will drive you out of your revenge
and turn all to a merriment, if you take not the heat.

---

274 *hearken a'th'end* (proverbial) see what
time will show

276–7 *Anon, anon, sir*. This is the response that drawers customarily
made as they rushed about serving
drinks. In *1 Henry IV*, II.4.20–100,
the Prince and Poins have a game
with the drawer Francis, making him
repeat the cry interminably. Here, as
soon as they speak these words Falstaff recognizes them, as if he recalled
the episode. In fact he had not arrived on the scene then, but doubtless an audience would not remember
this so exactly; possibly Shakespeare
also did not.

279 *Poins his*. The Q reading reproduced
here is a possessive construction

which would now be rendered by
'Poins's'. F has a comma after *Poins*,
which implies that Poins is the
brother of this *bastard son of the
King's*.

280 *sinful continents* (with a pun on the
meanings 'containers of sin' and
'sinful contents')

289 *compound* lump

290 *by this light* (a common oath, which
Falstaff then extends to refer to Doll
– *this light flesh and corrupt
blood*)

294 *if you take not the heat* if you do not
(as an iron does) take up the heat of
the moment so that you may give it
out again (that is, join in)

PRINCE HENRY You whoreson candle-mine you, how
vilely did you speak of me now, before this honest,
virtuous, civil gentlewoman!

HOSTESS God's blessing of your good heart, and so she
is, by my troth!

300 FALSTAFF Didst thou hear me?

PRINCE HENRY Yea, and you knew me, as you did when
you ran away by Gad's Hill; you knew I was at your
back, and spoke it on purpose to try my patience.

FALSTAFF No, no, no, not so; I did not think thou wast
within hearing.

PRINCE HENRY I shall drive you then to confess the
wilful abuse, and then I know how to handle you.

FALSTAFF No abuse, Hal, o' mine honour, no abuse.

PRINCE HENRY Not? To dispraise me, and call me
310 pantler, and bread-chipper, and I know not what?

FALSTAFF No abuse, Hal.

POINS No abuse?

FALSTAFF No abuse, Ned, i'th'world, honest Ned, none.
I dispraised him before the wicked that the wicked
might not fall in love with (turning to Prince Henry) thee
– in which doing, I have done the part of a careful friend
and a true subject, and thy father is to give me thanks
for it. No abuse, Hal; none, Ned, none; no, faith, boys,
none.

320 PRINCE HENRY See now whether pure fear and entire
cowardice doth not make thee wrong this virtuous
gentlewoman to close with us. Is she of the wicked? Is
thine hostess here of the wicked? Or is thy boy of the

---

295 candle-mine. Falstaff is so gross that
candles could be mined from him.
296 honest chaste
301–2 as . . . Gad's Hill. This recalls Falstaff's claim that he ran away at Gad's
Hill because he knew his opponent
was the Prince, and 'The lion will

not touch the true prince' (1 Henry
IV, II.4.265).
314 the wicked the unregenerate (a puritan idiom, Falstaff taking the guise
of a puritan preacher)
322 close with side with

wicked? Or honest Bardolph, whose zeal burns in his
nose, of the wicked?

POINS Answer, thou dead elm, answer.

FALSTAFF The fiend hath pricked down Bardolph irrecoverable, and his face is Lucifer's privy-kitchen,
where he doth nothing but roast malt-worms. For the
boy, there is a good angel about him, but the devil binds   330
him too.

PRINCE HENRY For the women?

FALSTAFF For one of them, she's in hell already, and
burns poor souls. For th'other, I owe her money, and
whether she be damned for that I know not.

324 *zeal* (another word with puritan asso-
ciations, immortalized in the name
Zeal-of-the-Land-Busy in Jonson's
Bartholomew Fair)

326 *dead elm.* Falstaff is no longer a *withered elder* (line 253) but a *dead elm*.
The elm is noted for its size and
notorious for the ease with which it
rots from the centre and collapses.
Traditionally it was the support of
the vine, as Falstaff is for the prod-
ucts of the vine.

327 *pricked* marked (as in a list)

328 *privy-kitchen* personal kitchen (presumably, as kitchens tend to be the
hottest part of a house, the hottest
part of hell)

329 *malt-worms* drunkards (those who
love 'the malt')
For as for

330 *good angel.* See the note to I.2.166.
binds. Q has 'blinds', F 'outbids', and
editors have offered a variety of interpretations of these words. But, as
the editor of the New Variorum edition puts it, 'It may be . . . that Shakespeare wrote something different
from both ["blinds" and "outbids"]
and that both are guesses'. The emendation suggested here, *binds*, is close

to the Q reading, and 'blinds' is a
very possible error for it; the Q compositor was prone to mistakes of this
kind (see the note to I.1.41; and in
the second Quarto of *Richard II*, on
which he worked, 'sparkes' is printed
as 'sparkles'). *Binds* is appropriate to
the context and also to Falstaff, who
is well versed in biblical matters and
religious language (see lines 314 and
324 of this scene, and the notes to
I.2.33, 34, and 191). Besides its
common meaning of 'make fast', *bind*
has a specific religious meaning;
when Christ says to Peter that he is
the rock upon which the Church will
be founded He tells him: 'whatsoever
thou shalt bind in earth shall be
bound in heaven, and whatsoever
thou shalt loose in earth shall be
loosed in heaven' (Matthew 16.19,
repeated at 18.18). Falstaff is suggesting that the boy is bound (1) in this
spiritual and ecclesiastical way to the
Devil, and (2) as an apprentice to 'a
devil', Bardolph. As the Prince says
at II.2.66–8, Falstaff was given the
boy Christian and he is now transformed into an ape – probably equivalent to a devil, for in the Middle

HOSTESS No, I warrant you.

FALSTAFF No, I think thou art not; I think thou art quit
for that. Marry, there is another indictment upon thee,
for suffering flesh to be eaten in thy house, contrary to
the law, for the which I think thou wilt howl.

340

HOSTESS All victuallers do so. What's a joint of mutton
or two in a whole Lent?

PRINCE HENRY You, gentlewoman —

DOLL What says your grace?

FALSTAFF His grace says that which his flesh rebels
against.

Peto knocks at door

HOSTESS Who knocks so loud at door? Look to th'door
there, Francis.

Enter Peto

PRINCE HENRY
Peto, how now, what news?

PETO

350

The King your father is at Westminster,
And there are twenty weak and wearied posts
Come from the north; and as I came along
I met and overtook a dozen captains,
Bare-headed, sweating, knocking at the taverns,

Ages the 'old ape' was the Devil (in
the poem *The Ancrene Riwle*), and in
Elizabethan times Antichrist was said
to be 'the Ape of our Lord Christ'.

334 *burns* infects (with venereal disease)

335 *damned*. Usury was forbidden by
Church and state.

337 *quit* (1) forgiven (in a religious
sense); (2) repaid

339 *suffering flesh to be eaten in thy house*
(1) allowing meat to be eaten in your
house (on fast days); (2) using your
house as a brothel. 'Flesh' could
mean sexual intercourse (as, for example, in the phrase 'exchange flesh',
The Winter's Tale, IV.4.278) or, in 'a

piece of flesh', a woman, especially a
prostitute.

340 *howl*. This probably picks up the
religious implications of what has
gone before and suggests howling in
hell.

341 *mutton* (1) sheep meat; (2) prostitute

345–6 *says that which his flesh rebels against*
utters a word — *gentlewoman* — which
serves to gloss over that which his
sexual appetite now finds repugnant

351 *posts* messengers travelling post-
haste

354 *Bare-headed* (indicative of the urgency of the captains' search: to go

And asking every one for Sir John Falstaff.

PRINCE HENRY
By heaven, Poins, I feel me much to blame,
So idly to profane the precious time
When tempest of commotion, like the south
Borne with black vapour, doth begin to melt
And drop upon our bare unarmèd heads.   360
Give me my sword and cloak. Falstaff, good night.

Exeunt Prince and Poins

FALSTAFF Now comes in the sweetest morsel of the
night, and we must hence and leave it unpicked.

Knocking within   *Exit Bardolph*

More knocking at the door?

Enter Bardolph

How now, what's the matter?

BARDOLPH
You must away to court, sir, presently.
A dozen captains stay at door for you.

FALSTAFF (*to Page*) Pay the musicians, sirrah. Farewell,
hostess; farewell, Doll. You see, my good wenches, how
men of merit are sought after; the undeserver may sleep,   370
when the man of action is called on. Farewell, good
wenches. If I be not sent away post, I will see you again
ere I go.

DOLL I cannot speak; if my heart be not ready to burst —
well, sweet Jack, have a care of thyself.

FALSTAFF Farewell, farewell.

Exit with Bardolph, Peto, Page, and musicians

bare-headed was very unusual)
356 *I feel me much to blame.* The Prince,
who has not entered very wholeheartedly into the action of this scene (in
contrast to his behaviour in the
equivalent scene of *1 Henry IV*),
begins now to feel positive guilt.
358 *the south* the south wind (supposed

to bring stormy weather)
363 *unpicked* unenjoyed
366 *presently* immediately
367 *stay* wait
368 *Pay the musicians.* Unless Falstaff's
purse has been replenished since
1.2.237 the musicians will fare badly.
372 *post* post-haste

HOSTESS Well, fare thee well. I have known thee these
twenty-nine years, come peascod-time, but an honester
and truer-hearted man – well, fare thee well

380 BARDOLPH (*at the door*) Mistress Tearsheet!

HOSTESS What's the matter?

BARDOLPH Bid Mistress Tearsheet come to my master.

HOSTESS O, run, Doll, run! Run, good Doll! Come! –
She comes blubbered. – Yea, will you come, Doll?

Exeunt

III.I   *Enter the King in his nightgown, followed by a page*

KING HENRY IV

Go call the Earls of Surrey and of Warwick –
But, ere they come, bid them o'er-read these letters
And well consider of them. Make good speed.

Exit page

378 *peascod-time* (the time when peas
form in their pods). 'In Peascod-time'
was a very popular tune in the sixteenth century. One of the ballads
most frequently sung to it was 'The
Lamentable Ballad of the Lady's
Fall', and that would be quite likely
to occur to an Elizabethan audience,
if not to the Hostess. The first verse
begins:

Mark well my heavy doleful tale,
    You loyal lovers all;
And heedfully bear in your breast
    A gallant lady's fall.

The tune is given by Chappell in
Popular Music of the Olden Time I
(1859), 198. The other song most
sung to the tune was 'The Ballad of
Chevy Chase'.

378–9 *an honester and truer-hearted man.*
Falstaff is, of course, anything but

honest and true-hearted. What is
more, as this scene has shown, the
Hostess knows that only too well.
Her words (as two nineteenth-
century editors, Charles and Mary
Clarke, put it very well) 'serve better
than pages of commentary' to indicate Sir John's powers of fascina-
tion.

384 *blubbered* with face tear-stained

III.I This scene was omitted in some
copies of Q. See the Account of the
Text, page 461. The King's speech is
curiously different in the Q and F versions; see collations lists 1 and 2 in the
Account of the Text.

(stage direction) *nightgown* dressing-gown
    followed by a page. On Q's reading,
    '*alone*', see the note to the opening
    stage direction of I.2. F has '*with a
    Page*'.

How many thousand of my poorest subjects
Are at this hour asleep! O sleep, O gentle sleep,
Nature's soft nurse, how have I frighted thee,
That thou no more wilt weigh my eyelids down
And steep my senses in forgetfulness?
Why rather, sleep, liest thou in smoky cribs,
Upon uneasy pallets stretching thee,   10
And hushed with buzzing night-flies to thy slumber,
Than in the perfumed chambers of the great,
Under the canopies of costly state,
And lulled with sound of sweetest melody?
O thou dull god, why liest thou with the vile
In loathsome beds, and leavest the kingly couch
A watch-case, or a common 'larum-bell?
Wilt thou upon the high and giddy mast
Seal up the ship-boy's eyes, and rock his brains
In cradle of the rude imperious surge,   20
And in the visitation of the winds,
Who take the ruffian billows by the top,
Curling their monstrous heads, and hanging them

---

5   *O sleep, O gentle sleep*. On many occasions Shakespeare comments on the difficulty with which sleep comes to the troubled mind. This half-line seems to echo the opening of a sonnet by Sir Philip Sidney, 'Come, sleep, O sleep, the certain knot of peace' (*Astrophil and Stella* 39), but with Shakespeare there is a very strong association between inability to sleep and those troubled by doubts as to the course of action they should adopt, whether they are rightly in authority – as is Henry V (*Henry V* IV.1.250–77) – or are usurpers (*Macbeth*, II.2.36–40). Even in this respect the association is not peculiar to Shakespeare (see the first note to line 31).

9   *cribs* hovels

10   *uneasy pallets* uncomfortable beds

13   *state* grandeur

15   *vile* lowly

17   *watch-case*. The meaning is not known. Some editors suggest that a sentry-box is meant; and the expression has also been interpreted as equating the king in his bed with the restless mechanism of a watch-case. The former meaning, if grounded in fact, would be simple and straightforward, but there is no firm evidence for it. The second suggestion is strained; but it would lead on naturally to the *common 'larum bell*, especially as in Shakespeare's time there were already watches which could sound an alarm.

21   *visitation* violent buffeting

With deafing clamour in the slippery clouds,
That with the hurly death itself awakes?
Canst thou, O partial sleep, give thy repose
To the wet sea-son in an hour so rude,
And in the calmest and most stillest night,
With all appliances and means to boot,
30   Deny it to a king? Then happy low, lie down!
Uneasy lies the head that wears a crown.

       Enter Warwick and Surrey

WARWICK
  Many good morrows to your majesty!

KING HENRY IV
  Is it good morrow, lords?

WARWICK
  'Tis one o'clock, and past.

---

24 *slippery* swiftly passing
25 *hurly* uproar
27 *sea-son*. Q has 'season', F 'Sea-Boy'. A sort of sense can be wrung from 'season', but it is more probably the *ship-boy* (line 19) who is referred to. 'Sea-son' is a trifle awkward; it sounds rather like elegant variation on Shakespeare's part, and he may have had second thoughts and changed 'son' to 'boy'. On the other hand, that is exactly the kind of change, from the unusual to the obvious, that is made by copyists.

Sea-son seems idiosyncratic enough to be Shakespeare's; 'sea-boy' could be his or anyone's.

29 *to boot* into the bargain
30 *happy low, lie down*. In Q the word *happy* is enclosed in parentheses, a device that was sometimes punctuational and sometimes indicated an aside. Neither usage seems appropriate here, and it has been suggested that *happy* was meant to be deleted, especially as there are twelve syllables in the line. The meaning may simply be 'you who are happy in being low-born, lie sleeping'; but it is just possible that the King addresses *lie down* to himself.

31 *Uneasy lies the head that wears a crown*. Erasmus had expressed this idea in his *Institutio Principis* (1516) and it was already proverbial in Shakespeare's time; but his phrasing has made it seem his own creation.

(stage direction) Q gives an entry here (and at v.2.42) for Blunt, but he has no lines in the play. However, a mute called Blunt is required to lead Colevile away at IV.3.74, and there would be no harm if a stage extra who played that part also appeared here, especially as at line 35 the King bids *good morrow to you all, my lords* (though 'all' could mean only two). Like Blunt, Surrey has no lines to speak, but the King calls for him by name in line 1. See the note to 1.1.16 and the Account of the Text, page 460.

KING HENRY IV

   Why then, good morrow to you all, my lords.
   Have you read o'er the letters that I sent you?

WARWICK

   We have, my liege.

KING HENRY IV

   Then you perceive the body of our kingdom
   How foul it is, what rank diseases grow,
   And with what danger, near the heart of it.   40

WARWICK

   It is but as a body yet distempered,
   Which to his former strength may be restored
   With good advice and little medicine.
   My lord Northumberland will soon be cooled.

KING HENRY IV

   O God, that one might read the book of fate,
   And see the revolution of the times
   Make mountains level, and the continent,
   Weary of solid firmness, melt itself
   Into the sea; and other times to see
   The beachy girdle of the ocean   50
   Too wide for Neptune's hips; how chance's mocks
   And changes fill the cup of alteration
   With divers liquors! 'Tis not ten years gone

---

42 *his* its
43 *little* a little
46 *the revolution of the times*. Although the King is concerned with rebellion, he means simply 'the changes wrought by the passage of the times', just as changes are seen with the progress of the seasons.
47 *continent* dry land
51 *chance's mocks*. The absence of the apostrophe in Q and F has led some editors to read 'chances' as a plural noun, either followed by a comma or with *mock* as a verb. But 'the

mockeries (or 'tricks') of chance' seems likely, especially with *changes* in line 52.
53 Q has three and a half lines here which do not appear in F. It has been suggested that they were censored from F because they are so pessimistic as to be offensive to Christians; but this is not wholly convincing. The complete passage (modernized) reads

With divers liquors! O, if this were
   seen,

Since Richard and Northumberland, great friends,
Did feast together, and in two years after
Were they at wars. It is but eight years since
This Percy was the man nearest my soul,
Who like a brother toiled in my affairs
And laid his love and life under my foot;
60   Yea, for my sake, even to the eyes of Richard
Gave him defiance. But which of you was by –
(*To Warwick*) You, cousin Nevil, as I may remember –
When Richard, with his eye brimful of tears,
Then checked and rated by Northumberland,
Did speak these words, now proved a prophecy?

The happiest youth, viewing his
     progress through,
What perils past, what crosses to
     ensue,
Would shut the book and sit him
     down and die.
'Tis not ten years gone,
Since Richard and Northumberland,
     great friends, . . .

It will be noted that the fifth of these lines not only is a half-line but also runs on exactly in metre *and in sense* from *With divers liquors!* Half- or part-lines are not an impossibility (see v.2.67 and v.5.75); but the passage omitted from F seems an awkward interpolation. A. R. Humphreys suggested that it was an addition made at some stage, perhaps marginally, to an early draft, since, if it were Shakespeare's final intention to retain it, he would surely have given more weight to the half-line, for instance by writing '*Tis* in full. On these grounds the passage is omitted here. See the Account of the Text, page 468, and the notes to IV.5.76–7 and 178.

53,55,56 *not ten years . . . two years . . . eight years.* The events which culmi-

nated in the affair at Gaultree Forest took place in 1405. A full decade would take one back well before the break between Richard and Northumberland; Richard was deposed in 1399 and the Battle of Shrewsbury took place in 1403.

61,66–7,71–3 *Gave him defiance . . . into corruption.* Shakespeare may here have in mind more than one scene of *Richard II.* When Richard is at Flint Castle, Northumberland obeys Bolingbroke's order to 'send the breath of parley | Into his ruined ears' (*Richard II*, III.3.33–4). Northumberland's face-to-face defiance of Richard comes in the deposition scene (IV.1.221–74). The words echoed here at lines 66–7 and 71–3 are part of Richard's speech to Northumberland at v.1.55–68.

62 *Cousin* (often used imprecisely for any blood relation or (as here) as a mark of friendliness between people not related to each other)
Nevil. The Earl of Warwick at this time was a Beauchamp, not a Neville; and he does not appear at all in *Richard II.*

64 *rated* berated

'Northumberland, thou ladder by the which
My cousin Bolingbroke ascends my throne' –
Though then, God knows, I had no such intent
But that necessity so bowed the state
That I and greatness were compelled to kiss –   70
'The time shall come' – thus did he follow it –
'The time will come that foul sin, gathering head,
Shall break into corruption' – so went on,
Foretelling this same time's condition,
And the division of our amity.

WARWICK

There is a history in all men's lives
Figuring the natures of the times deceased,

69 *necessity*. When Bolingbroke returns to England, breaking his banishment, he maintains, indeed swears, that he comes only for what is rightfully his, invoking the specious plea 'As I was banished, I was banished Hereford; | But as I come, I come for Lancaster' (*Richard II*, II.3.112–13). Even in the course of claiming what is his, before the confrontation with Richard, he orders the execution of Bushy and Green (III.1), an act which only the king (or a judge with the king's authority) might command. There is no question that he is a usurper, a fact which still troubles his son when, as Henry V, he prays before Agincourt: 'Not today, O Lord, | not today, think not upon the fault | My father made in compassing the crown!' (*Henry V*, IV.1.285–7). Henry IV blames Exton for Richard's murder but admits (*Richard II*, v.6.39) that he 'did wish him dead' (and in this play (IV.5.93) he accuses his son of wishing for his death with the words *Thy wish was father, Harry, to that thought*). It is unlikely that Shakespeare intended Henry to seem guiltless in encompassing the crown; his part in Richard's deposition and murder, his remorse, his son's sense of inherited guilt, run through the sequence of plays too insistently for him to escape blame (see also the note to IV.5.185). On the other hand he undoubtedly returned to an England despoiled, and this also Shakespeare graphically shows, particularly in the scene with the Gardeners in *Richard II* (III.4). To that extent, *necessity*, the needs of England, was something that Henry IV as Bolingbroke was forced to respond to. The meaning of 'necessity' is well illustrated in one of Oliver Cromwell's speeches to Parliament (1654): 'Necessity hath no law. Feigned necessities, imaginary necessities ... are the greatest cozenage that men can put upon the Providence of God, and make pretences to break known rules by.' The balance between self-seeking and selfless concerns is nicely held here. See also the note to lines 88, 89.

77 *Figuring the natures of the times deceased* reproducing the forms of the past

The which observed, a man may prophesy,
With a near aim, of the main chance of things
80   As yet not come to life, who in their seeds
And weak beginning lie intreasurèd.
Such things become the hatch and brood of time,
And by the necessary form of this
King Richard might create a perfect guess
That great Northumberland, then false to him,
Would of that seed grow to a greater falseness,
Which should not find a ground to root upon
Unless on you.

KING HENRY IV Are these things then necessities?
Then let us meet them like necessities,
90   And that same word even now cries out on us.
They say the Bishop and Northumberland
Are fifty thousand strong.

WARWICK   It cannot be, my lord.
Rumour doth double, like the voice and echo,
The numbers of the feared. Please it your grace
To go to bed. Upon my soul, my lord,
The powers that you already have sent forth
Shall bring this prize in very easily.
To comfort you the more, I have received
A certain instance that Glendower is dead.
100   Your majesty hath been this fortnight ill,
And these unseasoned hours perforce must add

---

79 *chance* outcome
80 *who* which
81 *intreasurèd* safely stored
83 *necessary form* inevitable pattern
88,89 *necessities*. Henry, perhaps a trifle ironically, repeats the word from line 69 to summarize Warwick's philosophical explanation of the inevitability of certain causes and the effects that follow.
99 *A certain instance* unquestionable evidence

Glendower is dead. Glendower supported the rebels in *1 Henry IV*. The historical Glendower did not die for another decade – after Henry IV, in fact, though Holinshed reports his death in 1409, four years after the events here dramatized. In 1405, however, Glendower's son was captured in a scuffle at Usk, and it may be this that Shakespeare had in mind.

101 *unseasoned* (late)

Unto your sickness.

KING HENRY IV   I will take your counsel.

And were these inward wars once out of hand,

We would, dear lords, unto the Holy Land.   *Exeunt*

Enter Justice Shallow and Justice Silence   III.2

SHALLOW Come on, come on, come on! Give me your
hand, sir, give me your hand, sir! An early stirrer, by

102 *take* accept
103 *inward* internal (civil)
      out of hand off our hands
104 *the Holy Land.* At the end of *Richard
      II* (v.6.49–50) Henry IV, full of re-
      morse for Richard's murder, says 'I'll
      make a voyage to the Holy Land |
      To wash the blood off from my
      guilty hand'. At the beginning of *1
      Henry IV* (1.1.19–21 and 100–101) he
      recalls his intention but is forced by
      rebellion at home to postpone his
      crusade. This levying of a force to
      fight for Jerusalem anticipates hist-
      orical events by about a decade.
      The historical Henry IV planned an
      expedition 'to recover the city of
      Jerusalem from the infidels' (as
      Holinshed puts it) in 1412 and ships,
      men, and materials were collected to
      this end. The King here refers to his
      proposed expedition, and at IV.4.1–
      10 he will report *Our navy is addressed,
      our power collected* in order to fight on
      higher fields. However, Henry was
      taken ill before he could leave, and
      the nearest he got to Jerusalem as
      King (for he had made a pilgrimage
      there as Duke of Lancaster in 1392–
      3) was the Jerusalem Chamber at
      Westminster, where he died (see the
      note to IV.5.234–9).

III.2 This is undoubtedly one of the

great comic scenes in English drama.
Its success depends at least as much
on the two justices as on Falstaff,
and it is possible that Shakespeare,
conscious of the decline in the fortunes of Falstaff, deliberately provided an alternative source of
comedy, one lacking the sourness
which characterizes much of Falstaff's part in this play. The scene is
set in Gloucestershire, though we
are not told that until IV.3.81 (see
the Introduction, page 437). Shakespeare may seem to be mocking
country life if the scene is taken out
of context; but if it is considered as
part of the play as a whole, its kindly
humour and warm humanity show a
marked contrast with the comic
scenes set in London and the events
at Gaultree Forest.

Q's opening stage direction brings
on the two justices alone, presumably
indicating that the prospective recruits should enter one by one as
their names are called. F, however,
brings them all on at once with the
justices. This has been thought to
reflect Elizabethan stage practice,
and it has been followed in a number
of modern productions. But the dialogue seems to suggest that the recruits appear individually: at line 95
Falstaff asks to see them, and at lines

the rood! And how doth my good cousin Silence?

SILENCE Good morrow, good cousin Shallow.

SHALLOW And how doth my cousin your bedfellow? And
your fairest daughter and mine, my god-daughter Ellen?

SILENCE Alas, a black woosel, cousin Shallow!

SHALLOW By yea and no, sir. I dare say my cousin
William is become a good scholar – he is at Oxford still,
is he not?

SILENCE Indeed, sir, to my cost.

SHALLOW 'A must then to the Inns o'Court shortly. I
was once of Clement's Inn, where I think they will talk
of mad Shallow yet.

SILENCE You were called 'lusty Shallow' then, cousin.

SHALLOW By the mass, I was called anything, and I
would have done anything indeed too, and roundly too.
There was I, and little John Doit of Staffordshire, and
black George Barnes, and Francis Pickbone, and Will
Squele, a Cotsole man – you had not four such swinge-
bucklers in all the Inns o'Court again. And I may say

98–9 Shallow says *Let them appear as
I call* and then asks for the first man
– *where is Mouldy?* Moreover, there is
no certainty that F represents stage
practice here, since it several times
gives entries long before the characters are required on stage. This *may*
reflect the use of actors' parts (see
pages 465–8), for although the parts
could provide the words said (and
added) they might prove inadequate
as a guide for allocating entries. If all
the recruits enter at the beginning of
the scene, the business associated
(quite properly) with them takes
away from the comedy of the two
justices, part visual, part verbal; and
it produces one guffaw from the audience instead of the sequence of

laughs that can begin with the justices' entry and continue as each recruit appears.

3 *rood* cross
cousin. See the first note to III.1.62.

7 *black woosel* black ousel (blackbird).
Ellen, alas, is not a blonde, and at
the time dark-haired girls were out
of fashion.

13 *Clement's Inn* (situated in the Strand;
one of the Inns of Chancery, which
prepared law students for the Inns of
Court and were considered inferior
to them)

15 *lusty* (1) lively; (2) lascivious

17 *roundly* thoroughly, without ceremony

20 *Cotsole* (for 'Cotswold')

20–21 *swinge-bucklers* swash-bucklers

to you, we knew where the bona-robas were, and had the best of them all at commandment. Then was Jack Falstaff, now Sir John, a boy, and page to Thomas Mowbray, Duke of Norfolk.

SILENCE This Sir John, cousin, that comes hither anon about soldiers?

SHALLOW The same Sir John, the very same. I see him break Scoggin's head at the court gate, when 'a was a crack, not thus high; and the very same day did I fight   30 with one Samson Stockfish, a fruiterer, behind Gray's Inn. Jesu, Jesu, the mad days that I have spent! And to see how many of my old acquaintance are dead!

SILENCE We shall all follow, cousin.

SHALLOW Certain, 'tis certain, very sure, very sure. Death, as the Psalmist saith, is certain to all; all shall die. How a good yoke of bullocks at Stamford fair?

SILENCE By my troth, I was not there.

SHALLOW Death is certain. Is old Double of your town living yet?   40

SILENCE Dead, sir.

SHALLOW Jesu, Jesu, dead! 'A drew a good bow, and dead! 'A shot a fine shoot. John o'Gaunt loved him well, and betted much money on his head. Dead! 'A would

---

22 *bona-robas* smarter prostitutes ('good stuff', as Florio put it in 1598)

29 *Scoggin.* A Henry Scogan was court-poet to Henry IV (and a friend of Chaucer); a John Scoggin served Edward IV as a jester, and his surname became synonymous with 'buffoon'.

30 *crack* (cheeky) lad

31 *Samson Stockfish. Samson* gives a fine impression of Shallow's boldness; but 'stockfish' is dried cod. For an Elizabethan audience a slight pause between the two names would give the right comic effect; but this must

largely be lost on an audience today.

31–2 *behind Gray's Inn* (in Gray's Inn Fields)

36 *Death, as the Psalmist saith* . . . (Psalm 89.48: 'What man is he that liveth and shall not see death?')

37 *How* what price is
Stamford fair. Stamford, in Lincoln-shire, was famous for its great horse and cattle fairs, held in February, Lent, and August.

43 *John o'Gaunt* (Henry IV's father). Here and later in the scene F spells out 'of'; Q uses the colloquial form 'a'. See the Introduction, page 452.

have clapped i'th'clout at twelve score, and carried you
a forehand shaft a fourteen and fourteen and a half,
that it would have done a man's heart good to see. How
a score of ewes now?

SILENCE Thereafter as they be; a score of good ewes may
be worth ten pounds.

SHALLOW And is old Double dead?

SILENCE Here come two of Sir John Falstaff's men, as I
think.

Enter Bardolph and one with him

SHALLOW Good morrow, honest gentlemen.

BARDOLPH I beseech you, which is Justice Shallow?

SHALLOW I am Robert Shallow, sir, a poor esquire of
this county, and one of the King's justices of the peace.
What is your good pleasure with me?

---

45 *clapped i'th'clout at twelve score.* We
cannot now tell whether hitting the
centre of a target (marked by a small
piece of cloth, a *clout*) at 240 yards
was, by the standards of the time,
easy, exceptional, or impossible. The
evidence we have is contradictory. It
seems unlikely that a countryman
would not know what a good shot
was, and though Shallow might be
exaggerating the range (see the next
note) he probably knows what he is
talking about here.

46 *a forehand shaft a fourteen and fourteen
and a half.* These distances are 280
and 290 yards, not impossible if an
arrow is shot high into the air; but
Shallow's point is that when Double
fired he aimed at his target by keeping it in sight above his bow hand
(shooting a *forehand shaft*), and this
seems very improbable. The comedy
is probably no deeper than a gentle
mockery of the old story-teller given

to exaggeration.

49 *Thereafter as they be* according to their
quality. The phrase has a country
ring about it; if it sounded strange to
a London audience it would have
helped to reinforce the sense of a
different locality.

54 SHALLOW. In Q, as first printed,
this speech (as well as the next) was
given to Bardolph. In the course of
printing his name was removed, and
when this portion of the play was
later reset (because of the insertion
of III.1) it was again omitted. F seems
to clear up the problem satisfactorily
by giving the speech to Shallow,
who, as the host, would be likely to
greet the new arrivals. If actors' parts
underlie F (see pages 465–8) one
would expect them to have given the
correct allocation of speeches.

56 *esquire* (a rank between gentleman and
knight)

BARDOLPH My captain, sir, commends him to you, my
captain Sir John Falstaff, a tall gentleman, by heaven,   60
and a most gallant leader.

SHALLOW He greets me well, sir; I knew him a good
backsword man. How doth the good knight? May I ask
how my lady his wife doth?

BARDOLPH Sir, pardon; a soldier is better accommodated
than with a wife.

SHALLOW It is well said, in faith, sir, and it is well said
indeed too. 'Better accommodated'! It is good, yea
indeed is it. Good phrases are surely, and ever were,
very commendable. 'Accommodated': it comes of   70
accommodo. Very good, a good phrase.

BARDOLPH Pardon, sir, I have heard the word – phrase
call you it? By this day, I know not the phrase, but I
will maintain the word with my sword to be a soldier-
like word, and a word of exceeding good command, by
heaven. Accommodated: that is, when a man is, as they
say, accommodated, or when a man is being whereby 'a
may be thought to be accommodated; which is an
excellent thing.

SHALLOW It is very just.   80

Enter Falstaff

Look, here comes good Sir John. Give me your good
hand, give me your worship's good hand. By my troth,
you like well, and bear your years very well. Welcome,
good Sir John.

FALSTAFF I am glad to see you well, good Master Robert

---

60 *tall* valiant
63 *backsword man* (one who fenced, for
  practice, with a stick with a basket-
  work hilt)
65 *accommodated* (seemingly a word
  coming into favour at the time, and
  Shallow immediately pounces on it.
  This points to the interest Shake-

speare's audience could be expected
  to have in new words.)
69 *phrases*. 'Phrase' could be used to
  mean a single word.
75 *word of exceeding good command* very
  good military term
80 *It is very just* that is very true
83 *like* thrive

Shallow. Master Surecard, as I think?

SHALLOW No, Sir John, it is my cousin Silence, in commission with me.

FALSTAFF Good Master Silence, it well befits you should
90   be of the peace.

SILENCE Your good worship is welcome.

FALSTAFF Fie, this is hot weather, gentlemen. Have you provided me here half a dozen sufficient men?

86 *Surecard*. Q gives the name as 'Soc-card', but that text is very unreliable with names (for example it has 'Bill-ingsgate' for 'Basingstoke' at II.1.168, and 'Weminster' for 'West-minster' at II.4.350). *Surecard* offers some sort of meaning (as do the names of other characters in this scene). It can mean a certainty (a trump card); and the great eighteenth-century editor Edmond Malone maintained that it was a word for 'boon companion' in the seven-teenth century, though no evidence for that statement has survived.

87 *Silence*. Here and in a number of other places this name is spelt 'Scilens' in Q. This very unusual spelling also occurs in a short section of the manu-script additions to the play *Sir Thomas More*, and many scholars adduce this similarity as part of the evidence for Shakespeare's having had a hand in the revision of that play. The unusual spelling (which is not known to occur elsewhere in the work of the man who set Q – and indeed in resetting part of this pas-sage he altered the spelling to 'Silens') suggests that the copy used in printing Q may have been Shake-speare's own manuscript. See also the Account of the Text, page 468.

87–8 *in commission* (as justice of the peace)

92–282 Falstaff also recruits men in

1 Henry IV, where he freely admits to having 'misused the King's press damnably' (IV.2.12–13). His beha-viour can look comic enough to us, but corrupt recruiting practices (which dated back at least to the time of the historic Henry IV's youth) were a matter of particular social concern at the end of the six-teenth century. The Vice element in Falstaff's character (see the Introduc-tion, page 445) may well have struck an Elizabethan audience in this re-spect, especially when he admits to having led his men where they were so 'peppered' that not three of them are left alive (*1 Henry IV*, v.3.35–7). This recruiting scene is in the main comic; but the comedy springs chiefly from the justices, who are well-intentioned, and the recruits, who are not all as mean as they may be made to appear (see lines 228–32), and it is to some extent counterbal-anced by the corrupt practices of Falstaff and Bardolph. In *1 Henry IV*, IV.2.13–34, Falstaff describes how he recruits only those able to buy themselves out of service, pocket-ing what they pay him and replacing them what with 'tattered prodigals'. It is the tattered prodigals we see here; the best physical specimen, Bullcalf, is allowed, together with Mouldy, to bribe his way out of service.

93 *sufficient* able

SHALLOW Marry, have we, sir. Will you sit?

FALSTAFF Let me see them, I beseech you.

SHALLOW Where's the roll? Where's the roll? Where's the roll? Let me see, let me see, let me see. So, so, so, so, so, so, so. Yea, marry, sir. Rafe Mouldy! Let them appear as I call, let them do so, let them do so. Let me see – where is Mouldy?   100

    Enter Mouldy

MOULDY Here, an't please you.

SHALLOW What think you, Sir John? A good-limbed fellow, young, strong, and of good friends.

FALSTAFF Is thy name Mouldy?

MOULDY Yea, an't please you.

FALSTAFF 'Tis the more time thou wert used.

SHALLOW Ha, ha, ha! Most excellent, i'faith! Things that are mouldy lack use! Very singular good, in faith, well said, Sir John, very well said.

FALSTAFF Prick him.   110

MOULDY I was pricked well enough before, an you could have let me alone. My old dame will be undone now for one to do her husbandry and her drudgery. You need not to have pricked me; there are other men fitter to go out than I.

FALSTAFF Go to! Peace, Mouldy; you shall go, Mouldy; it is time you were spent.

MOULDY Spent?

SHALLOW Peace, fellow, peace – stand aside. Know you where you are? For th'other, Sir John – let me see.   120
Simon Shadow!

---

103 *friends* family
110 *Prick him* mark him down on the list
111 *pricked.* Mouldy plays on *Prick* in line 110, using *pricked* with the meanings (1) grieved; (2) soured (mouldy), and with obvious sexual wordplay.
112 *dame* (probably 'wife', not 'mother',

in view of the sexual innuendoes in *undone* and *husbandry*)
117 *spent* used up (again with sexual innuendo – hence Mouldy's query in the next line)
120 *other* others
121 *Shadow.* The name refers to Shadow's thinness (he is wasted away

Enter Shadow

FALSTAFF Yea, marry, let me have him to sit under. He's like to be a cold soldier.

SHALLOW Where's Shadow?

SHADOW Here, sir.

FALSTAFF Shadow, whose son art thou?

SHADOW My mother's son, sir.

FALSTAFF Thy mother's son! Like enough, and thy father's shadow. So the son of the female is the shadow of the male; it is often so, indeed – but much of the father's substance!

SHALLOW Do you like him, Sir John?

FALSTAFF Shadow will serve for summer. Prick him, for we have a number of shadows fill up the muster-book.

SHALLOW Thomas Wart!

130

to nothing) and also suggests the practice of recruiting 'shadows' (see the note to line 134). Shadow might well have been played by Sincklo (see the note to the opening stage direction of v.4).

123 *cold* (1) cool; (2) cowardly

128–31 *Thy mother's son! ... substance!* This speech lacks the sprightliness of wit typical of the Falstaff of *1 Henry IV* (see the Introduction, page 449, above). This is a laboured invention dependent on the uncertainty of fatherhood and a play on Shadow's name. It is demonstrable that he is his mother's son, but his father may be a shadowy unreality; and the son cannot be more than an image (that is, the shadow) cast by the father, and images and shadows are without substance; there is little of Shadow's putative father to be found in him.

133 *serve* (1) serve as a soldier; (2) suffice, do well enough

134 *a number of shadows fill up the muster-*

book. The muster-book includes the names of some non-existent men (commonly called 'shadows') to enable Falstaff to claim more money than he is really entitled to. Compare Morton's comment on Percy and his army, I.1.192–3.

fill up to fill up

135 *Thomas Wart.* A list of men from Gloucestershire fit to serve the King in 1608 includes a Thomas Warter, who was a carpenter (see the note to lines 142–3), and being of 'lower stature', was 'fit to serve with a caliver' (at line 264 Wart begins caliver drill). This might all be coincidence (and the date of the muster-roll is a decade after the play was written); but as Shakespeare seems to have known the area well (see the note to V.1.33–4), it is possible that he knew Warter, who could have been bearing his caliver for some years before the date of the surviving roll.

Enter Wart

FALSTAFF Where's he?

WART Here, sir.

FALSTAFF Is thy name Wart?

WART Yea, sir.

FALSTAFF Thou art a very ragged Wart.   140

SHALLOW Shall I prick him, Sir John?

FALSTAFF It were superfluous, for his apparel is built upon his back, and the whole frame stands upon pins. Prick him no more.

SHALLOW Ha, ha, ha! You can do it, sir, you can do it; I commend you well. Francis Feeble!

Enter Feeble

FEEBLE Here, sir.

SHALLOW What trade art thou, Feeble?

FEEBLE A woman's tailor, sir.

SHALLOW Shall I prick him, sir?   150

FALSTAFF You may; but if he had been a man's tailor he'd ha' pricked you. Wilt thou make as many holes in an enemy's battle as thou hast done in a woman's petticoat?

---

140 *ragged*. As well as describing Wart's clothes, this could mean 'with projecting lumps' (as warts have).

142–3 *his apparel . . . upon pins.* Wart is so tattered that he cannot bear any further (physical) pricking. His clothes are like a loose timber frame held together on his back by *pins* (pegs or pieces of dowelling for joining timbers).

148 SHALLOW. Many editors give this speech to Falstaff, but Q and F both indicate that it is spoken by Shallow. The question is properly Falstaff's, but Shakespeare's allocation is perfectly natural: when several people are present at an interview it is not

uncommon for one person to ask another's questions. If actors' parts underlie F (see pages 465–8) a faulty allocation of speeches in Q should have been revealed and corrected in F.

149, 151 *A woman's tailor . . . a man's tailor.* Tailors were traditionally cowardly (hence the surprise of the tailor in the nursery story who kills nine, and the expression 'Nine tailors make a man'); but see lines 228–32. 'Tailor' also implied the sexual organs, male or female.

152 *pricked* clothed (with a sexual innuendo; see the previous note)

153 *battle* army

FEEBLE I will do my good will, sir; you can have no more.

FALSTAFF Well said, good woman's tailor! Well said, courageous Feeble! Thou wilt be as valiant as the wrathful dove, or most magnanimous mouse. Prick the woman's tailor well, Master Shallow; deep, Master Shallow.

FEEBLE I would Wart might have gone, sir.

FALSTAFF I would thou wert a man's tailor, that thou mightst mend him and make him fit to go. I cannot put him to a private soldier, that is the leader of so many thousands. Let that suffice, most forcible Feeble.

FEEBLE It shall suffice, sir.

FALSTAFF I am bound to thee, reverend Feeble. Who is next?

SHALLOW Peter Bullcalf o'th'green!

Enter Bullcalf

FALSTAFF Yea, marry, let's see Bullcalf.

BULLCALF Here, sir.

FALSTAFF 'Fore God, a likely fellow! Come, prick Bullcalf till he roar again.

BULLCALF O Lord, good my lord captain –

FALSTAFF What, dost thou roar before thou art pricked?

BULLCALF O Lord, sir, I am a diseased man.

FALSTAFF What disease hast thou?

BULLCALF A whoreson cold, sir, a cough, sir, which I caught with ringing in the King's affairs upon his coronation day, sir.

FALSTAFF Come, thou shalt go to the wars in a gown. We will have away thy cold, and I will take such order that thy friends shall ring for thee. Is here all?

SHALLOW Here is two more called than your number.

---

158 *magnanimous* courageous
163–4 *put him to* enlist him as
165 *thousands.* Evidently Feeble is lice-ridden.

179–80 *ringing ... coronation day* bell-ringing to celebrate the anniversary of the King's coronation
181 *gown* dressing-gown

You must have but four here, sir; and so, I pray you,
go in with me to dinner.

FALSTAFF Come, I will go drink with you, but I cannot
tarry dinner. I am glad to see you, by my troth, Master
Shallow.

SHALLOW O, Sir John, do you remember since we lay all   190
night in the Windmill in Saint George's Field?

FALSTAFF No more of that, Master Shallow.

SHALLOW Ha, 'twas a merry night! And is Jane Nightwork alive?

FALSTAFF She lives, Master Shallow.

SHALLOW She never could away with me.

FALSTAFF Never, never. She would always say she could
not abide Master Shallow.

SHALLOW By the mass, I could anger her to th'heart. She
was then a bona-roba. Doth she hold her own well?   200

FALSTAFF Old, old, Master Shallow.

SHALLOW Nay, she must be old, she cannot choose but
be old, certain she's old, and had Robin Nightwork by
old Nightwork before I came to Clement's Inn.

184–5 *two . . . four*. Commentators have
remarked that these numbers do not
tally, and that this is because Shakespeare was careless in such little matters. But there is nothing careless
here. At line 93 Falstaff mentions
half a dozen men (a general number,
from which he can select those he
wants); he sees five; at lines 242–3 it
is apparent that the precise number
to be taken from those available is
four, but, because he can make a
little money by releasing two men
and substituting for one of them, he
takes only three.

187–8 *I cannot tarry dinner* I cannot waste
time taking dinner (but he makes an
effort; and dramatic if not real time
is allowed for the delay)

191 *the Windmill in Saint George's Field*.

The Windmill may have been an inn;
but St George's Field lay close by
Southwark, which was noted for its
brothels.

192 *Master Shallow*. F has 'good' before
'Master', and then repeats 'No more
of that'. This may be what Shakespeare wrote; but it is the sort of
change that actors tend to introduce
and might stem from actors' parts
(see page 468).

196 *away with* endure, bear (probably
with a sexual innuendo)

200 *Doth she hold her own well?* Shallow
asks whether she withstands the rav-
ages of time (to which he and Falstaff
are succumbing) and, presumably,
disease. It is a little surprising that
Falstaff should still know of her after
so many years.

SILENCE That's fifty-five year ago.

SHALLOW Ha, cousin Silence, that thou hadst seen that that this knight and I have seen! Ha, Sir John, said I well?

FALSTAFF We have heard the chimes at midnight, Master Shallow.

210

SHALLOW That we have, that we have, that we have! In faith, Sir John, we have. Our watchword was 'Hem, boys!' Come, let's to dinner; come, let's to dinner. Jesus, the days that we have seen! Come, come.

Exeunt Falstaff, Shallow, and Silence

BULLCALF Good Master Corporate Bardolph, stand my friend — and here's four Harry ten shillings in French crowns for you. In very truth, sir, I had as lief be hanged, sir, as go. And yet for mine own part, sir, I do not care, but rather because I am unwilling, and, for mine own part, have a desire to stay with my friends; else, sir, I did not care, for mine own part, so much.

220

BARDOLPH Go to; stand aside.

MOULDY And, good Master Corporal Captain, for my old dame's sake stand my friend. She has nobody to do anything about her when I am gone, and she is old and cannot help herself. You shall have forty, sir.

BARDOLPH Go to; stand aside.

---

209 *We have heard the chimes at midnight.* This most evocative phrase is reminiscent of (and similar in meaning to) Pistol's *We have seen the seven stars* (II.4.182).

212–13 *Hem boys!* (a drinking cry)

215 *Corporate* (for 'Corporal'; Bullcalf mistakes the word in the manner of the Hostess)
   stand act as

216–17 *four Harry ten shillings in French crowns.* The ten-shilling pieces and the French crowns became current only in Tudor times (*Harry* is Henry VIII), and early in the reign of Eliza-

beth they were devalued. We should presumably compute Bullcalf's sum at the devalued rate, as that is the value an Elizabethan audience would understand. He is offering £1, which he would pay as five French crowns, formerly worth six shillings each but later only four shillings.

223 *Corporal Captain* (a neat mixture of precision — Corporal — and promotion — *Captain*)

226 *forty.* Mouldy offers forty shillings (£2), making with Bullcalf's £1 the £3 that Bardolph offers Falstaff at line 238.

FEEBLE By my troth, I care not; a man can die but once; we owe God a death. I'll ne'er bear a base mind. An't. be my destiny, so; an't be not, so. No man's too good   230
to serve's prince; and, let it go which way it will, he that dies this year is quit for the next.

BARDOLPH Well said; th'art a good fellow.

FEEBLE Faith, I'll bear no base mind.

Enter Falstaff and the Justices

FALSTAFF Come, sir, which men shall I have?

SHALLOW Four of which you please.

BARDOLPH (*aside to Falstaff*) Sir, a word with you. I have three pound to free Mouldy and Bullcalf.

FALSTAFF Go to, well.

SHALLOW Come, Sir John, which four will you have?   240

FALSTAFF Do you choose for me.

SHALLOW Marry, then, Mouldy, Bullcalf, Feeble, and Shadow.

FALSTAFF Mouldy and Bullcalf: for you, Mouldy, stay at home till you are past service; and for your part, Bullcalf, grow till you come unto it. I will none of you.

SHALLOW Sir John, Sir John, do not yourself wrong; they are your likeliest men, and I would have you served with the best.

FALSTAFF Will you tell me, Master Shallow, how to   250
choose a man? Care I for the limb, the thews, the stature, bulk, and big assemblance of a man? Give me

---

228–32 *a man . . . next*. Having been mocked for cowardice, Feeble now shows commendable spirit (and a fluent knowledge of popular proverbs).

229 *bear* have

245 *past service*. Falstaff is referring primarily not to the service of the King but to Mouldy's sexual service of his wife (a duty he has alluded to at line 113).

246 *come unto it* are matured enough for service (and when Bullcalf is no

longer a calf he will be capable of the same service as the *town bull*; see the note to II.2.151)

251–3 *Care I . . . spirit*. Should a soldier be chosen for his outward appearance or his spirit? Falstaff juxtaposes two contemporary approaches to recruiting, manipulating them dishonestly to suit his own purpose. See also the note to IV.1.155.

251 *thews* muscles

252 *assemblance*. The precise meaning is unsure. The word was used by

the spirit, Master Shallow. Here's Wart; you see what
a ragged appearance it is. 'A shall charge you, and
discharge you, with the motion of a pewterer's hammer,
come off and on swifter than he that gibbets on the
brewer's bucket. And this same half-faced fellow
Shadow; give me this man; he presents no mark to the
enemy – the foeman may with as great aim level at the
edge of a penknife. And for a retreat, how swiftly will
this Feeble the woman's tailor run off! O, give me the
spare men, and spare me the great ones. Put me a caliver
into Wart's hand, Bardolph.

BARDOLPH Hold, Wart, traverse. Thas! Thas! Thas!

Caxton a century before 2 *Henry IV*
was written, and it seems to combine
'appearance' and 'bodily frame'.

255 *with the motion of a pewterer's hammer*
(very rapidly)

256 *come off and on*. This is uncertain in
meaning; it may be a military metaphor, meaning 'retire and advance'
but with the sense of having a name
off the list and on (properly, on the
list, then off – just as advance should
take place before retiring).

256–7 *he that gibbets on the brewer's bucket*.
This is even more obscure than the
phrase before. To 'gibbet' is to hang
or be hung from a gibbet. *Bucket*
may mean a beam (from an old
French word, *buquet*), hence, it has
been suggested, a pig hung by the
heels after being slaughtered 'kicks
the bucket' (though equally convincing alternative explanations are offered for that phrase). It is conceivable that the expression is an antecedent to 'kicking the bucket' for
'dying', and as such implies 'a quick
release from earthly misery' – a meaning that is at least in accord with
Falstaff's images of swiftness. It has
also been suggested that a *brewer's*

bucket is a brewer's yoke for carrying
pails of liquor. See also the use of
bucket (probably for 'pail') at v.1.19.

257 *half-faced* thin-faced (like a profile –
'half-face' – on a coin)

259 *as great aim* as likely a target

261–2 *give me ... great ones*. Again this is
a parody of military writing of the
time, but it is also Falstaff's own
philosophy: he would have as his
men those who will not be missed,
so that he may more easily make
money out of them, and he must
stand clear of the great (such as the
Lord Chief Justice).

262 *caliver* (a light firearm)

264 *traverse. Thas!* ... 'Traverse' can
refer to bodily movement from side
to side, and some editors and producers have Wart engage in a little rapid
marching; but 'traverse' also means
to move the rifle or gun to a different
position, and although the first recorded use of the word in that sense
in the *O.E.D.* is of 1628, it may well
be the meaning here. *Thas!* probably
represents the unintelligible sound
barked out by those who drill troops
and could indicate Wart's taking aim
at first one group of the audience,

FALSTAFF Come, manage me your caliver. So, very well!
Go to, very good! Exceeding good! O, give me always
a little, lean, old, chopped, bald shot. Well said, i'faith!
Wait, th' art a good scab. Hold, there's a tester for thee.

SHALLOW He is not his craft's master; he doth not do it
right. I remember at Mile End Green, when I lay at   270
Clement's Inn — I was then Sir Dagonet in Arthur's
show — there was a little quiver fellow, and 'a would
manage you his piece thus, and 'a would about, and
about, and come you in, and come you in. 'Rah, tah,
tah!' would 'a say. 'Bounce!' would 'a say. And away
again would 'a go, and again would 'a come. I shall
ne'er see such a fellow.

FALSTAFF These fellows will do well, Master Shallow.
God keep you, Master Silence; I will not use many
words with you. Fare you well, gentlemen both; I thank   280

then a second, and a third. Both
instructions would fit arms-drill
better than foot-drill.

267 *chopped* dried up
   shot. A secondary meaning may be
   intended: a 'shot' was an animal left
   after the best of the flock or herd
   had been selected.
   Well said. This could mean 'Well
   done' (as at v.3.9). But Falstaff may
   be addressing it to himself; there are
   other instances of characters being
   intrigued with the language they use:
   compare *accommodated* (lines 65–79)
   and *occupy* (II.4.144–6).

268 *scab* (referring to Wart's name)
   rascal
   tester sixpence

270 *Mile End Green* (used as a drilling
   ground for citizens of London in
   Elizabethan times)
   lay lodged

271 *Sir Dagonet* (King Arthur's fool)

271–2 *Arthur's show* (an archery display
   held on Mile End Green by a society

of archers which named itself after
King Arthur and the Knights of the
Round Table)

272 *quiver* nimble

273–4 *manage you. . .come you in.* Elizabethan firearms took so long to
   reload that, in order to keep up a
   fairly continuous sequence of fire,
   the front rank of men, after firing,
   ran round to the back to reload
   whilst the second rank fired, and so
   on, until the first rank was ready
   again.

273 *piece* firearm

275 *Bounce!* This imitates the sound of a
   gun firing, and was also a catchword
   of the time. Robert Armin, in *A
   Nest of Ninnies* (1608), writes 'Bounce
   is the world's motto'; this line does
   not appear in the earlier version of
   the book published in 1600 (called
   Fool upon Fool), so presumably the
   word came into fashion about, or
   shortly after, the time of *1 Henry IV*.

you. I must a dozen mile tonight. Bardolph, give the
soldiers coats.

SHALLOW Sir John, the Lord bless you! God prosper
your affairs! God send us peace! At your return, visit
my house; let our old acquaintance be renewed. Peradventure I will with ye to the court.

FALSTAFF 'Fore God, would you would.

SHALLOW Go to; I have spoke at a word. God keep you!

FALSTAFF Fare you well, gentle gentlemen.

Exeunt Shallow and Silence

290   On, Bardolph, lead the men away.

Exeunt Bardolph and the recruits

As I return, I will fetch off these justices. I do see the
bottom of Justice Shallow. Lord, Lord, how subject we
old men are to this vice of lying! This same starved
justice hath done nothing but prate to me of the wildness
of his youth, and the feats he hath done about Turnbull
Street, and every third word a lie, duer paid to the
hearer than the Turk's tribute. I do remember him at
Clement's Inn, like a man made after supper of a
cheese-paring. When 'a was naked, he was for all the
300   world like a forked radish, with a head fantastically

288 *have spoke at a word* mean what I
    have said
291 *fetch off* delude, cozen
295-6 *Turnbull Street* (a haunt of thieves
    and prostitutes)
296 *duer* more punctiliously
297 *the Turk's tribute*. The tribute due to
    the Sultan of Turkey was said to be
    exacted with the utmost rigour. Com-
    pare v.2.47-8.
298-301 *like a man. . .knife*. Falstaff illus-
    trates the insignificance of Shallow
    by likening him to a man shaped in a
    moment's idleness from a scrap of
    cheese rind. He goes on to liken him
    to a radish (and radishes might ac-

company cheese, so the progression
is logical enough) with a split root
so that it looked like a man's legs;
above these a head is carved, but
there will be little room for a body.
So Shallow is mere waste (like the
rind of cheese) and a 'no-body' (like
the carved radish). Falstaff's dispar-
agement of Shallow is comic enough,
but, unfortunately for Falstaff, Shallow engages our sympathy in spite
of his silliness. Seeing his hospitality
so abused goes a little way to prepare
an audience for the rejection of
Falstaff.

carved upon it with a knife. 'A was so forlorn that his dimensions to any thick sight were invincible. 'A was the very genius of famine, yet lecherous as a monkey, and the whores called him mandrake. 'A came ever in the rearward of the fashion, and sung those tunes to the overscutched housewives that he heard the carmen whistle, and sware they were his fancies or his goodnights. And now is this Vice's dagger become a squire, and talks as familiarly of John o'Gaunt as if he had been sworn brother to him, and I'll be sworn 'a ne'er saw him but once in the tilt-yard, and then he burst his head for crowding among the marshal's men. I saw it and told John o'Gaunt he beat his own name, for you

310

301 *forlorn* meagre
302 *thick* dull, not acute
invincible. This is the reading of both Q and F, but editors have suggested that it is an error for 'invisible' (the two words could look alike in Elizabethan handwriting). If so, the misreading has produced a more difficult word instead of an obvious one – not the direction of change one expects. If it were certain that F's reading was produced independently of Q's, that would be very strong evidence that 'invincible' is correct. It is at least noteworthy that the scribe who prepared the manuscript for F did not make the very plausible substitution of 'invisible'. 'Invincible' suggests that only acute sight could overcome the limitations imposed by Shallow's puny dimensions.
304 *mandrake*. The point of the insult is that the mandrake (see the second note to 1.2.14) was thought to be a sexual stimulant, which, as represented by Shallow, even whores found excessive.
306 *overscutched housewives*. *Overscutched* means 'over-beaten'; *housewives* was

pronounced 'hussives', hence 'hussies'. Falstaff's implication is that a whore who has often been punished by beating (see v.4.5 and the note) has been long at the game and is of the lowest grade of prostitute. There may be a play on 'scut', technically the tail of the hare but also a term of abuse and meaning the female sexual organs.
306–7 *the carmen whistle*. Carters were famous for whistling and singing. The *Fitzwilliam Virginal Book* includes a piece by William Byrd called 'The Carman's Whistle'.
307 *fancies* fantasias
307–8 *good-nights* serenades
308 *Vice's dagger*. The Vice in the Morality plays traditionally brandished a thin wooden dagger.
311 *tilt-yard* tournament ground
311–12 *burst his head* had his head broken. Presumably Shallow, far from being a close friend of John of Gaunt, was so insignificant that he had to struggle among the crowd in order to see, and, getting among the officials (*the marshal's men*), was roughly pushed into place.

might have thrust him and all his apparel into an eel-skin – the case of a treble hautboy was a mansion for him, a court. And now has he land and beefs. Well, I'll be acquainted with him if I return, and't shall go hard but I'll make him a philosopher's two stones to me. If the young dace be a bait for the old pike, I see no reason in the law of nature but I may snap at him. Let time shape, and there an end.   *Exit*

320

IV.I   *Enter the Archbishop, Mowbray, and Hastings, with*
              their forces, within the Forest of Gaultree

ARCHBISHOP
   What is this forest called?

314-15 *eel-skin*. This (in slightly differing spellings) is the reading of the corrected Q and of F. However, the uncorrected Q reading, 'eele-shin', may be correct, for 'elsin' is a northern dialect word for a shoemaker's awl. Confusion of 'eel-skin' and 'elf-skin' occurs in *1 Henry IV* (see page 333), also with the implication of slightness.

315 *treble hautboy* (the smallest and narrowest of the hautboys, an early relation of the oboe)

316 *beefs* fat cattle

318 *a philosopher's two stones*. One of these stones, so the alchemists believed, would give eternal life, and the other would allow base metals to be turned into gold. Falstaff means to make Shallow his 'golden goose'.

319 *dace* (a small fish used as bait to catch pike)

320 *the law of nature* (the strong destroying the weak)

IV.I Q provides an entry here for '*Bardolfe*' (Lord Bardolph) but he has nothing to say; Shakespeare probably realized as he worked from the histories that Bardolph was in Scotland and took no part in the affair at Gaultree Forest. F provides an entry for Colevile (see the note to the opening stage direction of IV.3), and anticipates Westmorland's entry, though it also has a direction that he should enter at line 24.

(stage direction) *within the Forest of Gaultree*. This is Q's only mention of location. F's stage direction does not include it, and it is not necessary, as the first lines establish the locale. The forest is that referred to in the modern place name Sutton on the Forest (known as Sutton sub Galtris in 1242), about eight miles to the north of York.

HASTINGS

'Tis Gaultree Forest, an't shall please your grace.

ARCHBISHOP

Here stand, my lords, and send discoverers forth
To know the numbers of our enemies.

HASTINGS

We have sent forth already.

ARCHBISHOP   'Tis well done.
My friends and brethren in these great affairs,
I must acquaint you that I have received
New-dated letters from Northumberland,
Their cold intent, tenor, and substance, thus:
Here doth he wish his person, with such powers   10
As might hold sortance with his quality,
The which he could not levy; whereupon
He is retired to ripe his growing fortunes
To Scotland, and concludes in hearty prayers
That your attempts may overlive the hazard
And fearful meeting of their opposite.

MOWBRAY

Thus do the hopes we have in him touch ground
And dash themselves to pieces.

                    Enter a Messenger

HASTINGS   Now, what news?

MESSENGER

West of this forest, scarcely off a mile,
In goodly form comes on the enemy,   20
And, by the ground they hide, I judge their number
Upon or near the rate of thirty thousand.

---

3 *discoverers* scouts
8 *New-dated* of recent date
11 *hold sortance* be in accord
    quality rank
15 *overlive* survive

16 *opposite* adversary
17 *touch ground* strike bottom (as a
    ship against a rocky shore, hence
    line 18)

MOWBRAY

    The just proportion that we gave them out.
    Let us sway on and face them in the field.
        Enter Westmorland

ARCHBISHOP

    What well-appointed leader fronts us here?

MOWBRAY

    I think it is my lord of Westmorland.

WESTMORLAND

    Health and fair greeting from our general,
    The Prince, Lord John and Duke of Lancaster.

ARCHBISHOP

    Say on, my lord of Westmorland, in peace,
    What doth concern your coming.

30 WESTMORLAND   Then, my lord,
    Unto your grace do I in chief address
    The substance of my speech. If that rebellion
    Came like itself, in base and abject routs,
    Led on by bloody youth, guarded with rage,
    And countenanced by boys and beggary;
    I say, if damned commotion so appeared
    In his true, native, and most proper shape,
    You, reverend father, and these noble lords
    Had not been here to dress the ugly form
40   Of base and bloody insurrection
    With your fair honours. You, Lord Archbishop,
    Whose see is by a civil peace maintained,

---

23 *just proportion* exact number
   gave . . . out estimated
24 *sway on* advance
34 *guarded* ornamented
   rage. This is the reading of both Q
   and F. Most editors now emend to
   'rags', although they admit that Q
   and F are not necessarily wrong.
   'Guarded with rags' is a splendid
paradox; but *rage* is obviously in tune
with the general import of the passage. It could easily be a misreading
of 'rags'; but the fact that Q and F
agree lends support to *rage*, even
though we cannot be certain that F
has it from an independent source.
35 *countenanced* approved

Whose beard the silver hand of peace hath touched,
Whose learning and good letters peace hath tutored,
Whose white investments figure innocence,
The dove and very blessèd spirit of peace,
Wherefore do you so ill translate yourself
Out of the speech of peace that bears such grace
Into the harsh and boisterous tongue of war,
Turning your books to graves, your ink to blood,   50
Your pens to lances, and your tongue divine
To a loud trumpet and a point of war?

ARCHBISHOP

Wherefore do I this? So the question stands.
Briefly, to this end: we are all diseased,
And with our surfeiting and wanton hours
Have brought ourselves into a burning fever,
And we must bleed for it; of which disease

44 *good letters* erudition, scholarship
45 *figure* symbolize. For the heinousness of ecclesiastical support for rebellion, see the note to 1.1.201 and the second note to 1.2.34.
47 *translate* (with the additional meanings of 'transform' and, in a technical usage for the movement of bishops from one see to another, 'transfer')
52 *point of war* (short bugle or trumpet call given as a signal in the field)
54–7 *we are . . . for it.* It is commonplace in Elizabethan literature for disturbance in the state to be reflected in or explained as disturbance in some other sphere. Thus at IV.3.108 Falstaff speaks of *this little kingdom, man*, and strange births and disorder in the seasons are mentioned at IV.4.122–5. In *Richard II* England is a garden, full of possibilities for order and beauty (as seen by Gaunt) but rank and overgrown (as seen by the

Gardener). Here the Archbishop explains himself by reference to bodily disorders, their cause and cure.
57 *bleed* (in war and as patients were bled in the treatment of fever). King Richard, 'though no physician', argues that it 'is no month to bleed' when he is trying to avert conflict (*Richard II*, 1.1.153–7); and in line 60 here the Archbishop also disclaims the role of physician (but see lines 64–5). Richard's speech is mocking in tone (as the precise triple rhymes imply – 'incision' with 'physician'), but the Archbishop's dilemma is in theory more genuine, though whether he feels it very deeply is open to question. As a leader of the Church he is bound to advocate peace but, as he sees it, there is *a rough torrent of occasion* (line 72) which oppresses the peace and against which only force can prevail.

Our late King Richard being infected died.
But, my most noble lord of Westmorland,
60   I take not on me here as a physician,
Nor do I as an enemy to peace
Troop in the throngs of military men,
But rather show awhile like fearful war
To diet rank minds sick of happiness,
And purge th'obstructions which begin to stop
Our very veins of life. Hear me more plainly.
I have in equal balance justly weighed
What wrongs our arms may do, what wrongs we suffer,
And find our griefs heavier than our offences.
70   We see which way the stream of time doth run
And are enforced from our most quiet there
By the rough torrent of occasion,
And have the summary of all our griefs,
When time shall serve, to show in articles,
Which long ere this we offered to the King,
And might by no suit gain our audience.
When we are wronged, and would unfold our griefs,
We are denied access unto his person
Even by those men that most have done us wrong.
80   The dangers of the days but newly gone,
Whose memory is written on the earth
With yet-appearing blood, and the examples
Of every minute's instance, present now,

64 *rank* bloated
67 *justly* precisely
71 *our most quiet there*. This is F's reading
(lines 55–79 are not in Q); the sense
is awkward but not impossible, *there*
referring back to *the stream of time* in
line 70, and *most* used adjectivally, as
elsewhere in Shakespeare. Various
emendations for *there* have been sug-

gested, of which the best are 'shore'
and 'sphere'.
72 *occasion* events
73 *griefs* grievances
74 *articles* items listed in a deposition.
(See IV.2.36.)
78 *access* (accented on the second syllable)
83 *instance* entreaty

Hath put us in these ill-beseeming arms,
Not to break peace, or any branch of it,
But to establish here a peace indeed,
Concurring both in name and quality.

WESTMORLAND

Whenever yet was your appeal denied?
Wherein have you been gallèd by the King?
What peer hath been suborned to grate on you,   90
That you should seal this lawless bloody book
Of forged rebellion with a seal divine?

84 *Hath* (the singular form for the plural)

90 *suborned* traitorously induced
grate on harass

92–4 After line 92 an uncorrected version of Q has this line: 'And consecrate commotions bitter edge.'. After line 93, that uncorrected version has: 'To brother borne an houshold cruelty,'. Both lines are omitted from the corrected Q and from F. Some editors think these lines were excised by mistake during the proof-correction of Q, it being argued that the cut in Q which begins at line 101 should have begun at line 99. It will be noted that lines 99 and 100 begin with the same words as the lines quoted above (*And* and *To*). The reason for omitting lines 101–37 would doubtless be that they refer in too close detail to the deposition of Richard, a matter upon which Elizabeth was particularly sensitive. (See the Introduction, page 431.) It has been suggested that lines 99 and 100 were to be omitted because they are similarly objectionable; but they are so general, and so little different from what the Archbishop says in his immediately preceding speech, that this argument is difficult to accept. Certainly the passage is awkward. The Archbishop's declaration that it is the well-being of all – *the commonwealth* – that he seeks to defend seems peculiarly unctuous, but of course that may be what Shakespeare intended. The first line omitted reads well, but the second has been thought by other editors to be corrupt. In the manipulation of type, it was much harder to remove two lines from either side of an intervening line than two adjacent lines, so it is unlikely that a compositor would have removed the lines on either side of line 93 if his instruction was to remove two adjacent lines; but nothing is beyond the bounds of possibility. Certainly two lines were marked to be removed; certainly F, though elsewhere it restores many passages missing from Q, does not include these lines. Since a separate manuscript source must have been available to produce F, if only to supply the lines that it adds, and since there is no other firm evidence or convincing conjecture, these cuts made in the course of printing Q are observed in this edition.

ARCHBISHOP
  My brother general, the commonwealth,
  I make my quarrel in particular.
WESTMORLAND
  There is no need of any such redress,
  Or if there were, it not belongs to you.
MOWBRAY
  Why not to him in part, and to us all
  That feel the bruises of the days before,
  And suffer the condition of these times
100 To lay a heavy and unequal hand
  Upon our honours?
WESTMORLAND   O, my good lord Mowbray,
  Construe the times to their necessities,
  And you shall say, indeed, it is the time,
  And not the King, that doth you injuries.
  Yet for your part, it not appears to me
  Either from the King or in the present time
  That you should have an inch of any ground
  To build a grief on. Were you not restored

93 *brother general . . . commonwealth*. This reads awkwardly, and, coupled with the excision of the adjacent lines, seems to have caused some puzzlement to those who prepared Q and F. Q has no comma after *commonwealth*, suggesting that the Archbishop is addressing Westmorland as a brother army commander. F has a comma (as in this edition), indicating that *commonwealth* and *brother general* are in apposition. We cannot be certain that the comma is Shakespeare's; but it seems more likely that the Archbishop is claiming to be fighting on behalf of the general brotherhood of man, his fellow subjects.

94 *quarrel* reason for complaint

95–6 *There is . . . to you*. With superb arrogance Westmorland asserts that he, as authority's representative, can determine that no wrongs exist, and that if they did it would be for authority to decide if they needed redress. This is said by the man who, to seek redress of his own wrongs, was one of the first to join Bolingbroke against Richard, and it is wholly in accord with his duplicity here (however justifiable that may technically be; see the note to IV.2.121). In Holinshed it is Westmorland, not Lancaster, who tricks the rebels.

100 *unequal* unjust

101–37 *O, my . . . the King* (omitted in Q; see the note to lines 92–4)

102 *Construe the times to their necessities* interpret the present time according to the dictates of expediency

To all the Duke of Norfolk's signories,
Your noble and right well-remembered father's?   110

MOWBRAY

What thing, in honour, had my father lost
That need to be revived and breathed in me?
The King that loved him, as the state stood then,
Was force perforce compelled to banish him,
And then that Henry Bolingbroke and he,
Being mounted and both rousèd in their seats,
Their neighing coursers daring of the spur,
Their armed staves in charge, their beavers down,
Their eyes of fire sparkling through sights of steel,
And the loud trumpet blowing them together,   120
Then, then, when there was nothing could have stayed
My father from the breast of Bolingbroke,
O, when the King did throw his warder down,
His own life hung upon the staff he threw.
Then threw he down himself and all their lives
That by indictment and by dint of sword
Have since miscarried under Bolingbroke.

WESTMORLAND

You speak, Lord Mowbray, now you know not what.
The Earl of Hereford was reputed then
In England the most valiant gentleman.   130
Who knows on whom fortune would then have smiled?

109 *signories* estates. In *Richard II* Mowbray, Duke of Norfolk, is banished
(1.3), and his death abroad is reported
by Carlisle (IV.1.91–102); immediately before this (IV.1.87–9) Bolingbroke restores Norfolk's 'lands and
signories'.

114 *force perforce*. The same expression
appears at IV.4.46 and *Perforce must
move* at IV.5.35. F has 'forc'd,' for
force, but in Elizabethan handwriting
'e' is easily confused with 'd'.

116 *roused* raised (and excited)

117 *daring of the spur*. This probably

means that the horses were so keen
to be off that they dared the riders'
spurs to prick them into action.

118 *armed staves in charge* lances at the
ready
beavers visors (of their helmets)

123 *warder* mace. (Richard's dramatic
act, preventing the combat between
Mowbray and Bolingbroke, occurs
at 1.3.118 of *Richard II*.)

129 *Hereford*. F spells the word here in
three syllables (though a disyllable is
more appropriate for the metre) but
at line 136 as '*Herford*' (as is

But if your father had been victor there,
He ne'er had borne it out of Coventry;
For all the country, in a general voice,
Cried hate upon him, and all their prayers and love
Were set on Herford, whom they doted on,
And blessed, and graced, indeed more than the King.
But this is mere digression from my purpose.
Here come I from our princely general
140   To know your griefs, to tell you from his grace
That he will give you audience; and wherein
It shall appear that your demands are just,
You shall enjoy them, everything set off
That might so much as think you enemies.

MOWBRAY
But he hath forced us to compel this offer,
And it proceeds from policy, not love.

WESTMORLAND
Mowbray, you overween to take it so.
This offer comes from mercy, not from fear;
For lo, within a ken our army lies,
150   Upon mine honour, all too confident
To give admittance to a thought of fear.
Our battle is more full of names than yours,
Our men more perfect in the use of arms,
Our armour all as strong, our cause the best;
Then reason will our hearts should be as good.

---

commonly done in *Richard II*). Henry IV was known as Henry Boling-broke, Duke of Hereford, before he assumed John of Gaunt's title, Duke of Lancaster (see also the note to 1.3.82)

133 *ne'er had borne it out of* would never have carried the victory away from

143 *set off* set aside

146 *it proceeds from policy*. Events will show that Mowbray speaks prophetically here and at lines 181–2. 'Policy' could mean 'dissimulation'.

149 *a ken* sight

152 *battle* army
names. This may simply mean 'men', but it could mean 'men of distinction' (compare *Henry V*, IV.8.104).

155 *reason will* it stands to reason that. Falstaff has contrasted the physical and spiritual qualities of the soldier (see the note to III.2.251–3). Westmorland argues that in both respects his men are stronger than those of the rebels.

Say you not then our offer is compelled.

MOWBRAY

Well, by my will we shall admit no parley.

WESTMORLAND

 That argues but the shame of your offence;
 A rotten case abides no handling.

HASTINGS

 Hath the Prince John a full commission,   160
 In very ample virtue of his father,
 To hear and absolutely to determine
 Of what conditions we shall stand upon?

WESTMORLAND

 That is intended in the general's name.
 I muse you make so slight a question.

ARCHBISHOP

 Then take, my lord of Westmorland, this schedule,
 For this contains our general grievances.
 Each several article herein redressed,
 All members of our cause, both here and hence,
 That are ensinewed to this action   170
 Acquitted by a true substantial form
 And present execution of our wills –
 To us and to our purposes confined
 We come within our awful banks again,
 And knit our powers to the arm of peace.

WESTMORLAND

 This will I show the general. Please you, lords,
 In sight of both our battles we may meet,

160,165,170,190 *commission . . . question . . . action* (all pronounced '-i-on')
161 *In very ample virtue* with the full authority
163 *stand* insist
164 *intended in* signified by
165 *muse you make* am surprised you ask
166 *schedule* statement
167 *general* joint, common

168 *several* individual
170 *ensinewed to* joined together in
171–2 *Acquitted . . . our wills* – provided we are pardoned for this present action, and our demands being met, then . . .
174 *awful*. Q's spelling, 'aweful', points to the meaning.

At either end in peace – which God so frame! –
Or to the place of difference call the swords
Which must decide it.

180 ARCHBISHOP   My lord, we will do so.

Exit Westmorland

MOWBRAY

There is a thing within my bosom tells me
That no conditions of our peace can stand.

HASTINGS

Fear you not that. If we can make our peace
Upon such large terms, and so absolute,
As our conditions shall consist upon,
Our peace shall stand as firm as rocky mountains.

MOWBRAY

Yea, but our valuation shall be such
That every slight and false-derivèd cause,
Yea, every idle, nice, and wanton reason,
190 Shall to the King taste of this action;
That, were our royal faiths martyrs in love,
We shall be winnowed with so rough a wind
That even our corn shall seem as light as chaff,

---

178 *At either end. At*, the reading of both Q and F, is usually emended to 'And', giving the simple sense 'And either conclude' instead of the less obvious, but surely acceptable 'At either extremity'. Q's meaning cannot have puzzled whose who prepared the copy for F.
frame bring to pass.
179 *difference* battle
184 *large* generous, all-encompassing
185 *consist* insist
187 *our valuation* the way we are esteemed
189 *nice* trifling
wanton frivolous
191 *That, were our royal faiths martyrs in love* so that, even if our faithfulness

to the King was put to the test of dying for love of him
192–4 *We shall . . . partition.* For winnowing corn a gentle breeze was required, to blow off the lighter chaff, leaving the ears of corn for milling. The wind that will blow on the former rebels will be so rough that their virtues will be dismissed with their faults: even death in the King's cause would not suffice to prove their loyalty. Shakespeare may be making a contrast with one of the earliest rebels of Henry's reign, Aumerle, who is pardoned at the end of *Richard II*, and as Duke of York leads the van at Agincourt and is killed (*Henry V*, IV.6).

And good from bad find no partition.

ARCHBISHOP

No, no, my lord. Note this: the King is weary
Of dainty and such picking grievances,
For he hath found to end one doubt by death
Revives two greater in the heirs of life;
And therefore will he wipe his tables clean,
And keep no tell-tale to his memory   200
That may repeat and history his loss
To new remembrance. For full well he knows
He cannot so precisely weed this land
As his misdoubts present occasion.
His foes are so enrooted with his friends
That, plucking to unfix an enemy,
He doth unfasten so and shake a friend.
So that this land, like an offensive wife
That hath enraged him on to offer strokes,
As he is striking, holds his infant up,   210
And hangs resolved correction in the arm
That was upreared to execution.

HASTINGS

Besides, the King hath wasted all his rods
On late offenders, that he now doth lack
The very instruments of chastisement,
So that his power, like to a fangless lion,
May offer, but not hold.

ARCHBISHOP   'Tis very true;
And therefore be assured, my good Lord Marshal,

195–6 *weary . . . grievances* tired of finding
  fault at every opportunity, however
  trivial
197 *doubt* suspicion
198 *the heirs of life* those who survive the
  person executed
199 *tables* notebooks, records
201 *history* recount
203–4 *so precisely . . . occasion* eradicate
  from this land everything which his
  fears draw to his attention

208–12 *an offensive wife . . . execution.*
  Those who seek Shakespeare's biography in his writing suggest that
  there is personal experience here; but
  he evidently observed much, and
  there are no grounds for drawing
  this conclusion.
211 *hangs* suspends
213 *wasted* used up
217 *offer* threaten

If we do now make our atonement well,

220   Our peace will, like a broken limb united,
Grow stronger for the breaking.

MOWBRAY   Be it so.
Here is returned my lord of Westmorland.

Enter Westmorland

WESTMORLAND
The Prince is here at hand. Pleaseth your lordship
To meet his grace just distance 'tween our armies?

MOWBRAY
Your grace of York, in God's name then, set forward.

ARCHBISHOP
Before, and greet his grace! My lord, we come.

They go forward

IV.2   *Enter Prince John of Lancaster and his army*

PRINCE JOHN
You are well encountered here, my cousin Mowbray;
Good day to you, gentle Lord Archbishop;
And so to you, Lord Hastings, and to all.
My lord of York, it better showed with you
When that your flock, assembled by the bell,
Encircled you to hear with reverence
Your exposition on the holy text,

---

219 *atonement* reconciliation
224 *just distance* half-way. (See the headnote to IV.2.)
226 *Before* be forward, lead on (a usage
not found in the *O.E.D.*)

IV.2 Most editions mark a partial exit at
IV.1.226 and begin a new scene. The
traditional scene divisions are preserved
here for readers' convenience; but F,
which carefully divides the play into acts
and scenes, marks no division here and

none is required, since the action is continuous. Shakespeare's source, Holinshed, is uncertain as to what happened
and gives two versions; the second refers
to a meeting between the disputants 'just
in the midway between both the armies'
(compare *just distance 'tween our armies,*
IV.1.224). The rebels and Prince John
confront one another immediately in the
play, and the audience has to imagine
that the location has shifted to half-way
between the armies.

Than now to see you here an iron man,
Cheering a rout of rebels with your drum,
Turning the word to sword, and life to death.   10
That man that sits within a monarch's heart
And ripens in the sunshine of his favour,
Would he abuse the countenance of the king?
Alack, what mischiefs might he set abroach
In shadow of such greatness! With you, Lord Bishop,
It is even so. Who hath not heard it spoken
How deep you were within the books of God?
To us the speaker in His parliament,
To us th'imagined voice of God himself,
The very opener and intelligencer   20
Between the grace, the sanctities, of heaven
And our dull workings. O, who shall believe
But you misuse the reverence of your place,
Imply the countenance and grace of heaven
As a false favourite doth his prince's name,
In deeds dishonourable? You have taken up,
Under the counterfeited zeal of God,
The subjects of His substitute, my father,
And both against the peace of heaven and him
Have here up-swarmed them.

---

8 *iron* (1) armoured; (2) merciless
  man. Q reads 'man talking'. It could
  be that the compositor was half-
  anticipating the next word, *Cheering*,
  but it seems more likely that Shakespeare first wrote 'talking', then substituted 'cheering', but failed to
  cancel 'talking'.
10 *the word to sword* the word of God to
  war. In Shakespeare's time 'word'
  and 'sword' sounded similar.
13 *countenance* support, approval
14 *set abroach* open up
17 *the books of God* (1) works of divinity;
  (2) God's grace
18 *speaker.* The Speaker in Parliament

acts as intermediary between the
members and the sovereign, a part
of his role that was of much greater
significance in Tudor and Stuart
times than today.
20 *opener and intelligencer* interpreter and
  messenger
21 *sanctities* holiness (or 'saints')
22 *workings* perceptions
24 *Imply* insinuate. (F has the easier reading 'Employ'.)
26 *taken up* enlisted
28 *substitute* deputy. The sovereign was
  God's deputy on earth.
30 *up-swarmed them* raised them up in
  swarms

30   ARCHBISHOP   Good my lord of Lancaster,
      I am not here against your father's peace,
      But, as I told my lord of Westmorland,
      The time misordered doth, in common sense,
      Crowd us and crush us to this monstrous form
      To hold our safety up. I sent your grace
      The parcels and particulars of our grief,
      The which hath been with scorn shoved from the court,
      Whereon this Hydra son of war is born,
      Whose dangerous eyes may well be charmed asleep
40   With grant of our most just and right desires,
      And true obedience, of this madness cured,
      Stoop tamely to the foot of majesty.

   MOWBRAY
      If not, we ready are to try our fortunes
      To the last man.
   HASTINGS   And though we here fall down,
      We have supplies to second our attempt.
      If they miscarry, theirs shall second them,
      And so success of mischief shall be born,
      And heir from heir shall hold this quarrel up
      Whiles England shall have generation.

33 *misordered* disordered, confused
   in common sense as everyone can see
34 *monstrous form*. This can be glossed
   as 'distorted shape' or 'abnormal
   course', but the word *monstrous* suggests one of the terrible creatures
   which rise first from the sea and
   then from the earth in Revelation 13.
   This is the beast that stands for Antichrist, a role in which, as a rebel
   against God's deputy, the Archbishop finds himself, whether he
   likes it or not.
35 *hold . . . up* maintain
36 *parcels* details
   grief grievances
38 *Hydra* many-headed. Hydra was a
   many-headed snake of Lerna which

grew two heads for each one cut off.
39 *Whose dangerous . . . asleep*. Shakespeare has conflated Hydra, with its
   many heads (and doubtless eyes to
   go with them), and Argus, Juno's
   watchman, who had a hundred eyes
   and was charmed asleep by the music
   of Mercury.
44 *though* even if
46 *theirs shall second them*. This continues
   the many-headed Hydra idea, made
   specific at line 48, which also recalls
   the King's reported fear that one
   rebel killed *Revives two greater in the
   heirs of life* (IV.1. 197–8).
47 *success of mischief* a succession of
   disturbances
49 *generation* offspring

PRINCE JOHN

You are too shallow, Hastings, much too shallow,   50
To sound the bottom of the after-times.

WESTMORLAND

Pleaseth your grace to answer them directly
How far forth you do like their articles.

PRINCE JOHN

I like them all, and do allow them well,
And swear here, by the honour of my blood,
My father's purposes have been mistook,
And some about him have too lavishly
Wrested his meaning and authority.
My lord, these griefs shall be with speed redressed,
Upon my soul, they shall. If this may please you,   60
Discharge your powers unto their several counties,
As we will ours; and here, between the armies,
Let's drink together friendly and embrace,
That all their eyes may bear those tokens home
Of our restorèd love and amity.

ARCHBISHOP

I take your princely word for these redresses.

PRINCE JOHN

I give it you, and will maintain my word;

51 *sound the bottom* plumb the depths
54–65 *I like ... amity.* Holinshed remarks that when Westmorland saw the rebels' strength 'he subtly devised how to quail their purpose'. Shakespeare transfers the 'subtle device' to Prince John (though Westmorland is still party to the plan), in order, it has been suggested, to associate the duplicity with the royal household (see the Introduction, pages 439–40). Divorced from the horrors and exigencies of war, we may deplore Prince John's stratagem, but the fear of civil war was doubtless strong enough to allow an Elizabethan audience to accept any means of putting

down rebellion. The Council of Constance (1410–15, contemporaneous with the reign of Henry IV) had decreed that faith need not be kept in dealings with heretics; and in Elizabethan eyes rebels were in much the same category. Prince John could claim (as indeed he does at lines 112–14) that in undertaking to redress the grievances he does not promise to do so in any particular manner. He simply redresses them as he thinks fit, not as the rebels expect and desire. See also the note to line 121.
57 *lavishly* freely
61 *several* respective

And thereupon I drink unto your grace.

HASTINGS

Go, captain, and deliver to the army

70 This news of peace. Let them have pay, and part.

I know it will well please them. Hie thee, captain!

Exit a captain

ARCHBISHOP

To you, my noble lord of Westmorland!

WESTMORLAND

I pledge your grace – and if you knew what pains

I have bestowed to breed this present peace

You would drink freely; but my love to ye

Shall show itself more openly hereafter.

ARCHBISHOP

I do not doubt you.

WESTMORLAND   I am glad of it.

Health to my lord and gentle cousin, Mowbray.

MOWBRAY

You wish me health in very happy season,

80 For I am on the sudden something ill.

ARCHBISHOP

Against ill chances men are ever merry,

But heaviness foreruns the good event.

WESTMORLAND

Therefore be merry, coz, since sudden sorrow

Serves to say thus, 'Some good thing comes tomorrow.'

ARCHBISHOP

Believe me, I am passing light in spirit.

MOWBRAY

So much the worse, if your own rule be true.

Shouts within

PRINCE JOHN

The word of peace is rendered. Hark how they shout!

79 *happy* appropriate
80 *something* somewhat
81 *Against* in the face of

83 *coz* cousin (as at III.1.62)
85 *passing* exceptionally

MOWBRAY

    This had been cheerful after victory.

ARCHBISHOP

    A peace is of the nature of a conquest,

    For then both parties nobly are subdued,   90

    And neither party loser.

PRINCE JOHN   Go, my lord,

    And let our army be dischargèd too.   *Exit Westmorland*

    And, good my lord, so please you, let our trains

    March by us, that we may peruse the men

    We should have coped withal.

ARCHBISHOP   Go, good Lord Hastings,

    And, ere they be dismissed, let them march by.

                         Exit Hastings

PRINCE JOHN

    I trust, lords, we shall lie tonight together.

       Enter Westmorland

    Now, cousin, wherefore stands our army still?

WESTMORLAND

    The leaders, having charge from you to stand,

    Will not go off until they hear you speak.   100

PRINCE JOHN

    They know their duties.

       Enter Hastings

HASTINGS

    My lord, our army is dispersed already.

    Like youthful steers unyoked they take their courses

    East, west, north, south; or like a school broke up,

    Each hurries toward his home and sporting-place.

WESTMORLAND

    Good tidings, my lord Hastings – for the which

---

88 *had been* would have been. It is ironic that the contest in which Mowbray's father took part, and which opens this four-part dramatization of the dispute between the houses of York and Lancaster, was also 'resolved' without a blow being struck (*Richard II*, 1.3).

93 *trains* followers, armies

95 *coped* encountered, fought

I do arrest thee, traitor, of high treason;
And you, Lord Archbishop, and you, Lord Mowbray,
Of capital treason I attach you both.

MOWBRAY

110   Is this proceeding just and honourable?

WESTMORLAND

Is your assembly so?

ARCHBISHOP

Will you thus break your faith?

PRINCE JOHN   I pawned thee none.
I promised you redress of these same grievances
Whereof you did complain, which, by mine honour,
I will perform with a most Christian care.
But, for you rebels, look to taste the due
Meet for rebellion and such acts as yours.
Most shallowly did you these arms commence,
Fondly brought here, and foolishly sent hence.

120   Strike up our drums, pursue the scattered stray;
God, and not we, hath safely fought today.

---

107 *high treason*. This was defined in 1350–51, during the reign of Edward III, as an act 'compassing or imagining' the death of the king or his immediate family, killing his judges (who represented him in the administration of justice), levying war in the king's dominions, or aiding the king's enemies.

109 *capital treason*. This is not a specific charge: treason was a capital offence and the adjective is simply a reminder of the penalty.
attach arrest

115 *with a most Christian care*. We may take this ironically, but Prince John is doubtless sincere according to his interpretation of the Christian duty to rebels.

116 *look* expect

117 *and such ... yours*. See the second note to line 122.

118 *shallowly* without adequate consideration

119 *Fondly* ill-advisedly

120 *stray* strays, fleeing stragglers

121 *God ... today*. This is a traditional expression of indebtedness to God for victory. Henry V is even more forthright after Agincourt:

> be it death proclaimèd through our host
> To boast of this, or take that praise from God
> Which is his only.
>   *Henry V*, IV.8.113–15

But Henry's men fought against odds; Prince John has won by a trick, so it is not the military virtues of courage and resolution that he attributes to God, but the subtle device that quailed the rebels' purpose (see the note to lines 54–65).

Some guard these traitors to the block of death,
Treason's true bed and yielder-up of breath.   *Exeunt*

Alarum. Excursions. Enter Falstaff and Sir John   IV.3
Colevile

FALSTAFF What's your name, sir? Of what condition are
you, and of what place?

There is a similar, and certainly ironic, offer of praise to heaven at the end of Marlowe's play *The Jew of Malta*, in which victory is also gained by deceit. Prince John's stratagem is coldly efficient. There is nothing noble here, but nor has he risked the lives of his troops. His condemnation of the rebels is expressed in rhymed couplets, which, together with some alliteration, suggest a degree of self-satisfaction that prevents his winning our admiration. It is not long since he could swear, by the honour of his blood, that his father's purposes had been mistook (lines 55–6); and we have now seen *his* purposes 'honourably' mistook.

122 *Some guard* some (of you) escort
these traitors. This is F's reading: Q has 'this traitour' (and it omits F's *and such acts as yours* in line 117), but F is correct in suggesting that the Archbishop was not the only one of the rebels to be executed.

IV.3 F has no indication of a new scene here, despite the care with which it divides up the play; but '*Exeunt*' is marked at the end of IV.2 (F's IV.1), and that clearing of the stage technically ends the scene.

Like so much of *2 Henry IV*, this scene has a parallel in the First Part, in this case Falstaff's supposed killing of Hotspur (v.4).

(stage direction) *Alarum* (a call to arms)
Excursions (military attacks, sorties)
Sir John Colevile. In F. Colevile is also brought on at the beginning of IV.1 (see the note to line 65 below); no exit is provided for him, so that he would leave at the end of IV.2 (F's IV.1) and would then have to re-enter immediately. That there is a time lapse between the two scenes is apparent from line 24. Sir John Colevile of the Dale was a real person, but he is not mentioned in the histories as being involved in the affair at Gaultree Forest. With Hastings and others he was executed at Durham when the King, after settling matters in Yorkshire, moved north to attack the Earl of Northumberland. But it has been suggested that Colevile was pardoned, for a man of the same name fought with Henry V in the campaign in France which led to Agincourt; but names and descriptive adjuncts could be passed on like noble titles. No certain reason can be given for Shakespeare's choice of Colevile. He might with historical accuracy have chosen Sir John Lampley or Sir Robert Plumpton. It may be that he was simply attracted by the name (which might mean that he wished to engage the audience's sympathies for Colevile, especially in view of his resolute character); or he may have chosen it

COLEVILE I am a knight, sir, and my name is Colevile
of the Dale.

FALSTAFF Well then, Colevile is your name, a knight is
your degree, and your place the Dale. Colevile shall be
still your name, a traitor your degree, and the dungeon
your place – a place deep enough; so shall you be still
Colevile of the Dale.

10 COLEVILE Are not you Sir John Falstaff?

FALSTAFF As good a man as he, sir, whoe'er I am. Do
ye yield, sir, or shall I sweat for you? If I do sweat,
they are the drops of thy lovers, and they weep for thy
death. Therefore rouse up fear and trembling, and do
observance to my mercy.

COLEVILE I think you are Sir John Falstaff, and in that
thought yield me.

He kneels

FALSTAFF I have a whole school of tongues in this belly
of mine, and not a tongue of them all speaks any other
20 word but my name. An I had but a belly of any indifferency, I were simply the most active fellow in Europe;
my womb, my womb, my womb undoes me. Here
comes our general.

Retreat sounded

because it was also the name of a
contemporary Scottish spy of ill repute (which would make his defeat
by Falstaff redound more obviously
to the latter's credit). The first explanation seems more probable.

Since the eighteenth century editors
have expanded this stage direction to
indicate that Falstaff and Colevile
enter 'meeting'. The entry need not
be so arranged; for example, they
might well enter at sword-point, one
facing the other, Falstaff backing on
to the stage first, asking his questions
as Colevile appears. Such an entry,

with Falstaff backing away but tri-
umphing verbally and on the
strength of his reputation, would be
appropriate to his character.

1 *condition* rank

7–9 *dungeon . . . Dale.* The dale, like the
dungeon, is deep.

13–14 *they are . . . death.* Sweat-drops
become tears.

13 *lovers* friends

18–19 *I have . . . of mine.* Falstaff's fat-
ness speaks for itself in all lan-
guages.

20–21 *indifferency* ordinary kind

22 *womb* belly

Enter Prince John, Westmorland, and Blunt, with
soldiers

PRINCE JOHN

The heat is past; follow no further now.

Call in the powers, good cousin Westmorland.

                               Exit Westmorland

Now, Falstaff, where have you been all this while?

When everything is ended, then you come.

These tardy tricks of yours will, on my life,

One time or other break some gallows' back.

FALSTAFF I would be sorry, my lord, but it should be   30
thus. I never knew yet but rebuke and check was the
reward of valour. Do you think me a swallow, an arrow,
or a bullet? Have I in my poor and old motion the
expedition of thought? I have speeded hither with the
very extremest inch of possibility; I have foundered nine
score and odd posts; and here, travel-tainted as I am,
have in my pure and immaculate valour taken Sir John
Colevile of the Dale, a most furious knight and valorous
enemy. But what of that? He saw me, and yielded;
that I may justly say, with the hook-nosed fellow of   40
Rome, three words, 'I came, saw, and overcame.'

PRINCE JOHN It was more of his courtesy than your
deserving.

FALSTAFF I know not. Here he is, and here I yield him.

---

30 *but it should be* if it were not

31 *check* reproof

34 *expedition* speed

35–6 *foundered nine score and odd posts*
lamed 180 and more post-horses

40–41 *the hook-nosed fellow of Rome* (Julius
Caesar)

41 *three words.* Q reads 'there cosin'; F
omits both words. This emendation,
proposed by A. R. Humphreys seems
to provide what is required, since
the Latin of Caesar's famous saying
is precisely three words: *Veni, vidi,*

vici. As Professor Humphreys points
out, Falstaff would be unlikely to be
quite so impertinent as to address
Prince John as cousin, and in any
case he has little liking for him.

44 *Here . . . yield him.* Falstaff's gesture
makes an intriguing contrast with
Hotspur's behaviour which was the
source of Henry's complaint at the
beginning of *1 Henry IV* (1.1 and 3);
Hotspur refused to surrender his prisoners to the King (and indeed he
was duty-bound to surrender only

And I beseech your grace, let it be booked with the rest
of this day's deeds, or by the Lord I will have it in a
particular ballad else, with mine own picture on the
top on't, Colevile kissing my foot — to the which course
if I be enforced, if you do not all show like gilt twopences to me, and I in the clear sky of fame o'ershine
you as much as the full moon doth the cinders of the
element, which show like pins' heads to her, believe not
the word of the noble. Therefore let me have right, and
let desert mount.

PRINCE JOHN Thine's too heavy to mount.

FALSTAFF Let it shine, then.

PRINCE JOHN Thine's too thick to shine.

FALSTAFF Let it do something, my good lord, that may
do me good, and call it what you will.

PRINCE JOHN Is thy name Colevile?

COLEVILE It is, my lord.

PRINCE JOHN A famous rebel art thou, Colevile.

FALSTAFF And a famous true subject took him.

COLEVILE
I am, my lord, but as my betters are
That led me hither. Had they been ruled by me,

Mordake, who was of blood royal),
but Falstaff yields Colevile, whom he
was entitled to keep, without being
asked.

46-7 *a particular ballad* a ballad all about
me. In *1 Henry IV*, II.2.43-5, Falstaff
threatens to have ballads made on
his companions and 'sung to filthy
tunes'.

49-50 *show like gilt twopences to me* look
like counterfeit coins in comparison
with me. Twopenny pieces were
often gilded so that they could be
passed as half-crowns.

51-2 *the cinders of the element* the stars of
heaven

55 *heavy* troublesome (also punning on
Falstaff's weight)

57 *thick* (1) dim (as of a light); (2) thick
(of Falstaff's body)

60 *Colevile*. This was pronounced as
three syllables (see line 72), so some
editors arrange this and the next two
lines as two verse lines.

65 *Had they been ruled by me* if they had
taken my advice. Presumably Colevile
had more sense than to trust Prince
John. Some editors take this line as
evidence that he should be present
from the beginning of IV.1 (see the
note to the opening stage direction
of this scene), but he is given no
lines which would prove that the
rebel lords had the benefit of his
advice. His remark must refer to an
incident not dramatized, or it is

You should have won them dearer than you have.

FALSTAFF I know not how they sold themselves, but
thou like a kind fellow gavest thyself away gratis, and I
thank thee for thee.

Enter Westmorland

PRINCE JOHN
Now, have you left pursuit?   70

WESTMORLAND
Retreat is made and execution stayed.

PRINCE JOHN
Send Colevile with his confederates
To York, to present execution.
Blunt, lead him hence, and see you guard him sure.

Exit Blunt with Colevile

And now dispatch we toward the court, my lords.
I hear the King my father is sore sick.
Our news shall go before us to his majesty,
Which, cousin, you shall bear to comfort him,
And we with sober speed will follow you.

FALSTAFF My lord, I beseech you give me leave to go   80
through Gloucestershire, and when you come to court,
stand my good lord in your good report.

PRINCE JOHN
Fare you well, Falstaff. I, in my condition,
Shall better speak of you than you deserve.

Exeunt all but Falstaff

FALSTAFF I would you had the wit; 'twere better than

---

simply the general observation of a
soldier who feels he knows better
than his commanders.

71 *Retreat is made* the signal for retreat
has been sounded
stayed stopped

73 *present* instant

74 *Blunt.* See the note to the stage direction at III.1.31.

78 *cousin* (Westmorland)

82 *stand* act as

83 *in my condition.* Some editors gloss
condition as 'natural disposition', but
Prince John's natural disposition,
from what we have seen, is hardly to
speak better of anyone than he deserves. He may mean 'in my capacity'
(as victorious commander and therefore expected to speak well of his
troops).

your dukedom. Good faith, this same young sober-
blooded boy doth not love me, nor a man cannot make
him laugh – but that's no marvel, he drinks no wine.
There's never none of these demure boys come to any
proof, for thin drink doth so over-cool their blood, and
making many fish meals, that they fall into a kind of
male green-sickness; and then when they marry they
get wenches. They are generally fools and cowards –
which some of us should be too, but for inflammation.
A good sherris-sack hath a twofold operation in it. It
ascends me into the brain, dries me there all the foolish
and dull and crudy vapours which environ it, makes it
apprehensive, quick, forgetive, full of nimble, fiery, and
delectable shapes, which delivered o'er to the voice, the
tongue, which is the birth, becomes excellent wit. The
second property of your excellent sherris is the warming
of the blood, which before, cold and settled, left the
liver white and pale, which is the badge of pusillanimity
and cowardice; but the sherris warms it, and makes it

87–8 *a than cannot make him laugh.* Dr
Johnson commented: 'He who cannot be softened into gaiety cannot
easily be melted into sadness'.

90 *proof* fulfilment

92 *male green-sickness.* Green-sickness
(chlorosis) was a form of anaemia in
young girls.

93 *get wenches.* Falstaff, an advocate of
meat and strong drink (to him indicative of virility), argues that fish-eating
and thin drink make a man anaemic
and so capable of begetting only
girls. If there is a sexual innuendo in
*skill in the weapon is nothing with-
out sack* (lines 111-12), that would
tally with his assertion here. But
there was a proverb that 'Who goes
drunk to bed begets a girl', and this
Falstaff seems to belie.

94 *inflammation* passions inflamed with
drink

95 *sherris-sack* (the white wine from
Xeres, Spain: sherry; but see the note
to 1.2.199)

97 *crudy* curd-like, thick

98 *apprehensive* quick to apprehend or
respond
    forgetive (pronounced with the 'g'
    soft, as in 'forge') inventive

100 *becomes.* It is possible that the
subject of *becomes* is *shapes* (see the
note to 1.2.72-3), but probably Falstaff is loosely harking back to *good
sherris-sack* (line 95), which *becomes
excellent wit* by the process he has
described.

102-3 *the liver.* See the first note to
1.2.177.

course from the inwards to the parts' extremes. It illumineth the face, which, as a beacon, gives warning to all the rest of this little kingdom, man, to arm; and then the vital commoners, and inland petty spirits, muster me all to their captain, the heart, who, great and puffed up with this retinue, doth any deed of courage; and this valour comes of sherris. So that skill in the weapon is nothing without sack, for that sets it a-work, and learning a mere hoard of gold kept by a devil, till sack commences it and sets it in act and use. Hereof comes it that Prince Harry is valiant; for the cold blood he did naturally inherit of his father he hath like lean, sterile, and bare land manured, husbanded, and tilled, with excellent endeavour of drinking good and good store of fertile sherris, that he is become very hot and valiant. If I had a thousand sons, the first human principle I would teach them should be to forswear thin potations, and to addict themselves to sack.

Enter Bardolph

How now, Bardolph?

BARDOLPH The army is discharged all and gone.

FALSTAFF Let them go. I'll through Gloucestershire, and

105 *parts' extremes* bodily extremities

107 *this little kingdom, man.* See the note to IV.1.54-5.

108 *vital commoners . . . inland petty spirits.* Spirits of three kinds, natural, animal, and vital, were believed to permeate the blood and be carried by it to the various parts of the body, determining spiritual as well as physical characteristics.

111–14 *skill . . . use.* Falstaff argues that sack gives the soldier courage to use his weapon and enables the scholar to use his hoard of learning. There may also be a sexual innuendo, de-

spite the proverbial belief that drink prompts desire but inhibits performance; see the note to line 93.

113 *hoard of gold . . . devil.* Treasure was said to be guarded by devils or evil spirits.

114 *commences . . . act* (punning on the use of these words at Cambridge and Oxford Universities respectively for the conferring of degrees – enabling students to put to use their hoard of learning)

117 *husbanded* cultivated

120 *human* secular

there will I visit Master Robert Shallow, Esquire. I
have him already tempering between my finger and my
thumb, and shortly will I seal with him. Come away.

Exeunt

IV.4   *Enter the King, carried in a chair, Warwick, Thomas*
            Duke of Clarence, Humphrey Duke of Gloucester, and
            attendant lords

KING HENRY IV

Now, lords, if God doth give successful end
To this debate that bleedeth at our doors,
We will our youth lead on to higher fields,
And draw no swords but what are sanctified.

127 *tempering* (referring to the warming
of soft wax between the fingers
before using it to make a seal)
128 *seal with him* (1) come to an agreement with him; (2) mould him, like
wax, to my purpose

IV.4 We know from IV.5.233 that the
Jerusalem Chamber in Westminster
Abbey is the location of IV.4 and IV.5
(which form a single continuous scene:
see the headnote to IV.5). Events are
compounded: historically the affair at
Gaultree Forest dates from 1405, and
the victory at Bramham Moor (lines 97–
9) from 1408. Henry was with the forces
that marched north from York (when
the historical Colevile was executed; see
the note to the opening stage direction
of IV.3). By 1408 the last armed rebellion
of the reign had been put down, but
Henry was already suffering from what
was described as leprosy, visited on him,
according to 'foolish friars' (as Holinshed puts it), for his having executed the
Archbishop of York; but the disease was
probably congenital syphilis. He became
much more seriously ill in 1412 and by

the end of that year was incapacitated.
He died on 20 March 1413.

Q's stage direction gives the Earl of
Kent an entry here, but he has no lines
to speak. In 1413 he had been dead for
five years, and the title was then vacant
until 1461. Perhaps Shakespeare at first
thought Kent would be 'available' for
this scene because he was working from
events of 1405, 1408, and 1413 simultaneously, but then realized that Kent was
dead at the time of the King's illness and
dropped him. Alternatively he may have
confused the Lord Fauconbridge whose
name appears in the Q entry to 1.3 with
William Neville, also a Lord Fauconbridge, who was granted the title of Earl
of Kent in 1461.
(stage direction) *carried in a chair*. This is
    not in Q or F, but it makes the
    King's illness apparent and his faint-
    ing more practicable without over-
    dramatization.
    Clarence. Historically he was in France
    at this time.
2 *debate* struggle
3 *to higher fields* (on a crusade; see the
    note to III.1.104)

Our navy is addressed, our power collected,
Our substitutes in absence well invested,
And everything lies level to our wish;
Only we want a little personal strength,
And pause us till these rebels now afoot
Come underneath the yoke of government.   10

WARWICK
Both which we doubt not but your majesty
Shall soon enjoy.

KING HENRY IV   Humphrey, my son of Gloucester,
Where is the Prince your brother?

GLOUCESTER
I think he's gone to hunt, my lord, at Windsor.

KING HENRY IV
And how accompanied?

GLOUCESTER   I do not know, my lord.

KING HENRY IV
Is not his brother Thomas of Clarence with him?

GLOUCESTER
No, my good lord, he is in presence here.

CLARENCE
What would my lord and father?

KING HENRY IV
Nothing but well to thee, Thomas of Clarence.
How chance thou art not with the Prince thy brother?   20
He loves thee, and thou dost neglect him, Thomas.
Thou hast a better place in his affection

---

5 *addressed* made ready
6 *substitutes in absence* deputies
   invested empowered with authority
7 *level* accessible
20–48 *How chance . . . gunpowder*. This
   plea for brotherly accord is probably
   inspired by a passage in Stow's *The
   Annals of England* (1592), though in
   Stow the King gives his advice to
   Prince Henry, not Clarence. He says

he fears that after his death 'some
discord shall grow and arise between
thee and thy brother, Thomas Duke
of Clarence, whereby the realm may
be brought to destruction and
misery, for I know you both to be of
great stomach and courage'. Prince
Henry promises he will honour and
love his brothers above all men 'as
long as they be to me true'.

Than all thy brothers; cherish it, my boy,
And noble offices thou mayst effect
Of mediation, after I am dead,
Between his greatness and thy other brethren.
Therefore omit him not; blunt not his love,
Nor lose the good advantage of his grace
By seeming cold, or careless of his will.
For he is gracious, if he be observed;
He hath a tear for pity, and a hand
Open as day for melting charity;
Yet notwithstanding, being incensed, he is flint,
As humorous as winter, and as sudden
As flaws congealèd in the spring of day.
His temper therefore must be well observed.
Chide him for faults, and do it reverently,
When you perceive his blood inclined to mirth;
But, being moody, give him time and scope,
Till that his passions, like a whale on ground,
Confound themselves with working. Learn this, Thomas,
And thou shalt prove a shelter to thy friends,
A hoop of gold to bind thy brothers in,
That the united vessel of their blood,
Mingled with venom of suggestion,
As force perforce the age will pour it in,
Shall never leak, though it do work as strong
As aconitum or rash gunpowder.

27 *omit* neglect
30 *observed* humoured
34 *humorous*. There is probably some wordplay here. The word means 'capricious', which accords with *sudden*, but there may be a suggestion of another meaning of 'humorous': 'moist'. This is appropriate to winter, and also suggests one of the four bodily humours controlling the mental disposition.

35 *Flaws congealèd* icy squalls
   spring of day daybreak
41 *Confound* destroy
   working exertion
45 *suggestion* suspicion
48 *aconitum* (aconite or wolf's bane, to the Elizabethans a poison: its medicinal qualities were not discovered till much later)
   rash violent

CLARENCE
 I shall observe him with all care and love.
KING HENRY IV
 Why art thou not at Windsor with him, Thomas?   50
CLARENCE
 He is not there today; he dines in London.
KING HENRY IV
 And how accompanied? Canst thou tell that?
CLARENCE
 With Poins, and other his continual followers.
KING HENRY IV
 Most subject is the fattest soil to weeds,
 And he, the noble image of my youth,
 Is overspread with them; therefore my grief
 Stretches itself beyond the hour of death.
 The blood weeps from my heart when I do shape
 In forms imaginary th'unguided days
 And rotten times that you shall look upon   60
 When I am sleeping with my ancestors.
 For when his headstrong riot hath no curb,
 When rage and hot blood are his counsellors,
 When means and lavish manners meet together,
 O, with what wings shall his affections fly
 Towards fronting peril and opposed decay!
WARWICK
 My gracious lord, you look beyond him quite.
 The Prince but studies his companions
 Like a strange tongue, wherein, to gain the language,

52 *Canst thou tell that?* These words
appear only in F. Like those at lines
120 and 132 they could have been
added merely to fill out a line and
may not be Shakespeare's.
54 *fattest* most fertile
58 *blood weeps from my heart.* It was
thought that every sigh caused a
drop of blood to drain from the heart.
64 *lavish* unrestrained
65 *affections* inclinations
66 *fronting* confronting
 opposed hostile
67 *look beyond him.* Warwick protests that
the King exaggerates the Prince's current misdemeanours – goes too far.

70   'Tis needful that the most immodest word
        Be looked upon and learnt, which, once attained,
        Your highness knows, comes to no further use
        But to be known and hated. So, like gross terms,
        The Prince will, in the perfectness of time,
        Cast off his followers, and their memory
        Shall as a pattern or a measure live
        By which his grace must mete the lives of other,
        Turning past evils to advantages.

KING HENRY IV
        'Tis seldom when the bee doth leave her comb
        In the dead carrion.
                Enter Westmorland
80   Who's here? Westmorland?

WESTMORLAND
        Health to my sovereign, and new happiness
        Added to that that I am to deliver!
        Prince John your son doth kiss your grace's hand.
        Mowbray, the Bishop Scroop, Hastings, and all
        Are brought to the correction of your law.
        There is not now a rebel's sword unsheathed,

75 *Cast off his followers.* This suggests
that the coldness of blood which Falstaff finds in the Lancasters (iv.3.
114–20) will play its part in determining Prince Henry's behaviour,
despite all the sack that Falstaff has
induced him to drink. It anticipates
the rejection of Falstaff, and it looks
back to the plan of action Prince
Henry outlined for himself in *1 Henry
IV*, 1.2.193–215 (but see pages 233–
5). See also iv.5.155 and v.2.125–9
below.
77 *mete* appraise
   other others
79–80 *'Tis seldom . . . carrion.* This may
recall Judges 14.8, where Samson,

turning aside from his path, saw a
swarm of bees which had made
honey in the carcase of a lion. The
meaning of the King's words is that
Prince Henry is unlikely to renounce
his pleasure, however corrupt; but
an Elizabethan audience might well
remember that the circumstances of
the honey and the lion led to
Samson's famous riddle: 'Out of the
eater came meat, and out of the
strong came sweetness' (Judges
14.14), 'the strong' being the dead
lion, the carrion; and the association
of corruption with sweetness could
readily be linked with the myth of
the regenerate Hal.

But Peace puts forth her olive everywhere.
The manner how this action hath been borne
Here at more leisure may your highness read,
With every course in his particular.   90

KING HENRY IV
O Westmorland, thou art a summer bird,
Which ever in the haunch of winter sings
The lifting up of day.
    Enter Harcourt
                Look, here's more news.

HARCOURT
From enemies heaven keep your majesty,
And, when they stand against you, may they fall
As those that I am come to tell you of!
The Earl Northumberland and the Lord Bardolph,
With a great power of English and of Scots,
Are by the shrieve of Yorkshire overthrown.
The manner and true order of the fight   100
This packet, please it you, contains at large.

KING HENRY IV
And wherefore should these good news make me sick?
Will Fortune never come with both hands full,

---

90 *every course in his particular*. The general sense is clear enough – 'each incident in every detail' – but the word *course* is not easily glossed precisely. It has been explained as 'proceeding' and as 'phase', but what might be implied is the meaning used in bear-baiting, where a course was one of a succession of attacks. This meaning is used by Shakespeare (in *Macbeth*, v.6.11–12, and *King Lear*, III.7.53), and it would be appropriate here, since the insurrection put down at Gaultree was one of a series of attacks 'baiting' Henry IV.
his its

92 *haunch* hind part, latter end (an expression one would expect to be comic, like 'the buttock of the night', *Coriolanus*, II.1.48–9)

93 (stage direction) *Harcourt* (Shakespeare's creation)

97–9 *The Earl . . . overthrown*. This refers to the Battle of Bramham Moor (1408), in which the historic Northumberland at last behaved with distinction – and was killed. Shakespeare allows him no glory. See also the headnote to I.1.

99 *shrieve* sheriff

101 *at large* in full

But wet her fair words still in foulest terms?
She either gives a stomach and no food –
Such are the poor, in health – or else a feast
And takes away the stomach – such are the rich
That have abundance and enjoy it not.
I should rejoice now at this happy news,
And now my sight fails, and my brain is giddy.
O me! Come near me. Now I am much ill.

GLOUCESTER
Comfort, your majesty!

CLARENCE   O my royal father!

WESTMORLAND
My sovereign lord, cheer up yourself, look up.

WARWICK
Be patient, Princes. You do know these fits
Are with his highness very ordinary.
Stand from him, give him air; he'll straight be well.

CLARENCE
No, no, he cannot long hold out these pangs.
Th'incessant care and labour of his mind
Hath wrought the mure that should confine it in
So thin that life looks through and will break out.

GLOUCESTER
The people fear me, for they do observe
Unfathered heirs and loathly births of nature.

---

104 *wet her fair words still in foulest terms?*
F has 'write' for *wet* and 'Letters' for
terms. As A. R. Humphreys puts it,
the F reading 'seems a little glib and
may indicate botching', but to explain the Q reading 'requires three
specialized interpretations in nine
words', that is, *wet* as a variant of
'wit', meaning 'bequeath'; *words* as
'that which is granted'; *terms* as 'conditions' (though that is not very 'specialized'). These interpretations were
proposed by Hilda M. Hulme in *Ex-
plorations in Shakespeare's Language*
(1962).

still always
105 *stomach* appetite
113 *look up* cheer up
119 *wrought the mure* made the wall
120 *and will break out* (omitted from Q;
see the note to line 52)
121 *fear* alarm
122–5 *Unfathered heirs . . . between*. Disturbance in the state is reflected in unusual events in nature (see the note to
IV.1.54–7). Prince Henry makes a
point of the return to normality in
terms of ebb and flood at V.2.129–33.
122 *Unfathered heirs* children unnaturally

The seasons change their manners, as the year
Had found some months asleep and leaped them over.

CLARENCE

The river hath thrice flowed, no ebb between,
And the old folk, time's doting chronicles,
Say it did so a little time before
That our great-grandsire, Edward, sicked and died.

WARWICK

Speak lower, Princes, for the King recovers.

GLOUCESTER

This apoplexy will certain be his end.   130

KING HENRY IV

I pray you take me up, and bear me hence
Into some other chamber. Softly, pray.

They take up the King and lay him on a bed
Let there be no noise made, my gentle friends,   IV.5

conceived, specifically by partheno-
genesis. Such 'virgin births' could be
miraculous, but the offspring could
be (like the *loathly births of nature*)
monstrous, ill-formed creatures and
were sometimes said to result from
the intercourse of a witch and an
incubus (evil spirit).

125–8 *The river . . . died.* Holinshed states
that the Thames flowed three times
'and no ebbing between' on 12 October 1412. But there is no record of
any such events in conjunction with
the death of Edward III.

132 *Softly, pray* (omitted from Q; see the
note to line 52)

IV.5 As at IV.2 and IV.3, F does not
mark a new scene here. The action is
continuous and the move to *some other
chamber* could easily be represented by
movement across the stage. Otherwise, a
formal change of scene would have to

be made in the middle of the King's
speech, which is absurd. However, as
most editors mark a new scene at this
point, the tradition is again followed
here for readers' convenience.

Except perhaps at line 107, Shakespeare makes nothing of Holinshed's detailed account of an event of 1412, when
the Prince, seeking to remove Henry
IV's suspicions that he wished to usurp
the throne, knelt before him, gave him a
dagger, and invited him to kill him,
saying 'that his life was not so dear to
him that he wished to live one day with
his [the King's] displeasure'. *The Famous
Victories of Henry the Fifth* bases a scene
on this (see the Introduction, page 435).

The incident of the Prince's removal
of the crown is briefly described in Holinshed, where those attending the King
believe him dead and so inform the
Prince, who then takes away the crown.
In *The Famous Victories of Henry the Fifth*

Unless some dull and favourable hand
Will whisper music to my weary spirit.

WARWICK

Call for the music in the other room.

KING HENRY IV

Set me the crown upon my pillow here.

CLARENCE

His eye is hollow, and he changes much.

WARWICK

Less noise, less noise!

Enter Prince Henry

PRINCE HENRY Who saw the Duke of Clarence?

CLARENCE I am here, brother, full of heaviness.

10 PRINCE HENRY How now, rain within doors, and none
abroad? How doth the King?

GLOUCESTER Exceeding ill.

PRINCE HENRY Heard he the good news yet? Tell it him.

GLOUCESTER

He altered much upon hearing it.

---

the pattern of the incident is closer to
Shakespeare's version; and although the
speeches are much briefer there is some
similarity of tone, with especially close
parallels in the Prince's answer to the
King (lines 139–77). In Samuel Daniel's
poem *The First Four Books of the Civil
Wars between the Two Houses of Lancaster
and York* (see the Introduction, page
434), Henry (not the Prince, as in lines
24–9 here) addresses the crown, and the
interchange between father and son after
the King has awoken includes the advice
closely paralleled in lines 204–15.

2 *dull.* This hardly goes with *hand.* It
may be a transferred epithet, describing the music and meaning 'inducing
drowsiness'.

6 *changes* turns pale

9 *heaviness* sadness

10–17 Editions, including Q and F, vary
in the treatment of these lines as
prose or verse. The arrangement here
allows for a movement from the pro-
saic to the poetic; Prince Henry's
comment at lines 15–16 deliberately
jars in content and tone with the
verse immediately before and after.

14 *altered.* Good news might be expected
to bring an alteration for the better,
not for the worse, as is here implied.
But at IV.4.102 the King has said
*wherefore should these good news make me
sick?,* and although the Prince was
not then present, his response here
continues that train of thought.

PRINCE HENRY If he be sick with joy, he'll recover
    without physic.

WARWICK
    Not so much noise, my lords. Sweet Prince, speak low;
    The King your father is disposed to sleep.

CLARENCE
    Let us withdraw into the other room.

WARWICK
    Will't please your grace to go along with us?   20

PRINCE HENRY
    No, I will sit and watch here by the King.
                              Exeunt all but Prince Henry
    Why doth the crown lie there upon his pillow,
    Being so troublesome a bedfellow?
    O polished perturbation! Golden care!
    That keepest the ports of slumber open wide
    To many a watchful night! Sleep with it now!
    Yet not so sound, and half so deeply sweet,
    As he whose brow with homely biggen bound
    Snores out the watch of night. O majesty!
    When thou dost pinch thy bearer, thou dost sit   30
    Like a rich armour worn in heat of day,
    That scaldest with safety. By his gates of breath
    There lies a downy feather which stirs not;
    Did he suspire, that light and weightless down
    Perforce must move. My gracious lord! My father!
    This sleep is sound indeed; this is a sleep
    That from this golden rigol hath divorced
    So many English kings. Thy due from me
    Is tears and heavy sorrows of the blood,

25 *ports* gates
28 *biggen* nightcap
32 *gates of breath* (mouth and nose)
33 *downy*. Q spells this 'dowlny', and F
    has 'dowlney'; both spell *down* in line
    34 'dowlne'. Like the Q spelling

'Scilens', this has been taken to be of
Shakespearian   origin   (see   the
Account of the Text, page 468).

34 *suspire* breathe
37 *rigol* circle

40   Which nature, love, and filial tenderness
Shall, O dear father, pay thee plenteously.
My due from thee is this imperial crown,
Which, as immediate from thy place and blood,
Derives itself to me.

        He puts the crown on his head

                Lo where it sits,
Which God shall guard, and put the world's whole
      strength
Into one giant arm, it shall not force
This lineal honour from me. This from thee
Will I to mine leave, as 'tis left to me.   *Exit*

KING HENRY IV

Warwick! Gloucester! Clarence!

    Enter Warwick, Gloucester, Clarence, and attendant
    lords

CLARENCE

Doth the King call?

50 WARWICK   What would your majesty?

KING HENRY IV

Why did you leave me here alone, my lords?

CLARENCE

We left the Prince my brother here, my liege,
Who undertook to sit and watch by you.

KING HENRY IV The Prince of Wales? Where is he?
Let me see him. He is not here.

WARWICK

This door is open; he is gone this way.

GLOUCESTER

He came not through the chamber where we stayed.

---

43 *as immediate from* as I am next in line
   to
44 *Derives itself* descends
50 After *your majesty?*, F adds 'how fares

your Grace?'. This could be authorial, but it could well be an actor's
interpolation, especially if actors'
parts underlie F (see page 467).

KING HENRY IV Where is the crown? Who took it from
my pillow?

WARWICK

When we withdrew, my liege, we left it here.   60

KING HENRY IV

The Prince hath ta'en it hence. Go, seek him out.
Is he so hasty that he doth suppose
My sleep my death?
Find him, my lord of Warwick; chide him hither.

Exit Warwick

This part of his conjoins with my disease,
And helps to end me. See, sons, what things you are.
How quickly nature falls into revolt
When gold becomes her object!
For this the foolish over-careful fathers
Have broke their sleep with thoughts,   70
Their brains with care, their bones with industry;
For this they have engrossed and pillèd up
The cankered heaps of strange-achievèd gold;
For this they have been thoughtful to invest
Their sons with arts and martial exercises;
When, like the bee tolling from every flower,

---

65 *part* action
70 *thoughts* worries
72 *engrossed* collected *pillèd* pillaged. F has
'pyl'd' (that is 'piled'), which makes
easier sense; but Q's reading, followed
here, has an appropriate forcefulness.
75 *arts and martial exercises*. Arts and
arms were the two branches of a
gentleman's education.
76 *tolling* levying (a toll – that is, the
pollen)
76–7 *flower, | Our ... wax*. F reads
'flower | The vertuous Sweetes,' the
line being completed with 'our
Thighes packt with Wax'. This disturbs the lineation as far as line 80,
and if 'The virtuous sweets' is in-

cluded in a modern edition it has to
be made a half-line on its own; the
lineation can then follow that of Q.
The source of 'The virtuous sweets'
is not easily determined. It seems
unlikely that Shakespeare, or even
the most insensitive of writers,
would deliberately add it and allow
it to dislocate the following lines,
especially as the addition also dis-
rupts the sense; and it does not sound
like an actor's interpolation. It is conceivable that Shakespeare started a
modification, did not complete it,
and failed to score out this phrase,
so that it was mistakenly included
in F.

Our thighs packed with wax, our mouths with honey,
We bring it to the hive; and like the bees
Are murdered for our pains. This bitter taste
80   Yields his engrossments to the ending father.

Enter Warwick

Now where is he that will not stay so long
Till his friend sickness have determined me?

WARWICK

My lord, I found the Prince in the next room,
Washing with kindly tears his gentle cheeks,
With such a deep demeanour in great sorrow,
That tyranny, which never quaffed but blood,
Would, by beholding him, have washed his knife
With gentle eye-drops. He is coming hither.

KING HENRY IV

But wherefore did he take away the crown?

Enter Prince Henry

90   Lo where he comes. Come hither to me, Harry. –
Depart the chamber, leave us here alone.

Exeunt all except King Henry IV and Prince Henry

PRINCE HENRY

I never thought to hear you speak again.

KING HENRY IV

Thy wish was father, Harry, to that thought.

79 *Are murdered*. It is not the worker
bees but the drones that are murdered, as Shakespeare knew, since he
refers to the killing of the 'lazy yawning drone' in *Henry V*, 1.2.204.
79–80 *This . . . engrossments*. Proverbially
the bee produces sweetness from
even the bitterest flowers. Shakespeare reverses the normal course of
nature (compare IV.4.121–5), and he
also inverts the syntax: *engrossments*
('accumulations') is the subject of the
sentence and *taste* is the object. *Yields*
is either the singular form for the
plural (see the note to 1.2.72–3) or an
error, induced by *taste*.
80 *ending* dying
82 *determined* put an end to
84 *kindly* natural (filial)
86–8 *tyranny . . . eye-drops*. The Prince's
sorrow would move even those who
normally drink nothing but blood.
86 *tyranny* cruelty (and the tyrant
himself)
quaffed drank
93 *Thy wish was father . . . to that thought*
(an idea already proverbial in Shakespeare's time)

I stay too long by thee, I weary thee.
Dost thou so hunger for mine empty chair
That thou wilt needs invest thee with my honours
Before thy hour be ripe? O foolish youth!
Thou seekest the greatness that will overwhelm thee.
Stay but a little, for my cloud of dignity
Is held from falling with so weak a wind   100
That it will quickly drop; my day is dim.
Thou hast stolen that which after some few hours
Were thine without offence, and at my death
Thou hast sealed up my expectation.
Thy life did manifest thou lovedst me not,
And thou wilt have me die assured of it.
Thou hidest a thousand daggers in thy thoughts,
Which thou hast whetted on thy stony heart,
To stab at half an hour of my life.
What, canst thou not forbear me half an hour?   110
Then get thee gone, and dig my grave thyself,
And bid the merry bells ring to thine ear
That thou art crownèd, not that I am dead.
Let all the tears that should bedew my hearse
Be drops of balm to sanctify thy head;
Only compound me with forgotten dust.
Give that which gave thee life unto the worms.
Pluck down my officers, break my decrees;
For now a time is come to mock at form —

95 *chair* throne
99 *dignity* high estate. *Cloud* suggests
    both its height and its insubstantial
    nature.
100 *so weak a wind*. The wind was said to
    hold up the clouds; the King's breath
    sustains his life and thus his
    kingship.
101 *dim* (1) weak; (2) darkening to its
    close
104 *sealed up* confirmed

107 *a thousand daggers*. This is a common
    enough expression, but it may reflect
    the story of Prince Henry and the
    dagger (see the headnote to this
    scene).
116 *compound* mix
118 *Pluck down my officers* (perhaps a sug-
    gestion that Prince Henry will dis-
    miss the Lord Chief Justice)
119 *form* decorum, law and order

120   Harry the Fifth is crowned! Up, vanity!
Down, royal state! All you sage counsellors, hence!
And to the English court assemble now,
From every region, apes of idleness!
Now, neighbour confines, purge you of your scum!
Have you a ruffian that will swear, drink, dance,
Revel the night, rob, murder, and commit
The oldest sins the newest kind of ways?
Be happy, he will trouble you no more.
England shall double gild his treble guilt;
130   England shall give him office, honour, might;
For the fifth Harry from curbed licence plucks
The muzzle of restraint, and the wild dog
Shall flesh his tooth on every innocent.
O my poor kingdom, sick with civil blows!
When that my care could not withhold thy riots,
What wilt thou do when riot is thy care?
O, thou wilt be a wilderness again,
Peopled with wolves, thy old inhabitants!

PRINCE HENRY (*kneels*)
    O, pardon me, my liege! But for my tears,
140   The moist impediments unto my speech,
I had forestalled this dear and deep rebuke
Ere you with grief had spoke and I had heard
The course of it so far. There is your crown,
And He that wears the crown immortally

---

120 *vanity* worthlessness, futility
124 *confines* territories
125 *dance*. Dancing was often associated with such vices as drinking and swearing, and it was frequently included in puritan attacks on the stage.
133 *flesh* initiate in bloodshed (as at 1.1.149)
135–6 *When that ... thou*. Lines 135–6 are addressed to the Prince (but *thou*

in line 137 is England). *Care* implies 'caring for', 'looking after', and 'being anxious or uneasy'. *Thy riots* are the excesses of wantonness and debauchery of which the Prince stands accused; the *riot* (line 136) is the public violence and disorder that the King foresees when England is in the Prince's care. But see v.5.65.

141 *dear* grievous

Long guard it yours! If I affect it more
Than as your honour and as your renown,
Let me no more from this obedience rise,
Which my most inward true and duteous spirit
Teacheth this prostrate and exterior bending.
God witness with me, when I here came in   150
And found no course of breath within your majesty,
How cold it struck my heart! If I do feign,
O, let me in my present wildness die,
And never live to show th'incredulous world
The noble change that I have purposèd!
Coming to look on you, thinking you dead,
And dead almost, my liege, to think you were,
I spake unto this crown as having sense,
And thus upbraided it: 'The care on thee depending
Hath fed upon the body of my father;   160
Therefore thou best of gold art worse than gold.
Other, less fine in carat, is more precious,
Preserving life in medicine potable;
But thou, most fine, most honoured, most renowned,
Hast eat thy bearer up.' Thus, my most royal liege,
Accusing it, I put it on my head,
To try with it, as with an enemy
That had before my face murdered my father,
The quarrel of a true inheritor.
But if it did infect my blood with joy   170
Or swell my thoughts to any strain of pride,

---

145 *affect* aspire to
147 *obedience* obeisance (kneeling)
155 *The noble change that I have purposèd.*
  See the note to IV.4.75.
161 *thou best of gold art worse than gold.*
  The *best of gold* is the crown; coupled
  with the *care* it brings, it is *worse than
  gold.* In lines 164–5 the crown itself is
  seen as having eaten the King up,

and in line 168 it is treated as his
murderer.
162 *carat* quality
163 *medicine potable* aurum potabile (a
  liquid supposed to contain gold, credited with great medicinal powers)
167 *try* fight out
169 *quarrel* aversion, hostility
171 *strain* tendency

If any rebel or vain spirit of mine
Did with the least affection of a welcome
Give entertainment to the might of it,
Let God for ever keep it from my head,
And make me as the poorest vassal is
That doth with awe and terror kneel to it!

KING HENRY IV

God put it in thy mind to take it hence,
That thou mightst win the more thy father's love,
180   Pleading so wisely in excuse of it!
Come hither, Harry; sit thou by my bed,
And hear, I think, the very latest counsel
That ever I shall breathe. God knows, my son,
By what by-paths and indirect crooked ways
I met this crown, and I myself know well
How troublesome it sat upon my head.
To thee it shall descend with better quiet,

173 *affection* inclination
178 In F this speech begins with the line 'O my Sonne!', and the Prince's reply (line 220) begins with 'My gracious Liege:'. Neither of these half-lines appears in Q; they echo the opening of the Prince's speech at line 139, and they may well be actors' interpolations (see the note to line 50).
182 *latest* last
184 *crooked* (one syllable) devious. The guilt and self-justification of the usurper hang heavily over King Henry's speech.
185 *I met this crown.* The word *met* suggests that the King would like to argue that he did not seek the crown – as if he found it unclaimed and put it on (rather as the Prince has just done, technically usurping his father's crown). Richard by no means gave the crown to Henry. In *Richard II* York and Bolingbroke urge Rich-

ard to resign the crown (IV.1.179, 189, and 199), but Richard, in a dramatic moment, holds the crown in his hand, places Bolingbroke's hand on the other side, and bids him seize it (lines 181–2). Any member of an audience who had seen *Richard II* would have no doubt that Henry IV did not merely 'meet' the crown. And an audience might remember Falstaff's superbly sardonic comment when the rebel Worcester protests that he has 'not sought the day of this dislike'; Falstaff remarks 'Rebellion lay in his way, and he found it' (*1 Henry IV*, V.1.26–8). However Henry might rationalize his actions, however much he might vow a pilgrimage to the Holy Land, and however bad the state of England under Richard, he usurped the throne and he knew it (see, for example, line 189). See also the note to III.1.69.

Better opinion, better confirmation,
For all the soil of the achievement goes
With me into the earth. It seemed in me   190
But as an honour snatched with boisterous hand,
And I had many living to upbraid
My gain of it by their assistances,
Which daily grew to quarrel and to bloodshed,
Wounding supposèd peace. All these bold fears
Thou seest with peril I have answerèd,
For all my reign hath been but as a scene
Acting that argument. And now my death
Changes the mood, for what in me was purchased
Falls upon thee in a more fairer sort,   200
So thou the garland wearest successively.
Yet though thou standest more sure than I could do,
Thou art not firm enough, since griefs are green;
And all my friends, which thou must make thy friends,
Have but their stings and teeth newly ta'en out,
By whose fell working I was first advanced,
And by whose power I well might lodge a fear
To be again displaced; which to avoid,
I cut them off, and had a purpose now

188 *opinion* reputation
189 *soil of the achievement* moral taint of
my success (punning on *soil* as
'earth')
191 *snatched.* What was *met* is now
snatched, a description more in line
with King Richard's demand that
Henry seize the crown (see the note
to line 185).
boisterous (two syllables). The word
means not only 'energetic' but also
'violent'; Henry means the first but
implies the second.
195 *fears* objects of fear
198 *argument* subject-matter (of a play)
199 *purchased.* Again Henry means one
thing ('fairly bought') but implies
another (the legal meaning, 'acquired

otherwise than by inheritance or
descent').
201 *garland* crown (with the implication
that it can be worn meritoriously)
successively by right of succession
203 *griefs* grievances
green fresh (and still growing)
204 *my.* Q and F read 'thy', but *my* is
surely intended. If Q alone had 'thy',
it could be attributed to the compositor, who was inclined to make similar
errors in setting *Richard II.* If F's
'thy' comes from a source independent of Q, it could be that Shakespeare
himself made a mistake, perhaps anticipating the *thy* later in the line (a
type of error that is common).
207 *lodge* harbour

210   To lead out many to the Holy Land,
         Lest rest and lying still might make them look
         Too near unto my state. Therefore, my Harry,
         Be it thy course to busy giddy minds
         With foreign quarrels, that action hence borne out
         May waste the memory of the former days.
         More would I, but my lungs are wasted so
         That strength of speech is utterly denied me.
         How I came by the crown, O God forgive,
         And grant it may with thee in true peace live!

PRINCE HENRY
220   You won it, wore it, kept it, gave it me;
         Then plain and right must my possession be,
         Which I with more than with a common pain
         'Gainst all the world will rightfully maintain.

                  *Enter Prince John of Lancaster, Warwick, and
                  attendant lords*

KING HENRY IV
         Look, look, here comes my John of Lancaster.

PRINCE JOHN
         Health, peace, and happiness to my royal father!

KING HENRY IV
         Thou bringest me happiness and peace, son John,
         But health, alack, with youthful wings is flown
         From this bare withered trunk. Upon thy sight
         My worldly business makes a period.
         Where is my lord of Warwick?

230 PRINCE HENRY   My lord of Warwick!

KING HENRY IV
         Doth any name particular belong
         Unto the lodging where I first did swoon?

211–12 *look | Too near unto* pay too much
attention to (and consider usurping)
213–14 *busy giddy minds | With foreign quar-
rels.* The Prince quickly takes this
advice, for at v.5.108–11 Prince John

is prophesying an expedition to
France.
215 *waste* weaken. (Compare *wasted* in
the next line.)
220 See the note to line 178.
229 *period* conclusion

WARWICK
 'Tis called Jerusalem, my noble lord.
KING HENRY IV
 Laud be to God! Even there my life must end.
 It hath been prophesied to me, many years,
 I should not die but in Jerusalem,
 Which vainly I supposed the Holy Land.
 But bear me to that chamber; there I'll lie;
 In that Jerusalem shall Harry die.   *Exeunt*

                 Enter Shallow, Falstaff, Bardolph, and the Page   V.I
SHALLOW By cock and pie, sir, you shall not away to-
 night. What, Davy, I say!
FALSTAFF You must excuse me, Master Robert Shallow.
SHALLOW I will not excuse you; you shall not be excused;
 excuses shall not be admitted; there is no excuse shall
 serve; you shall not be excused. Why, Davy!
                 Enter Davy
DAVY Here, sir.
SHALLOW Davy, Davy, Davy, Davy! Let me see, Davy;
 let me see, Davy; let me see – yea, marry, William cook,
 bid him come hither. Sir John, you shall not be excused.   10
DAVY Marry, sir, thus: those precepts cannot be served;

---

233 *Jerusalem*. The Jerusalem Chamber in Westminster Abbey took its name from inscriptions round the fireplace mentioning Jerusalem.

234-9 *Even there ... Harry die*. Holinshed recounts the legend that it had been prophesied that Henry would die in Jerusalem, the implication being that his death would occur during his proposed crusade (see the note to III.I.104).

V.I.I *By cock and pie* (a mild oath, meaning 'By God and the book of church services', *pie* being the ordinal of the Roman Catholic Church)

9 *William cook* William the cook

11–12 *those precepts...wheat*. Davy is torn in two ways. It is his duty not only to provide for his master's guests but also to see that the day-to-day work of the farm is carried on and that the process of law continues (even to the point of protecting an *arrant knave*; see line 36).

and again, sir – shall we sow the hade land with wheat?

SHALLOW With red wheat, Davy. But for William cook –
are there no young pigeons?

DAVY Yes, sir. Here is now the smith's note for shoeing
and plough-irons.

SHALLOW Let it be cast and paid. Sir John, you shall not
be excused.

DAVY Now, sir, a new link to the bucket must needs be
had. And, sir, do you mean to stop any of William's
wages, about the sack he lost at Hinckley fair?

SHALLOW 'A shall answer it. Some pigeons, Davy, a
couple of short-legged hens, a joint of mutton, and any
pretty little tiny kickshaws, tell William cook.

DAVY Doth the man of war stay all night, sir?

SHALLOW Yea, Davy. I will use him well; a friend
i'th'court is better than a penny in purse. Use his men

20

Whilst the master can be wholly wrapped up in the excitement of receiving his guests, Davy has to keep his feet on the ground.

11 *precepts* writs

12 *hade land* headland (that is, the strip of land left when ploughing so that the plough could be turned without disordering the furrows; it could be worked only after all tasks on the rest of the field had been completed). This is Q's spelling; F uses the more 'correct' version 'head-land'.

13 *red wheat* (late wheat, with a reddish tinge, unlike the white wheat of the main crop)

14 *pigeons*. In Shakespeare's time pigeons (doves) were a source of fresh meat, especially in winter. The large dove-cote at his mother's house at Wilmcote, near Stratford-upon-Avon, can still be seen.

15 *note* invoice

17 *cast* added up

19 *link* (either a rope or chain, or part of one)
bucket. This may mean 'pail', but it could be 'yoke' (see the note to III.2.256–7).

21 *Hinckley* (a market town some thirty miles north-east of Stratford-upon-Avon)

22 *answer* answer for, make amends for

23 *short-legged hens* (preferable to those with long legs, because they had more and better flesh)

24 *tiny*. F reads 'tine' here and 'tyne' at v.3.56, an example of the tendency for a later edition to make a difficult word easier, for at the time when 2 *Henry IV* was written, 'tine' was the more common version of the word. 'Tiny' is first recorded in 1598 and 1599, and 'tine' seems to have dropped out fairly quickly thereafter, perhaps because the second syllable added to the sense of diminutiveness.
kickshaws (from the French *quelques choses*) fancy extra dishes

well, Davy, for they are arrant knaves, and will backbite.

DAVY No worse than they are backbitten, sir, for they
have marvellous foul linen.   30

SHALLOW Well conceited, Davy – about thy business,
Davy.

DAVY I beseech you, sir, to countenance William Visor of
Woncot against Clement Perkes o'th'Hill.

SHALLOW There is many complaints, Davy, against that
Visor; that Visor is an arrant knave, on my knowledge.

DAVY I grant your worship that he is a knave, sir; but yet
God forbid, sir, but a knave should have some countenance at his friend's request. An honest man, sir, is able
to speak for himself, when a knave is not. I have served   40
your worship truly, sir, this eight years, and if I cannot
once or twice in a quarter bear out a knave against an
honest man, I have little credit with your worship. The
knave is mine honest friend, sir; therefore, I beseech
you, let him be countenanced.

SHALLOW Go to; I say he shall have no wrong. Look
about, Davy.   *Exit Davy*

---

29 *backbitten* (by lice)
31 *Well conceited* very witty
33–4 *William Visor ... o'th'Hill.* It is
not possible to be certain of these
identifications, but 'Woncot' is a
local pronunciation for Woodman-
cote in Gloucestershire, and a family
named Visor (or Vizard) lived there
in the early seventeenth century; the
nearby Stinchcombe Hill could be
th'Hill, and there was a Perkis (or
Purchase) family there. Shakespeare
almost certainly knew this area: in
Richard II, when Bolingbroke is
marching through Gloucestershire,
Hotspur, asked how far it is to Berkeley Castle, replies that it stands
'by yon tuft of trees' (II.3.53); and
Berkeley can be seen in a copse less

than four miles from Stinchcombe
Hill.
42 *bear out* help
44 *honest friend* good friend (not implying
that he is either honest or good in
anything but his friendship with
Davy)
46 *shall have no wrong* shall be fairly
treated. It has been suggested that
Shakespeare is depicting petty corruption of the magistracy here. This
argument is partly based on an accusation made in the House of Commons
in 1601 that a justice of the peace
would for half a dozen chickens 'dis-
pense with a whole dozen of penal
statutes'. Doubtless there was dis-
honesty among justices, but Shakespeare's point here is surely the

Where are you, Sir John? Come, come, come, off with
your boots. Give me your hand, Master Bardolph.

50   BARDOLPH I am glad to see your worship.

SHALLOW I thank thee with all my heart, kind Master
Bardolph; (*to the Page*) and welcome, my tall fellow.
Come, Sir John.

FALSTAFF I'll follow you, good Master Robert Shallow.

Exit Shallow

Bardolph, look to our horses.

Exeunt Bardolph and Page

If I were sawed into quantities, I should make four
dozen of such bearded hermits' staves as Master Shallow. It is a wonderful thing to see the semblable
coherence of his men's spirits and his. They, by
60   observing him, do bear themselves like foolish justices;
he, by conversing with them, is turned into a justice-like
servingman. Their spirits are so married in conjunction,
with the participation of society, that they flock together
in consent, like so many wild geese. If I had a suit to

reverse. Shallow is shown to be
rather silly and very naïve, but basically kind and human; Davy is concerned only to ensure that his friend
has a fair hearing – which Shallow
grants.

46–7 *Look about* look sharp!

52 *tall* (1) lofty (ironically, the Page
being small); (2) valiant

56 *quantities* little pieces

58 *a wonderful thing.* Falstaff's comments
suggest that he is being purely ironic,
yet there is much to be admired in
the relationships Shakespeare dramatizes in Gloucestershire. Bolingbroke
imagined executive efficiency could
replace the mystique of kingship, and
Touchstone thought his court wit
superior to the natural sympathy and
understanding of the shepherd Corin;
so Falstaff imagines his cunning and

worldly wisdom are superior to the
good-natured folly of Shallow and
the dutifulness of Davy.

58–9 *semblable coherence* close correspondence

61 *conversing* associating

62 *married in conjunction* intimately united

63 *with the participation of society* by their
participating with one another, associating together

64–8 *If I had . . . servants.* Falstaff explains how to present a request indirectly. Had he a favour (*suit*) to beg
of Shallow he would humour his
servants, stressing in what close confidence they were with their master; if
he wanted something of the servants,
he would flatter (*curry with*) their
master that he (Shallow) had them
wholly in his control.

Master Shallow, I would humour his men with the imputation of being near their master; if to his men, I would curry with Master Shallow that no man could better command his servants. It is certain that either wise bearing or ignorant carriage is caught, as men take diseases, one of another; therefore let men take heed   70
of their company. I will devise matter enough out of this Shallow to keep Prince Harry in continual laughter the wearing out of six fashions, which is four terms, or two actions, and 'a shall laugh without intervallums. O, it is much that a lie with a slight oath, and a jest with a sad brow, will do with a fellow that never had the ache in his shoulders! O, you shall see him laugh till his face be like a wet cloak ill laid up!

SHALLOW (*within*) Sir John!

FALSTAFF I come, Master Shallow, I come, Master   80
Shallow.   *Exit*

66 *near* intimate with
69 *carriage* behaviour
70–71 *let men take heed of their company* (a proverbial saying; Falstaff apparently fails to recognize its relevance to Prince Henry)
73, 74 *six fashions ... four terms ... two actions*. Four law *terms* make up the lawyer's year. Falstaff sees fashions changing rapidly – a new one every two months – but *actions* (lawsuits) proceeding slowly, a single action taking two terms. The legal references (and the Latin word *intervallums*) may have been designed to appeal to law students in the audience.
74 *intervallums* intervals
76 *sad* serious, grave

76–7 *never had the ache in his shoulders*. Falstaff may mean simply that Shallow has never had to bear the problems of the 'real' (city) world on his shoulders and so is not bowed down with pain. But he may refer to experience of another kind: 'ache' was used of the pain of venereal disease (as in 'incurable bone-ache', *Troilus and Cressida*, V.I.21), and although Shallow has known whores (III.2.193–4 and 304) he seems to have escaped venereal disease.
76 *ache*. The noun (but not the verb) was pronounced 'aitch' in Shakespeare's time.
78 *like a wet cloak ill laid up* creased like a wet cloak that was not properly hung up to dry

V.2   *Enter Warwick and the Lord Chief Justice*

WARWICK

How now, my Lord Chief Justice, whither away?

LORD CHIEF JUSTICE

How doth the King?

WARWICK

Exceeding well; his cares are now all ended.

LORD CHIEF JUSTICE

I hope, not dead.

WARWICK   He's walked the way of nature,

And to our purposes he lives no more.

LORD CHIEF JUSTICE

I would his majesty had called me with him.

The service that I truly did his life

Hath left me open to all injuries.

WARWICK

Indeed I think the young King loves you not.

LORD CHIEF JUSTICE

10   I know he doth not, and do arm myself

To welcome the condition of the time,

Which cannot look more hideously upon me

Than I have drawn it in my fantasy.

>   *Enter Prince John of Lancaster, Clarence, Gloucester*
>   *and attendant lords*

WARWICK

Here come the heavy issue of dead Harry.

O that the living Harry had the temper

Of he, the worst of these three gentlemen!

How many nobles then should hold their places

---

v.2.7–8 *The service . . . injuries.* The Lord
Chief Justice fears that Prince Henry,
now King Henry V, will seek revenge
for his action against him (see 1.2.54 and
the note). His fears resemble those expressed by the dead king at IV.5.118–38,

especially in the first line of that passage,
Pluck down my officers, break my decrees.
13 *fantasy* wildest imaginings
14 *heavy issue* sorrowful descendants
15 *temper* disposition

That must strike sail to spirits of vile sort!

LORD CHIEF JUSTICE

O God, I fear all will be overturned.

PRINCE JOHN

Good morrow, cousin Warwick, good morrow.   20

GLOUCESTER *and* CLARENCE

Good morrow, cousin.

PRINCE JOHN

We meet like men that had forgot to speak.

WARWICK

We do remember, but our argument
Is all too heavy to admit much talk.

PRINCE JOHN

Well, peace be with him that hath made us heavy.

LORD CHIEF JUSTICE

Peace be with us, lest we be heavier.

GLOUCESTER

O, good my lord, you have lost a friend indeed,
And I dare swear you borrow not that face
Of seeming sorrow – it is sure your own.

PRINCE JOHN

Though no man be assured what grace to find,   30
You stand in coldest expectation.
I am the sorrier; would 'twere otherwise.

CLARENCE

Well, you must now speak Sir John Falstaff fair,
Which swims against your stream of quality.

LORD CHIEF JUSTICE

Sweet Princes, what I did I did in honour,
Led by th'impartial conduct of my soul.

---

18 *strike sail* submit
22 *forgot to* forgotten how to
23 *our argument* the subject of our conversation
30 *to find* to expect
31 *coldest expectation* bleakest anticipation
34 *your stream of quality* the current of your dignity

And never shall you see that I will beg
A raggèd and forestalled remission.
If truth and upright innocency fail me,
I'll to the King my master that is dead,
And tell him who hath sent me after him.

WARWICK
Here comes the Prince.
    Enter King Henry V, attended by Blunt and others

LORD CHIEF JUSTICE
Good morrow, and God save your majesty!

KING HENRY V
This new and gorgeous garment, majesty,
Sits not so easy on me as you think.
Brothers, you mix your sadness with some fear.
This is the English, not the Turkish court;
Not Amurath an Amurath succeeds,

38 *raggèd* mean, beggarly
   forestalled remission. This is a little difficult to interpret. The Lord Chief Justice has yet to be accused by the new king of having performed his office incorrectly, and *forestalled* is probably to be taken as 'intercepted' – he will not ask pardon before a charge has even been laid against him – but it could also mean 'that will certainly be refused'.

42 (stage direction) *Blunt.* See the note to the stage direction at III.1.31. Q's direction is retained (and expanded) here because it seems unlikely that the King would enter unattended (as in F).

44–5 *This new and gorgeous garment, majesty,* | *Sits not so easy on me.* This suggests an understanding of kingship that Shakespeare also demonstrates in the lines in *Henry V* beginning 'And what have kings that privates have not too, | Save ceremony' (IV.1.231 onwards), and the passage in *Richard II*, IV.1, where Richard proceeds to 'undo' himself,

separating from himself the insignia of kingship until, when he has completed this task, '"God save King Henry," unkinged Richard says' (IV.1.219). The notion that king and man were not indissolubly united runs as an undercurrent through all four plays of this sequence; and in the political affairs of the Stuarts it was to be fought out soon after, and disastrously for Charles I. Kingship is like a garment that can be put on and off; and, as Shakespeare shows in his characterization of Macbeth, kingly garments may not fit a usurper.

48 *Amurath* (a topical allusion to a current example of tyranny: in 1574 Sultan Murad III, known as Amurath, on succeeding his father, killed all his brothers; and his successor did the same when he came to the throne in 1596. Amurath was the subject of a play, *The Courageous Turk*, performed at Oxford in 1619.)

But Harry Harry. Yet be sad, good brothers,
For, by my faith, it very well becomes you.   50
Sorrow so royally in you appears
That I will deeply put the fashion on
And wear it in my heart. Why then, be sad;
But entertain no more of it, good brothers,
Than a joint burden laid upon us all.
For me, by heaven, I bid you be assured,
I'll be your father and your brother too.
Let me but bear your love, I'll bear your cares.
Yet weep that Harry's dead, and so will I;
But Harry lives, that shall convert those tears   60
By number into hours of happiness.

PRINCES

We hope no otherwise from your majesty.

KING HENRY V

You all look strangely on me – and (*to Lord Chief Justice*)
    you most;
You are, I think, assured I love you not.

LORD CHIEF JUSTICE

I am assured, if I be measured rightly,
Your majesty hath no just cause to hate me.

KING HENRY V

No?
How might a prince of my great hopes forget
So great indignities you laid upon me?
What! Rate, rebuke, and roughly send to prison   70
Th'immediate heir of England? Was this easy?
May this be washed in Lethe and forgotten?

LORD CHIEF JUSTICE

I then did use the person of your father;

---

52 *deeply* profoundly and seriously
63 *strangely on me* as if I were a stranger
65 *measured* judged
70 *Rate* admonish
71 *easy* insignificant
72 *Lethe* (a river in Hades (the under-world); to drink it – not to be *washed in* it – brought forgetfulness)
73 *use the person of* represent. The expression is technically exact; judges represent the king in administering justice.

The image of his power lay then in me
And in th'administration of his law.
Whiles I was busy for the commonwealth,
Your highness pleasèd to forget my place,
The majesty and power of law and justice,
The image of the King whom I presented,
80   And struck me in my very seat of judgement;
Whereon, as an offender to your father,
I gave bold way to my authority
And did commit you. If the deed were ill,
Be you contented, wearing now the garland,
To have a son set your decrees at naught?
To pluck down justice from your awful bench?
To trip the course of law, and blunt the sword
That guards the peace and safety of your person?
Nay, more, to spurn at your most royal image,
90   And mock your workings in a second body?
Question your royal thoughts, make the case yours;
Be now the father and propose a son,
Hear your own dignity so much profaned,
See your most dreadful laws so loosely slighted,
Behold yourself so by a son disdained;
And then imagine me taking your part,
And in your power soft silencing your son.
After this cold considerance sentence me,

74 *image* symbol
79 *presented* represented
84 *garland* crown. See the note to
    IV.5.201.
86 *awful*. See the note to IV.1.174.
87 *sword*. In the coronation service the
    Archbishop officiating offers the sov-
    ereign the Sword of Spiritual Justice
    and says 'With this sword do justice';
    it is then worn briefly by the sover-
    eign and carried naked before him

for the rest of the ceremony. It is to
this sword that the Lord Chief Justice refers. See also lines 103 and
114.
90 *your workings in a second body* duties as
    carried out by your representative
92 *propose* imagine. This passage recalls
    the play-acting of *1 Henry IV*, II.4.
97 *soft* gently, quietly
98 *considerance* reflection

And, as you are a king, speak in your state
What I have done that misbecame my place,   100
My person, or my liege's sovereignty.

KING HENRY V

You are right justice, and you weigh this well.
Therefore still bear the balance and the sword,
And I do wish your honours may increase
Till you do live to see a son of mine
Offend you and obey you, as I did.
So shall I live to speak my father's words:
'Happy am I, that have a man so bold
That dares do justice on my proper son;
And not less happy, having such a son   110
That would deliver up his greatness so
Into the hands of justice.' You did commit me –
For which I do commit into your hand
Th'unstained sword that you have used to bear,
With this remembrance: that you use the same
With the like bold, just, and impartial spirit
As you have done 'gainst me. There is my hand.
You shall be as a father to my youth;
My voice shall sound as you do prompt mine ear,
And I will stoop and humble my intents   120
To your well-practised wise directions.
And, Princes all, believe me, I beseech you,

---

99 *in your state* from your throne, in
your capacity as king
102 *right justice.* There is no punctuation
between these words in Q and F.
Some modern editors (but not all)
add a comma after *right*. The more
difficult reading preferred here gives
the sense 'justice itself'.
weigh consider, judge

103 *still bear the balance and the sword.* See
the first note to the stage direction at
1.2.52.
109 *proper* own
115 *remembrance* reminder
119–21 *My voice ... directions.* A good
monarch was advised, among many
other things, to listen to and act
upon the advice of elder statesmen.

My father is gone wild into his grave,
For in his tomb lie my affections;
And with his spirits sadly I survive
To mock the expectation of the world,
To frustrate prophecies, and to raze out
Rotten opinion, who hath writ me down
After my seeming. The tide of blood in me
130 Hath proudly flowed in vanity till now.
Now doth it turn, and ebb back to the sea,
Where it shall mingle with the state of floods,
And flow henceforth in formal majesty.
Now call we our high court of parliament,
And let us choose such limbs of noble counsel
That the great body of our state may go
In equal rank with the best-governed nation;
That war, or peace, or both at once, may be
As things acquainted and familiar to us;
140 In which you, father, shall have foremost hand.
Our coronation done, we will accite,

123–4 *My father . . . affections*. The obvious implication is that Prince Henry's youthful wildness has been buried with his father, but there is a sense in which Henry IV's wildness – his guilt in usurping the throne – is also buried. Compare IV.5.184–5. Several interpretations of *affections* are possible, and one need not exclude the others. 'Natural disposition' – that which will be modified by cultivation and civilizing influences – may be implied; or the reference may be to the Prince's (past) inclinations – the *riots*, excess, mentioned by Henry IV at IV.5.135 – or, simply, to lusts.

125 *sadly* gravely

126 *mock* disprove

129 *After my seeming* according to my outward appearance. (See the note to IV.4.75.)

130 *proudly* overbearingly, unreasonably

131 *Now . . . sea*. Nature is returning to normality. Compare IV.4.122–5 (especially 125) and the notes.

132 *state of floods* majesty of the oceans

134 *we*. Only now does the new king adopt the royal plural. His father was quicker to use it (*Richard II*, IV.1.90), and even quicker to execute justice as if he were already king (*Richard II*, III.1).

135 *limbs* members (of the body politic)

141 *accite* summon

As I before remembered, all our state.
And, God consigning to my good intents,
No prince nor peer shall have just cause to say,
God shorten Harry's happy life one day!   *Exeunt*

Enter Falstaff, Shallow, Silence, Davy, Bardolph,   V.3
   and the Page

SHALLOW Nay, you shall see my orchard, where, in an
   arbour, we will eat a last year's pippin of mine own
   graffing, with a dish of caraways, and so forth – come,
   cousin Silence – and then to bed.

FALSTAFF 'Fore God, you have here a goodly dwelling,
   and a rich.

SHALLOW Barren, barren, barren; beggars all, beggars
   all, Sir John – marry, good air. Spread, Davy, spread,
   Davy, well said, Davy.

FALSTAFF This Davy serves you for good uses – he is   10
   your servingman and your husband.

SHALLOW A good varlet, a good varlet, a very good
   varlet, Sir John – by the mass, I have drunk too much
   sack at supper – a good varlet. Now sit down, now sit
   down – come, cousin.

SILENCE Ah, sirrah! quoth 'a, we shall
   (*sings*)   *Do nothing but eat, and make good cheer,*
         And praise God for the merry year,

---

142 *remembered* mentioned
   state men of rank, government
143 *consigning to* endorsing

v.3.3 *graffing* grafting
   caraways (sweetmeats containing cara-
   way seeds)
8 *Spread* lay the cloth on the table. Compare *cover*, II.4.10.
9 *well said* well done. Compare III.2.267.

11 *husband* husbandman, steward
16 *Ah, sirrah!* (an exclamation addressed
   to the world in general and no one
   in particular)
17–22 Silence's songs are set as prose in
   Q and F, except for the one at lines
   32–5, which F prints as verse. All of
   them sound traditional, but only the
   one at lines 73–5 has been identified;
   it is from a drinking song called

> *When flesh is cheap and females dear,*
20 *And lusty lads roam here and there,*
> *So merrily,*
> *And ever among so merrily.*

FALSTAFF There's a merry heart, good Master Silence!
I'll give you a health for that anon.

SHALLOW Give Master Bardolph some wine, Davy.

DAVY Sweet sir, sit – I'll be with you anon. Most sweet
sir, sit; master page, good master page, sit. Proface!
What you want in meat, we'll have in drink; but you
must bear; the heart's all.   *Exit*

30 SHALLOW Be merry, Master Bardolph; and, my little
soldier there, be merry.

SILENCE (*sings*)
> *Be merry, be merry, my wife has all,*
> *For women are shrews, both short and tall.*
> *'Tis merry in hall, when beards wags all,*
> *And welcome merry Shrovetide! Be merry, be merry.*

FALSTAFF I did not think Master Silence had been a man
of this mettle.

SILENCE Who, I? I have been merry twice and once ere
now.

> *Enter Davy*

Monsieur Mingo which Orlando di Lasso
set to music. Its popularity can be
gauged from the fact that snatches
from it appear in plays by Nashe,
Jonson, Chapman, and Marston. The
music is reprinted on page 486.
19 *flesh.* See the note to II.4.339.
22 *ever among* all the while
27 *Proface!* may it do you good (a polite
formula before eating or drinking,
derived from the French *bon prou vous
fasse*)
28 *want* lack
29 *bear* put up with things

34 *wags* (the singular form for the plural)
38–9 *I have . . . now.* As Silence is drinking, *merry* may mean 'slightly tipsy';
or, as his song at lines 32–5 suggests,
it may mean 'happy'. A third possibility is that he claims he can, on occasion, be amusing. In the theatre
Silence certainly is a source of laughter, but not because he is himself
witty; the nearest he gets to wit is at
lines 89–90 and that may be accidental. The formula *twice and once* was
evidently a stock type of inversion
suggesting frequency.

DAVY (*to Bardolph*) There's a dish of leather-coats for   40
you.

SHALLOW Davy!

DAVY Your worship? I'll be with you straight. (*To Bardolph*) A cup of wine, sir?

SILENCE (*sings*)
> A cup of wine that's brisk and fine,
> And drink unto thee, leman mine,
> And a merry heart lives long-a.

FALSTAFF Well said, Master Silence.

SILENCE An we shall be merry, now comes in the sweet
o'th'night.   50

FALSTAFF Health and long life to you, Master Silence.

SILENCE (*sings*)
> Fill the cup, and let it come,
> I'll pledge you a mile to th'bottom.

SHALLOW Honest Bardolph, welcome! If thou wantest
anything and wilt not call, beshrew thy heart. (*To the
Page*) Welcome, my little tiny thief, and welcome indeed,
too! I'll drink to Master Bardolph, and to all the
cabileros about London.

DAVY I hope to see London once ere I die.

BARDOLPH An I might see you there, Davy –   60

SHALLOW By the mass, you'll crack a quart together – ha!
will you not, Master Bardolph?

BARDOLPH Yea, sir, in a pottle-pot.

---

40 *leather-coats* russet apples (which have rough skins)

46 *leman* sweetheart, lover

52 *let it come* (a drinking cry) pass it round

53 *a mile to th'bottom* (another drinking term: Silence undertakes to drain the cup even if it is a mile deep)

55 *beshrew thy heart*. See the note to II.3.45.

56 *tiny*. See the first note to V.1.24.
thief wretch. (Lady Percy uses the word affectionately of Hotspur in *1 Henry IV*, III.1.229.)

58 *cabileros* gallants

59 *once* one day

63 *pottle-pot* two-quart tankard (twice the amount that Shallow has mentioned)

SHALLOW By God's liggens, I thank thee. The knave
will stick by thee, I can assure thee that; 'a will not out,
'a; 'tis true bred!

BARDOLPH And I'll stick by him, sir.

SHALLOW Why, there spoke a king. Lack nothing! Be
merry!

One knocks at door

70   Look who's at door there, ho! Who knocks?

Exit Davy

FALSTAFF (*to Silence, seeing him drink*) Why, now you
have done me right.

SILENCE (*sings*)

> *Do me right,*
> *And dub me knight:*
> *Samingo.*

Is't not so?

FALSTAFF 'Tis so.

SILENCE Is't so? Why then, say an old man can do
somewhat.

Enter Davy

80   DAVY An't please your worship, there's one Pistol come
from the court with news.

FALSTAFF From the court? Let him come in.

Enter Pistol

How now, Pistol?

PISTOL Sir John, God save you!

FALSTAFF What wind blew you hither, Pistol?

PISTOL Not the ill wind which blows no man to good.

---

64 *By God's liggens.* The origin of this
oath is not known.
65 *out* drop out
72 *done me right* done the right thing by
me (by drinking as much as I have).
'Do me right' was a common drinking challenge.
73–5 See the note to lines 17–22. *Dub*

me knight refers to the Elizabethan
practice of 'knighting' whoever
drank the most or drank urine; *Sa-
mingo* is probably a corruption of 'Sir
Mingo' (*mingo* is Latin for 'I
urinate').
79 *somewhat* something worth doing (as
a drinker)

Sweet knight, thou art now one of the greatest men in this realm.

SILENCE By'r lady, I think 'a be, but goodman Puff of Barson.   90

PISTOL

Puff?

Puff i'thy teeth, most recreant coward base!

Sir John, I am thy Pistol and thy friend,

And helter-skelter have I rode to thee,

And tidings do I bring, and lucky joys,

And golden times, and happy news of price.

FALSTAFF I pray thee now, deliver them like a man of this world.

PISTOL

A foutre for the world and worldlings base!

I speak of Africa and golden joys.   100

FALSTAFF

O base Assyrian knight, what is thy news?

---

87 *greatest* (1) most important (because Prince Henry is King); (2) largest (which meaning Silence takes up in his comment; whether he is being deliberately witty or comically uncomprehending is not clear, but the latter seems more likely)

89 *but* apart from
   goodman (title for those, such as yeomen and farmers, below the rank of gentleman)

90 *Barson.* No particular place is necessarily intended; but there is a Barston between Solihull and Coventry, some fifteen miles north-east of Stratford-upon-Avon, and a Barcheston (sometimes pronounced Barston) twelve miles to the south-east.

92 *recreant* one who has broken faith or yielded in battle

93–6 *Sir John . . . price.* Pistol has a new verse style: for the moment he has abandoned his rant and lets fly a joyous jingle.

97–8 *like a man of this world* (that is, in plain words)

99 *A foutre for* (an indecent expression of contempt)

101–2 *O base Assyrian . . . thereof.* Falstaff joins in Pistol's game, imitating his style. No particular *Assyrian knight* is referred to; Assyrians were thought of as brigands by the Elizabethans, and that occupation is close enough to Pistol's. An old ballad telling the story of *Cophetua*, an African king who 'cared not for womenkind' but saw, loved, and married a beautiful beggar-girl, was published in 1612. Shakespeare also refers to it in *Love's Labour's Lost* (1.2.106, IV.1.67), *Romeo and Juliet* (II.1.14), and *Richard II* (V.3.79).

Let King Cophetua know the truth thereof.

SILENCE (*sings*)
> *And Robin Hood, Scarlet, and John.*

PISTOL

Shall dunghill curs confront the Helicons?
And shall good news be baffled?
Then, Pistol, lay thy head in Furies' lap.

SHALLOW   Honest gentleman, I know not your breeding.

PISTOL   Why then, lament therefor.

SHALLOW   Give me pardon, sir. If, sir, you come with
110   news from the court, I take it there's but two ways,
either to utter them or conceal them. I am, sir, under
the King, in some authority.

PISTOL

Under which king, Besonian? Speak, or die.

SHALLOW

Under King Harry.

PISTOL   Harry the Fourth, or Fifth?

SHALLOW

Harry the Fourth.

PISTOL   A foutre for thine office!

104 *Shall dunghill curs confront the Helicons?*
The *Helicons* were the Muses. Pistol,
still incensed at Silence's mention of
Puff, turns on the poor old man
again and complains of his singing a
line of a ballad in competition with
the outpourings of one who is (or
has) a true muse, Pistol himself.

105 *baffled*. This was a fairly new word
in Shakespeare's time, and its meaning was uncertain and shifting. Its
primary sense is related to the public
disgracing of a knight who had committed perjury – the *recreant* that
Pistol calls Silence (line 92), though
he is a justice of the peace, not a
knight; Pistol may be accusing
Silence of treating the news with

contempt. But Shakespeare may have
had in mind the sense 'confounded'
or 'foiled': Silence, by joining in, is
hindering the telling of the news (although the chief hindrance is, of
course, Pistol himself).

106 *Furies* (in classical mythology, aveng-
ing goddesses; see also v.5.37)

108 *therefor* for that

113–15 *Under which king . . . thine office!*
Shallow's office as justice of the
peace has automatically terminated
on the death of the King.

113 *Besonian* knave (literally 'raw recruit'; the word, from Italian, gives
an excellent high-sounding impression)

Sir John, thy tender lambkin now is King;
Harry the Fifth's the man. I speak the truth —
When Pistol lies, do this, and fig me, like
The bragging Spaniard.

FALSTAFF What, is the old King dead?

PISTOL

As nail in door! The things I speak are just.   120

FALSTAFF Away, Bardolph, saddle my horse! Master
Robert Shallow, choose what office thou wilt in the land,
'tis thine. Pistol, I will double-charge thee with dignities.

BARDOLPH O joyful day! I would not take a knighthood
for my fortune.

PISTOL What, I do bring good news?

FALSTAFF Carry Master Silence to bed. Master Shallow,
my lord Shallow — be what thou wilt — I am fortune's
steward! Get on thy boots; we'll ride all night. O sweet
Pistol! Away, Bardolph!   *Exit Bardolph*   130
Come, Pistol, utter more to me, and withal devise
something to do thyself good. Boot, boot, Master
Shallow! I know the young King is sick for me. Let us
take any man's horses — the laws of England are at my

118–19 *do this . . . Spaniard. Fig me* is a
variant of *foutre* (line 99), and Pistol
accompanies it with the traditional
gesture (*this*), putting the thumb between the first and middle fingers.
This originated in Spain, hence *The
bragging Spaniard.*
120 *just* exact, true
123 *double-charge.* Pistol will be doubly
loaded with honours. The expression
plays on his name.
133 *sick* longing
134 *take any man's horses.* Falstaff does
not mean to steal the horses, but to
ride post-haste, hiring horses on the
strength of the King's name. The
owners will forgo only hiring fees,
not the horses themselves. Neverthe-

less, in taking the King's name so,
Falstaff presumes too much; the outcome for him (and for Shallow) is
sadder and more serious than was
the outcome for Prince Henry in presuming to take the crown before his
father's death.
134–6 *the laws of England are at my commandment . . . woe to my Lord Chief
Justice!* This 'terrible sentence', as
William Empson described it, might
be guaranteed to shock an Elizabethan audience, which would be ap-
palled that the law could be held in
contempt by sectional interests. Falstaff's comic role would not protect
him here; his attitude would be rejected, and it is no coincidence that

commandment. Blessed are they that have been my friends, and woe to my Lord Chief Justice!

PISTOL
Let vultures vile seize on his lungs also!
'Where is the life that late I led?' say they;
Why, here it is. Welcome these pleasant days!

Exeunt

V.4   *Enter Beadles dragging in Hostess Quickly and Doll Tearsheet*

HOSTESS No, thou arrant knave! I would to God that I might die, that I might have thee hanged. Thou hast

---

he is given these lines at this point. Even if an Elizabethan audience had missed all the earlier signals (as modern audiences are liable to do), King Henry's rejection some eighty lines later would come as no surprise to them after Falstaff's words here. Shakespeare gives a similar sentiment to Northumberland: *Let order die!* (I.I.154); Northumberland and Falstaff are two aspects of Rebellion, Northumberland the political rebel, Falstaff 'that reverend Vice, that grey Iniquity' (see *1 Henry IV*, II.4.441 and the note to 131–2). Falstaff's attitude is apparent to the Lord Chief Justice as early as II.1.128–9 when he says *You speak as having power to do wrong.*

137 *Let vultures vile seize on his lungs also!* Pistol may be alluding to Tityus (whose liver was gnawed by vultures) or Prometheus (whose liver was gnawed by an eagle). He makes the same reference in *The Merry Wives of Windsor*, I.3.80: 'Let vultures gripe thy guts!' Similar expressions occur in other plays of the period, which no doubt are again Pistol's source

here, rather than a reading of the classics themselves.

138 *Where is the life that late I led?* (a line, also quoted in *The Taming of the Shrew*, IV.I.126, from a poem, now lost, in which a lover laments the loss of his freedom).

v.4 We now approach the end of the play, and two important events are to be dramatized: the coronation of Henry V and the rejection of Falstaff; one is a matter for rejoicing and the other (however much it is deserved) a matter for regret. Shakespeare now introduces a little scene, partly to allow dramatic time for Falstaff and Shallow's journey (though even the strewing of rushes at the beginning of v.5 would suffice for that). Adapters have often omitted this scene, but its sordidness is essential. To remove it is to romanticize the end of the play (indeed, the whole play) and to lose that vital contrast between the pomp of coronation and the other side of the coin – Hal's past and Falstaff's present. See the Introduction, pages 428–31.

(stage direction) Q has '*Enter Sincklo and three or foure officers*' (with no

drawn my shoulder our of joint.

FIRST BEADLE The constables have delivered her over
to me, and she shall have whipping-cheer, I warrant
her; there hath been a man or two killed about her.

DOLL Nut-hook, nut-hook, you lie! Come on, I'll tell
thee what, thou damned tripe-visaged rascal, an the
child I go with do miscarry, thou wert better thou hadst
struck thy mother, thou paper-faced villain.   10

HOSTESS O the Lord, that Sir John were come! I would
make this a bloody day to somebody. But I pray God
the fruit of her womb miscarry!

FIRST BEADLE If it do, you shall have a dozen of cushions
again – you have but eleven now. Come, I charge you

---

mention of the Hostess and Doll).
John Sincklo's name appears in other
plays, *3 Henry VI*, *The Taming of the
Shrew*, Marston's *The Malcontent*, and
the 'plot' (the outline indicating entries) of *2 Seven Deadly Sins*. It seems,
from the part he plays here (see lines
8, 10, 18, 20, 27–30) and the other
roles for which he is named, that he
was unusually thin and pale, and it is
suspected that Shakespeare wrote a
number of other small parts with
him specifically in mind: possibly
Snare (II.1) and Shadow (III.2) in
this play, and the Apothecary in
Romeo and Juliet, Pinch in *The Comedy
of Errors*, and Holofernes in *Love's
Labour's Lost*. Sincklo is not among
the 'Principall Actors' listed at the
beginning of the first Folio, probably
because he was only a small-part
actor.

Beadles (minor parish officers, responsible for punishing petty crim-
inals)

3 *drawn my shoulder out of joint*. Constables
and other officers had a reputation
for grabbing their victims' shoulders
vigorously.

5 *whipping-cheer* whipping fare, all the
whipping she wants (whipping being
the punishment meted out to
whores)

6 *about her* (either 'because of her' or 'in
her company')

7 *Nut-hook* (literally, a hooked stick like
a shepherd's crook, used for drawing
down branches; applied to beadles
and constables, perhaps because they,
like the nut-hook, catch hold of what
they are after)

8 *tripe-visaged*. If this is a specific rather
than a general insult, the Beadle's
face is presumably pale and pock-
marked, like tripe.

8–9 *the child I go with*. Doll maintains
that she is pregnant, probably in the
hope that this will save her from
rough handling. The Beadle is not
taken in, and in lines 14–15 he implies that she has stuffed her dress
with a cushion.

12–13 *I pray ... miscarry*. As at line 24,
the Hostess says the opposite of what
she means.

both, go with me, for the man is dead that you and
Pistol beat amongst you.

DOLL I'll tell you what, you thin man in a censer, I will
have you as soundly swinged for this – you bluebottle
20   rogue, you filthy famished correctioner, if you be not
swinged I'll forswear half-kirtles.

FIRST BEADLE Come, come, you she knight-errant,
come!

HOSTESS O God, that right should thus overcome might!
Well, of sufferance comes ease.

DOLL Come, you rogue, come, bring me to a justice.

HOSTESS Ay, come, you starved bloodhound.

DOLL Goodman death, goodman bones!

HOSTESS Thou atomy, thou!

30   DOLL Come, you thin thing, come, you rascal!

FIRST BEADLE Very well.   *Exeunt*

V.5   *Enter three Grooms, strewers of rushes*
FIRST GROOM More rushes, more rushes!

17 *amongst* between
18 *thin man in a censer*. Censers (perfum-
ing pans) often had figures embossed
on them in low relief.
19 *swinged* thrashed
bluebottle. Elizabethan beadles wore a
blue livery.
20 *correctioner* (an official of the House
of Correction, Bridewell)
21 *forswear half-kirtles* give up wearing
skirts. A kirtle was a bodice and
skirt, a half-kirtle the skirt part.
22 *knight-errant* (here, one who errs at
night: a prostitute)
24 *right . . . might*. See the note to lines
12–13.
25 *of sufferance comes ease*. The Hostess

may be confusing 'sufferance' and
'suffering', though in Elizabethan
English the words were closer in
meaning than they are now. The
phrase is proverbial, the Hostess comforting herself that her suffering will
earn her freedom from pain at some
future date.
29 *atomy*. The Hostess means 'anatomy'
(which F prints) but she uses – rather
appropriately – the Elizabethan word
for 'atom'.
30 *rascal* (young lean deer; Doll has already used the term at II.4.39)

v.5 There is a strange difference between the arrangement of this scene in F

SECOND GROOM The trumpets have sounded twice.
THIRD GROOM 'Twill be two o'clock ere they come from
the coronation. Dispatch, dispatch!

Exeunt

Trumpets sound, and the King and his train pass over
the stage. After them enter Falstaff, Shallow, Pistol,
Bardolph, and the Page

and in Q. Q has a procession to the coronation and then another for the return (as reproduced here); F misses out the first procession. If actors' parts underlie the F text (see the Account of the Text, pages 465–8), the omission would be understandable, for the procession involves no lines for the actors to speak. It might be expected that, if Q were being at all closely consulted, the first procession would be picked up from it, but possibly whoever left it out was in some way misled by the Third Groom's speech with its reference to coming *from* the coronation (see the note to lines 3–4). F might represent a cut – even a cut made by Shakespeare – but it seems reasonable to expect that, having gone to the trouble of arranging and providing for one procession, the company would wish to delight the audience with more than one sight of the spectacle.

Henry VIII, performed some fifteen years after *2 Henry IV*, also includes a coronation procession (IV.1.36). From the way in which it is described it seems clear that Shakespeare's company had appropriate ceremonial costumes for it; and we know from details of expenditure that plays in Shakespeare's time were often sumptuously dressed, so it is very probable that the procession in *2 Henry IV* was lavishly presented.

There is also a christening procession in *Henry VIII*, and the dialogue (v.4) and the stage direction (v.5) suggest that it came down steps at one side of the stage, past the groundlings standing in front of the stage, forcing them back out of the way, up steps at the other side of the stage, and then, as F's direction puts it, '*The Troope passe once about the Stage*'. In this way part of the audience would become 'extras' in the stage production; and there would be full opportunity for all the audience to see every detail of the procession. In *2 Henry IV* the procession may have done no more than 'passe ouer the stage', as Q has it; but it would be surprising if an opportunity for pageantry were not used to the full in the Elizabethan theatre.

1 *rushes* (strewn on floors or, as here, in the street as a mark of deference)

3–4 *two o'clock ... from the coronation.* Since (in Q's version of the scene) the King is about to appear on his way to the Abbey, it is strange that the Groom should speak of his return. If, as in F, the first procession is cut, there is no need for such haste – and F does not include the words *Dispatch, dispatch* (it also omits the

FALSTAFF Stand here by me, Master Shallow; I will make the King do you grace. I will leer upon him as 'a comes by, and do but mark the countenance that he will give me.

PISTOL God bless thy lungs, good knight!

10 FALSTAFF Come here, Pistol, stand behind me. (*To Shallow*) O, if I had had time to have made new liveries, I would have bestowed the thousand pound I borrowed of you. But 'tis no matter; this poor show doth better; this doth infer the zeal I had to see him.

SHALLOW It doth so.

FALSTAFF It shows my earnestness of affection –

PISTOL It doth so.

FALSTAFF My devotion –

PISTOL It doth, it doth, it doth!

20 FALSTAFF As it were, to ride day and night, and not to deliberate, not to remember, not to have patience to shift me –

SHALLOW It is best, certain.

Third Groom himself, his two lines being given to the First Groom). There may be an authorial error here.

6 *grace* honour
  leer upon him. Falstaff would be expected to bow his head as the King passes, but he proposes to cast a sly glance (*leer*) at him to attract his attention.

12 *bestowed* laid out

15, 17, 19 SHALLOW ... PISTOL ... PISTOL. These lines are distributed here as in F. Q gives line 15 to Pistol and agrees with F in giving him lines 17 and 19. Many editors follow F at line 15 and reassign lines 17 and 19 to Shallow. But if the tentative suggestion that actors' parts underlie the F text (see page 468) is correct, then F's allocations have a claim to

be respected. The difficulty is that line 19, if not line 17 too, is reminiscent of Shallow's habit of repeating what he says several times in succession. However, Falstaff has just called up Pistol to stand behind him, and it is surely not beyond Pistol to mimic the old justice. Most of his language imitates that of plays he has heard and there would be a certain humour in his now imitating the language of a character in the play in which he is appearing. It is also more effective on the stage to have dialogue shared between more than two of the characters appearing together, and Pistol's mocking of Shallow's mode of speech would provide a useful scrap of interaction.

22 *shift me* change my clothes

FALSTAFF But to stand stained with travel, and sweating
with desire to see him, thinking of nothing else, putting
all affairs else in oblivion, as if there were nothing else
to be done but to see him.

PISTOL 'Tis *semper idem,* for *obsque hoc nihil est*; 'tis all
in every part.

SHALLOW 'Tis so, indeed.   30

PISTOL

My knight, I will inflame thy noble liver,
And make thee rage.
Thy Doll, and Helen of thy noble thoughts,
Is in base durance and contagious prison,
Haled thither
By most mechanical and dirty hand.
Rouse up Revenge from ebon den with fell Alecto's
      snake,
For Doll is in. Pistol speaks naught but truth.

FALSTAFF I will deliver her.

      The trumpets sound

---

28 *semper idem ... est.* The two Latin
tags mean 'ever the same' and 'apart
from this there is nothing'. *Obsque* is
an error for *absque*, but it is impossible to tell whether the blame lies
with Shakespeare, Pistol, or the
compositor.

28-9 *'tis all in every part.* It is not clear
what this means, and probably it was
not absolutely clear in the copy or to
the compositors. It is usually explained as an English proverb
roughly equivalent to the sense of
the Latin: ''Tis all in all and all in
every part'. Q does not have *all*, and
F has either restored what Q left out
or added it to bring it close to a
proverb of the day. Shakespeare may
have intended ''tis in every part',

Pistol adapting the proverb to his
own use as he does with the plays he
quotes from.

31 *liver.* See the first note to 1.2.177.

33 *Helen.* The name of Helen of Troy
was often used for wives and mistresses. But its application to Doll is
absurd, and it must sharply remind
an audience that the prostitute hauled
away, cursing, in the last scene is
Falstaff's Doll.

34 *contagious* foul, injurious to life (other
than by disease)

36 *mechanical* of a mechanic (labourer)

37 *Alecto's snake.* Alecto was one of the
Furies (see the note to v.2.106), who
were described as having snakes
writhing in their hair.

38 *in* in prison

PISTOL

40   There roared the sea, and trumpet-clangour sounds.

> *Enter the King and his train, the Lord Chief Justice*
> *among them*

FALSTAFF God save thy grace, King Hal, my royal Hal!

PISTOL The heavens thee guard and keep, most royal
imp of fame!

FALSTAFF God save thee, my sweet boy!

KING HENRY V My Lord Chief Justice, speak to that
vain man.

LORD CHIEF JUSTICE Have you your wits? Know you
what 'tis you speak?

FALSTAFF

My King! My Jove! I speak to thee, my heart!

KING HENRY V

50   I know thee not, old man. Fall to thy prayers.
How ill white hairs becomes a fool and jester.
I have long dreamt of such a kind of man,
So surfeit-swelled, so old, and so profane,
But being awaked I do despise my dream.
Make less thy body hence, and more thy grace;
Leave gormandizing; know the grave doth gape
For thee thrice wider than for other men.
Reply not to me with a fool-born jest.

43 *imp* (an obsolete word for a descendant of a noble house).
46 *vain* foolish. There is something particularly chilling in having the Lord
Chief Justice, of all people, *speak to*
Falstaff.
50 *I know thee not, old man.* The rejection
of Falstaff is discussed in the Introduction, pages 446–8. Henry as king
has adopted a new style of speech,
just as he has put on a *new and gorgeous
garment* (V.2.44). He speaks with a
new authority, taking on the judicial
accent of the Lord Chief Justice,

whose advice he has said he will
now take (V.2.119): *My voice shall
sound as you do prompt mine ear.*
56–8 *the grave . . . fool-born jest.* An
eighteenth-century editor, William
Warburton, described this as 'one of
Shakespeare's grand touches of
nature'. For a brief moment the King
slips back into his former self, jesting
about Falstaff's bulk (though a trifle
sardonically); and then, before Falstaff can respond in like kind, he
pulls himself together: *Reply not to
me . . .*

Presume not that I am the thing I was,
For God doth know, so shall the world perceive,   60
That I have turned away my former self;
So will I those that kept me company.
When thou dost hear I am as I have been,
Approach me, and thou shalt be as thou wast,
The tutor and the feeder of my riots;
Till then I banish thee, on pain of death,
As I have done the rest of my misleaders,
Not to come near our person by ten mile.
For competence of life I will allow you,
That lack of means enforce you not to evils;   70
And as we hear you do reform yourselves,
We will, according to your strengths and qualities,
Give you advancement. (*To the Lord Chief Justice*) Be
it your charge, my lord,
To see performed the tenor of my word.
Set on.   *Exeunt King and his train*

FALSTAFF Master Shallow, I owe you a thousand pound.

SHALLOW Yea, marry, Sir John, which I beseech you to
let me have home with me.

FALSTAFF That can hardly be, Master Shallow. Do not
you grieve at this. I shall be sent for in private to him.   80
Look you, he must seem thus to the world. Fear not
your advancements; I will be the man yet that shall
make you great.

SHALLOW I cannot perceive how, unless you give me
your doublet, and stuff me out with straw. I beseech
you, good Sir John, let me have five hundred of my
thousand.

---

65 *riots* (a word the King's father has
used about him — for example at
IV.4.62 and IV.5.135)

69 *competence of life* sufficient for living
comfortably

71 *we* (the royal plural; see V.2.134 and
the note)

79 *That can hardly be*. There is no good
reason why Shallow cannot have his
money back, for even Falstaff has
not had time to *bestow* it yet (see lines
11–13).

FALSTAFF Sir, I will be as good as my word. This that
you heard was but a colour.

90   SHALLOW A colour that I fear you will die in, Sir John.

FALSTAFF Fear no colours. Go with me to dinner. Come,
Lieutenant Pistol; come, Bardolph. I shall be sent for
soon at night.

> *Enter the Lord Chief Justice and Prince John, with officers*

LORD CHIEF JUSTICE
Go, carry Sir John Falstaff to the Fleet.
Take all his company along with him.

FALSTAFF
My lord, my lord —

LORD CHIEF JUSTICE
I cannot now speak; I will hear you soon.
Take them away.

89 *but a colour* only a pretence
90 *colour* (1) appearance; (2) halter ('collar')
  die (1) die (by hanging); (2) dye (*colour*)
92 *Lieutenant*. Pistol's promotion may be a gift that Falstaff feels he can bestow at no cost to himself.
93 *soon at night* (a common Elizabethanism) towards evening
94-5 *carry Sir John . . . with him*. This detail is added by Shakespeare, and it has been suggested that it is an act of personal revenge by the Lord Chief Justice. But the Fleet prison had not then acquired its bad reputation, and Queen Elizabeth was accustomed to send there courtiers who had displeased her. It has also been pointed out that the banishment from

the court could not immediately be made effective whilst the coronation festivities were in progress, and that being held in the Fleet would be an interim measure until the Lord Chief Justice had time to hear Falstaff and his followers, which, as he says, will be soon. Nevertheless, all explanations made, the action of the play does not require Falstaff's imprisonment (still less Shallow's), and, if it is a kind of joke, as has also been suggested, it is pretty sour, coming hard on the rejection. The imprisonment of Falstaff and his companions, even if it is brief, and less uncomfortable than we might imagine, is nonetheless a reminder of the cold Lancastrian wind that is blowing through the land.

PISTOL

> *Si fortuna me tormenta, spero me contenta.*
>> *Exeunt all but Prince John and*
>> *the Lord Chief Justice*

PRINCE JOHN

I like this fair proceeding of the King's.   100
He hath intent his wonted followers
Shall all be very well provided for,
But all are banished till their conversations
Appear more wise and modest to the world.

LORD CHIEF JUSTICE

And so they are.

PRINCE JOHN

The King hath called his parliament, my lord.

LORD CHIEF JUSTICE

He hath.

PRINCE JOHN

I will lay odds that, ere this year expire,
We bear our civil swords and native fire
As far as France. I heard a bird so sing,   110
Whose music, to my thinking, pleased the King.
Come, will you hence?   *Exeunt*

99 *Si fortuna . . . contenta.* See the note to
  II.4.176.
103 *conversations* behaviour
108–10 *ere this year . . . France.* See

IV.5.213–14 and the note.
109 *civil swords* swords recently engaged
  in civil strife

EPILOGUE

First, my fear; then, my curtsy; last, my speech.

  My fear is your displeasure; my curtsy, my duty;
and my speech, to beg your pardons. If you look for a
good speech now, you undo me, for what I have to say
is of mine own making; and what indeed I should say
will, I doubt, prove mine own marring. But to the
purpose, and so to the venture. Be it known to you, as it
is very well, I was lately here in the end of a displeasing
play, to pray your patience for it, and to promise you a
10 better. I meant indeed to pay you with this, which, if
like an ill venture it come unluckily home, I break, and

Epilogue Many editors have assigned the Epilogue to a dancer because of the references in lines 17–18 and 32. There is no evidence that there was any such dancer, but there was certainly a member of Shakespeare's company who was famous for his dancing: the clown, William Kemp. We know that Kemp played Dogberry in *Much Ado About Nothing*, probably written a year or so after *2 Henry IV* but published in the same year (1600). It cannot be more than a guess, but it seems at least likely that this Epilogue, either wholly or in part, was spoken by Kemp (but see the note to lines 21–2).

After a line of introduction, the Epilogue is divided into three paragraphs, which may represent three stages of development. The first paragraph could be the original Epilogue. In Q (as in this edition) it concludes with an indication that the speaker kneels to pray for the Queen; in F this is transferred to the very end of the Epilogue. There are epilogues in other plays – for example, in *A Nice Wanton* (an interlude published

in 1560 but written in the reign of Edward VI) – that invite the audience to pray for the sovereign, and one would expect that to mark the conclusion of this Epilogue. The second paragraph might be an extension of the first, but it could be a complete Epilogue in its own right. The last paragraph is introduced in a way that may suggest that it is an addition, but it must have been written before *Henry V* (see the note to line 27). All three paragraphs might have been used on their own on different occasions. Thus the reference in lines 8–9 to *a displeasing play* could only be made when it recalled some particular event known to the audience (unless the company had a habit of performing displeasing plays).

1 *curtsy* bow (by either sex)

6 *doubt* fear

7 *venture* attempt (at his speech)

8–9 *a displeasing play.* This has not been identified. See also the headnote above.

11 *ill venture* unsuccessful expedition
  break (1) break my promise; (2) go bankrupt

you, my gentle creditors, lose. Here I promised you I would be, and here I commit my body to your mercies. Bate me some, and I will pay you some, and, as most debtors do, promise you infinitely. And so I kneel down before you – but, indeed, to pray for the Queen.

If my tongue cannot entreat you to acquit me, will you command me to use my legs? And yet that were but light payment, to dance out of your debt. But a good conscience will make any possible satisfaction,   20 and so would I. All the gentlewomen here have forgiven me. If the gentlemen will not, then the gentlemen do not agree with the gentlewomen, which was never seen in such an assembly.

One word more, I beseech you. If you be not too much cloyed with fat meat, our humble author will continue the story, with Sir John in it, and make you merry with fair Katherine of France – where, for anything I know, Falstaff shall die of a sweat, unless already 'a be killed with your hard opinions; for Oldcastle died   20 martyr, and this is not the man. My tongue is weary; when my legs are too, I will bid you good night.

14 *Bate me* let me off
21–2 *All the gentlewomen here have forgiven me.* J. Dover Wilson suggested that this might appropriately be spoken by the Page.
27 *with Sir John in it.* Falstaff does not appear in *Henry V* (though his death is mentioned). Consequently this part of the Epilogue could hardly have been written after Shakespeare had started *Henry V*, probably within a year of completing *2 Henry IV*. At

this point he evidently expected Falstaff's fortunes to revive; why they did not can only be conjectured.
29 *sweat* (plague or venereal disease)
30 *Oldcastle.* It is very surprising that Shakespeare's use of the name Oldcastle in the original version of *1 Henry IV* (see the Introduction, page 445) should have seemed again to need explanation. Someone, however, must have thought a disclaimer essential.

HENRY V

Introduction

Henry V is Shakespeare's ninth and last English historical play, apart from *King Lear* and *Cymbeline*, which treat of pseudo-history, and the late *Henry VIII*, in which he collaborated with John Fletcher. In the English historical sequence it is crucially placed. *Richard II* and the *Henry IV* plays look towards it, towards England's unity restored after usurpation and division, and Henry's emergence as true ruler from the ambiguous promise of Prince Hal. Equally, the earlier-written tetralogy of *Henry VI* and *Richard III* had shown the tragic consequences following upon Henry's premature death. So the play of triumph shines like an hour of glory between two periods of storm.

It can be dated with pleasing precision. Its fifth chorus confidently expects that 'the General of our gracious Empress' will shortly return to London, 'Bringing rebellion broachèd on his sword' (v. Chorus. 30,32) – that is, that the Earl of Essex, triumphant in Ireland against Tyrone, will soon be greeted in the capital by the rejoicing citizens. Essex had left England in March 1599; he came back in September, having failed in his mission; and the play is therefore coincident with the mood of patriotic expectancy so vivid in the spring but extinguished by the autumn. In Shakespeare's career it marks the masterful flow of his full and confident power, evolved through almost a decade of rich and varied composition.

It was not the first time that Henry's reign had been treated in drama. *Tarlton's Jests* (*c.* 1600), a collection of anecdotes about a famous comedian who died in 1588, mentions 'a play of Henry the Fifth, wherein the judge was to take a box on the ear'. This refers to the apocryphal but cherished legend that Prince Hal assaulted the Lord Chief Justice and was sent to prison. In 1592, Thomas Nashe's comic story, *Pierce Penilesse*, celebrated a scene Nashe had clearly found delightful though it is not exactly paralleled in surviving plays on Henry's reign:

... what a glorious thing it is to have Henry the Fifth represented on the stage leading the French King prisoner, and forcing both him and the Dauphin to swear fealty.

The diary of Philip Henslowe the theatre manager records thirteen performances of a new play, *harey the v*, between November 1595 and July 1596. And a chaotic, garbled text of an anonymous drama, *The Famous Victories of Henry the Fifth*, entered for publication in the Stationers' Register on 14 May 1594, is extant, though only in an edition of 1598. How these plays related to each other is not clear, nor indeed how *The Famous Victories* relates to *Henry V*; there are resemblances between these two latter which prove that Shakespeare owed the anonymous drama much, though the debt is probably to some earlier, better version rather than to the surviving scrap-heap of mangled incidents and illiterate text.

The popularity of the subject hardly needs explaining. Not only did Henry's reign stand out to later generations by contrast with the preceding troubles of Richard II and Henry IV, and the succeeding disasters of Henry VI, but Henry's almost miraculous conversion from wild youth to ideal king was an article of faith going back to chronicles contemporary with Henry himself. The king reborn from evil to good, and leading a heroic campaign to a famous victory, was irresistibly attractive. Edward Hall's chronicle, *The Union of the Two Noble and Illustre Fameilies of Lancaster and Yorke* (1548), entitles the reign 'The Victorious Acts of King Henry the Fifth', celebrates its hero as king, warrior, justiciary, and shepherd of his people, in an astonishing *catena* of praise, and concludes:

He was merciful to offenders, charitable to the needy, indifferent [impartial] *to all men, faithful to his friends, and fierce to his enemies, toward God most devout, toward the world moderate, and to his realm a very father.*

It is not surprising that the renown of 'Henry the Fifth, too famous to live long', 'Henry the Fifth, that made all France to quake', 'Henry the Fifth, | Who made the Dauphin and the French to stoop', sounds like a tolling bell through the calamities of the *Henry VI* trilogy:

> *Glory is like a circle in the water,*
> *Which never ceaseth to enlarge itself*
> *Till by broad spreading it disperse to naught.*
> *With Henry's death the English circle ends;*
> *Dispersèd are the glories it included.*
>
> *1 Henry VI*, 1.2.133–7

For Tudor chroniclers and poets Henry's prowess had the quality of myth, like that also of Edward III and the Black Prince, 'Making defeat on the full power of France' (1.2.107): that had been the era when, though for a short while only, England had found her destiny. Henry's reign figures as an Homeric adventure in Samuel Daniel's *Fowre Bookes of the Civile Wars* (1595):

> *O what eternal matter here is found,*
> *Whence new immortal Iliads might proceed.*

Years later, praising Michael Drayton's poems, and in particular his *Battaile of Agincourt* (1627), Ben Jonson likened Drayton's own achievement to Homer's, since he had commemorated England's valour and written verses which

> *strike the bravest heat*
> *That ever yet did fire the English blood!*
> *Our right in France! if rightly understood.*
> *There, thou art Homer! . . .*
> *So shall our English youth urge on, and cry*
> *'An Agincourt! an Agincourt! or die!'*

Henry V has much of epic character, for epic presents, through a story of adventure, a symbolic crisis in a nation's life such as matures it into knowledge of its own being, temperament, and destiny. The manner in which Shakespeare expresses this epic spirit (while at the same time qualifying it and relating it to the unideal truths of human life) makes this one of his most memorable and exciting plays, that which more than any other breathes the spirit of Elizabethan courage and pride and shows him in happy command of his powers. It comes particularly into its own in times of national peril.

It is, in a way, self-conscious, not in the sense of being embarrassed by its own character (though some critics have taken its chorus-apologetics very solemnly) but in that of standing as a great manifesto or demonstration, proudly doctrinal and exemplary. If it is epic in manner, that is partly because out of the miscellaneous chronicle-events of Henry's reign it makes a clear theme of high adventure, partly because its stress is narrative rather than psychological (the story of the heroic company under its leader), but mostly because England as well as England's King is its principal character. In a general sense, England is the hero of all the histories; Shakespeare writes of his country's fate. But this is especially so in *Henry V*. Commenting on the lines in the prologue (3-4) –

> *A kingdom for a stage, princes to act,*
> *And monarchs to behold the swelling scene –*

Dr Johnson rather oddly remarked, 'Shakespeare does not seem to set distance enough between the performers and spectators'; and in his final observation he wondered 'why the intelligence given by the chorus is more necessary in this play than in many others where it is omitted'. The answer is that Shakespeare wants to *cancel* the distance between performers and spectators – this is a play of a very special sort; and it is through the chorus that this is attempted, the epic note sounded, and the particular function exerted (besides that of clarifying the narrative sequence) of conveying the exhilarated involvement of Henry's people and Henry's land – and so of Elizabeth's.

Likewise, the Archbishop's parable of the ordered hive, while not universally admired (one critic thinks Shakespeare must have had 'fun', 'making such a fool of his Archbishop'), is meant as a genuine celebration of national harmony; England must be virtually a Chosen Land to be presented thus. The analogy between hive and kingdom is admittedly not original; it comes from Pliny and Virgil through Sir Thomas Elyot's *The Boke named the Governour* (1531), a treatise by Chelidonius translated as *Of the Institution and Firste Beginning of Christian Princes* (1571), Lyly's *Euphues* (1578), and other channels. But Shakespeare treats it in no perfunctory spirit; he gives it a lively and captivating beauty. Here in *Henry V*, as distinct from the political rifts of the other histories, the obedient kingdom is achieved, and the ideal order of Church and State affirmed not only as doctrine but as reality. When Henry, 'Being free from vainness and self-glorious pride' (v. Chorus.20), gives thanks for victory to God, it is England, the beneficiary of God's favour, who joins in *Non Nobis* and *Te Deum* for her salvation. The Chorus apologizes for the theatre's defects less because Shakespeare 'distressfully realized' that his stage could not do what he wanted (the phrase is Granville-Barker's) than because only 'The brightest heaven of invention' and a corresponding imaginative elation in his hearers could match his great theme.

Such is the basic creed and the dominant assumption of the play. As it unfolds, however, it is much more variegated than the above sketch of the epic hero leading a devoted country to triumph would suggest. The nature of kingship, the motives of war, and the qualities of political allegiance are presented with a sense of the tensions that stretch between ideal and reality, and make a political order human. *Henry V* is peculiarly interesting in treating this situation. It stands, brilliantly, for the excitements of heroism and victory, and for the gratification of national pride. At the same time it admits elements which suggest the dark underside of war and policy. Yet in doing so it shows no radical irony, though it provides material which may be used for radically ironical judgements (and Hazlitt, for one, is radically ironical when he criticizes it in *Characters of Shakespeare's Plays*). Within the whole context of the play the ironies seem no more than passing and incidental shadowings to the dominant heroic zest, reminders of human frailties above which the heroism stands sturdily.

Shakespeare's plots may require Romans or kings, Dr Johnson observes in his *Preface to Shakespeare*, 'but he thinks only on men'. The material for this play presented a considerable difficulty – how to make *man* a character whose accepted role it was to be essentially *king*. A being virtually superhuman (and hyperbolically presented so by the Archbishop in the first scene) may well prove a mere mechanism, even if an exhilarating one (as Tamburlaine is). One recalls Sir Leslie Stephen's comment on another ideal hero, the Sir Charles Grandison of Richardson's novel:

The greatest man is perhaps one who is so equably developed that he has the strongest faculties in the most perfect equilibrium, and is apt to be somewhat uninteresting to the rest of mankind.

As a dramatic personality Henry is far from being the fullest of Shakespeare's creations, even if the field of comparison be restricted to the history plays; in situations which are virtually pre-established he behaves in predictable ways, with such mastery that the result is immensely effective, but effective in a manner which falls short of nourishing the imagination deeply. Yet he certainly holds the attention.

For his material Shakespeare went to Holinshed's *Chronicles* and *The Famous Victories of Henry the Fifth*. Traces of other works may be found, too; the more important particulars are noted in the commentary. There seem to be recollections of *Edward III* (1596), the anonymous play about Henry's great ancestor, victor of Crécy and Poitiers. Either Elyot's *The Boke named the*

Governour or Lyly's *Euphues* suggested some important analogies (see 1.2.180–204, and the notes thereon). Henry's night-visit to his camp may derive from Tacitus's *Annals*, translated by Richard Grenewey in 1598; in this, Germanicus, like Henry, disguises himself to test the morale of his troops in danger. Fluellen's devotion to the military art of the Romans is strikingly like the similar devotion expressed by Thomas Digges, in his treatise *Stratioticos* (1579); this is discussed further on page 679. Yet though memories, conscious and subconscious, would certainly come to Shakespeare's mind from books he had read, it seems unlikely that (as some scholars believe) he deliberately sought widely for material in earlier works. In *Richard II* and *Henry IV* he had been influenced by Daniel's poem, *The Civile Wars between the two Houses of Lancaster and Yorke* (1595), but Daniel's treatment of Henry V was perfunctory and offered nothing to the purpose save for a eulogy of the King found equally in Holinshed. Shakespeare, then, seems to have put his play together substantially from two convenient works, one of serious history (Holinshed's *Chronicles*) and the other of popular serio-comic dramatization (*The Famous Victories*).

Holinshed's work must actually have been open before him as he wrote, and it is interesting to observe both where his discipleship was close (and sometimes caused him to take over particulars which in the play create critical difficulties) and where he varied importantly. He followed his source in hundreds of details and expressions, through the main tenor and indeed through much of the phrasing of the historical scenes. In the 'Salic law' harangue the transcription is slavish – this is one of the points where excessive fidelity creates a critical problem, that of interpreting aright the Archbishop's longwindedness. But in general the borrowing is spirited and vivid enough to awaken wonder that Shakespeare could follow common prose so closely and yet produce fine poetry. His mind is everywhere attentive to what he reads, yet almost everywhere freshly creative. Holinshed ends with a panegyric on Henry which gave Shakespeare the lead both for the

Archbishop's eulogy at the beginning and the Epilogue's plaudits at the end. A number of features which critics of Henry cite to prove him hypocritical derive, hardly modified at all, from Holinshed, in whose pages they certainly have no disparaging intention. These features include Henry's religious zeal, with the recurrent appeals to God; confident belief in the rightness of his cause, with reiterated assertions of his just title; the conviction that the guilt of bloodshed lies on the French for resisting his claim and not on him for prosecuting it; and the assumption that since he is morally right at all points those opposing him must be morally wrong. Dubious though these traits are to a sceptical eye, Shakespeare takes them over smoothly enough; he remains discreetly reticent over one or two shady manoeuvres, as though he judged (as well he might) that his play would succeed best if Englishmen were not too evidently seen to behave dishonourably. Holinshed, for instance, tells how the Archbishop deliberately schemes to distract Henry from the Church's revenues by instigating him to attack France: Shakespeare, though he starts his play with the threat to the Church, muffles that problem behind the question of Henry's war and, while recognizing the Archbishop's dubious aims (I.I.75–9), treats them more casually than does his source. Holinshed, further, introduces the tennis-balls insult as a separate incident, earlier than the council of war, and itself a main cause of the conflict; Shakespeare prefers *The Famous Victories'* version, that it is subsequent to the council, an aggravation of the quarrel, but only a confirmatory detail after the establishment of Henry's legal claim and his resolve for invasion.

Other interesting modifications of Holinshed are the following. Holinshed presents the French King as lunatic, so that affairs must be directed by the Dauphin: in the play, as in *The Famous Victories*, the French King directs matters throughout, and so (this is not in *The Famous Victories*) the Dauphin can be characterized as a modish gallant. Holinshed records no repentant speeches from Cambridge, Scroop, and Grey; Shakespeare invents these farewell addresses so that even the would-be

traitors may acknowledge how the hand of God guards the
country's safety. In Holinshed's pages the citizens of Harfleur
suffer terribly before they yield, and the town is then sacked
and depopulated: in Shakespeare's, the mere threat of horrors
ensures their surrender, and mercy is then shown to them all.
In the chronicle, Henry himself supervises the execution of a
(nameless) soldier for theft: in the play, he approves but does
not personally enforce the hanging of his old acquaintance,
Bardolph. Holinshed relates in detail the English strategy at
Agincourt: Shakespeare ignores it, even the famous prowess of
the English bowmen, in favour of heroic oratory which gives
the spirit rather than the tactical particulars of the battle. And
finally, again like the author of *The Famous Victories* but unlike
Holinshed, Shakespeare omits the five years (1415-20) of cam-
paigning between Agincourt and the Treaty of Troyes (as
indeed he does everything in Henry's reign which does not
relate to Agincourt), and so gives his play a clearer course and
greater impetus. His treatment of Holinshed is, therefore,
equally striking for close indebtedness and for constructive
independence. Summarizing all the above changes one may say
that their effect is to clarify Henry's motives, improve the
morality of his cause, disengage the Agincourt campaign from
the many other concerns of his reign, enhance the force and
spirit of the action, and treat the whole in terms of human
passion and thought.

As for *The Famous Victories*, crude though it was it clearly
afforded Shakespeare guidance. In it the King, dismissing his
scapegrace companions (as at the end of *2 Henry IV*), at once
consults the Archbishop, who vouches for the justice of his
claim though without mentioning the Salic law. The council of
war is followed immediately by the tennis-balls scene, after
which Henry prepares for speedy invasion; as in *Henry V*, the
theme of speed is prominent. There is a clownish leave-taking
of husband and wife, which inspired that in *Henry V* (II.3). The
French King directs the French campaign, while the Dauphin
foolishly thinks Henry 'young and wild-headed' but is warned

that he is 'a haughty and high-minded Prince'. The French soldiers (though not, as in *Henry V*, the leaders) dice for prisoners, in pidgin English. The English low comics, garbling French tags, mix farcically in the Agincourt scenes, and Derick the clown captures a French soldier, as Pistol does Monsieur Le Fer. The action passes straight from Agincourt to Troyes, and Henry woos Katherine 'in plain terms', not like 'those countries [that] spend half their time in wooing'. Poor though it is, then, *The Famous Victories* furnished elements not less integral to Shakespeare's play than those from Holinshed, and this brief inspection of his original materials may serve to suggest how shrewd in selection, constructive in assimilation, and intelligent in adjustment his mind was.

What no sources seem to have given him, except for the incalculable influence of his reading of books and his observation of men, are the inspirations from which he evolved his account of the death of Falstaff, the comedy of Fluellen and of his fellow captains, the episode of Katherine and Alice (boldly presented entirely in French), and the wonderful night-scene before Agincourt (save that, as aforesaid, the germ of this may have come from Tacitus). These components, varied in manner but all richly humane in quality, are the contribution of Shakespeare's own creative fertility.

Fluellen, above all, is the play's most delightful offering. All four captains, Gower, Macmorris, Jamy, and he, serve Henry well; in them, the constituent peoples of Britain unite behind the King and yet, most entertainingly, preserve their national idiosyncrasies. The play would be much poorer were Henry heading an army merely of likeminded loyalists, the Bedfords, Exeters, Erpinghams, and the rest. Instead, he leads a various host with independent minds, likely at any moment to break out into disputes, yet bound together not only by danger but also by trueheartedness; the quarrelsomeness of the French is of a different nature altogether. So the argument between Fluellen and Macmorris (III.2), with Gower and Jamy intervening, is not just incidental comedy; it proves their fine, vehement spirits and their devotion to the war in hand. Fluellen may owe something to Shakespeare's contemporary, the Welsh soldier Sir Roger Williams, or alternatively to Sir John Smythe, Williams's opponent in a debate on ancient and modern warfare; scholars dispute the matter. His antiquarian pedantry about the Roman disciplines, however, seems to derive from a work on military tactics already mentioned, the *Stratioticos* of Thomas Digges (1579), which perhaps came to Shakespeare's notice when republished in 1590 by his fellow Stratfordian Richard Field, who was to bring out *Venus and Adonis* in 1593. Digges commends 'the ancient Roman discipline for the wars' and 'the most noble government of the Romans (who in military virtue surmounteth all other)'; nowadays, he protests, 'all those Roman orders' are held obsolete, whereas they are more valid than ever they were in the past; it was when Rome's original military discipline was corrupted under the Emperors that her power collapsed – Fluellen's court of appeal, one recalls, is to 'the *pristine* wars of the Romans' (III.2.79). To find the phrases of the ancient obscure book of military science coming so delightfully to life on Fluellen's lips is to sense what Shakespeare's transforming power could do from a few hints. Yet even without this enlivening recognition Fluellen's temper of pedantry, patriotism, generosity, and touchiness unfailingly endears him.

The night-scene before Agincourt, another superb invention, is discussed in the last pages of this Introduction. It works, like that of the four captains, to show that Henry's troops are human beings, not ciphers; at this moment above all Shakespeare remembers the common lot and, to repeat Dr Johnson, 'thinks only on men'.

For Pistol, Nym, Bardolph, the Hostess, and the Boy, *The Famous Victories* gave Shakespeare some sort of cue, though a crude one. The comedy they provide here does not work so richly as that of their counterparts in *Henry IV*. Yet even to think that, like Falstaff, they might have been dropped from the action altogether is to realize how desirable is their ripe ignominy, always human and touching in its nonsense and noise. It is they who feel for Falstaff, and move us as they do so more than anything else in the play; we feel for them, too, as war and disease and disgrace cut them brutally off, one by one, who once warmed themselves gratefully in the solar mirth of Falstaff.

It is appropriate to turn to evaluations of the play.

> *Small time, but in that small most greatly lived*
> *This star of England*

– so the Epilogue confidently sums up. Yet a drama based on invasion of a foreign land (even if, by definition, justified invasion) may be morally and emotionally unpalatable, and not a few critics find *Henry V* so. There is disagreement about nearly all aspects of the play – about the value of the choruses, the tenor of many major speeches, the motives and morals of prelates and courtiers, Henry's handling of the ambassadors and of the traitorous Scroop, his threats to Harfleur, his debate with his soldiers, his massacre of the French, and his wooing of Katherine. Contention extends to the total interpretation of how the play takes war, honour, kingship, and allegiance. To include it among Shakespeare's problem plays would seem extravagant, yet its apparent simplicity masks a good many problems of assessment, so that one of its shrewdest critics, Mr Derek Traversi, can remark in *Shakespeare from 'Richard II' to 'Henry V'* that it has been 'most generally popular when imperfectly understood'. It is, as he observes, among Shakespeare's simpler plays, without poetic subtlety or symbolical complexity; its plot is clear historical narrative, and its purpose the recognizable one of studying the conditions of kingship. Yet there lurk ambiguities enough for a wide liberty of interpretation.

The play raises fewer questions in the theatre than in the study – impetus carries one over obstacles, whereas deliberation makes them seem larger than they are. It raises interestingly the problem of criticizing a dramatic action, being second only to *Hamlet* in this respect: how much analytical going back and forth over the evidence is admissible when the very nature of dramatic art is to carry the narrative vigorously onwards? Dover Wilson has observed (not the only critic to do so, but the one to make the point most sharply) that *Henry V* is a work 'which men of action have been wont silently to admire, and literary men . . . volubly to condemn', and he believes that he himself learnt more about its hero from Wavell's *Life of Allenby* than from all the critics together. He recalls, too, how in 1914–15 the play suddenly revealed its enormous power; and in 1945 the film version with Sir Laurence Olivier again proved how well it could match a time of mortal danger and of saving courage. At such moments, and seeing it acted, one yields to the drive of the action; this is something Shakespeare has made integral to its effects. A fateful pressure is the dominant theme: to move fast, to work with energy, is its characteristic:

> *with reasonable swiftness add*
> *More feathers to our wings;*   1.2.307–8

> *For England his approaches makes as fierce*
> *As waters to the sucking of a gulf.*   II.4.9–10

> *Dispatch us with all speed, lest that our King*
> *Come here himself to question our delay,*
> *For he is footed in this land already.*   II.4.141–3

> *Thus with imagined wing our swift scene flies*
> *In motion of no less celerity*
> *Than that of thought.*   III.Chorus.1–3

The play's dynamism as it passes on the stage allows little time for thought, and the Chorus, as presenter of events, delivers us over, unreflecting, to those heroic assumptions which are its creed. And, basically, this is right; the play's aim is to celebrate heroic actions under a heroic king.

Hazlitt, humanitarian and republican, in his *Characters of Shakespeare's Plays* held that Shakespeare, while believing Henry to be the heroic prince and king of good fellows, had *unwittingly* glorified a self-seeking and brutal autocrat, licensed by a Machiavellian Archbishop 'to rob and murder in circles of latitude and longitude abroad', and had thereby exposed 'the hidden motives that actuate princes and their advisers'.

Henry [Hazlitt continues], *because he did not know how to govern his own kingdom, determined to make war upon his neighbour's. Because his own title to the crown was doubtful, he laid claim to that of France. Because he did not know how to exercise the enormous power which had just dropped into his hands to any one good purpose, he immediately undertook (a cheap and obvious resource of sovereignty) to do all the mischief he could.*

And more to the same purpose; for Hazlitt the whole baronial Middle Ages amounted to 'accomplished barbarism'. Yet when Hazlitt asks, 'How then do we like him [Henry]?' he answers,

We like him in the play. There he is a very amiable monster, a very splendid pageant ... We take a very romantic, heroic, patriotic, and poetical delight in the boasts and feats of our younger Harry, as they appear on the stage and are confined to lines of ten syllables.

In other words, we enjoy as dramatic adventure what in historical reality was iniquitous. And with this lively formulation of Hazlitt's we approach the problem of interpreting the play: is Shakespeare offering us merely 'romantic, heroic, patriotic, and poetical delight', is he on the other hand exposing the unabashed Machiavellianism of power, or is he glorifying the heroic while still acknowledging the unheroic, thereby making the heroic the more valid, as pure metal and base alloy combine in a tougher and more dependable product?

When *Henry V* is looked at closely, certain features complicate the impression of simple zest and conviction the unreflecting reader is likely to form. If these features are now to be discussed at some length, the reason is not that the play is radically uncertain in its aims; even with its ambiguities it remains powerful and assured. As Dr Johnson remarked in his *Life of Gray*, 'by the common sense of readers uncorrupted with literary prejudices, after all the refinements of subtlety and the dogmatism of learning, must finally be decided all claim to poetical honours'. Common sense long ago decided that the play's subject is unambiguous valour and that its spirit is expressed in Henry's Agincourt speech. It works splendidly – as before observed – at a speed which prevents awkward questions, and it is charged with a rich and compelling emotion. Before Agincourt in particular it achieves a humanity and honesty, as well as a sense of great peril and noble courage, which live in the mind as its valid message. Mr Traversi puts the matter well, in *Shakespeare from 'Richard II' to 'Henry V'*:

Should we need a word to describe the best positive values of this play, that which distinguishes it from mere patriotic rhetoric on the one side and sardonic pessimism on the other (and both moods are constituent parts of it), it would be ... honesty, which can offer loyalty while maintaining independence of judgement, and which is brought out, as much as the cruelty which balances it, by the sombre circumstances of war which no merely patriotic show of rhetoric or romantic comradeship in death can conceal.

The first problem is that of Henry's claim to the throne of France. This, historically speaking, depended on the fact that his great-great-grandmother Isabella, Edward II's Queen, was the daughter of Philip IV of France and granddaughter of Philip III, from whom also Princess Katherine descended (by marrying Katherine Henry reinforced his supposed right). But the historical basis of this claim is, for criticism of the play, far less important than the fact that in Shakespeare's time it was held without question to be valid. To hold, as Hazlitt did, that Henry was guilty of aggression against another man's rightful domain is irrelevant to critical judgement. The Archbishop's prominence and Henry's earnest injunctions to him 'justly and religiously' to state the case are meant as proof that the claim is lawful and French resistance to it unlawful, so that by contumacy France provokes an 'impious war' not only against her rightful sovereign but against God, the source of royal authority. The scepticism of later ages makes this assumption hard to credit, as the nationalism of later ages makes it hard to accept that the French are the aggressors for standing their ground. But there is no doubt that the play is based on an honest faith in these assumptions. Should one concede to a work of art tenets which affront one's convictions? If one wholly declines, art can never work its disturbing reorganizations. If one wholly accepts, one quits one's bases of moral evaluation. One needs to give the work its chance, in a willing suspension (if necessary) of disbelief in its premises, and judge whether the result justifies the concession. Certainly *Henry V* takes it as proven that Henry is in the right. The question then is whether this belief is imaginatively brought home, as well as doctrinally reiterated. It is hard to think that, in any deep sense, this is so. The Archbishop's persuasives to war, the nobles' zest for re-enacting ancient prowess, the recurrent genuflections to God – these convince more as gestures in the game of power than as moral validations. What can be said is that Shakespeare does much, by the splendid surface vigour which hustles out of the way the teasing questions beneath, to convince us that the participants themselves, and Henry above all, believe in their cause, and that while we watch the play we should do so too. This is the concession which the vigour of Shakespeare's handling exacts of us, though he himself in the zest of composition probably never realized there was a problem at all. Energy here does duty for insight, eloquence for imagination. One recalls Yeats's aphorism – 'Out of our quarrel with ourselves we make poetry; out of our quarrel with others, we make only rhetoric'. The application to *Henry V* is not precise, yet there is a sense in which the play, opposing patriotism to an external enemy, simplifies its attitudes into those suited to challenge and defiance, and finds its idiom to be rhetoric – wonderful rhetoric, certainly, but rhetoric in the sense that words are directed to calculated effects.

The second problem is that the play's basic assumptions seem to be the uncritical patriotism of the chronicles. With this one cannot in normal times feel as happy as when the blast of war blows in one's ears, and many who dislike the play find here their principal ground of objection. In the first chorus, for example, 'The brightest heaven of invention' is to be ascended so that the warlike Harry shall 'Assume the port of Mars' – the sense is of a bearing grandly put on; 'famine, sword, and fire' are to crouch behind him 'for employment'. No irony is hinted, though this is (if one thinks about it) a disagreeable light in which to present heroic leadership; nor can the speech be taken as eye-opening realism, for the Chorus is in a high state of exhilaration. At once there follows the clerics' statecraft, received by Henry as honest and intelligent discourse. How is one to take this? – sceptically? – derisively? – realistically (this is how things are done in the political game)? – or, as the play seems to require, in earnest? Shakespeare, as has already been said, presents things less openly against Canterbury than Holinshed had done or, moreover, than Drayton was to do in his *Battaile of Agincourt*, where the Archbishop works a calculated diversionary intrigue in the interest of the Church:

> *His working soul projecteth many a thing,*
> *Until at length, out of the strength of wit,*
> *He found a war with France must be the way*
> *To dash this bill, else threat'ning their decay.*

Shakespeare does not linger upon this duplicity, just as he leaves unrecalled the Machiavellian advice given to Prince Hal by Henry IV on his death-bed, that, to avert dissension at home, he should (*2 Henry IV*, IV.5.214)

> *busy giddy minds*
> *With foreign quarrels . . .*

No hint of this appears in the play. Shakespeare, then, means his clerics to argue truly (whatever the motive), as he has meant his prologue to be unambiguous. The trouble is that the 'Salic law' speech falls as far short of proving their *bona fides* as it does of achieving poetic charm. Unrivalled for tedium throughout Shakespeare's works it would, admittedly, be more interesting to subjects of the first Elizabeth than to those of the second, since the accessions of Queen Mary, Queen Elizabeth herself, and the prospective King James depended on the validity of succession in the female line; a similar Salic law argument occurs at the beginning of *Edward III*, when Edward presses his claim to the French throne. Exeter is later to assure us that Henry's right is not based on pettifogging legalism:

> *'Tis no sinister nor no awkward claim*
> *Picked from the worm-holes of long-vanished days,*
> *Nor from the dust of old oblivion raked . . .*   II.4.85–7

But since, by following Holinshed too closely, this is just what Shakespeare made the claim sound like in the Archbishop's mouth, he unintentionally cast into doubt what is not meant to be in doubt at all (and so gave the makers of the film version the chance to turn the whole thing into satire) – the legality of Henry's claim.

Then, from the prosaism of his lecture, the Archbishop breaks out with evident relish into bloodthirstiness, exhorting the King to 'Stand for your own, unwind your bloody flag' (I.2.101), and describing how Edward III smiled to see the Black Prince 'Forage in blood of French nobility'. His language is gross and his mood zestfully brutal as he urges 'blood and sword and fire' upon Henry. The Bishop of Ely is no more felicitous; the King, he asserts, 'Is in the very May-morn of his youth' (the image suggests a generous gaiety and idealism), and so 'Ripe for exploits and mighty enterprises' – what better than war? The lords follow the clerics; Henry's fellow-kings, Exeter proclaims, expect him to rouse himself; his subjects, Westmorland declares, wait to invade France in body as they have already done in spirit. All this comes from Holinshed, but what passes muster on the historical page comes to questionable life in the Shakespearian context. To a modern taste such adjurations are admissible only as satire; one invokes against them Ezra Pound's *Hugh Selwyn Mauberley*:

> *There died a myriad,*
> *And of the best, among them,*
> *For an old bitch gone in the teeth,*
> *For a botched civilisation.*

Yet outlooks and circumstances change; one should not, because of modern experience, judge that the play ridicules war-makers, for its whole tenor is to make the action enormously worth the pain and effort. Shakespeare's first scenes are often significant, and unambiguously so, of his plays' main bearings. Are these scenes of questionable diplomacy pointers to a cynical world, indices of a general hypocrisy, with their arguments so tricky to assess that one critic thinks they 'dazzle us with their brilliance' while another takes them for the chicane with which Henry must learn to deal? Working briskly from his sources, Shakespeare probably thinks the arguments good ones, even if voiced by a worldly prelate, and the encouragements to war patriotic ones, even if uttered by boisterous barons. Henry is certainly not surrounded by paladins of virtue – this is a tough, stirring drama, and it is grounded in the recognizable realities of power – but his counsellors are meant as vigorous and effective statesmen. Having taken the best advice he can get, and being convinced that that advice is correct (as by Shakespeare's lights it was), Henry prepares to fight and (the play unquestioningly holds) is completely justified in doing so.

*

Some features, certainly, ought to be taken as the offshoots of dramatic exuberance rather than as psychologically or morally important; at first sight, and at the speed at which stage action passes, they seem straightforward, at second sight so curious as to imply an ironic intention, and yet on final consideration hardly definable as anything but unironic. When, for example, the Archbishop eulogizes Henry, first one believes what he says about the King's virtues; next one reflects that such fulsomeness must be specious; and yet finally one concludes that, this being the first we hear about Henry, and Shakespeare not usually puzzling his audience with false trails, the eulogy, however extravagant, must be truly meant. Likewise when Henry woos Katherine: one thinks first that he is hearty and honest; next that only a crude nature could be so jocular ('lubberly' is Dr Tillyard's word), and also that he is shrewdly using Katherine to secure his ends; but finally that Shakespeare really means this 'king of good fellows' performance to be genuine love. This fluctuation of possible judgements helps to explain the diversity of opinions about the play. At such points the dramatic intention is best served by taking the material at its face value.

This, however, does not always produce a reasonable answer. It does not do so, for instance, over the massacre of the French prisoners (IV.6.35–8, IV.7.1–10). The massacre was, in fact, a military necessity, and by examining the historical circumstances one can defend it as such. Yet Shakespeare not only neglects Holinshed's description of it as 'a dolorous decree and pitiful proclamation' but allows it to seem an act of almost casual ruthlessness, and moreover glosses it with Fluellen's ludicrous outburst, 'Kill the poys and the luggage?', and with Gower's odd explanation that, because cowards who fled from the battle had done the pillage, Henry has 'most worthily' had the throats cut of brave men who had been captured fighting. In this context, 'O, 'tis a gallant King!' is not the happiest of comments. To treat so dreadful an incident in such a spirit is irresponsible, and the mood of approving gusto in which it is mentioned forbids one to explain it as savage realism. How is one to take Shakespeare's lack of concern? As a demonstration of war's horrors? – but so little is made of it. As insensibility? – but Shakespeare is not usually insensible. As unquestioning endorsement of Henry's leadership? – if so, it is unhappily done. As the carelessness of haste? – probably so; Shakespeare treats the incident as one among many, and passes readily to the Irish bull of Fluellen's Welsh paralogism, that Henry is like Alexander because Alexander when drunk wrongly killed Cleitus, and Henry when sober rightly dismissed Falstaff.

In some respects, indeed, the play is 'popular' in a limiting sense, in endorsing uncritical patriotism with what has been called 'a determined "one-eyedness"' about England's interests. The French must be frisky and confident, vainglorious and yet reported to 'shake in their fear'; the English must succeed incredibly against odds (few faces remain straight in a modern theatre when, as against the French ten thousand, their losses are announced as twenty-nine); Katherine must be wooed bluffly as befits the hearty English nature. Double-think, common in popular politics, is not unknown; Scotland invading England is a weasel, but England invading France is an eagle. (This seems to be caught from *Edward III*, 1.1.94, 1.2.90, where England is 'the eagle's nest' and the invading Scots are 'stealing foxes'.) Henry, having decided to invade France even before the Dauphin's insult, then treats that insult as if it occasioned the war, and blames on the Dauphin the 'wasteful vengeance' to follow – Henry, that is, invades France only because he would be legally wrong not to do so, *but* he invades France because he has been insulted and will avenge himself even unto those 'yet ungotten and unborn' (1.2.288). (This particular confusion arises, probably, because Holinshed gives the former motive for invasion, *The Famous Victories* the latter, and Shakespeare works too quickly to reconcile them.) The second chorus, having evoked an army in which

> *honour's thought*
> *Reigns solely in the breast of every man,*

passes without a hint of irony to the motive of plunder:

> *crowns and coronets,*
> *Promised to Harry and his followers.*

When the conspirators appeal for mercy, Henry answers, in effect, that he would have been merciful had they themselves been so, *but* that in any case he could not be merciful since England's safety requires their deaths (II.2.79–80, 174–7). (Here again the confusion results from too indiscriminate a following of Holinshed: no duplicity on Henry's part is implied.)

These are some of the inconsistencies which in the study invite, and have received, sinister interpretations. On the stage they pass unnoticed; the force of the action, like a torrent bearing all before it, sweeps incoherences out of sight. In a sense, they scarcely matter. Why, then, pausing over the text, does one not simply ignore them? The answer relates to the nature of the play. *Henry V* is concerned with moral vindications of national interest and policy, and so undertakes to explain and to justify all that is done in the nation's name. In explanations one expects rational consistency, yet here the patriotic *parti pris* overrides impartial reason. Plays are not, of course, exercises in logic, but it is because *Henry V* argues so much that flaws in the argument may seem significant; it really is felt to matter, more than in the other plays (even the other histories), whether or not acts and their vindications can stand scrutiny. Even so, such inconsistencies in it are signs not (as many critics have supposed) of Henry's politic hypocrisy but of Shakespeare's sharing with his public some of the stock responses to so loaded a subject as the French wars. His imagination was engaged at a brilliantly effective level for dramatic excitement; it was not engaged at the deeper levels of thoughtfulness of which he had already elsewhere shown himself capable.

*

What are the play's attitudes to war? More than any other of Shakespeare's works it takes war as its theme; elsewhere war is incidental even when, as in much of *Henry VI* and *King John*, it forms the staple of the action. Here it offers virtually the whole substance of interest – its causes, the ritual of embassies and ultimata, the mobilizing and the strategy, the discipline, heroism, and horror. War's terrors are recognized, formidably, as in the threats to Harfleur, Williams's recital of wounds and death, and Burgundy's lament over the ruined state of France. Yet the prevailing impression is one which at first warrants the 'romantic, heroic, patriotic, and poetical delight' of Hazlitt's playful phrase; *this* war, if not war in general, seems not only a necessary but an exhilarating exercise of policy. Does this impression survive a closer study?

Shakespeare was not in general an enthusiastic militarist; the previous history plays prove this truth. That here, despite its acknowledged awfulness, war is a matter of celebration is something the chronicles, popular tradition, and the great name of Agincourt rendered all but inevitable. One cannot expect Shakespeare to dodge the accepted data of his story; an anti-war *Henry V* is (or certainly would have been then) quite inconceivable. Since military valour and victory are the theme, and since these are bound here to be treated with approval, Shakespeare could not handle them as he would shortly do in *Troilus and Cressida*; had he, against all likelihood, done such a thing, the resulting play would certainly have been – as the *Troilus and Cressida* Quarto observes of that work – 'never staled with the stage, never clapper-clawed with the palms of the vulgar'.

What then does Shakespeare do? He produces some remarkable multiple effects, which can in one reading be taken as plain patriotic enthusiasm, in another as horrific realism, and in a third as a powerful and valid relationship of these two. This multiplicity of effect may be examined in some of the most famous episodes. In the first place there is the 'Once more unto the breach' oration, widely assumed to express the healthy zest of battle and the joy of martial heroics. So exuberantly compelling is it that, unless one reflects, it seems like a first instalment of the great Agincourt manner: indeed, it finishes in the spirit of Agincourt, with soldier humour ('now attest | That those whom you called fathers did beget you', III.1.22–3), with exhortations and comradeliness ('And you, good yeomen . . .'), with the eager valour of the 'noble lustre' in the eyes, and with the resounding slogan-climax. Nothing, certainly, could be better done. But what precisely is going on? Is one to take any attitude to it other than the impetuous-enthusiastic? To start with, there is the note of desperation; the breach is to be attacked *again*, until English corpses fill the gap (after how many failures?). Then, in a series of extraordinary hyperboles, there emerge like frightful caricatures the beast-violences of action, the histrionic strains of whipped-up ferocity (as when modern soldiers force from constrained throats the insane screams expected at bayonet-drill). The language incites to an appalling *show* ('imitate . . . stiffen . . . disguise . . . lend'), with the frenzy of staring eyeballs and craggy brows. Is the intention really so overtly enthusiastic as it at first seems? Is it, on the other hand, savagely (though covertly) critical of war? Is Shakespeare, as a skilful playwright, making the most of the do-or-die heroics? – certainly this is a famous theatrical moment. Or is he seriously bringing home what, under the heroics, war really means, that (as with Macbeth before the murder of Duncan) one must – against the use of nature – 'bend up | Each corporal agent to this terrible feat'? The speech deserves its fame, not because it prompts a surge of vicarious valour in the unreflecting but because it combines the complex elements outlined above. It is desperate, appalling, and inspiring at once; it makes war awful, but with an awfulness which only victory can compensate for, so that those who hear it shall be swept out of their tremors (except for Nym, Pistol, and the Boy) into a berserk frenzy of assault (though still the town remains untaken – see III.3). Shakespeare is not glorifying war; he is, brilliantly, conveying what war requires from leaders and followers in times of desperate danger.

More ambiguous is the equally famous ultimatum to Harfleur (III.3.1–43). Henry's oath as he asserts his will to win –

> *as I am a soldier,*
> *A name that in my thoughts becomes me best –*

would in other contexts go down well. It would fit his Agincourt speech; General Montgomery might have cited it before El Alamein. But at Harfleur it introduces with what seems a horrifying *relish* the threats with which Henry menaces the town. Perhaps, one reflects, Shakespeare, honest about war's horrors, is shocking the moral sense so that it sees what war means; perhaps, further, he is drawing the tragic contrast between the normally humane man and the enforcedly brutal leader. The trouble is that the speech gives no sign of these assumptions; Henry proudly invokes his soldiership as the warranty for the fiendishness soldiership commits, a warranty accompanied by a disavowal not only of responsibility ('when you yourselves are cause') but even of regret:

> *What is it then to me, if impious war,*
> *Arrayed in flames, like to the prince of fiends,*
> *Do with his smirched complexion all fell feats*
> *Enlinked to waste and desolation?*

War and policy, it is true, call at times for cruelty, as at other times for clemency; moreover, within the terms of the play Henry's threats, however bloodthirsty (and indeed because they are so bloodthirsty), never materialize – the town yields and the townsmen are shown mercy. Henry's ferocity thereby justifies itself as both essential and effective; threats are his ultimate weapon, and they save his army at the moment when 'winter [is] coming on, and sickness growing | Upon our soldiers' (III.3.55–6). Expedient ruthlessness is essential. Is there, then, a valid criticism not against the threat of horrors but against Henry's horrific zest in threatening them, and against what seems Shakespeare's invitation to approve without moral qualms so stirring a leader? 'As the embodiment of worldly success,' an earlier editor of the play remarked, '[Henry is] entitled to our unreserved admiration'. But a proper response is more complex than this. One might argue that, with very serious but very covert irony, Shakespeare here offers a profound criticism of the whole nature of war; and so, in a sense, he does – but it is not a criticism of *Henry's* war. Rather, he presents his King as both a cool and a passionate man. The coolness reckons that threats, if violent enough, will carry the day; the passion generates the extraordinary force of melodramatic realization the speech achieves. Henry is master of his strategy, and speaks with a well-judged purpose. But, as in the great leader they must do, his passions kindle from his judgements and make him, when need requires, in the highest degree bloody, bold, and resolute. As for his apparent relish, which in real life would indicate a sadistically exciting hysteria, in the simpler conditions of Elizabethan drama it simply means that Shakespeare is writing as strongly as he can; any relish is the author's, and it is an artistic, not a moral (or immoral), relish. Henry speaks with a frightening urgency; war is a nightmare as well as an adventure, and if soldiers are heroes they can also be brutes.

Is there, perhaps, a developing theme in the play's sense of war, by which it moves from the unintelligent fervour of prelates and peers (indeed, of the whole nation, as the choruses interpret it) to the informed realization of butchery, so that peace, willingly forsaken at the outset, is again revered at the close, and war, having been painfully experienced, is known for what it is? There is indeed a general trend of this kind; the play realizes these truths as it develops through Act III into the grimmer attitudes of Act IV. Yet the movement is uncertain. Henry is already conscious in Act I (as who could not be?) of the sufferings war causes:

> *For God doth know how many now in health*
> *Shall drop their blood in approbation*
> *Of what your reverence shall incite us to.*   I.2.18–20

Yet Act IV has not so accepted war's realities as to deny itself the sentimental-elegiac death-scene of York and Suffolk. Act V shows Henry carrying into his wooing the soldierly manner of which he is so proud, and the Epilogue rejoices in the rewards of victory. One reflects again that Shakespeare's sources, and popular expectation, allowed him no real chance of revaluing Henry's war even had he wished to do so, and the play's splendid vigour does not in the least suggest that he did. The point is not that he could or should have rejected Elizabethan notions of a cherished heroic episode, and the excited attitudes these naturally provoked; it is rather that his treatment of the war shows far more insights into its necessary accompaniments and consequences than do the chronicles or patriotic poems, while still accepting without question the popular case for the war, the popular zest that went with it, and the popular sense of triumph that resulted from it. None of his plays shows him better as the skilled professional, the writer who can measure his material against the interests of his audience and provide the maximum dramatic gratification. He is certainly too captivated by his theme to be *merely* turning out an efficient product; the play is too grand, the poetry too powerful, the realization too moving, for such a limiting judgement to hold good. Yet sheer professional zest in face of so gripping and famous a story makes him write to the top of his bent *for each immediate purpose*, and one understands the play better by recognizing this than by seeking to draw all its parts into convincing psychological, symbolical, or moral coherence. Just this same characteristic, of writing for the greatest immediate effect, marks his treatment also of action and character; this will be the next subject for discussion. The result is a play which works superbly as a dramatic sequence but which, on the moral plane, teasingly offers and then withdraws (as if uncertain whether they belong with the heroic theme) a series of tentatives towards an altogether deeper realization of its subject.

*

The acceptance of the chronicles' popular reading of events results in an enormously effective yet an episodic drama rather than one integrated from a centre. 'Pageant-like' is the word often applied to its practice of showing off each scene as a separate entity, rather than developing the action organically from the impulses of characters who progressively know more about themselves; development of action is something more than mere sequence of actions. Yet 'pageant-like' needs qualifying; the play holds together much better than that word would suggest. To some degree (though a small one), the low comedy satirically reacts to the high history, and so makes a pattern with it. Act II, for instance, shows lofty patriotism in its chorus and second scene but base rapacity in its first and third, and the cynic might say (though Shakespeare would probably reject the view) that these are not quite as antithetical as they seem. Immediately after 'God for Harry, England, and Saint George!' (III.1.34) there enter the discreditable Bardolph, Pistol, and Nym, like a sardonic comment. The degree of such interaction, however, does not go far towards establishing organic form, as it does in *Henry IV*, though certainly it affords a diverting variety of effect. Much more telling in producing coherence is the speed and thrust with which the action drives forward, each episode pressing on and looking towards the event. The play generates unity by its impetus.

Shakespeare shapes the material well. He assumes that the whole significance of Henry's reign is to lead to Agincourt and Troyes, and he uses the choruses brilliantly to link and explain the action. The episodic nature of the plot arises not because the events fall apart – they are connected and consecutive – but because the serious action consists of successive demonstrations rather than a germination and growth of part into part, connected by moral significance, such as make 'dramatic poems' of *Othello* and *Macbeth* and *King Lear* – or, should these comparisons be unfair, of *Richard II* and either part of *Henry IV*. The plot is extremely simple, without an 'inner' dimension.

*

From the nature of plot to that of characterization: how is Henry himself handled? In 1886 R. G. Moulton delivered to the New Shakspere Society a paper comparing the presentation of Henry's character with that of Macbeth's; Henry, he decided, is complete from the beginning, whereas Macbeth 'develops as the seed grows into the tree; the tree may be *potentially* present in the seed, but the passage from that potential to the actual is not a matter depending upon external observation but is a succession of changes in the substance of the organism itself'. This overstates the 'given' nature of Henry; from Act I we should hardly predict the much more interesting figure of Act IV, and Dover Wilson's introduction to the New Cambridge edition, arguing for a deepening personality as Agincourt draws near, provides the right counterbalance. Moulton's point is, though, not precisely that nothing new is revealed about Henry as the play proceeds but that what is presented is a series of stances, each powerful and effective, but not evincing that subtle, inward development of personality we look for in Shakespeare's great figures. King-as-counsellor, King-as-spokesman, King-as-patriot, King-as-warrior, King-as-wooer – these were some of the predetermined attitudes in which Henry needed to be displayed. And there comes to mind what Coleridge said about predetermined (or mechanic) and organic forms, during his lecture, 'Shakespeare a Poet Generally', in the *Lectures and Notes on Shakespeare*. The passage runs:

The form is mechanic, when on any given material we impress a predetermined form, not necessarily arising out of the properties of the material...The organic form, on the other hand, is innate; it shapes, as it develops, itself from within, and the fullness of its development is one and the same with the perfection of its outward form. Such as the life is, such is the form.

Is Henry V's 'form', or his play's 'form', in this sense 'mechanic'? Has the heroic model King of the chronicles proved hard to animate as an inwardly-motivated dramatic person? Holinshed presents the King as beloved, strong, just, bountiful, diligent, constant in temperament, enduring and valiant, 'of life without spot', 'of person and form . . . rightly representing his heroical affects, . . . a majesty . . . that both lived and died a pattern in princehood, a lode-star' (compare 'This star of England'; Epilogue. 6), 'and mirror of magnificence' (compare 'the mirror of all Christian kings'; 2. Chorus. 6).

Such a character might daunt the boldest dramatist, but Shakespeare is quite undaunted; he seems to welcome the chance of creating the hero and the man, just as in *Richard III*, facing an earlier problem of predetermined characterization, he had welcomed the chance of creating the great villain. Within a few months he would tackle the still harder problem of Caesar, the state figure so commanding that one cannot feel sure what sort of man lives within the imperial frame. Shakespeare surmounts the difficulty better with Henry than with Caesar, displaying him much more fully and variously. But does he mean Henry to combine majesty and humanity in harmonious union? Or is the majesty at odds with the humanity? If so, is the strain treated sympathetically, or objectively, or ironically? All these positions have been maintained.

Shakespeare's problem is to humanize and animate an accepted hero, and to show how a man can be a king, a king a man. What no one could predetermine was the success with which, in the moving address to Scroop, the night-scene self-examination before Agincourt, and the Agincourt speech itself, he would achieve all this, and this achievement gives the play at these moments a deeply human passion. So, designed though it must be to show Henry in this light and in that, *Henry V* is much more than a series of tableaux. It is vigorous in forwarding events, forceful in the asserting and urging of views (there is an intellectual drama as well as a historical one), and at its best successful in presenting not only an able but a deeply human ruler. It remains true, however, that Henry is on exhibition; each scene in which he figures is designed to show his quality, even though this is done not statically but dynamically.

But is there also something subtler going on, a searching

critique of power, unillusioned though unsatirical? Some critics have thought so. This critique might, in essence, be summed up in Henry's own words,

> *What infinite heart's ease*
> *Must kings neglect that private men enjoy!*
>
> IV.1.229–30

Does the royal office deprive its holder not only of his own private heart's ease but of the common humanity of heart's ease with other men? Presented in the Archbishop's panegyric as the essence of wisdom and grace, Henry must fill the part of the great king, centre of Church and State – yet at what expense of human naturalness and spontaneity? If one may put it so, kings are born free, yet are everywhere to be found in chains. The reverence in which Henry is held (so the argument goes) is vitiated by adulation; the imposing dispositions of his council do not conceal Machiavellianism; the heroics of war involve corruption and cruelty; the kingly authority ('a paradise | T' envelop and contain celestial spirits') must ignore such human attachments as once were felt for Falstaff and Bardolph (the wonderful treatment of Falstaff's death suggests how much has been, even if unavoidably, lost; and Henry's detachment over Bardolph's hanging reflects his now official status); and the King must yield periodically to outbursts of passion which betray the tension between kingly control and human emotion.

All this is interestingly observed. Certainly the difference is profound between a Tamburlaine, superhumanly wielding a heartless command, and Henry, ruling well yet bound to the political and social realities; the good king, working in the human conditions of politics, is affected by them in a way the tyrant is not. He can neither on the one hand override his subjects' rights, nor on the other be swayed from his duty by personal affections. On the whole, *Henry V* recognizes the problems of kingly position but does not stress the tension between office and man; after all, it makes a particular point of

the fact that Henry is surrounded by his brothers, his good
friends, and his devoted subjects. Certainly a king must sometimes act as ordinary humanity would not; he must reject a
Falstaff, hang a Bardolph, threaten innocent citizens, and order
prisoners to be killed. Yet the play offers virtually no criticism
at these points; if Henry has 'run bad humours' on Falstaff and
'killed his heart' (II.1.116, 84) yet for Nym he is 'a good king'
(II.1.120) and for Pistol 'a bawcock, and a heart of gold'
(IV.1.44). Had it been Shakespeare's point that kings must
forgo their finer feelings he would have made this clear, even if
an ironic commentator like Falconbridge in *King John* had been
needed to do so. He seems quite satisfied with Henry as he is,
and sturdily sure that provided he rules well he is all that could
be desired.

In two great scenes, however – that with Scroop, and that
leading from the soldiers' debate before the battle (together
with Henry's 'ceremony' speech) up to Henry's prayer – Henry
as man feels the burdens of kingship profoundly, and the play
takes on a moving gravity as he reveals what the loss of his
heart's ease means. Yet these are passing phases only, soon
superseded by the zest of leadership or by triumph in war and
love. Elsewhere, Henry willingly accords with what is expected
of a monarch, and indeed his finest quality as commander is the
naturalness with which, uncondescendingly, he is on terms as
man to man with those he leads. A comradely spirit, stemming
from him, unites the English army from general to private,
while on the French side the bickering leaders are worlds
removed from their despised peasants. The play, then, is on the
whole about unity (rather than division) between Henry's
kingly and human natures, as it is about unity between him and
his subjects.

So the theory that Shakespeare here penetrates into the
ironic intricacies of politics or of the political man, in a spirit
either coolly objective or wisely grave, is too ingenious. Indeed,
so little does the play really explore the subtleties of kingship
that some critics have judged Shakespeare to be deliberately

reducing the witty, sceptical, intelligent Prince Hal into the mere 'king of good fellows' who can deal handily with practical matters and is (whatever the Archbishop says) an average man writ large. So limited did Granville-Barker find Henry, in intellect and psychology, that in 'From *Henry V* to *Hamlet*' he suggested that Shakespeare had lost interest in the man of action and so turned, with Brutus and Hamlet, from the unreflective to the reflective hero. Yet limited though he is in inward interest there is more than enough about Henry to keep one wholly engaged by him. By turns sensitive, violent, and thoughtful, he is frank, honest, confident, shrewd, eminently good-hearted and resilient, and the play fully makes out its case that he is, in war and peace alike, a good king. One comes back, then, repeatedly to a central position among conflicting views, that the play is best interpreted rather simply. It is not quite so plain a tale of heroism as the more complacent used to think; neither on the other hand is it an ironically evaluated critique of ambiguous politics, such as current criticism is inclined to hold. It is essentially a play for the popular taste, but popular taste has now fewer romantic predilections and more toughness of quality than it used to have and it takes *Henry V* as relating real heroism to the real grimness of war and the real conditions of life.

The last question about the play concerns the manner of its writing. Does Shakespeare believe wholeheartedly in his subject, and address himself to it with zest, or does he, as one critic thinks, 'audibly brace himself [for a] not very congenial effort' as he faces a theme and character 'lacking in true humanity'? Is he, as has further been suggested, so uncomfortable that the play hides intellectual paucity behind a façade of oratory, reduces a courtly, witty Prince into a war-machine King, is casual in its comedy, and often falls slack in its verse?

The verse is not, in fact, slack, except in the 'Salic law' rigmarole. It is usually strong and interesting, forthright and uncomplicated, at its best animated, eloquent, and rich. Yet mostly it is the style of speech-making rather than of personal idiosyncrasy, that idiosyncrasy which is felt, for instance, throughout *Henry IV*, where the movement, texture, and meaning of the words simultaneously express inner complexes of feeling. In its attitude to style-making, though not in its particular styles, *Henry V* harks back to *Richard II*, aiming to put the content demonstratively on show. Most of its serious speeches are addresses with an aim in mind. This is appropriate to its material, to the demonstrative nature of plot and character, and it is extremely well done. In a story traditionally so concerned with the King's status, from a King who, it must always be made evident, has emerged into ability and wisdom, the necessary utterance will express not the complexities of personality but a demonstrative eloquence. One fires with admiration and pleasure at it, yet senses that on the whole one is being, as it were, set alight by design.

Henry's speech to the conspirators, and particularly to Scroop, is a case in point. A richly-felt and moving address, it sounds the tenor of tragic emotion as Henry discovers that one so trusted has proved so false. Yet the humiliation of Cambridge, Grey, and Scroop must be a formal public occasion, as that of Falstaff had been, and for the same reason, that the fault committed affects Henry's public station, and the world must understand this. Like much that Henry is bound by his office to do it needs to be set forth. To say this is to define but not to disparage it; it is excellently managed (even if 'managed' is, indeed, the word that significantly comes to mind). It creates a particular tone which the scene needs, that of reconciliation in tragic parting, through grief shared between King and conspirators, so that even their intended treachery ends in prayers for the safety of the land. Henry's speech is heartfelt, tender, and dignified. Yet its unusual length, and the relationship between speaker and hearer it necessarily imposes, that of authority *ex cathedra* and submissive penitent, cannot but promote a sense of occasion, unanswerable and final. The 'ceremony' speech preceding Agincourt has some of the same qualities; though a soliloquy, it is really a public address, eloquent and memorable. Not that it satisfies every reader: John Palmer calls it a 'most ingenuous apologia' and proposes to defend Shakespeare from the charge of approving 'moral humbug' only on the grounds that he is making clear, as a matter of natural fact, the attitudinizing habitual to the political man. Such a reaction is extravagant; Dr Johnson, who recognized moral humbug when he saw it, thought the speech 'very striking and solemn', and observed in his notes on the play, 'Something like this, on less occasions, every breast has felt'. In face of Agincourt, affected by the scepticism of Williams, Henry senses the truth underlying commonplaces about the 'hard condition, | Twin-born with greatness' (IV.1.226–7), and though his speech echoes his father's sentiment, 'Uneasy lies the head that wears a crown' (*2 Henry IV*, III.1.31), he speaks from his own awareness. Yet, eloquent though he is, this again is the speech of status; even in its very privacy it discourses to the audience about kingly cares and humble content. Tell-tale phrases, it is true, betray an unexpected petulance or self-pitying extravagance – phrases like 'every fool, whose sense no more can feel | But his own wringing' (this comes coarsely, after the honest realism of Williams), 'horrid night, the child of hell', 'the wretched slave . . . all night | Sleeps in Elysium' (said of the toiling peasant dead to the world with weariness in his hovel), or 'with profitable labour' (said of the peasant's hard-earned pittance). These touches of irrationality may be signs that Henry is under strain, and the actor may certainly treat them as such; the speech is not without Shakespeare's humanizing psychology. Yet on the whole Henry is going through an understood exercise; even the soliloquy is oratorical, and occasional false notes suggest that a case is being made.

The serious speeches must accord with what is expected. Nevertheless, even through this formidable apparatus of the demonstrative there shows much of spirited and brilliant verse; whatever the play's intellectual and psychological conditions, Shakespeare was evidently writing with pleasure. And at important points qualities emerge that, rather than being merely accomplished, are deep and true. Of this, in the smaller compass, all that relates to Falstaff's cronies as they learn of his illness, to the Hostess as she narrates his death, to the Boy as his wit brightens the scene until he goes down in the slaughter, and to Fluellen in everything he says and does is an example. This is all sensitive and humane, not in the least disguised behind the public gesture. In the larger compass, most of what bears upon Henry himself when he is gravely tested is imaginative and right. The fourth chorus is in a different manner from its precursors, superior even to the third in significance of atmosphere and mood. Henry is now to be not only leader but friend, and the language becomes tender in evoking the endangered English and the 'little touch of Harry in the night' which is to hearten them. This crucial eve before Agincourt gives all that could be asked for. The English commanders and soldiers know and fundamentally trust each other (the lifelike lower-rank cynicism is something quite different from disloyalty or untrustworthiness), and Henry's debate with his men is of the greatest interest. Critics who dislike him, or think him only a superb operator, hit him hardest here; for one of them the discussion is disappointingly 'sober and rational'; for another, Henry's arguments are 'squirming sophistry'; for a third, his conscience is 'incapable of even so much as an honest piece of reasoning'. If so, Shakespeare has missed his mark completely, for he gives no sign of meaning the King to show up poorly; leading his men in a cause by definition just, Henry is meant to be morally right and to make his case fairly. In fact, he argues with skill, but lucidly and honestly, even if (as with Scroop) he goes on so long that what began as debate ends in argumentative monopoly. The acuteness with which he follows the argument through and the sharpness and concentration of the argument itself are signs of an unexpectedly earnest engagement with the subject at a level of hypothesis of which one would not have thought him capable. As Dr Johnson observes on the passage, 'the whole argument is well followed, and properly concluded'.

As for the speech before Agincourt, fame has made its every phrase so familiar that one can hardly hope to see it objectively at all. But familiarity breeds compulsion, not contempt. At each re-hearing it reaffirms its sway, almost against one's will, and renews that exultancy which it is its purpose to effect. Is this merely the climactic activation of stock responses? To some degree, yes; these are (and they are no worse for it) those 'images which find a mirror in every mind, and thoughts to which every bosom returns an echo', of which Johnson wrote in the *Life of Gray*. Technically, there is also the excitement of the supreme expected occasion; this is the crowning exercise of all those in which Henry must direct his words to a prescribed end. But as he does so he creates the sense that he is at one with the occasion and with his own truest feelings. The thoughts come with ease and power, borne along infallibly by the rhythmical flow and resonant melody of the lines, and heightened by the heady refrain about St Crispin's day. The daring paradox by which the very fewness of his soldiers is made to sound a source of strength is carried off with irresistible conviction; the mounting vision of victory and fame is offered in words both heroic and human; and from the initial stress on the King's own honour there spread out widening circles of contagious emulation, until all his men feel the spell of brotherhood, their thoughts lifted beyond present peril to the prospect of honour, old age, and brave memories. This comment merely rewrites flatly what Henry says exaltingly; the great thing about the exaltation is that it blends itself with intimate human feeling, with neighbourliness, and humour, and hope, and proper pride.

To sum up, then: if this discussion has been a good deal concerned with possible dissatisfactions or critical disagreements that is because the grounds on which, at one point or another, serious critics have disagreed or been dissatisfied need to be recognized. Yet one cannot but conclude that much of the criticism is based on false premises (such as those of much later historical and moral criteria), or is hypercritical, or springs from seeking more deeply-involved moral judgements than seem to be there. Naïve, in a sense, the play requires one to be, willingly naïve rather than innocent. It would be innocent to rise from it feeling idealistic about policy or war (that 'continuation of policy by other means', as Clausewitz called it); the underside of such things is sufficiently revealed, though at times in an oddly incidental, or accidental, manner. Naïve in a way one needs to be, for the play to work. One must give one's scepticism a day off and let one's gusto serve instead, though it will at times prove a disturbing gusto, as at others exhilarating. There must be a preparedness to go along with the play's fine confidence about what it is doing — it rarely hesitates in its onward action or its compulsive style. If one yields to its conviction, the result will be a slight anaesthetizing of the intellect but a marked exhilaration in the pulse, a stirring of pleasure in eloquence, and a very human sense of what men are like when danger brings out their better natures.

Further Reading

Anyone working on *Henry V* must owe an especial debt to John Dover Wilson for his New Cambridge edition. His dramatic, linguistic, and historical scholarship illuminates all the play's technical aspects; equally, his generous knowledge of men interprets its spirit and meaning as, surely, Shakespeare meant them to be interpreted. An editor coming after him cannot fail to salute one

Who laboured here, though with the greater art.

Sources and Historical Background

The sources are well presented and analysed in W. G. Boswell-Stone, *Shakespeare's Holinshed* (1896, 1907) and G. Bullough, *Narrative and Dramatic Sources of Shakespeare*, volume iv (1962). A very satisfactory edition for following the historical narrative is *Shakespeare's Holinshed: An Edition of Holinshed's Chronicle (1587)*, selected, edited, and annotated by Richard Hosley (New York, 1968). *The Famous Victories of Henry the Fifth* is available in Bullough (above) or in facsimiles (Shakspere-Quarto series, edited by C. Praetorius and P. A. Daniel, 1887; Tudor Facsimile Texts, edited by J. S. Farmer, 1913). The anonymous play of *Edward III*, which offers points of resemblance, is reprinted by G. C. Moore Smith (Temple Dramatists, 1897), J. S. Farmer (Tudor Facsimile Texts, 1910), C. F. Tucker Brooke, *The Shakespeare Apocrypha* (1918), and W. A. Armstrong, *Elizabethan History Plays* (1965). The actual historical events are related in C. L. Kingsford, *Henry V* (1901), J. H. Wylie, *The Reign of Henry V*, volume ii (1919), and E. F. Jacob, *Henry V and the*

Invasion of France (1947). Elizabethan views of this phase of history are surveyed in E. M. W. Tillyard, *Shakespeare's History Plays* (1944; Penguin Books, 1962), L. B. Campbell, *Shakespeare's 'Histories': Mirrors of Elizabethan Policy* (1947), K. J. Holzknecht, *The Backgrounds of Shakespeare's Plays* (1950 – a compact account of Elizabethan interest in the past, Shakespeare's treatment of history, and the presentation of kingship), and the editions by J. Dover Wilson (New Cambridge, 1947) and J. H. Walter (Arden, 1954).

Texts

There are facsimiles of the 1600 'Bad' Quarto by C. Praetorius (Shakspere-Quarto series, 1886) and W. W. Greg (Shakespeare Quarto series, 1957); reprints in the (old) Cambridge Shakespeare, volume iv (1864, 1891), and by Brinsley Nicholson for the New Shakspere Society (1875, with the Folio text following; 1877, with Quarto and Folio texts in parallel), and Ernest Roman (*Shakespeare Reprints* iii, Marburg, 1908, with the first and third Quarto and first Folio texts on the same page). Facsimiles of the first Folio text are available in the first Folio facsimiles (for example, edited by Sidney Lee, 1902; edited by Kökeritz and Prouty, 1955; edited by Charlton Hinman (the Norton Facsimile), 1968), and separately (edited by J. Dover Wilson, 1931). There are scholarly analyses of textual matters in E. K. Chambers, *William Shakespeare*, volume i (1930), W. W. Greg, *The Shakespeare First Folio* (1955), and the editions by J. Dover Wilson (New Cambridge, 1947) and J. H. Walter (Arden, 1954); both these editions argue for an original version 'with Sir John in it'. John Munro's London Shakespeare edition, volume iv (1957), skilfully and compactly examines textual matters and the range of critical opinion.

Critical Estimates

Several critics and editors survey the competing views of their precursors; the New Cambridge and London Shakespeare editions (above) do this well. The New Cambridge also offers a fine appraisal of the play's spirit and Henry's qualities, and the Arden usefully sets the play against the conventions of epic and of the Renaissance prince. The New Cambridge is informative also on stage history, but the best account of this is in A. C. Sprague, *Shakespeare's Histories: Plays for the Stage* (1964), a fascinating study of the play in performance, and what actors and critics have made of it. J. Dover Wilson and T. C. Worsley's *Shakespeare's Histories at Stratford, 1951* (1952) is a lively illustrated record of the *Richard II – Henry V* sequence in performance, with a stimulating anthology of critical viewpoints.

Critical studies divide, roughly, into those which accept and those which reject the play's proffered enthusiasm for Henry. Those which accept do so either unreservedly or with the admission of flaws which nevertheless are held to leave Henry largely unimpaired. Those which reject do so because Shakespeare is thought to have failed in percipience (to have succumbed to jingoism, or worship of crude success, or typecasting which he cannot humanize) or because, it is argued, the enthusiasm is merely ostensible and really masks an unillusioned analysis (whether comic, ironic, or tragic) of the inevitable Machiavellianism of 'policy'. A rough tabulation of views would go as follows (the more striking are starred *):

(a) *Unreserved approval of Henry*: G. G. Gervinus, *Shakespeare Commentaries*, volume i (1863); * H. N. Hudson, *Shakespeare: His Life, Art, and Characters*, volume i (1880); F. E. Schelling, *The English Chronicle Play* (1902); John Bailey, *Shakespeare* (1929) – cogent, though rather downright-commonsensical; Charles Williams, 'Henry V', in *Shakespeare Criticism* 1919–1935, edited by Anne Ridler (1936); * J. Middleton Murry, *Shakespeare* (1936) – this brings the play's glowing spirit imaginatively across; * J. Dover Wilson, New Cambridge edition (1947); * Rose A. Zimbardo, 'The Formalism of *Henry V*', in *Shakespeare Encomium*, edited by Anne Paolucci (1964).

(b) *Qualified approval of Henry*: * A. C. Bradley, 'The Rejection of Falstaff', in *Oxford Lectures on Poetry* (1909); * E. E. Stoll, *Poets and Playwrights* (1930); * M. M. Reese, *The Cease of Majesty* (1961) – an extract appears in *Shakespeare's Histories: An Anthology of Modern Criticism*, edited by William A. Armstrong (Penguin Shakespeare Library, 1972); * S. C. Sen Gupta, *Shakespeare's Historical Plays* (1964); H. M. Richmond, *Shakespeare's Political Plays* (1967) – harsh on Henry at the start, but just to his growing maturity; * Gareth Lloyd Evans, *Shakespeare II* (1969).

(c) *Discontent (moral and/or aesthetic) with Henry*: * W. Hazlitt, *Characters of Shakespeare's Plays* (1817) – Hazlitt, however, praises the poetry; H. Granville-Barker, 'From *Henry V* to *Hamlet*' (1925), revised in *Aspects of Shakespeare* (1933) and *Studies in Shakespeare*, edited by P. Alexander (1964); Mark van Doren, *Shakespeare* (1939); * U. M. Ellis-Fermor, *The Frontiers of Drama* (1945) – this is a brief but brilliant contention that in Henry the King-as-ruler has entirely displaced the King-as-human-being; * Honor Matthews, *Character and Symbol in Shakespeare's Plays* (1962).

(d) *The play as unillusioned political analysis*: A. C. Swinburne, *A Study of Shakespeare* (1880) – a few pages only; * W. B. Yeats, 'At Stratford-on-Avon', in *Ideas of Good and Evil* (1903); Gerald Gould, 'A New Reading of *Henry V*' (in *The English Review*, vol. 29, 1929) – this takes the play as anti-war satire and Henry as 'the perfect hypocrite'; H. B. Charlton, *Shakespeare, Politics and Politicians* (1929); * J. Palmer, *Political Characters of Shakespeare* (1945); H. C. Goddard, *The Meaning of Shakespeare*, volume i (1951) – a provocative view, very hostile to Henry, spoilt by prejudiced interpretation and the importation of extraneous evidence; * D. A. Traversi, *Shakespeare from 'Richard II' to 'Henry V'* (1957); R. W. Battenhouse, '*Henry V* as Heroic Comedy', in *Essays on Shakespeare and Elizabethan Drama*, edited by R. Hosley (1963) – rather extravagant in comment but interesting in taking the play as 'heroic comedy' when others – for example Traversi – offer it as potential tragedy;

* Z. Stříbrný, '*Henry V* and History', in *Shakespeare in a Changing World*, edited by A. Kettle (1964) – an excellent essay.

(e) Brief but interesting comments may be sampled in G. B. Shaw, '*Henry IV*', in *Our Theatre in the Nineties*, volume ii (1931), in *Plays and Players*, selected by A. C. Ward (1952), and in *Shaw on Shakespeare*, edited by Edwin Wilson (1962; Penguin Shakespeare Library, 1969); A. P. Rossiter, 'Ambivalence: the Dialectic of the Histories', in *Angel with Horns* (1951); P. Alexander, introduction to Collins' Classics edition (1955) – also in *Introductions to Shakespeare* (1964); L. C. Knights, *Shakespeare: the Histories* (1962).

(f) Brian Vickers, *The Artistry of Shakespeare's Prose* (1968), analyses the prose qualities well. * *Shakespeare: 'Henry V': A Casebook* (1969), edited by Michael Quinn, gathers critical commentaries since the eighteenth century: it includes, in full or in part, the discussions listed above by Bradley, Charlton, Ellis-Fermor, Gould, Granville-Barker, Hazlitt, Matthews, Shaw, Sprague, Stoll, Stříbrný, Tillyard, Traversi, Van Doren, Walter, Williams, Yeats, and Zimbardo.

An Account of the Text

The earliest text, that of 1600, is a 'bad' Quarto, that is, one derived from Shakespeare's manuscript only by an irregular process resulting in much corruption. Second and third Quartos followed in 1602 and 1619 (misdated 1608); each is a reprint of the first, with even less authority. The first Folio edition, of 1623, provides the text on which all later reprints have been based. It was set up from Shakespeare's manuscript, though clearer, better punctuated, and freer from irregularities than several other texts so derived; Shakespeare may have worked with more care than usual.

The evidence for this authenticity is presented by John Dover Wilson in the New Cambridge edition. It consists of apparent Shakespearian spellings transmitted into the text (such as 'vp-peer'd' for 'up'ard' [II.3.24], 'Deules' and 'Deule' for 'devils' and 'devil' [II.3.30, 33], 'Moth' for 'mote' [IV.1.174], and 'vawting' for 'vaulting' [V.2.137]), misprints resulting from Shakespeare's kind of script (for instance, 'name' for 'mare' [II.1.22], 'Straying' for 'Straining' [III.1.32], 'Leuitie' for 'lenitie' [III.6.109], and 'nam'd' for 'name' [IV. Chorus. 16]). There are variations in the designating of characters, to be expected from an author in the process of composition; the Hostess, for instance, appears as '*Quickly*', '*Hostesse*', and '*Woman*'; Fluellen is sometimes '*Welch*'; '*King*' stands for Henry and for Charles of France – in V.2 there is a mixture of '*King*', '*France*', '*England*', and '*French King*', which needs editorial regularization. Characters may be introduced in stage directions and then given nothing to do in the scene; conversely, others may play a part without having been introduced. There are also stage directions which sound like authorial notes rather than exact instructions (for example, 'Enter two Bishops' [1.2.6]; 'Enter the King and all his Traine before the Gates' [III.3.0]; 'Drum and Colours. Enter the King and his poore Souldiers' [III.6.84]; 'Enter the French Power, and the English Lords' [V.2.276]). The Folio text, then, is the indisputable authority.

The Quarto text is much shorter, some 1620 lines as against some 3380. It omits many passages, three complete scenes (1.1; III.1; and IV.2), and the prologue, choruses, and epilogue. The surviving verse approximates roughly to that of the Folio, though the sense is often garbled and the metre irregular; at times it is no more than paraphrase. The prose scenes fare still worse; printed in irregular lines capitalized as if verse, they give a scrappy rendering of the corresponding parts of the original, sometimes conveying no more than the gist of the Folio version. The Quarto does, however, furnish some apparently authentic readings lost in the Folio, including two whole lines (II.1.101 and IV.3.48), and it preserves the verse form of Pistol's speeches, nearly all of which the Folio gives as prose (see Collations, pages 716–17). It also includes several oaths, over and above those which appear in the Folio (see Collations, page 724). Since the 'copy' for several plays was to varying extents expurgated before the Folio was printed, some of these oaths may have been cut from the authentic text. Nine of them, out of the total of fifteen, come from Fluellen, and this may be significant of a cutting down of his exuberance. Unfortunately, so corrupt is the Quarto text that one cannot tell whether Shakespeare or the unauthorized compiler put them into Fluellen's mouth. Some, at least, are probably genuine expressions of his Welsh fieriness, but which are which cannot be ascertained. (Any expurgation to which Henry V may have been subjected was clearly incomplete; many oaths remain, particularly – though not solely – those that are serious and reverent.)

The brevity of the Quarto doubtless owes something to the forgetfulness of those compiling it. The text seems to be a reported one, written down from recitation probably by disloyal actors (the proper course was for the performing company to sell an authentic text to a publisher of its choice, when it judged such a sale advisable). Scholars have tried to assess the degrees of accuracy in various parts of the Quarto so as to ascertain which actors may have been involved, but the discussion has proved inconclusive. The Quarto's deficiencies probably result also from heavy cutting of the original text to produce a shortened version for a provincial tour – in any case, the full text would need some pruning before it could be staged, though not nearly as much as it gets in the Quarto. This condensation saves eleven acting parts and much acting time. The phrasal changes are botchings to compensate for imperfect memory, and auditory errors resulting from a reporter's mishearings (for example, 'the function' for 'defunction' [1.2.58], 'Inger' for 'Lingare' [1.2.74], 'Foraging' for 'Forage in' [1.2. 110], 'England' for 'inland' [1.2.142], 'a thing' for 'a sin' [11.4.74], 'shout' for 'suit' [111.6.76], 'partition' for 'perdition' [111.6.95], and 'de la Brute' for 'Delabreth' [1v.8.91]).

When a reading in the Quarto agrees with that in the Folio this agreement is strong evidence for correctness, since it has survived the hazards of abbreviation, recollection, and reporting. Now and then the Quarto offers a better reading than the Folio, but its authority is of the slightest, and the Folio reading must prevail unless clearly erroneous.

COLLATIONS

The following lists are selective, not comprehensive. They include the more noteworthy variants but omit many minor changes which are insignificant in the determination of the true reading, changes such as obvious misprints, trifling omissions, small variations in word order, and grammatical details not affecting the sense. Only the more interesting of editorial regularizations of the French passages have been recorded; to collate in full would have meant citing nearly every word.

Variants between the first Quarto and first Folio texts, which
are very numerous indeed since the Quarto is so irregular, have
been noted only when the Quarto variant has been accepted,
either in the present or in several earlier editions, or when it is
unusually interesting; the interest may lie in its offering a
possibly correct alternative to the accepted reading, or in its
revealing compositorial vagaries or other operations in textual
transmission (auditory errors, verbal alternatives, and the like).

When a reading in the text exceeds a word or two, only its
opening and closing words are quoted for identification, but
the whole passage is to be taken as representing the variant
version. Q1, Q2, and Q3 mean the first, second, and third
Quarto editions (1600,1602,1619); F1, F2, F3, and F4 mean the
first, second, third, and fourth Folio editions (1623, 1632,
1663–4, 1685). 'J. Dover Wilson, 1947' and 'J. H. Walter, 1954'
mean the New Cambridge and new Arden editions respectively,
by those editors.

I

(a) *Variants*: The following readings in the present text derive
from Q1, not from F1. Each represents the Q1 form in
modernized spelling; if, though derived from Q1, it differs
interestingly the actual Q1 form follows, in brackets. Each Q1
reading is followed by the F1 variant, unmodernized and
unbracketed. Later interesting variants, if any, come last, in
brackets.

I.2.	183	True:] *not in* F1
	209	several] *not in* F1
	213	End] And
II.1.	22	mare] name
	26	NYM] *not in* F1
		How now, mine host Pistol?] (*Nim.* How do you
		my Hoste? Q1) *In* F1 *this is a continuation of*

Bardolph's speech at line 25.

	69	thee defy] defie thee
	101	NYM I shall have . . . betting?] *not in* F1
	112	came] come
II.2.	147	Henry] *Thomas*
	176	you have] you (you three F2)
II.3.	15	fingers' ends] fingers end
III.6.	30	her] his
	109	lenity] Leuitie
IV.1.	35	*Qui va là?*] (Ke ve la? Q1) *Che vous la?*
	301	friends] friend
IV.3.	13–14	And yet I do thee wrong . . . valour.] Q1 *locates this correctly, though making Clarence the speaker of lines 12–14 and garbling the text.* F1 *makes this a continuation of Bedford's speech at line 11.*
	48	And say, 'These wounds . . . day.'] *not in* F1
IV.5.	11	Let's die in honour] (Lets dye with honour Q1) Let vs dye in (Let us die instant) (Let's die in harness) (Let's die in arms)
	15	Whilst by a] (Why least by a Q1) Whilst a base
V.1.	85	swear] swore

(b) *Metrical Speeches*: The following metrical speeches (from Pistol) appear in Q1 as verse (though sometimes so erratically that the verse form may be accidental), and in F1 as prose. Editors follow Q1 in presenting them as verse, though basing the text on F1. It is not clear in Q1 and F1 whether several one-line speeches are meant as verse or prose. They are given as verse in this edition if they sound histrionic. Metrical speeches which are not in Q1 and which F1 gives as prose are listed on page 720.

II.1.	27–9	Base tike, call'st thou me host? . . . lodgers.
	43–50	'*Solus*', egregious dog? . . . follow.
	68–76	'*Couple a gorge!*' . . . enough.
	102–8	A noble shalt thou have . . . hand.

II.3.	44–53	Come, let's away . . . blood to suck!
III.6.	20–21	Captain, I thee beseech . . . well.
	24–8	Bardolph, a soldier firm . . . stone–
	38–48	Fortune is Bardolph's foe . . . requite.
IV.1.	37–8	Discuss unto me . . . popular?
	44–8	The King's a bawcock . . . name?
IV.4.	47–8	Tell him my fury . . . take.
	63–4	As I suck blood . . . me!
V.1.	18–20	Ha, art thou bedlam . . . leek.
	76–83	Doth Fortune play the housewife . . . steal;

2

(a) *Variants*: The following readings in the present text (given first) originate in editions later than F1; if proposed by a modern editor, they are identified in brackets. The F1 variant comes next, unmodernized and unbracketed. Other interesting variants, whether earlier than F1 or later, come last, in brackets; the sources are given of such of them as originate in the Quartos or the later Folios, or in modern scholarly editions.

I.2.	94	imbare] imbarre (imbace Q1: embrace Q3: imbar F3)
	163	her] their (your Q1)
	208–9	Come to one mark . . . town,] *one line in* F1, *with* 'several' *omitted*
II.1.	34	drawn] hewne (here)
	76–7	enough. | Go to!] enough to go to.
	79	you, Hostess] your Hostesse
II.2.	87	him] *not in* F1
	114	All] And
	139	mark the] make thee
	159	I] *not in* F1
II.3.	16	'a babbled] a Table
II.4.	107	privèd] (J. H. Walter, 1954); priuy (pining Q1)

III. Chorus 4 Hampton] Douer

    6 fanning] fayning

III.1.   7 conjure] (J. H. Walter, 1954); commune (summon)

   17 noblest] Noblish (noble)

   24 men] me

   32 Straining] Straying

III.2. 114 hear] heard

III.3.   32 heady] headly (deadly)

   35 Defile] Desire

   54 all. For . . . uncle,] all for vs, deare Vnckle.

III.4. 7–13 KATHERINE De hand. Et les doigts?

     ALICE Les doigts? Ma foi, j'oublie les doigts, mais je me souviendrai. Les doigts? Je pense qu'ils sont appelés de fingres; oui, de fingres.

     KATHERINE La main, de hand; les doigts, de fingres. Je pense que je suis le bon écolier; j'ai gagné deux mots d'anglais vitement. Comment appelez-vous les ongles?] F1 *gives to Alice* 'Et les doigts?' (*line 7*), *to Katherine* 'Les doigts? Ma foi, j'oublie' *down to* 'oui, de fingres' (*lines 8–10*), *to Alice* 'La main, de hand' *down to* 'le bon écolier' (*lines 11–12*), *and to Katherine the remainder.*

   38 N'avez-vous pas déjà] *N'aue vos y desia*

III.5. 11 *Mort Dieu! Ma vie!*] Mort du ma vie (Mordeu ma via [at line 5] Q1, mor du [at line 11] Q1)

   26 Lest poor we] (This edition); Poore we (Poore we may F2)

   46 Knights] Kings

III.7. 12 pasterns] postures

   63 *et la truie*] *es la leuye*

IV. Chorus 16 name] nam'd

   27 Presenteth] Presented

IV.1. 92 Thomas] *John*

  174 mote] Moth

	226–30	We must bear all ... enjoy!] *six lines in* F1, *ending* 'beare all. | ... Greatnesse, | ... sence | ... wringing. | ... neglect, | ... enjoy?'
	238	What is thy soul of adoration?] What? is thy Soule of Odoration?
	284	if] of (lest); or (J. Dover Wilson, 1947)
	284–5	numbers | Pluck] numbers: | Pluck
	293–5	Toward heaven, to pardon blood ... do,] *four lines in* F1, *ending* 'blood: | ... Chauntries, | ... still | ... doe:'
IV.2.	9	dout] doubt
	58	guidon. To the field! | I will] Guard: on | To the field, I will
IV.4.	4	*Calitie*] (This edition); Qualtitie (Quality F4) *Calen o*] calmie
	15	Or] for
	35	*à cette heure*] asture
	51–2	*l'avez promis*] *layt a promets*
	55	*remerciments*] *remercious* *suis tombé*] *intombe*
	65	*Suivez*] *Saaue*
IV.6.	34	mistful] mixtfull
IV.7.	76	their] with (the)
	123	'a live] aliue
V.Chorus	10	with wives] Wiues
V.2.	12	England] Ireland
	50	all] withall
	54–5	as ... wildness,] all ... wildnesse.
	77	cursitory] (J. Dover Wilson, 1947); curselarie (cursenary Q1: cursorary Q3)
	93	Haply] Happily
	186–7	*que vous parlez, il est meilleur*] *ques vous parleis, il & melieus*
	317	never] *not in* F1
	326	then] *not in* F1

(b) *Metrical Speeches*: The following speeches (mostly from Pistol) have been arranged as verse by editors, though they are given as prose in F1. There is either nothing or very little in Q1 to correspond to them. Metrical speeches given as verse in Q1 but as prose in F1 are listed on pages 716–17.

II.1.	64–5	Give me thy fist . . . tall.
	118–19	Nym, thou hast spoke . . . corroborate.
II.3.	3–6	No, for my manly heart . . . therefor.
III.2.	6–10	The plainsong is most just . . . fame.
	14–19	If wishes would prevail . . . bough.
	22–5	Be merciful, great Duke . . . chuck!
IV.1.	54–5	Tell him I'll knock his leek . . . day.
IV.4.	4–5	*Calitie! Calen o* . . . Discuss.
	7–11	O Signieur Dew . . . ransom.
	14–16	Moy shall not serve . . . blood!
	19–21	Brass, cur? . . . brass?
	23–5	Say'st thou me so . . . name.
	37–9	*Owy, cuppele gorge, permafoy* . . . sword.

(c) *Act- and Scene-Divisions*: Q1 has no Act- and scene-divisions at all. F1 has '*Actus Primus. Scæna Prima*' before 1.1 but marks no later scenes. It puts '*Actus Secundus*' before III.Chorus, '*Actus Tertius*' before IV.Chorus, '*Actus Quartus*' before IV.7, and '*Actus Quintus*' before V.Chorus. Editors have amended the Act-divisions and inserted scene-numbers as in the present text.

(d) *Stage Directions*: The wording of the stage directions in this text follows as closely as practicable that in F1. Amendments and additions have been made only when necessary to clarify the action or to assimilate the entry and exit directions to it. The following stage directions, introduced by editors, differ sufficiently from those of F1 to qualify for recording; added *Exits* and *Exeunts*, when self-evident, are not listed, nor are characters' names when these merely regularize entry and exit

directions. The reading in the present text is given first, that of
F1 second.

I.2.	6	*Enter the Archbishop . . . Ely*] *Enter two Bishops.*
	222	*Exeunt some attendants*] *Not in* F1
II.1.	33	*Nym draws his sword*] *Not in* F1
	42	*He sheathes his sword*] *Not in* F1
	59	*They both draw*] *Not in* F1
	62	*He draws*] *Not in* F1
	63	*Pistol and Nym sheathe their swords*] *Not in* F1
	97	*He sheathes his sword*] *Not in* F1
	108	*Nym sheathes his sword*] *Not in* F1
II.2.	181	*Exeunt Cambridge, Scroop, and Grey, guarded*] *Exit.*
II.3.	56	*He kisses her*] *Not in* F1
II.4.	67	*Exeunt Messenger and certain lords*] *Not in* F1
III.2.	21	*He drives them forward*] *Not in* F1
	27	*Exeunt all but the Boy*] *Exit.*
	53	*Enter Fluellen, Gower following*] *Enter Gower.*
III.3.	0	*Some citizens . . . walls.*] *Not in* F1.
IV.1.	222	*Exeunt Soldiers*] *Exit Souldiers. [after line 217]*
IV.8.	73	*He gives him a paper*] *Not in* F1
	101	*The Herald gives him another paper*] *Not in* F1
V.1.	33–4	*He strikes him again*] *Not in* F1
V.2.	271–2	*He kisses her*] *Not in* F1
	276	*Enter the French King . . . Lords*] *Enter the French Power, and the English Lords.*

3

The following list contains some of the more interesting and
important variants (whether earlier or later than F1) and proposed emendations not accepted in the present text. The reading
of this edition is (unless otherwise identified) that of F1,
modernized; it is followed by the rejected variants, unmodernized. The sources are given of such variants as originate in the

Quartos or later Folios or in modern scholarly editions. When no source is given, the reading is one proposed by an earlier editor which has not gained general acceptance. Only a small selection of the very numerous Q1 variants is offered.

I.I.	49	wonder] wand'rer
I.2.	72	find] fine Q1
	99	man] sonne Q1
	112	pride] power Q1
	142	Our inland] your *England* Q1
	165	sumless] shipless Q1
	166	ELY] *Lord* Q1: WESTMORLAND
	173	'tame] spoyle Q1: tear taint
	175	crushed] curst Q1: crude
	199	kneading] lading Q1
	208	Come] flye Q1
	234	waxen] paper Q1
	244	is] are Q1
	255	spirit] study Q1
II. Chorus	20	But see, thy fault France hath in thee found out, | A nest] But see thy fault! France hath in thee found out | A nest
	31	we'll] well
	32	distance, force] distance while we force
II.I.	49	take] talke Q1
	49–50	Pistol's cock is up, | And flashing fire will follow] *Pistolls* flashing firy cock is vp Q1
	80	face] nose Q1
	111	that's] (that F1) theres Q1
II.2.	118	tempered] tempted
II.3.	14	play with] talk of Q1
	24	knees,] knees, and they were as cold as any stone Q1
	39	hell] hell fire Q1
	50	*Caveto*] cophetua Q1
	59	Adieu!] adieu. | *Pist.* Keepe fast thy buggle boe. Q1

II.4.	57	his mountain] his mounting his mighty
III.5.	15	Where] whence Q1
	54	captive chariot] chariot, captive (J. Dover Wilson, 1947)
III.6.	59	FLUELLEN Very good.] *Flew.* That is very well. | *Pist.* I say the fig within thy bowels and thy durty maw. | *Exit Pistoll.* | *Fle.* Captain *Gour*, cannot you hear it lighten & thunder? Q1
	76	suit] shout Q1
III.7.	14	*chez*] qui a avec
IV.1.	65	fewer] lewer Q1: lower Q3
IV.3.	44	shall see] outliues ⎫ *These* Q1 *variants occur in the*
		and live] and sees ⎭ *corresponding line, 41.*
	105	crasing] grazing
	128–9	thou wilt once more come again for a ransom] thou'lt once more come again for ransom
IV.4.	64	Follow me] Follow me cur Q1
IV.5.	14	base pander] bace leno Q1
	16	contaminated] contamuracke Q1
	18	our lives] our liues | Vnto these English, or else die with fame Q1
IV.6.	15	He cries] And cryde Q1
		my] deare Q1
	37–8	kill his prisoners! | Give the word through.] kill his prisoner. | *Pist.* Couple gorge. Q1
IV.8.	79–111	KING HENRY This note doth tell ... Thine!] Q1 *gives this passage as a continuation of Exeter's speech but prefixes 'Exe.' also to* 'Tis wonderful' *in line 111.* Q3 *continues lines 79–99 to Exeter (*'This note doth tell ... Lestrake'*) and then gives lines 100–101 to the King (*'Here was a royal fellowship ... dead?'*), lines 102–5 to Exeter (*'Edward the Duke of York ... five and twenty'*), and lines 105–11 to the King (*'O God, Thy arm was here! ... Thine!'*).*
	123	enclosed] enterred Q1

v.1.   77   Doll] Nell (*See textual note.*)

v.2. 180–2   *Je – quand sur le possession . . . mienne.*] Let me see,
Saint *Dennis* be my speed. | Quan *France* et mon.
| *Kate.* Dat is, when *France* is yours. | *Harry.* Et
vous ettes amoy. | *Kate.* And I am to you. |
Harry. Douck *France* ettes a vous: | *Kate.* Den
France sall be mine. | *Harry.* Et Ie suyues a vous.
| *Kate.* And you will be to me. Q1 (*See textual
note*)

222   untempering] untempting

252   *d'une – notre Seigneur – indigne*] (*d'une nostre Seigneur
indignie* F1) d'une vostre indigne d'une de votre
seigneurie indigne

4

The following list shows the oaths that occur in Q1 but not in
F1; the F1 reading, which is that also of the present text, is
given first, modernized. On this difference between the two
texts, see 'An Account of the Text', p. 713. A few more oaths
occur in parts of Q1 to which nothing in F1 corresponds.

II.1.   28   Now by this hand] Now by gads lugges

II.3.   7   Would I were with him] God be with him

40   Well] Well, God be with him

III.2.   3   Pray thee] Before God

20   Up to the breach] Godes plud vp to the breaches

III.6.   3   I assure you, there is] By Iesus thers

13   in my very conscience] by Iesus

62   I'll assure you] By Iesus

102   but his nose] But god be praised, now his nose

IV.1.   76   If the enemy] Godes sollud [*sic*], if the enemy

88–9   I think we shall never see] God knowes whether
we shall see

192   You pay him then] Mas youle pay him then

IV.7.   1   Kill the poys] Godes plud kil the boyes

	66	How now, what means] Gods will what meanes
iv.8.	62	By this day and this light] By Iesus
v.1.	38	I say] by Iesu
v.2.	272	You have withcraft] Before God *Kate*, you have witchcraft

5

The following are the more interesting of the stage-direction variants between Q1 and F1. The Q1 directions are given first.

i.2.	0	Q1, *Enter King* Henry, Exeter, 2. *Bishops, Clarence, and other Attendants*]. F1, *Enter the King, Humfrey, Bedford, Clarence, Warwick, Westmerland, and Exeter. [after line 6] Enter two Bishops.*
ii.1.	23	Q1, *Enter* Pistoll *and Hostes Quickly, his wife*]. F1, *Enter Pistoll, & Quickly.*
ii.2.	0	Q1, *Enter Exeter and Gloster*]. F1, *Enter Exeter, Bedford, & Westmerland.*
	11	Q1, *Enter the King and three Lords*]. F1, *Sound Trumpets. Enter the king, Scroope, Cambridge, and Gray.*
ii.4.	0	Q1, *Enter King of* France, Bourbon, Dolphin, and others.] F1, *Flourish. Enter the French King, the Dolphin, the Dukes of Berry and Britaine.*
iii.2.	21	Q1, *Enter* Flewellen *aud* [sic] *beates them in.*] F1, *Enter Fluellen.*
	27	Q1 *[after line 53]*, Exit Nim, Bardolfe, Pistoll, *and the Boy*]. F1 *[after line 27]*, Exit.
iii.3.	0	Q1, *Enter the King and his Lords alarum.*] F1, *Enter the King and all his Traine before the Gates.*
iii.4.	0	Q1, *Enter Katherine, Allice.*] F1, *Enter Katherine and an old Gentlewoman.*
iii.5.	0	Q1, *Enter King of* France *Lord Constable, the*

Dolphin, and Bourbon.] F1, *Enter the King of France, the Dolphin, the Constable of France, and others.*

III.6.   o   Q1, *Enter* Gower.] F1, *Enter Captaines, English and Welch, Gower and Fluellen.*

84   Q1, *Fnter* [sic] *King,* Clarence, Gloster *and others.*] F1, *Drum and Colours. Enter the King and his poore Souldiers.*

III.7.   o   Q1, *Enter* Burbon, Constable, Orleance, Gebon. F1, *Enter the Constable of France, the Lord Ramburs, Orleance, Dolphin, with others.*

IV.1.   34   Q1, *Enter the King disguised, to him* Pistoll.] F1, *[at line 1] Enter the King, Bedford, and Gloucester. [at line 34] Enter Pistoll.*

83   Q1, *Enter three Souldiers.*] F1, *Enter three Souldiers, Iohn Bates, Alexander Court, and Michael Williams.*

IV.3.   o   Q1, *Enter* Clarence, Gloster, Exeter, and Salisburie.] F1, *Enter Gloucester, Bedford, Exeter, Erpingham with all his Hoast: Salisbury, and Westmerland.*

78   Q1, *Enter the Herald from the French.*] F1, *Tucket. Enter Montioy.*

IV.4.   o   Q1, *Enter Pistoll, the French man, and the Boy.*] F1, *Alarum. Excursions. Enter Pistoll, French Souldier, Boy.*

IV.5.   o   Q1, *Enter the foure French Lords.*] F1, *Enter Constable, Orleance, Burbon, Dolphin, and Ramburs.*

IV.6.   o   Q1, *Enter the King and his Nobles,* Pistoll.] F1, *Alarum. Enter the King and his trayne, with Prisoners.*

IV.7.   52   Q1, *Enter King and the Lords.*] F1, *Alarum. Enter King Harry and Burbon with prisoners. Flourish.*

V.2.   o   Q1, *Enter at one doore, the King of* England *and his Lords. And at the other doore, the King of* France, *Queene* Katherine, *the Duke of* Burbon, *and others.*] F1, *Enter at one doore, King Henry, Exeter, Bedford, Warwicke, and other Lords. At another,*

Queene Isabel, the King, the Duke of Bourgongne, and other French.

98 Q1, *Exit King and the Lords. Manet,* Hrry [*sic*]. Katherine, *and the Gentlewoman.*] F1, *Exeunt omnes. Manet King and Katherine.*

276 Q1, *Enter the King of France, and the Lordes.*] F1, *Enter the French Power, and the English Lords.*

Genealogical Tables

TABLE I. *Henry V and the Throne of France*

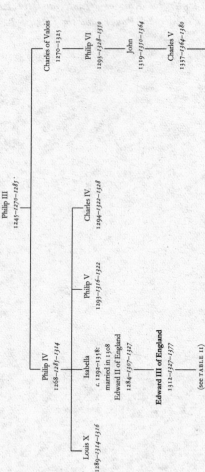

Philip III
1245–1270–1285

Philip IV
1268–1285–1314

Isabella
c. 1292–1358:
married in 1308
Edward II of England
1284–1307–1327

Louis X
1289–1314–1316

Philip V
1293–1316–1322

Charles IV
1294–1322–1328

Edward III of England
1312–1327–1377

(see TABLE II)

Charles of Valois
1270–1325

Philip VI
1293–1328–1350

John
1319–1350–1364

Charles V
1337–1364–1380

Charles VI
1368–1380–1422

Louis the Dauphin
1396–1415

Katherine
1401–1438:
married in 1420
Henry V of England
1387–1413–1422

Charles VII
1403–1422–1461

NOTE: Names in heavy type are those of persons in or closely relevant to the play. Italicized dates are those of reigns; other dates are those of births and deaths. Collateral kindred irrelevant to Henry's claim to the French crown have been omitted; nor has any attempt been made to illustrate the Archbishop's Salic Law speech. The 'Lewis the Tenth' of that speech (I.2.77) was in fact Louis IX, nor the Louis X shown above. The point at issue between the kings of France and those of England was whether the latter, descending from Philip IV through Isabella (the senior line) had a stronger claim than the descendants of Charles of Valois (the junior line). When Louis X died in 1316, Isabella was debarred by law from succeeding and from transmitting the right to succeed, whereupon her younger brothers succeeded and then her cousin, Philip VI.

TABLE II. *Claimants to the Throne of England*

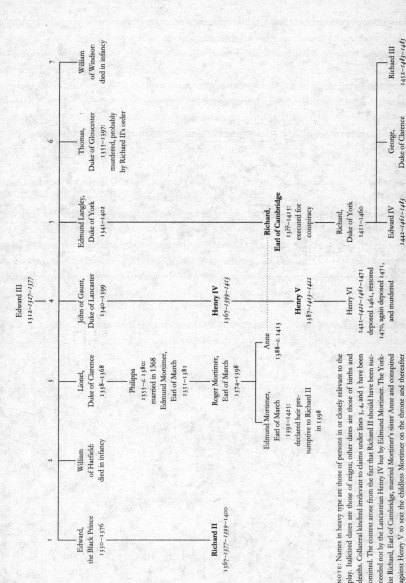

NOTE: Names in heavy type are those of persons in or closely relevant to the play. Italicized dates are those of reigns; other dates are those of births and deaths. Collateral kindred irrelevant to claims under lines 3, 4, and 5 have been omitted. The contest arose from the fact that Richard II should have been succeeded not by the Lancastrian Henry IV but by Edmund Mortimer. The Yorkist Richard, Earl of Cambridge, married Mortimer's sister Anne and conspired against Henry V to seat the childless Mortimer on the throne and thereafter have his own descendants succeed – this is the motive very obliquely hinted at in II.2.155–7.

KING HENRY THE FIFTH

The Characters in the Play

Chorus

KING HENRY THE FIFTH
DUKE OF GLOUCESTER
DUKE OF BEDFORD   brothers of the King
DUKE OF CLARENCE
DUKE OF EXETER, uncle of the King
DUKE OF YORK, cousin of the King
EARL OF SALISBURY
EARL OF WESTMORLAND
EARL OF WARWICK
EARL OF HUNTINGDON
ARCHBISHOP OF CANTERBURY
BISHOP OF ELY
RICHARD EARL OF CAMBRIDGE
HENRY LORD SCROOP   conspirators against the King
SIR THOMAS GREY
SIR THOMAS ERPINGHAM
CAPTAIN FLUELLEN
CAPTAIN GOWER   officers in the King's army
CAPTAIN JAMY
CAPTAIN MACMORRIS

References to plays by Shakespeare not yet available in the New Penguin Shakespeare are to Peter Alexander's edition of the *Complete Works*, London, 1951.
The Characters in the Play No list of these is provided in the Quarto or Folio. Many editions omit the Duke of Clarence and the Earl of Huntingdon, since, though they are passingly addressed in the final scene (v.2.84–5), neither is given anything at all to say. They are included here as having at least an action to perform, whereas Talbot, mentioned at iv. 3.54, says and does nothing whatever, and so is omitted from this list.

JOHN BATES
ALEXANDER COURT } soldiers in the King's army
MICHAEL WILLIAMS

BARDOLPH
NYM
PISTOL } camp-followers in the King's army
BOY

HOSTESS of an Eastcheap tavern, formerly Mistress Quickly,
   now married to Pistol
An English Herald

CHARLES THE SIXTH, King of France
LEWIS, the Dauphin
DUKE OF BURGUNDY
DUKE OF ORLEANS
DUKE OF BRITAINE
DUKE OF BOURBON
CHARLES DELABRETH, the Constable of France
GRANDPRÉ } French Lords
RAMBURES
THE GOVERNOR OF HARFLEUR
MONTJOY, a French Herald
AMBASSADORS to the King and Queen of France
MONSIEUR LE FER, a French soldier
ISABEL, Queen of France
KATHERINE, daughter of the King and Queen of France
ALICE, a lady attending on her

Lords, ladies
Officers, soldiers, citizens, messengers, and attendants

PROLOGUE

Flourish. Enter Chorus

CHORUS

O for a Muse of fire, that would ascend
The brightest heaven of invention,
A kingdom for a stage, princes to act,
And monarchs to behold the swelling scene!
Then should the warlike Harry, like himself,
Assume the port of Mars, and at his heels,
Leashed in like hounds, should famine, sword, and fire

Locations The action takes place in England and France.

Prologue Shakespeare has various formal conclusions to his plays (songs, dances, and epilogues), but formal openings occur only (apart from probably un-Shakespearian examples in *Henry VIII* and *Pericles*) in *Romeo and Juliet*, *2 Henry IV*, *Henry V*, and *Troilus and Cressida*. That to *Romeo and Juliet*, a sonnet, is followed by a second chorus-sonnet to Act II, and then by nothing further. That to *Troilus and Cressida* provides a lofty introduction to the theme and (as in *Henry V*) admits that a play is limited in what it can show. *2 Henry IV* is the only play other than *Henry V* to have an authentic Shakespearian prologue and epilogue; from it Shakespeare may have realized that in a history play a prologue surveying a great sweep of events could have a special value. He puts this realization to splendid use in *Henry V* by furnishing every Act with a chorus and by

using his epilogue (as he does not in *2 Henry IV*) to sum up the great story, thus stressing the play's epic nature.

(stage direction) *Flourish* fanfare. The Folio has flourishes before Acts II and III only; they are inserted here before each Act for uniformity.

1 *a Muse of fire* inspiration as brilliant and aspiring as the highest and brightest of the four elements. At III.7. 20–21 the Dauphin's horse is 'pure air and fire', as contrasted with the 'dull elements of earth and water'; and in a famous phrase Drayton described Marlowe's poetic 'raptures' as 'All air, and fire' (*Epistle to Henry Reynolds, Esquire, Of Poets and Poesie*).

5 *like himself* with all his true attributes

6 *port* bearing

7 *Leashed in*. A 'leash' was a trio of dogs on a lead. *famine, sword, and fire*. In Holinshed the Archbishop urges Henry to wage war with blood, sword, and fire, and replying to the

Crouch for employment. But pardon, gentles all,
The flat unraisèd spirits that hath dared
10   On this unworthy scaffold to bring forth
So great an object. Can this cockpit hold
The vasty fields of France? Or may we cram
Within this wooden O the very casques
That did affright the air at Agincourt?
O, pardon! since a crookèd figure may
Attest in little place a million,
And let us, ciphers to this great account,
On your imaginary forces work.
Suppose within the girdle of these walls
20   Are now confined two mighty monarchies,
Whose high uprearèd and abutting fronts
The perilous narrow ocean parts asunder.
Piece out our imperfections with your thoughts:
Into a thousand parts divide one man,
And make imaginary puissance.
Think, when we talk of horses, that you see them
Printing their proud hoofs i'th'receiving earth;
For 'tis your thoughts that now must deck our kings,
Carry them here and there, jumping o'er times,
30   Turning th'accomplishment of many years

French ambassador Henry threatens to do so. The presentation of the King here perhaps echoes Henry's declaration, when besieging Rouen, 'that the goddess of battle, called Bellona, had three handmaidens, ever of necessity attending upon her, as blood, fire, and famine' (Holinshed, *Chronicles of England*, 1587, III.567); similarly *1 Henry VI*, IV.2.11 – 'Lean famine, quartering steel, and climbing fire'.

8 *gentles* gentlefolk

9 *hath*. Plural nouns with singular verbs, and vice versa, are frequent in Elizabethan English.

11 *cockpit* round theatre (the 'wooden O' of line 13). Shakespeare may refer to the existing Curtain Theatre or to the Globe, which was under construction while he was writing the play.

12 *vasty* spacious

15 *crookèd* curved (like the nought which turns 100,000 into 1,000,000)

17 *ciphers* figures of no value
account (1) sum total; (2) narrative

28 *deck our kings* adorn our supposed kings like real ones

30 *many years*. The play covers events between 1414 and 1420.

Into an hour-glass: for the which supply,
Admit me Chorus to this history,
Who Prologue-like your humble patience pray,
Gently to hear, kindly to judge, our play.   *Exit*

                    Enter the Archbishop of Canterbury and the   I.I
                    Bishop of Ely

CANTERBURY

My lord, I'll tell you. That self bill is urged
Which in th'eleventh year of the last King's reign
Was like, and had indeed against us passed,
But that the scambling and unquiet time
Did push it out of farther question.

ELY

But how, my lord, shall we resist it now?

CANTERBURY

It must be thought on. If it pass against us,
We lose the better half of our possession;
For all the temporal lands which men devout
By testament have given to the Church   10
Would they strip from us; being valued thus –
As much as would maintain, to the King's honour,
Full fifteen earls, and fifteen hundred knights,
Six thousand and two hundred good esquires;
And, to relief of lazars and weak age,
Of indigent faint souls past corporal toil,
A hundred almshouses right well supplied;
And, to the coffers of the King beside,
A thousand pounds by th'year. Thus runs the bill.

ELY

This would drink deep.

CANTERBURY   'Twould drink the cup and all.   20

1.1.4 *scambling* turbulent. Because of civil   14 *esquires* candidates for knighthood,
disorders, a bill proposed by Lollard   attending on a knight
lords to dispossess the clergy was   15 *lazars* lepers
withdrawn from Parliament in 1413.

ELY

But what prevention?

CANTERBURY

The King is full of grace and fair regard.

ELY

And a true lover of the holy Church.

CANTERBURY

The courses of his youth promised it not.
The breath no sooner left his father's body
But that his wildness, mortified in him,
Seemed to die too. Yea, at that very moment,
Consideration like an angel came
And whipped th'offending Adam out of him,
30   Leaving his body as a paradise
T'envelop and contain celestial spirits.
Never was such a sudden scholar made;
Never came reformation in a flood
With such a heady currance scouring faults;
Nor never Hydra-headed wilfulness
So soon did lose his seat, and all at once,
As in this King.

ELY   We are blessèd in the change.

CANTERBURY

Hear him but reason in divinity,

22 *full of grace.* The chronicles present Henry as reformed from his wild youth by a deeply religious redemption; the play reflects this throughout.

26 *mortified.* This is the accepted word for the old sinning self ('th'offending Adam') dying before the onset of grace. The Archbishop uses many Biblical and theological phrases.

28 *Consideration* spiritual self-examination (a stronger sense than the modern one)

28–31 *like an angel came . . . T'envelop and contain celestial spirits* (like the angel sent by God to drive the sinning Adam – and Eve – out of Eden or Paradise, which thereafter was left to blessed spirits only)

34 *currance* current

35 *Hydra-headed* manifold and proliferating. The Hydra was a many-headed monster encountered by Hercules; each head, when cut off, grew two more, until a burning brand was thrust into the stump.

38 *reason in divinity.* Henry, according to Holinshed, was an able theological disputant; he argued matters of faith with the Lollard Sir John Oldcastle, imprisoned for heresy.

And all-admiring, with an inward wish,
You would desire the King were made a prelate.   40
Hear him debate of commonwealth affairs,
You would say it hath been all in all his study.
List his discourse of war, and you shall hear
A fearful battle rendered you in music.
Turn him to any cause of policy,
The Gordian knot of it he will unloose,
Familiar as his garter; that, when he speaks,
The air, a chartered libertine, is still,
And the mute wonder lurketh in men's ears
To steal his sweet and honeyed sentences.   50
So that the art and practic part of life
Must be the mistress to this theoric —
Which is a wonder how his grace should glean it,
Since his addiction was to courses vain,
His companies unlettered, rude, and shallow,
His hours filled up with riots, banquets, sports,
And never noted in him any study,
Any retirement, any sequestration,
From open haunts and popularity.

ELY

The strawberry grows underneath the nettle,   60

46 *Gordian knot* seemingly insoluble
problem. The peasant Gordius devised so intricate a knot that, tradition held, whoever undid it would
rule over Asia: Alexander cut it with
his sword. By implication, Henry out-
does Alexander by untying it, and
that easily.

48 *The air, a chartered libertine, is still.*
'This line is exquisitely beautiful'
(Johnson). The rich eloquence of this
eulogy does much to save the Archbishop's hyperboles from seeming
specious.
chartered libertine free spirit licensed
to roam abroad

51–2 *the art and practic part of life* |

Must be the mistress to this theoric
practical skill and experience must
govern his theoretical knowledge

55 *rude* coarse

58–9 *sequestration,* | *From open haunts
and popularity* keeping aloof from
places of common resort and from
mixing with the people

60–62 *The strawberry grows underneath the
nettle . . . of baser quality.* The Bishops
of Ely had a celebrated strawberry-
garden in Holborn, referred to in
Richard III (III.4.32–3). T. Hill's *Profitable Arte of Gardeninge* (1572) observes that 'Strawberry . . . aptly
groweth in shadowy places, and
rather joyeth under the shadow of

And wholesome berries thrive and ripen best
Neighboured by fruit of baser quality:
And so the Prince obscured his contemplation
Under the veil of wildness, which, no doubt,
Grew like the summer grass, fastest by night,
Unseen, yet crescive in his faculty.

CANTERBURY
It must be so, for miracles are ceased;
And therefore we must needs admit the means
How things are perfected.

ELY   But, my good lord,

70 How now for mitigation of this bill
Urged by the Commons? Doth his majesty
Incline to it, or no?

CANTERBURY   He seems indifferent,
Or rather swaying more upon our part
Than cherishing th'exhibiters against us;
For I have made an offer to his majesty –
Upon our spiritual Convocation,
And in regard of causes now in hand,
Which I have opened to his grace at large
As touching France – to give a greater sum

80 Than ever at one time the clergy yet
Did to his predecessors part withal.

ELY
How did this offer seem received, my lord?

CANTERBURY
With good acceptance of his majesty,
Save that there was not time enough to hear,
As I perceived his grace would fain have done,
The severals and unhidden passages

other herbs, than by growing alone';
and Montaigne describes refined
plants as growing best near coarse
ones, since the latter absorb the 'ill
savours' of the ground (*Essays*,
III.9).

66 *crescive in his faculty* increasing
   through its natural capacity
72 *indifferent* impartial
74 *exhibiters* proposers of the bill
86 *severals* details
   unhidden passages clear lines of descent

Of his true titles to some certain dukedoms,
And generally to the crown and seat of France,
Derived from Edward, his great-grandfather.

ELY

What was th'impediment that broke this off? 90

CANTERBURY

The French ambassador upon that instant
Craved audience, and the hour, I think, is come
To give him hearing. Is it four o'clock?

ELY

It is.

CANTERBURY

Then go we in to know his embassy;
Which I could with a ready guess declare
Before the Frenchman speak a word of it.

ELY

I'll wait upon you, and I long to hear it. *Exeunt*

Enter the King, Gloucester, Bedford, Clarence, Exeter, I.2
Warwick, Westmorland, and attendants

KING HENRY

Where is my gracious Lord of Canterbury?

EXETER

Not here in presence.

KING HENRY   Send for him, good uncle.

WESTMORLAND

Shall we call in th'ambassador, my liege?

KING HENRY

Not yet, my cousin; we would be resolved,
Before we hear him, of some things of weight
That task our thoughts, concerning us and France.

1.2.4 *cousin.* The word is often used
loosely for 'kinsman', but in fact
Westmorland was Henry's cousin by
marriage.
be resolved come to a solution

Enter the Archbishop of Canterbury and the Bishop
of Ely

CANTERBURY

God and His angels guard your sacred throne,
And make you long become it!

KING HENRY   Sure, we thank you.

My learnèd lord, we pray you to proceed,
10   And justly and religiously unfold
Why the law Salic that they have in France
Or should or should not bar us in our claim.
And God forbid, my dear and faithful lord,
That you should fashion, wrest, or bow your reading,
Or nicely charge your understanding soul
With opening titles miscreate, whose right
Suits not in native colours with the truth;
For God doth know how many now in health
Shall drop their blood in approbation
20   Of what your reverence shall incite us to.
Therefore take heed how you impawn our person,
How you awake our sleeping sword of war.
We charge you in the name of God, take heed;
For never two such kingdoms did contend
Without much fall of blood, whose guiltless drops

9–32 *My learnèd lord, we pray you to proceed*
... As pure as sin with baptism. The
religious note is evidence of Henry's
earnest moral sense. Holinshed
stresses his care before embarking on
a course of action – 'He never enterprised anything before he had fully
debated and forecast all the main
chances that might happen, which
done, with all diligence and courage
he set his purpose forward.'

11 *the law Salic.* This was the supposed
law by which the crown of France
could descend only through males.
Edward III (1.1.11–41) also has a discourse on the Salic law in relation to
Edward's claim to France.

15 *nicely charge your understanding soul*
sophistically burden your soul with
guilt by knowingly misrepresenting
the case

19 *approbation* putting to the proof

20 *incite* induce (without the present
sense of instigation). This is an example of the ambiguous diction which
haunts this diplomacy – Henry can
hardly be implying that the Archbishop is wilfully persuading him
into war, yet the modern sense of
the word creates suspicions about
the Archbishop's proceedings.

21 *impawn* pledge, commit (by offering
a guarantee of moral justification)

Are every one a woe, a sore complaint
'Gainst him whose wrongs gives edge unto the swords
That makes such waste in brief mortality.
Under this conjuration speak, my lord,
For we will hear, note, and believe in heart   30
That what you speak is in your conscience washed
As pure as sin with baptism.

CANTERBURY

Then hear me, gracious sovereign, and you peers,
That owe yourselves, your lives, and services
To this imperial throne. There is no bar
To make against your highness' claim to France
But this, which they produce from Pharamond:
'*In terram Salicam mulieres ne succedant*' –
'No woman shall succeed in Salic land';
Which Salic land the French unjustly gloze   40
To be the realm of France, and Pharamond
The founder of this law and female bar.
Yet their own authors faithfully affirm
That the land Salic is in Germany,
Between the floods of Sala and of Elbe;
Where Charles the Great, having subdued the Saxons,
There left behind and settled certain French,
Who, holding in disdain the German women
For some dishonest manners of their life,
Established then this law: to wit, no female   50
Should be inheritrix in Salic land;
Which Salic, as I said, 'twixt Elbe and Sala,

26–8 *sore complaint ... mortality* grave
accusation against him who wrongfully wages war, so destroying the
brief lives of men

33–95 *Then hear me, gracious sovereign, and
you peers ... Usurped from you and your
progenitors.* This address follows Holinshed so closely as to become quite
tiresome, yet one need not assume
that Shakespeare is satirizing the

Archbishop or statecraft. Tedious
though it is to modern ears, it conveyed to Elizabethan hearers all the
facts needed to prove that Henry
was right in his claim, and absolute
faith in the rightness of his claim is
the play's very basis.

37 *Pharamond* (legendary king of the
Salian Franks)

49 *dishonest* unchaste

Is at this day in Germany called Meisen.
Then doth it well appear the Salic law
Was not devisèd for the realm of France;
Nor did the French possess the Salic land
Until four hundred one-and-twenty years
After defunction of King Pharamond,
Idly supposed the founder of this law,
60   Who died within the year of our redemption
Four hundred twenty-six; and Charles the Great
Subdued the Saxons, and did seat the French
Beyond the river Sala, in the year
Eight hundred five. Besides, their writers say,
King Pepin, which deposèd Childeric,
Did, as heir general, being descended
Of Blithild, which was daughter to King Clothair,
Make claim and title to the crown of France.
Hugh Capet also — who usurped the crown
70   Of Charles the Duke of Lorraine, sole heir male
Of the true line and stock of Charles the Great —
To find his title with some shows of truth,
Though in pure truth it was corrupt and naught,
Conveyed himself as th'heir to th'Lady Lingare,
Daughter to Charlemain, who was the son
To Lewis the Emperor, and Lewis the son
Of Charles the Great. Also King Lewis the Tenth,
Who was sole heir to the usurper Capet,
Could not keep quiet in his conscience,
80   Wearing the crown of France, till satisfied
That fair Queen Isabel, his grandmother,
Was lineal of the Lady Ermengare,
Daughter to Charles the foresaid Duke of Lorraine;

66 *heir general* legal heir whether through
    male or female line
72 *find* provide
    shows specious appearances
74 *Conveyed himself* passed himself off
75 *Charlemain*. Hall and Holinshed, fol-

lowed by Shakespeare, give this
name in error for Charles the Bald.
77 *Lewis the Tenth*. This is an error, in
Holinshed and Shakespeare, for
Louis the Ninth. Hall is correct.

By the which marriage the line of Charles the Great
Was re-united to the crown of France.
So that, as clear as is the summer's sun,
King Pepin's title, and Hugh Capet's claim,
King Lewis his satisfaction, all appear
To hold in right and title of the female;
So do the kings of France unto this day,   90
Howbeit they would hold up this Salic law
To bar your highness claiming from the female,
And rather choose to hide them in a net
Than amply to imbare their crookèd titles
Usurped from you and your progenitors.

KING HENRY
May I with right and conscience make this claim?

CANTERBURY
The sin upon my head, dread sovereign!
For in the Book of Numbers is it writ,
When the man dies, let the inheritance
Descend unto the daughter. Gracious lord,   100
Stand for your own, unwind your bloody flag,
Look back into your mighty ancestors.
Go, my dread lord, to your great-grandsire's tomb,
From whom you claim; invoke his warlike spirit,
And your great-uncle's, Edward the Black Prince,
Who on the French ground played a tragedy,
Making defeat on the full power of France,

88 *appear* are plainly seen
94 *imbare* reveal to view. This explanation, though not very satisfactory,
seems the best one can do with the
Quarto's 'imbace' and the first
Folio's 'imbarre'. Some editions read
'imbar' and interpret it as 'fence
around', but it is hard to think that
the French kings preferred to hide
behind deceit rather than take steps
to defend their title. In a comparable
situation in *Edward III* (1.1.76),

Edward rejects the King of France's
claim, saying 'Truth hath pulled the
visard from his face.'
99–100 *When the man dies, let the inherit-
ance | Descend unto the daughter.*
Numbers 27.8 reads, 'If a man die
and have no son, then ye shall turn
his inheritance unto his daughter.'
Shakespeare omits 'and have no son'.
103 *great-grandsire* Edward III. Victorious at Crécy in 1346, he died in
1377.

Whiles his most mighty father on a hill
Stood smiling to behold his lion's whelp
110　Forage in blood of French nobility.
O noble English, that could entertain
With half their forces the full pride of France,
And let another half stand laughing by,
All out of work and cold for action!

ELY

Awake remembrance of these valiant dead,
And with your puissant arm renew their feats.
You are their heir, you sit upon their throne,
The blood and courage that renowned them
Runs in your veins; and my thrice-puissant liege
120　Is in the very May-morn of his youth,
Ripe for exploits and mighty enterprises.

EXETER

Your brother kings and monarchs of the earth
Do all expect that you should rouse yourself,
As did the former lions of your blood.

WESTMORLAND

They know your grace hath cause and means and
　　might –
So hath your highness. Never King of England
Had nobles richer and more loyal subjects,
Whose hearts have left their bodies here in England
And lie pavilioned in the fields of France.

CANTERBURY

130　O, let their bodies follow, my dear liege,

---

108 *on a hill.* Holinshed tells how
Edward III watched from 'a windmill hill', as the Black Prince waged
the battle of Crécy: the play of
Edward III treats of the incident
(III.5.1–2).
114 *for action* for want of action
120 *the very May-morn of his youth.* Henry
was 27; the prime of youth (the
Roman *juventus*) was held to lie between 20 and 35.

123–4 *rouse . . . lions.* To 'rouse' was a
hunting term for disturbing a large
animal from its lair, as in 1 *Henry IV*
– 'rouse a lion' (1.3.198); *Titus Andronicus* – 'rouse the proudest pan-
ther' (II.2.21); Marlowe, *Tamburlaine*,
Part One – 'As princely lions when
they rouse themselves' (1.2.52).
126 *So hath your highness* so indeed you
have (with an emphasis on 'hath')

With blood and sword and fire to win your right!
In aid whereof we of the spiritualty
Will raise your highness such a mighty sum
As never did the clergy at one time
Bring in to any of your ancestors.

KING HENRY
We must not only arm t'invade the French
But lay down our proportions to defend
Against the Scot, who will make road upon us
With all advantages.

CANTERBURY
They of those marches, gracious sovereign,   140
Shall be a wall sufficient to defend
Our inland from the pilfering borderers.

KING HENRY
We do not mean the coursing snatchers only,
But fear the main intendment of the Scot,
Who hath been still a giddy neighbour to us;
For you shall read that my great-grandfather
Never went with his forces into France
But that the Scot on his unfurnished kingdom
Came pouring, like the tide into a breach,
With ample and brim fullness of his force,   150
Galling the gleanèd land with hot assays,
Girding with grievous siege castles and towns;
That England, being empty of defence,
Hath shook and trembled at th'ill neighbourhood.

CANTERBURY
She hath been then more feared than harmed, my
    liege;
For hear her but exampled by herself:

136–9 *We must not only arm t'invade the*
French . . . With all advantages. Henry's
moral sense is satisfied; his practical
sense must now ensure his kingdom's
safety.
140 *marches* borders
145 *still* constantly

151 *gleaned* stripped (of defenders)
    assays assaults
155 *feared* frightened
156 *hear her but exampled by herself* note
    the examples she can provide from
    her own history

When all her chivalry hath been in France,
And she a mourning widow of her nobles,
She hath herself not only well defended
160   But taken and impounded as a stray
The King of Scots, whom she did send to France
To fill King Edward's fame with prisoner kings,
And make her chronicle as rich with praise
As is the ooze and bottom of the sea
With sunken wrack and sumless treasuries.

ELY

But there's a saying very old and true:
   'If that you will France win,
   Then with Scotland first begin.'
For once the eagle England being in prey,
170   To her unguarded nest the weasel Scot
Comes sneaking, and so sucks her princely eggs,
Playing the mouse in absence of the cat,
To 'tame and havoc more than she can eat.

EXETER

It follows then the cat must stay at home;
Yet that is but a crushed necessity,
Since we have locks to safeguard necessaries,
And pretty traps to catch the petty thieves.
While that the armèd hand doth fight abroad,

160 *taken and impounded as a stray* taken into custody like a strayed animal

161–2 *The King of Scots, whom she did send to France . . . kings.* King David II of Scotland was captured at Neville's Cross in 1346 while the main English army was in France. A story circulated, not in fact true, that he was sent to Edward III's camp at Calais, and the supposed episode occurs in the play of *Edward III* (v.1.63).

166–73 *But there's a saying very old and true . . . than she can eat.* In the Quarto this is spoken by '*Lord*', in the Folio by the Bishop of Ely. The corresponding speech in Holinshed is by Westmorland, and in *The Famous Victories* both the Archbishop and the Earl of Oxford have versions of it. In view of this uncertainty it seems best to follow the Folio, though many editors change to Westmorland.

173 *'tame* attame, broach, break into (a sense still current in country usage; compare Wright, *English Dialect Dictionary*, 'tame')

175 *Yet that is but a crushed necessity* yet the conclusion that that is necessary is a forced one

Th'advisèd head defends itself at home;
For government, though high, and low, and lower,   180
Put into parts, doth keep in one consent,
Congreeing in a full and natural close,
Like music.
CANTERBURY True: therefore doth heaven divide
The state of man in divers functions,
Setting endeavour in continual motion;
To which is fixèd as an aim or butt
Obedience; for so work the honey-bees,
Creatures that by a rule in nature teach

180–83 *For government, though high, and low, and lower . . . Like music.* These lines seem echoes of Elyot's *The Boke named the Governour* – 'In everything is order, and without order may be nothing stable or permanent: and it may not be called order, except it do contain in it degrees, high and base, according to the merit or estimation of the thing that is ordered' (Book I, chapter i), and 'Music, . . . how necessary it is for the better attaining the knowledge of a public weal: which . . . is made of an order of estates and degrees, and by reason thereof containeth in it a perfect harmony' (Book I, chapter vii).

181–2 *parts . . . consent . . . close.* These are musical terms for the separate melodies combining in a concluding cadence; *consent* unites the senses of 'agreement' and 'concent' (singing together). There may be an echo of Lyly's *Euphues* (see following note also), for, telling how bees delight in 'sweet and sound music', Lyly says they are called the Muses' birds, 'because they follow not the sound but the consent' (*Works*, ed. Bond, II.45).

187 *the honey-bees.* Elyot illustrates the need for a just ruler and obedient subjects from 'a little beast, which of all others is most to be marvelled at, I mean the bee' (*The Governour*, Book I, chapter ii), and he describes the ordered hive in a way which closely anticipates Shakespeare. But Lyly, in *Euphues*, may be the source; he tells how the commonwealth of bees 'live under a law' and 'choose a King, whose palace they frame both brave in show, and stronger in substance'. They call a parliament 'for laws, statutes, penalties, choosing officers', and 'every one hath his office, some trimming the honey, some working the wax, one framing hives, another the combs'. They 'keep watch and ward, as living in a camp to others', and their King 'goeth up and down, entreating, threatening, commanding' (*Works*, ed. Bond, II.45). Shakespeare's bees are still more anthropomorphic, performing all the functions of citizens; but the degree of similarity is striking. The idea goes back to Plato, Virgil, and Pliny.

188–9 *Creatures that by a rule in nature teach . . . to a peopled kingdom.* Elyot describes the bee as 'left to man by nature, as it seemeth, a perpetual figure of a just governance or rule' (*The Governour*, Book I, chapter ii).

The act of order to a peopled kingdom.
190   They have a king, and officers of sorts,
Where some, like magistrates, correct at home;
Others, like merchants, venture trade abroad;
Others, like soldiers, armed in their stings,
Make boot upon the summer's velvet buds;
Which pillage they with merry march bring home
To the tent-royal of their emperor;
Who, busied in his majesty, surveys
The singing masons building roofs of gold,
The civil citizens kneading up the honey,
200   The poor mechanic porters crowding in
Their heavy burdens at his narrow gate,
The sad-eyed justice, with his surly hum,
Delivering o'er to executors pale
The lazy yawning drone. I this infer,
That many things, having full reference
To one consent, may work contrariously,
As many arrows loosèd several ways
Come to one mark,
As many several ways meet in one town,
210   As many fresh streams meet in one salt sea,
As many lines close in the dial's centre;
So may a thousand actions, once afoot,
End in one purpose, and be all well borne
Without defeat. Therefore to France, my liege!
Divide your happy England into four;
Whereof take you one quarter into France,
And you withal shall make all Gallia shake.
If we, with thrice such powers left at home,
Cannot defend our own doors from the dog,
220   Let us be worried, and our nation lose
The name of hardiness and policy.

190 *sorts* different ranks
207 *loosèd several ways* shot from several
directions
211 *dial's* sundial's

220 *worried* shaken, savaged (as by a dog;
see also II.2.83)
221 *hardiness and policy* courage and
statesmanship

KING HENRY

    Call in the messengers sent from the Dauphin.

                     Exeunt some attendants

    Now are we well resolved, and by God's help

    And yours, the noble sinews of our power,

    France being ours, we'll bend it to our awe,

    Or break it all to pieces. Or there we'll sit,

    Ruling in large and ample empery

    O'er France and all her almost kingly dukedoms,

    Or lay these bones in an unworthy urn,

    Tombless, with no remembrance over them.   230

    Either our history shall with full mouth

    Speak freely of our acts, or else our grave,

    Like Turkish mute, shall have a tongueless mouth,

    Not worshipped with a waxen epitaph.

        Enter Ambassadors of France

    Now are we well prepared to know the pleasure

    Of our fair cousin Dauphin; for we hear

    Your greeting is from him, not from the King.

AMBASSADOR

    May't please your majesty to give us leave

    Freely to render what we have in charge,

    Or shall we sparingly show you far off   240

    The Dauphin's meaning and our embassy?

KING HENRY

    We are no tyrant, but a Christian king,

    Unto whose grace our passion is as subject

    As is our wretches fettered in our prisons:

    Therefore with frank and with uncurbèd plainness

    Tell us the Dauphin's mind.

AMBASSADOR   Thus then, in few:

    Your highness, lately sending into France,

    Did claim some certain dukedoms, in the right

---

225 *ours* our just possession

234 *Not worshipped with a waxen epitaph*
    not honoured with even the most
    perishable memorial

243 *grace* spiritual virtue (as being a
    Christian king)

244 *is our wretches* (singular verb and
    plural subject again)

Of your great predecessor, King Edward the Third.
250 In answer of which claim, the Prince our master
Says that you savour too much of your youth,
And bids you be advised there's naught in France
That can be with a nimble galliard won;
You cannot revel into dukedoms there.
He therefore sends you, meeter for your spirit,
This tun of treasure; and, in lieu of this,
Desires you let the dukedoms that you claim
Hear no more of you. This the Dauphin speaks.

KING HENRY
What treasure, uncle?

EXETER   Tennis-balls, my liege.

KING HENRY
260 We are glad the Dauphin is so pleasant with us.
His present, and your pains, we thank you for.
When we have matched our rackets to these balls,
We will in France, by God's grace, play a set
Shall strike his father's crown into the hazard.
Tell him he hath made a match with such a wrangler
That all the courts of France will be disturbed
With chases. And we understand him well,
How he comes o'er us with our wilder days,
Not measuring what use we made of them.
270 We never valued this poor seat of England,
And therefore, living hence, did give ourself
To barbarous licence; as 'tis ever common
That men are merriest when they are from home.
But tell the Dauphin I will keep my state,

253 *galliard* dance (in lively triple time)
255 *meeter* more fitting
262 *rackets* (1) tennis-rackets; (2) noises (of gunfire)
264 *crown* (1) coin; (2) royal crown
     hazard (1) aperture in a tennis-court into which if the ball was struck it was unplayable; (2) jeopardy
265 *wrangler* (1) opponent; (2) disputant. (The 'hazard' in tennis was a great source of contention.)
266 *courts* (1) tennis-courts; (2) royal courts
267 *chases* (1) points forfeited at tennis when a ball was allowed to bounce twice; (2) pursuits

Be like a king, and show my sail of greatness,
When I do rouse me in my throne of France.
For that I have laid by my majesty,
And plodded like a man for working-days;
But I will rise there with so full a glory
That I will dazzle all the eyes of France,   280
Yea, strike the Dauphin blind to look on us.
And tell the pleasant Prince this mock of his
Hath turned his balls to gun-stones, and his soul
Shall stand sore chargèd for the wasteful vengeance
That shall fly with them: for many a thousand widows
Shall this his mock mock out of their dear husbands;
Mock mothers from their sons, mock castles down;
And some are yet ungotten and unborn
That shall have cause to curse the Dauphin's scorn.
But this lies all within the will of God,   290
To whom I do appeal, and in whose name,
Tell you the Dauphin, I am coming on,
To venge me as I may, and to put forth
My rightful hand in a well-hallowed cause.
So get you hence in peace; and tell the Dauphin
His jest will savour but of shallow wit
When thousands weep more than did laugh at it.
Convey them with safe conduct. Fare you well.

Exeunt Ambassadors

EXETER
This was a merry message.
KING HENRY
We hope to make the sender blush at it.   300

---

274 *keep my state* live up to my royal
   dignity
275 *sail* full swell
279 *I will rise there with so full a glory.*
   The metaphor is the frequent sun-
   image of royalty.
282 *pleasant* jocular
283 *gun-stones* cannon-balls (originally of
   stone)

290–94 *But this lies all within the will of
   God . . . well-hallowed cause.* Shakespeare continually brings Henry back
   to reverence for God's will; the religious references are not at all meant
   as perfunctory – they establish the
   war as a 'well-hallowed cause', approved by God.

Therefore, my lords, omit no happy hour
That may give furtherance to our expedition;
For we have now no thought in us but France,
Save those to God, that run before our business.
Therefore let our proportions for these wars
Be soon collected, and all things thought upon
That may with reasonable swiftness add
More feathers to our wings; for, God before,
We'll chide this Dauphin at his father's door.
310   Therefore let every man now task his thought
That this fair action may on foot be brought.   *Exeunt*

II   *Flourish. Enter Chorus*
    CHORUS
Now all the youth of England are on fire,
And silken dalliance in the wardrobe lies.
Now thrive the armourers, and honour's thought
Reigns solely in the breast of every man.
They sell the pasture now to buy the horse,
Following the mirror of all Christian kings
With wingèd heels, as English Mercuries.
For now sits expectation in the air,
And hides a sword from hilts unto the point
10   With crowns imperial, crowns and coronets,

---

305 *proportions* appointed forces
308 *God before* with God leading us

II. *Chorus* 2 *silken dalliance* silk-robed
    pleasure and idleness
6 *the mirror of all Christian kings*. Hall
    calls Henry the 'mirror of Christen-
    dom', Holinshed 'a lode-star in
    honour' (compare Epilogue. 6 –
    'This star of England') and 'mirror
    of magnificence'.

8–11 *For now sits expectation in the air ...*
    Harry and his followers. The motives
    here, of personal aggrandisement, are
    less altruistic than the 'honour's
    thought' of line 3 but no irony seems
    intended; the honour sought is
    worldly renown and its accompani-
    ment of worldly splendour.
9 *hilts.* Since the hilt was made of several
    parts it was often spoken of in the
    plural, as it is also at II.1.61.

Promised to Harry and his followers.
The French, advised by good intelligence
Of this most dreadful preparation,
Shake in their fear, and with pale policy
Seek to divert the English purposes.
O England! model to thy inward greatness,
Like little body with a mighty heart,
What mightst thou do, that honour would thee do,
Were all thy children kind and natural!
But see, thy fault France hath in thee found out,   20
A nest of hollow bosoms, which he fills
With treacherous crowns; and three corrupted men –
One, Richard Earl of Cambridge, and the second,
Henry Lord Scroop of Masham, and the third,
Sir Thomas Grey, knight, of Northumberland –
Have, for the gilt of France – O guilt indeed! –
Confirmed conspiracy with fearful France;
And by their hands this grace of kings must die,
If hell and treason hold their promises,
Ere he take ship for France, and in Southampton.   30
Linger your patience on, and we'll digest
Th'abuse of distance, force a play.
The sum is paid; the traitors are agreed;
The King is set from London; and the scene
Is now transported, gentles, to Southampton.
There is the playhouse now, there must you sit,
And thence to France shall we convey you safe
And bring you back, charming the narrow seas
To give you gentle pass; for, if we may,

14 *policy* intrigue (the subversion of lines 20–30)
16 *model* image in miniature
19 *kind*. The senses of 'filial' and 'loving' are combined.
27 *fearful* frightened
28 *this grace of kings* this king who most honours the title (an echo, perhaps, of Chapman, *Seaven Bookes of the Ili-* *ades of Homere*, 1598, Book I, sig. C2ʳ – 'with her [Chryseis] the grace of kings wise Ithacus ascended too')
29 *hell and treason*. Henry being the mirror of all Christian kings, treason against him is diabolic.
31–2 *digest | Th'abuse* stomach the flouting
32 *force a play* produce a play by cramming its events into a small compass

40   We'll not offend one stomach with our play.
      But till the King come forth, and not till then,
      Unto Southampton do we shift our scene.   *Exit*

II.1   *Enter Corporal Nym and Lieutenant Bardolph*
      BARDOLPH Well met, Corporal Nym.
      NYM Good morrow, Lieutenant Bardolph.
      BARDOLPH What, are Ancient Pistol and you friends yet?
      NYM For my part, I care not. I say little; but when time
      shall serve, there shall be smiles – but that shall be as it
      may. I dare not fight, but I will wink and hold out mine
      iron. It is a simple one, but what though? It will toast
      cheese, and it will endure cold as another man's sword
      will – and there's an end.
10   BARDOLPH I will bestow a breakfast to make you friends,
      and we'll be all three sworn brothers to France. Let't
      be so, good Corporal Nym.
      NYM Faith, I will live so long as I may, that's the certain
      of it; and when I cannot live any longer, I will do as I

41–2 *But till the King come forth, and not
till then . . . our scene.* This looks like
an afterthought; possibly the chorus
ended at line 40 and was followed by
scene 2, scene 1 being inserted later
and the extra couplet being added to
explain the delay in reaching Southampton. Needing to dispose of Falstaff before the King embarks for
France, Shakespeare may have felt
that a low-life scene was wanted here
to prepare for scene 3.

II.1 (stage direction) *Corporal Nym.*
Nym occurs in *The Merry Wives of
Windsor* (date uncertain) but not in
Henry IV. The name means 'taker',
'thief'; compare the pun at line 105.
Lieutenant Bardolph. Bardolph was a
corporal in *2 Henry IV* and becomes
one again at III.2.3.

3 *Ancient* ensign, standard-bearer.
Thomas Digges in *Stratioticos* (1579)
defines the qualifications of an
ensign, and Pistol should be measured against these: 'above all other
[he ought] to have honourable respect of his charge, and to be no less
careful and jealous thereof, than
every honest and honourable gentleman should be of his wife . . . Let
the Ensign be a man of good
account, honest and virtuous' (pages
93–4).

6 *wink* close my eyes
7 *What though* what of that
8 *endure cold.* When not hot (toasting
cheese) it stays cold (with inactivity).
11 *sworn brothers* faithful comrades (in
thieving; strictly, companions-in-
arms sworn to the laws of chivalry)

may. That is my rest, that is the rendezvous of it.

BARDOLPH It is certain, Corporal, that he is married to Nell Quickly, and certainly she did you wrong, for you were troth-plight to her.

NYM I cannot tell; things must be as they may. Men may sleep, and they may have their throats about them at that time, and some say knives have edges: it must be as it may – though patience be a tired mare, yet she will plod – there must be conclusions – well, I cannot tell.

Enter Pistol and Hostess Quickly

BARDOLPH Here comes Ancient Pistol and his wife. Good Corporal, be patient here.

NYM How now, mine host Pistol?

PISTOL

Base tike, call'st thou me host?
Now by this hand I swear I scorn the term;
Nor shall my Nell keep lodgers.

HOSTESS No, by my troth, not long; for we cannot lodge and board a dozen or fourteen gentlewomen that live honestly by the prick of their needles but it will be thought we keep a bawdy-house straight.

Nym draws his sword

O well-a-day, Lady, if he be not drawn now! We shall see wilful adultery and murder committed.

BARDOLPH Good Lieutenant! Good Corporal! Offer nothing here.

NYM Pish!

PISTOL

Pish for thee, Iceland dog! thou prick-eared cur of

15 *rest* stake in the game
rendezvous last resort
26 *How now, mine host Pistol!* In the Folio, this forms the end of Bardolph's speech, but the Quarto allots the corresponding words to Nym, and he rather than the inoffensive Bardolph seems the proper target of Pistol's wrath.

27–9 *Base tike, call'st thou me host ... lodgers.* The first Folio gives most of Pistol's verses as prose: see Collation lists on pages 716–17, 720.
36 *Lieutenant.* As an ensign, Pistol was in effect a sub-lieutenant; at III.6.12 he is 'aunchient lieutenant'.
39 *Iceland dog.* Nym is evidently shaggy: 'Iceland dogs, curled and rough all

Iceland!

40 HOSTESS Good Corporal Nym, show thy valour, and put
up your sword.

NYM Will you shog off? I would have you *solus*.

He sheathes his sword

PISTOL

'*Solus*', egregious dog? O viper vile!
The '*solus*' in thy most mervailous face!
The '*solus*' in thy teeth and in thy throat,
And in thy hateful lungs, yea, in thy maw, perdy!
And, which is worse, within thy nasty mouth!
I do retort the '*solus*' in thy bowels,
For I can take, and Pistol's cock is up,
50 And flashing fire will follow.

NYM I am not Barbason; you cannot conjure me. I have
an humour to knock you indifferently well. If you grow
foul with me, Pistol, I will scour you with my rapier,
as I may, in fair terms. If you would walk off, I would

over . . . by reason of the length of
their hair, make show neither of face
nor of body' (A. Fleming, *Of English
Dogges*, 1576). They were kept as lap-
dogs.

40–41 *show thy valour, and put up your
sword.* The Hostess is given, in this
play and in *2 Henry IV*, to self-
contradictory remarks.

42 *solus* alone (theatre Latin). Pistol, a
shaky linguist, takes it as an insult;
or he may take Nym to mean 'I'd
prefer you unmarried' (compare line
70).

44 *mervailous.* F1's form is worth retain-
ing as more fitting to the metre than
'marvellous'. The spelling may be
Shakespeare's normal one (similar
spellings occur in other Shakespeare
plays) or it may represent Pistol's
idiosyncratic diction.

49 *take* (1) take offence, or take fire; (2)
strike
cock is up trigger is cocked

(with a bawdy quibble)

51 *Barbason.* This also occurs in *The
Merry Wives of Windsor* (II.2.265)
among 'the names of fiends'; it is of
uncertain origin. Reginald Scot's *Dis-
coverie of Witchcraft* (1584) names
among principal devils one 'Marbas
alias Barbas', who 'appeareth in the
form of a mighty lion; but at the
commandment of a conjuror cometh
up in the form of a man and answer-
eth fully as touching anything which
is hidden or secret' (page 378). Shakespeare may have half-recalled this.
conjure exorcize. (Pistol's threats in
lines 43–8 sound like the rigmaroles
used for conjuring or exorcizing
devils.)

53 *foul* (1) abusive; (2) dirty (of a pistol
barrel)
scour (1) thrash; (2) clean out. (Nym
will run his sword through Pistol as
if it were a scouring-rod.)

prick your guts a little, in good terms, as I may, and
that's the humour of it.

PISTOL

O braggart vile, and damnèd furious wight!
The grave doth gape, and doting death is near:
Therefore exhale!

They both draw

BARDOLPH Hear me, hear me what I say! He that strikes   60
the first stroke, I'll run him up to the hilts, as I am a
soldier.

He draws

PISTOL

An oath of mickle might, and fury shall abate.

Pistol and Nym sheathe their swords

Give me thy fist, thy forefoot to me give;
Thy spirits are most tall.

NYM I will cut thy throat one time or other, in fair terms,
that is the humour of it.

PISTOL

'*Couple a gorge!*'
That is the word. I thee defy again!
O hound of Crete, think'st thou my spouse to get?   70
No, to the spital go,
And from the powdering tub of infamy
Fetch forth the lazar kite of Cressid's kind,
Doll Tearsheet she by name, and her espouse.

---

59 *exhale* draw (a Pistolian extravagance;
used normally of the sun drawing
phosphorescent vapours from the
earth)

63 *mickle* much

65 *tall* valiant

68 *Couple a gorge!* Pistol has prepared
some useful tags for the campaign;
compare IV.4.37 and end of note to
IV.6.37.

70 *hound of Crete* (species of shaggy dog,
like 'Iceland dog', II.1.39)

72 *powdering tub* (properly) vat for salting

meat; (colloquially) sweating tub
used in treating venereal disease

73 *lazar kite of Cressid's kind* leprous
whore. In Henryson's *Testament of
Cresseid* (written late fifteenth century; printed 1532) the God of Love
strikes the faithless Cressida with leprosy; 'kites of Cressid's kind' was a
proverbial phrase, kites being birds
of prey. In 2 *Henry IV* Doll is haled
off to prison for brothel-violence
with Pistol.

I have, and I will hold, the quondam Quickly
For the only she; and – *pauca*, there's enough.
Go to!
　　　Enter the Boy

BOY　Mine host Pistol, you must come to my master – and
　you, Hostess: he is very sick, and would to bed. Good
80　Bardolph, put thy face between his sheets, and do the
　office of a warming-pan. Faith, he's very ill.

BARDOLPH　Away, you rogue!

HOSTESS　By my troth, he'll yield the crow a pudding one
　of these days; the King has killed his heart. Good
　husband, come home presently.　　　*Exit with Boy*

BARDOLPH　Come, shall I make you two friends? We must
　to France together: why the devil should we keep knives
　to cut one another's throats?

PISTOL
　Let floods o'erswell, and fiends for food howl on!

90　NYM　You'll pay me the eight shillings I won of you at
　betting?

PISTOL
　Base is the slave that pays!

NYM　That now I will have; that's the humour of it.

PISTOL
　As manhood shall compound. Push home!
　　　They draw

BARDOLPH　By this sword, he that makes the first thrust,
　I'll kill him! By this sword, I will.

PISTOL
　Sword is an oath, and oaths must have their course.

76　*pauca* in few words
77　(stage direction) *Enter the Boy*. The
　Boy is Falstaff's page, given him by
　Prince Hal in *2 Henry IV* (1.2.15).
81　*warming-pan*. Bardolph's red nose is
　the subject of repeated jests in *Henry
　IV* and *Henry V*.
83　*yield the crow a pudding* die (a prover-
　bial phrase, originally applied to a

dead animal whose flesh the crows
would peck; *pudding* = stuffed guts, as
in 'black pudding')
85　*presently* at once
92　*Base is the slave that pays*! The phrase
　was proverbial.
94　*As manhood shall compound* in the way
　a brave man settles such differences

He sheathes his sword

BARDOLPH Corporal Nym, an thou wilt be friends, be
friends: an thou wilt not, why then be enemies with me
too. Prithee put up.   100

NYM I shall have my eight shillings I won of you at betting?

PISTOL

A noble shalt thou have, and present pay;
And liquor likewise will I give to thee,
And friendship shall combine, and brotherhood.
I'll live by Nym, and Nym shall live by me.
Is not this just? For I shall sutler be
Unto the camp, and profits will accrue.
Give me thy hand.

     Nym sheathes his sword

NYM I shall have my noble?

PISTOL

In cash most justly paid.   110

NYM Well then, that's the humour of't.

     Enter Hostess

HOSTESS As ever you came of women, come in quickly
to Sir John. Ah, poor heart! he is so shaked of a burning
quotidian tertian that it is most lamentable to behold.
Sweet men, come to him.

NYM The King hath run bad humours on the knight, that's
the even of it.

PISTOL

Nym, thou hast spoke the right;
His heart is fracted and corroborate.

NYM The King is a good king, but it must be as it may: he   120

---

101 *I shall have my eight shillings I won of
you at betting?* This is not in the Folio
but editors supply it from the Quarto
as necessary to Pistol's reply.

102 *noble* coin worth 6s. 8d. (less than
Pistol owes, but with the advantage
of 'present pay')

106 *sutler* provision-seller. Pistol does
not in fact figure in this lucrative role.

114 *quotidian tertian.* This is typical Hostess's confusion; a quotidian ague
caused a fit daily, a tertian every
third day.

116 *run bad humours on* upset by his
displeasure

117 *even* plain truth

119 *corroborate* (strictly, strengthened,
but Pistolian for) broken

passes some humours and careers.

PISTOL

Let us condole the knight; for, lambkins, we will live.

Exeunt

II.2   *Enter Exeter, Bedford, and Westmorland*

BEDFORD

Fore God, his grace is bold to trust these traitors.

EXETER

They shall be apprehended by and by.

WESTMORLAND

How smooth and even they do bear themselves!
As if allegiance in their bosoms sat,
Crownèd with faith and constant loyalty.

BEDFORD

The King hath note of all that they intend,
By interception which they dream not of.

EXETER

Nay, but the man that was his bedfellow,
Whom he hath dulled and cloyed with gracious
          favours –

10   That he should, for a foreign purse, so sell
His sovereign's life to death and treachery!

Sound trumpets. Enter the King, Scroop, Cambridge,
Grey, and attendants

KING HENRY

Now sits the wind fair, and we will aboard.
My Lord of Cambridge, and my kind Lord of
          Masham,
And you, my gentle knight, give me your thoughts.
Think you not that the powers we bear with us
Will cut their passage through the force of France,

---

121 *passes some humours and careers* lets
himself go when he feels like it. To
'pass the career' in horsemanship was
to do a short gallop at full stretch.

II.2.4–5 *As if allegiance in their bosoms sat,*
| Crownèd with faith and constant
loyalty as if fealty ruled their natures
under the crown of faith and loyalty

Doing the execution and the act
For which we have in head assembled them?

SCROOP

No doubt, my liege, if each man do his best.

KING HENRY

I doubt not that, since we are well persuaded   20
We carry not a heart with us from hence
That grows not in a fair consent with ours,
Nor leave not one behind that doth not wish
Success and conquest to attend on us.

CAMBRIDGE

Never was monarch better feared and loved
Than is your majesty. There's not, I think, a subject
That sits in heart-grief and uneasiness
Under the sweet shade of your government.

GREY

True: those that were your father's enemies
Have steeped their galls in honey, and do serve you   30
With hearts create of duty and of zeal.

KING HENRY

We therefore have great cause of thankfulness,
And shall forget the office of our hand
Sooner than quittance of desert and merit
According to the weight and worthiness.

SCROOP

So service shall with steelèd sinews toil,
And labour shall refresh itself with hope
To do your grace incessant services.

KING HENRY

We judge no less. Uncle of Exeter,
Enlarge the man committed yesterday   40
That railed against our person. We consider
It was excess of wine that set him on,
And on his more advice we pardon him.

---

18 *in head* as an armed force
34 *quittance* due recompense
40 *Enlarge* set at liberty
43 *his more advice* his thinking better of it

SCROOP

That's mercy, but too much security.
Let him be punished, sovereign, lest example
Breed, by his sufferance, more of such a kind.

KING HENRY

O, let us yet be merciful.

CAMBRIDGE

So may your highness, and yet punish too.

GREY

Sir,

50   You show great mercy if you give him life
After the taste of much correction.

KING HENRY

Alas, your too much love and care of me
Are heavy orisons 'gainst this poor wretch!
If little faults, proceeding on distemper,
Shall not be winked at, how shall we stretch our eye
When capital crimes, chewed, swallowed, and digested,
Appear before us? We'll yet enlarge that man,
Though Cambridge, Scroop, and Grey, in their dear
            care
And tender preservation of our person
60   Would have him punished. And now to our French
            causes:
Who are the late commissioners?

CAMBRIDGE

I one, my lord.
Your highness bade me ask for it today.

SCROOP

So did you me, my liege.

GREY

And I, my royal sovereign.

---

44 *security* confidence
53 *orisons* pleas
54 *on distemper* from a disordered condition (the 'temper' being the proper
   balance of the disposition)

61 *late commissioners* persons lately appointed to the commission to act for
   the King during his absence. This
   handing out of supposed 'commis-
   sions' does not occur in the sources.

KING HENRY
    Then, Richard Earl of Cambridge, there is yours;
    There yours, Lord Scroop of Masham; and, sir knight,
    Grey of Northumberland, this same is yours.
    Read them, and know I know your worthiness.
    My Lord of Westmorland, and uncle Exeter,   70
    We will aboard tonight. – Why, how now, gentlemen?
    What see you in those papers, that you lose
    So much complexion? Look ye, how they change!
    Their cheeks are paper. – Why, what read you there
    That have so cowarded and chased your blood
    Out of appearance?
CAMBRIDGE   I do confess my fault,
    And do submit me to your highness' mercy.
GREY, SCROOP
    To which we all appeal.
KING HENRY
    The mercy that was quick in us but late
    By your own counsel is suppressed and killed.   80
    You must not dare, for shame, to talk of mercy,
    For your own reasons turn into your bosoms
    As dogs upon their masters, worrying you.
    See you, my Princes, and my noble peers,
    These English monsters! My Lord of Cambridge here –
    You know how apt our love was to accord
    To furnish him with all appertinents
    Belonging to his honour; and this man
    Hath, for a few light crowns, lightly conspired,
    And sworn unto the practices of France,   90
    To kill us here in Hampton: to the which
    This knight, no less for bounty bound to us

79 *quick* alive
85 *English monsters*. The conspirators'
treachery is the more 'monstrous' in
that they are *English*; 'monsters' (mon-
strosities) were commonly shown as
exotic marvels.
87 *appertinents* things appertaining
90 *practices* plots

Than Cambridge is, hath likewise sworn. But O,
What shall I say to thee, Lord Scroop, thou cruel,
Ingrateful, savage, and inhuman creature?
Thou that didst bear the key of all my counsels,
That knew'st the very bottom of my soul,
That almost mightst have coined me into gold,
Wouldst thou have practised on me, for thy use?
100 May it be possible that foreign hire
Could out of thee extract one spark of evil
That might annoy my finger? 'Tis so strange
That, though the truth of it stands off as gross
As black and white, my eye will scarcely see it.
Treason and murder ever kept together,
As two yoke-devils sworn to either's purpose,
Working so grossly in a natural cause
That admiration did not whoop at them.
But thou, 'gainst all proportion, didst bring in
110 Wonder to wait on treason and on murder:
And whatsoever cunning fiend it was
That wrought upon thee so preposterously
Hath got the voice in hell for excellence.
All other devils that suggest by treasons
Do botch and bungle up damnation
With patches, colours, and with forms, being fetched
From glistering semblances of piety;
But he that tempered thee bade thee stand up,
Gave thee no instance why thou shouldst do treason,
120 Unless to dub thee with the name of traitor.

99 *practised on* plotted against
107 *so grossly in a natural cause* so glaringly
  for their natural ends
108 *That admiration did not whoop at them*
  that they caused no outcry of surprise
109 *proportion* natural order
110 *Wonder to wait on* astonishment to
  accompany
112 *so preposterously* in a manner so invert-
  ing the natural order
114 *suggest* instigate
115 *botch and bungle up damnation* clumsily
  disguise the damnable deeds they
  incite to
118 *tempered thee* wrought thee to his
  will

If that same demon that hath gulled thee thus
Should with his lion gait walk the whole world,
He might return to vasty Tartar back,
And tell the legions, 'I can never win
A soul so easy as that Englishman's.'
O, how hast thou with jealousy infected
The sweetness of affiance! Show men dutiful?
Why, so didst thou. Seem they grave and learnèd?
Why, so didst thou. Come they of noble family?
Why, so didst thou. Seem they religious?   130
Why, so didst thou. Or are they spare in diet,
Free from gross passion or of mirth or anger,
Constant in spirit, not swerving with the blood,
Garnished and decked in modest complement,
Not working with the eye without the ear,
And but in purgèd judgement trusting neither?
Such and so finely bolted didst thou seem:
And thus thy fall hath left a kind of blot
To mark the full-fraught man and best endued
With some suspicion. I will weep for thee;   140
For this revolt of thine, methinks, is like
Another fall of man. Their faults are open.
Arrest them to the answer of the law;
And God acquit them of their practices!
EXETER I arrest thee of high treason, by the name of
Richard Earl of Cambridge.
I arrest thee of high treason, by the name of Henry Lord
Scroop of Masham.
I arrest thee of high treason, by the name of Thomas
Grey, knight, of Northumberland.   150

---

122 *his lion gait* his devil's stride (an
echo of 1 Peter 5.8 – 'your adversary
the devil, as a roaring lion, walketh
about seeking whom he may de-
vour'.)
123 *vasty* wide and waste (the two senses
are combined)

Tartar Tartarus (the hell of classical
mythology)
126 *jealousy* suspicion
134 *complement* the qualities which make
the complete man
137 *bolted* sifted, refined

SCROOP

Our purposes God justly hath discovered,
And I repent my fault more than my death,
Which I beseech your highness to forgive,
Although my body pay the price of it.

CAMBRIDGE

For me, the gold of France did not seduce,
Although I did admit it as a motive
The sooner to effect what I intended.
But God be thankèd for prevention,
Which I in sufferance heartily will rejoice,
160   Beseeching God and you to pardon me.

GREY

Never did faithful subject more rejoice
At the discovery of most dangerous treason
Than I do at this hour joy o'er myself,
Prevented from a damnèd enterprise.
My fault, but not my body, pardon, sovereign.

KING HENRY

God quit you in His mercy! Hear your sentence.
You have conspired against our royal person,
Joined with an enemy proclaimed, and from his coffers
Received the golden earnest of our death;
170   Wherein you would have sold your King to slaughter,
His princes and his peers to servitude,
His subjects to oppression and contempt,
And his whole kingdom into desolation.
Touching our person seek we no revenge,

151–65 *Our purposes God justly hath discovered . . . pardon, sovereign.* The plotters
receive their sentences in a manner
which strengthens the nation's unity
under God.
155–7 *For me, the gold of France did not
seduce . . . what I intended.* Holinshed
attributes the plotters' treachery to
bribes received from the French

King but says further that Cambridge's motive was basically to seat
on the throne the legitimate claimant
Edmund Mortimer, Earl of March
(the Mortimer of *1 Henry IV* and *1
Henry VI*), who was expected to die
and be succeeded by Cambridge's
heirs as next in line.
169 *earnest* part-payment in advance

But we our kingdom's safety must so tender,
Whose ruin you have sought, that to her laws
We do deliver you. Get you therefore hence,
Poor miserable wretches, to your death;
The taste whereof God of His mercy give
You patience to endure, and true repentance   180
Of all your dear offences. Bear them hence.
    Exeunt Cambridge, Scroop, and Grey, guarded
Now, lords, for France; the enterprise whereof
Shall be to you, as us, like glorious.
We doubt not of a fair and lucky war,
Since God so graciously hath brought to light
This dangerous treason lurking in our way
To hinder our beginnings. We doubt not now
But every rub is smoothèd on our way.
Then forth, dear countrymen! Let us deliver
Our puissance into the hand of God,   190
Putting it straight in expedition.
Cheerly to sea! The signs of war advance!
No King of England if not King of France!
       Flourish. Exeunt

   Enter Pistol, Hostess, Nym, Bardolph, and Boy II.3
HOSTESS Prithee, honey-sweet husband, let me bring thee
  to Staines.
PISTOL
 No, for my manly heart doth earn.
 Bardolph, be blithe! Nym, rouse thy vaunting veins!
 Boy, bristle thy courage up! For Falstaff, he is dead,
 And we must earn therefor.

175 *tender* tend, watch over	191 *expedition* speedy motion
181 *dear* dire	192 *signs* banners
183 *like* equally	
184 *lucky* fortunate	II.3.3 *earn* yearn, grieve
188 *rub* impediment	

BARDOLPH Would I were with him, wheresome'er he is, either in heaven or in hell!

HOSTESS Nay, sure, he's not in hell: he's in Arthur's bosom, if ever man went to Arthur's bosom. 'A made a finer end, and went away an it had been any christom child; 'a parted e'en just between twelve and one, e'en at the turning o'th'tide; for after I saw him fumble with the sheets, and play with flowers, and smile upon his fingers' ends, I knew there was but one way; for his nose was as sharp as a pen, and 'a babbled of green fields. 'How now, Sir John?' quoth I, 'What, man, be o'good cheer!' So 'a cried out, 'God, God, God!' three or four times. Now I, to comfort him, bid him 'a should not think of God — I hoped there was no need to trouble himself with any such thoughts yet. So 'a bade me lay more clothes on his feet; I put my hand into the bed, and felt them, and they were as cold as any stone;

9 *Arthur's* Abraham's (compare Luke 16.22 — 'the beggar died, and was carried by the angels into Abraham's bosom'). The Hostess merges the biblical heaven with the Arthurian Isle of Avalon, whither her knightly patron has gone to join the company of the Round Table.

11 *a finer end* as fine an end as can be imagined (and certainly finer than going to hell)
an as if
christom newly christened (and so in perfect innocence). The Hostess amalgamates 'christen' and 'chrisom', a chrisom child being one dying within a month of birth, during which time it wore the white chrisom cloth put on it at its christening. Bunyan's Mr Badman is reported to have 'died like a lamb, or, as they call it, like a chrisom-child'.

13 *turning o'th'tide*. There is an ancient and widespread belief that a man at the point of death will die as the flood tide turns to the ebb.

13–17 *for after I saw him fumble with the sheets ... fields*. Many writers from classical antiquity onwards list similar details as signs of approaching death. Dover Wilson cites Thomas Lupton, *A Thousand Notable Things* (1578), Book IX — 'If the forehead of the sick wax red, and his nose wax sharp, if he pull straws or the clothes of his bed, these are most certain tokens of death.'

16–17 *'a babbled of green fields*. This reading, originated by Theobald in his edition of 1733, for the Folio's 'a Table of greene fields' is perhaps the most famous of Shakespeare emendations. The Quarto reads 'talk of floures'.

then I felt to his knees, and so up'ard and up'ard, and
all was as cold as any stone.

NYM They say he cried out of sack.

HOSTESS Ay, that 'a did.

BARDOLPH And of women.

HOSTESS Nay, that 'a did not.

BOY Yes, that 'a did, and said they were devils incarnate.   30

HOSTESS 'A could never abide carnation, 'twas a colour
he never liked.

BOY 'A said once, the devil would have him about women.

HOSTESS 'A did in some sort, indeed, handle women; but
then he was rheumatic, and talked of the Whore of
Babylon.

BOY Do you not remember, 'a saw a flea stick upon Bardolph's nose, and 'a said it was a black soul burning in
hell?

BARDOLPH Well, the fuel is gone that maintained that   40
fire — that's all the riches I got in his service.

---

25 *as cold as any stone.* 'Such is the end of Falstaff, from whom Shakespeare had promised us in his epilogue to *Henry IV* that we should receive more merriment . . . But whether he could contrive no train of adventures suitable to his character, or could match him with no companions likely to quicken his humour, or could open no new vein of pleasantry, and was afraid to continue the same strain lest it should not find the same reception, he has here for ever discarded him, and made haste to dispatch him, perhaps for the same reason for which Addison killed Sir Roger, that no other hand might attempt to exhibit him. Let meaner authors learn from this example, that it is dangerous to sell the bear which is yet not hunted; to promise to the public what they have not written' (Johnson).

26 *of* against. Falstaff is making his 'finer end' by ruing his excesses.

35 *rheumatic.* This is a Quicklyism for lunatic, delirious; in *2 Henry IV* she calls Falstaff and Doll 'as rheumatic as two dry toasts' (II.4.54–5), though the 'rheumatic humour' was in fact cold and damp.

35–6 *Whore of Babylon* the Church of Rome (in Protestant interpretation of the scarlet woman of Revelation 17. 3–9, 'great Babylon, the mother of whoredom and abominations of the earth', drunken with the blood of the martyrs, and riding a seven-headed beast symbolizing seven mountains on which she sits). This no doubt put 'rheumatic' into the Hostess's mind, Rome being pronounced 'Room'.

41 *riches.* There is word-play on the normal sense and on 'rich' as red(-faced, -nosed); compare Lodge, *A*

NYM Shall we shog? The King will be gone from Southampton.

PISTOL

Come, let's away. My love, give me thy lips.
Look to my chattels and my movables.
Let senses rule. The word is 'Pitch and pay!'
Trust none;
For oaths are straws, men's faiths are wafer-cakes,
And Holdfast is the only dog, my duck.

50   Therefore, *Caveto* be thy counsellor.
Go, clear thy crystals. Yoke-fellows in arms,
Let us to France, like horse-leeches, my boys,
To suck, to suck, the very blood to suck!

BOY And that's but unwholesome food, they say.

PISTOL

Touch her soft mouth, and march.

BARDOLPH Farewell, Hostess.

        He kisses her

NYM I cannot kiss, that is the humour of it; but adieu.

PISTOL

Let housewifery appear. Keep close, I thee command.

HOSTESS Farewell! Adieu!   *Exeunt*

Looking Glasse for London – 'you and
I have been tossing many a good
cup of ale, your nose is grown very
rich.'

42 *shog* be off

46 *Let senses rule* keep your wits about
you
Pitch and pay pay as you go, cash
down, no credit (a proverbial
phrase)

48 *wafer-cakes* (flimsy as) thin pastry

49 *Holdfast is the only dog.* This echoes

the proverb, 'Brag is a good dog,
but Holdfast is a better.'

50 *Caveto* beware

54 *And that's but unwholesome food.* Compare Andrew Boorde, *Dyetary of
Helth* (1542) – 'The blood of all
beasts and fowls is not praised, for it
is hard of digestion.'

58 *housewifery* careful housekeeping

59 *Farewell! Adieu!* This is the last we
see of the Eastcheap company in its
familiar haunts.

Flourish. Enter the French King, the Dauphin, the
Dukes of Berri and Britaine, the Constable and others   II.4

FRENCH KING
Thus comes the English with full power upon us,
And more than carefully it us concerns
To answer royally in our defences.
Therefore the Dukes of Berri and of Britaine,
Of Brabant and of Orleans, shall make forth,
And you, Prince Dauphin, with all swift dispatch,
To line and new repair our towns of war
With men of courage and with means defendant;
For England his approaches makes as fierce
As waters to the sucking of a gulf.   10
It fits us then to be as provident
As fear may teach us, out of late examples
Left by the fatal and neglected English
Upon our fields.
DAUPHIN   My most redoubted father,
It is most meet we arm us 'gainst the foe;
For peace itself should not so dull a kingdom,
Though war nor no known quarrel were in question,
But that defences, musters, preparations,
Should be maintained, assembled, and collected,
As were a war in expectation.   20
Therefore, I say, 'tis meet we all go forth
To view the sick and feeble parts of France:
And let us do it with no show of fear –
No, with no more than if we heard that England
Were busied with a Whitsun morris-dance;

II.4 (stage direction) *Britaine* Brittany,
Bretagne. Shakespeare's spelling indicates the required pronunciation (in
line 4, for instance).
7 *line* strengthen
10 *gulf* whirlpool (compare IV.3.82)
13 *fatal and neglected* fatally underrated
25 *Whitsun morris-dance.* Morris-dances

were held at Whitsuntide or on 1
May as spring festivities, by performers with blackened faces and bell-
hung costumes. The name refers to
their supposed Moorish origin,
though the characters presented persons in the Robin Hood and other
medieval stories.

For, my good liege, she is so idly kinged,
Her sceptre so fantastically borne
By a vain, giddy, shallow, humorous youth,
That fear attends her not.

CONSTABLE   O, peace, Prince Dauphin!
30   You are too much mistaken in this King.
Question your grace the late ambassadors,
With what great state he heard their embassy,
How well supplied with noble counsellors,
How modest in exception, and withal
How terrible in constant resolution,
And you shall find his vanities forespent
Were but the outside of the Roman Brutus,
Covering discretion with a coat of folly;
As gardeners do with ordure hide those roots
40   That shall first spring and be most delicate.

DAUPHIN
Well, 'tis not so, my Lord High Constable;
But though we think it so, it is no matter.
In cases of defence, 'tis best to weigh
The enemy more mighty than he seems.
So the proportions of defence are filled;
Which of a weak and niggardly projection
Doth like a miser spoil his coat with scanting
A little cloth.

FRENCH KING Think we King Harry strong;
And, Princes, look you strongly arm to meet him.
50   The kindred of him hath been fleshed upon us,

28 *humorous* capricious
34 *modest in exception* reasonable in rais-
    ing objections
36 *forespent* formerly indulged
37 *Brutus*. Lucius Junius Brutus feigned
    stupidity (*brutus* = stupid) as a safe-
    guard while planning to expel the
    tyrannous Tarquinius Superbus, last
    King of Rome; he became one of the
first consuls, in 509 BC.
40 *delicate* fine (in quality) and sensitive
45 *So the proportions of defence are filled*
    thus the necessary defensive forces
    are fully provided
46 *of a weak and niggardly projection* if
    planned too scantily
50 *fleshed* inured to carnage

And he is bred out of that bloody strain
That haunted us in our familiar paths.
Witness our too much memorable shame
When Crécy battle fatally was struck,
And all our princes captived by the hand
Of that black name, Edward, Black Prince of Wales;
Whiles that his mountain sire, on mountain standing,
Up in the air, crowned with the golden sun,
Saw his heroical seed, and smiled to see him,
Mangle the work of nature, and deface   60
The patterns that by God and by French fathers
Had twenty years been made. This is a stem
Of that victorious stock; and let us fear
The native mightiness and fate of him.
        Enter a Messenger

MESSENGER
Ambassadors from Harry King of England
Do crave admittance to your majesty.

FRENCH KING
We'll give them present audience. Go and bring them.
                Exeunt Messenger and certain lords
You see this chase is hotly followed, friends.

DAUPHIN
Turn head, and stop pursuit, for coward dogs
Most spend their mouths when what they seem to   70
        threaten
Runs far before them. Good my sovereign,
Take up the English short, and let them know
Of what a monarchy you are the head.

---

54 *Crécy battle*. Of Henry's campaign Holinshed writes, 'At length the King
approached the river Seine, and . . .
came . . . where his great-grandfather
King Edward the Third a little
before had stricken the battle of
Crécy.' Crécy was fought in 1346.

57 *mountain sire*. 'Mountain' may be an

error by attraction from 'mountain
standing'. If correct, it presumably
means 'of more than human stature'.
on mountain standing. Compare 1.2.108,
note.

69 *Turn head* stand at bay (a hunting
term)

Self-love, my liege, is not so vile a sin
As self-neglecting.

Enter lords, with Exeter and train

FRENCH KING   From our brother of England?

EXETER

From him; and thus he greets your majesty:
He wills you, in the name of God Almighty,
That you divest yourself, and lay apart
The borrowed glories that by gift of heaven,
By law of nature and of nations, 'longs
To him and to his heirs — namely, the crown,
And all wide-stretchèd honours that pertain
By custom and the ordinance of times
Unto the crown of France. That you may know
'Tis no sinister nor no awkward claim
Picked from the worm-holes of long-vanished days,
Nor from the dust of old oblivion raked,
He sends you this most memorable line,
In every branch truly demonstrative,
Willing you overlook this pedigree;
And when you find him evenly derived
From his most famed of famous ancestors,
Edward the Third, he bids you then resign
Your crown and kingdom, indirectly held
From him, the native and true challenger.

FRENCH KING

Or else what follows?

EXETER

Bloody constraint; for if you hide the crown
Even in your hearts, there will he rake for it.
Therefore in fierce tempest is he coming,

77–95 *He wills you, in the name of God Almighty . . . true challenger.* Exeter is to be taken as voicing not a propagandist manifesto but a God-approved claim.

83 *ordinance of times* time-honoured usage

85 *sinister* illegitimate (associated with the 'bar sinister' of irregular descent)
    awkward perverse

90 *overlook* look over

99 *fierce* (two syllables)

In thunder and in earthquake, like a Jove,   100
That, if requiring fail, he will compel;
And bids you, in the bowels of the Lord,
Deliver up the crown, and to take mercy
On the poor souls for whom this hungry war
Opens his vasty jaws; and on your head
Turning the widows' tears, the orphans' cries,
The dead men's blood, the privèd maidens' groans,
For husbands, fathers, and betrothèd lovers
That shall be swallowed in this controversy.
This is his claim, his threatening, and my message –   110
Unless the Dauphin be in presence here,
To whom expressly I bring greeting too.

FRENCH KING

For us, we will consider of this further.
Tomorrow shall you bear our full intent
Back to our brother of England.

DAUPHIN   For the Dauphin,
I stand here for him. What to him from England?

EXETER

Scorn and defiance, slight regard, contempt,
And anything that may not misbecome
The mighty sender, doth he prize you at.
Thus says my King: an if your father's highness   120
Do not, in grant of all demands at large,
Sweeten the bitter mock you sent his majesty,
He'll call you to so hot an answer of it
That caves and womby vaultages of France
Shall chide your trespass, and return your mock

---

100 *Jove*. The Greek Zeus, Roman Jupiter or Jove, was lord of the heavens,
ruler of gods and men. His weapon
was the thunderbolt.
101 *requiring* demanding
102 *in the bowels of the Lord*. The phrase
originates in Philippians 1.8, but here
echoes Holinshed – '[Henry] ex-

horted the French King in the
bowels of Jesu Christ, to render him
that which was his own, whereby
effusion of Christian blood might be
avoided.'
107 *privèd* bereaved
124 *womby vaultages* hollow recesses

In second accent of his ordinance.

DAUPHIN
Say, if my father render fair return,
It is against my will, for I desire
Nothing but odds with England. To that end,
130   As matching to his youth and vanity,
I did present him with the Paris balls.

EXETER
He'll make your Paris Louvre shake for it,
Were it the mistress court of mighty Europe:
And, be assured, you'll find a difference,
As we his subjects have in wonder found,
Between the promise of his greener days
And these he masters now. Now he weighs time
Even to the utmost grain; that you shall read
In your own losses, if he stay in France.

FRENCH KING
140   Tomorrow shall you know our mind at full.
           Flourish

EXETER
Dispatch us with all speed, lest that our King
Come here himself to question our delay,
For he is footed in this land already.

FRENCH KING
You shall be soon dispatched with fair conditions.
A night is but small breath and little pause
To answer matters of this consequence.   *Exeunt*

---

126 *second accent* echo
   ordinance ordnance, cannon
131 *Paris balls* tennis-balls (so called because the game came to England
   from the French capital)
132 *Louvre*. The spelling 'Louer' (that

is, Lover) in the Quarto and Folio
suggests a pronunciation quibbling
on 'mistress court' in line 133.
136 *greener* less mature
140 (stage direction) *Flourish*. This is to
mark the King's rising.

Flourish. Enter Chorus   III

CHORUS

Thus with imagined wing our swift scene flies
In motion of no less celerity
Than that of thought. Suppose that you have seen
The well-appointed King at Hampton pier
Embark his royalty, and his brave fleet
With silken streamers the young Phoebus fanning.
Play with your fancies, and in them behold
Upon the hempen tackle ship-boys climbing;
Hear the shrill whistle which doth order give
To sounds confused; behold the threaden sails,   10
Borne with th'invisible and creeping wind,
Draw the huge bottoms through the furrowed sea,
Breasting the lofty surge. O, do but think
You stand upon the rivage and behold
A city on th'inconstant billows dancing;
For so appears this fleet majestical,
Holding due course to Harfleur. Follow, follow!
Grapple your minds to sternage of this navy,
And leave your England, as dead midnight still,
Guarded with grandsires, babies, and old women,   20
Either past or not arrived to pith and puissance.
For who is he whose chin is but enriched
With one appearing hair that will not follow
These culled and choice-drawn cavaliers to France?
Work, work your thoughts, and therein see a siege:
Behold the ordnance on their carriages,
With fatal mouths gaping on girded Harfleur.
Suppose th'ambassador from the French comes back;

III. *Chorus* 1 *imagined wing* wing of ima-
    gination
5 *brave* gaily decked
6 *the young Phoebus fanning* fluttering
    against the early-morning sun
12 *bottoms* hulls
17 *Harfleur* (accented on the first syllable

throughout; spelt 'Harflew(e)' in the
Folio)
18 *Grapple your minds to sternage of this
navy* let your thoughts seize the sterns
of these ships (and be drawn to
France)

Tells Harry that the King doth offer him
30   Katherine his daughter, and with her. to dowry,
Some petty and unprofitable dukedoms.
The offer likes not; and the nimble gunner
With linstock now the devilish cannon touches,

> *Alarum, and chambers go off*

And down goes all before them. Still be kind,
And eke out our performance with your mind.   *Exit*

> *Alarum. Enter the King, Exeter, Bedford, Gloucester,*
III.1   *other lords, and soldiers with scaling-ladders*

KING HENRY

Once more unto the breach, dear friends, once more,
Or close the wall up with our English dead!
In peace there's nothing so becomes a man
As modest stillness and humility:
But when the blast of war blows in our ears,
Then imitate the action of the tiger;
Stiffen the sinews, conjure up the blood,
Disguise fair nature with hard-favoured rage;
Then lend the eye a terrible aspect;
10   Let it pry through the portage of the head
Like the brass cannon; let the brow o'erwhelm it
As fearfully as doth a gallèd rock
O'erhang and jutty his confounded base,
Swilled with the wild and wasteful ocean.
Now set the teeth, and stretch the nostril wide,

---

32 *likes* pleases
33 *linstock* ignited stick (the staff holding
    the gunner's lighted match)
(stage direction) *chambers* small cannon
    (for giving salutes, or for theatre use)

III.1.7 *conjure.* Almost all editions follow
    Rowe's 'summon' (for the Folio's

'commune'), but, as the new Arden
edition argues, 'conjure' is graphically closer and quite as appropriate.
8 *hard-favoured* hard-featured
10 *portage* port-holes, embrasures
12 *gallèd* fretted (by the sea)
13 *jutty his confounded base* beetle over its
    ruined base

Hold hard the breath, and bend up every spirit
To his full height! On, on, you noblest English,
Whose blood is fet from fathers of war-proof! –
Fathers that, like so many Alexanders,
Have in these parts from morn till even fought,   20
And sheathed their swords for lack of argument.
Dishonour not your mothers; now attest
That those whom you called fathers did beget you!
Be copy now to men of grosser blood,
And teach them how to war. And you, good yeomen,
Whose limbs were made in England, show us here
The mettle of your pasture; let us swear
That you are worth your breeding – which I doubt not;
For there is none of you so mean and base
That hath not noble lustre in your eyes.   30
I see you stand like greyhounds in the slips,
Straining upon the start. The game's afoot!
Follow your spirit, and upon this charge
Cry, 'God for Harry, England, and Saint George!'

Exeunt. Alarum, and chambers go off

Enter Nym, Bardolph, Pistol, and Boy   III.2

BARDOLPH On, on, on, on, on! To the breach, to the
breach!

NYM Pray thee, Corporal, stay – the knocks are too hot,
and, for mine own part, I have not a case of lives. The

---

18 *fet* fetched, derived
   of war-proof tested in war
21 *argument* further opposition
27 *mettle of your pasture* quality of your
   nurture
31 *slips* leashes (for restraining dogs
   before releasing them)

III.2.3 *Pray thee, Corporal, stay.* It is amusing to have Nym's antiheroics imme-

diately after Henry's valiant rant, but
too much should not be made of
them as ironic deflation: cowardly
camp-followers out for loot are part
of war but are not authorities on its
values. The play demands heroism
even though it admits the reasonable
case against heroics which the soldiers present in IV.1.
4 *case* set

humour of it is too hot, that is the very plainsong of it.

PISTOL

>The plainsong is most just; for humours do abound.
>Knocks go and come; God's vassals drop and die;
>>>And sword and shield,
>>>>In bloody field,
>>>>>Doth win immortal fame.

BOY Would I were in an alehouse in London! I would give all my fame for a pot of ale, and safety.

PISTOL And I:

>>>If wishes would prevail with me,
>>>My purpose should not fail with me,
>>>>But thither would I hie.

BOY

>>>As duly,
>>>>But not as truly,
>>>As bird doth sing on bough.

Enter Fluellen

FLUELLEN Up to the breach, you dogs! Avaunt, you cullions!

He drives them forward

PISTOL

>Be merciful, great Duke, to men of mould!
>Abate thy rage, abate thy manly rage,
>Abate thy rage, great Duke!
>Good bawcock, bate thy rage! Use lenity, sweet chuck!

NYM These be good humours! Your honour wins bad humours.   *Exeunt all but the Boy*

BOY As young as I am, I have observed these three swashers. I am boy to them all three, but all they three, though they would serve me, could not be man to me;

5 *humour of it* way it's going
very plainsong simple truth (tune un-
adorned by harmonies)
6 *humours* bad humours, rages
21 *cullions* rascals
22 *mould* mortal clay
25 *bawcock* fine fellow (French, 'beau

coq')
26 *These be good humours*! This is a fine
way to carry on!
26–7 *wins bad humours* makes everyone
angry
29 *swashers* blusterers, swashbucklers

for indeed three such antics do not amount to a man. For Bardolph, he is white-livered and red-faced; by the means whereof 'a faces it out, but fights not. For Pistol, he hath a killing tongue, and a quiet sword; by the means whereof 'a breaks words, and keeps whole weapons. For Nym, he hath heard that men of few words are the best men; and therefore he scorns to say his prayers, lest 'a should be thought a coward; but his few bad words are matched with as few good deeds, for 'a never broke any man's head but his own, and that   40 was against a post, when he was drunk. They will steal anything, and call it purchase. Bardolph stole a lute-case, bore it twelve leagues, and sold it for three half-pence. Nym and Bardolph are sworn brothers in filching, and in Calais they stole a fire-shovel – I knew by that piece of service the men would carry coals. They would have me as familiar with men's pockets as their gloves or their handkerchers: which makes much against my manhood, if I should take from another's pocket to put into mine; for it is plain pocketing up of wrongs. I   50 must leave them, and seek some better service. Their villainy goes against my weak stomach, and therefore I must cast it up.   *Exit*

    Enter Fluellen, Gower following

GOWER Captain Fluellen, you must come presently to the mines. The Duke of Gloucester would speak with you.

FLUELLEN To the mines? Tell you the Duke, it is not so good to come to the mines, for, look you, the mines is not according to the disciplines of the war. The con-cavities of it is not sufficient; for, look you, th'athversary,

---

31 *antics* buffoons
35 *breaks words* (1) bandies words (not blows); (2) breaks his word
36–7 *men of few words are the best men*. 'Few words are best' was proverbial.
42 *purchase* booty
46 *carry coals* (1) do any dirty work; (2)

put up with insults (a proverbial phrase)
50 *pocketing up of wrongs*. This quibbles on the usual sense, 'putting up with insults'.
53 *cast it up*. This is a quibble.
58 *disciplines of the war* military science

60   you may discuss unto the Duke, look you, is digt him-
     self four yard under the countermines. By Cheshu, I
     think 'a will plow up all, if there is not better directions.

GOWER The Duke of Gloucester, to whom the order of the
     siege is given, is altogether directed by an Irishman, a
     very valiant gentleman, i'faith.

FLUELLEN It is Captain Macmorris, is it not?

GOWER I think it be.

FLUELLEN By Cheshu, he is an ass, as in the world; I
     will verify as much in his beard. He has no more
70   directions in the true disciplines of the wars, look you,
     of the Roman disciplines, than is a puppy-dog.

          Enter Captain Macmorris and Captain Jamy

GOWER Here 'a comes, and the Scots captain, Captain
     Jamy, with him.

FLUELLEN Captain Jamy is a marvellous falorous gentle-
     man, that is certain, and of great expedition and
     knowledge in th'aunchient wars, upon my particular
     knowledge of his directions. By Cheshu, he will maintain
     his argument as well as any military man in the world, in
     the disciplines of the pristine wars of the Romans.

80 JAMY I say gud-day, Captain Fluellen.

FLUELLEN Good-e'en to your worship, good Captain
     James.

GOWER How now, Captain Macmorris, have you quit the

60–61 *is digt himself four yard under the*
countermines. Fluellen presumably
means to say 'has dug himself countermines four yards under (our
mines)'.

62 *plow up all, if there is not better direc-*
tions. The Folio is inconsistent in its
indications of dialect ('plow',
'better'), which the actor will doubtless regularize.

70–71 *the true disciplines of the wars ...*
the Roman disciplines. For apparent

echoes of Thomas Digges's *An Arith-*
meticall Militare Treatise, named Strati-
oticos see the Introduction, p. 679.

71 (stage direction) *Enter Captain Mac-*
morris and Captain Jamy. The addition
of the Irishman and the Scot to the
Englishman and the Welshman sym-
bolizes the wide provenance of forces
under Henry's command.

75 *expedition* readiness (in argument)

81 *Good-e'en* good evening (but used any
time after noon)

mines? Have the pioneers given o'er?

MACMORRIS By Chrish, la, 'tish ill done! The work ish give over, the trompet sound the retreat. By my hand I swear, and my father's soul, the work ish ill done: it ish give over. I would have blowed up the town, so Chrish save me, la, in an hour. O, 'tish ill done, 'tish ill done – by my hand, 'tish ill done!   90

FLUELLEN Captain Macmorris, I beseech you now, will you voutsafe me, look you, a few disputations with you, as partly touching or concerning the disciplines of the war, the Roman wars, in the way of argument, look you, and friendly communication? – partly to satisfy my opinion, and partly for the satisfaction, look you, of my mind – as touching the direction of the military discipline, that is the point.

JAMY It sall be vary gud, gud feith, gud captens bath, and I sall quit you with gud leve, as I may pick occasion: that   100 sall I, marry.

MACMORRIS It is no time to discourse, so Chrish save me! The day is hot, and the weather, and the wars, and the King, and the Dukes – it is no time to discourse, the town is beseeched, and the trumpet call us to the breach, and we talk, and, be Chrish, do nothing; 'tis shame for us all: so God sa' me, 'tis shame to stand still, it is shame, by my hand – and there is throats to be cut, and works to be done, and there ish nothing done, so Chrish sa' me, la!

JAMY By the mess, ere theise eyes of mine take them-   110 selves to slomber, ay'll de gud service, or ay'll lig i'th'grund for it, ay, or go to death! And ay'll pay't as valorously as I may, that sall I suerly do, that is the breff and the long. Marry, I wad full fain hear some question 'tween you tway.

FLUELLEN Captain Macmorris, I think, look you, under your correction, there is not many of your nation –

MACMORRIS Of my nation? What ish my nation? Ish a
villain, and a bastard, and a knave, and a rascal. What
120   ish my nation? Who talks of my nation?

FLUELLEN Look you, if you take the matter otherwise
than is meant, Captain Macmorris, peradventure I shall
think you do not use me with that affability as in discretion you ought to use me, look you, being as good a
man as yourself, both in the disciplines of war, and in
the derivation of my birth, and in other particularities.

MACMORRIS I do not know you so good a man as myself.
So Chrish save me, I will cut off your head.

GOWER Gentlemen both, you will mistake each other.

130   JAMY Ah, that's a foul fault!

A parley is sounded

GOWER The town sounds a parley.

FLUELLEN Captain Macmorris, when there is more
better opportunity to be required, look you, I will be
so bold as to tell you, I know the disciplines of war; and
there is an end.   *Exeunt*

III.3   *Some citizens of Harfleur appear on the walls. Enter*
the King and all his train before the gates

KING HENRY

How yet resolves the Governor of the town?
This is the latest parle we will admit:
Therefore to our best mercy give yourselves,

---

118 *Of my nation?* Macmorris may be so
inflammable that he catches fire
before he even understands what is
being said, or he may think that
Fluellen is accusing the Irish of being
present only in small numbers.

III.3.1–43 *How yet resolves the Governor . . .*
be thus destroyed? The modern reader
is not likely to applaud what looks
like Henry's unholy relish in so ruth-

lessly depicting war's horrors and
then blaming the proposed victims
for provoking them. But the play
takes him to be in the right and his
foes to be in the wrong, his army is
in peril, and as commander he must
shake his opponents' nerve; having
done so he shows mercy. The apparent sadism is only Shakespeare's
vividness in description.

Or, like to men proud of destruction,
Defy us to our worst; for, as I am a soldier,
A name that in my thoughts becomes me best,
If I begin the battery once again,
I will not leave the half-achievèd Harfleur
Till in her ashes she lie burièd.
The gates of mercy shall be all shut up,   10
And the fleshed soldier, rough and hard of heart,
In liberty of bloody hand shall range
With conscience wide as hell, mowing like grass
Your fresh fair virgins, and your flowering infants.
What is it then to me, if impious war,
Arrayed in flames, like to the prince of fiends,
Do, with his smirched complexion, all fell feats
Enlinked to waste and desolation?
What is't to me, when you yourselves are cause,
If your pure maidens fall into the hand   20
Of hot and forcing violation?
What rein can hold licentious wickedness
When down the hill he holds his fierce career?
We may as bootless spend our vain command
Upon th'enraged soldiers in their spoil
As send precepts to the leviathan
To come ashore. Therefore, you men of Harfleur,
Take pity of your town and of your people
Whiles yet my soldiers are in my command,
Whiles yet the cool and temperate wind of grace   30
O'erblows the filthy and contagious clouds
Of heady murder, spoil, and villainy.
If not, why, in a moment look to see
The blind and bloody soldier with foul hand
Defile the locks of your shrill-shrieking daughters;

---

4 *proud of destruction* elated with the prospect of death
24 *bootless* vainly
31 *O'erblows* blows away

contagious. Pestilence was supposed to
drop from the clouds – here the pestilence of hysterical cruelty dropping
from the clouds of war.

Your fathers taken by the silver beards,
And their most reverend heads dashed to the walls;
Your naked infants spitted upon pikes,
Whiles the mad mothers with their howls confused
Do break the clouds, as did the wives of Jewry
At Herod's bloody-hunting slaughtermen.
What say you? Will you yield, and this avoid?
Or, guilty in defence, be thus destroyed?

Enter the Governor on the wall

GOVERNOR
Our expectation hath this day an end.
The Dauphin, whom of succours we entreated,
Returns us that his powers are yet not ready
To raise so great a siege. Therefore, great King,
We yield our town and lives to thy soft mercy.
Enter our gates, dispose of us and ours,
For we no longer are defensible.

KING HENRY
Open your gates.   *Exit Governor*
              Come, uncle Exeter,
Go you and enter Harfleur; there remain,
And fortify it strongly 'gainst the French.
Use mercy to them all. For us, dear uncle,
The winter coming on, and sickness growing
Upon our soldiers, we will retire to Calais.
Tonight in Harfleur will we be your guest;
Tomorrow for the march are we addressed.

Flourish, and enter the town

40–41 *as did the wives of Jewry . . . slaughter-men.* Matthew 2.16–18 – 'Then Herod . . . sent forth, and slew all the children that were in Bethlehem . . . In Rama was there a voice heard, lamentation, weeping, and great mourning.'

43 *guilty in defence* guilty because defending yourselves in a wrongful cause.

54 *Use mercy to them all.* Shakespeare diverges markedly from Holinshed, who relates that even after the surrender 'the town [was] sacked, to the great gain of the Englishmen.'

55 *sickness growing.* 'The number of his people was much minished by the flix [flux] and other fevers' (Holinshed).

58 *addressed* prepared

Enter Katherine and Alice, an old gentlewoman III.4

KATHERINE Alice, tu as été en Angleterre, et tu parles bien le langage.

ALICE Un peu, madame.

KATHERINE Je te prie, m'enseignez – il faut que j'apprenne à parler. Comment appelez-vous la main en anglais?

ALICE La main? Elle est appelée de hand.

KATHERINE De hand. Et les doigts?

ALICE Les doigts? Ma foi, j'oublie les doigts, mais je me souviendrai. Les doigts? Je pense qu'ils sont appelés de fingres; oui, de fingres. 10

KATHERINE La main, de hand; les doigts, de fingres. Je pense que je suis le bon écolier; j'ai gagné deux mots d'anglais vitement. Comment appelez-vous les ongles?

ALICE Les ongles? Nous les appelons de nailès.

KATHERINE De nailès. Écoutez: dites-moi si je parle bien – de hand, de fingres, et de nailès.

ALICE C'est bien dit, madame. Il est fort bon anglais.

KATHERINE Dites-moi l'anglais pour le bras.

ALICE De arm, madame.

KATHERINE Et le coude? 20

ALICE D'elbow.

KATHERINE D'elbow. Je m'en fais la répétition de tous les mots que vous m'avez appris dès à présent.

ALICE Il est trop difficile, madame, comme je pense.

KATHERINE Excusez-moi, Alice; écoutez – d'hand, de fingre, de nailès, d'arma, de bilbow.

III.4.1–58 The French text in this edition has been regularized, but not fully corrected, in many details. The Folio version is, however, sufficiently comprehensible to suggest that the origi-

nal script was tolerably accurate.
14 *nailès*. The Folio spelling 'Nayles' throughout (save for line 41, 'Maylees') suggests disyllabic pronunciation.

ALICE D'elbow, madame.

KATHERINE O Seigneur Dieu, je m'en oublie! D'elbow.
Comment appelez-vous le col?

30 ALICE De nick, madame.

KATHERINE De nick. Et le menton?

ALICE De chin.

KATHERINE De sin. Le col, de nick; le menton, de sin.

ALICE Oui. Sauf votre honneur, en vérité, vous prononcez
les mots aussi droit que les natifs d'Angleterre.

KATHERINE Je ne doute point d'apprendre, par la grace
de Dieu, et en peu de temps.

ALICE N'avez-vous pas déjà oublié ce que je vous ai
enseigné?

40 KATHERINE Non, je réciterai à vous promptement:
d'hand,
de fingre, de mailès —

ALICE De nailès, madame.

KATHERINE De nailès, de arm, de ilbow —

ALICE Sauf votre honneur, d'elbow.

KATHERINE Ainsi dis-je: d'elbow, de nick, et de sin.
Comment appelez-vous le pied et la robe?

ALICE Le foot, madame, et le count.

KATHERINE Le foot, et le count? O Seigneur Dieu! Ils
sont mots de son mauvais, corruptible, gros, et impu-
50 dique, et non pour les dames d'honneur d'user. Je ne
voudrais prononcer ces mots devant les seigneurs de
France pour tout le monde. Foh! Le foot et le count!
Néanmoins, je réciterai une autre fois ma leçon en-
semble: d'hand, de fingre, de nailès, d'arm, d'elbow, de
nick, de sin, de foot, le count.

ALICE Excellent, madame!

KATHERINE C'est assez pour une fois. Allons-nous à
dîner.   *Exeunt*

---

47 *count* (pronounced, more or less,
'coont', as 'gown' was, more or less,
'goon')

49–50 *mots de son mauvais ... impudique.*

Katherine associates the words with
the vulgar French '*foutre*' (coition;
compare '*figo*' at III.6.56, note) and
'*con*' (female organ).

Enter the King of France, the Dauphin, the Duke of   III.5
Britaine, the Constable of France, and others

FRENCH KING

'Tis certain he hath passed the River Somme.

CONSTABLE

And if he be not fought withal, my lord,
Let us not live in France: let us quit all,
And give our vineyards to a barbarous people.

DAUPHIN

O Dieu vivant! Shall a few sprays of us,
The emptying of our fathers' luxury,
Our scions, put in wild and savage stock,
Spirt up so suddenly into the clouds,
And overlook their grafters?

BRITAINE

Normans, but bastard Normans, Norman bastards!   10
Mort Dieu! Ma vie! If they march along
Unfought withal, but I will sell my dukedom
To buy a slobbery and a dirty farm
In that nook-shotten isle of Albion.

CONSTABLE

Dieu de batailles! Where have they this mettle?
Is not their climate foggy, raw, and dull,
On whom, as in despite, the sun looks pale,

III.5.2 *withal* with
5 *sprays* (bastard) offshoots
6 *luxury* lust
9 *overlook their grafters* look down on those from whom they were transplanted
11 *Mort Dieu! Ma vie!* The Quarto reads 'Mordeu ma via' and the Folio 'Mort du ma vie', which many editors render as 'Mort de ma vie'. At IV.5.3 the Quarto has 'Mor du ma vie' and the

Folio 'Mor Dieu ma vie'. '*Vie*' here is a disyllable.
13 *slobbery* sloppy
14 *nook-shotten* 'having many sharp turns or angles' (Wright, *English Dialect Dictionary*), angular, crooked (with the figurative implication of 'angular', 'perverse', in temper as well as shape)
15 *batailles* (a trisyllable)
17 *as in despite* as if despising them

Killing their fruit with frowns? Can sodden water,
A drench for sur-reined jades, their barley broth,
Decoct their cold blood to such valiant heat?
And shall our quick blood, spirited with wine,
Seem frosty? O, for honour of our land,
Let us not hang like roping icicles
Upon our houses' thatch, whiles a more frosty people
Sweat drops of gallant youth in our rich fields! –
Lest poor we call them in their native lords.

DAUPHIN

By faith and honour,
Our madams mock at us, and plainly say
Our mettle is bred out, and they will give
Their bodies to the lust of English youth,
To new-store France with bastard warriors.

BRITAINE

They bid us to the English dancing-schools,
And teach lavoltas high and swift corantos,
Saying our grace is only in our heels,
And that we are most lofty runaways.

FRENCH KING

Where is Montjoy the Herald? Speed him hence,
Let him greet England with our sharp defiance.

18–20 *Can sodden water ... heat?* Can
their cold blood be so warmed up by
their barley-brew (ale), the stewed-up
liquor of the malt-and-water mash
they give their weary horses?
18 *sodden* boiled
19 *drench* drink
  sur-reined over-ridden. (For an *Edward
III* echo, see III.7.148 below, 'out of
beef', note.)
23 *roping* hanging rope-like
26 *Lest poor we*. The first Folio reads
'Poor we', which is defective; the
second Folio reads 'Poor we may',
which mends the metre but is unau-

thoritative and a jolt in sense. The
proposed reading maintains the train
of thought ('Let us not hang ...
Lest ...').
29 *bred out* exhausted by breeding
33 *lavoltas* dances with high capers
  corantos dances with quick running
steps
34–5 *grace ... heels ... lofty runaways*.
Quibbles abound; the sense is, 'The
only thing that distinguishes us is
our agility (in dancing, or in fleeing),
and we are lofty (high-born, or high-
leaping) performers in running
(corantos, or away from danger)'.

Up, Princes, and with spirit of honour edged,
More sharper than your swords, hie to the field!
Charles Delabreth, High Constable of France,   40
You Dukes of Orleans, Bourbon, and of Berri,
Alençon, Brabant, Bar, and Burgundy,
Jaques Chatillon, Rambures, Vaudemont,
Beaumont, Grandpré, Roussi, and Faulconbridge,
Foix, Lestrake, Bouciqualt, and Charolois,
High Dukes, great Princes, Barons, Lords, and Knights,
For your great seats, now quit you of great shames.
Bar Harry England, that sweeps through our land
With pennons painted in the blood of Harfleur!
Rush on his host, as doth the melted snow   50
Upon the valleys, whose low vassal seat
The Alps doth spit and void his rheum upon!
Go down upon him, you have power enough,
And in a captive chariot into Rouen
Bring him our prisoner.
CONSTABLE This becomes the great.
Sorry am I his numbers are so few,
His soldiers sick, and famished in their march;
For I am sure, when he shall see our army,
He'll drop his heart into the sink of fear,
And for achievement offer us his ransom.   60
FRENCH KING
Therefore, Lord Constable, haste on Montjoy,
And let him say to England that we send
To know what willing ransom he will give.

40–45 *Charles Delabreth High Constable
. . . and Charolois.* These names occur
in Holinshed's list of the French
lords captured or slain at Agincourt,
save for Berri and Charolois, who
take part in the council of war but
not in the battle. Holinshed spells
Burgundy 'Burgognie' (Folio 'Burgo-

nie'), Faulconbridge 'Fauconberge'
(earlier 'Fauconbridge'), and Foix
'Fois' (Folio 'Loys'); Lestrake (Holinshed) becomes 'Lestrale' in the Folio,
which most editors follow.

60 *for achievement* as his sole accomplishment, instead of victory

Prince Dauphin, you shall stay with us in Rouen.

DAUPHIN

Not so, I do beseech your majesty.

FRENCH KING

Be patient, for you shall remain with us.
Now forth, Lord Constable, and Princes all,
And quickly bring us word of England's fall. *Exeunt*

III.6 *Enter Captains, English and Welsh (Gower and Fluellen)*

GOWER How now, Captain Fluellen? Come you from
the bridge?

FLUELLEN I assure you, there is very excellent services
committed at the bridge.

GOWER Is the Duke of Exeter safe?

FLUELLEN The Duke of Exeter is as magnanimous as
Agamemnon, and a man that I love and honour with my
soul, and my heart, and my duty, and my live, and my
living, and my uttermost power. He is not – God be
10   praised and blessed! – any hurt in the world, but keeps

---

64 *Prince Dauphin, you shall stay with us in
Rouen.* Shakespeare here follows Holinshed, who reports that the French
King forbade the Dauphin to fight.
In III.7, IV.2, and IV.5, however, the
Dauphin is taking part, as he evidently was also in the *Henry V* play
mentioned by Nashe (see the Introduction, p. 670) and in the episode
Shakespeare had referred to when
Henry 'made the Dauphin and the
French to stoop' (*3 Henry VI*,
I.I.108). The idea may have originated in a later remark of Holinshed's, that the French mob who
pillaged the English camp would
have been punished 'if the Dauphin
had longer lived'.

III.6.1–2 *the bridge.* The keeping of the
bridge over the River Ternoise was
essential for the English march to
Calais. Holinshed records that
Henry, 'doubting [fearing] lest if the
same bridge should be broken it
would be greatly to his hindrance,
appointed certain captains, with their
bands, to go thither with all speed
before him, and to take possession
thereof, and to keep it, till his coming
thither. Those that were sent, finding
the Frenchmen busy to break down
the bridge, assailed them so vigorously that they discomfited them, and
took and slew them; and so the
bridge was preserved.'

6 *magnanimous* great-souled (the literal
sense)

the bridge most valiantly, with excellent discipline. There is an aunchient lieutenant there at the pridge, I think in my very conscience he is as valiant a man as Mark Antony, and he is a man of no estimation in the world, but I did see him do as gallant service.

GOWER What do you call him?

FLUELLEN He is called Aunchient Pistol.

GOWER I know him not.

Enter Pistol

FLUELLEN Here is the man.

PISTOL

Captain, I thee beseech to do me favours.   20
The Duke of Exeter doth love thee well.

FLUELLEN Ay, I praise God, and I have merited some love at his hands.

PISTOL

Bardolph, a soldier firm and sound of heart,
And of buxom valour, hath, by cruel fate,
And giddy Fortune's furious fickle wheel,
That goddess blind,
That stands upon the rolling restless stone –

FLUELLEN By your patience, Aunchient Pistol: Fortune is painted blind, with a muffler afore her eyes, to signify   30
to you that Fortune is blind; and she is painted also with a wheel, to signify to you, which is the moral of it, that she is turning, and inconstant, and mutability, and variation; and her foot, look you, is fixed upon a spherical stone, which rolls, and rolls, and rolls. In good truth, the poet makes a most excellent description of it: Fortune is an excellent moral.

---

12 *aunchient lieutenant*. Compare II.1.36, note.
25 *buxom* sturdy
26–8 *And giddy Fortune's furious fickle wheel . . . restless stone*. Pistol mixes up two traditional emblems of Fortune,

as the power turning the wheel on which men rise and fall, and as the blindfold figure balancing upon the rolling stone of change and chance.
37 *moral* allegorical figure

PISTOL

    Fortune is Bardolph's foe, and frowns on him;
    For he hath stolen a pax, and hangèd must 'a be –
40   A damnèd death!
    Let gallows gape for dog; let man go free,
    And let not hemp his windpipe suffocate.
    But Exeter hath given the doom of death
    For pax of little price.
    Therefore go speak – the Duke will hear thy voice;
    And let not Bardolph's vital thread be cut
    With edge of penny cord and vile reproach.
    Speak, Captain, for his life, and I will thee requite.

FLUELLEN Aunchient Pistol, I do partly understand your
50   meaning.

PISTOL

    Why then, rejoice therefor!

FLUELLEN Certainly, Aunchient, it is not a thing to
    rejoice at, for if, look you, he were my brother, I would
    desire the Duke to use his good pleasure, and put him to
    execution; for discipline ought to be used.

PISTOL

    Die and be damned! and *figo* for thy friendship.

---

38 *Fortune is Bardolph's foe, and frowns on him*. This echoes the familiar tag, 'Fortune's my foe', and the ballad line, 'Fortune, my foe! Why dost thou frown on me?'

39 *pax* little picture of the Crucifixion, kissed by communicants at Mass. Holinshed's word is 'pix', the box for the consecrated wafers at communion.

41 *Let gallows gape for dog*. Animals were sometimes hanged for misdemeanours; compare the phrase, 'Hangdog look', and Dekker's *Honest Whore*, Part One – 'Now you look like an old he-cat, going to the gallows'

(II.1.131–2).

42 *let not hemp his windpipe suffocate*. Holinshed relates that 'a soldier took a pix out of a church, for which he was apprehended, and the King not once removed till the box was restored, and the offender strangled.' In the play Henry does not thus personally insist on his old companion's execution, but the impersonal way in which he receives the news in line 104 marks the gulf which separates his old from his new life.

56 *figo* fig. The phrase has lost its original coarseness, by which it meant the rude gesture, supposedly Spanish in

FLUELLEN It is well.

PISTOL

The fig of Spain! *Exit*

FLUELLEN Very good.

GOWER Why, this is an arrant counterfeit rascal, I 60
remember him now – a bawd, a cutpurse.

FLUELLEN I'll assure you, 'a uttered as prave words at
the pridge as you shall see in a summer's day. But it is
very well; what he has spoke to me, that is well, I
warrant you, when time is serve.

GOWER Why, 'tis a gull, a fool, a rogue, that now and then
goes to the wars, to grace himself at his return into
London under the form of a soldier. And such fellows
are perfect in the great commanders' names, and they
will learn you by rote where services were done: at such 70
and such a sconce, at such a breach, at such a convoy;
who came off bravely, who was shot, who disgraced,
what terms the enemy stood on; and this they con
perfectly in the phrase of war, which they trick up with
new-tuned oaths: and what a beard of the general's
cut and a horrid suit of the camp will do among foaming
bottles and ale-washed wits is wonderful to be thought
on. But you must learn to know such slanders of the
age, or else you may be marvellously mistook.

FLUELLEN I tell you what, Captain Gower; I do perceive 80
he is not the man that he would gladly make show to
the world he is. If I find a hole in his coat, I will tell
him my mind. (*Drum within*) Hark you, the King is
coming, and I must speak with him from the pridge.

---

origin (compare line 58), of thrusting
the thumb between the clenched fingers or into the mouth.

66–79 *'tis a gull, a fool, a rogue . . . marvellously mistook.* Satire on the tricks of
bogus soldiers is common in Eliza-

bethan literature.
71 *sconce* fort, earthwork
82 *find a hole in his coat* find a weak spot
in him (a proverbial phrase)
84 *speak with him* tell him my news

Drum and colours. Enter the King and his poor soldiers, with Gloucester

God pless your majesty!

KING HENRY

How now, Fluellen, cam'st thou from the bridge?

FLUELLEN Ay, so please your majesty. The Duke of Exeter has very gallantly maintained the pridge. The French is gone off, look you, and there is gallant and most prave passages. Marry, th'athversary was have possession of the pridge, but he is enforced to retire, and the Duke of Exeter is master of the pridge. I can tell your majesty, the Duke is a prave man.

KING HENRY What men have you lost, Fluellen?

FLUELLEN The perdition of th'athversary hath been very great, reasonable great. Marry, for my part, I think the Duke hath lost never a man, but one that is like to be executed for robbing a church, one Bardolph, if your majesty know the man: his face is all bubukles, and whelks, and knobs, and flames o'fire; and his lips blows at his nose, and it is like a coal of fire, sometimes plue, and sometimes red; but his nose is executed, and his fire's out.

KING HENRY We would have all such offenders so cut off: and we give express charge, that in our marches through the country there be nothing compelled from the villages, nothing taken but paid for, none of the

---

99–101 *his face . . . fire.* Shakespeare may be recalling Chaucer's Summoner, with his 'fire-reed' face blotched with 'whelkes white' and 'knobbes sitting on his chekes'.

99 *bubukles* sores, tumours. Fluellen combines '*bubo*' (Latin, abscess) and '*charbucle*' (a variant of carbuncle).

100 *whelks* pimples

104–10 *We would have all such offenders so cut off . . . soonest winner.* Commentators unwilling to allow Henry any

motives but those of cold expediency cite this speech as evincing mere calculating policy, but Shakespeare is unreservedly adopting Holinshed's tribute to the English army as observing strict discipline before Agincourt, even in difficult straits – 'Yet in this great necessity the poor people of the country were not spoiled, nor anything taken of them without payment, nor any outrage or offence done.'

French upbraided or abused in disdainful language;
for when lenity and cruelty play for a kingdom, the
gentler gamester is the soonest winner.   110

    Tucket. Enter Montjoy

MONTJOY You know me by my habit.

KING HENRY Well then, I know thee: what shall I know
of thee?

MONTJOY My master's mind.

KING HENRY Unfold it.

MONTJOY Thus says my King: 'Say thou to Harry of
England, Though we seemed dead, we did but sleep.
Advantage is a better soldier than rashness. Tell him
we could have rebuked him at Harfleur, but that we
thought not good to bruise an injury till it were full   120
ripe. Now we speak upon our cue, and our voice is
imperial: England shall repent his folly, see his weakness,
and admire our sufferance. Bid him therefore consider
of his ransom, which must proportion the losses we
have borne, the subjects we have lost, the disgrace we
have digested; which in weight to re-answer, his petti-
ness would bow under. For our losses, his exchequer is
too poor; for th'effusion of our blood, the muster of his
kingdom too faint a number; and for our disgrace, his
own person kneeling at our feet but a weak and worth-   130
less satisfaction. To this add defiance: and tell him for
conclusion, he hath betrayed his followers, whose
condemnation is pronounced.' So far my King and
master; so much my office.

---

110 (stage direction) *Tucket* (a preliminary trumpet signal)
   Montjoy. Like 'Garter' in Britain, this
is the title of the chief herald of
France, not a personal name.
111 *You know me by my habit.* This is a
terse, discourteous opening, which
Henry answers in the same vein.
   habit herald's tabard

118 *Advantage* the restraint which awaits
a favourable opportunity
120 *bruise an injury* (1) squeeze out an
abscess; (2) hit back at the cause of
our harm
123 *admire our sufferance* be astonished to
find that our patience was not caused
by weakness

KING HENRY
What is thy name? I know thy quality.
MONTJOY Montjoy.
KING HENRY
Thou dost thy office fairly. Turn thee back,
And tell thy King I do not seek him now,
But could be willing to march on to Calais
140 Without impeachment: for, to say the sooth,
Though 'tis no wisdom to confess so much
Unto an enemy of craft and vantage,
My people are with sickness much enfeebled,
My numbers lessened, and those few I have
Almost no better than so many French;
Who when they were in health, I tell thee, Herald,
I thought upon one pair of English legs
Did march three Frenchmen. Yet forgive me, God,
That I do brag thus! This your air of France
150 Hath blown that vice in me – I must repent.
Go, therefore, tell thy master here I am;
My ransom is this frail and worthless trunk;
My army but a weak and sickly guard:
Yet, God before, tell him we will come on,
Though France himself, and such another neighbour,
Stand in our way. There's for thy labour, Montjoy.
Go bid thy master well advise himself:
If we may pass, we will; if we be hindered,
We shall your tawny ground with your red blood
160 Discolour: and so, Montjoy, fare you well.

138–45 *tell thy King I do not seek him now
. . . so many French.* In Holinshed,
Henry replies, 'Mine intent is to do
as it pleaseth God. I will not seek
your master at this time; but if he or
his seek me, I will meet with them,
God willing . . . And yet wish I not
any of you so unadvised as to be the

occasion that I dye your tawny
ground with your red blood' (compare lines 158–60). He does not, however, admit his army's plight, as he
so frankly does here.
140 *impeachment* impediment (French,
'*empêchement*')
sooth truth

The sum of all our answer is but this:
We would not seek a battle as we are,
Nor, as we are, we say we will not shun it.
So tell your master.

MONTJOY
I shall deliver so. Thanks to your highness.　　　*Exit*

GLOUCESTER
I hope they will not come upon us now.

KING HENRY
We are in God's hand, brother, not in theirs.
March to the bridge; it now draws toward night.
Beyond the river we'll encamp ourselves,
And on tomorrow bid them march away.　　　*Exeunt*　170

Enter the Constable of France, the Lord Rambures,　III.7
Orleans, Dauphin, with others

CONSTABLE Tut! I have the best armour of the world.
Would it were day!

ORLEANS You have an excellent armour; but let my horse
have his due.

CONSTABLE It is the best horse of Europe.

ORLEANS Will it never be morning?

DAUPHIN My Lord of Orleans, and my Lord High
Constable, you talk of horse and armour?

ORLEANS You are as well provided of both as any prince
in the world.　　　10

DAUPHIN What a long night is this! I will not change my
horse with any that treads but on four pasterns. *Ça, ha!*
He bounds from the earth as if his entrails were hairs —

III.7 (stage direction) *Dauphin.* For the
Dauphin's presence at Agincourt,
contrary to the chronicles, see
III.5.64, note.
12 *but on four pasterns* merely on natural
hooves. The pastern is the part of

the foot between the fetlock and
hoof.
13 *as if his entrails were hairs* as if he were
a tennis-ball (stuffed, as tennis-balls
were, with hair)

le cheval volant, the Pegasus, *chez les narines de feu!*
When I bestride him, I soar, I am a hawk. He trots the
air; the earth sings when he touches it; the basest horn
of his hoof is more musical than the pipe of Hermes.

ORLEANS He's of the colour of the nutmeg.

DAUPHIN And of the heat of the ginger. It is a beast for
Perseus: he is pure air and fire; and the dull elements of
earth and water never appear in him, but only in
patient stillness while his rider mounts him. He is
indeed a horse, and all other jades you may call beasts.

CONSTABLE Indeed, my lord, it is a most absolute and
excellent horse.

DAUPHIN It is the prince of palfreys; his neigh is like the
bidding of a monarch, and his countenance enforces
homage.

ORLEANS No more, cousin.

DAUPHIN Nay, the man hath no wit that cannot, from the
rising of the lark to the lodging of the lamb, vary
deserved praise on my palfrey. It is a theme as fluent as
the sea: turn the sands into eloquent tongues, and my
horse is argument for them all. 'Tis a subject for a

---

14 *Pegasus, chez les narines de feu* Pegasus
(the winged horse of classical fable),
with fiery nostrils. Some editors correct Shakespeare's *chez* to the more
orthodox *avec*.

17 *the pipe of Hermes*. Hermes, or Mercury, invented the musical pipe and
with it charmed asleep the many-eyed
monster Argus.

18 *nutmeg* dull brown. Horses' colours
were thought to reflect their temperaments. 'A good horse cannot be of a
bad colour' was proverbial.

20 *Perseus*. A son of Zeus; his winged
sandals bore him through the air to
destroy the Gorgon, Medusa.
air and fire. Compare Prologue 1,
note; also *Antony and Cleopatra*,

v.2.287–8 – 'I am fire and air; my
other elements | I give to baser life.'

23 *all other jades you may call beasts* all
other horses are poor specimens,
merely animals

26 *palfreys* saddle-horses ('for ordinary
riding, esp. for ladies' [*Oxford English
Dictionary*], as distinguished from
war-horses). The Dauphin errs in no-
menclature, unless Shakespeare is implying effeminacy in him, which the
context by no means suggests.

30–31 *from the rising of the lark to the
lodging of the lamb*. 'To go to bed with
the lamb and rise with the lark' was
proverbial.

34 *argument* theme for discourse

Sovereign to reason on, and for a sovereign's sovereign
to ride on; and for the world, familiar to us and unknown, to lay apart their particular functions and
wonder at him. I once writ a sonnet in his praise, and
began thus: 'Wonder of nature —'.

ORLEANS I have heard a sonnet begin so to one's mistress. 40

DAUPHIN Then did they imitate that which I composed
to my courser, for my horse is my mistress.

ORLEANS Your mistress bears well.

DAUPHIN Me well, which is the prescript praise and
perfection of a good and particular mistress.

CONSTABLE Nay, for methought yesterday your mistress.
shrewdly shook your back.

DAUPHIN So perhaps did yours.

CONSTABLE Mine was not bridled.

DAUPHIN O, then belike she was old and gentle, and you 50
rode like a kern of Ireland, your French hose off, and in
your strait strossers.

CONSTABLE You have good judgement in horsemanship.

DAUPHIN Be warned by me, then: they that ride so, and
ride not warily, fall into foul bogs. I had rather have my
horse to my mistress.

CONSTABLE I had as lief have my mistress a jade.

DAUPHIN I tell thee, Constable, my mistress wears his
own hair.

38–40 *I once writ a sonnet ... mistress.*
The idea may come from *Edward III*,
where Edward orders a poem of sur-
passing praise and, when the poet
asks about the intended recipient, replies, 'Thinkest thou I did bid thee
praise a horse?' (1.2.92).

43 *bears* carries her riders

44 *prescript* prescribed

47 *shrewdly* sharply (with a quibble on
'shrewishly')

49 *bridled.* There is a quibble on the

bridle worn by a horse and the bridle
or gag used to quiet a shrew.

51 *kern* light-armed Irish soldier
French hose wide breeches

52 *strait strossers* tight trousers (the skin
of the bare legs)

57 *jade* (1) low-grade horse, hack; (2)
trollop

59 *own hair* (that is, as distinct from
human mistresses decked out with
false hair; compare *The Merchant of
Venice*, III.2.92–5 – 'So are those

60   CONSTABLE I could make as true a boast as that, if I had
     a sow to my mistress.

     DAUPHIN '*Le chien est retourné à son propre vomissement,*
     et la truie lavée au bourbier': thou mak'st use of anything.

     CONSTABLE Yet do I not use my horse for my mistress, or
     any such proverb so little kin to the purpose.

     RAMBURES My Lord Constable, the armour that I saw
     in your tent tonight – are those stars or suns upon it?

     CONSTABLE Stars, my lord.

     DAUPHIN Some of them will fall tomorrow, I hope.

70   CONSTABLE And yet my sky shall not want.

     DAUPHIN That may be, for you bear a many super-
     fluously, and 'twere more honour some were away.

     CONSTABLE E'en as your horse bears your praises,
     who would trot as well were some of your brags
     dismounted.

     DAUPHIN Would I were able to load him with his desert!
     Will it never be day? I will trot tomorrow a mile, and
     my way shall be paved with English faces.

     CONSTABLE I will not say so, for fear I should be faced
80   out of my way; but I would it were morning, for I
     would fain be about the ears of the English.

     RAMBURES Who will go to hazard with me for twenty
     prisoners?

crispèd snaky golden locks, | Which
make such wanton gambols with the
wind | Upon supposèd fairness, often
known | To be the dowry of a second
head.')

62–3 *Le chien . . . bourbier.* 2 Peter 2.22 –
'The dog is turned to his own vomit
again, and the sow that was washed
to her wallowing in the mire.' The
sentence was proverbial, and Shakespeare had already made powerful
use of it in *2 Henry IV* (1.3.97–9)
when the Archbishop calls the popu-
lace 'thou common dog', and contin-

ues, '[thou] didst . . . disgorge | Thy
glutton bosom of the royal Richard;
| And now thou wouldst eat thy
dead vomit up'.

71 *a many* a lot

79–80 *faced out of my way* (1) put out of
countenance; (2) driven off by
(enemy) faces

82 *go to hazard* play dice; *hazard* was so
called because of its tricky rules. Compare Holinshed – 'The [French] soldiers the night before had played
[that is, played for] the Englishmen
at dice.'

CONSTABLE You must first go yourself to hazard ere you
have them.

DAUPHIN 'Tis midnight: I'll go arm myself   *Exit*

ORLEANS The Dauphin longs for morning.

RAMBURES He longs to eat the English.

CONSTABLE I think he will eat all he kills.

ORLEANS By the white hand of my lady, he's a gallant   90
prince.

CONSTABLE Swear by her foot, that she may tread out
the oath.

ORLEANS He is simply the most active gentleman of
France.

CONSTABLE Doing is activity, and he will still be doing.

ORLEANS He never did harm, that I heard of.

CONSTABLE Nor will do none tomorrow: he will keep that
good name still.

ORLEANS I know him to be valiant.   100

CONSTABLE I was told that, by one that knows him better
than you.

ORLEANS What's he?

CONSTABLE Marry, he told me so himself, and he said he
cared not who knew it.

ORLEANS He needs not; it is no hidden virtue in him.

CONSTABLE By my faith, sir, but it is; never anybody
saw it but his lackey. 'Tis a hooded valour, and when it
appears it will bate.

ORLEANS Ill will never said well.   110

CONSTABLE I will cap that proverb with 'There is flattery
in friendship.'

ORLEANS And I will take up that with 'Give the devil
his due!'

---

89 *he will eat all he kills* (a proverbial tag)
92 *tread out* (1) dance away; (2) tread
into extinction
108 *hooded* concealed (like a hawk under
the hood that subdues it)

109 *bate*. This is a quibble: (1) flutter its
wings for action (referring to a
hawk); (2) dwindle (referring to the
Dauphin's valour).

CONSTABLE Well placed! There stands your friend for the
devil. Have at the very eye of that proverb with 'A pox
of the devil!'

ORLEANS You are the better at proverbs by how much
'A fool's bolt is soon shot.'

120 CONSTABLE You have shot over.

ORLEANS 'Tis not the first time you were overshot.

Enter a Messenger

MESSENGER My Lord High Constable, the English lie
within fifteen hundred paces of your tents.

CONSTABLE Who hath measured the ground?

MESSENGER The Lord Grandpré.

CONSTABLE A valiant and most expert gentleman. Would
it were day! Alas, poor Harry of England! He longs not
for the dawning as we do.

ORLEANS What a wretched and peevish fellow is this King
130 of England, to mope with his fat-brained followers so far
out of his knowledge.

CONSTABLE If the English had any apprehension, they
would run away.

ORLEANS That they lack; for if their heads had any
intellectual armour, they could never wear such heavy
head-pieces.

RAMBURES That island of England breeds very valiant
creatures: their mastiffs are of unmatchable courage.

ORLEANS Foolish curs, that run winking into the mouth
140 of a Russian bear, and have their heads crushed like
rotten apples! You may as well say that's a valiant flea
that dare eat his breakfast on the lip of a lion.

CONSTABLE Just, just: and the men do sympathize with
the mastiffs in robustious and rough coming on,

---

121 *overshot* (1) outshot, outdone; (2)
mistaken

130 *mope* go blundering about

131 *knowledge* familiar bearings

132 *apprehension* (1) understanding; (2)
sense of fear

138 *mastiffs*. English mastiffs were
famous for bull- and bear-baiting.

143 *sympathize with* resemble

leaving their wits with their wives; and then, give them
great meals of beef, and iron and steel; they will eat
like wolves, and fight like devils.

ORLEANS Ay, but these English are shrewdly out of beef.

CONSTABLE Then shall we find tomorrow they have only
stomachs to eat, and none to fight. Now is it time to   150
arm. Come, shall we about it?

ORLEANS
It is now two o'clock: but, let me see – by ten
We shall have each a hundred Englishmen.   *Exeunt*

Flourish. Enter Chorus   IV

CHORUS
Now entertain conjecture of a time
When creeping murmur and the poring dark
Fills the wide vessel of the universe.
From camp to camp, through the foul womb of night,
The hum of either army stilly sounds,
That the fixed sentinels almost receive
The secret whispers of each other's watch.
Fire answers fire, and through their paly flames
Each battle sees the other's umbered face.
Steed threatens steed, in high and boastful neighs,   10
Piercing the night's dull ear; and from the tents
The armourers, accomplishing the knights,
With busy hammers closing rivets up,
Give dreadful note of preparation.

---

148 *shrewdly* severely
out of beef. This seems to echo *Edward
III* (III.3.159–62) when the King of
France says of the English soldiers,
'but scant them of their chines of
beef, | . . . | And presently they are
as resty stiff | As 'twere a many

over-ridden jades' (compare 'sur-
reined jades' at III.5.19, above).

IV. *Chorus* 9 *battle* army
umbered shadowed
12 *accomplishing* putting the finishing
touches to

The country cocks do crow, the clocks do toll,
And the third hour of drowsy morning name.
Proud of their numbers, and secure in soul,
The confident and over-lusty French
Do the low-rated English play at dice,
20 And chide the cripple tardy-gaited night
Who like a foul and ugly witch doth limp
So tediously away. The poor condemnèd English,
Like sacrifices, by their watchful fires
Sit patiently, and inly ruminate
The morning's danger; and their gesture sad,
Investing lank-lean cheeks and war-worn coats,
Presenteth them unto the gazing moon
So many horrid ghosts. O now, who will behold
The royal Captain of this ruined band
30 Walking from watch to watch, from tent to tent,
Let him cry, 'Praise and glory on his head!'
For forth he goes and visits all his host,
Bids them good morrow with a modest smile,
And calls them brothers, friends, and countrymen.
Upon his royal face there is no note
How dread an army hath enrounded him,
Nor doth he dedicate one jot of colour
Unto the weary and all-watched night,
But freshly looks, and overbears attaint
40 With cheerful semblance and sweet majesty;
That every wretch, pining and pale before,
Beholding him, plucks comfort from his looks.
A largess universal, like the sun,
His liberal eye doth give to every one,
Thawing cold fear, that mean and gentle all
Behold, as may unworthiness define,

17 *secure* carefree
25 *gesture sad* grave demeanour
26 *Investing* enveloping
39 *overbears attaint* conquers any blemish
(of weariness)

45 *mean and gentle* humble and high-born
46 *as may unworthiness define* as far as our
unworthy efforts may present it

A little touch of Harry in the night.
And so our scene must to the battle fly;
Where – O for pity! – we shall much disgrace,
With four or five most vile and ragged foils,   50
Right ill-disposed in brawl ridiculous,
The name of Agincourt. Yet sit and see,
Minding true things by what their mockeries be.   *Exit*

Enter the King, Bedford, and Gloucester   IV.I
KING HENRY
Gloucester, 'tis true that we are in great danger:
The greater therefore should our courage be.
Good morrow, brother Bedford. God Almighty!
There is some soul of goodness in things evil,
Would men observingly distil it out;
For our bad neighbour makes us early stirrers,
Which is both healthful, and good husbandry.
Besides, they are our outward consciences,
And preachers to us all, admonishing
That we should dress us fairly for our end.   10
Thus may we gather honey from the weed,
And make a moral of the devil himself.
    Enter Erpingham
Good morrow, old Sir Thomas Erpingham!
A good soft pillow for that good white head

49–53 *we shall much disgrace . . . their mockeries be*. Stage-battles were often satirized; compare Sidney's *An Apologie for Poetrie* – 'Two armies fly in represented with four swords and bucklers, and then what hard heart will not receive it for a pitched field?' Jonson is equally derisive in the prologue to *Every Man In His Humour* about 'three rusty swords' set to fight the Wars of the Roses.

IV.I This admirable scene shows the 'little touch of Harry in the night' in relationship with the various ranks which form the army, the King's brothers, generals, camp-followers, captains, and common soldiers.

7 *husbandry* management

10 *dress us* prepare ourselves. Holinshed reports that though the English were 'hungry, weary, sore travelled, and vexed with many cold diseases', yet they took holy communion and made confession; compare lines 172–80, below.

Were better than a churlish turf of France.

ERPINGHAM

Not so, my liege – this lodging likes me better,
Since I may say, 'Now lie I like a king.'

KING HENRY

'Tis good for men to love their present pains
Upon example: so the spirit is eased;
And when the mind is quickened, out of doubt
The organs, though defunct and dead before,
Break up their drowsy grave and newly move
With casted slough and fresh legerity.
Lend me thy cloak, Sir Thomas. Brothers both,
Commend me to the princes in our camp;
Do my good morrow to them, and anon
Desire them all to my pavilion.

GLOUCESTER   We shall, my liege.

ERPINGHAM

Shall I attend your grace?

KING HENRY   No, my good knight.
Go with my brothers to my lords of England.
I and my bosom must debate a while,
And then I would no other company.

ERPINGHAM

The Lord in heaven bless thee, noble Harry!

                            Exeunt all but the King

KING HENRY

God-a-mercy, old heart, thou speak'st cheerfully.
        Enter Pistol

PISTOL

    Qui va là?

KING HENRY   A friend.

---

23 *With casted slough* like a snake after it
has cast its dead skin (before which
it is torpid)

34 *God-a-mercy* I thank thee (strictly,

'God have mercy', but confused with
'gramercy' ['graunt mercy', that is,
great thanks])

PISTOL

    Discuss unto me, art thou officer,

    Or art thou base, common, and popular?

KING HENRY I am a gentleman of a company.

PISTOL

    Trail'st thou the puissant pike?   40

KING HENRY Even so. What are you?

PISTOL

    As good a gentleman as the Emperor.

KING HENRY Then you are a better than the King.

PISTOL

    The King's a bawcock, and a heart of gold,

    A lad of life, an imp of fame;

    Of parents good, of fist most valiant.

    I kiss his dirty shoe, and from heartstring

    I love the lovely bully. What is thy name?

KING HENRY Harry le Roy.

PISTOL

    Le Roy? A Cornish name. Art thou of Cornish crew?   50

KING HENRY No, I am a Welshman.

PISTOL

    Know'st thou Fluellen?

KING HENRY Yes.

PISTOL

    Tell him I'll knock his leek about his pate

    Upon Saint Davy's day.

KING HENRY Do not you wear your dagger in your cap

    that day, lest he knock that about yours.

---

39 *gentleman of a company* non-commissioned officer

40 *Trail'st thou the puissant pike?* That is, are you in the infantry? (The pike was carried by holding it below the point, trailing the butt along the ground.)

44 *bawcock* fine fellow (French, '*beau coq*'); compare III.2.25.

45 *imp* scion, son. Pistol calls the King 'most royal imp of fame' in *2 Henry IV*, v.5.43.

48 *lovely bully* splendid fellow

55 *Saint Davy's day* 1 March (the Welsh national day, when Welshmen wear their national emblem to mark the supposed anniversary of their victory over the Saxons on that date in AD 540).

PISTOL

Art thou his friend?

KING HENRY And his kinsman too.

PISTOL

60   The *figo* for thee then!

KING HENRY I thank you. God be with you!

PISTOL

My name is Pistol called.   *Exit*

KING HENRY It sorts well with your fierceness.

Enter Fluellen and Gower

GOWER Captain Fluellen!

FLUELLEN So! In the name of Jesu Christ, speak fewer. It is the greatest admiration in the universal world, when the true and aunchient prerogatifes and laws of the wars is not kept. If you would take the pains but to examine the wars of Pompey the Great, you shall find, 70   I warrant you, that there is no tiddle-taddle nor pibble-pabble in Pompey's camp. I warrant you, you shall find the ceremonies of the wars, and the cares of it, and the forms of it, and the sobriety of it, and the modesty of it, to be otherwise.

GOWER Why, the enemy is loud, you hear him all night.

FLUELLEN If the enemy is an ass, and a fool, and a prating coxcomb, is it meet, think you, that we should also, look you, be an ass, and a fool, and a prating cox-comb? In your own conscience now?

80   GOWER I will speak lower.

FLUELLEN I pray you and beseech you that you will.

Exeunt Gower and Fluellen

---

60 *figo*. Compare III.6.56, note.
65 *fewer*. The Folio reads 'fewer', the Quarto 'lewer' ('lower' in the third Quarto). Since Gower has spoken only two words, and later promises to 'speak lower', many editors read 'lower' here. But Fluellen's reproof

is against 'tiddle-taddle' and 'pibble-pabble', and the comedy is in his loquacious warning to the taciturn Gower to speak less.
66 *admiration* cause of astonishment
67 *prerogatifes* due rights

KING HENRY
  Though it appear a little out of fashion,
  There is much care and valour in this Welshman.
        Enter three soldiers, John Bates, Alexander Court,
        and Michael Williams

COURT Brother John Bates, is not that the morning which
  breaks yonder?

BATES I think it be; but we have no great cause to desire
  the approach of day.

WILLIAMS We see yonder the beginning of the day, but I
  think we shall never see the end of it. Who goes there?

KING HENRY A friend.   90

WILLIAMS Under what captain serve you?

KING HENRY Under Sir Thomas Erpingham.

WILLIAMS A good old commander, and a most kind
  gentleman. I pray you, what thinks he of our estate?

KING HENRY Even as men wrecked upon a sand, that
  look to be washed off the next tide.

BATES He hath not told his thought to the King?

KING HENRY No, nor it is not meet he should. For
  though I speak it to you, I think the King is but a man,
  as I am: the violet smells to him as it doth to me; the   100
  element shows to him as it doth to me; all his senses have
  but human conditions. His ceremonies laid by, in his
  nakedness he appears but a man; and though his
  affections are higher mounted than ours, yet when they
  stoop, they stoop with the like wing. Therefore, when
  he sees reason of fears, as we do, his fears, out of doubt,

82 *out of fashion* (1) out of the expected
  form or shape; (2) unconventional in
  manner
93–4 *A good old commander . . . gentleman.*
  The various ranks on the English
  side know and trust each other.
99–107 *I think the King is but a man . . . as*
  ours are. In a sense the King is quibbling in equating the reactions of
  'the King' to his own as supposedly

those of an ordinary man; yet what
  he says is in fact true – the King is a
  human being, though with the extra
  weight of responsibility.
101 *element* sky
104 *affections are higher mounted* feelings
  soar higher
105 *stoop* descend (the falconry word for
  the hawk's swoop on its prey)

be of the same relish as ours are: yet, in reason, no
man should possess him with any appearance of fear,
lest he, by showing it, should dishearten his army.

110   BATES He may show what outward courage he will, but I
believe, as cold a night as 'tis, he could wish himself in
Thames up to the neck; and so I would he were, and
I by him, at all adventures, so we were quit here.

KING HENRY By my troth, I will speak my conscience of
the King: I think he would not wish himself anywhere
but where he is.

BATES Then I would he were here alone; so should he be
sure to be ransomed, and a many poor men's lives
saved.

120   KING HENRY I dare say you love him not so ill to wish
him here alone, howsoever you speak this to feel other
men's minds. Methinks I could not die anywhere so
contented as in the King's company, his cause being
just and his quarrel honourable.

WILLIAMS That's more than we know.

BATES Ay, or more than we should seek after; for we know
enough if we know we are the King's subjects. If his
cause be wrong, our obedience to the King wipes the
crime of it out of us.

130   WILLIAMS But if the cause be not good, the King himself
hath a heavy reckoning to make, when all those legs,
and arms, and heads, chopped off in a battle, shall join
together at the latter day, and cry all, 'We died at such
a place'; some swearing, some crying for a surgeon,
some upon their wives left poor behind them, some upon
the debts they owe, some upon their children rawly left.
I am afeard there are few die well that die in a battle, for

---

113 *at all adventures* whatever might
come of it
114 *my conscience* (1) what I honestly believe; (2) what I actually know (a
slight quibble)
123–4 *his cause being just.* The moral bear-

ing of this discussion, and the validity of the King's case, depend on the
justice of his cause; this assertion is
not a mere official gloss but a funda-
mental tenet of the play.
133 *the latter day* the Day of Judgement

how can they charitably dispose of anything when
blood is their argument? Now, if these men do not die
well, it will be a black matter for the King that led   140
them to it, who to disobey were against all proportion
of subjection.

KING HENRY So, if a son that is by his father sent about
merchandise do sinfully miscarry upon the sea, the
imputation of his wickedness, by your rule, should be
imposed upon his father that sent him; or if a servant,
under his master's command, transporting a sum of
money, be assailed by robbers, and die in many irreconciled iniquities, you may call the business of the master
the author of the servant's damnation. But this is not so.   150
The King is not bound to answer the particular endings
of his soldiers, the father of his son, nor the master of
his servant; for they purpose not their death when they
purpose their services. Besides, there is no king, be
his cause never so spotless, if it come to the arbitrement
of swords, can try it out with all unspotted soldiers.
Some, peradventure, have on them the guilt of pre-
meditated and contrived murder; some, of beguiling
virgins with the broken seals of perjury; some, making
the wars their bulwark, that have before gored the   160
gentle bosom of peace with pillage and robbery. Now,
if these men have defeated the law, and outrun native
punishment, though they can outstrip men they have no
wings to fly from God. War is His beadle, war is His

138 *charitably* in Christian charity
141–2 *proportion of subjection* due relation
of subject to ruler
143–54 *So, if a son . . . services.* This argument has been thought sophistical
on the grounds that Williams's hypothesis is that the King's cause may
not be good, whereas Henry's answer
is concerned only with the soldiers'
possible misdemeanours. But by all
the hypotheses of the play Henry's
cause is righteous. If his soldiers die
in sin, therefore, the sin must result

from their own wrongdoings, not
from their fighting wrongfully. For
Dr Johnson's comment, see the Introduction, pp. 704–5. As in the address
to Scroop, Henry presses his arguments so long as to suggest that he
enjoys rhetorical virtuosity, but what
he actually says is perfectly valid.
148–9 *irreconciled* unabsolved
155–6 *arbitrement of* settlement by
164 *beadle* officer of the law (a minor
functionary who whipped offenders)

vengeance; so that here men are punished for before-
breach of the King's laws, in now the King's quarrel.
Where they feared the death, they have borne life away;
and where they would be safe, they perish. Then if
they die unprovided, no more is the King guilty of their
170   damnation than he was before guilty of those impieties
for the which they are now visited. Every subject's duty
is the King's, but every subject's soul is his own.
Therefore should every soldier in the wars do as every sick
man in his bed, wash every mote out of his conscience;
and dying so, death is to him advantage; or not dying,
the time was blessedly lost wherein such preparation
was gained; and in him that escapes, it were not sin to
think that, making God so free an offer, He let him
outlive that day to see His greatness, and to teach others
180   how they should prepare.

WILLIAMS 'Tis certain, every man that dies ill, the ill
    upon his own head – the King is not to answer it.

BATES I do not desire he should answer for me, and yet I
    determine to fight lustily for him.

KING HENRY I myself heard the King say he would not
    be ransomed.

WILLIAMS Ay, he said so, to make us fight cheerfully:
    but when our throats are cut he may be ransomed, and
    we ne'er the wiser.

190   KING HENRY If I live to see it, I will never trust his word
    after.

WILLIAMS You pay him then! That's a perilous shot out
    of an elder-gun, that a poor and a private displeasure
    can do against a monarch! You may as well go about to

169 *unprovided* unprepared (for death)
175 *death is to him advantage*. This echoes
    Philippians 1.21 in the Genevan and
    Bishops' Bible versions – 'Christ is to
    me life, and death is to me advantage.'
181–2 *'Tis certain ... the King is not to*
    answer it. Williams assents because he
    is convinced, not because he is

browbeaten.
183 *I do not desire he should answer for me* I do
    not want him to have to answer for
    me (that is, I hope I shan't be killed)
192 *You pay him then!* Well, you *are*
    going to pay him out, aren't you!
193 *elder-gun* pop-gun (made from a
    hollow elder stick)

turn the sun to ice, with fanning in his face with a pea-
cock's feather. You'll never trust his word after! Come,
'tis a foolish saying.

KING HENRY Your reproof is something too round. I
should be angry with you, if the time were convenient.

WILLIAMS Let it be a quarrel between us, if you live.   200

KING HENRY I embrace it.

WILLIAMS How shall I know thee again?

KING HENRY Give me any gage of thine, and I will wear
it in my bonnet: then, if ever thou dar'st acknowledge it,
I will make it my quarrel.

WILLIAMS Here's my glove: give me another of thine.

KING HENRY There.

WILLIAMS This will I also wear in my cap. If ever thou
come to me and say, after tomorrow, 'This is my glove,'
by this hand, I will take thee a box on the ear.   210

KING HENRY If ever I live to see it, I will challenge it.

WILLIAMS Thou dar'st as well be hanged.

KING HENRY Well, I will do it, though I take thee in the
King's company.

WILLIAMS Keep thy word. Fare thee well.

BATES Be friends, you English fools, be friends! We have
French quarrels enow, if you could tell how to reckon.

KING HENRY Indeed, the French may lay twenty French
crowns to one they will beat us, for they bear them on
their shoulders; but it is no English treason to cut   220
French crowns, and tomorrow the King himself will be
a clipper.   *Exeunt Soldiers*

Upon the King! Let us our lives, our souls,

198 *round* blunt
210 *take* give
218-19 *lay twenty French crowns* (1) bet
    twenty écus (about 6s. each); (2) ven-
    ture twenty French heads
220-21 *but it is no English treason to cut
    French crowns.* For an Englishman to
    clip bits off English coins, or English
    skulls, would be treasonable, but for

him to do so to the French is not so
at all.
223-77 *Upon the King! . . . best advantages.*
    Johnson has a characteristic note —
    'There is something very striking and
    solemn in this soliloquy . . . Some-
    thing like this, on less occasions,
    every breast has felt. Reflection and
    seriousness rush upon the mind upon

Our debts, our careful wives,
Our children, and our sins, lay on the King!
We must bear all. O hard condition,
Twin-born with greatness, subject to the breath
Of every fool, whose sense no more can feel
But his own wringing! What infinite heart's ease
230   Must kings neglect that private men enjoy!
And what have kings that privates have not too,
Save ceremony, save general ceremony?
And what art thou, thou idol ceremony?
What kind of god art thou, that suffer'st more
Of mortal griefs than do thy worshippers?
What are thy rents? What are thy comings-in?
O ceremony, show me but thy worth!
What is thy soul of adoration?
Art thou aught else but place, degree, and form,
240   Creating awe and fear in other men?
Wherein thou art less happy, being feared,
Than they in fearing.
What drink'st thou oft, instead of homage sweet,
But poisoned flattery? O, be sick, great greatness,
And bid thy ceremony give thee cure!
Thinks thou the fiery fever will go out
With titles blown from adulation?
Will it give place to flexure and low bending?
Canst thou, when thou command'st the beggar's knee,
250   Command the health of it? No, thou proud dream,
That play'st so subtly with a king's repose.
I am a king that find thee, and I know

the separation of a gay company, and especially after forced and unwilling merriment.' All the same, there is something of the oratorical display in its *parti pris* – or perhaps, more humanly, a touch of petulance suggesting tense nerves.

224 *careful* anxious
229 *wringing* aches and pains

238 *thy soul of adoration* the real nature of the adoration offered thee
246 *Thinks thou* (a frequent second-person singular form for verbs ending in a dental or guttural consonant)
247 *blown from adulation* inflated by the wind of flattery

'Tis not the balm, the sceptre, and the ball,
The sword, the mace, the crown imperial,
The intertissued robe of gold and pearl,
The farcèd title running fore the king,
The throne he sits on, nor the tide of pomp
That beats upon the high shore of this world –
No, not all these, thrice-gorgeous ceremony,
Not all these, laid in bed majestical,   260
Can sleep so soundly as the wretched slave,
Who, with a body filled, and vacant mind,
Gets him to rest, crammed with distressful bread;
Never sees horrid night, the child of hell,
But, like a lackey, from the rise to set,
Sweats in the eye of Phoebus, and all night
Sleeps in Elysium; next day after dawn
Doth rise and help Hyperion to his horse;
And follows so the ever-running year
With profitable labour to his grave: 270
And but for ceremony, such a wretch,
Winding up days with toil, and nights with sleep,
Had the fore-hand and vantage of a king.
The slave, a member of the country's peace,
Enjoys it, but in gross brain little wots
What watch the king keeps to maintain the peace,
Whose hours the peasant best advantages.

---

253 *balm . . . ball* oil of consecration . . .
orb of sovereignty (given to the monarch at coronation)

256 *farcèd* stuffed up

266 *Phoebus* (the sun-god)

267 *Elysium* (the place of ideal happiness
– in classical mythology, the abode
of the virtuous dead)

268 *Hyperion* (the father of the sun-god
– often taken for the sun-god
himself)

270 *profitable labour.* The King is rather
forcing his argument; the labour of
the 'wretched slave' is hardly to be

called 'profitable'.

273 *fore-hand* superiority

274 *member of the country's peace* partici-
pant in the peace the country enjoys
under proper rule. 'The King's [or,
God's] peace' was a legal term for
'peaceful recognition of the authority, . . . and acceptance of the protection, of a king or lord' (*Oxford
English Dictionary*).

277 *advantages* (1) benefits from (if 'peasant' is the subject); or (2) benefits (if
'hours' is the subject – with the frequent plural noun and singular verb)

Enter Erpingham

ERPINGHAM
    My lord, your nobles, jealous of your absence,
    Seek through your camp to find you.

KING HENRY   Good old knight,
280   Collect them all together at my tent.
    I'll be before thee.

ERPINGHAM   I shall do't, my lord.   *Exit*

KING HENRY
    O God of battles, steel my soldiers' hearts;
    Possess them not with fear; take from them now
    The sense of reckoning, if th'opposèd numbers
    Pluck their hearts from them. Not today, O Lord,
    O not today, think not upon the fault
    My father made in compassing the crown!
    I Richard's body have interrèd new,
    And on it have bestowed more contrite tears
290   Than from it issued forcèd drops of blood.
    Five hundred poor I have in yearly pay,
    Who twice a day their withered hands hold up
    Toward heaven, to pardon blood: and I have built
    Two chantries where the sad and solemn priests
    Sing still for Richard's soul. More will I do,
    Though all that I can do is nothing worth,
    Since that my penitence comes after all,
    Imploring pardon.

            Enter Gloucester

GLOUCESTER
                        My liege!

278 *jealous of* anxious about
285–98 *Not today, O Lord ... Imploring*
    pardon. At this crisis of the war Henry
    admits the moral problem underlying
    his reign – whether God will visit
    upon him the consequences of Rich-
    ard II's deposition and murder by
    Henry IV, or whether his own succes-
    sion is religiously validated by the
justice of his rule.
294 *Two chantries.* Henry founded the
    religious houses of Bethlehem at
    Sheen and of Sion at Twickenham,
    on opposite sides of the Thames, but
    there seems no evidence that this
    was done to expiate Richard's fate.
295 *still* continually

KING HENRY My brother Gloucester's voice? Ay,
    I know thy errand, I will go with thee.   300
    The day, my friends, and all things stay for me.

                                                  Exeunt

      Enter the Dauphin, Orleans, Rambures, and others   IV.2

ORLEANS
    The sun doth gild our armour: up, my lords!

DAUPHIN
    Montez à cheval! My horse! *Varlet! Lacquais!*
    Ha!

ORLEANS
      O brave spirit!

DAUPHIN   *Via! Les eaux et la terre!*

ORLEANS
    Rien puis? L'air et le feu?

DAUPHIN   *Ciel,* cousin Orleans!
      Enter the Constable
    Now, my Lord Constable!

CONSTABLE
    Hark how our steeds for present service neigh!

DAUPHIN
    Mount them and make incision in their hides,
    That their hot blood may spin in English eyes
    And dout them with superfluous courage, ha!

RAMBURES
    What, will you have them weep our horses' blood?   10
    How shall we then behold their natural tears?
      Enter a Messenger

MESSENGER
    The English are embattled, you French peers.

IV.2.3–4 *Via! Les eaux et la terre!* . . .
Ciel, cousin Orleans! In the Folio these
speeches read, '*Via les ewes & terre.*'
– '*Rien puis le air & feu.*' – '*Cein,*
Cousin *Orleance.*' The sense is, prob-
ably, 'Away! [over] water and land!'

– 'Nothing more? Not air and fire?'
– '[Yes,] Heaven itself!'
9 *dout* put out
  superfluous courage blood (identified
  with valour) of which our horses
  have more than they need

CONSTABLE

To horse, you gallant Princes, straight to horse!
Do but behold yon poor and starvèd band,
And your fair show shall suck away their souls,
Leaving them but the shales and husks of men.
There is not work enough for all our hands,
Scarce blood enough in all their sickly veins
To give each naked curtle-axe a stain

20 That our French gallants shall today draw out,
And sheathe for lack of sport. Let us but blow on
    them,
The vapour of our valour will o'erturn them.
'Tis positive 'gainst all exceptions, lords,
That our superfluous lackeys, and our peasants,
Who in unnecessary action swarm
About our squares of battle, were enow
To purge this field of such a hilding foe,
Though we upon this mountain's basis by
Took stand for idle speculation:

30 But that our honours must not. What's to say?
A very little little let us do,
And all is done. Then let the trumpets sound
The tucket sonance and the note to mount;
For our approach shall so much dare the field
That England shall couch down in fear and yield.

       Enter Grandpré

GRANDPRÉ

Why do you stay so long, my lords of France?
Yon island carrions, desperate of their bones,

---

16 *shales* shells, outer cases
19 *curtle-axe* cutlass
26 *squares* formations (in square form)
27 *hilding* good-for-nothing
29 *speculation* onlooking
33 *tucket sonance* trumpet flourish (as signal for military or stage action)
34 *dare the field* (1) defy the foe; (2) daze

the prey (a fowling term, 'to dare' being to dazzle or fascinate birds so that they can be captured)
37 *carrions* corpses for birds to scavenge. A parallel notion to that here and in lines 49–50 occurs in *Edward III* (IV.5.49–51) – 'these ravens for the carcasses | Of those poor English

Ill-favouredly become the morning field.
Their ragged curtains poorly are let loose,
And our air shakes them passing scornfully.   40
Big Mars seems bankrupt in their beggared host,
And faintly through a rusty beaver peeps.
The horsemen sit like fixèd candlesticks,
With torch-staves in their hand; and their poor jades
Lob down their heads, dropping the hides and hips,
The gum down-roping from their pale-dead eyes,
And in their pale dull mouths the gimmaled bit
Lies foul with chawed grass, still and motionless;
And their executors, the knavish crows,
Fly o'er them all, impatient for their hour.   50
Description cannot suit itself in words
To demonstrate the life of such a battle
In life so lifeless as it shows itself.

CONSTABLE

They have said their prayers, and they stay for death.

DAUPHIN

Shall we go send them dinners, and fresh suits,
And give their fasting horses provender,
And after fight with them?

CONSTABLE

I stay but for my guidon. To the field!

that are marked to die | Hover
about.' (Compare 'If we are marked
to die . . .', IV.3.20, below.)
39 *curtains* banners
40 *passing* more than
42 *beaver* visor
43–4 *candlesticks,* | *With torch-staves in*
their hand. Candlesticks were sometimes made in the form of horsemen,
the candle being the lance held upright; in *The White Devil* (III.1.69–70),
Webster writes, 'he showed like a
pewter candlestick, fashioned like a
man in armour, holding a tilting-staff

in his hand.'
45 *Lob* droop
47 *gimmaled* jointed (of twin parts). The
Folio spelling is 'Iymold'. 'Gymould
mayle' occurs in *Edward III* (I.2.29).
49 *their executors* the disposers of their
remains
49–50 *the knavish crows,* | *Fly o'er them*
all. See line 37, above, note.
52–3 *To demonstrate the life of such a*
battle | *In life so lifeless as it shows*
itself to set forth what such an army is
like in such a lifeless state as it is in
58 *guidon* pennant (the commander's

I will the banner from a trumpet take,
60   And use it for my haste. Come, come away!
The sun is high, and we outwear the day.   *Exeunt*

IV.3   *Enter Gloucester, Bedford, Exeter, Erpingham with*
        all his host; Salisbury and Westmorland

GLOUCESTER
Where is the King?

BEDFORD
The King himself is rode to view their battle.

WESTMORLAND
Of fighting men they have full three-score thousand.

EXETER
There's five to one: besides, they all are fresh.

SALISBURY
God's arm strike with us! 'Tis a fearful odds.
God bye you, Princes all: I'll to my charge.
If we no more meet till we meet in heaven,
Then joyfully, my noble Lord of Bedford,
My dear Lord Gloucester, and my good Lord Exeter,
10   And my kind kinsman, warriors all, adieu!

BEDFORD
Farewell, good Salisbury, and good luck go with thee!

sign). Many editions, following the
Folio, read 'guard: on', but the detail
clearly derives from Holinshed, who
writes, 'The Duke of Brabant, when
his standard was not come, caused a
banner to be taken from a trumpet
[compare line 59] and fastened to a
spear, the which he commanded to
be borne before him instead of his
standard.'
59   *trumpet* trumpeter

IV.3.3–4   *three-score thousand . . . five to one.*
This would make the English army
12,000, though in line 76 it is 5,000;
Shakespeare neglects details which in

performance will go unnoticed. Holinshed numbers the French at 60,000
but makes the proportion six to one.
6   *God bye you* God be with you (Folio,
'God buy' you.'). Various forms of
the phrase include 'God be wi' you',
'God buy ye', and 'Goodbye'.
7–10   *If we no more meet till we meet in*
heaven . . . adieu! This seems to foreshadow *Julius Caesar*, v.i.114–18 –
'whether we shall meet again I know
not. | Therefore our everlasting fare-
well take . . . | If we do meet again,
why, we shall smile. | If not, why
then this parting was well made.'

EXETER

   Farewell, kind lord: fight valiantly today –
   And yet I do thee wrong to mind thee of it,
   For thou art framed of the firm truth of valour.

                        Exit Salisbury

BEDFORD

   He is as full of valour as of kindness,
   Princely in both.

     Enter the King

WESTMORLAND   O that we now had here
   But one ten thousand of those men in England
   That do no work today!

KING HENRY   What's he that wishes so?
   My cousin Westmorland? No, my fair cousin.
   If we are marked to die, we are enow   20
   To do our country loss: and if to live,
   The fewer men, the greater share of honour.
   God's will! I pray thee wish not one man more.
   By Jove, I am not covetous for gold,
   Nor care I who doth feed upon my cost;
   It yearns me not if men my garments wear;
   Such outward things dwell not in my desires.
   But if it be a sin to covet honour,
   I am the most offending soul alive.
   No, faith, my coz, wish not a man from England: 30
   God's peace! I would not lose so great an honour

16–18 *O that we now had here . . . no work today*. In Holinshed this speech is given merely to 'one of the host', and Westmorland is not at Agincourt. Shakespeare, however, makes him one of the main supporters of the Bolingbroke line and a leader in the battle.

18 *work* fighting (as often in Shakespeare)

22 *The fewer men, the greater share of honour.* 'The more danger, the more honour' was proverbial. In *Edward III* the King refuses to send a single man to reinforce the Black Prince, who is in mortal peril, so as not to diminish his glory (III.5.40).

28–9 *But if it be a sin to covet honour . . . soul alive.* This recalls Hotspur's greed for honour in *I Henry IV*, but whereas Hotspur wished, rantingly, 'to wear | Without corrival all her dignities' (1.3.206–7), Henry speaks in a comradely way which encourages emulation.

As one man more methinks would share from me
For the best hope I have. O, do not wish one more!
Rather proclaim it, Westmorland, through my host,
That he which hath no stomach to this fight,
Let him depart: his passport shall be made,
And crowns for convoy put into his purse.
We would not die in that man's company
That fears his fellowship to die with us.
40 This day is called the Feast of Crispian:
He that outlives this day, and comes safe home,
Will stand a-tiptoe when this day is named,
And rouse him at the name of Crispian.
He that shall see this day, and live old age,
Will yearly on the vigil feast his neighbours,
And say, 'Tomorrow is Saint Crispian.'
Then will he strip his sleeve, and show his scars,
And say, 'These wounds I had on Crispin's day.'
Old men forget; yet all shall be forgot,
50 But he'll remember, with advantages,
What feats he did that day. Then shall our names,
Familiar in his mouth as household words,
Harry the King, Bedford and Exeter,
Warwick and Talbot, Salisbury and Gloucester,
Be in their flowing cups freshly remembered.
This story shall the good man teach his son;
And Crispin Crispian shall ne'er go by,

40 *the Feast of Crispian.* 25 October is
the day of Saints Crispinus and Crispianus (compare line 57), who fled
from Rome under Diocletian's oppression but were martyred in AD
287.
48 *And say, 'These wounds I had on
Crispin's day.'* This line occurs in the
Quarto only but sounds authentic.
49 *yet* yet even should the time come
when
50 *with advantages* with additions (a hu-

morous touch typical of the comradely warmth so abundant in this
speech)
51 *our names.* As also in line 60, Henry
seems to speak primarily to and for
his leaders; yet the spirit of his address goes far beyond the leaders
only – if it is *their* names which will
be remembered, it is the common
soldiers who, with a sense of fellowship, will celebrate the remembrance.

From this day to the ending of the world,
But we in it shall be rememberèd –
We few, we happy few, we band of brothers: 60
For he today that sheds his blood with me
Shall be my brother; be he ne'er so vile,
This day shall gentle his condition;
And gentlemen in England now abed
Shall think themselves accursed they were not here,
And hold their manhoods cheap, whiles any speaks
That fought with us upon Saint Crispin's day.
         Enter Salisbury
SALISBURY
My sovereign lord, bestow yourself with speed.
The French are bravely in their battles set,
And will with all expedience charge on us.   70
KING HENRY
All things are ready, if our minds be so.
WESTMORLAND
Perish the man whose mind is backward now!
KING HENRY
Thou dost not wish more help from England, coz?
WESTMORLAND
God's will, my liege, would you and I alone,
Without more help, could fight this royal battle!
KING HENRY
Why, now thou hast unwished five thousand men,
Which likes me better than to wish us one.
You know your places. God be with you all!
         Tucket. Enter Montjoy

61–3 *he today that sheds his blood with me ... his condition.* The 'happy few', who in line 60 seem to be Henry's immediate entourage, are here extended to cover all who shed or endanger their blood with him, and therefore to embrace all in his small force.

69 *bravely* handsomely (since, Holinshed remarks, the French 'made a great show', in contrast to the sombre English)

70 *expedience* celerity

MONTJOY

    Once more I come to know of thee, King Harry,
80   If for thy ransom thou wilt now compound,
    Before thy most assurèd overthrow:
    For certainly thou art so near the gulf
    Thou needs must be englutted. Besides, in mercy,
    The Constable desires thee thou wilt mind
    Thy followers of repentance, that their souls
    May make a peaceful and a sweet retire
    From off these fields, where, wretches, their poor bodies
    Must lie and fester.

KING HENRY   Who hath sent thee now?

MONTJOY

    The Constable of France.

KING HENRY

90   I pray thee bear my former answer back:
    Bid them achieve me, and then sell my bones.
    Good God, why should they mock poor fellows thus?
    The man that once did sell the lion's skin
    While the beast lived, was killed with hunting him.
    A many of our bodies shall no doubt
    Find native graves; upon the which, I trust,
    Shall witness live in brass of this day's work.
    And those that leave their valiant bones in France,
    Dying like men, though buried in your dunghills,
100   They shall be famed; for there the sun shall greet them,
    And draw their honours reeking up to heaven,
    Leaving their earthly parts to choke your clime,
    The smell whereof shall breed a plague in France.
    Mark then abounding valour in our English,

---

80 *compound* come to terms
91 *achieve* (1) gain; (2) kill, finish off
93–4 *The man that once did sell the lion's skin . . . hunting him.* The idea is proverbial, deriving from Aesop's fable of the hunter who sold a bear's skin before he had killed the animal; in the fable he himself escaped death, but only narrowly. (Compare II.3.25, note.)
104 *abounding.* There is a quibble-suggestion of 'rebounding'.

That being dead, like to the bullet's crasing,
Break out into a second course of mischief,
Killing in relapse of mortality.
Let me speak proudly: tell the Constable
We are but warriors for the working-day;
Our gayness and our gilt are all besmirched   110
With rainy marching in the painful field.
There's not a piece of feather in our host —
Good argument, I hope, we will not fly —
And time hath worn us into slovenry.
But, by the mass, our hearts are in the trim;
And my poor soldiers tell me, yet ere night
They'll be in fresher robes, or they will pluck
The gay new coats o'er the French soldiers' heads,
And turn them out of service. If they do this —
As, if God please, they shall — my ransom then   120
Will soon be levied. Herald, save thou thy labour;
Come thou no more for ransom, gentle Herald.
They shall have none, I swear, but these my joints,
Which if they have as I will leave 'em them
Shall yield them little, tell the Constable.

MONTJOY

I shall, King Harry. And so fare thee well:
Thou never shalt hear herald any more.   *Exit*

KING HENRY

I fear thou wilt once more come again for a ransom.
      Enter York

---

105 *crasing* shattering. Many editors
amend to 'grazing' but both Quarto
and Folio agree on 'crasing', and no
change is needed.
107 *in relapse of mortality* by a deadly
rebound
111 *painful* toilsome
117 *or they will* even if they have to
119 *turn them out of service* demobilize
them by removing their liveries. A
servant or soldier wore his master's
liveried coat, which was stripped off

when he left. There is a semi-quibble
on the two kinds of service.
122 *gentle* noble
123–5 *They shall have none, I swear, but
these my joints . . . yield them little.* Holinshed reports that, when the French
herald asked what ransom he would
give, Henry replied 'that his dead
carcass should rather be prize to the
Frenchmen than that his living body
should pay any ransom'.

YORK

130   My lord, most humbly on my knee I beg
The leading of the vaward.

KING HENRY

Take it, brave York. Now, soldiers, march away:
And how Thou pleasest, God, dispose the day!

Exeunt

IV.4   *Alarum. Excursions. Enter Pistol, French Soldier, Boy*

PISTOL

Yield, cur!

FRENCH SOLDIER *Je pense que vous êtes le gentilhomme de
bonne qualité.*

PISTOL

Calitie! 'calen o custure me!'
Art thou a gentleman? What is thy name? Discuss.

FRENCH SOLDIER

O Seigneur Dieu!

PISTOL

O Signieur Dew should be a gentleman:
Perpend my words, O Signieur Dew, and mark.

131 *vaward* vanguard. Henry 'appointed a vaward, of the which he made captain Edward Duke of York, who of an haughty courage had desired that office' (Holinshed).

IV.4 (stage direction) *Excursions* sorties

2–3 *Je pense que vous . . . qualité.* The Folio's French in this scene has been regularized but not completely corrected. Verbs and pronouns in the second person vacillate between singular and plural forms.

4 *Calitie . . . me.* The Folio reads, 'Qualtitie calmie custure me.' 'Qualtitie' is doubtless meant as a parrot-echo of

'qualité' (Folio, '*qualitee*'), but misspelt in printing. By sound-association it prompts Pistol to an Irish refrain ('*Cailin ōg a' stor*' [= 'Maiden, my treasure']) of an Elizabethan song, given in Clement Robinson's *Handefull of Pleasant Delites* (1584).

8 *Perpend* ponder. Shakespeare uses the word five times, always with speakers who are mock-solemn – Touchstone in *As You Like It,* the Clown in *Twelfth Night* – or pompous-pretentious – Pistol here, Falstaff in *The Merry Wives of Windsor*, and Polonius in *Hamlet.*

O Signieur Dew, thou diest on point of fox,
Except, O Signieur, thou do give to me   10
Egregious ransom.

FRENCH SOLDIER *O, prenez miséricorde! Ayez pitié de*
moy!

PISTOL

Moy shall not serve: I will have forty moys,
Or I will fetch thy rim out at thy throat
In drops of crimson blood!

FRENCH SOLDIER *Est-il impossible d'échapper la force de*
ton bras?

PISTOL

Brass, cur?
Thou damnèd and luxurious mountain goat,   20
Offer'st me brass?

FRENCH SOLDIER *O, pardonne-moy!*

PISTOL

Say'st thou me so? Is that a ton of moys?
Come hither, boy: ask me this slave in French
What is his name.

BOY *Écoutez: comment êtes-vous appelé?*

FRENCH SOLDIER *Monsieur le Fer.*

BOY He says his name is Master Fer.

PISTOL Master Fer! I'll fer him, and firk him, and ferret

---

9 *fox* sword. The maker's mark, a wolf,
on fine steel swords was mistaken
for a fox.

11 *Egregious* extraordinary

13 *moy*. This, now spelt 'moi', rhymes in
sixteenth-century usage with other
words in '-oy' – for example, with
'destroy' in *Richard II* (v.3.119–20).
Compare 'le Roy' at iv.1.49.

14 *Moy*. Pistol takes this to be a coin;
the word occurs in French and English for a measure of quantity (about
a bushel).

15 *rim* midriff, diaphragm

18 *bras* (pronounced 'brass' in French of
the time)

20 *luxurious* lascivious
   mountain goat savage lecher (the goat
   being a symbol of lustfulness)

22 *pardonne-moy*. The Folio's '*perdonne
   moy*' is probably meant to be pronounced as the second person singular, phonetically very close to Pistol's
   'a ton of (o') moys'.

29 *fer* (a meaningless echo-word)
   firk trounce
   ferret worry (as a ferret worries its
   prey)

30   him. Discuss the same in French unto him.

BOY I do not know the French for fer, and ferret, and firk.

PISTOL

Bid him prepare, for I will cut his throat.

FRENCH SOLDIER *Que dit-il, monsieur?*

BOY *Il me commande à vous dire que vous faites vous prêt,
car ce soldat içi est disposé tout à cette heure de couper
votre gorge.*

PISTOL

Owy, cuppele gorge, permafoy,

Peasant, unless thou give me crowns, brave crowns;

Or mangled shalt thou be by this my sword.

40 FRENCH SOLDIER *O, je vous supplie, pour l'amour de Dieu,
me pardonner! Je suis le gentilhomme de bonne maison.
Gardez ma vie, et je vous donnerai deux cents écus.*

PISTOL

What are his words?

BOY He prays you to save his life. He is a gentleman of a
good house, and for his ransom he will give you two
hundred crowns.

PISTOL

Tell him my fury shall abate, and I

The crowns will take.

FRENCH SOLDIER *Petit monsieur, que dit-il?*

50 BOY *Encore qu'il est contre son jurement de pardonner aucun
prisonnier; néanmoins, pour les écus que vous l'avez
promis, il est content à vous donner la liberté, le franchise-
ment.*

FRENCH SOLDIER *Sur mes genoux je vous donne mille
remercîments; et je m'estime heureux que je suis tombé
entre les mains d'un chevalier, je pense, le plus brave,
vaillant, et très distingué seigneur d'Angleterre.*

PISTOL

Expound unto me, boy.

BOY He gives you upon his knees a thousand thanks; and

60   he esteems himself happy that he hath fallen into the

hands of one – as he thinks – the most brave, valorous, and thrice-worthy signieur of England.

PISTOL

As I suck blood, I will some mercy show.
Follow me! *Exit*

BOY *Suivez-vous le grand capitaine.* (*Exit French Soldier*)
I did never know so full a voice issue from so empty a heart; but the saying is true, 'The empty vessel makes the greatest sound.' Bardolph and Nym had ten times more valour than this roaring devil i'th'old play, that everyone may pare his nails with a wooden dagger; and they are both hanged – and so would this be, if he durst steal anything adventurously. I must stay with the lackeys, with the luggage of our camp. The French might have a good prey of us, if he knew of it, for there is none to guard it but boys. *Exit*

70

Enter the Constable, Orleans, Bourbon, Dauphin, and IV.5
Rambures

CONSTABLE *O diable!*

63 *As I suck blood.* The characteristic ejaculation which at II.3.53, among Pistol's cronies, was merely predatory is here meant to terrify the enemy.
I will some mercy show. Pistol is breaking military law. Thomas Digges's *Stratioticos* (1579) declares, 'Every soldier shall present such prisoners as are taken to their captain immediately at their return to the camp, and none shall either kill them or license them to depart' (pages 278–9).
69–70 *roaring devil . . . wooden dagger.* This refers to what was apparently a popular morality-play incident. The Clown in *Twelfth Night* sings of 'the

old Vice . . . | Who with dagger of lath . . . | Cries, "Ah, ha!" to the Devil', and who offers to 'Pare [his] nails' (IV.2.120–26). Samuel Harsnet's *Declaration of Popish Impostures* (1603) refers to 'the old church-plays, when the nimble Vice would skip up nimbly like a jackanapes into the Devil's neck, and ride the Devil a course, and belabour him with his wooden dagger, till he made him roar' (pages 114–15).
73–5 *The French might have a good prey . . . boys.* This hints at the massacre to follow (IV.7.1–4); Falstaff's page is to follow his dead master.

ORLEANS *O seigneur! Le jour est perdu, tout est perdu!*

DAUPHIN

Mort Dieu! Ma vie! All is confounded, all

Reproach and everlasting shame

Sits mocking in our plumes. *O méchante fortune!*

    A short alarum

Do not run away!

CONSTABLE   Why, all our ranks are broke.

DAUPHIN

O perdurable shame! Let's stab ourselves.

Be these the wretches that we played at dice for?

ORLEANS

Is this the King we sent to for his ransom?

BOURBON

10   Shame, and eternal shame, nothing but shame!

Let's die in honour! Once more back again!

And he that will not follow Bourbon now,

Let him go hence, and with his cap in hand,

Like a base pander, hold the chamber-door

Whilst by a slave, no gentler than my dog,

His fairest daughter is contaminated.

CONSTABLE

Disorder that hath spoiled us, friend us now!

Let us on heaps go offer up our lives.

ORLEANS

We are enow yet living in the field

20   To smother up the English in our throngs,

If any order might be thought upon.

IV.5.3 *Mort Dieu! Ma vie!* Compare III.5.11, note.

7 *perdurable* (accented on the first syllable)

11 *in honour! Once.* The Folio reads 'in once', a word evidently having dropped out. The Quarto's version of line 23 is 'Lets dye with honour, our shame doth last too long', and this probably supplies the omission. Other suggestions are 'in harness' and 'in arms'.

23 *Let life be short, else shame will be too long.* 'Better die with honour than live with shame' was proverbial.

BOURBON
    The devil take order now! I'll to the throng.
    Let life be short, else shame will be too long.   *Exeunt*

    Alarum. Enter the King and his train, Exeter and   IV.6
    others, with prisoners

KING HENRY
    Well have we done, thrice-valiant countrymen;
    But all's not done – yet keep the French the field.

EXETER
    The Duke of York commends him to your majesty.

KING HENRY
    Lives he, good uncle? Thrice within this hour
    I saw him down; thrice up again, and fighting.
    From helmet to the spur all blood he was.

EXETER
    In which array, brave soldier, doth he lie,
    Larding the plain; and by his bloody side,
    Yoke-fellow to his honour-owing wounds,
    The noble Earl of Suffolk also lies.   10
    Suffolk first died; and York, all haggled over,
    Comes to him, where in gore he lay insteeped,
    And takes him by the beard, kisses the gashes
    That bloodily did yawn upon his face.
    He cries aloud, 'Tarry, my cousin Suffolk!
    My soul shall thine keep company to heaven.
    Tarry, sweet soul, for mine, then fly abreast,
    As in this glorious and well-foughten field
    We kept together in our chivalry!'
    Upon these words I came and cheered him up;   20
    He smiled me in the face, raught me his hand,
    And, with a feeble grip, says, 'Dear my lord,

IV.6.8 *Larding* enriching (with the liquor   11 *haggled* hacked
    of his blood)   21 *raught* reached
9 *owing* owning

Commend my service to my sovereign.'
So did he turn, and over Suffolk's neck
He threw his wounded arm, and kissed his lips,
And so espoused to death, with blood he sealed
A testament of noble-ending love.
The pretty and sweet manner of it forced
Those waters from me which I would have stopped;
30   But I had not so much of man in me,
And all my mother came into mine eyes
And gave me up to tears.

KING HENRY   I blame you not;
For, hearing this, I must perforce compound
With mistful eyes, or they will issue too.

      Alarum

But hark! what new alarum is this same?
The French have reinforced their scattered men.
Then every soldier kill his prisoners!
Give the word through.   *Exeunt*

IV.7   *Enter Fluellen and Gower*

FLUELLEN Kill the poys and the luggage? 'Tis expressly
against the law of arms; 'tis as arrant a piece of knavery,

---

28 *pretty* comely (without the present
'dainty' sense)

31 *my mother* my softer feelings

33–4 *compound | With mistful eyes* allow
my eyes to become misty

35–8 *But hark! what new alarum is this
same? ... Give the word through.* Elegiac sentiment turns suddenly to
brutal reality.

37 *Then every soldier kill his prisoners! Had*
Shakespeare explained this savage
order as Holinshed does, that is, as a
grievous but necessary measure to
save the small English army from
disaster under renewed attack, ham-
pered as it was by hordes of prisoners, Henry would have been spared
some hostile criticisms from commentators, but he seems unaware that
any exoneration is needed. The following comments from Fluellen and
Gower are no help; Gower thinks
the massacre justified because the
King's tents have been plundered,
and Fluellen's outburst turns it to
comedy, as does a piece of apparent
stage business preserved in the
Quarto where, after Henry's order,
Pistol (present but hitherto speechless) ends the scene with his tag line,
'Couple gorge'.

mark you now, as can be offert – in your conscience now, is it not?

GOWER 'Tis certain there's not a boy left alive, and the cowardly rascals that ran from the battle ha' done this slaughter. Besides, they have burnt and carried away all that was in the King's tent, wherefore the King most worthily hath caused every soldier to cut his prisoner's throat. O, 'tis a gallant King!   10

FLUELLEN Ay, he was porn at Monmouth, Captain Gower. What call you the town's name where Alexander the Pig was born?

GOWER Alexander the Great.

FLUELLEN Why, I pray you, is not 'pig' great? The pig, or the great, or the mighty, or the huge, or the magnanimous, are all one reckonings, save the phrase is a little variations.

GOWER I think Alexander the Great was born in Macedon; his father was called Philip of Macedon, as I take it.   20

FLUELLEN I think it is in Macedon where Alexander is porn. I tell you, Captain, if you look in the maps of the 'orld, I warrant you sall find, in the comparisons between Macedon and Monmouth, that the situations, look you, is both alike. There is a river in Macedon, and there is also moreover a river at Monmouth – it is called Wye at Monmouth, but it is out of my prains what is the name of the other river; but 'tis all one, 'tis alike as my fingers is to my fingers, and there is salmons in both. If you mark Alexander's life well, Harry of Monmouth's   30 life is come after it indifferent well; for there is figures in all things. Alexander, God knows and you know, in his rages, and his furies, and his wraths, and his cholers, and his moods, and his displeasures, and his indignations, and also being a little intoxicates in his prains, did in his ales and his angers, look you, kill his best friend Cleitus.

IV.7.31, 42 *figures* parallels

GOWER Our King is not like him in that: he never killed
any of his friends.

40   FLUELLEN It is not well done, mark you now, to take the
tales out of my mouth, ere it is made and finished. I
speak but in the figures and comparisons of it. As
Alexander killed his friend Cleitus, being in his ales
and his cups, so also Harry Monmouth, being in his
right wits and his good judgements, turned away the
fat knight with the great-belly doublet – he was full of
jests, and gipes, and knaveries, and mocks: I have forgot
his name.

GOWER Sir John Falstaff.

50   FLUELLEN That is he. I'll tell you, there is good men porn
at Monmouth.

GOWER Here comes his majesty.

> *Alarum. Enter King Henry and Bourbon, with prisoners;*
> *also Warwick, Gloucester, Exeter, and others. Flourish*

KING HENRY

I was not angry since I came to France
Until this instant. Take a trumpet, Herald;
Ride thou unto the horsemen on yon hill.
If they will fight with us, bid them come down,
Or void the field: they do offend our sight.

42–51 *As Alexander killed his friend Clei-*
tus . . . Monmouth. Inflamed with wine
after a banquet, Alexander quarrelled
with his friend and commander Cleitus in 328 BC and killed him. That
this incident should be used as a
(ludicrously fallacious) parallel to
Henry's dismissal of Falstaff is curious. The apparent purpose is to poke
fun at Fluellen's illogic, but in this
reminder of Falstaff's fate some critics detect an implicit criticism by
Shakespeare of Henry's ruthlessness.
Yet the tone is too light to carry
such an implication; as with the
French prisoners, comedy enters not
to attract attention to but to divert it
from the King's harshness (necessary
in both cases, and specifically
approved by Fluellen and Gower).
Falstaff is so sunk in the past that
Fluellen cannot even recall his name.
46 *great-belly doublet.* The doublet had a
stuffed 'belly' or lower part. Considered as a real person Falstaff would
hardly have needed padding, but
Shakespeare's mind goes back to the
actor who performed the part.
54 *trumpet* trumpeter

If they'll do neither, we will come to them,
And make them skirr away as swift as stones
Enforcèd from the old Assyrian slings.   60
Besides, we'll cut the throats of those we have,
And not a man of them that we shall take
Shall taste our mercy. Go and tell them so.

Enter Montjoy

EXETER

Here comes the Herald of the French, my liege.

GLOUCESTER

His eyes are humbler than they used to be.

KING HENRY

How now, what means this, Herald? Know'st thou not
That I have fined these bones of mine for ransom?
Com'st thou again for ransom?

MONTJOY   No, great King;
I come to thee for charitable licence,
That we may wander o'er this bloody field   70
To book our dead, and then to bury them,
To sort our nobles from our common men.
For many of our princes – woe the while! –
Lie drowned and soaked in mercenary blood;
So do our vulgar drench their peasant limbs
In blood of princes, and their wounded steeds
Fret fetlock-deep in gore, and with wild rage
Yerk out their armèd heels at their dead masters,
Killing them twice. O, give us leave, great King,
To view the field in safety, and dispose   80
Of their dead bodies!

KING HENRY   I tell thee truly, Herald,
I know not if the day be ours or no;
For yet a many of your horsemen peer

59 *skirr* scurry
67 *fined* pledged
77 *Fret* struggle
78 *Yerk* kick, strike
83 *peer* appear

And gallop o'er the field.

MONTJOY   The day is yours.

KING HENRY

Praisèd be God, and not our strength, for it!
What is this castle called that stands hard by?

MONTJOY

They call it Agincourt.

KING HENRY

Then call we this the field of Agincourt,
Fought on the day of Crispin Crispianus.

90 FLUELLEN Your grandfather of famous memory, an't
please your majesty, and your great-uncle Edward the
Plack Prince of Wales, as I have read in the chronicles,
fought a most prave pattle here in France.

KING HENRY They did, Fluellen.

FLUELLEN Your majesty says very true. If your majesties
is remembered of it, the Welshmen did good service in a
garden where leeks did grow, wearing leeks in their
Monmouth caps, which your majesty know to this hour
is an honourable badge of the service; and I do believe
100 your majesty takes no scorn to wear the leek upon Saint
Tavy's day.

KING HENRY

I wear it for a memorable honour;
For I am Welsh, you know, good countryman.

FLUELLEN All the water in Wye cannot wash your
majesty's Welsh plood out of your pody, I can tell you

97 *garden where leeks did grow*. It is not clear whether Fluellen refers to the battle of AD 540 (compare IV.1.55, note) or to Crécy; the episode he cites has not been traced. Shakespeare may have gathered a tradition from Welshmen in London, as he seems to have done for details of Glendower's character in *1 Henry IV*.

98 *Monmouth caps* round brimless caps (originally made at Monmouth)

99–101 *and I do believe . . . day*. Dover Wilson cites Francis Osborne, *Works* (8th edition, 1682, page 610), as evidence of distinguished support for Fluellen – 'Nor did he [the Earl of Essex] fail to wear a leek on St David's Day, but besides would upon all occasions vindicate the Welsh inhabitants and own them for his countrymen, as Queen Elizabeth usually was wont, upon the first of March.'

that. God pless it and preserve it, as long as it pleases
His grace, and His majesty too!

KING HENRY Thanks, good my countryman.

FLUELLEN By Jeshu, I am your majesty's countryman, I
care not who know it; I will confess it to all the 'orld. 110
I need not to be ashamed of your majesty, praised be
God, so long as your majesty is an honest man.

KING HENRY
God keep me so!
       Enter Williams
                 Our heralds go with him.
Bring me just notice of the numbers dead
On both our parts.   *Exeunt Heralds with Montjoy*
                 Call yonder fellow hither.

EXETER Soldier, you must come to the King.

KING HENRY Soldier, why wear'st thou that glove in thy
cap?

WILLIAMS An't please your majesty, 'tis the gage of one
that I should fight withal, if he be alive.   120

KING HENRY An Englishman?

WILLIAMS An't please your majesty, a rascal that
swaggered with me last night: who, if 'a live and ever
dare to challenge this glove, I have sworn to take him a
box o'th'ear: or if I can see my glove in his cap, which he
swore as he was a soldier he would wear if alive, I will
strike it out soundly.

KING HENRY What think you, Captain Fluellen, is it
fit this soldier keep his oath?

FLUELLEN He is a craven and a villain else, an't please   130
your majesty, in my conscience.

KING HENRY It may be his enemy is a gentleman of
great sort, quite from the answer of his degree.

FLUELLEN Though he be as good a gentleman as the

---

105 *Welsh plood.* Henry's great-grand-
mother was Welsh, and he himself
born at Monmouth.

133 *sort* rank

from the answer of his degree exempt
from answering one of his station
134-5 *as good . . . as the devil is.* The idea
was traditional, the devil being of

devil is, as Lucifer and Belzebub himself, it is necessary, look your grace, that he keep his vow and his oath. If he be perjured, see you now, his reputation is as arrant a villain and a Jack-sauce as ever his black shoe trod upon God's ground and His earth, in my conscience, la!

140 KING HENRY Then keep thy vow, sirrah, when thou meet'st the fellow.

WILLIAMS So I will, my liege, as I live.

KING HENRY Who serv'st thou under?

WILLIAMS Under Captain Gower, my liege.

FLUELLEN Gower is a good captain, and is good knowledge and literatured in the wars.

KING HENRY Call him hither to me, soldier.

WILLIAMS I will, my liege.   *Exit*

KING HENRY Here, Fluellen, wear thou this favour for
150 me, and stick it in thy cap. When Alençon and myself were down together, I plucked this glove from his helm. If any man challenge this, he is a friend to Alençon, and an enemy to our person: if thou encounter any such, apprehend him, an thou dost me love.

FLUELLEN Your grace doo's me as great honours as can be desired in the hearts of his subjects. I would fain see the man that has but two legs that shall find himself aggriefed at this glove, that is all: but I would fain see it once, and please God of His grace that I might see.

160 KING HENRY Know'st thou Gower?

FLUELLEN He is my dear friend, an please you.

KING HENRY Pray thee go seek him, and bring him to my tent.

---

the highest rank among angels; compare *King Lear*, III.4.139 – 'The prince of darkness is a gentleman.'
138 *Jack-sauce* saucy knave
149–54 *Here, Fluellen, wear this favour ... dost me love.* Henry's jest involves

straightfaced lying, but not more so than many a leg-pull, soldierly or other, and he at once ensures that no harm shall follow (lines 165–77). Fluellen's gratification is very funny (lines 155–9).

FLUELLEN I will fetch him. *Exit*

KING HENRY
My Lord of Warwick, and my brother Gloucester,
Follow Fluellen closely at the heels.
The glove which I have given him for a favour
May haply purchase him a box o'th'ear.
It is the soldier's: I by bargain should
Wear it myself. Follow, good cousin Warwick. 170
If that the soldier strike him, as I judge
By his blunt bearing he will keep his word,
Some sudden mischief may arise of it;
For I do know Fluellen valiant,
And, touched with choler, hot as gunpowder,
And quickly will return an injury.
Follow, and see there be no harm between them.
Go you with me, uncle of Exeter. *Exeunt*

Enter Gower and Williams IV.8

WILLIAMS I warrant it is to knight you, Captain.
Enter Fluellen

FLUELLEN God's will and His pleasure, Captain, I
beseech you now, come apace to the King. There is
more good toward you, peradventure, than is in your
knowledge to dream of.

WILLIAMS Sir, know you this glove?

FLUELLEN Know the glove? I know the glove is a glove.

WILLIAMS I know this; and thus I challenge it.
He strikes him

FLUELLEN 'Sblood! an arrant traitor as any's in the
universal world, or in France, or in England! 10

GOWER How now, sir? You villain!

168 *haply* perhaps

IV.8.1 *I warrant it is to knight you, Captain.*
The comradely tone between the sol-
dier and his captain is characteristic
of the English army, whereas the
French are widely divided into
nobles, peasants, and mercenaries.

WILLIAMS Do you think I'll be forsworn?

FLUELLEN Stand away, Captain Gower: I will give treason
his payment into plows, I warrant you.

WILLIAMS I am no traitor.

FLUELLEN That's a lie in thy throat. I charge you in his
majesty's name, apprehend him: he's a friend of the
Duke Alençon's.

Enter Warwick and Gloucester

WARWICK How now, how now, what's the matter?

20 FLUELLEN My Lord of Warwick, here is — praised be
God for it! — a most contagious treason come to light,
look you, as you shall desire in a summer's day. Here is
his majesty.

Enter the King and Exeter

KING HENRY How now, what's the matter?

FLUELLEN My liege, here is a villain and a traitor, that,
look your grace, has struck the glove which your majesty
is take out of the helmet of Alençon

WILLIAMS My liege, this was my glove, here is the fellow
of it; and he that I gave it to in change promised to wear
30 it in his cap. I promised to strike him if he did. I met
this man with my glove in his cap, and I have been as
good as my word.

FLUELLEN Your majesty hear now, saving your majesty's
manhood, what an arrant, rascally, beggarly, lousy knave
it is. I hope your majesty is pear me testimony and
witness, and will avouchment, that this is the glove of
Alençon that your majesty is give me, in your conscience,
now.

KING HENRY Give me thy glove, soldier. Look, here is the
40 fellow of it.
'Twas I indeed thou promisèd'st to strike,
And thou hast given me most bitter terms.

16 *lie in thy throat*. A lie in the throat
was one uttered deliberately and inex-
cusably; a lie in the teeth was a
degree less grave and objectionable.
36 *avouchment* assurance

FLUELLEN An please your majesty, let his neck answer for
it, if there is any martial law in the world.

KING HENRY How canst thou make me satisfaction?

WILLIAMS All offences, my lord, come from the heart:
never came any from mine that might offend your
majesty.

KING HENRY It was ourself thou didst abuse.

WILLIAMS Your majesty came not like yourself: you   50
appeared to me but as a common man – witness the
night, your garments, your lowliness; and what your
highness suffered under that shape, I beseech you take
it for your own fault, and not mine; for had you been
as I took you for, I made no offence: therefore, I beseech your highness, pardon me.

KING HENRY
Here, uncle Exeter, fill this glove with crowns,
And give it to this fellow. Keep it, fellow,
And wear it for an honour in thy cap
Till I do challenge it. Give him the crowns;   60
And, Captain, you must needs be friends with him.

FLUELLEN By this day and this light, the fellow has
mettle enough in his belly. Hold, there is twelve pence
for you, and I pray you to serve God, and keep you out
prawls, and prabbles, and quarrels, and dissensions,
and I warrant you it is the better for you.

WILLIAM I will none of your money.

FLUELLEN It is with a good will: I can tell you it will serve
you to mend your shoes. Come, wherefore should you
be so pashful? – your shoes is not so good; 'tis a good   70
silling, I warrant you, or I will change it.
          Enter an English Herald
KING HENRY Now, Herald, are the dead numbered?

46–56 *All offences ... pardon me.* The
honest rightness of Williams's answers is admirable, a further sign of
the manliness existing between all
ranks in the King's army and evinced
when Henry rewards him and takes
care to reconcile him to Fluellen.

HERALD
  Here is the number of the slaughtered French.
      He gives him a paper

KING HENRY
  What prisoners of good sort are taken, uncle?

EXETER
  Charles Duke of Orleans, nephew to the King;
  John Duke of Bourbon, and Lord Bouciqualt;
  Of other lords and barons, knights and squires,
  Full fifteen hundred, besides common men.

KING HENRY
  This note doth tell me of ten thousand French
80 That in the field lie slain. Of princes, in this number,
  And nobles bearing banners, there lie dead
  One hundred twenty-six: added to these,
  Of knights, esquires, and gallant gentlemen,
  Eight thousand and four hundred; of the which,
  Five hundred were but yesterday dubbed knights.
  So that, in these ten thousand they have lost,
  There are but sixteen hundred mercenaries;
  The rest are princes, barons, lords, knights, squires,
  And gentlemen of blood and quality.
90 The names of those their nobles that lie dead:
  Charles Delabreth, High Constable of France,
  Jaques of Chatillon, Admiral of France,
  The Master of the Cross-bows, Lord Rambures,
  Great Master of France, the brave Sir Guichard
          Dauphin,
  John Duke of Alençon, Antony Duke of Brabant,
  The brother to the Duke of Burgundy,
  And Edward Duke of Bar: of lusty earls,
  Grandpré and Roussi, Faulconbridge and Foix,
  Beaumont and Marle, Vaudemont and Lestrake.
100 Here was a royal fellowship of death!

75-99 *Charles Duke of Orleans, nephew to
the King ... Vaudemont and Lestrake.*

This transcribes Holinshed nearly
word for word.

Where is the number of our English dead?
> *The Herald gives him another paper*

Edward the Duke of York, the Earl of Suffolk,
Sir Richard Kikely, Davy Gam, esquire;
None else of name; and of all other men
But five-and-twenty. O God, Thy arm was here!
And not to us, but to Thy arm alone,
Ascribe we all! When, without stratagem,
But in plain shock and even play of battle,
Was ever known so great and little loss
On one part and on th'other? Take it, God,   110
For it is none but Thine!

FLUELLEN   'Tis wonderful!

KING HENRY

Come, go we in procession to the village:
And be it death proclaimèd through our host
To boast of this, or take that praise from God
Which is His only.

FLUELLEN Is it not lawful, an please your majesty, to tell
how many is killed?

KING HENRY

Yes, Captain, but with this acknowledgement,
That God fought for us.

FLUELLEN Yes, my conscience, He did us great good.   120

KING HENRY

Do we all holy rites:
Let there be sung *Non Nobis* and *Te Deum*,
The dead with charity enclosed in clay;

---

103 *Kikely* (spelt thus in Holinshed;
'*Ketly*' in the Folio)

105 *five-and-twenty*. Holinshed gives this
figure 'as some do report', though
he also records 'other writers of
greater credit' as reckoning 'above
five or six hundred' English dead.
Modern historians estimate about
7,000 French dead and 400–500 English, a discrepancy striking enough.
By uncritically accepting an absurd

figure, Shakespeare, contrary to the
realism he had shown in *Henry IV*,
seems to capitulate to the 'miraculous' view of Henry.

108 *even* equal

122 *Non Nobis . . . Te Deum*. These are
the opening words of Psalm 115 (part
of 113 in the Vulgate), 'Give praise
not unto us, O God', and of the
canticle *Te Deum laudamus*, 'We praise
Thee, O God'.

And then to Calais, and to England then,
Where ne'er from France arrived more happy men.

Exeunt

V   *Flourish. Enter Chorus*

CHORUS
    Vouchsafe to those that have not read the story
    That I may prompt them; and of such as have,
    I humbly pray them to admit th'excuse
    Of time, of numbers, and due course of things,
    Which cannot in their huge and proper life
    Be here presented. Now we bear the King
    Toward Calais. Grant him there: there seen,
    Heave him away upon your wingèd thoughts
    Athwart the sea. Behold, the English beach
10   Pales in the flood with men, with wives, and boys,
    Whose shouts and claps outvoice the deep-mouthed
         sea,
    Which like a mighty whiffler fore the King
    Seems to prepare his way. So let him land,
    And solemnly see him set on to London.
    So swift a pace hath thought that even now
    You may imagine him upon Blackheath,
    Where that his lords desire him to have borne
    His bruisèd helmet and his bended sword
    Before him through the city. He forbids it,
20   Being free from vainness and self-glorious pride,
    Giving full trophy, signal, and ostent
    Quite from himself to God. But now behold,

---

v. *Chorus* 3–4 *th'excuse* | *Of time.* Be-
tween Agincourt (1415) and the
Treaty of Troyes five years elapsed;
compare lines 38–41, note.
10 *Pales* fences (as with palings)

12 *whiffler* attendant (whose job it is to
clear the way)
21 *full trophy, signal, and ostent* every
token, sign, and display of honour

In the quick forge and working-house of thought,
How London doth pour out her citizens:
The Mayor and all his brethren in best sort,
Like to the senators of th'antique Rome,
With the plebeians swarming at their heels,
Go forth and fetch their conquering Caesar in:
As, by a lower but loving likelihood,
Were now the General of our gracious Empress –   30
As in good time he may – from Ireland coming,
Bringing rebellion broachèd on his sword,
How many would the peaceful city quit
To welcome him! Much more, and much more cause,
Did they this Harry. Now in London place him –
As yet the lamentation of the French
Invites the King of England's stay at home.
The Emperor's coming in behalf of France
To order peace between them; and omit
All the occurrences, whatever chanced,   40
Till Harry's back-return again to France.
There must we bring him; and myself have played
The interim, by remembering you 'tis past.
Then brook abridgement, and your eyes advance,

23 *working-house* place of industry
25–8 *The Mayor and all his brethren in best sort ... Caesar in.* 'The mayor of London, and the aldermen, apparelled in orient grained scarlet, and four hundred commoners clad in beautiful murrey [cloth of mulberry colour], well mounted, and trimly horsed, with rich collars, and great chains, met the king on Blackheath, rejoicing at his return' (Holinshed).
25 *in best sort* of the highest station
29 *lower but loving likelihood* like probability, less exalted but eagerly desired
30–32 *the General of our gracious Empress ... on his sword.* For Essex's expedition to suppress Tyrone, see the In-

troduction, page 669. Begun early in 1599, the play reflects the vigorous military preparations and confidence which launched the enterprise.
38–41 *The Emperor's coming ... France.* The Emperor Sigismund came to England to negotiate on behalf of France in May, 1416; further English invasions of France took place in 1416–19; and the Treaty of Troyes was signed in 1420. The play recognizes no appreciable interval between the events of IV.8 and those of V.1 (Dr Johnson indeed thought that V.1 should be the last scene of Act IV).
43 *remembering* reminding

After your thoughts, straight back again to France.

Exit

V.I   *Enter Fluellen and Gower*

GOWER Nay, that's right; but why wear you your leek
today? Saint Davy's day is past.

FLUELLEN There is occasions and causes why and wherefore in all things. I will tell you ass my friend, Captain
Gower: the rascally, scauld, beggarly, lousy, pragging
knave Pistol – which you and yourself and all the world
know to be no petter than a fellow, look you now, of no
merits – he is come to me and prings me pread and salt
yesterday, look you, and bid me eat my leek. It was in a
place where I could not breed no contention with him;
but I will be so bold as to wear it in my cap till I see
him once again, and then I will tell him a little piece of
my desires.

Enter Pistol

GOWER Why, here he comes, swelling like a turkey-cock.

FLUELLEN 'Tis no matter for his swellings nor his turkey-
cocks. God pless you, Aunchient Pistol! you scurvy,
lousy knave, God pless you!

PISTOL

Ha, art thou bedlam? Dost thou thirst, base Troyan,
To have me fold up Parca's fatal web?
Hence! I am qualmish at the smell of leek.

FLUELLEN I peseech you heartily, scurvy, lousy knave,
at my desires, and my requests, and my petitions, to eat,
look you, this leek. Because, look you, you do not love
it, nor your affections, and your appetites, and your
digestions, doo's not agree with it, I would desire you to
eat it.

10

20

---

v.i.5 *scauld* scurvy
18 *bedlam* lunatic
     Troyan (often, like Corinthian, Eph-
     esian, Greek, etc., used for a boon

companion, but here, in effect,
knave)
19 *Parca's fatal web* the web of life (spun
and cut by the three Parcae or Fates)

PISTOL

  Not for Cadwallader and all his goats!

FLUELLEN There is one goat for you. (*He strikes him*)
  Will you be so good, scauld knave, as eat it?

PISTOL

  Base Troyan, thou shalt die!   30

FLUELLEN You say very true, scauld knave, when God's
  will is. I will desire you to live in the meantime, and
  eat your victuals – come, there is sauce for it. (*He strikes
  him again*) You called me yesterday mountain-squire,
  but I will make you today a squire of low degree. I pray
  you fall to – if you can mock a leek, you can eat a leek.

GOWER Enough, Captain, you have astonished him.

FLUELLEN I say, I will make him eat some part of my leek,
  or I will peat his pate four days. Bite, I pray you, it is
  good for your green wound and your ploody coxcomb.   40

PISTOL Must I bite?

FLUELLEN Yes, certainly, and out of doubt, and out of
  question too, and ambiguities.

PISTOL By this leek, I will most horribly revenge – I eat
  and eat, I swear –

FLUELLEN Eat, I pray you; will you have some more
  sauce to your leek? There is not enough leek to swear
  by.

PISTOL Quiet thy cudgel, thou dost see I eat.

FLUELLEN Much good do you, scauld knave, heartily.   50
  Nay, pray you throw none away, the skin is good for
  your broken coxcomb. When you take occasions to see
  leeks hereafter, I pray you mock at 'em, that is all.

PISTOL Good!

27 *Cadwallader* (a famous seventh-century Welsh warrior)
34 *mountain-squire* squire of the barren Welsh hills
35 *squire of low degree* (an allusion to the title of a medieval romance)
37 *astonished* stupefied
40 *green* fresh
  coxcomb fool's head
52 *broken* wounded (not 'fractured')

FLUELLEN   Ay, leeks is good. Hold you, there is a groat to
heal your pate.

PISTOL   Me a groat?

FLUELLEN   Yes, verily and in truth you shall take it, or I
have another leek in my pocket which you shall eat.

60   PISTOL   I take thy groat in earnest of revenge.

FLUELLEN   If I owe you anything, I will pay you in
cudgels — you shall be a woodmonger, and buy nothing
of me but cudgels. God bye you, and keep you, and heal
your pate.   *Exit*

PISTOL

All hell shall stir for this!

GOWER   Go, go, you are a counterfeit cowardly knave.
Will you mock at an ancient tradition, begun upon an
honourable respect, and worn as a memorable trophy
of predeceased valour, and dare not avouch in your
70   deeds any of your words? I have seen you gleeking and
galling at this gentleman twice or thrice. You thought,
because he could not speak English in the native garb,
he could not therefore handle an English cudgel. You
find it otherwise, and henceforth let a Welsh correction
teach you a good English condition. Fare ye well. *Exit*

PISTOL

Doth Fortune play the housewife with me now?
News have I that my Doll is dead i'th'spital

---

55 *groat* fourpenny piece

60 *earnest* first instalment (as a pledge
that a bargain will be fulfilled)

67–9 *an ancient tradition . . . valour.* Compare IV.1.55, note.

70–71 *gleeking and galling* mocking and
jeering

76 *housewife* hussy, jade (pronounced
'hussif')

77 *Doll.* Both the Quarto and the Folio
read 'Doll', but, since Doll Tearsheet
was Falstaff's woman and Nell
Quickly Pistol's, many editors
change to 'Nell'. Some argue that
Falstaff originally appeared in *Henry*

V (as promised in the epilogue to *2
Henry IV*) and that his part was later
transferred to Pistol, 'Doll' remaining unchanged through an oversight
though it should have been altered
to 'Nell'. The theory is unlikely, and
'Doll' is probably a mere slip, arising
from the similarity of the two
women's positions and names. Apart
from many difficulties in envisaging
Falstaff in France, this speech and
the action preceding it are very appropriate to Pistol, very inappropriate
to Falstaff.

spital hospital

Of malady of France,
And there my rendezvous is quite cut off.
Old I do wax, and from my weary limbs   80
Honour is cudgellèd. Well, bawd I'll turn,
And something lean to cutpurse of quick hand.
To England will I steal, and there I'll – steal;
And patches will I get unto these cudgelled scars,
And swear I got them in the Gallia wars.   *Exit*

> *Enter, at one door, King Henry, Exeter, Bedford,* V.2
> *Gloucester, Clarence, Warwick, Westmorland, Hunt-*
> *ingdon, and other Lords; at another, the French King,*
> *Queen Isabel, the Princess Katherine, Alice, and*
> *other French, the Duke of Burgundy and his train*

KING HENRY
Peace to this meeting, wherefor we are met!
Unto our brother France, and to our sister,
Health and fair time of day. Joy and good wishes
To our most fair and princely cousin Katherine;
And, as a branch and member of this royalty,
By whom this great assembly is contrived,
We do salute you, Duke of Burgundy;
And, Princes French, and peers, health to you all!

FRENCH KING
Right joyous are we to behold your face,
Most worthy brother England: fairly met!   10
So are you, Princes English, every one.

---

78 *malady of France* venereal disease
79 *rendezvous* refuge
83–5 *To England will I steal ... Gallia
   wars.* 'The comic scenes of *The History of Henry the Fourth* and *Fifth* are
   now at an end, and all the comic
   personages are now dismissed. Falstaff and Mrs Quickly are dead; Nym

and Bardolph are hanged; Gadshill
was lost immediately after the robbery; Poins and Peto have vanished
since, one knows not how; and Pistol
is now beaten into obscurity. I believe every reader regrets their departure' (Johnson).

QUEEN ISABEL

So happy be the issue, brother England,
Of this good day, and of this gracious meeting,
As we are now glad to behold your eyes –
Your eyes which hitherto have borne in them,
Against the French that met them in their bent,
The fatal balls of murdering basilisks.
The venom of such looks, we fairly hope,
Have lost their quality, and that this day
20   Shall change all griefs and quarrels into love.

KING HENRY

To cry 'Amen' to that, thus we appear.

QUEEN ISABEL

You English Princes all, I do salute you.

BURGUNDY

My duty to you both, on equal love,
Great Kings of France and England! That I have
        laboured
With all my wits, my pains, and strong endeavours,
To bring your most imperial majesties
Unto this bar and royal interview,
Your mightiness on both parts best can witness.
Since, then, my office hath so far prevailed
30   That face to face, and royal eye to eye,
You have congreeted, let it not disgrace me
If I demand, before this royal view,
What rub or what impediment there is
Why that the naked, poor, and mangled peace,
Dear nurse of arts, plenties, and joyful births,
Should not in this best garden of the world,

---

v.2.17 *The fatal balls of murdering basilisks*.
Basilisks were: (1) fabulous reptiles
(hatched by a serpent from a cockatrice's egg) which killed by projecting a venomous influence from their
eye-balls; (2) large cannon (originally

marked   with   the   device   of   a
basilisk).
27 *bar* tribunal
31 *congreeted* greeted each other
33 *rub* hindrance

Our fertile France, put up her lovely visage?
Alas, she hath from France too long been chased,
And all her husbandry doth lie on heaps,
Corrupting in it own fertility.   40
Her vine, the merry cheerer of the heart,
Unprunèd dies; her hedges even-pleached,
Like prisoners wildly overgrown with hair,
Put forth disordered twigs; her fallow leas
The darnel, hemlock, and rank fumitory
Doth root upon, while that the coulter rusts
That should deracinate such savagery.
The even mead, that erst brought sweetly forth
The freckled cowslip, burnet, and green clover,
Wanting the scythe, all uncorrected, rank,   50
Conceives by idleness, and nothing teems
But hateful docks, rough thistles, kecksies, burs,
Losing both beauty and utility;
And as our vineyards, fallows, meads, and hedges,
Defective in their natures, grow to wildness,
Even so our houses and ourselves and children
Have lost, or do not learn for want of time,
The sciences that should become our country,
But grow like savages – as soldiers will
That nothing do but meditate on blood –   60
To swearing and stern looks, diffused attire,
And everything that seems unnatural.
Which to reduce into our former favour
You are assembled; and my speech entreats

---

40 *it* its (the old genitive form)
42 *even-pleached* evenly layered, plaited
44 *fallow leas* unsown arable land
45 *The darnel, hemlock, and rank fumitory.*
These are weeds particularly liable to
grow on cultivated land; in *King Lear*
they are included among 'the idle
weeds that grow | In our sustaining
corn' (IV.4.3–6).

46 *coulter* blade in front of the
ploughshare
51 *teems* abounds
52 *kecksies* (plants with) dry hollow innu-
trient stems
61 *diffused* disordered
63 *reduce into our former favour* restore to
the favourable aspect we used to
show

That I may know the let why gentle peace
Should not expel these inconveniences,
And bless us with her former qualities.

KING HENRY

If, Duke of Burgundy, you would the peace
Whose want gives growth to th'imperfections
Which you have cited, you must buy that peace
With full accord to all our just demands,
Whose tenors and particular effects
You have, enscheduled briefly, in your hands.

BURGUNDY

The King hath heard them, to the which as yet
There is no answer made.

KING HENRY   Well then, the peace
Which you before so urged lies in his answer.

FRENCH KING

I have but with a cursitory eye
O'erglanced the articles. Pleaseth your grace
To appoint some of your Council presently
To sit with us once more, with better heed
To re-survey them, we will suddenly
Pass our accept and peremptory answer.

KING HENRY

Brother, we shall. Go, uncle Exeter,
And brother Clarence, and you, brother Gloucester,
Warwick, and Huntingdon, go with the King;
And take with you free power to ratify,
Augment, or alter, as your wisdoms best
Shall see advantageable for our dignity,
Anything in or out of our demands,
And we'll consign thereto. Will you, fair sister,
Go with the Princes, or stay here with us?

65 *let* hindrance
68 *would* would have
77 *cursitory* cursory
79 *presently* immediately

82 *accept and peremptory answer* decision
and definitive reply
90 *consign* sign jointly

QUEEN ISABEL
  Our gracious brother, I will go with them.
  Haply a woman's voice may do some good,
  When articles too nicely urged be stood on.

KING HENRY
  Yet leave our cousin Katherine here with us;
  She is our capital demand, comprised
  Within the fore-rank of our articles.

QUEEN ISABEL
  She hath good leave.

> *Exeunt all but Henry, Katherine, and Alice*

KING HENRY   Fair Katherine, and most fair,
  Will you vouchsafe to teach a soldier terms
  Such as will enter at a lady's ear   100
  And plead his love-suit to her gentle heart?

KATHERINE Your majesty shall mock at me; I cannot
  speak your England.

KING HENRY O fair Katherine, if you will love me soundly
  with your French heart, I will be glad to hear you confess
  it brokenly with your English tongue. Do you like me,
  Kate?

KATHERINE *Pardonnez-moi*, I cannot tell wat is 'like me'.

KING HENRY An angel is like you, Kate, and you are like
  an angel.   110

KATHERINE *Que dit-il? que je suis semblable à les anges?*

ALICE *Oui, vraiment, sauf votre grâce, ainsi dit-il.*

KING HENRY I said so, dear Katherine, and I must not
  blush to affirm it.

KATHERINE *O bon Dieu! Les langues des hommes sont
  pleines de tromperies.*

KING HENRY What says she, fair one? that the tongues of
  men are full of deceits?

---

94 *When articles too nicely urged be stood on*
when items are insisted upon too
particularly

96 *capital* principal. The marriage was in
fact the first article of the Treaty of
Troyes; compare lines 97, 326.

ALICE *Oui*, dat de tongues of de mans is be full of deceits —
120   dat is de *Princesse*.
KING HENRY The Princess is the better Englishwoman.
I'faith, Kate, my wooing is fit for thy understanding. I
am glad thou canst speak no better English; for if thou
couldst, thou wouldst find me such a plain king that
thou wouldst think I had sold my farm to buy my crown.
I know no ways to mince it in love, but directly to say,
'I love you': then if you urge me farther than to say,
'Do you, in faith?' I wear out my suit. Give me your
answer, i'faith, do; and so clap hands, and a bargain.
130   How say you, lady?
KATHERINE *Sauf votre honneur*, me understand well.
KING HENRY Marry, if you would put me to verses, or to
dance for your sake, Kate, why, you undid me. For the
one, I have neither words nor measure; and for the
other, I have no strength in measure, yet a reasonable
measure in strength. If I could win a lady at leapfrog,
or by vaulting into my saddle with my armour on my
back, under the correction of bragging be it spoken, I
should quickly leap into a wife. Or if I might buffet for
140   my love, or bound my horse for her favours, I could lay
on like a butcher, and sit like a jackanapes, never off.

121 *is the better Englishwoman* qualifies as
a good Englishwoman (in preferring
plain dealing)
124 *such a plain king*. Johnson expressed
surprise that 'Shakespeare now gives
the King nearly such a character as
he made him formerly ridicule in
Percy' (*1 Henry IV*), but, as the
nineteenth-century editor S. W.
Singer rejoined, 'Shakespeare only
meant to characterize English downright sincerity; and surely the previous habits of Henry . . . do not make
us expect great refinement or polish
in him upon this occasion, especially
as fine speeches would be lost upon
the Princess from her imperfect com-

prehension of his language.'
134 *measure* (skill in) metre
135 *I have no strength in measure* I am no
good at dancing
136–41 *If I could win . . . never off*. Among
other praises of Henry, Holinshed
writes: 'In wrestling, leaping, and
running, no man [was] well able to
compare with him.' As Prince Hal,
when fully armed for war Henry
'vaulted with such ease into his seat'
that he seemed the angelic rider of a
fiery Pegasus, to 'witch the world
with noble horsemanship' (*1 Henry
IV*, IV.I.107–10).
141 *jackanapes* monkey

But, before God, Kate, I cannot look greenly, nor gasp
out my eloquence, nor I have no cunning in protestation:
only downright oaths, which I never use till urged, nor
never break for urging. If thou canst love a fellow of this
temper, Kate, whose face is not worth sunburning, that
never looks in his glass for love of anything he sees
there, let thine eye be thy cook. I speak to thee plain
soldier. If thou canst love me for this, take me; if not,
to say to thee that I shall die is true – but for thy love,   150
by the Lord, no – yet I love thee too. And while thou
liv'st, dear Kate, take a fellow of plain and uncoined
constancy; for he perforce must do thee right, because
he hath not the gift to woo in other places. For these
fellows of infinite tongue, that can rhyme themselves
into ladies' favours, they do always reason themselves
out again. What! A speaker is but a prater, a rhyme is
but a ballad. A good leg will fall; a straight back will
stoop; a black beard will turn white; a curled pate will
grow bald; a fair face will wither; a full eye will wax   160
hollow: but a good heart, Kate, is the sun and the moon
– or rather, the sun, and not the moon; for it shines
bright and never changes, but keeps his course truly.
If thou would have such a one, take me; and take me,
take a soldier; take a soldier, take a king. And what

142 *greenly* like a green, callow, youth
146 *not worth sunburning* one that the sun
could not make worse. A sunburnt
face was thought unbecoming; compare *Troilus and Cressida* – 'The Gre-
cian dames are sunburnt and not
worth | The splinter of a lance'
(1.3.282–3).
148 *be thy cook* serve me up to your taste
149–51 *If thou canst love me for this . . .
thee too.* This cheerful mockery of
romantic extravagance finds a close
parallel in Rosalind's common-sense
to Orlando, in *As You Like It*
(IV.1.83–94).

152 *uncoined* (1) unalloyed, genuine; (2)
not put into circulation
155–6 *rhyme themselves into ladies' favours.*
Henry deriding rhyming wooers recalls Benedick admitting that he 'was
not born under a rhyming planet'
(*Much Ado About Nothing*, V.2.36),
Berowne claiming that, being
'honest', he would never 'write a
thing in rhyme' (*Love's Labour's Lost*,
IV.3.177), and Hotspur ridiculing
Glendower's 'mincing poetry' (*1
Henry IV*, III.1.134).
158 *but a ballad.* Ballads were often mere
doggerel, and scorned as such.

say'st thou then to my love? Speak, my fair, and fairly,
I pray thee.

KATHERINE Is it possible dat I sould love de *ennemi* of
France?

170 KING HENRY No, it is not possible you should love the
enemy of France, Kate; but in loving me you should
love the friend of France, for I love France so well that
I will not part with a village of it – I will have it all mine:
and Kate, when France is mine, and I am yours, then
yours is France, and you are mine.

KATHERINE I cannot tell wat is dat.

KING HENRY No, Kate? I will tell thee in French, which
I am sure will hang upon my tongue like a new-married
wife about her husband's neck, hardly to be shook off.
180 *Je – quand sur le possession de France, et quand vous avez
le possession de moi,* – let me see, what then? Saint Denis
be my speed! – *donc vôtre est France, et vous êtes mienne.*
It is as easy for me, Kate, to conquer the kingdom as to
speak so much more French. I shall never move thee in
French, unless it be to laugh at me.

KATHERINE *Sauf votre honneur, le français que vous
parlez, il est meilleur que l'anglais lequel je parle.*

KING HENRY No, faith, is't not, Kate; but thy speaking
of my tongue, and I thine, most truly-falsely, must
190 needs be granted to be much at one. But Kate, dost
thou understand thus much English – canst thou love
me?

KATHERINE I cannot tell.

KING HENRY Can any of your neighbours tell, Kate?
I'll ask them. Come, I know thou lovest me; and at
night, when you come into your closet, you'll question

180–82 *Je – quand sur le possession* ...
mienne. The Quarto suggests a lively
stage adaptation of this; see the Collation on page 724.

181 *Saint Denis.* Henry appeals to the
patron saint of France.
189 *truly-falsely* true-heartedly but incorrectly

this gentlewoman about me; and I know, Kate, you will to her dispraise those parts in me that you love with your heart. But, good Kate, mock me mercifully; the rather, gentle Princess, because I love thee cruelly. 200 If ever thou beest mine, Kate, as I have a saving faith within me tells me thou shalt, I get thee with scambling, and thou must therefore needs prove a good soldier-breeder. Shall not thou and I, between Saint Denis and Saint George, compound a boy, half French, half English, that shall go to Constantinople and take the Turk by the beard? Shall we not? What say'st thou, my fair flower-de-luce?

KATHERINE I do not know dat.

KING HENRY No, 'tis hereafter to know, but now to 210 promise. Do but now promise, Kate, you will endeavour for your French part of such a boy, and for my English moiety take the word of a king and a bachelor. How answer you, *la plus belle Katherine du monde, mon très cher et devin déesse?*

KATHERINE Your majestee 'ave *fausse* French enough to deceive de most *sage demoiselle* dat is *en France.*

KING HENRY Now fie upon my false French! By mine honour, in true English, I love thee, Kate: by which honour I dare not swear thou lovest me, yet my blood 220 begins to flatter me that thou dost, notwithstanding the poor and untempering effect of my visage. Now beshrew my father's ambition! He was thinking of civil wars when he got me; therefore was I created with a stubborn outside, with an aspect of iron, that when I come to woo

---

202 *scambling* fighting
206 *Constantinople.* The city did not fall to the Turks until 1453, thirty-one years after Henry died, but its recovery was thereafter a project which haunted Christian leaders. The 'boy' whom Henry foresees winning it was in fact the incompetent Henry VI under whom England suffered the Wars of the Roses.
214–15 *mon très cher et devin déesse.* Henry's French is, as Katherine says, '*fausse*'.
222 *untempering* unsoftening

ladies I fright them. But in faith, Kate, the elder I wax, the better I shall appear. My comfort is, that old age, that ill layer-up of beauty, can do no more spoil upon my face. Thou hast me, if thou hast me, at the worst; and thou shalt wear me, if thou wear me, better and better; and therefore tell me, most fair Katherine, will you have me? Put off your maiden blushes, avouch the thoughts of your heart with the looks of an empress, take me by the hand, and say, 'Harry of England, I am thine': which word thou shalt no sooner bless mine ear withal but I will tell thee aloud, 'England is thine, Ireland is thine, France is thine, and Henry Plantagenet is thine' – who, though I speak it before his face, if he be not fellow with the best king, thou shalt find the best king of good fellows. Come, your answer in broken music – for thy voice is music, and thy English broken; therefore, Queen of all, Katherine, break thy mind to me in broken English – wilt thou have me?

KATHERINE Dat is as it shall please de *Roi mon père*.

KING HENRY Nay, it will please him well, Kate – it shall please him, Kate.

KATHERINE Den it sall also content me.

KING HENRY Upon that I kiss your hand, and I call you my Queen.

KATHERINE *Laissez, mon seigneur, laissez, laissez! Ma foi, je ne veux point que vous abaissiez votre grandeur en baisant la main d'une – notre Seigneur – indigne serviteur. Excusez-moi, je vous supplie, mon très puissant seigneur.*

KING HENRY Then I will kiss your lips, Kate.

KATHERINE *Les dames et demoiselles pour être baisées devant leur noces, il n'est pas la coutume de France.*

KING HENRY Madam my interpreter, what says she?

---

228 *ill layer-up* wrinkler (like a 'wet cloak ill laid up', *2 Henry IV*, v.1.82)
230 *thou shalt wear me, if thou wear me* you will find me suiting you, if you take me

240–41 *broken music*. This quibbles on the technical term for music arranged for wind and string instruments.

ALICE Dat it is not be de fashion *pour les* ladies of *France* —
I cannot tell wat is *baiser en* Anglish.

KING HENRY To kiss.   260

ALICE Your majestee *entendre* bettre *que moi.*

KING HENRY It is not a fashion for the maids in France to
kiss before they are married, would she say?

ALICE *Oui, vraiment.*

KING HENRY O Kate, nice customs curtsy to great kings.
Dear Kate, you and I cannot be confined within the
weak list of a country's fashion. We are the makers of
manners, Kate, and the liberty that follows our places
stops the mouth of all find-faults — as I will do yours for
upholding the nice fashion of your country in denying   270
me a kiss; therefore, patiently, and yielding. (*He kisses
her*) You have witchcraft in your lips, Kate: there is
more eloquence in a sugar touch of them than in the
tongues of the French Council, and they should sooner
persuade Harry of England than a general petition of
monarchs. Here comes your father.

          *Enter the French King and Queen, Burgundy, and
          English and French Lords*

BURGUNDY God save your majesty! My royal cousin,
teach you our Princess English?

KING HENRY I would have her learn, my fair cousin, how
perfectly I love her, and that is good English.   280

BURGUNDY Is she not apt?

KING HENRY Our tongue is rough, coz, and my condition
is not smooth; so that, having neither the voice nor the
heart of flattery about me, I cannot so conjure up the
spirit of love in her that he will appear in his true
likeness.

BURGUNDY Pardon the frankness of my mirth, if I answer
you for that. If you would conjure in her, you must
make a circle; if conjure up love in her in his true like-

---

265 *nice* punctilious, finicky
267 *list* limits
268 *places* (high) rank

289 *make a circle* (that is, as if for magical
    rites; with a bawdy quibble also)

290   ness, he must appear naked and blind. Can you blame
her, then, being a maid yet rosed over with the virgin
crimson of modesty, if she deny the appearance of a
naked blind boy in her naked seeing self? It were, my
lord, a hard condition for a maid to consign to.

KING HENRY Yet they do wink and yield, as love is blind
and enforces.

BURGUNDY They are then excused, my lord, when they
see not what they do.

KING HENRY Then, good my lord, teach your cousin to
300   consent winking.

BURGUNDY I will wink on her to consent, my lord, if you
will teach her to know my meaning: for maids, well
summered and warm kept, are like flies at Bartholomew
tide, blind, though they have their eyes, and then they
will endure handling, which before would not abide
looking on.

KING HENRY This moral ties me over to time and a hot
summer; and so I shall catch the fly, your cousin, in the
latter end, and she must be blind too.

310   BURGUNDY As love is, my lord, before it loves.

KING HENRY It is so; and you may, some of you, thank
love for my blindness, who cannot see many a fair
French city for one fair French maid that stands in my
way.

FRENCH KING Yes, my lord, you see them perspectively,
the cities turned into a maid; for they are all girdled
with maiden walls, that war hath never entered.

KING HENRY Shall Kate be my wife?

---

290 *blind* (1) sightless (like blind Cupid);
(2) oblivious of all else

303 *summered* nurtured (as cattle are in
summer pastures)

303–4 *Bartholomew-tide* 24 August (when
the flies supposedly feel the late
summer's warmth and grow sluggish)

307 *This moral ties me over* this reflection
means I must wait

315 *perspectively* as if in a perspective (an
optical device which showed different images when viewed from different angles)

FRENCH KING So please you.

KING HENRY I am content, so the maiden cities you talk   320
of may wait on her: so the maid that stood in the way
for my wish shall show me the way to my will.

FRENCH KING
We have consented to all terms of reason.

KING HENRY
Is't so, my lords of England?

WESTMORLAND
The King hath granted every article:
His daughter first, and then, in sequel, all,
According to their firm proposèd natures.

EXETER
Only he hath not yet subscribèd this:
Where your majesty demands that the King of France,
having any occasion to write for matter of grant, shall   330
name your highness in this form, and with this addition,
in French, *Notre très cher fils Henri, Roi d'Angleterre,*
Héritier de France: and thus in Latin, *Praeclarissimus*
filius noster Henricus, Rex Angliae et Haeres Franciae.

FRENCH KING
Nor this I have not, brother, so denied
But your request shall make me let it pass.

KING HENRY
I pray you then, in love and dear alliance,
Let that one article rank with the rest,
And thereupon give me your daughter.

320–21 *so the maiden cities . . . her.* As
lover, Henry insists on Katherine for
his wife; but as King, standing for
his country's rights, he demands all
that is due to his crown.

328 *subscribèd* signed in agreement

330 *matter of grant* conferment of lands
or titles

332–3 *très cher . . . Praeclarissimus.* The
discrepancy in meaning between the
French and the Latin words ('most
beloved . . . most renowned') arises
since 'praeclarissimus' is a misprint
in Shakespeare's sources for 'prae-
charissimus' (that is, 'praecarissimus',
'most beloved').

FRENCH KING

340   Take her, fair son, and from her blood raise up
Issue to me, that the contending kingdoms
Of France and England, whose very shores look pale
With envy of each other's happiness,
May cease their hatred, and this dear conjunction
Plant neighbourhood and Christian-like accord
In their sweet bosoms, that never war advance
His bleeding sword 'twixt England and fair France.

LORDS Amen!

KING HENRY

Now welcome, Kate; and bear me witness all
350   That here I kiss her as my sovereign Queen.
     Flourish

QUEEN ISABEL

God, the best maker of all marriages,
Combine your hearts in one, your realms in one!
As man and wife, being two, are one in love,
So be there 'twixt your kingdoms such a spousal
That never may ill office, or fell jealousy,
Which troubles oft the bed of blessèd marriage,
Thrust in between the paction of these kingdoms
To make divorce of their incorporate league;
That English may as French, French Englishmen,
360   Receive each other, God speak this 'Amen'!

ALL Amen!

KING HENRY

Prepare we for our marriage; on which day,
My Lord of Burgundy, we'll take your oath,
And all the peers', for surety of our leagues.

342 *pale* white (the chalk cliffs)
354 *spousal* married union
355 *ill office* malevolent interference
357 *paction* compact (Folio, 'Pation')
358 *incorporate* united (as marriage makes man and wife one flesh)
363–4 *My Lord of Burgundy, we'll take your oath,* | *And all the peers'.* In *The Famous Victories of Henry the Fifth* Burgundy and the Dauphin take their oaths on the stage; see also the Introduction, page 670, for Nashe's reference to a similar incident.

Then shall I swear to Kate, and you to me,
And may our oaths well kept and prosperous be!

Sennet. Exeunt

EPILOGUE

Enter Chorus

CHORUS

Thus far, with rough and all-unable pen,
Our bending author hath pursued the story,
In little room confining mighty men,
Mangling by starts the full course of their glory.
Small time, but in that small most greatly lived
This star of England. Fortune made his sword,
By which the world's best garden he achieved,
And of it left his son imperial lord.
Henry the Sixth, in infant bands crowned King
Of France and England, did this King succeed, 10
Whose state so many had the managing
That they lost France, and made his England bleed:
Which oft our stage hath shown; and, for their sake,
In your fair minds let this acceptance take. *Exit*

---

366 (stage direction) *Sennet* trumpet signal

Epilogue 2 *Our bending author.* Compare *Hamlet* – 'For us, and for our tragedy, | Here stooping to your clemency, | We beg your hearing patiently' (III.2.144–5). Possibly Shakespeare himself was the Chorus and here spoke in his own person.

5 *Small time.* Henry died at thirty-five, having reigned nine years (1413–22).

Discover more about our forthcoming books through Penguin's FREE newspaper...

Penguin
Quarterly

It's packed with:

- exciting features
- author interviews
- previews & reviews
- books from your favourite films & TV series
- exclusive competitions & much, much more...

Write off for your free copy today to:
Dept JC
Penguin Books Ltd
FREEPOST
West Drayton
Middlesex
UB7 0BR
NO STAMP REQUIRED

READ MORE IN PENGUIN

In every corner of the world, on every subject under the sun, Penguin represents quality and variety – the very best in publishing today.

For complete information about books available from Penguin – including Puffins, Penguin Classics and Arkana – and how to order them, write to us at the appropriate address below. Please note that for copyright reasons the selection of books varies from country to country.

In the United Kingdom: Please write to *Dept. JC, Penguin Books Ltd, FREEPOST, West Drayton, Middlesex UB7 OBR*

If you have any difficulty in obtaining a title, please send your order with the correct money, plus ten per cent for postage and packaging, to *PO Box No. 11, West Drayton, Middlesex UB7 OBR*

In the United States: Please write to *Penguin USA Inc., 375 Hudson Street, New York, NY 10014*

In Canada: Please write to *Penguin Books Canada Ltd, 10 Alcorn Avenue, Suite 300, Toronto, Ontario M4V 3B2*

In Australia: Please write to *Penguin Books Australia Ltd, 487 Maroondah Highway, Ringwood, Victoria 3134*

In New Zealand: Please write to *Penguin Books (NZ) Ltd,182–190 Wairau Road, Private Bag, Takapuna, Auckland 9*

In India: Please write to *Penguin Books India Pvt Ltd, 706 Eros Apartments, 56 Nehru Place, New Delhi 110 019*

In the Netherlands: Please write to *Penguin Books Netherlands B.V., Keizersgracht 231 NL–1016 DV Amsterdam*

In Germany: Please write to *Penguin Books Deutschland GmbH, Friedrichstrasse 10–12, W–6000 Frankfurt/Main 1*

In Spain: Please write to *Penguin Books S. A., C. San Bernardo 117–6° E–28015 Madrid*

In Italy: Please write to *Penguin Italia s.r.l., Via Felice Casati 20, 1–20124 Milano*

In France: Please write to *Penguin France S. A., 17 rue Lejeune, F–31000 Toulouse*

In Japan: Please write to *Penguin Books Japan, Ishikiribashi Building, 2–5–4, Suido, Bunkyo-ku, Tokyo 112*

In Greece: Please write to *Penguin Hellas Ltd, Dimocritou 3, GR–106 71 Athens*

In South Africa: Please write to *Longman Penguin Southern Africa (Pty) Ltd, Private Bag X08, Bertsham 2013*

READ MORE IN PENGUIN

A CHOICE OF CLASSICS

Francis Bacon	**The Essays**
George Berkeley	**Principles of Human Knowledge/Three Dialogues between Hylas and Philonous**
James Boswell	**The Life of Samuel Johnson**
Sir Thomas Browne	**The Major Works**
John Bunyan	**The Pilgrim's Progress**
Edmund Burke	**Reflections on the Revolution in France**
Frances Burney	**Evelina**
Margaret Cavendish	**The Blazing World and Other Writings**
William Cobbett	**Rural Rides**
William Congreve	**Comedies**
Thomas de Quincey	**Confessions of an English Opium Eater**
	Recollections of the Lakes and the Lake Poets
Daniel Defoe	**A Journal of the Plague Year**
	Moll Flanders
	Robinson Crusoe
	Roxana
	A Tour through the Whole Island of Great Britain
Henry Fielding	**Amelia**
	Jonathan Wild
	Joseph Andrews
	Tom Jones
John Gay	**The Beggar's Opera**
Oliver Goldsmith	**The Vicar of Wakefield**

READ MORE IN PENGUIN

A CHOICE OF CLASSICS

William Hazlitt	**Selected Writings**
George Herbert	**The Complete English Poems**
Thomas Hobbes	**Leviathan**
Samuel Johnson/	
James Boswell	**A Journey to the Western Islands of Scotland and The Journal of a Tour of the Hebrides**
Charles Lamb	**Selected Prose**
George Meredith	**The Egoist**
Thomas Middleton	**Five Plays**
John Milton	**Paradise Lost**
Samuel Richardson	**Clarissa**
	Pamela
Earl of Rochester	**Complete Works**
Richard Brinsley	
Sheridan	**The School for Scandal and Other Plays**
Sir Philip Sidney	**Selected Poems**
Christopher Smart	**Selected Poems**
Adam Smith	**The Wealth of Nations**
Tobias Smollett	**The Adventures of Ferdinand Count Fathom**
	Humphrey Clinker
Laurence Sterne	**The Life and Opinions of Tristram Shandy**
	A Sentimental Journey Through France and Italy
Jonathan Swift	**Gulliver's Travels**
	Selected Poems
Thomas Traherne	**Selected Poems and Prose**
Sir John Vanbrugh	**Four Comedies**

BY THE SAME AUTHOR

The plays in these collections are accompanied by notes and an introduction to each text, making them of particular value to students,
scholars and theatre-goers.

Four Tragedies
Hamlet · Othello · King Lear · Macbeth

The theme of the great Shakespearian tragedies is the fall from grace
of a great man due to a flaw in his nature. Whether it is the ruthless
ambition of Macbeth or the folly of Lear, the irresolution of Hamlet
or the suspicion of Othello, the cause of the tragedy – even when it is
the murder of a king – is trifling compared with the calamity it
unleashes.

Four Comedies
*The Taming of the Shrew · A Midsummer Night's Dream · As You
Like It · Twelfth Night*

Shakespearian comedy has as much to do with the structure and
movement of the drama as with the wit of its dialogue or the humour
of its characters. In these four comedies there is a near-tragic crisis at
which disaster or happiness may ensue, but the overriding force of
goodwill and the power of understanding, love and generosity brings
us through to a joyful conclusion.

and

Three Roman Plays
Julius Caesar · Antony and Cleopatra · Coriolanus